THE NEW OXFORD HISTORY
OF ENGLAND

General Editor · J. M. ROBERTS

The Later Tudors

ENGLAND

1547–1603

―――

PENRY WILLIAMS

CLARENDON PRESS · OXFORD

1995

Oxford University Press, Walton Street, Oxford OX2 6DP

Oxford New York
Athens Auckland Bangkok Bombay
Calcutta Cape Town Dar es Salaam Delhi
Florence Hong Kong Istanbul Karachi
Kuala Lumpur Madras Madrid Melbourne
Mexico City Nairobi Paris Singapore
Taipei Tokyo Toronto
and associated companies in
Berlin Ibadan

Oxford is a trade mark of Oxford University Press

Published in the United States
by Oxford University Press Inc., New York

First published 1995

British Library Cataloguing in Publication Data
Data available

Library of Congress Cataloging-in-Publication Data
Williams, Penry.
The later Tudors : England, 1547–1603 / Penry Williams.
p. cm. — (New Oxford history of England)
Includes bibliographical references (p.).
1. Great Britain—History—Elizabeth, 1558–1603. 2. Great
Britain—History—Tudors, 1485–1603. 3. England—Civilization—16th
century. 4. Tudor, House of. I. Title. II. Series.
DA955.W4895 1995
942.05—dc20 95-8886
ISBN 0-19-822820-1

1 3 5 7 9 10 8 6 4 2

Typeset by Best-set Typesetter Ltd., Hong Kong
Printed in Great Britain
on acid-free paper by
Butler & Tanner Ltd., Frome

IN MEMORY OF JUNE

1926–1991

General Editor's Preface

The first volume of Sir George Clark's *Oxford History of England* was published in 1934. Undertaking the General Editorship of a *New Oxford History of England* forty-five years later it was hard not to feel overshadowed by its powerful influence and well-deserved status. Some of Clark's volumes (his own among them) were brilliant individual achievements, hard to rival and impossible to match. Of course, he and his readers shared a broad sense of the purpose and direction of such books. His successor can no longer be sure of doing that. The building-blocks of the story, its reasonable and meaningful demarcations and divisions, the continuities and discontinuities, the priorities of different varieties of history, the place of narrative—all these things are now much harder to agree upon. We now know much more about many things, and think about what we know in different ways. It is not surprising that historians now sometimes seem unsure about the audience to which their scholarship and writing are addressed.

In the end, authors should be left to write their own books. None the less, the *New Oxford History of England* is intended to be more than a collection of discrete or idiosyncratic histories in chronological order. Its aim is to give an account of the development of our country in time. Changing geographical limits suggest it is hard to speak of that solely as a history of England. Yet the core of the institutional story which runs from Anglo-Saxon times to our own is the story of the State structure built round the English monarchy, the only continuous articulation of the history of those peoples we today call British. Certainly the emphasis of individual volumes will vary. Each author has been asked to bring forward what he or she sees as the most important topics explaining the history under study, taking account of the present state of historical knowledge, drawing attention to areas of dispute and to matters on which final judgement is at present difficult (or, perhaps, impossible) and not merely recapitulating what has recently been the fashionable centre of professional debate. But each volume, allowing for its special approach and proportions, must also provide a comprehensive account, in which politics is always likely to be prominent. Volumes have to be demarcated chronologically but continuities must not be obscured; vestigially or not, copyhold survived into the 1920s and the Anglo-Saxon shires until the 1970s. Any one volume should be an entry-point to the understanding of processes only slowly unfolding, sometimes across centuries. My hope is that in the end we shall have, as the outcome, a set of standard and authoritative histories, embodying the scholarship of a generation, and not mere compendia in which the determinants are lost to sight among the detail.

J. M. ROBERTS

Preface

In writing a general book on the second half of the sixteenth century in England, I have thought it essential to provide the reader with a strong narrative core which could carry the story of the development and survival of the English state and the Anglican Church from the accession of Edward VI to the death of Elizabeth I. I have tried to integrate into that narrative as many aspects of late Tudor England as I could, even if this meant some overlapping with the thematic sections. Rather than separating foreign and domestic history into different chapters, I have combined them as far as possible into the broad strand of the narrative. Only in that way can the full complexity of events be understood. Since Scotland was not then part of the English kingdom I have omitted its history except for its effect upon England. Ireland presented me with a problem. To corral Irish history into a separate chapter would have made it difficult to understand the interplay between Ireland and England; and I therefore decided on setting the Irish scene briefly in chapter one, telling the Irish story in the narrative chapters, and summing up the significance of the period for Ireland in the last. I have avoided a specific chapter on economic history, believing that it is properly seen both in the context of society and within the narrative.

The plates are intended to illustrate the written word and I have given cross-references in the text to specific pictures.

I have tried, not altogether successfully, to be economical with my footnotes. I have given the sources of quotations and references to statutes and proclamations; and I have also indicated when I have relied particularly heavily on the work of other historians; but I am aware that I have not always given credit where it was due. Indeed, in a book of this kind, that would be impossible, so great is my debt to the labours of others.

I have many specific debts to acknowledge. The Warden and Fellows of New College granted me four terms of sabbatical leave during the writing of this book and provided me with a congenial intellectual environment for more than thirty years. Successive fellows' secretaries in New College grappled bravely with my handwriting until I learned to use a word-processor. Tony Morris of the Oxford University Press encouraged me over several years, while he and Anna Illingworth have skilfully seen the book through the processes of publication. Friends, colleagues, and pupils have contributed in many ways. In particular, Ian Archer, Mark Byford, Helen Cobb (now Helen Hackelt), Ralph Houlbrooke, the late Jennifer Loach,

Tony Nuttall, David Palliser, Alastair Parker, and Blair Worden have read and commented on parts or all of the book and have made invaluable suggestions. John Roberts invited me to write it and thereafter provided exactly the right measure of encouragement, criticism, and stimulus. Sylvia Platt not only read the whole text in typescript, but supported me in many other ways during the final laborious stages. Lastly, my wife June helped and encouraged me during most of the writing and indeed for many years before that: to her memory this book is dedicated.

PENRY WILLIAMS

Contents

Plates

Maps and Tables

Acknowledgements to the Illustrations

Plates 1, 3a, 5b, 5c are reproduced by courtesy of the National Portrait Gallery, London; plate 2a by permission of Westminster Cathedral Treasury; plates 2b, 4a, 5a, 7b, 8a, 10, 11a, 11b, 12, 15, 16, 17a, 17b by permission of the Bodleian Library, University of Oxford; plate 3b by permission of the Victoria & Albert Museum, London; plate 4b by courtesy of the Marquess of Salisbury and Courtauld Institute of Art; plates 6, 8b are copyright British Museum; plates 7a, 9a are reproduced by permission of Country Life Picture Library; plate 9b by permission of Oxfordshire Photographic Archive; plate 13 by permission of the Fitzwilliam Museum, Cambridge; plate 14 by permission of the Master & Fellows of Magdalene College, Cambridge.

Maps 1, 2, and table 5 are reproduced by permission of Dr Joan Thirsk, Dr Peter Bowden, and Cambridge University Press from Joan Thirsk (ed.), *Agrarian History of England and Wales*, iv. *1500–1640* (Cambridge, 1967); tables 1–4 by permission of Professor Steve Rappaport and Cambridge University Press from Steve Rappaport, *Worlds within Worlds* (Cambridge, 1987); map 6 by permission of Dr Michael Bush and Edward Arnold (publisher) Limited, from Michael Bush, *The Government Policy of Protector Somerset* (London, 1975); maps 7 and 8 by permission of Oxford University Press from T. W. Moody *et al.* (eds.), *New History of Ireland*, ix. *Maps* (Oxford, 1984).

Abbreviations

APC	*The Acts of the Privy Council of England*, ed. J. R. Dasent (46 vols., London, 1890–1964)
BIHR	*Bulletin of the Institute of Historical Research*; known from 1987 onwards as *Historical Research*
BL	British Library
Birch, *Memoirs*	Thomas Birch, *Memoirs of the Reign of Queen Elizabeth, from the Year 1581 until her Death* (2 vols., London, 1754)
Camden, *Annals*	William Camden, *Annals of Queen Elizabeth*, trans. H. Norton (London, 1635)
Chronicle of Edward VI	*The Chronicle and Political Papers of Edward VI*, ed. W. K. Jordan (London, 1966)
Chronicle of Queen Jane	*The Chronicle of Queen Jane, and of two years of Queen Mary*, ed. J. G. Nichols, Camden Soc. 48 (London, 1850)
Collins, *Letters*	Arthur Collins (ed.), *Letters and Memorials of State . . . Written and Collected by Sir Henry Sidney* (2 vols., London, 1746)
CSP Dom.	*Calendar of State Papers, Domestic*
CSP Ire.	*Calendar of State Papers, Ireland*
CSP Scot.	*Calendar of State Papers, Scotland*
CSP Span.	*Calendar of State Papers, Spanish*
CSP Ven.	*Calendar of State Papers, Venetian*
Devereux, *Letters*	W. B. Devereux, *Lives and Letters of the Devereux Earls of Essex* (2 vols., London, 1853)
DNB	Leslie Stephen and Sidney Lee (eds.), *The Dictionary of National Biography* (63 vols., London, 1885–1900)
EcHR	*Economic History Review*
EHR	*English Historical Review*
Foxe	John Foxe, *Acts and Monuments of the English Church* (better known as *The Book of Martyrs*),

	ed. S. R. Cattley and George Townshend (8 vols., London, 1837–41)
Hartley, *Proceedings*	T. E. Hartley (ed.), *Proceedings in the Parliaments of Elizabeth I*, i: *1559–81* (Leicester, 1981)
Haynes, *State Papers*	Samuel Haynes and William Murdin, *Collection of State Papers . . . left by William Cecil, Lord Burghley* (2 vols., London, 1740–59)
HJ	*Historical Journal*
HMC	Historical Manuscripts Commission
Leland, *Itinerary*	*The Itinerary of John Leland in or about the Years 1535–1543*, ed. L. Toulmin Smith (5 vols., London, 1907–10)
Leland, *Itinerary in Wales*	*Leland's Itinerary in Wales*, ed. L. Toulmin Smith (London, 1906)
Neale, *Parliaments*	J. E. Neale, *Elizabeth I and her Parliaments* (2 vols., London, 1953, 1957)
Proclamations	P. L. Hughes and J. F. Larkin (eds.), *Tudor Royal Proclamations* (3 vols., New Haven, Conn., 1964–9)
PRO	Public Record Office
Read, *Burghley*	Conyers Read, *Lord Burghley and Queen Elizabeth* (London, 1960)
Read, *Cecil*	Conyers Read, *Mr Secretary Cecil and Queen Elizabeth* (London, 1955)
Read, *Walsingham*	Conyers Read, *Mr Secretary Walsingham and the Policy of Queen Elizabeth* (3 vols., Oxford, 1925)
Rymer, *Foedera*	Thomas Rymer, *Foedera, conventiones, literae et . . . acta publica* (20 vols., London, 1727–35)
STC	*A Short Title Catalogue of Books Printed in England, Scotland, and Ireland . . . 1475–1640*, comp. A. W. Pollard and G. R. Redgrave (2nd edn., 3 vols., London, 1976–1991)
Strype, *Ecclesiastical Memorials*	John Strype, *Ecclesiastical Memorials, Relating Chiefly to Religion and the Reformation of it . . .* (3 vols., Oxford, 1822)
Spedding, *Bacon*	James Spedding et al. (eds.), *The Letters and the Life of Francis Bacon* (7 vols., London,

	1862–74). These are vols. viii–xiv of Spedding *et al.* (eds.), *The Works of Francis Bacon* (14 vols., London, 1857–74)
TED	R. H. Tawney and Eileen Power (eds.), *Tudor Economic Documents* (3 vols. London, 1924)
VCH	*The Victoria History of the Counties of England* (Westminster, 1900–). This work is generally known as *The Victoria County History*

NOTE ON SPELLING

In referring to the royal house of Scotland I have used the spelling preferred by Scottish historians: Stewart. In referring to the same family when it was reigning in England I have used the normal English spelling: Stuart.

I have modernized all prose quotations but have preserved the original spelling in quoting from poets, although I have adopted modern conventions for u, v, i, and j. Spenser, especially, was particular about his spelling. However, I have followed twentieth-century practice in modernizing the works of Shakespeare, for which I have used the Arden edition.

CHAPTER I

Introduction

1. THE FACE OF BRITAIN[1]

In sixteenth-century England sheep outnumbered humans by two or three
to one. Foreign visitors were struck by the country's sparse population and
its broad green pastures. The Venetian ambassador wrote in the reign of
Henry VII that 'the population of this island does not appear to me to bear
any proportion to her fertility and riches'.[2] In an imaginary debate between
French and English heralds the Frenchman declared that 'while France is
a world of people . . . a great part of [England] is waste desert and savage
ground, not inhabited nor th'earth tilled'. By 'desert and savage ground' he
almost certainly referred to woodlands and forests, then generally regarded
as primitive wildernesses. An Italian traveller complained that English
farmers were 'so lazy and slow that they do not bother to sow more wheat
than is necessary for their own consumption; they prefer to let the ground
be transformed into pasture for the use of the sheep that they breed in large
numbers.' George Rainsford, an Englishman describing his own country to
King Philip in 1556, praised it by boasting that it 'has every kind of animal
except the elephant, the camel, the mule and the ass. . . . They have sheep
and other beasts in great quantity because one fourth of the country is
pasture.'[3]

The human population was certainly small. Before the Black Death
England had probably between 4.5 and 6 million inhabitants. By the middle
of the fifteenth century the total had sunk to perhaps 2 million; and although it had begun to recover in the early years of the sixteenth, it was still,
at about 2.8 million in 1547, well below the peak reached in the early

[1] The purpose of this section is to give a brief pictorial account of England, Wales, and
Ireland in 1547: a fuller analysis of society follows in Ch. 6.
[2] *The Relation . . . of the Isle of England about the Year 1500 . . .* , ed. G. A. Sneyd,
Camden Soc. 37 (London, 1847), 10.
[3] *TED* iii. 5–6; *Two Italian Accounts of Tudor England*, ed. and trans. C. V. Malfatti
(Barcelona, 1953), 4; 'George Rainsford's *Rittratto d'Ingilterra (1556)*', ed. P. S. Donaldson,
Camden Soc., 4th ser., 27 (London, 1979), 92.

fourteenth.[4] By contemporary European standards English population density was low. Whereas Italy may have had some 114 inhabitants per square mile, the Netherlands 100, and France 90, England averaged only about 50, roughly equal with Spain. (In 1970 there were 820 persons per square mile in England.) There were as many as 100 people per square mile in thickly inhabited parts, but only a sparse 15 in the uplands of Wales; and even within a single county there were great differences, for the richer parts of Devon averaged 100, the poorer only 20–30 per square mile. Broadly speaking, the density of both population and wealth was higher in the region lying south of a line drawn from the Wash to the Severn Estuary than elsewhere. People and wealth were most heavily concentrated in the cloth-making districts of the south-west—Wiltshire, Gloucestershire, Somerset—and in East Anglia, the Home Counties, and Kent. The poorest counties lay in the north-west and in Wales.

Sparse as the population was in 1547, it had probably been growing from the early years of the century and was to grow more substantially, at an average rate of some 150,000 people every five years, until about 1640. By 1603 the population of England had reached 4 million, an increase of 50 per cent over the previous fifty years. The recovery was interrupted by serious harvest failures in 1555 and 1556, and by savage influenza epidemics in 1557 and 1558, which may have reduced the population by as much as 5 per cent over five years; but unlike the persistent epidemics of the fourteenth and fifteenth centuries, the 'Marian' influenza was short-lived in its effect. For twenty-five years, from 1561 to 1586, the annual growth rate of 1 per cent was resumed, adding 800,000 to the population. After 1586 the increase slowed to half its previous rate but was not seriously interrupted by the harvest failures of the mid-1590s. The increase seems to have come to an end around 1640, but the mortality crises of the fourteenth century were not repeated: population remained fairly static for the next hundred years, after which it again began to grow. Elsewhere in Europe during the early modern era periodic famines and epidemics severely cut back population and prevented that long-term increase with which England was favoured.

Following the serious epidemics of 1557–9 the death rate remained relatively low from 1561 until the end of Elizabeth's reign: it was highest in

[4] Population figures are derived from E. A. Wrigley and R. S. Schofield, *The Population History of England, 1541–1871: A Reconstruction* (London, 1981), *passim*, esp. pp. 207–15, and from D. M. Palliser, *The Age of Elizabeth: England under the Later Tudors, 1547–1603* (London, 1983), ch. 2. Population statistics become more abundant and reliable with the introduction of parish registers in 1538; but registers have not survived in large numbers for the sixteenth century and figures are at best approximate and at worst unreliable.

the quinquennium 1561–5, at 32.90 deaths per 1,000, averaging only 25 per 1,000 for the whole period 1561–1601. The expectation of life at birth, in spite of heavy infant mortality, was correspondingly high, at an average of 37 years. The birth rate kept steadily ahead of the death rate, averaging 34.5 per 1,000 in 1561–86, and then slackening a little to 32.2 in the final years of the century. Such figures acquire more meaning when compared with other times and other countries. In England in 1976 the death rate was 15 per 1,000, the birth rate 11.8, and expectation of life at birth was 69 years for men and 75 for women. Thus the Elizabethan population was sustained by a birth rate nearly three times our own and a death rate less than double. The use of contraceptives and the advance of medical science have combined to reduce the pressures of birth and of death upon the demography of Western Europe. At the other extreme, in the Indian subcontinent between 1901 and 1911, the death rate was 42 per 1,000, the birth rate 47 per 1,000, and the expectation of life at birth only 24 years: that is a typical 'high-pressure' system. Comparisons with other European countries in the sixteenth century are made difficult by paucity of evidence; but in early eighteenth-century France birth and death rates both seem to have been around 40 per 1,000. English society was, by the standards of early modern Europe, shaped by a relatively 'low-pressure' demographic system. A critical element in this was the late average age of first marriage for women: about 25 years. This allowed relatively few years for child-bearing and also left a high proportion of women unmarried, about 25 per cent towards the end of the sixteenth century. By contrast, in Eastern Europe around 1900, the mean age at first marriage for women was 20 years and only about 5 per cent remained permanently single. In the 'high-pressure' systems of Eastern Europe and Asia, and even of early modern France, population always threatened to rise too rapidly ahead of resources, producing recurrent and drastic mortality crises. English population increased gradually, the checks upon its growth operating in a relatively benign way through changes in the age of marriage and the fertility rate.

The explanation for the upturn in English population from the stagnation of the later Middle Ages to the steady, modest, but nevertheless significant growth of the Elizabethan period has yet to be found, for, in the absence of parish registers for the centuries before 1538, we are deprived of our most reliable source for population statistics. Monastic evidence suggests that the death rate was declining during the latter part of the fifteenth century and was still low in the early years of the sixteenth; births were probably running ahead of deaths already. After 1520 the death rate may have risen slightly, but not sufficiently to catch up with births; and

after 1600 the increase in population slowed as the resources available to
feed the people neared their limit.

Nine-tenths of the population lived in the countryside, either in small
market towns, or in villages, hamlets, and isolated farms. Although travellers noticed the extensive pastures, the landscape was in fact immensely
varied: contrasting patterns of settlement mingled with one another, even
within a single shire. Traditionally, England and Wales have been seen as
divided into highland and lowland zones; north and west of a line from
Weymouth to Teeside was upland pastoral country; south and east was the
lowland region of mixed farming. This distinction holds broadly true, but
there were many areas of arable and valley pasture in the uplands and
several varieties of lowland farming.[5]

In much of Wales, the north-west, and the south-west, bare pastoral
uplands predominated. In Northumberland arable land was in retreat during the sixteenth century: thin crops of barley and oats were grown in small
enclosed fields, while most of the uplands were rough open grazing, where
cattle were bred for fattening in the lowlands and sheep pastured for their
wool and their meat; settlements lay in scattered hamlets or isolated farm-
steads. The Welsh scene was more varied. John Leland, the greatest of early
Tudor topographers, said that in the north of Glamorgan he found 'many
hills . . . and woods good plenty', but 'few villages or corn except in a few
small valleys'; in the mountains there were 'some red deer, kids plenty, oxen
and sheep'. In the southern part of Glamorgan—the Vale—there was
'meetly good corn ground . . . and very good fruit for orchards'. Rice
Merrick, a Glamorgan man, spoke of the 'many great hills and high mountains' of the northern part, fit for 'great breeding of cattle, horses and sheep'
and for 'nourishing and bringing up tall, mighty and active men'. On
the evidence of Leland's description and of place-names, the Glamorgan
mountains, now bare slopes of rough grass, bracken, bilberries and heather,
were in many parts thickly wooded: not until the nineteenth century did the
combined appetites of sheep and of industry demolish the trees. Where
sheep are almost exclusively pastured today, there were in the sixteenth
century at least as many cattle—'the best means unto wealth that this shire
doth afford', according to John Speed. In North Wales Leland confined
his travels largely to the coastal strip and the valleys. In part of Denbighshire he found 'many bogs, rocky hills and moorish ground, and the soil
is too cold to have good corn, yet in diverse places it beareth oats and some
rye'. The bleak moorlands and mountains, attractive to travellers from the

[5] See Maps 1 and 2.

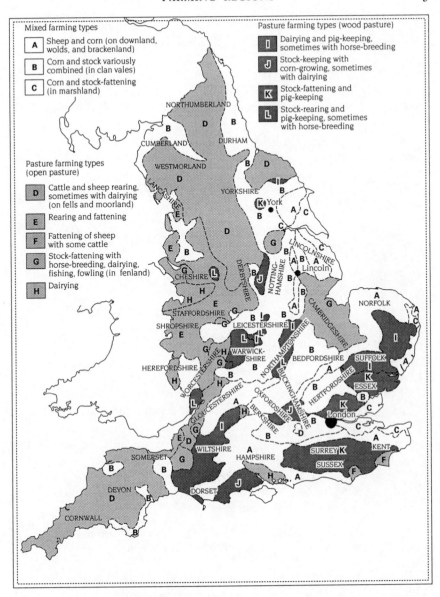

Mixed farming types

A Sheep and corn (on downland, wolds, and brackenland)

B Corn and stock variously combined (in clan vales)

C Corn and stock-fattening (in marshland)

Pasture farming types (open pasture)

D Cattle and sheep rearing, sometimes with dairying (on fells and moorland)

E Rearing and fattening

F Fattening of sheep with some cattle

G Stock-fattening with horse-breeding, dairying, fishing, fowling (in fenland)

H Dairying

Pasture farming types (wood pasture)

I Dairying and pig-keeping, sometimes with horse-breeding

J Stock-keeping with corn-growing, sometimes with dairying

K Stock-fattening and pig-keeping

L Stock-rearing and pig-keeping, sometimes with horse-breeding

MAP 1. The farming regions of England

romantic era onwards, seemed harsh and repellent to Leland and his contemporaries.[6]

---

[6] Leland, *Itinerary in Wales*, 16–26; Glanmor Williams, 'The economic life of Glamorgan, 1536–1642', in G. Williams (ed.), *Glamorgan County History*, iv (Cardiff, 1974), 1–6.

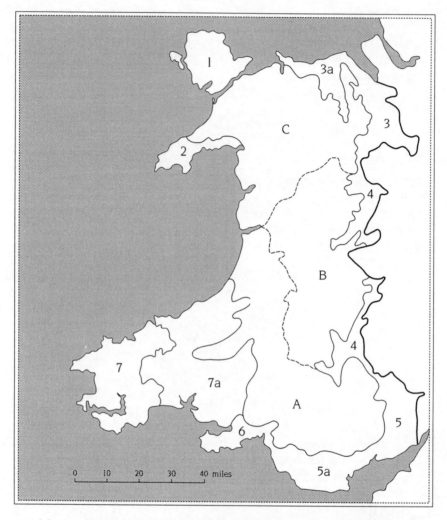

MAP 2. The farming regions of Wales. Areas 1–7 show mixed-farming
lowlands; areas A–C show pastoral stock-rearing uplands

On downland country, like the Lincolnshire wolds or the Sussex and
Wiltshire downs, sheep and grain were raised together in a well-tried
symbiosis. The sheep were pastured on the uplands during the day and then
folded on the arable of down slopes during the night so that they might
manure the land. The damp valley bottoms were mostly used as meadows
for hay and permanent grazing. Villages were small, but rich graziers often
owned extensive sheep-walks on the hills. Barley and wheat produced the
main source of revenue for the small farmer, who kept sheep mainly to

manure the ploughland. A few cows were kept, but they took second place to the ubiquitous sheep.

In some parts of England rich farming land lay side by side with barren heaths, for instance in northern Norfolk and in the region around Windsor, Ascot, and Bagshot. The soil was too poor for more than occasional cultivation and was generally left as rough pasturage for sheep. As on the downs, the sheep grazed on the common by day and were folded on the arable at night. But the soil was much less promising than in the downland. Early in the eighteenth century Daniel Defoe depicted Bagshot Heath in sombre terms: 'not only poor, but even quite sterile, given up to barrenness, horrid and frightful to look on, not only good for little, but good for nothing; much of it is a sandy desert . . . ; passing this heath in a windy day, I was so far in danger of smothering with the clouds of sand . . . that I could neither keep it out of my mouth, nose or eyes . . . the product of it feeds no creatures, but some very small sheep'.[7] It was probably little different in the reign of Elizabeth; and the Norfolk Breckland is still an inhospitable country of gorse and bracken today.

The fens and marshlands of Somerset, Kent, Essex, and Lincolnshire looked damp, cold, and forbidding. To outsiders the Lincolnshire fenland seemed a 'mere quaqmire', but those who lived in it knew the contrary, for the fenland contained a great deal of excellent pasture and a small amount of arable.[8] The economy rested mainly on the rearing and fattening of stock, with cattle, used both for dairying and for beef, holding primary place. Sheep were less important than in upland districts, but most farmers had some horses and a few pigs. Although the bulk of the population lived from pasture farming, incomes were usefully supplemented by fishing and fowling. Altogether the fenland was a prosperous region with many well-to-do small farmers, few very wealthy ones, and still fewer gentlemen or nobles: 'the want of gentlemen here to inhabit' was a constant worry to the government. Yet the fen-dwellers were proud of their country. Defending it in the next century against the undertakers who wished to drain the region, they wrote that 'the Fens breed infinite number of serviceable horses', that 'we breed and feed great store of young cattle', that 'we have the richest corn land in *England*', that 'we keep great flocks of sheep', and 'that we have many thousand cottagers, which live on our Fens, which otherwise must go abegging'.[9]

The neighbouring marshlands of Lincolnshire lay along the coast between the mouth of the Humber and the Wash, the saltmarsh next to the

[7] W. G. Hoskins, *The Making of the English Landscape* (London, 1955), 110.
[8] Joan Thirsk, *English Peasant Farming* (London, 1957), *passim*.
[9] Ibid. 30.

sea, and the clay middle-marsh inland. The region was drier than the fenland and had been settled earlier, but the process of land reclamation was still going on. There was ample meadow and pasture, and much more arable than in the fenland. Leland wrote that 'there is good wheat and beans in most parishes of the low marsh in Lindsey'.[10] But, valuable as the arable was, the real basis of the marshland economy lay in the rearing and fattening of cattle and sheep. The average farmer of the marshland was distinctly richer than his counterpart in the fenland and the key to his prosperity lay in the combination of relatively large areas of both pasture and arable.

Fenlands and marshlands covered only small areas of England; traditionally the typical settlement of lowland England was the nucleated village of about forty families with large open arable fields and common pastures. Their houses were clustered together in the centre of the open fields, and their holdings interspersed one with another in the arable area, which was divided into two, three, four, or occasionally even more open fields, partitioned into strips, cultivated on a strict system of crop rotation. Beyond the open fields was the common pasture or waste. On the most usual system, the three-field pattern, each arable field, perhaps 300 to 900 acres in size, followed the sequence of winter-sown wheat or rye, spring-sown barley, oats or peas and beans, and fallow. Sheep and cattle were pastured on the common waste, the fallow, and, for a brief time after harvest, on the stubble before ploughing. The meadows, usually lying along the banks of a river or stream, were principally cropped for hay. This, with many variations, is known as the fielden system of mixed farming in 'champion' regions. It was found in the coastal zones of the north-east and north-west, in east Yorkshire, and, above all, in the Midlands. In Wales it predominated in Anglesey, the lowlands of Pembrokeshire and Glamorgan, and in parts of the border country. Corn was the principal source of livelihood and strict by-laws governed the cultivation of the land. Dates of opening or closing the meadows for grazing, and of allowing animals onto the stubble, had to be strictly observed. Stints were laid down for the number of animals that could be pastured by the holders of each tenement. Leland gave a general view of typical fielden country on his journey through Leicestershire: 'the country betwixt Deane and Staunton plentiful of corn and exceeding fair and large meadows on both sides of Welland'; from Rockingham to Staunton 'there was in sight little wood as in a county all champion'.[11]

However, many lowland regions presented a quite different picture. These were the forest or woodland-pasture areas, distinct in topography, economy, and settlement from the fielden country.[12] Many counties con-

---

[10] Leland, *Itinerary*, iv. 34.　　[11] Ibid. i. 13.　　[12] See Map 1.

tained both fielden and woodland regions. Leland, having described Leicestershire as 'all champion', later corrected his account by telling his readers to 'mark that such part of Leicestershire as is lying by south and east [is] champion, and hath little wood. And such part of Leicestershire as lyeth by west and north hath much wood.' Suffolk was also a county 'of two several conditions of soil, the one champion, which yields for the most part sheep and some corn, the other enclosed pasture grounds employed most to grazing and dairy'.[13] Southern Warwickshire was mostly 'champion' country; the north, especially the Forest of Arden, was woodland. The woodland-pasture settlements were generally situated on heavy, wet clay soils, better suited for grazing cattle or pigs than sheep. Corn was grown largely for subsistence, and the main profits were drawn from dairying or from the fattening of stock. The fields had mostly been enclosed at an early date; settlements were scattered in hamlets or isolated farms and cottages. Since there was generally an abundant supply of common pasture, the woodland and forest regions could often support large numbers of immigrants and squatters. The eighteenth-century agriculturalist, William Marshall, gives an admirable picture of the woodland region of south-east Norfolk: 'the enclosures are, in general, small, and the hedges high and full of trees. This has a singular effect in travelling through the country: the eye seems ever on the verge of a forest, which is, as it were by enchantment, continually changing into enclosures and hedgerows'. Although the trees would probably have been denser in the sixteenth century than in Marshall's day, the general impression would otherwise have been the same.[14]

In almost every county of England and Wales the deer parks of nobles and gentlemen caught the eye. John Leland, travelling in the 1530s, usually mentioned them: he counted fifteen large parks in Leicestershire alone, and was especially impressed by the 'fair large park . . . six miles in compass' built by the Marquis of Dorset near Groby.[15] Christopher Saxton's maps of the Elizabethan counties are dotted with the fenced-off parks of the substantial landowners. William Harrison, writing fifty years later than Leland, asserted that there were a hundred parks in Kent and in Essex, twenty even in the bishopric of Durham, 'wherein great plenty of fallow deer is cherished and kept'.[16] However, the great fashion for emparking declined after 1550, and although some new parks were being made in the second half of the century, as many others were being converted to arable or pasture. Sixteenth-century parks were essentially kept for sport: they were heavily

[13] Leland, *Itinerary*, i. 21–2; ii. 47.
[14] William Marshall, *The Rural Economy of Norfolk* (2 vols., London, 1787), 303.
[15] Leland, *Itinerary*, i. 18.
[16] William Harrison, *Description of England*, ed. F. J. Furnivall (London, 1877), 303.

stocked, as Leland observed, with deer. Their owners were not much interested in the aesthetic possibilities of landscapes, and the parks which now embellish the English countryside were the creation of later centuries, when landowners competed with each other to achieve the picturesque.

If we take 2,000 inhabitants to be the minimum size for a town, then town-dwellers made up only about 10 per cent of the population in 1547, and a little more in 1603. Foreigners were usually dismissive of English towns: the Venetian Ambassador wrote in 1497–8 that apart from London, Bristol, and York, 'there are scarcely any towns of importance in the Kingdom'.[17] But London, compassing two cities in one, the City of London and the City of Westminster, was the seat of government,the usual abode of the royal Court, the most important trading post, and the main centre of financial operations. With a growing population of between 55,000 and 70,000 in 1547, it was outstripped by only about a dozen European towns, notably Naples, Paris, Milan, Venice, and Genoa. In numbers and in riches it towered above its English competitors. The next biggest city, Norwich, then had only 12,000 inhabitants and was assessed for taxes at only one-ninth the London amount.

Foreign travellers marvelled at London. One visitor wrote of it in 1497: 'it is defended by handsome walls . . . Within these stands a very strongly defended castle . . . There are also other great buildings, and especially a beautiful and convenient bridge over the Thames, of many marble arches, which has on it many shops built of stone and mansions and even a church of considerable size. Nowhere have I seen a finer or more richly built bridge.' He and others were struck by the luxury and prosperity of the city. Nicander Nucius, a Greek, remarked that 'throughout the city a large number of mansions are built for the residences of the nobles and mer-chants, and lofty halls ornamented with floral paintings are erected'.[18] The Venetian ambassador in 1497–8 reported that 'London abounds with every article of luxury'. In particular it had a 'wonderful quantity of wrought silver'; and there were fifty-two goldsmiths' shops in the Strand alone. The only complaint was about the condition of the streets, which were so badly paved that they were full of 'a vast amount of evil-smelling mud'.[19]

Apart from London there had, in the 1520s, been fifteen regional centres, with populations of 4,000–12,000; Norwich, Bristol, York, Salisbury, Exeter, Newcastle, and Coventry were the leaders in this group. Below

---

[17] *Relation . . . of the Isle of England*, 41.

[18] *Two Italian Accounts*, ed. Malfatti, 32, citing Andreas Franciscus; *The Second Book of the Travels of Nicander Nucius of Corcyra*, ed. J. A. Cranmer, Camden Soc. 17 (London, 1841), 10; below, p. 18, for information on Nucius.

[19] *Relation . . . of the Isle of England*, 42; *Two Italian Accounts*, ed. Malfatti, 34.

them were about eighteen substantial towns with populations between 3,000 and 4,000, and a further group of about fifty whose inhabitants numbered between 2,000 and 3,000. Many market-towns had fewer than 2,000 inhabitants and would today be regarded as villages. The great majority of English towns were in the midlands, the south, and the east; in the north only York, Newcastle, Durham, Carlisle, and Hull were of any importance. Most provincial towns had been in decline for several decades before the death of Henry VIII: the phrase 'sore decayed' is reiterated throughout Leland's account of his travels. Poor harvests and high prices, plague, the decline of the urban textile industry, and the competition of London all helped to reduce the wealth of most medium-sized and small towns, making them less attractive to the immigrants on whom they depended to keep up their populations. There were a few exceptions: Hull, in Leland's words, 'waxed very rich' and Newcastle upon Tyne immediately impressed him: 'the strength and magnificence of the walling of this town far passeth all the walls of the cities of England and of most of the towns of Europe'. Some of the small textile towns were also prospering. Trowbridge, said Leland, 'flourished by drapery';[20] Lavenham, with a small population, was enriched by the huge fortune of the Spring family. Yet these were rare exceptions in the middle of the sixteenth century, although in its last quarter some provincial towns began to grow and prosper. But London maintained its dominance throughout.

Of the buildings in early Tudor England foreign observers were most struck by the churches. 'There is not a parish church in the Kingdom so mean as not to possess crucifixes, candlesticks, censers, patens and cups of silver . . .', wrote the Venetian ambassador.[21] The church plate was to disappear soon after the accession of Edward VI, sold by the parish authorities or confiscated by the Crown. In London eighty-nine parishes had sold between them £10,000 worth of church goods before the confiscation began, effective confirmation of the Venetian's comment. Little of this survives for our own eyes. Yet the splendour of the buildings is still to be seen in villages like Lavenham and Long Melford—where the wealth of the cloth industry had enabled local men to build superb perpendicular churches— in Henry VII's chapel at Westminster with its elaboration of fan vaulting, and in the cathedrals which had long dominated urban landscapes. But by 1547 some great ecclesiastical buildings had been destroyed. The Venetian ambassador in 1554 reported that London 'is much disfigured by the ruins of a multitude of churches and monasteries belonging heretofore to friars and nuns': these 'bare, ruin'd quiers' had no romantic appeal for him. Many

[20] Leland, *Itinerary*, v. 60, i. 136.   [21] *Relation . . . of the Isle of England*, 29.

of the abbeys had been deliberately razed to the ground, at great cost and with considerable difficulty, by a government that was anxious to render them uninhabitable. Others suffered from the greed of local men, seeking cheap building materials. One of these, rebuked by his son, defended himself with this reply: 'What should I do? Might not I as well as others have some profit of the spoil of the Abbey? For I did see all would away; and therefore I did what others did.' Some abbeys had been saved by conversion to other uses: at Malmesbury, said Leland, 'the whole lodgings of the abbey be now longing [i.e. belonging] to one Stump, an exceeding rich clothier that bought them of the King' and had filled them with 'looms to weave cloth'.[22]

The castles of English noblemen were also crumbling. Except in the north of England many had already been taken over by the Crown, which maintained a few, but allowed the majority to fall into ruin. Landowners, too, were now less interested than before in preserving bleak and draughty fortifications. Leland comments on the large numbers of decaying castles: at Kimbolton, for instance, he records that Sir Richard Wingfield 'builded new fair lodgings and galleries upon the old foundations of the castle'.[23] The most impressive secular buildings of the early Tudor period were royal palaces: Henry VII's palace of Richmond, Hampton Court, begun by Wolsey and completed by Henry VIII, and above all Nonsuch in Surrey, where Henry destroyed a whole village in order to erect the most sumptuous Renaissance palace in England. Next to the royal palaces the most splendid dwellings were episcopal residences. Leland counted seven houses belonging to the Bishop of Durham, failing to notice an eighth. The palace at Bishop Auckland particularly impressed him with 'its divers pillars of black marble, speckled with white, and [an] exceeding fair great chamber'.[24] As the castles of England began to crumble, the age of country-house building was beginning: Layer Marney in Essex, Hengrave Hall in Suffolk, Compton Wynyates in Warwickshire, and many other mansions already ornamented the landscape by 1547. But the great surge of private building was still to come: the massive prodigy houses of the courtiers were built on fortunes made under Edward VI and Elizabeth; and the profits of landownership and farming were converted into the manors and farm-houses of Elizabethan and Jacobean England. Even before the accession of Henry VII, better-off farmers had begun to build substantial houses, and by

[22] Margaret Aston, 'English ruins and English history', *Journal of the Warburg and Courtauld Institute*, 36 (1973), *passim*; Leland, *Itinerary*, i. 132.

[23] Leland, *Itinerary*, i. 2.

[24] Felicity Heal, *Of Prelates and Princes: A Study of the Economic and Social Position of the English Episcopate* (Cambridge, 1980), 40.

the reign of Elizabeth these houses, together with the grander edifices of magnates and gentlemen, were new features of a landscape which in most other respects was largely unchanging.

Until the sixteenth century only the larger buildings of England and Wales—cathedrals, churches, castles, palaces, and a few manor houses— were constructed of stone. Most houses, certainly the homes of the lesser gentry, yeomen, and husbandmen, were timber framed, with an infill of mud, plaster, wattle, and occasionally brick. Today half-timbered houses are looked upon as a rarity, found only in regions where trees, in particular oaks, survived the depredations of recent centuries, principally in the eastern and south-eastern counties and in the west. But until the end of the sixteenth century the supply of timber was sufficient over most of the country to construct a whole range of houses from simple cruck-built dwellings—some of them still visible in Herefordshire—to post-and-truss or box-frame houses. Some of these houses were immensely elaborate, with intricate and profuse carvings, others were no more than temporary hovels, which had to be rebuilt in every generation. Until the middle of the sixteenth century brick buildings were rare: even town houses were made with wooden frames and consequently vulnerable to fire. Hull was remarkable and remarked upon by Leland for a town wall 'made all of brick, as most parts of the houses of the town . . . was'.[25] The brick buildings of the fifteenth century—Eton College and Tattershall Castle, Lincolnshire, for instance—are memorable for their rarity. In the first half of the sixteenth century brick was more often used in large manor houses, to splendid effect at Compton Wynyates; and in the second half elaborate polychromatic effects were produced, as in the Second Court at St John's College, Cambridge, while in some counties, Berkshire for example, brick building became common in the market towns. Stone for cathedrals, churches, castles, and palaces was usually quarried locally and gave these great buildings their particular regional quality: the golden oolite limestone of the Cotswolds and of Oxford, resplendent in its colleges; the red Devonian sandstones of Shropshire and Cheshire; the flint of Suffolk, Berkshire, and Hampshire.

No picture of Tudor England should be confined to the land. The large coastline was broken by dozens of little creeks and harbours, in addition to such major ports as Newcastle, Hull, Lynn, Yarmouth, Dover, Southampton, Exeter, Bristol, and, above all, London. English fishermen from the south-west were sailing far into the Atlantic during the fifteenth century. The export trade in wool and cloth ensured that the port of

[25] Leland, *Itinerary*, i. 47.

London was crowded with ships. Coastal trade from one English port to another was an essential artery of economic life: in this connection the sea has been well described as 'merely a river round England, a river with peculiar dangers, peculiar conditions and peculiar advantages'.[26] In the east-coast ports alone there were 240 ships in 1544, most of them relatively small, below 100 tons. In Cornwall, according to Richard Carew, there were 'cock-boats for passengers, sein-boats for taking of pilchard, fisher-boats for the coast, barges for sand, lighters for burden, and barks and ships for traffic'. In the first half of the sixteenth century England had lagged behind in the search for new lands. The promising start made by Cabot's voyages had not been followed up and one English entrepreneur lamented to Henry VIII that 'of the four parts of the world, it seemeth that three parts are discovered by other princes'.[27] However, by 1547 England was poised to enter the great surge of exploration.

There was a constant movement of information, people and goods within sixteenth-century England. News could be sent surprisingly quickly: on the death of Elizabeth, Sir Robert Carey, with a relay of post-horses stationed for him along the route, reached Edinburgh from London in three days, averaging about 150 miles each day. His achievement was an exceptional response to exceptional circumstances. Yet even in normal times royal couriers could bring a letter from Plymouth to London in two days, from Dover to London in twenty-four hours. Couriers moved rapidly, changing horses as they went, although ordinary travellers would consider twenty or thirty miles a day a reasonable stint. There was a well-established system of roads—rough, muddy, and unsurfaced, admittedly—mostly radiating out from London. Hostile comments on these abound: 'a foul and noisome slough'; 'so gulled with the fall of water that passengers cannot pass'; 'very noisome and tedious to travel'. But in spite of the discomforts and hazards of travel men and women of all classes were willing to undergo its hardships, and the poor quality of the roads may have been the result of greater use. The royal Court went regularly on stately progress. Nobles and the richer gentlemen moved from one residence to another and made prolonged visits to London. Carriers and chapmen took goods from place to place, early in the century by packhorse, but increasingly after 1550 by wagon and cart. Young men and women travelled from country parishes to the towns in the hope of social betterment, while the destitute wandered along the roads in a desperate attempt to stay alive. Probably the least mobile groups were the lesser gentry and the yeomen

[26] T. S. Willan, *River Navigation in England* (Oxford, 1936), 5.
[27] Richard Carew, *The Survey of Cornwall*, ed. F. E. Halliday (London, 1953), 112; *TED* ii. 21.

farmers. Those above and below them in the social scale were often on the move in pursuit of patronage, entertainment, lawsuits, trade, employment, and charity.

The movement of goods was much slower. Heavy commodities like grain, wool, and coal were more cheaply transported by river or by sea than over land. But travel by water was slow: it took two weeks for a ship to reach London from Newcastle. Rivers complemented the road system as a means of transport: in the second half of the sixteenth century there were 685 miles of navigable rivers. For most people the important journey was the regular trip to the local market with their produce: most corn-growing villages lay within six miles of their nearest market. Livestock, driven on the hoof, could be moved more easily than produce, and the average radius for the catchment area of a cattle market was eleven miles, although in some regions people might travel forty miles or more with their animals. Yet drovers were also taking cattle over much longer distances from the upland zone to midland markets like Coventry, Northampton, and Market Harborough, where they were fattened and then driven on to London.

Such was the general appearance of England in 1547: more densely inhabited by sheep than by men; its countryside intricately varied; a pre-dominantly rural landscape with only one great city; its major buildings of locally quarried stone, the others of timber; the sea a passage round its coasts and a route to the wider world.

Ireland was an alien country to sixteenth-century Englishmen. Fynes Moryson, secretary to the Lord Deputy of Ireland, wrote that 'the land . . . is uneven, mountainous, soft, watery, woody, and open to winds and floods of rain, and so fenny as it has bogs upon the very tops of mountains, not bearing man or beast, but dangerous to pass'.[28] Yet it had its attractions. Thomas Smith, writing to encourage colonial settlement, de-scribed Ireland as a land 'that floweth with milk and honey, a fertile soil truly if there be any in Europe, whether it be manured to corn or left to grass'.[29] English soldiers and settlers were drawn to the land but repelled by its people. To Edmund Spenser it was a country to which gods and god-desses had once resorted:

> In her sweet streams, Diana used oft
> (After her sweatie chace and toilsome play)

[28] Fynes Moryson, *A Description of Ireland*, cited in H. Morley (ed.), *Ireland under Elizabeth and James I* (1890), 419; David Beers Quinn, *The Elizabethans and the Irish* (Ithaca, NY, 1966), 76.   [29] Quinn, *Elizabethans and the Irish*, 58.

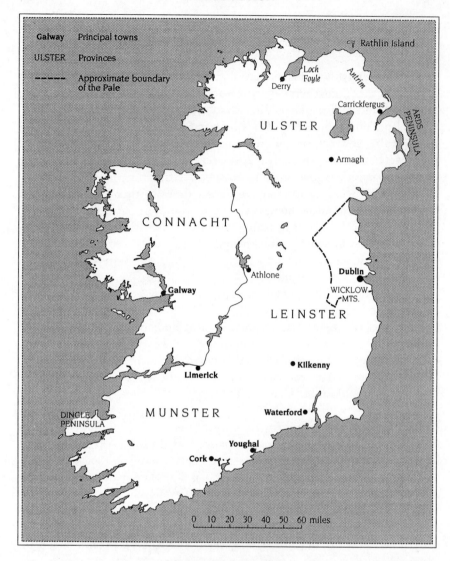

MAP 3. Tudor Ireland

> To bathe her selfe; and after, on the soft
> And downy grass, her dainty limbs to lay
> In covert shade . . .

Then everything went wrong. The 'foolish god', Faunus, saw Diana naked and she at once departed from Ireland in fury, laying a curse upon the island:

to weet, that Wolves, where she was wont to space,
Should harbour'd be, and all those Woods deface,
And Thieves should rob and spoile that Coast around.[30]

Unfortunately, we depend upon English writers for descriptions of Ireland in the Tudor century; and they saw the country with the eyes of soldiers and colonists. To soldiers Ireland was a theatre of war obstructed by inhospitable mountains, lakes, bogs, and thick woods; to settlers it was an Arcadia poorly cultivated by 'rude' inhabitants. Certainly, the people were few in number: probably a little over 1 million in 1600, at a density of 20 to the square mile compared with 50 in England. While cultivation was not so neglected as the English made out, the region north and west of a line drawn from Carrickfergus through Athlone to Limerick, the Gaelic world, was predominantly pastoral. Settlements were scattered, and live-stock was moved from place to place according to the practice of 'booleying', or transhumance, going up to the higher pastures in summer. The herds of cattle were reputedly very large: the Earl of Tyrone was alleged to possess 120,000 milking cows in the 1590s, with even larger numbers of 'barren kine'. Although there was some arable land, mainly producing oats, the Gaelic diet consisted largely of dairy products and meat.[31]

The south and east of Ireland was not dissimilar to parts of England, except in the wild regions of south-west Munster and in the Wicklow mountains that loom still over Dublin and were then the territories of Gaelic chiefs. In the Pale, southern Wexford, Kilkenny, and Tipperary mixed farming predominated, organized in the manorial system, with wheat as the principal crop.[32] Irish towns were much smaller than their English counterparts; and the Irish were, even more than the English, a rural people. Apart from Kilkenny, all the towns were on the coast: Dublin, Waterford, Youghal, Cork, Limerick, Galway. Ulster had virtually no towns in 1600, apart from the decayed city of Armagh and the military settlement of Carrickfergus. Even Dublin was still small and undeveloped: one observer described it as similar but inferior to Bristol.[33]

[30] Edmund Spenser, *Poetical Works*, ed. J. C. Smith and E. de Selincourt (Oxford, 1912), 394–400: *Two Cantos of Mutabilitie*, vi. stanzas 42, 55.

[31] See Map 3.

[32] The Pale was the area surrounding Dublin in which the writ of the English government generally ran: it consisted of the five counties of Dublin, Meath, Louth, Kildare, and Westmeath.

[33] Below, Ch. 3, s. 4, for the political situation in Ireland; Ch. 6, for a more detailed account of English society; and Ch. 13, for a discussion of overseas enterprise. I have omitted Scotland from this survey, since it was then a foreign country.

2. THE EVIDENCE

During the sixteenth century, especially in its latter half, the materials for writing the history of England became more abundant than before. Most of the main sources later used by medievalists continued to be produced, some of them greatly expanded in volume and detail, while new types of evidence became available. The topographical survey of the country just attempted was made possible partly by the observations of foreign and native travellers. Such observations had been made in earlier times, notably by Giraldus Cambrensis in the twelfth century and by William Worcester in the fifteenth; but the writers of the sixteenth century were more numerous and more thorough. The Venetian ambassador sent his masters an account of the country in 1497–8, later published as *The Relation . . . of the Isle of England*. Polydore Vergil, an Italian who came to England as a papal tax collector in 1502 and stayed until 1553, wrote a major history of Britain, the *Anglica historia*, which was prefaced by a short geographical account of the island. Nicander Nucius, a Greek who visited England with an embassy from Charles V, produced a history of the reign of Henry VIII, with a description of England itself; and subsequent ambassadors, mostly from Venice, compiled useful reports on English topography, customs, and government.[34] But most of these men saw only a small part of the country, mainly the roads from Dover to London and from London to Oxford; their descriptions of London are drawn directly from their own observation, but much of the rest is derivative. This is certainly not true of the greatest native topographer of the early Tudor period, John Leland. Between 1534 and 1543 he travelled most of England and Wales with the intention of 'seeing thoroughly all those parts of this . . . opulent and ample realm', so that the glory of Britain might 'flourish through the world'. Sadly, before he had finished the work, 'by a most pitiful occasion [he] fell besides his wits', and there remains of his projected survey only eight manuscript volumes, soon to become 'moth eaten, mouldy and rotten', but happily edited with meticulous care almost four centuries later.[35] He was followed in the second half of the century by a band of dedicated topographers and historians. William Camden, founder of the Society of Antiquaries, combined scholarly enquiry with a tour of Hadrian's Wall and other monuments to produce his *Britannia* in 1586; John Stow, a London tailor, published his *Survey of London* in 1598; Christopher Saxton's atlas provided a notable panorama of the shires. Almost every county had its devoted chorographer, William

[34] *Relation . . . of the Isle of England*, *passim*; Polydore Vergil, *Anglica historia*, ed. Denys Hay, Camden Soc., 3rd ser., 74 (London, 1950), *passim*.
[35] Leland, *Itinerary*, i. introd. pp. xli, xlii, xiv.

Lambard in Kent, Richard Carew in Cornwall, George Owen in Pembrokeshire among the most eminent.

A major new category of official records was begun in 1509: the State Papers, the archives of the Secretary of State.[36] From 1558 they became increasingly voluminous, and those in the Public Record office are supplemented by the collections of William Cecil and his son, Robert, the former in the Lansdowne Manuscripts of the British Library, the latter at Hatfield House. The State Papers mostly record letters and memoranda received by the Secretary of State, less often those dispatched by him. To some extent this gap is filled by the Register of the Privy Council, begun in 1540, a letter-book of outgoing correspondence. The historian of Tudor England thus has access to a new wealth of information fed to the government in ever growing quantity as well as to much of the government's own response. Yet much of the process of policy-making is concealed in the official record, to be occasionally and only partially revealed in the gossip of courtiers and the reports of foreign ambassadors. These diplomatic dispatches, contained in the State Papers Spanish and Venetian, and in French archives, provide valuable and sometimes vivid information: but they need to be used with care, for ambassadors usually had a distorted vision of English affairs and were often supplied with carefully doctored intelligence.

The records of Parliament became significantly fuller in the second half of the century. The House of Lords' Journals were well established by the time the Journals of the House of Commons began in 1547; they were both to develop gradually into comprehensive records of proceedings. From 1563 no parliamentary session is without at least one private diary of its debates, adding colour and detail to the official account. These do, however, tempt the historian into concentrating upon the 'newsworthy' items selected by the diarist, to the detriment of equally important, but less dramatic, aspects of business, such as legislation. The records of lawcourts, substantial for the Middle Ages, became even more voluminous in the sixteenth century. To the archives of King's Bench and Common Pleas were added those of Star Chamber, Requests, Chancery, and Exchequer at the centre, Quarter Sessions and assizes in the shires. Because they are in English and less wedded to medieval formulas, the proceedings of Star Chamber dramatically illuminate some of the feuds and disputes of the period. Like parliamentary diaries they have until lately drawn attention away from the less accessible records of the older courts. However, the great series of law reports, beginning with those of Justice Spelman in the reign

---

[36] On source-material, G. R. Elton, *England 1200–1640*, in the series *The Sources of History* (London, 1969), *passim*. The State Papers for the period after 1547 were divided in the nineteenth century into the two categories of foreign and domestic.

of Henry VIII and culminating with those of Edward Coke, helps to redress the balance.

In the course of the century the English, especially well-to-do males, became more literate. Not only could about 30 per cent of men sign their names in 1600, but reading books and writing letters was by then a natural part of life for gentry and merchants. Fifteenth-century England has been illuminated for us by some great collections of family letters, especially those of the Pastons, Stonors, and Celys, but these are a precious rarity. The reign of Henry VIII is documented by the superb volumes of Lisle letters, but there are few other major private collections.[37] By the second half of the century, however, scarcely a county in England does not yield up a rich hoard of family correspondence, and there are five or six valuable series for Wales. Pre-eminent among them all are the letters and papers of Nathaniel Bacon of Stiffkey in Norfolk, running to about 4,000 documents for the years 1562–1622.[38] To these family archives can be added the letters written by courtiers like Rowland White, John Chamberlain, and Michael Hickes, which document the personalities and politics of the royal Court. In the last twenty years of Elizabeth's reign the production of official, semi-official, and private papers suddenly became abundant. We know far more about political and social affairs for the period from 1580 to 1603 than for the previous forty years.

This later period saw the creation of the English professional theatre, the production of the plays of Shakespeare, Marlowe, and their rivals, and the writing of such great epics as Edmund Spenser's *The Faerie Queene* and Philip Sidney's *Arcadia*. Literary sources are notoriously difficult to use as historical evidence: the dramatic and the unusual are too easily and too often mistaken for the normal. Yet, carefully approached, plays and poems can reveal the attitudes and feelings of Elizabethan writers and the society to which they belonged. We can also know what many Elizabethans looked like—or wanted to look like. From Holbein's day onwards portraiture caught the eye of fashion. Much of the work produced by his successors is crude and wooden, but such foreign visitors as Eworth, the Gheeraerts, and the de Gritzes painted portraits of high quality, while English artists, led by Nicholas Hillyard and Isaac Oliver, triumphed in the art of the miniature.

Surprisingly, perhaps, the advances in literacy were not matched by advances in numeracy. The men of the sixteenth century were little, if at all, more numerate than their medieval predecessors. Partly for that reason, partly through the inadequacies of government machinery, the statistics

---

[37] *The Lisle Letters*, ed. M. St C. Byrne (6 vols., Chicago, 1981), *passim*.

[38] In process of being edited by A. Hassell Smith and others for the Centre of East Anglian Studies and the Norfolk Record Society.

that they produced were primitive and unreliable: the tax returns for Elizabeth's reign are so inaccurate as to be almost useless for measuring wealth, and customs records are seriously misleading about trading figures. The accounts of the Exchequer hide as much as they reveal about the government's finances. However, records produced for non-statistical purposes—parish registers, wills, and inventories—are more amenable to quantitative analysis. The government first ordered parish registers to be kept in 1538, and they survive in growing numbers from about 1550. Wills and inventories had been made since the early Middle Ages, but were few in number until the sixteenth century: then 'the thin stream . . . became a flood when the authority of the state was placed behind that of the Church'.[39] Parish registers have allowed the use of sophisticated techniques in historical demography, while wills and their accompanying inventories make possible an assessment of the living standards of all but the very poor.

Historians of the later sixteenth century have many advantages denied to their medieval colleagues. They can discover more about the processes of politics and government. Social and political life in the localities is revealed by new kinds of evidence. Literature opens windows on attitudes and aspirations; portraiture upon image and appearance. Parish registers and wills provide the raw material for reconstructing the fundamental progression of birth, copulation, and death. One source of evidence is rare in the sixteenth century, but becomes common in the seventeenth: diaries and autobiographies. Ralph Josselin, Samuel Pepys, and John Evelyn have few counterparts in the Elizabethan age. In consequence there are virtually no men or women whom we can know with real intimacy.

3. 1547–1603: AN OVERVIEW

The fifty-six years between the death of Henry VIII and the accession of James I began and ended with decades of tension and disturbance, decades apparently threatening to the whole English polity. Between 1547 and 1558 the rule of a boy was followed, after a brief struggle for the succession, by that of England's first queen regnant since Matilda in the twelfth century. Expensive wars against the Scots and the French undermined royal finances and robbed England of her last continental foothold, Calais. Rioting in 1548 was followed in 1549 by risings over much of England. Debasement of the coinage eroded faith in the currency. Oscillations of the export trade in cloth set off bankruptcies and unemployment. Bad harvests in 1555 and 1556 pushed the price of grain to unprecedented heights. Rapid and contradictory changes in religious doctrine and liturgy provoked opposition from

[39] M. W. Barley, *The English Farmhouse and Cottage* (London, 1961), 39.

Catholic and Protestant zealots, while the Church's standing sank in the eyes of a bewildered population.

During the last decade of the century the government again faced the combined assaults of war, inflation, religious contention, and harvest failure. England was fully committed to war against Spain, whose rebuilt navy seemed to present a constant threat of invasion; expeditionary forces had to be dispatched to the aid of our allies in France and the Low Countries. By 1598 rebellion in Ireland had gathered such powerful momentum that the island seemed likely to be lost to the Crown. The government's continuous demands for taxation and for troops provoked protests from the shires, already discontented at the corruption of royal agents. The Church was threatened on both flanks, by Protestant radicals and by the agents of the Counter-Reformation. At Court the stable balance of factions appeared to be upset by the increasingly acrimonious disputes between the Cecils and the Earl of Essex, disputes which ended only with the Earl's execution in 1601.

Yet neither decade inflicted serious and lasting damage on the social and political order. The risings of 1549 were quelled without undue difficulty. The overthrow of Somerset was accomplished without bloodshed. Northumberland's attempt to divert the succession collapsed with only a hint of civil war. Mary's regime, although hardly popular, achieved most of its initial objectives and never looked, even at the end, in danger of being overthrown. The harvests of the mid-1550s and the mid-1590s inflicted terrible sufferings upon the poor, but nowhere in England set off the large-scale risings that terrified landowners and governments in the rest of Europe during those decades. Elizabeth crushed the Presbyterian movement and effectively contained the Catholic threat, while Essex's revolt collapsed into black comedy in twenty-four hours. The shires, in spite of their grumbling, produced the money and the men required for war; both the O'Neill revolt and a Spanish expeditionary force were defeated and Ireland was subjugated—for the time being. Above all, the succession crisis at the death of Elizabeth was solved dextrously and peacefully.

Yet until James Stewart ascended the throne in 1603, the problem of the succession had hung over late Tudor England. Under all three monarchs from 1547, the legal heir to the throne was known to be hostile to the religious stance of the incumbent. Mary and Elizabeth each reversed the ecclesiastical settlements that they found on their accession; and for thirty years Elizabeth's closest heir was a Catholic, Mary Stewart. After her death in 1587, the succession lay open and undecided. Although there was a general presumption that James would succeed, no one could be certain of this. It is a tribute to the stability of the regime and the skill of the ruling clique that civil war was averted and that James succeeded without question or disturbance.

His accession, following soon after the defeat of the Irish rebels, marked the end, but not for long, of the British Problem—the dangers from Ireland and Scotland—which had troubled English rulers for centuries. Under Edward VI, and in the early years of Elizabeth, Scotland was the more serious threat. The Privy Council was preoccupied with the French presence in Scotland and with the security of the northern border. From 1570, however, French influence in Scotland was reduced and the Protestant lords established a hold—if occasionally a weak one—upon the country. With the execution of Mary Stewart and the achievement of effective government in Scotland by her son, James VI, the problem of the north was confined to lawlessness and raiding. James's interest in the English throne was too strong to allow him to be tempted into any flirtation with Elizabeth's enemies. But while the Scottish problem was on the way to solution, during the second half of Elizabeth's reign the Irish question became more intractable and dangerous. The bellicose policy of the English government under Edward VI and Mary, combined with the insensitive enforcement of the Protestant settlement upon the Irish, drew together both the Anglo-Irish and the Gaelic lords into hostility to the Crown and alliance with the Counter-Reformation. Conquest and colonization under Elizabeth ignited a series of risings, culminating in the Tyrone rebellion and the Spanish landing at Kinsale. With Mountjoy's victory and the surrender of the Ulster lords, all Ireland was—for the moment—subjected to English domination. The British Problem seemed to be solved; but events between 1638 and 1642 were to show that the solution was temporary and incomplete. In effect the problem had changed rather than disappeared.

Although religious differences divided Englishmen under Edward, Mary, and Elizabeth, the nation was prepared, in 1549, 1553, and 1559, to acquiesce in the form of worship imposed by the monarch. England in 1558 was certainly not Protestant, but the Anglican settlement was enforced effectively enough in the next forty-five years to ensure that on the death of Elizabeth there could be no return to Roman Catholicism. Although the Church of England seemed to many a long way from being the reformed Church of their aspirations, it had won the loyalty of the political nation. Archbishop Laud and James II were both to find that the fabric of the Church could not be altered and that the religious reversals accomplished by the later Tudors had become impossible in the seventeenth century. Fear and hatred of popery dominated the attitudes of most Englishmen and by 1603 Catholics themselves had come to accept the Protestant establishment.

The Protestant triumph was largely confined to the ruling élite and the more prosperous classes. This did not mean that its effects were superficial, for the Reformation fundamentally altered the attitudes of many towards religion. The Bible and Foxe's *Book of Martyrs* (first published in English in 1563) were widely read and provided a common culture, at least for the literate. The availability of books made possible the household worship which complemented the traditional liturgy. The influence of the laity over ecclesiastical affairs became stronger. Having acquired impropriated livings with their monastic estates, landowners held the right of presentation to many benefices. Secular courts and lay commissioners gained increasing hold over the enforcement of the religious settlement, while bishops and other clerical officers lost authority. The clergy ceased to be a group set apart from the rest of society, the celibate guardians of ritual. They were being assimilated into lay society, increasingly taking on the characteristics of a profession. Their principal task was to teach their flocks the truths of Christianity by word and example, rather than to perform the miraculous transformation of bread and wine into the body and blood of Christ: they were now essentially pastors. Officially at least this change in the status of the clergy was accompanied by the suppression of the 'magical' elements in religion and by the elimination of religious ritual from secular life. The saints were deprived of their special functions; the ties between the agrarian year and the Christian calendar were loosened; civic ceremonies lost their religious attributes. However, although the Protestant Church was firmly established at the official level, its influence over the population at large is harder to assess. Probably the majority of educated people genuinely accepted it; but the response of humbler men and women varied. Attendance at church was often irregular and many of the poor had only vague notions of basic Christian teaching: magic, witchcraft, and superstition were still common. Nevertheless, by the end of the century Protestant teaching was making some headway among the less well-to-do, at least in those towns and villages fortunate enough to have devout and active ministers.

Compared with the momentous upheavals in religion, the institutions of central government were relatively stable and unchanging between 1547 and 1603. Authority over government finance, dispersed among several departments under Henry VIII, was largely concentrated into the hands of the Exchequer under Edward VI and Mary; but control of revenue and expenditure, though more stringent than it had been before the reforms of Thomas Cromwell, remained loose. The Privy Council, established as the central agency of executive government in the 1530s and 1540s, regained that position after some uncertainty in the early years of Edward VI. The office of Secretary of State, raised to pre-eminence by Cromwell, lost ground under his successors, but was restored to its dominant role under William Cecil. Parliament, considered by some historians to have acquired under Mary and Elizabeth new powers and greater ambitions, changed little in procedure, organization, or authority during those reigns. We know more about its debates, but that should not deceive us into thinking it more important than before. Nor should we regard it as primarily a constitutional check upon the Crown. As an opposition it was less effective than it had been in the fourteenth and fifteenth centuries. In the second half of the sixteenth it continued to operate, as it had done under Henry VIII, as an element in the large co-operative system of government. The crucial feature of the central government was the long period of stability under Elizabeth: continuity was as important as reform in establishing an effective machine.

Changes were more apparent and more significant at the level of local government. With the gradual establishment of lieutenancies from 1549 onwards, the military government of the shires acquired a permanent command structure which it had previously lacked. The Lords Lieutenant began to take over general supervision of county government, collecting loans and enforcing order. Other commissions were devised for specific tasks: the discovery of recusants, the suppression of piracy, and so on. The tasks of local rulers became heavier and more complex, but they were not all laid upon the shoulders of the justices of the peace. A diversified system of local rule emerged, with the formal and the informal, the permanent and the *ad hoc* agencies operating together.

This reorganization of county government was accompanied by a diffusion of regional and local power. The great magnates who had dominated much of England at the beginning of the century were weaker than they had been by 1547; in 1603 they were fewer and weaker still. Many great houses disappeared; others were robbed of their local powers; others chose to exercise their influence at Court rather than in the shires. County government fell increasingly into the hands of groups of gentry families, who often squabbled among themselves for pre-eminence.[40]

In 1547 the country was already experiencing the inflationary pressures that continued for another century. Initially they seemed threatening to property owners as well as to the poor. But from about 1570 landowners found ways of increasing their revenues, especially their rents, more rapidly than prices. For squires and yeomen the next fifty years were a golden age:

[40] See Maps 4 and 5.

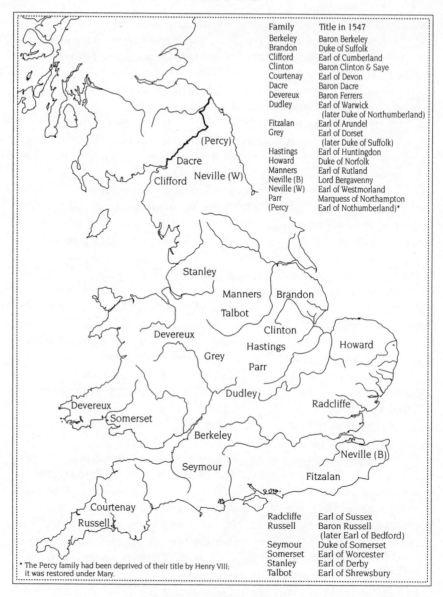

Family	Title in 1547
Berkeley	Baron Berkeley
Brandon	Duke of Suffolk
Clifford	Earl of Cumberland
Clinton	Baron Clinton & Saye
Courtenay	Earl of Devon
Dacre	Baron Dacre
Devereux	Baron Ferrers
Dudley	Earl of Warwick
	(later Duke of Northumberland)
Fitzalan	Earl of Arundel
Grey	Earl of Dorset
	(later Duke of Suffolk)
Hastings	Earl of Huntingdon
Howard	Duke of Norfolk
Manners	Earl of Rutland
Neville (B)	Lord Bergavenny
Neville (W)	Earl of Westmorland
Parr	Marquess of Northampton
(Percy	Earl of Nothumberland)*

Radcliffe	Earl of Sussex
Russell	Baron Russell
	(later Earl of Bedford)
Seymour	Duke of Somerset
Somerset	Earl of Worcester
Stanley	Earl of Derby
Talbot	Earl of Shrewsbury

* The Percy family had been deprived of their title by Henry VIII;
it was restored under Mary.

MAP 4. Principal noble families in 1547

rents were high, prices were good, wages were low. But the poorer members of society were vulnerable to the increase in population and prices; low wages lagged behind high prices. Although a combination of domestic industry, agricultural wages, and the produce of smallholdings enabled

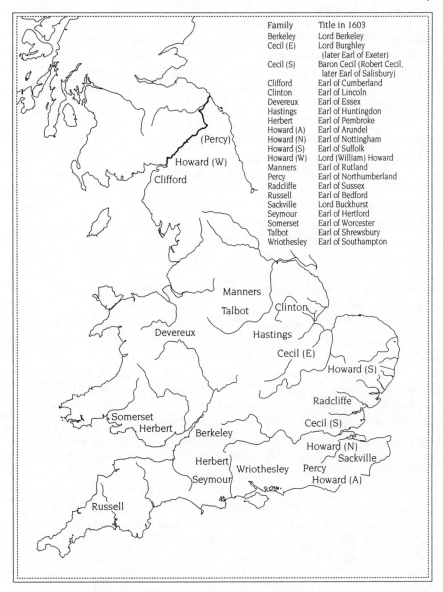

Family	Title in 1603
Berkeley	Lord Berkeley
Cecil (E)	Lord Burghley (later Earl of Exeter)
Cecil (S)	Baron Cecil (Robert Cecil, later Earl of Salisbury)
Clifford	Earl of Cumberland
Clinton	Earl of Lincoln
Devereux	Earl of Essex
Hastings	Earl of Huntingdon
Herbert	Earl of Pembroke
Howard (A)	Earl of Arundel
Howard (N)	Earl of Nottingham
Howard (S)	Earl of Suffolk
Howard (W)	Lord (William) Howard
Manners	Earl of Rutland
Percy	Earl of Northumberland
Radcliffe	Earl of Sussex
Russell	Earl of Bedford
Sackville	Lord Buckhurst
Seymour	Earl of Hertford
Somerset	Earl of Worcester
Talbot	Earl of Shrewsbury
Wriothesley	Earl of Southampton

MAP 5. Principal noble families in 1603

some labourers to achieve a fair level of subsistence, for many the outlook was harsh: uncertain employment, recurrent harvest failures, and the onset of disease all contributed to misery. The differences of wealth and poverty were accentuated. A growing diversity of manufactures testified to the beginnings of a consumer society, in which the families of landowners, prosperous yeomen, professional men, merchants, and shopkeepers were living more comfortable lives than before. At the same time, smallholders and urban workers were in many cases forced into a degrading dependence and poverty. The age of the country house was also the age of the poor laws.

The growing gulf between rich and poor was matched by an increasing contrast between London and the provincial towns. During the first half of the sixteenth century London grew in riches and in numbers, while many of the provincial manufacturing and trading centres, like York and Coventry, were in decline. The growth of London continued under the later Tudors until by 1600 it was ten times the size of its nearest rival and its population had risen to about 150,000. Finance, trade, government, law, drama, the royal Court, and fashionable society were increasingly focused upon London, which became an urban community totally unlike any other in England and equalled only by half a dozen cities in the rest of Europe. Other towns had begun some recovery under Elizabeth, but their modest prosperity could not match the riches and influence of the capital.

English society, at least in its upper reaches, was becoming educated and literate. The sons of nobles, gentlemen, clergy, and merchants were going in greater numbers than before to the universities and the Inns of Court. The printing industry, concentrated in London, Oxford, and Cambridge, produced a growing volume of books, pamphlets, and broadsheets. The outlook of the landowning classes was reflected in their patronage of theatrical companies and country-house poets. The concentration of population in London and the growing sophistication of that population provided an audience for writers and for the theatre. As the traditional mystery plays of the provincial towns died, the professional theatre of London rose like a phoenix. However, education was not confined to the capital or to the propertied classes: there was a substantial increase in the number of 'petty schools' and grammar schools in the second half of the sixteenth century, especially in southern England; and even some smallholders and artisans were reading the works of popular history and religion produced by the printing presses.

Relations between England and the rest of the world were changing. The death of Henry VIII saw the effective end of English attempts to recover a European empire, although the campaign that he began dragged on for a few more years. In 1558 England lost Calais, the last remnant of her possessions in France and the traditional outlet for exports of raw wool. Between 1551 and 1585 Antwerp, the principal staple for English trade in manufactured cloth, declined. In consequence, English merchants began to look further afield for their trade, and commercial links were developed with Russia, the Baltic, North Africa, the Near East, Asia, and the Americas. Explorers opened the routes to distant lands, while cartographers and travellers increased English awareness of a wider world. As word spread of the riches of the Spanish and Portuguese empires, adventurous sea captains penetrated their commercial monopolies. The Iberian powers, whose geographical position had favoured them in the early stages of European exploration and expansion, were unable to repel the intruders. The voyages of Hawkins and Drake were only the most celebrated of countless enterprises.

While Elizabethan sailors pioneered new openings for English trade and laid the foundations for England's navy, her first and most important line of defence, on land England could put into the field only small and poorly equipped armies, puny beside the might of the Habsburgs. At sea English ships were a match for any hostile fleet; but the English navy was essentially a joint-stock concern formed from the ships of the Queen, the merchants, and the privateers. The switch of English power from landed to naval forces was of immense consequence for the future; but the significance of English seafarers in Elizabeth's reign can easily be overrated. Long-distance trade with the Near East and with Asia was considerably more glamorous than the established commerce with northern Europe; but in 1600 it was still much less important in bulk and in value. The Elizabethan plans to found English colonies in Ireland and in America were imaginative and exciting; yet they were mostly failures. Elaborate schemes were formed to colonize south-west Ireland in the 1580s, but few English farmers were willing to transport their families to that unwelcoming and poverty-stricken land. An American colony established at Roanoke Island in the 1580s had disappeared without trace by 1590. Only under James I were permanent plantations established in Ireland and colonies built in America.

The contest with Spain was more immediately successful. In 1547 Spain was still England's natural ally, France her traditional enemy. Although there was evident hostility to the Spanish King and his entourage under Mary, the alignment of English policy remained little changed until about 1568. Then English diplomacy gradually became hostile to Spain, while seeking alliance with the French. Fear that Philip II would establish absolute rule in the Low Countries drew England into the European conflict and in 1585 Elizabeth was forced reluctantly into open, though limited, war. The English role remained primarily naval and defensive. In spite of the massively greater resources of Spain, English arms were successful in ward-ing off invasion. By 1598 the Spanish were beginning to withdraw from their burdensome military commitments, and by the death of Elizabeth it was evident that peace was at hand. England had survived a series of major onslaughts from the most powerful state in Europe.

CHAPTER 2

The Rule of Protector Somerset

1. THE HENRICIAN INHERITANCE

When Henry VIII died in the early hours of Friday 28 January 1547 he had dominated his kingdom for thirty-eight years. Most members of his own generation were dead and few could remember England without this masterful and unscrupulous political giant, under whose rule immense changes were brought about in government, Church, and society. The ecclesiastical apparatus of the realm was brought under royal control in the 1530s. Convocation surrendered its capacity to enact ecclesiastical laws without the consent of the Crown; the pope was deprived of his jurisdiction, revenues, and authority, which were transferred to the king, now 'Supreme Head in earth of the Church of England'; archbishops and bishops became the servants of their monarch as well as of their Maker; and monastic houses and friaries were dissolved, their riches seized by the Crown, which was able for a time to double its revenue. Although Henry disavowed any sympathy with heresy, every parish was ordered to purchase a copy of the Great Bible in English, and reforming divines like Thomas Cranmer were promoted to high office.

The monarch's control over his subjects was tightened by a series of important statutes. An Act of 1534 declared it treason to 'pronounce the King our sovereign lord should be heretic, schismatic, tyrannical, infidel, or usurper', and further enacted that the mere spoken word, without any other overt act, could incur the penalties of treason.[1] Private franchises and jurisdictions were greatly reduced by a statute of 1536; the powers of Marcher lords were diminished; and the English system of county government was established in Wales.[2] In Ireland English Lord Deputies were appointed and an English garrison was stationed in the Pale. The Dublin

---

[1] 26 Henry VIII c. 13.

[2] 26 Henry VIII c. 24. Marcher lords were established along the borders of England and Wales, and in central and southern Wales. Until 1536 they had considerable independence from the Crown and wielded wide powers of jurisdiction.

administration was subordinated to London, and in 1541 Henry VIII was declared King of Ireland, where before he had been merely Lord.

Under Henry's aegis the image of monarchy acquired unprecedented grandeur. In his youth the King's superb physical presence generated the glamour which his father had lacked, and even when he was old, obese, and racked with arthritis, the impression of splendour persisted. In 1540 the chronicler Edward Hall ecstatically wrote of Henry's entry into Greenwich with the plain-looking Anne of Cleves: 'Oh, what a sight was this to see so goodly a Prince and so noble a King to ride with so fair a lady. . . . I think no creature could see them but his heart rejoiced.'³ Holbein's portraits of the monarch fixed the image of Henry for all time, while pageants, processions, and tournaments provided the lavish and living theatre in which the King played out his role. The great royal palaces—Hampton Court, Whitehall, Nonsuch—formed a magnificent backdrop to the royal presence.

In spite of this accretion of royal power and presence, Henry's last years were darkened by costly wars and vicious intrigue at Court. War with Scotland began auspiciously when James V of Scotland died of grief after the crushing English victory at Solway Moss, leaving only a six-day-old daughter, Mary Stewart, to inherit the Scottish throne. The English triumph in the field was followed by diplomatic success when the regency government of Scotland agreed to the Treaty of Greenwich, under which Mary was to marry Henry's heir, the Prince Edward, thus making possible a union of the two realms, with England as the dominant partner. These hopes were short-lived. The French, determined that Scotland should not become an English satellite, won over the Scottish Regent and persuaded him to have the treaty annulled. Successive invasions by English troops only reaffirmed Scottish hostility; and by the time of Henry's death Scotland was firmly tied to the French alliance.

Alongside his Scottish undertaking, Henry conducted a series of campaigns against France. In 1544 he led a massive army across the Channel with the proclaimed object of capturing Paris; in the event he took Boulogne but achieved nothing more. Fighting continued for a further two years, stretching the royal finances to their limit, until Henry reluctantly made peace with the French by the Treaty of Camp in 1546. The English were to keep Boulogne for eight years and then return it to the French; the Scots were to be included in the peace only if they agreed to observe the Treaty of Greenwich, which they refused to do. Henry's last wars left a legacy of foreign debt, eroded capital, debased coinage, and the enmity of both France and Scotland.

³ L. B. Smith, *Henry VIII, the Mask of Royalty* (London, 1971), 51.

Domestic dissension accompanied the pressures of war. The progress of reformed doctrines, albeit slow, produced uncertainty and dispute: Queen Catherine Parr, Archbishop Cranmer, and Bishop Gardiner of Winchester all became the targets of religious intrigues at Court. Secular rivalries played as significant, perhaps more significant, a role in conflicts at the centre of power. In the winter of 1546, as Henry's health grew more precarious, two groups of nobles and courtiers manœuvred for position. The Howards—Thomas, 3rd Duke of Norfolk, and his son Henry, Earl of Surrey—headed the oustanding noble dynasty in England. Against them were ranged Queen Catherine Parr and her brother William, Earl of Essex; Edward Seymour, Earl of Hertford, brother-in-law to Henry and maternal uncle to the young Prince Edward; Thomas Seymour, Hertford's brother; John Dudley, Lord Lisle, Admiral of England; and Sir William Paget, Secretary of State. Somewhat detached from both groups was Stephen Gardiner, Bishop of Winchester, conservative in religion, cautious in politics.

The final contest for power began in December 1546, when Norfolk and Surrey were arrested and charged with political conspiracy. Surrey was executed; his father, saved by the fortunate chance of the King's death, spent the next seven years in the Tower. A parallel attack was mounted on Gardiner for refusing to exchange land with the Crown. He went unpunished, but was forbidden access to the King. The ground was now cleared for the consolidation of power by Seymour and his allies. The 'politic shifts' by which they proceeded were conducted in the dark recesses of the Court, and especially in the Privy Chamber, its innermost sanctum. What happened can never be precisely known: historians have to make do with the most plausible conjectures from the available evidence.[4] After the fall of the Howards control at Court lay with the Seymours (Hertford and his brother), Lisle, and Paget; with Thomas Wriothesley, the Lord Chancellor; and with Sir Anthony Denny and Sir William Herbert, two gentlemen of the Privy Chamber, who controlled access to the King. Denny kept the 'dry stamp' by which Henry's signature could be applied to documents without his having to sign them himself: it was a considerable weapon. Although Wriothesley was not a committed member of any faction and Lisle was ultimately concerned with his own advancement, the others were reliable adherents of Edward Seymour. By statute Henry was empowered to decide

---

[4] H. Miller, 'Henry VIII's unwritten will', in E. W. Ives *et al.* (eds.), *Wealth and Power in Tudor England* (London, 1978), 87–105; G. R. Elton, *Reform and Reformation: England 1509–1558* (London, 1977), 328–32; E. W. Ives, 'Henry VIII's Will: a forensic conundrum', *HJ* 35 (1992), 779–804. For another interpretation see Smith, *Henry VIII*, chs. 11, 12; and on the role of the Court in politics, below, Ch. 5 s. 1.

in his will both the succession to the throne and the membership of the royal Council which would govern in Edward's name as long as he was a minor. On 26 December Henry ordered his existing will to be brought and approved a revision of it on the 30th; the will was probably then signed by the application of the dry stamp. In its final form it laid down that the throne should pass to Prince Edward, Princess Mary, and Princess Elizabeth, in that order, and then, if they had no heirs, to Lady Frances Grey, Henry's niece, and her descendants. The Stewart dynasty was implicitly excluded. On Henry's death the country was to be ruled by a Council of sixteen, who were also executors of the will; the Council should decide matters by majority vote, aided by twelve assistants. The Council contained all Edward Seymour's principal allies—Lisle, Paget, Denny, Herbert—and was 'reformist' in its religious balance: the most notable omission was the name of Stephen Gardiner.[5]

While the Seymour faction was establishing its power it also obtained more tangible rewards from the King. The evidence for this operation comes largely from depositions made by Paget, Denny, and Herbert after Henry's death, but it seems in the main to be reliable. Henry was persuaded to grant lands to the innermost courtiers and to promise them titles of nobility. Edward Seymour, for example, was to have a dukedom and estates worth £800 per annum. After Henry's death, many of the Howard lands, which the King had intended for Prince Edward, were also distributed, with Norfolk's offices, to the victorious courtiers. The operation, designed to buttress the power of Edward Seymour and his friends, and to complete the destruction of the Howards, demonstrates the tight hold exercised by the dominant faction over power at Court.[6]

When Henry died on 28 January 1547 the new Council kept his death secret for three days, closing the ports while they assumed authority. Paget, the most skilful political manager at Court, conducted the process by which Edward Seymour was made Lord Protector and governor of the young King's person. In return, as Paget later reminded him, the new Protector promised 'to follow mine advice in all your proceedings more than any other man's'.[7] The Council's appointment of a Protector was not, strictly speaking, contrary to Henry's will; indeed it was a sensible and practical step, warranted by the precedents of 1422 and 1483, when royal uncles, Humfrey of Gloucester and Richard of Gloucester, had each become Protector during the minorities of Henry VI and Edward V respectively. On 17 February new titles of nobility were bestowed on Edward Seymour, who

[5] Rymer, *Foedera*, xv. 110–17.
[6] Miller, 'Henry VIII's unwritten will', *passim*; *APC* ii. 15–22.
[7] Strype, *Ecclesiastical Memorials*, ii/2, appendix HH.

became Duke of Somerset; on Lisle, now Earl of Warwick; on Wriothesley, now Earl of Southampton; and on others. The assumption of power, and of its fruits, by the ruling clique had so far been smoothly managed, but rough going was soon encountered. Four men had taken direction of affairs, but each, in the sound judgement of the Imperial Ambassador, Francois van der Delft, aimed for his own advancement. Somerset had office and authority, but lacked personal appeal; Lisle was courageous and popular, thanks to his liberality and splendour; the other two, Paget and Wriothesley, were experienced administrators and politicians, but had not the social standing to attain supreme power.[8] Somerset could rely upon Paget, but his relations with the other two were at best uneasy.

The first squall came early in February, when Somerset's ambitious and reckless brother, Thomas Seymour, demanded that he be appointed Governor of the young King, a position that would have given him regular access to the royal person. Somerset had already reserved this post for himself and, as a compromise, gave his brother a place on the Council. Possibly Thomas Seymour had been put up to make his claim by Warwick, in the hope of securing his own progress by making bad blood between the brothers. Of that we cannot be sure; but relations between them were from that day uneasy and ultimately disastrous for the younger brother. The next threat to Somerset's ambitions came from Southampton, the Lord Chancellor, who controlled the great seal, the essential instrument of authority. Although he has usually been regarded as a religious conservative, opposed to the reforming attitudes of the Protector, it is more likely that he suspected Somerset's ambitions and distrusted his abilities. Somerset quickly struck at him: soon after Henry's death, Southampton was accused of illegally issuing judicial commissions, a charge which had no substance but provided an excuse for depriving him of office. That done, Somerset secured letters patent enabling him to appoint privy councillors on his own authority. By this step, a clear breach of Henry's will, Somerset now had virtually the power of a king.[9]

2. SOMERSET AND GOVERNMENT

On his accession to the throne Edward VI was only 9 years old. Brought up until the age of 6 'among the women', as he records in his own *Chronicle*, he had then been entrusted to the care of two prominent scholars, Richard Cox and John Cheke. By the age of 8 he was capable of writing a letter in Latin

[8] *CSP Span.* ix: *1547–1549*, 18–21.
[9] A. J. Slavin, 'The fall of Lord Chancellor Wriothesley', *Albion*, 7 (1975), 265–86. D. E. Hoak, *The King's Council in the Reign of Edward VI* (Cambridge, 1976), 34–53, 231–41.

and knew by heart 'four books of Cato'. Beyond the details of his education, we know little of his character at this stage. From the moment of Henry's death Somerset made sure that the young King was kept close to himself and his formidable wife, or to his own political allies. Edward's life, after he ascended the throne, was played out mainly in the Privy Chamber, the focus of the Court's political life, to which access was closely guarded by the four principal gentlemen of the Chamber, of whom the most important was Sir Michael Stanhope, Somerset's brother-in-law. Until the Protector's fall in October 1549, Edward was a cypher in politics, exercising little influence of his own. He was like the king on a chessboard, having small room for manœuvre, but crucial to the development of the game. Control of his person determined the possession of power.[10]

Although Somerset's claims to the Protectorship were beyond challenge, he was personally unsuited to the exercise of such high authority. Born into a Wiltshire landed family, he had risen rapidly at Court, becoming Esquire of the Body to Henry VIII in 1530. The King's marriage to Somerset's sister Jane in 1536 raised him from the rank of courtier to a viscountcy and membership of the Privy Council. During Henry's last years he had led two successful invasions into Scotland and had been made Lieutenant of the Kingdom while Henry was campaigning in France during the summer of 1544. Luck had been on his side, but so had high personal ambition and military ability. Beyond that he was ruthless and grasping. He had built up his landed estates by driving hard bargains and pursuing his claims relentlessly in the law courts. Thomas Cromwell, not himself a man easily manipulated, said of him: 'this man will be by no measures entreated'.[11] Van der Delft, writing in February 1547, commented that Somerset was 'looked down upon by everybody as a dry, sour, opinionated man'.[12] In the next two years he fully bore out that description. To those near him he was arrogant, bad-tempered, tactless, and authoritarian. Paget, acting the candid friend, urged him to listen to others and to put a curb on his tongue. Sir Richard Lee, after a rebuke from Somerset, had come to Paget's chamber weeping, 'almost out of his wits and out of heart'. 'Your Grace', wrote Paget, 'is grown in great choleric fashion, whensoever you are contraried in that which you have conceived in your head.'[13]

Having secured authority to appoint men to the Privy Council, Somerset was released by letters patent at the end of 1547 from the obligation even to secure its consent to his decisions. During 1548 and the early months of

[10] For the Privy Chamber, below, Ch. 5 s. 1; for Edward's later role in politics, below, Ch. 3 ss. 1, 2, 5.

[11] M. L. Bush, 'The Lisle-Seymour land dispute', *HJ* 9 (1966), 255–74.

[12] *CSP Span.* ix. 18–21.   [13] Strype, *Ecclesiastical Memorials*, ii/2, 427–9.

1549 he virtually ignored the Council, which he expected simply to ratify his proposals. The Protector preferred to rule through a small group of carefully chosen administrators and intellectuals, mostly dependent on himself, the most important of whom was Sir William Paget, Secretary of State at the time of Somerset's elevation to power. His skill and experience made him indispensable to Somerset, who tolerated his outspoken criticism. In June 1547 Paget, having ceased to be Secretary, had been appointed instead to the profitable but less arduous posts of Comptroller of the Household and Chancellor of the Duchy of Lancaster, and was now able to devote all his talents to politics and diplomacy. His companion as Secretary, Sir William Petre, was less influential. Excluded from the Council by Henry's will, he was restored to membership in March 1547. After Paget resigned from the secretaryship, Petre remained in sole charge of the office until the appointment of Sir Thomas Smith nine months later. Petre was a shadowy figure, essentially a political survivor, who weathered successive crises and kept his hold on office from 1544 until he resigned in 1557. His fellow secretary, Smith, appointed in April 1548, was altogether more interesting. After a distinguished academic career at Cambridge, where he taught Greek and became Professor of Civil Law, he moved into government circles in the first three months of the new reign, quickly becoming personal secretary to Somerset, Clerk to the Privy Council, and Master of Requests. He was an exceptionally able administrator and a man with profound insight into the economic problems of the time, which he analysed in his *Discourse of the Common Weal*.[14] Unfortunately he alienated many important politicians by his arrogance and never achieved the influence over Somerset which his abilities deserved. William Cecil, a more subtle politician, who became the dominant servant of the Crown under Elizabeth, first appeared as a member of Somerset's retinue during the Scottish campaign of 1547; a year later, in September 1548, he achieved his first office as personal secretary to the Protector. Little is known of his political activities at this time, but the number of his correspondents shows that he was already a man of influence. The most controversial member of Somerset's entourage was John Hales, an outspoken proponent of social reform. Holder of a lucrative post in Chancery, Hales was the most active of the enclosure commissioners in 1548 and the author of three radical but unsuccessful parliamentary bills for the redress of agrarian abuses.[15]

[14] Sir Thomas Smith, *A Discourse of the Commonweal of the Realm of England*, ed. Mary Dewar (Charlottesville, Va., 1969), *passim*; on the authorship see id. 'The authorship of the "Discourse of the Commonweal"', *EcHR*, 2nd ser. 19 (1966), 388–400.

[15] Below, pp. 48–9.

Somerset's neglect of the Council and reliance upon administrators of little social standing—however remarkable their talents—was risky. But it was also understandable, for the great men of the Council were ambitious, quarrelsome, and untrustworthy. Thomas Seymour, Somerset's younger brother, was on strained, if not hostile, terms with the Protector from the beginning of the reign; and his open pursuit of power threatened the political balance. Warwick was more covertly self-seeking, but his popularity and military esteem made him more dangerous. Southampton, excluded from power, was not content to stay in retirement; and Arundel disliked the Protector's reforming views on religion. The Council, with its divisive factions, was thus a difficult instrument to control; but Somerset was unwise to treat its members as he did, allowing them little voice in government and bestowing few of the rewards of patronage.

Somerset's authoritarian style of government revealed itself in his use of proclamations: commands issued nominally by the personal authority of the monarch, validated by the Great Seal, and publicly proclaimed. His proclamations—seventy-six in a little over two and a half years—were decreed at a higher annual rate than in any other period of the sixteenth century, indicating his reliance upon this instrument of rule. According to Paget, he would even have preferred to use proclamations in the religious settlement, by-passing Parliament: 'as for matters of religion, your Grace thought they might, if need were, be ordered by the King's Majesty's authority'.[16] In the event, Somerset was dissuaded from this course of action; and his use of proclamations was generally within the bounds of the law. That is not to say that they were unimportant or uncontentious: the Injunctions of 1547 and the Order for Communion of 1548 were, as we shall see, important stages in the religious changes of the reign; and some proclamations on less inflammatory matters, such as the wool and cloth trades, showed a mild disregard for statutory authority.

In apparent contrast to Somerset's autocratic style of government was his relaxation of the law. In the first Parliament of the reign many of Henry VIII's statutes were repealed, the preamble to the Act of Repeal announcing that 'as in tempest or winter one course and garment is convenient, in calm or warm weather a more liberal . . . or lighter garment may and ought to be followed and used'.[17] Accordingly, much of the Henrician extension of treason, the heresy laws, and all Henrician statutes creating new felonies were repealed. Further clauses were added by the Commons to strengthen

[16] Paget to Somerset, 25 Dec. 1548, printed by B. L. Beer, 'A critique of the Protectorate', *Huntington Library Quarterly*, 34 (1971), 277–83. See R. W. Heinze, *The Royal Proclamations of the Tudor Kings* (Cambridge, 1976), 200–3.

[17] 1 Edward VI c. 12.

the position of defendants in treason trials, although it remained possible for men to be convicted of treason on the ground of spoken words alone. Paget commented that although in Henry's time 'all things were too straight [i.e. strict], . . . now they are too loose', for every man had been given liberty to do and speak as he pleased. The consequences, he insisted, were dangerous: 'the governor not feared; the noblemen contempted; the gentlemen despised'.[18] In relaxing the laws Somerset seems to have been following the precedent of Henry VIII, who had needed to secure popularity at the start of his reign and had won it by reversing some of his father's harsh policies. Somerset's repeal Act evidently had the same objective, and he needed popularity more than Henry had done, because he was Protector rather than monarch, because he was not personally liked, because his style of government divorced him from the support of his peers, and because he was dangerously exposed to pressure from Protestants and from Parliament. But he evidently pushed his measures too far for a tough-minded adviser like Paget.

3. SCOTLAND

The most urgent problem facing the Protector was the success of the Catholic, pro-French party in Scotland, linked with the threat from France, whose new monarch, Henry II, was hostile to England and determined to win back Boulogne. Preparations for a major Scottish campaign were made by the English government from early summer, 1547. On 30 August Somerset himself reached Berwick at the head of 16,000 men, and three days later Clinton sailed with the fleet for the Firth of Forth. On the battlements at Berwick Somerset told of a dream, in which he had returned from Scotland to a warm welcome from the King, 'but yet him thought he had done nothing at all in this voyage'.[19] The dream reveals Somerset's overriding concern with Scotland and the uncertainty of his mind. His campaign, however, was marked by no such uncertainty. On 10 September, by brilliantly exploiting his enemy's mistakes, he defeated a poorly armed and badly led Scottish army at Pinkie, nine miles east of Edinburgh. The victory enabled Somerset to put into operation his strategy of establishing English garrisons in Scottish castles, and in the course of the next year about two dozen such garrisons were installed. Some extended English control of the border country further into Scotland; others were placed on or near the coastal stretch between Berwick and Edinburgh; and a few were

[18] Beer, 'Critique of the Protectorate', 280.
[19] W. Patten, 'The Expedition into Scotland', in A. F. Pollard (ed.), *Tudor Tracts, 1532–1588* (London, 1903), 82.

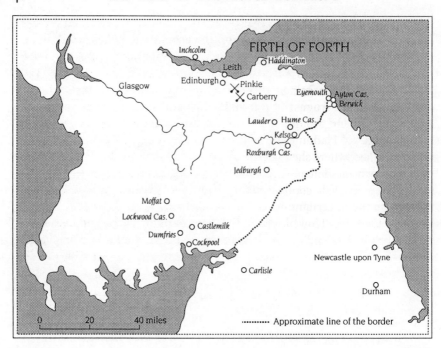

MAP 6. Scotland and the English border. Principal garrisons established by
Somerset are shown in *italics*

located in more distant parts, on the rivers Forth and Tay. Much the most
important was Haddington, fifteen miles east of Edinburgh, which was
manned by 2,500 troops and served as the principal base for military operations in Scotland. The garrisons were intended to protect England's friends
among the Scottish lords, to promote the Protestant cause, to put pressure
on the Scottish government to agree to the marriage of Princess Mary with
Edward VI, and to unite the Scots and English 'under the indifferent old
name of Britains again'. The garrisons were not a means of imposing
English rule, nor were they initially intended to punish or exploit the Scots:
they were paid for by English, not Scottish, taxes. In theory the policy was
imaginatively conceived. In practice it was rendered hopeless by the weakness and unreliability of the 'English party' in Scotland and, above all, by
the arrival of French troops at Leith in June 1548. Paget, for one, thought
the policy ill-conceived and urged Somerset to build no more fortresses,
levying an army instead to repel the French. His advice was ignored and
from the moment the French landed the possibility of winning over the
Scots by 'assurance' was negligible. The English then put increasing emphasis upon military reprisals: 'from henceforward', wrote John Luttrell,

commander of one of the garrisons, 'there is no hope of any practice for friendship to be ministered, but rather an extreme plague with fire and sword which shall reduce them to poverty and submission . . .'.[20] But the English could not afford sufficient fire or swords for the purpose, and gradually the French gained the initiative. Remaining formally at peace with England until August 1549, they nevertheless exerted military pressure in Scotland and around Boulogne. In the summer of 1548 they began the long siege of Haddington and shortly afterwards Mary Stewart was taken to France, where she married the Dauphin. By the winter the English troops were on the defensive. But defeat was not inevitable: gloomy as the reports from English commanders generally were, their pessimism was matched by the uncertainties of the French, who were finding their commitment expensive. However, when men and money were needed to suppress risings in England during the summer of 1549, the Scottish garrisons were depleted. In August of that year the French laid siege to Boulogne. Paget urged Somerset to make peace in Scotland, assuring him that it would be no dishonour to abandon Haddington, 'but rather a wisdom and so reputed throughout the world'.[21] This time Paget's advice was heard; the garrison abandoned Haddington in September and it was apparent to all that Somerset's Scottish policy had collapsed. His successors were left to make the peace. The policy had cost an immense sum—£580,000 in two years—and many lives. It achieved nothing at all. Ironically, Somerset's one sensible decision, the withdrawal of the Haddington garrison, became one of the major charges against him after his fall.

4. RELIGION

The most influential and far-reaching measures of Somerset's Protectorate were the changes in religion. Although the faction-fighting at Court during the last years of Henry VIII had not been primarily concerned with spiritual issues, the leadership of the Church itself had been seriously divided between orthodox 'conservatives' under Gardiner and 'reformers' led by Cranmer. In some parts of England the death of Henry was followed by popular agitation for reform: the Imperial ambassador reported in September 1547 that 'the populace around London are too much attached to the sects and clamour for novelties of all sorts', and later that 'the great crucifix . . . on the altar of St Paul's was a few days ago cast down by force

---

[20] M. L. Bush, *The Government Policy of Protector Somerset* (London, 1975), 32. See ibid., ch. 5 for Somerset's Scottish policy. Map 6, for location of the garrisons.

[21] B. L. Beer (ed.), *Letters of William Paget*, Camden Soc., Camden Miscellany 25 (London, 1974), 77.

of instruments, several men being wounded in the process and one killed.
There is not a single crucifix now remaining in the other churches . . .'.[22]
Popular ballads attacked the pretensions of the priests who

> . . . also undertake
> Right holy things to make,
> Yea, God within a cake . . .[23]

Images, the claims of the priesthood, transubstantiation, prayers for
the dead, chantries, and clerical celibacy were all targets for popular
abuse, while within the Church clerical leaders debated the nature of the
Eucharist, the sources of ecclesiastical authority, and the doctrine of justification by faith.

Yet it would be wrong to attribute the progress of reform under Somerset
mainly to popular or clerical pressure.[24] Mary Tudor was soon to show that
a determined monarch could easily restore religious orthodoxy. Under
Somerset, as under Northumberland, Mary, and indeed Elizabeth, the
government decided. There is little doubt that Somerset himself favoured
the Protestant faith, though it is less clear how radical his views were.
Although he supported reform, he was equally determined that the government should remain fully in control. He was not harsh in repressing opposition: the two most prominent conservatives, Gardiner and Bonner, were
given plenty of chance to conform; and no heretics were burned. But
neither did he favour toleration.

The first step in the process of reform was taken in July 1547, when
Injunctions were issued in the King's name and a general visitation ordered
for the whole of the Church. The Injunctions were conservative in appearance, for the most part ordering the clergy to perform their spiritual duties,
but they indicated clearly the direction in which the government was moving.[25] The superstitious worship of images was condemned; no man was to
be discouraged from reading the Bible; the sprinkling of holy water was
forbidden; processions was abolished. The *Homilies*, issued in the same
year, were to be read in all churches. Many of these homilies were uncontentious, but the Homily on Salvation set out in unequivocal terms the
doctrine of justification by faith alone and thus aligned the English Church
with the reformed confessions of Europe. It is not surprising that Bishops
Gardiner and Bonner protested against the Injunctions and were both, for
a time, imprisoned.

[22] *CSP Span.* ix. 148, 222.
[23] Strype, *Ecclesiastical Memorials*, ii/2, 333.
[24] As in W. K. Jordan, *Edward VI: The Young King* (London, 1968), 153.
[25] *Proclamations*, i, no. 287.

Edward's first Parliament was convened in the autumn of 1547 and pushed the programme further. The heresy acts, the Henrician Act of Six Articles, and the censorship statutes were repealed. This produced a dramatic outpouring of books: nearly 400 were published during the Protectorate, 160 of which were controversial religious works: one 'conservative', and 159 Protestant. Although Somerset denied Gardiner's accusation that he was responsible for this, he supported some of the more respectable Protestant writers and preachers, such as Hugh Latimer, John Hooper, Thomas Becon, and William Turner. At the same time the government denounced any attempt by private individuals to introduce change or stir up controversy. Reform was to be conducted under the firm control of secular authority. The first positive step towards change was taken with the Act 'against such as shall unreverently speak against the sacrament'.[26] In its title conservative, the statute nevertheless opened the way for liturgical change by permitting the laity to receive both the bread and the wine in the communion service.

The Act for the dissolution of chantries put into effect a statute of 1545 which had lapsed with the death of Henry VIII. However, whereas the earlier measure had been proposed for avowedly fiscal reasons, the Edwardian Act explicitly condemned the 'superstition and errors in Christian religion' created by 'vain opinions of purgatory and masses satisfactory': its principal intention was to end the saying of Masses for the dead, although it also abolished all religious 'fraternities, brotherhoods and guilds'.[27] The dissolution of the chantries, unlike the earlier destruction of the monasteries, left no stark, ruined monuments; but chantries—foundations for saying Masses for the souls of the donor and his friends—and fraternities or guilds—associations of lay men and women intended to provide for their members appropriate funerals and prayers after death—had figured largely in the communal life of the time; and their wealth, amounting to some £600,000, was considerable. Fraternities enabled lay persons to participate in the affairs of the Church, and many of them gave charitable support to members who had fallen on hard times. The suppression of chantries and fraternities had therefore a major social, economic, and religious effect. In York 100 chantries disappeared together with all religious guilds, including the Corpus Christi Guild, which produced the Mystery Plays. These institutions and their ceremonies touched the lives of parishioners more closely than had the monasteries, and their dissolution was a landmark in the shift of civic life from the religious to the secular. Yet their destruction was accomplished with surprising ease. Twenty years earlier they had still been

---

[26] 1 Edward VI c. 1.   [27] 1 Edward VI c. 14.

attracting significant support from donors and testators, but by 1547 the hostility of the Henrician government towards such religious institutions had eroded confidence in their future.

Early in 1548 the government followed up the parliamentary statutes with two measures issued on the authority of King and Council alone. The injunctions of the previous summer had allowed images to remain, provided that they were not worshipped superstitiously. This compromise had produced uncertainty and contention: 'almost in no places of the realm is any sure quietness, but where all images be wholly taken away and pulled down already', pronounced the Council when ordering the bishops to remove all religious images.[28] Official sanction was thus given to the destruction of the sculptures and the roods which had been the splendour of English churches for centuries. In March the Council issued the Order of Communion, to put into effect the statute of 1547 ordering the provision of both bread and wine to the laity.[29] The measure was, however, of much wider importance than this. Inserted into the Latin Mass was a liturgical section in English for administering communion to the laity. While the Mass had before been primarily a communion of the priest witnessed by the laity, the whole congregation was now allowed to participate more fully in the service. Probably the Order was designed as the first stage in abolishing services at which the priest was the only communicant; and it is not surprising that Coverdale called it 'the first fruits of godliness'.

This was the prelude to the most significant religious measure of Somerset's regime, the introduction of the Prayer Book of 1549. A committee under the leadership of Cranmer met in September 1548 to begin work on the new liturgy, which was presented to Parliament in December and given statutory sanction in the Act of Uniformity early the following year. The First Prayer Book of Edward VI was in many ways remarkably conservative, for much of its form and content were based upon the liturgy of a Catholic reformer, Cardinal Quinones. The provision of a service wholly in English was not necessarily a Protestant step, although the resounding and evocative prose of Thomas Cranmer, its principal author, was to be one of the glories of the Church of England for centuries. But the omissions from the Prayer Book, rather than any specific elements within it, marked its Protestant character. The communion service contained few rubrics laying down the ceremonial which was to accompany the prayers. Probably its authors intended that most of the gestures and actions should be omitted, although few were specifically forbidden: the elevation of the host was, however, expressly prohibited; and the Catholic doctrine of the sacrifice of

[28] Jordan, *Edward VI: The Young King*, 184.   [29] 1 Edward VI c. 1.

the Mass—the belief that Christ's sacrifice at Calvary was re-enacted in the service by the priest—was entirely absent.[30]

The 1549 Prayer Book was variously interpreted at the time and has been subject to many different opinions since. Some twentieth-century historians have even seen in it a reformed Catholic or an Erasmian service rather than a Protestant.[31] The uncertainty is understandable, partly because the rubrics were few and much was left to the discretion of the officiating priest, and partly because a great deal of the book's significance lay in what it did not say rather than in what it did. However, the attitude of Cranmer, who wrote it, is certain: he no longer believed in transubstantiation, as he made clear in the House of Lords debate in December 1548.

Why then was the Book ambiguous and open to contradictory interpretations? One reason may have been the caution urged by Somerset's political advisers: Paget pointed out that it was important not to alienate the Emperor Charles V when England was at war with the Scots and threatened by the French. Moderate reformers saw the Book as an interim measure intended to wean laity and clergy gradually away from the traditional rites until they were ready to accept an unequivocally Protestant service: for example, Martin Bucer, the great German reformer exiled in England, considered it a concession to the 'infirmities of the age', designed to be temporary; and he believed that more preliminary instruction was needed before a fully reformed rite could be imposed. Yet the Book was pleasing to few. Gardiner objected to many of its features, although he was prepared to use it under orders from the Crown, while some radical Protestants refused to communicate unless it was amended. Whether or not its authors intended it to be temporary, as seems probable, the Book's reception ensured that it would not long survive unaltered.

In the same session Parliament carried the statute allowing the marriage of priests.[32] The measure was strongly, but ineffectively, opposed in the House of Lords and met biting opposition from conservative clerics in the country. Nevertheless, many clergy took advantage of it in the four years before Mary's first Parliament repealed it. Probably few of these married from Protestant conviction: domestic happiness and convenience weighed more strongly than doctrine, but the long-term effect upon the clergy was

---

[30] The 1549 Prayer Book can conveniently be studied in E. C. S. Gibson (ed.), *The First and Second Prayer Books of Edward VI* (London, 1st edn. 1910; refs. here to edn. of 1964), *passim*; see pp. 212–30 for the communion service.

[31] E.g. James Kelsey McConica, *English Humanists and Reformation Politics* (Oxford, 1965), ch. 8.

[32] 2 & 3 Edward VI c. 21.

important. They were no longer a group set apart and they now had family responsibilities to consider.

In terms of doctrine and liturgy Somerset's reforms were cautious and conciliatory; but his regime destroyed much of the traditional imagery and ritual in parishes throughout England. By the time of his fall the images of saints had been removed from all London churches and from the majority elsewhere. Mostly this had been done by royal visitation and commission, sometimes by spontaneous action. Ancient ceremonies, such as the blessing of candles at Candlemas, the use of ashes on Ash Wednesday, 'creeping to the cross' on Good Friday, were abolished; and popular festivities like the Plough Monday jollifications in January disappeared from many parishes. Traditional religion was on the retreat well before the more radical changes in liturgy were introduced under Northumberland.

5. SOCIAL AND AGRARIAN POLICY

The political and religious drama of Somerset's protectorate was played out at a time of social dislocation and distress. The essence of the agrarian changes and their consequences lay in the pressure of growing population on the available land, which rendered some men homeless and enabled landlords to raise rents.[33] Increasing demand for wool encouraged the keeping of great sheep flocks, which not only encroached on the arable land but pushed the cattle and other livestock belonging to poorer farmers off the commons. The agrarian struggle has often been represented as one between tillage and pasture; equally important was the competition for grazing between sheep bred for wool and cattle bred for milk and cheese. Indeed, in the years of Somerset's rule there was no shortage of corn, for harvests were good; the serious dearth was in milk, butter, and cheese, important elements in the diet of the poor. Enclosure of common land for parks and for pasture, overstocking of commons by rich sheep-owners, and the closing of rights of way were all sources of grievance. The number of unemployed vagrants seemed to be increasing, a challenge to the forces of order and to obligations of charity. Throughout the 1540s sporadic peasant rioting disturbed rural society.

Preachers, pamphleteers, and ballad writers were vociferous in their denunciation of poverty. An anonymous pamphleteer condemned 'The decay of England only by a great multitude of sheep'. William Forrest's ballad, 'The Pleasant Poesye of Princelie Practise', demanded a reduction in rents:

---

[33] See below, Ch. 6, *passim* for analysis of social problems.

These raging rents must be looked upon,
And brought unto th'old accustomed rent,
As they were let at forty years agone:
Then shalbe plenty and most men content,
Though great possessioners list not t'assent:
Yet, better it were their rents to bring under,
Than thousands, thousands to perish for hunger.

Henry Brinklow denounced the depopulation of villages: 'for by your oppressors and extortioners, how be the towns and villages decayed? Where as were viii, x, xii, yea xvi households and more, is now but a sheep house and ii or iii shepherds'.[34]

The response of Somerset's government to these grievances has long been debated by historians. In one tradition he appears as a liberal hero, born before his time, generous to a fault, sympathetic to the poor, anxious to widen areas of opportunity in English life. This idealized portrait has been effectively demolished by later writers: Somerset's personal greed and harshness make it unacceptable.[35] One authority considers Somerset's social policy to have been entirely subordinated to the needs of the Scottish war: faced with a crisis of inflation, the Protector had either to restore the coinage or to attack enclosure; the first solution was impossible, because the government needed the fiscal profits of debasement, and Somerset therefore turned to the second.[36] This analysis seems altogether too simple. Inflation was only one of many social grievances, and, thanks to good harvests, was not immediately pressing. Nor does it seem realistic to envisage Somerset as consciously choosing between two contrary policies: there is no evidence that such a choice was debated, and such clear-cut alternatives were seldom presented to sixteenth-century politicians. Admittedly, the restoration of the coinage, advocated by Sir Thomas Smith, was not feasible for a government at war; but that does not in itself explain why Somerset took the initiative against enclosing landlords.

What *was* his social policy? The first major measure, the Vagrancy Act of 1547, hardly accords with the 'liberal' picture of Somerset's government.[37] Any man or woman refusing work was to be treated as a vagabond, branded with a 'V', and condemned to slavery for two years. Although the bill was

[34] *TED* iii. 43; H. Brynkelow, *The Complaynt of Roderick Mors*, ed. J. M. Cooper, Early English Text Society (London, 1874), 48–9.
[35] For the 'liberal' view see A. F. Pollard, *England under Protector Somerset* (London, 1900), *passim*, and Jordan, *Edward VI: The Young King, passim*; Bush, *Government Policy*, provides the most complete rebuttal so far.
[36] Bush, *Government Policy, passim*. On debasement and inflation see below, Ch. 3 s. 2.
[37] 1 Edward VI c. 3. C. S. L. Davies, 'Slavery and Protector Somerset: the Vagrancy Act of 1547', *EcHR* 19 (1966), 533–49.

probably not originally proposed by the government, it seems to have been adopted by Somerset, and some of its clauses on slavery reflect the ideas of Sir Thomas Smith, a close associate of the Protector. The statute was a harsh response to the problem of vagrancy, which seemed to be on the increase and was alarming many men inside and outside government circles. Its authors, entirely unsympathetic to the destitute, produced the most repressive poor law of the century, which was repealed two years later because of its severity.

The two sets of enclosure commissions, issued in 1548 and 1549, accord more closely with the traditional image of Somerset as a friend to the poor. Only the Midlands Commision of 1548, under John Hales, was put into execution. Its object, in Hales's words, was 'only to enquire, and not to hear and determine': it was designed so that the government should be better informed on the extent of the problem. Somerset might seem only to have been enforcing existing statutes and enquiring into their breach, operating in effect a traditional policy with the support of his Council.[38] But the only precedent for enclosure commissions, those issued by Wolsey in 1517–18, had been unpopular with landlords and in many ways successful in limiting their excesses. The high rhetoric with which Hales addressed the juries of inquiry could not fail to disturb landlords:

Towns, villages and parishes do daily decay in great numbers; houses of husbandry and poor men's habitation be utterly destroyed everywhere, and in no small number; husbandry and tillage, which is the very paunch of the commonwealth, . . . greatly abated . . . All this groweth through the great dropsy and the insatiable desire of riches of some men, that be so much given to their own private profit, that they pass nothing on to the commonwealth . . .[39]

What then were the origins of Somerset's social measures? They are surely to be found in the writings of men like Thomas Smith, John Hales, Hugh Latimer, and Thomas Becon, all of them close to the Protector and all incensed at the dislocation of society. It is certainly false to describe them as a 'commonwealth party', for their ideas were various and they were in no sense a party. Some, like Latimer, inveighed against greed in general terms: to him and others the problem was essentially moral. Hales and Smith were much more concerned to diagnose social ills and to propose specific remedies. Of the two Smith was the more interesting thinker, entirely original in his perception that the problem could be solved, not by forcing men to forgo enrichment, but by inducing them through economic incentive to act in the common interest.[40] Yet in the circumstances of 1549 his proposals

---

[38] Bush, *Government Policy*, ch. 3.
[39] Strype, *Ecclesiastical Memorials*, ii/2, 352.
[40] Smith, *Discourse of the Commonweal*, *passim*.

were hardly practicable. Hales's analysis was more superficial, but, in its condemnation of depopulating landlords, more attractive; and his solution, although it failed dismally, was not entirely unrealistic, as Wolsey's measures had shown. But if the policy sprang largely from a desire to remedy the ills of the commonwealth, how do we account for the apparent contrast between the Vagrancy Act of 1547 and the enclosure commissions? Both aimed at the same end: the preservation of order in the body of the commonwealth, an order made precarious in time of war and threatened alike by vagrants *and* by depopulating landlords. Somerset was not a liberal friend of the poor, but a man prepared to use stern measures both against vagrants and against landowners if either seemed to endanger the social fabric.

Somerset has probably been best known in succeeding centuries for his social policy, particularly when the 'liberal' assessment of the protectorate was dominant. Subsequent controversy has made it difficult to get that policy into perspective. Almost certainly social and economic problems were not the matters which most preoccupied the Duke: war, diplomacy, and, in particular, Scotland were his main concerns. Yet social policy was no mere subsidiary of his Scottish project. It arose from a genuine concern that the structure of the commonwealth was threatened and it needs to be judged in its own right. The dilemma was that a campaign against depopulation would alienate the landed classes if successful and create frustration, born of disappointed hope, among the peasantry if it failed. In the end, without having any of the success achieved by Wolsey's commission, it managed to do both, and some of Somerset's colleagues were understandably antagonistic. Worse was to come next year. The activities of Somerset, Hales, and like-minded men did little to solve agrarian problems: rather they helped to foment the risings of 1549 and to set in train the fall of the Protector.

6. 1549: RIOT AND REVOLT

In the spring of 1549 reports came in of riots and uprisings over most of the southern English counties. Generally they seem to have been a response to a proclamation against enclosures issued by Somerset in April. The commons pulled down fences and broke open parks in eager anticipation of official action. The government met this first challenge by offering pardons and sending trusted noblemen down to the shires to settle matters by pacification. The Earl of Arundel set up an informal court in Sussex, where he heard grievances, punishing both oppressive landlords and unruly peasants. He was able to report to the Council that 'these parts remain well as may be in a quavering quiet'.[41] By the end of May this first outbreak had been settled by peaceful means and the government could feel relatively safe. The calm was short-lived.

Early in June more serious disturbances broke out in the south-west. The traditional leaders in Devon and Cornwall had been members of the Courtenay family, but their authority had been destroyed in 1538 by the execution for treason of Henry Courtenay, Marquis of Exeter, and the confiscation of his lands. In his place the Crown had tried to establish Sir John (later Lord) Russell, a soldier and diplomat who had built his career on service to the monarch. But Russell had not been able to assume the influence of the Courtenays, and in consequence the two counties lacked a firm authority. For two years Cornwall had been in a state of disturbance. In 1548 William Body, lessee of the archdeaconry, while touring the county with a commission for the removal of images from churches, had been murdered at Helston by an angry crowd demanding that no new laws be enacted until King Edward reached the age of 24. That protest had received little support from other parts of Cornwall and had been easily suppressed by local officers. But it was a warning of worse to come. Next year the government ordered that the new Prayer Book be read in all parish churches on Whitsunday, 9 June. A protest meeting under the mayor of Bodmin issued a summons to all Cornishmen to muster and defend their liberties. Within a day or two the rebels had acquired two leaders of some social standing: Humfrey Arundell, a quarrelsome soldier from a minor branch of an important county family; and John Winslade, a member of the middling gentry. Arundell took command, set up a camp, and dispatched a force to capture St Michael's Mount.

Meanwhile, or Thursday 6 June, an independent outburst had occurred at Sampford Courtenay in north Devon, led by William Harper, the parish priest, William Underhill, a tailor, and William Segar, a labourer. Harper was 'prevented' from saying the new service on Whitsunday, probably with his own connivance; men assembled at Sampford; and the authority of the local justices collapsed. Soon after, a rash gentleman, William Hellyons, tried to suppress the protest and was murdered. Gradually news of the rising spread to other villages, in the over-coloured words of John Hooker, 'as a cloud carried with a violent wind and as a thunderclap sounding through the whole country'.[42] Within ten days the Devonshire rebels had camped at Crediton, a few miles north of Exeter. Here they were joined,

[41] N. Pocock, *Troubles connected with the Prayer Book of 1549*, Camden Soc., NS 37 (London, 1884), 14.
[42] Julian Cornwall, *The Revolt of the Peasantry, 1549* (London, 1977), 67.

towards the end of June, by the men of Cornwall. On 2 July the rebels began the siege of Exeter.

The south-western rebels drew up articles containing their demands. These articles are marked by a peremptory tone, most of them opening with the uncompromising words 'we will have'. They are overwhelmingly religious. The rebels demanded the re-enactment of the Six Articles of 1539, the saying of Mass in Latin, the hanging of the sacrament over the high altar, communion of the laity only at Easter and then only in one kind, baptism on weekdays as well as on Sundays, the distribution of holy bread and holy water, prayers for the dead, and suppression of the vernacular Bible. They refused to receive the new services, which they likened to 'a Christmas game'. They also demanded that half the abbey and chantry lands should be given back to the Church and used to set up places for devout persons, and that gentlemen should keep only one retainer for each £66 of landed income.[43] These two last articles are signs of a distinct hostility towards the gentry, hostility which was evident in the actions and attitudes of the rebels. Although the articles probably reflect the views of the leaders and of the priests who were influential in the rising, rather than those of the rank-and-file, it is impossible to avoid the conclusion that the principal motives were religious. But hostility to the landed classes was real enough, aroused by the arrogance of the gentry and their servants, and by the role of the leading gentlemen in imposing the religious changes. And economic discontents were present, behind the religious protest. For the rebels made two demands not included in the final version of their articles: one was for the repeal of the tax on sheep, unpopular in a pastoral region; the other for a remedy for the scarcity of victuals.

A month after the outbreak of the south-western revolt the government was faced with very different risings in East Anglia. The best known of these, Kett's revolt, had its origins at Wymondham, near Norwich, where a traditional play was performed each summer. Worked up by rumours that enclosures had been destroyed elsewhere, a group under the leadership of Robert Kett, a tanner and minor landowner, went to throw down the hedges of an unpopular local lawyer. That done, they marched on Norwich, gaining numbers as they went. The city authorities temporized with the 'rebels', who passed round Norwich to camp on Mousehold Heath, north-east of the town. Several thousand men were 'inkenneled', as they described it, on the heath, assembled to petition the government about their grievances. Within a few days of the Wymondham rising, other groups were encamped at

---

[43] Ibid. 115, for a complete set of the articles.

Ipswich and Bury St Edmunds in Suffolk, and at Downham Market in Norfolk; later, the Ipswich camp moved to Melton and a new one was formed at King's Lynn. The risings need to be set against the agrarian background of East Anglia, which was divided into three main farming regions. Two of these, one in the north and west, the other in the south and south-east, consisted of light soil, devoted to corn-growing and the pasturing of sheep. Here prevailed the peculiarly East Anglian institution of the foldcourse, by which lords of manors had the right to pasture sheep on the common fields. The arrangement gave rise to considerable friction, the tenants complaining that their lands were over-grazed. Between these two regions was one of woodland-pasture, stretching over southern Norfolk and northern Suffolk. Here small farmers had long been concerned about the encroachment by landlords on the common pastures. Over the whole of East Anglia large landowners were building up big sheep flocks, some of them several thousands strong. In the sheep-corn regions tenants enclosed their lands in an attempt to keep out the lord's sheep; in the woodland-pasture region the lords did the enclosing, mainly of commons. This difference of attitude helps to explain why, when the destruction of hedges had sparked off the risings, enclosures received little attention in the formal demands of the insurgents. The main attention of the rebel articles issued by Kett and his followers focused upon the sheep flocks of the lords. They petitioned that 'no lord of no manor shall common upon the commons', that freeholders and copyholders were to take all the profits of commons, and that 'no lord, knight, esquire or gentleman do graze nor feed any bullocks or sheep, if he may spend forty pounds a year by his lands, but only for the provision of his house'. The 'rebels' wanted all copyhold rents to be reduced to the level of 1485 and prayed that 'all bond men may be free for God made all free with his precious blood-shedding'.[44] This last clause, and perhaps much else in the East Anglian protest, may well have arisen from hostility to the Duke of Norfolk, whose estates contained many bondmen. Norfolk had been an unusually severe landowner, whose imprisonment at the end of Henry's reign removed the central core of power in the region: his unpopularity helped to provoke the risings, while his absence aided their progress.

The articles of Kett's 'rebels' represent the outlook of small tenant farmers, not of landless labourers or the destitute. But that does not make them 'conservative': the demands about commons would have destroyed the pastoral economy of the big landlords. Their actions show a combination of restraint and radicalism, for while they were distinctly hostile to

---

[44] BL Harleian MS 304 fo. 75.

gentlemen, they stopped short of killing, choosing instead to humiliate. They set up an organized form of government over most of East Anglia, claiming to act on the King's behalf, and complaining against the corruption of the local officials. The orderly procedures of the 'rebel' camps were striking: not until the government used force did they become violent. Kett's men did not see themselves as rebels. Their articles were moderate in tone, each one beginning 'we pray that . . .', in contrast to the peremptory demands of the men of the south-west. They were content to camp in force, occupying East Anglia and making no effort to march on London. But their non-violent, law-abiding attitudes should not mislead us into thinking them deferential or 'conservative': they hated the gentry and they wanted a very different society from the one they knew. It would still be hierarchical, but the lords and gentlemen would be prevented from using the commons and exploiting small farmers.

East Anglia, Devon, and Cornwall were not the only regions that 'stirred' in the summer of 1549. Risings broke out during July in Oxfordshire and Buckinghamshire, according to Somerset 'by instigation of sundry priests for these matters of religion'. The dissolution of the chantries seems to have been the immediate provocation of a rising at Seamer in Yorkshire, where there was also a strong element of hostility to the gentry: according to later and hostile reports the leaders intended to kill gentlemen and promised spoils to the poor in order to recruit support. There were also risings in Essex, Hertfordshire, and Hampshire serious enough to evoke official letters from the King to the assembled commons in those counties. In London the Mayor and aldermen became nervous, ordering a curfew, followed by proclamation of martial law; but there is no evidence of serious trouble.

Somerset's initial response to the south-western and East Anglian risings was placatory. He offered pardons to those who submitted and sent local notables to pacify the regions. He was desperately overstretched, facing uprisings in much of southern England, a war with Scotland, and the threat of war with France. It was sensible to try again the conciliatory policy which had succeeded in May; but unwisely he chose in July to issue a new commission for redressing enclosures, which seemed to some of his councillors to be encouraging the 'rebels'. At the same time letters were sent in the King's name, reprimanding the commons for their disobedience, but promising redress of genuine grievances and the summoning of Parliament, to enact the necessary legislation, one month earlier than it was due to meet. In spite of the tone of heavy rebuke this was a remarkable concession to armed protest.[45]

---

[45] *Proclamations*, i, no. 338. BL Additional MS 48018 fos. 388–90.

Within two weeks of the rising at Bodmin, Sir Peter Carew, a Devonshire soldier of fortune, was sent by the government to persuade the south-western rebels to submit. Carew was not the man for patient negotiation and his actions only exacerbated the tension. A more influential, though scarcely more effective figure, Lord Russell, was then dispatched with a small force and instructions to discover the causes of the revolt, remedy them if poss-ible, and 'bring the people with gentleness to . . . conformity'.[46] If that was impossible, he was to levy troops and repress the disobedient. Where Carew was hot-headed, Russell was cautious. He was understandably reluctant to attack the rebels until he was assured of superior numbers. Since he was facing perhaps 8,000 rebels, 3,000 of whom were well armed, this was reasonable. His refusal to move until he was assured of superiority in numbers was, however, irritating to the government, which desperately needed a quick end to the revolt. A somewhat acrimonious correspondence followed between Russell and Somerset. The Protector urged rapid action and gave lessons in tactics. Russell took offence at the implied criticism and demanded reinforcements. By the end of July Lord Grey of Wilton had arrived with 250 cavalry and 350 infantry, fresh from suppressing the risings of Oxfordshire and Buckinghamshire. These and other bands brought Russell's total to more than 3,000, of whom nearly half were foreign professional mercenaries. At last he was ready to move. He defeated the rebels in hard fighting at Clyst St Mary, just east of Exeter, on 4 August and relieved the city two days later. The rest of the month was spent in suppressing pockets of resistance, hanging ringleaders, and parcelling out their lands.

York Herald reached Norwich on 21 July and offered a pardon to the 'rebels' there. Kett replied that pardons were offered only to wrongdoers and protested that he was innocent. The herald then declared him a traitor. From this point Kett and his followers knew that they must fight. William Parr, Marquis of Northampton, was appointed by the Council to lead a force against them. He left London about 26 July and dispersed the camp at Bury on his way, while Sir Anthony Wingfield put down the rising at Melton. With Suffolk secure, the government forces were in a stronger position to deal with Kett. Unfortunately, Northampton, whose force amounted only to some 1,000 men, ignored the Council's instructions to avoid battle and entered Norwich. Here he was trapped by the 'rebels', who rushed the city's defences. Northampton lost 100 men, including Lord Sheffield, one of his senior commanders, and retreated hastily from the

---

[46] Pocock, *Troubles*, 8, 10.

scene. By this time the 'rebels' were beginning to get out of control and several houses were looted and burned before Kett was able to reimpose his authority. The Council was now compelled to devote more resources to the suppression of Mousehold camp. Royal ships were sent to take over the defence of Yarmouth. The Earl of Warwick was appointed to lead a new force, and on 24 August he reached Norwich with 8,500 men, most of them untrained English levies. The next day, reinforced by 1,100 German mercenaries, he felt strong enough to attack. Kett by now realized his weakness, and cut off from his source of food, he decided to retreat. At a place called Dussindale, no longer identifiable, Warwick's troops caught up with the 'rebel' army and destroyed it.

By the end of August all the risings had been put down and the government was in control. About 3,000 men had been killed at Dussindale and at least as many of the south-western rebels had died in battle. Brutal executions were carried out in Devon and Cornwall by Russell's provost-marshal, Sir Anthony Kingston. Elsewhere the reprisals were less drastic; only four of the Suffolk 'rebels' are known to have been hanged; Lord Grey hanged about fifteen in Oxfordshire, including two priests from their church steeples; Warwick executed forty-nine 'rebels' when he entered Norwich and several more after the battle. The ringleaders of both main risings—Arundell, Winslade, Robert Kett, and three others—were tried and convicted in London.

The two main uprisings were very different. The south-western movement was without doubt a rebellion: its demands were uncompromisingly stated and diametrically opposed to government policy. By contrast, Kett considered himself to be acting in support of the government. Both, however, showed a considerable degree of organization and there was very little violence away from the fields of battle. Both suffered in the end from the same weakness: they had little support from nobles or major gentry. This did not prevent the leaders from organizing their forces effectively, but it did mean that they had no one to speak for them at Court. They showed that they could tie down royal armies and frighten royal commanders. But in the end they were defeated by Italian and German professionals, who turned the scales on the battlefield. The year 1549 left a legacy of hatred. In 1550 a Norwich man complained that 'as sheep or lambs are a prey to the wolf or lion, so are the poor men to the rich men'.[47] The ruling classes were frightened and angry. Sir John Cheke, later Secretary of State, attacked the 'rebels' in hysterical tones: 'do ye not see', he demanded of them, 'how for

[47] Walter Rye (ed.), *Depositions taken before the Mayor and Aldermen of Norwich* (Norwich, 1905), 22–5.

the maintenance of these ungodly rabblements, not only cities and villages, but also shires and countries be utterly destroyed?'[48]

The immediate sequel to the uprisings was the fall of Protector Somerset. His social policy was probably not the most important cause of his unpopularity with his fellow councillors, and he was certainly no friend to rebellion; but he was blamed for what happened. Paget, always the candid friend, rhetorically asked Somerset what was the cause of the disturbances? 'Your own lenity, your softness, your opinion to be good to the poor,' he replied to his own question.[49] Somerset's enclosure commissions and the high rhetoric employed by Hales had probably helped to detonate uprisings and were certainly thought by many landowners to have done so. From Kent it was reported that an agitator named Latimer—not the famous Hugh Latimer—was touring the shire, Somerset's 'name in his mouth'. The gentlemen of the county, hearing that the Protector had pardoned some of the agitators, 'think my Lord's Grace [Somerset] rather to will the decay of the gentlemen than otherwise'.[50] Not only had Somerset lost the trust of his fellow landowners; he had put arms into the hands of his rivals when he gave command of armies to Warwick, Russell, and Herbert.

7. THE FALL OF SOMERSET

Even before the uprisings of 1549, Somerset's political authority had been shaken by the treason and execution of his younger brother. Thomas Seymour, created Baron Sudeley and Lord Admiral of England in 1547, was attractive, quarrelsome, foolish, and insanely ambitious. Early in the reign, urged on perhaps by the Earl of Warwick, he had demanded the office of Governor to the young King, claiming that it was improper for the elder of the King's uncles to be both Protector and Governor, while the younger had nothing.[51] Somerset's refusal opened a breach between the brothers which was soon widened by the hostility of his Duchess towards her brother-in-law; but the principal agent of catastrophe was Sudeley himself. After failing to become Governor, he wooed the Queen Dowager, Catherine Parr, whom he married four months after the death of her husband, Henry VIII. He also worked on the feelings of Edward, providing him with extra pocket-money, which Somerset kept tightly rationed, and encouraging him

[48] Sir John Cheke, *The Hurt of Sedition*, printed in R. Holinshed, *Chronicles* (6 vols., London, 1808), iii. 987–1011, esp. p. 998.

[49] Strype, *Ecclesiastical Memorials*, ii/2, 429–37 (letter of 7 July 1549).

[50] F. W. Russell, *Kett's Rebellion in Norfolk* (London, 1854), 202–3. B. L. Beer and R. J. Nash, 'Hugh Latimer and the Lusty Knave of Kent', *BIHR*, 52 (1979), 175–8.

[51] G. W. Bernard, 'The downfall of Sir Thomas Seymour', in G. W. Bernard (ed.), *The Tudor Nobility* (Manchester, 1992), 212–40.

to take power into his own hands. At the same time he made a play for the affections of Princess Elizabeth, then 14, and may even have proposed marriage to her after Catherine's death in September 1548. His ambitions stretched beyond the royal Court. He tried, with some success, to win over members of both Houses of Parliament to his side, obstructing some of Somerset's legislation; he recruited local nobles, gentlemen, and yeomen; and there is some evidence that he planned to kidnap Edward and Elizabeth and take them to his castle at Holt, Denbighshire. In January 1549 Sudeley was arrested and the Council opened a prolonged and exacting enquiry into his affairs. Since the judges had some doubts about a trial at common law, he was condemned for treason by Act of Attainder and executed with the consent of his own brother. Some contemporary accounts suggest that Somerset's authority was impaired by this episode; according to the chronicler Hayward he was considered by many nobles to be 'a blood-sucker, a murderer, a parasite, a villain' for his treatment of his brother; but this may be part of a programme of self-justification by his successors in office.[52] Sudeley's activities show how widely power was dispersed during a royal minority, between the king, the royal family, the Council, Parliament, the nobility and gentry in the shires; and how uneasy Somerset had become in his hold on authority.

Some time in August 1549 the Earl of Warwick and other leading noblemen decided that Somerset's rule must be ended. Warwick himself, the Earls of Arundel and Southampton, and William Paulet, Lord St John, visited Princess Mary to enlist her support. While Warwick was the ultimate victor in the coming struggle, Southampton was probably as important in forming the conspiracy. Although Mary refused to be drawn, the conspirators continued with their plans.[53] Early in October they were ready to strike. Warwick had probably kept in being part of the force with which he had defeated the Norfolk rebels; Russell and Herbert were encamped with their army in Wiltshire; and the councillors had assembled their retainers in London. The charges brought against Somerset were many and wide-ranging. Some of the conspirators—the Earl of Arundel for instance—may have been impelled by religion. Certainly there were rumours that Somerset's opponents intended to restore the old religion and to make Mary Regent. But Mary herself had given no support to the second objective and it is unlikely that religious conservatism played a major role. The Protector's social policy touched the leading councillors more closely. In itself the policy was traditional, but the energetic inquiries of Hales made it seem more threatening than it was. When the uprisings broke out in 1549

[52] Read, *Cecil*, 54.   [53] *CSP. Span.* ix. 445.

even Somerset's closest associates blamed him for encouraging and prolonging rebellion. The war had gone badly in Scotland, where English
troops had been forced to withdraw from Haddington, while across the
Channel French troops were threatening Boulogne. The government was
bankrupt and Somerset's military policy was in disarray. Most important of
all perhaps, the Protector had failed to observe the rules of wise political
conduct. His neglect of the Privy Council—doing 'things of most weight
and importance by himself alone'—and his arrogant manner were matched
by niggardliness.[54] Somerset did well out of his Protectorship, his sumptuous buildings in the Strand and at Sion House standing as lavish testimony
to his greed. Outside the ranks of his own cronies few men profited and after
his first year of office Somerset was mean with gifts of Crown lands. He was
also tactless enough to offend powerful and sensitive colleagues. He turned
down a request from Warwick for two offices to be granted to one of his
sons, and gave them instead to one of his own secretaries. Lord Russell had
been hurt by Somerset's criticism of his conduct in the south-west. The
Marquis of Northampton was aggrieved at Somerset's refusal to help him
secure a divorce.

The dislodgment of the Protector, when it came, was swift. The two
sides openly mustered their forces at the beginning of October; eleven days
later Somerset was on his way to the Tower. In late September Somerset
and his Duchess had been hunting in Hampshire, and although reports of
plotting had probably reached him there, he took no immediate action.
However, on Tuesday 1 October he was sufficiently alarmed to ride to
Hampton Court, where the King was in residence, and to issue a proclamation ordering a general muster to defend Edward and the Protector.
Handbills were distributed accusing the conspirators of plotting 'the utter
impoverishing and undoing of all the commons'. Somerset ordered Russell
and Herbert to march with their troops to his aid. By Sunday 6 October his
opponents, who included most of the privy councillors, had mobilized
several thousand horsemen and foot-soldiers in London. They issued their
own proclamation, justifying their action and insisting on their peaceable
intentions. Somerset ordered the fortification of Hampton Court, accused
Warwick of seeking the throne, sent an officer to capture the Tower, and
dispatched Secretary Petre to negotiate with the councillors in London.
Although men were rallying to his side at Hampton Court he had not
enough food to maintain them and had to send many away. Then came
news that the Tower had been secured by the London councillors and that
Petre had changed sides. Somerset abandoned Hampton Court and re-

[54] Pocock, *Troubles*, 115.

treated with the King to Windsor. Here he found little food or drink and it became obvious that he could not hold out for long. Only three council-lors—Archbishop Cranmer, Sir William Paget, and Secretary Smith—remained loyal to him; while seventeen councillors out of twenty-five signed the proclamation in London. Russell and Herbert, commanding a large force in Wiltshire, refused to come to the Protector's aid and thus removed his last hope of resistance. At Windsor, Paget, who had probably been in touch with the conspirators, advised Somerset to submit and urged the London councillors to be reasonable: 'temporize your determination', he begged them. The London Council responded by sending Sir Philip Hoby, an experienced diplomat, to Windsor with a promise that Somerset's life would be spared. Secret messages, detailing charges of treason against Somerset, were sent at the same time to those at Windsor whose loyalty to the Protector was thought to be weakening. Lord William Howard, com-mander of the royal bodyguard, a man unwisely trusted by Somerset, distributed these charges to 'all the good fellows of credit' while the 'mul-titude went to the houses of office [i.e. the lavatories] in the morning, turning in a moment all the Court . . .'. Within an hour those who had proclaimed that they would fight with Somerset to the death were uttering abuse against him: in treachery timing is all. Howard blew a trumpet and allowed all Somerset's troops to depart. Paget, relieved at the outcome and almost certainly involved in the plotting of the final stages, fell to his knees, clasping the Duke and saying the Judas words: 'Oh my lord, ye see now what my lords be!' That day, Thursday 10 October, the Protector was put in custody. His lack of a reliable and independent power base, his reluctance to use force in his own defence, the threats of the London councillors, and the desertion of men like Petre, Howard, and Paget brought him down. Within nine days the most powerful man in England had been toppled without the shedding of blood. The Protectorate was finished; but there was as yet no knowing what would replace it.[55]

[55] For contemporary accounts of Somerset's fall see especially A. J. A. Malkiewicz (ed.), 'An eye-witness's account', *EHR* 70 (1955), 600–9; P. F. Tytler, *England under the Reigns of Edward VI and Mary* (London, 1839), i. 238–40.

CHAPTER 3

The Rule of Northumberland

I. THE ACHIEVEMENT OF POWER

On 14 October 1549 Somerset was consigned to the Tower. During the next few weeks signs of disagreement were evident among his opponents and early in November the Imperial Ambassador, Van der Delft, was reporting a split within the Council.[1] The chief protagonists were Thomas Wriothesley, Earl of Southampton, and John Dudley, Earl of Warwick. Having co-operated in the overthrow of the Protector, neither would take second place in government. Southampton, who had been restored to the Council early in 1549, was the most experienced administrator among the conspirators and appeared at first the most likely to triumph. Bishop John Ponet, writing some years later, commented that initially he seemed to occupy the commanding heights of power: 'every man repaireth to Wriothesley, honoureth Wriothesley, sueth unto Wriothesley . . . and all things be done by his advice'. His rival, Warwick, was an effective military commander who had achieved swift and decisive victory over the Norfolk rebels. Ponet called him 'the ambitious and subtle Alcibiades of England'; Mary described him as 'the most unstable man' in the realm.[2] Another assessment of his character, by the diplomat Richard Morison, is more illuminating: 'Warwick had such a head that he seldom went about anything, but he conceived three or four purposes beforehand.'[3] He was, in short, a master of improvisation.

Van der Delft saw the confrontation as a struggle between Catholic and Protestant factions. Warwick, he alleged, had dissembled with his fellow conspirators before the coup, promising to restore the true faith, but had then thrown off the mask and gained supremacy with the help of Protestant allies.[4] However, it is unlikely that any of Somerset's principal opponents,

[1] *CSP Span.* ix. 468.
[2] John Poynet, *A Short Treatise of Politike Power* (n.p., 1556; repr. 1639), 62. In modern facsimile edn. (Amsterdam, 1972), I. iii. *CSP Span.* x. 6.
[3] W. K. Jordan, *Edward VI: The Threshold of Power* (London, 1970), 260.
[4] *CSP Span.* x. 5–11.

with the possible exception of Arundel, were strongly committed to any religious cause. Southampton and Warwick were *politiques*, willing to accept and enforce the doctrines and liturgy laid down by law; both of them, together with Arundel and St John, had sought the support of Princess Mary; and Southampton and Warwick may have hoped, in vain as it turned out, that a profession of Catholic faith would gain her backing and with it that of Charles V. On the other side, Edward VI was known to be sympathetic to reformed doctrines, so that a display of Protestant zeal might appeal to him. Religion, while probably not a prime cause of the conflict, to some extent determined its course. In the opinion of one modern historian Southampton's party struck first, leading Warwick to suspect that they supported Princess Mary as Regent and forcing him to fight back; but it seems equally plausible to believe that Warwick began the campaign by taking a Protestant stance to win the favour of the King. It is often impossible in such manœuvres to determine who makes the first move, and in any event the decisive one was Warwick's achievement of control over the young King.[5]

Edward was still at this stage a child, but he was growing in maturity and held the keys to power. His education was as intense as ever. He was learning Latin, Greek, and French, and was being encouraged to develop an interest in matters of state. Over the next few years he wrote a series of 'position papers' on such topics as the procedure of the Privy Council and the reform of abuses in Church and state. From April 1550 his *Chronicle* becomes much more detailed than before, with almost daily entries: it is a remarkable, perhaps unique, record of political events by a reigning monarch.[6] While it is difficult to know how much of the *Chronicle* and the 'position papers' were his own work, they indicate the ways in which his mind was being formed by his mentors. Edward was a long way from being the sickly child of legend, for until his last months he was active and healthy, enjoying courtly entertainment and display, taking part in the hunt. In his *Chronicle* entry for 19 June 1550, for instance, he gives a vivid description of a mock sea battle at Deptford, where a fort built on a lighter in the Thames was assaulted by four pinnaces, 'with clods, squibs, canes of fire, darts made for the nonce, and bombards'. The entry for 20 July 1551 recounts with obvious pleasure the visit of the French Marshal, St André, to Hampton Court, where 'he [St André] came to see mine arraying and saw my bedchamber and went a-hunting with hounds and saw me shoot and saw

---

[5] D. E. Hoak, *The King's Council in the Reign of Edward VI* (Cambridge, 1976), ch. 7. I have followed Professor Hoak's interpretation for much of the way, but do not agree with him on every issue.

[6] *Chronicle of Edward VI, passim.*

all my guard shoot together'.[7] Although Edward was probably a convinced Protestant by the time of Somerset's fall, there is little sign in his *Chronicle* of religious devotion; and he may have been less of a bigot than is sometimes thought.

The key to Warwick's hold over Edward lay in the Privy Chamber, where the King performed public duties and where access to him was strictly controlled by the gentlemen on duty. Soon after Somerset's imprisonment four new gentlemen of the Privy Chamber were appointed: one was Warwick's own brother, Sir Andrew Dudley, and another was Sir Thomas Darcy, a loyal supporter of the Dudley cause. In February of the following year Darcy was appointed Vice-Chamberlain and Captain of the Guard; and when he was made Lord Chamberlain in 1551, he was succeeded in both those offices by Sir John Gates, an Essex landowner, who remained true to Warwick until the end.[8] Gates controlled the dry stamp of Edward's signature and with it much of the authority of the King. Warwick's son-in-law, Sir Henry Sidney, a young man eight years older than Edward, entered the Privy Chamber in April 1550, was brought up with the King, and became one of his close friends. An unknown official of the French Ambassador's household has left a vivid, if exaggerated, description of the way in which Edward was manipulated by Warwick: the King, he wrote, 'revered [Warwick] as if he were himself one of his subjects'. Warwick had placed in the royal household 'Master Gates', 'who was his intimate friend and [the] principal instrument which he used' to persuade the King without revealing that a proposal had come from Warwick himself. 'All of the others who were in the Chamber of the said [King] were creatures of the Duke [i.e. Warwick].'[9]

Within six weeks of the coup against Somerset Warwick extended his influence by placing two of his supporters in the Privy Council, Bishop Goodrich of Ely and Henry Grey, Marquis of Dorset and later Duke of Suffolk. At the end of November William Paget, the ablest of Somerset's allies, came over to Warwick, to be rewarded with a peerage a few weeks later. Southampton and Arundel now struck back. According to an anonymous contemporary they hoped to implicate Warwick in the charges being prepared against Somerset, declaring them 'both worthy to die'. Warwick was warned of the plot by Lord St John, who told him to 'beware how he did prosecute the Lord Protector's death, for he could suffer himself for the

---

[7] *Chronicle of Edward VI*, 36, 73.

[8] D. E. Hoak, 'The King's Privy Chamber, 1547–1553', in D. J. Guth and J. W. McKenna (eds.), *Tudor Rule and Revolution: Essays for G. R. Elton from his American Friends* (Cambridge, 1982), 87–108.

[9] Hoak, *King's Council*, 123.

same'. Warwick then determined to save Somerset and turn the attack against his opponents. At the next Council meeting, 'with a warlike visage', he declared to Southampton: 'he that seeketh his [Somerset's] blood would have mine also.'[10] In January 1550 Arundel and Southampton were banned from Court; St John was rewarded with the earldom of Wiltshire and Russell with the earldom of Bedford. Shortly after, Somerset was released from the Tower in a bid to gain his support, and Warwick became Lord President of the Council. Not until October 1551 was his victory marked by his promotion to the title of Duke of Northumberland.[11] But from the beginning of 1550 until July 1553 he was the most powerful man in England. He had triumphed in part through his ascendancy over the King, in part through winning over such prominent councillors as St John, Russell, and Paget. Fortune, too, was on his side, for although both he and Southampton were ill during the crucial months, he was well enough to convene Council meetings at his own house, while Southampton was in such poor health that he died in the summer of 1550. The outcome of this brief contest, crucial for English history, was decided by a small group of courtiers and councillors, operating within the royal Court and at Warwick's house in Holborn. Like the initial overthrow of Somerset himself, it was resolved without violence or bloodshed.

Given control of the King and his Household, Northumberland was well placed to dominate the central machinery of government. As Lord President he was empowered to nominate and to dismiss members of the Privy Council, and to summon its meetings. His own supporters— Bishop Goodrich, the Duke of Suffolk, Lord Darcy, Sir John Gates, Sir William Cecil—became councillors; his opponents—Southampton, Arundel, Bishop Tunstall, and others—were quickly and relatively painlessly removed from the Council within the first six months of 1550. Cecil, appointed Secretary in September 1550, was described by the Imperial Ambassador as being Northumberland's man; he was the liaison officer between the Duke, the Council, and the royal Household. Control over policy, administration, and patronage was restricted to a small group of about twenty councillors, who attended meetings regularly, together with six or so senior members of the Household. Men like Darcy and Gates belonged to both groups; Cecil linked the two; Northumberland presided over all. Of the men who counted most, six were soldiers, courtiers, and landed magnates: Northumberland himself, Somerset (until October 1551),

[10] BL Additional MS 48126, fos. 15–16. I am grateful to Dr G. W. Bernard for allowing me to use his transcript. See Hoak, *King's Council*, 255–6.

[11] For the rest of this chapter I have, for the sake of simplicity, referred to him as Northumberland, although it is not strictly accurate to do so before October 1551.

Suffolk, Bedford, Herbert (later Earl of Pembroke), Lord Admiral Clinton, and Northampton. Two were bishops: Cranmer and Goodrich. Five were primarily administrators: St John (later Marquis of Winchester), Cecil, Paget (until October 1551), Mason, and Petre. Three had risen through positions in the royal Household, especially from the Privy Chamber: Darcy, Gates, and Sidney.

Northumberland's personal reputation has not stood high since the day of his fall in 1553. He was understandably hated by those whom he brought down under Edward and the disastrous consequences of his attempted coup in 1553 led Protestants to damn him as a wicked and corrupt schemer. Yet in 1547 the Imperial Ambassador had described him as a man of 'high courage', in great favour with people and nobles owing to his 'liberality and splendour'. Ambitious and calculating he undoubtedly was; but he had the presence and perhaps the charm to draw men to his side.[12]

Tightly as he controlled the machinery of power in Court and Council, his situation, especially in 1550–1, did not seem wholly secure. Discontent was reported from the shires, while there was growing tension within the ruling group. The troubles of 1549 had left murmurs of sedition: a Norwich man was charged with recalling the good days on Mousehold Heath in 1549 and claiming that 'it was a merry world when we were yonder eating of mutton'.[13] The harvests of 1549, 1550, and 1551 were bad and the price of wheat in 1549–50 was almost double the level of the previous year. Debasement of the coinage in 1549 and 1551, followed by attempts to restore its value, destroyed faith in the currency, and in July 1551 the sweating sickness fell upon London.[14] Edward VI described the shocking swiftness of its attack: 'if one took cold, he died within three hours . . . Also if he slept the first six hours . . . then he raved and should die raving.'[15] Foul weather and disease were no fault of the government, but their effects made men wonder whether God was visiting England with punishment for her shortcomings.

The register of the Privy Council, the reports of ambassadors, and the *Chronicle* of the young King record constant uprisings or rumours of risings. Jehan Scheyfve, the new Imperial Ambassador, wrote in June 1550 that 10,000 peasants—an absurd estimate—had gathered at Sittingbourne in Kent; and Edward recorded a conspiracy in Essex later that month. In the following year Scheyfve reported great hostility in London towards foreign merchants, who were blamed for high prices; and Edward noted a

[12] *CSP Span.* ix. 19–20.
[13] W. Rye (ed.), *Depositions taken before the Mayor and Aldermen of Norwich* (Norwich, 1905), 22.
[14] Below, p. 70.   [15] *Chronicle of Edward VI*, 71.

conspiracy of Londoners who 'thought to rise on May Day against the strangers of the City'.[16] In October Scheyfve told Charles V that 'the commons and peasantry in various parts of the kingdom are once more inclined to rise, because of the everlasting instability and debasement of the coinage and the high prices of commodities'.[17]

The Council took harsh and effective measures to suppress unrest. The Parliament of 1549–50 carried a statute against unlawful assembly, under which the penalty of treason could be imposed if twelve or more persons assembled for longer than one hour with the purpose of demanding an alteration in the law.[18] Censorship, relaxed under Somerset, was reimposed by proclamation: nothing was to be printed nor any play performed unless first licensed by the King himself or six of his Council.[19] Military force was mobilized. In April 1550 the King issued licences for members of the Council and certain gentlemen of the Privy Chamber to keep in all 2,340 retainers. During July the government, faced with the problem of disbanded soldiers returning from Boulogne, resolved the difficulty by forming them into troops, 100 or 200 strong, under the command of local gentry in the southern and eastern counties. At the end of the year the Council devised a scheme for the nucleus of a standing army: selected councillors were to command bands of mounted men-at-arms, paid by the government. Somerset was allocated 100, and twelve other councillors fifty each, 'for the surety of His Majesty's person as for the stay of unquiet subjects'. Scheyfve interpreted the plan as designed to demonstrate the strength of the government and 'to rob the peasantry of all hope'.[20] Full mustering of the men-at-arms was, however, postponed until Somerset had been safely lodged again in the Tower. On 7 December Edward watched them parade, 'all well-armed men', 'the horses all great and fair'. Scheyfve was more sceptical: 'most of them were lightly armed and only middling-well accoutred . . . the troops were clumsy and unseasoned'.[21] The men-at-arms do not seem to have been used in action; but they provided a reserve of force in the capital. They were disbanded, to save money, in the autumn of 1552. In the provinces the Privy Council appointed Lords Lieutenant, most of whom were councillors, to take charge of the counties and to prevent unrest.

The privy councillors, and particularly Northumberland, have been accused of being so moved by hysterical fears and imagined plots that they neglected essential business. Probably their fears were indeed exaggerated; but there is ample confirmation from men on the spot and from ambassado-

[16] Ibid. 59.   [17] *CSP Span.* x. 381.   [18] 3 & 4 Edward VI c. 5.
[19] *Proclamations*, i, no. 371.
[20] *Chronicle of Edward VI*, 50; *APC* iii. 225; *CSP Span.* x. 279, 300.
[21] *Chronicle of Edward VI*, 100; *CSP Span.* x. 408.

rial reports that the times were unquiet. In the circumstances that was to be expected. Scheyfve, no great admirer of Northumberland's regime, commented that 'such great precautions have been taken against the possibility of an insurrection that the malcontents are unable to assemble'.[22] Following the risings of 1549, the Council would have been negligent had it relaxed its vigilance; and that vigilance prevented any actual rising of the populace.

More alarming to the government than popular revolt were the threats of dissension within its own ranks. In an attempt to gain Somerset's support against his own rivals, Northumberland had secured the Duke's restoration to the Council in April 1550 and had married his eldest son, John Dudley, to Somerset's daughter. Yet relations between the two men were never comfortable, and in the autumn there were rumours that Somerset was trying to win back personal support and, less credibly, that Northumberland planned to divorce his wife and marry Princess Elizabeth. Then in April 1551 there were reports of conspiracies against the Council in London and the north: the Earls of Derby and Shrewsbury were said to be involved with Somerset in plots to overthrow Northumberland. For the time being, however, the dissension was quelled and the councillors held banquets on four successive days to demonstrate their harmony. But six months later, on 16 October, Somerset was arrested and charged with having plotted to imprison Northumberland, seize the Tower, and stir up the people of London. One of Northumberland's henchmen, Sir Thomas Palmer, 'confessed' that Somerset, Arundel, and others had planned to assassinate their fellow-councillors at a banquet. The evidence against Somerset was defective and his peers rejected the charge of treason, finding him guilty only of felony. Since this was still a capital offence, it may not have been much consolation to Somerset; but the verdict was a blow to Northumberland. Although the more dramatic charges were almost certainly false, it is possible—even likely—that Somerset and his allies were involved in plans of some sort to unseat Northumberland, perhaps through the manipulation of Parliament.

Somerset was publicly executed on 22 January 1552 before a large and emotional gathering. When it was over 'a great crowd assembled all day long . . . talking about the Duke and bewailing his death. Those who could come near washed their hands in his blood . . .'.[23] Arundel and Paget were brought down with him. Arundel never came to trial, but after he had confessed to being party to the 'conspiracy' he was fined and set free in

[22] Jordan, *Edward VI: The Threshold of Power*, ch. 3. For reports of disturbances see e.g. Haynes, *State Papers*, 114 (report by Lord Admiral Clinton and Sir John Harington of troubles in the East Midlands); *CSP Span*. x. 381 (report of 10 Oct. 1551).

[23] *CSP Span*. x. 453.

December 1552; and he was restored to the Council shortly before Edward's death in 1553. Even Northumberland could find no evidence with which to convict Paget of treason, and the charges against him were altered to malversation of public money, to which he confessed during his trial: he, too, was fined and then pardoned. Northumberland was now without any serious rival for power. Although there were reports of dissension between him and Pembroke, the latter posed no threat to the Dudley ascendancy. The real danger lay in the future, with the failing health of the King, upon whose life and favour Northumberland was utterly dependent.

The ruthless manœuvres of October 1551 to January 1552 were brilliantly masked at Court by elaborate feasting. The King kept an open table at Greenwich over Christmas 'to win the hearts of the gentry'. A tournament was arranged between eighteen challengers, drawn from the leading nobles and courtiers; and a Lord of Misrule was appointed with a following of 100 people, who paraded through the Court carrying a representation of the sacrament, 'which they wetted and perfumed in most strange fashion'.[24] Northumberland seems now to have been pushing the young King into the public light in order to shelter himself from the repercussions of Somerset's death. Scheyfve reported of Edward that 'he seems to be a likely lad of quick, ready and well developed mind; remarkably so for his age . . . Northumberland, whom he seems to love and fear, is beginning to grant him a great deal of freedom, in order to dispel the hostility felt for [himself].'[25] Edward was not averse to the limelight; and in the summer of 1552 he made a successful progress through the southern counties. It was a sign both of restored order in the provinces and of Edward's emergence as an active monarch.

2. GOVERNMENT AND POLICY UNDER NORTHUMBERLAND

Northumberland's social policy has often been regarded as harsh and unfeeling towards the poor, especially in comparison with the supposedly 'liberal' measures of Protector Somerset. But this judgement is unfair. The brutal 'slavery Act' of 1547 was repealed in the parliamentary session of 1549–50 on the ground that it was too fierce to be enforced;[26] and two years later Parliament enacted a new Poor Law, which ordered the appointment in every parish of offical collectors who would 'gently ask' parishioners for alms and distribute these among the poor.[27] Those who refused to give would be reprimanded by the priest and, if necessary, by the bishop. This was the first statutory provision of administrative machinery for poor relief

[24] Ibid. 43–4; *Chronicle of Edward VI*, 103–5.   [25] *CSP Span.* x. 437–8.
[26] Above, Ch. 2 s. 5.   [27] 5 & 6 Edward VI c. 2.

since a short-lived Act of 1536; and although it probably had little practical effect, it stands as a landmark, albeit a small one, in the process by which free-lance begging was discouraged and local parish officers were charged with supporting the deserving poor.

The successive poor harvests of 1549, 1550, and 1551 threatened to raise food prices to a dangerous level, and the Council tried to ensure the supply of food at reasonable cost. Statutes prohibited the sale of corn before it came to the open market and two ambitious proclamations sought to control prices in detail. The first of these, issued in October 1550, fixed the maximum price of best white wheat at 13s. 4d. per quarter, and the second, promulgated a year later, dealt with livestock, pricing the 'greatest lean ox' at £2, veal and mutton at 1½d. per lb.[28] Neither was successful. The first rated prices at so low a point that farmers simply refused to sell in the open market; as the diplomat, Sir John Mason, shrewdly observed: 'I have seen so many experiences of such ordinances; and ever the end is dearth and lack of the thing that we seek to make a good cheap.'[29] A slightly more serious effort was made to enforce the proclamation on meat, but after only two months it was withdrawn with the promise of parliamentary legislation to follow, a promise that was never fulfilled.

Although Northumberland's Parliaments did little to deal with enclosure, that little was not particularly favourable to landlords. The tax on sheep and cloth was repealed, not as a concession to major graziers, but because it brought in little revenue and was resented by rich and poor sheep farmers alike. A modest Act of 1549–50 confirmed the Statute of Merton, which permitted landlords to cultivate waste ground provided that sufficient pasture was left.[30] A later Act ordered the appointment of commissioners to inquire into the amount of land under plough; but no such commissioners were appointed.[31] The law governing enclosure thus remained fundamentally unchanged, and actions could still be and were brought in the Court of Exchequer against enclosing landlords. The new regime differed from its predecessor in employing a more emollient tone and in avoiding the use of enclosure commissioners.

Somerset's ruinous administrative and financial legacy was dealt with more actively by Northumberland. The Privy Council was brought back into the centre of government from the periphery to which it had, for much of the protectorate, been relegated by Somerset. Paget, the most experienced of the councillors, drew up rules for its conduct which determined its procedure for the rest of the reign. His 'advice' ranged from moral exhortation to voting methods. 'The council to love one another as brethren or

[28] *Proclamations*, i, nos. 366, 380.   [29] *TED* ii. 188.
[30] 3 & 4 Edward VI c. 3.   [31] 5 & 6 Edward VI c. 5.

dear friends' was his optimistic beginning before he moved to more practical matters. Six councillors were always to attend at Court, of whom two
should be great officers of state and a third should be one of the Secretaries.
The Council should meet regularly for public business on at least three days
each week from 7 a.m. until dinner and from 2 p.m. until 4 p.m.; private
petitions would be heard on Sunday afternoons. Requests for offices and
other forms of patronage would be decided by vote on Sundays, each
councillor to have a white and a black ball for ballotting.[32] This exacting
routine was by no means the end of a councillor's business. During the last
eighteen months of Edward's reign at least sixteen commissions for the
restoration of the royal finances were issued, recovery of the debts owed to
the King and payment of debts owed by him becoming a major concern.
One of the most important commissions was set up in December 1551 for
calling in the King's debts, and three months later it was given the additional task of examining the operation of all the revenue departments. In
five months it produced a remarkably detailed analysis of royal revenue and
expenditure, with a long list of defects in the financial administration. Its
labours were perhaps more impressive than its achievements, for few of its
proposals were adopted. More significant was a separate discussion of the
total reorganization of the financial departments, with a view to bringing
the work of all the revenue courts under the direct supervision of the
Exchequer.[33] A statute carried in Edward's last Parliament authorized the
King to dissolve or unite all the courts by letters patent.[34] In the event the
actual changes were made under Mary, but the groundwork had been laid
under Northumberland. The work of extracting money from the King's
debtors, cutting down expenses, and tightening the accounting system went
forward slowly and painfully. Its results have yet to be examined fully by
historians, but it seems reasonably well established that by 1553 most of the
King's foreign loans, totalling about £130,000, had been repaid. 'I am sure
you would be glad to have his Majesty out of debt', Northumberland told
the Council in 1551; and two years later he had, through the work of men
like the Marquis of Winchester and Sir Walter Mildmay, come near to
achieving that end.[35]

The most formidable secular problem confronting Northumberland was
the state of the coinage. Successive debasements since 1542 had produced
coins lighter in weight and fuller of base metal than before. By the end of

[32] *Letters of William Lord Paget*, ed. B. L. Beer, Camden Soc., Camden Miscellany, 25
(London, 1974), 98–100.
[33] Below, Ch. 5 s. 5; J. D. Alsop, 'The Revenue Commission of 1552', *HJ* 22 (1979),
511–33.
[34] 7 Edward VI c. 2.   [35] Hoak, *King's Council*, 207.

1550 the so-called 'silver' coins were two-thirds their original weight and only 50 per cent silver: they contained therefore only one-third the quantity of silver in equivalent coins minted before 1542. By adulterating and diminishing the coins the Crown had made profits, between 1542 and 1551, of £1,200,000, equal to the sums raised by sale of Crown lands between 1534 and 1554 and more than the total cost of the Scottish campaigns. The operation, a gigantic fraud on the public, was essential for financing the Crown's wars; but its success depended upon acceptance of debased coins at their face value. Once the nominal and intrinsic values of the currency diverged too far the Crown could no longer persuade men to sell silver for minting. Furthermore, critics were denouncing the new coins: Latimer poured scorn on the 'pretty little shilling' issued in 1549 and Sir Thomas Smith blamed the debasement for rising prices.

Early in 1551 Northumberland determined to restore the true value of the coinage. At the same time he indulged in one final bout of debasement, issuing coins with only 25 per cent silver content in the spring of that year just as he was announcing measures to revalue the currency. Not unnaturally, suspicion and confusion resulted; and this was exacerbated by the method used for revaluation, known as 'calling down' the currency. A proclamation of April 1551 declared that from the following August the teston, or shilling, would be valued at 9d. and the groat, the fourpenny piece, at 3d; a later proclamation in August brought down the values at once to 6d. and 2d. respectively. This was an administratively simple device for increasing the quantity of silver in the coinage, by which there would, after August, be as much silver in coins of 6d. face value as there had been before in coins of 12d.: the silver content was thus doubled without any of the trouble and expense of reminting. Two months later, however, the mints began to issue new coins which conformed very nearly to the pre-1542 standard. Northumberland's objectives were laudable, indeed their achievement was essential to the establishment of economic confidence, but unfortunately his methods were clumsy and, to a large degree, ineffective. Yet, although he has been blamed for raising extra profit for the Crown by debasement after he had decided to restore the currency, the Crown's needs were desperate and the amount involved—about £120,000—not such as to imperil the larger operation. More serious was the decision to announce the 'calling down' of the coinage four months before it was due. From the moment of the proclamation no one wished to possess currency that would soon lose 25 per cent of its face value, and rumours spread that further 'calling down' was being considered. The government denied this in July and then did exactly that in August. The effect was to prevent producers from selling their goods for cash, except at a high price, and to generate uncertainty about the currency. Instead of falling in response to the revaluation of the currency, prices remained high. Although the coins issued in October were of far higher standard than before, the currency remained in confusion, with debased and standard coins circulating together. Northumberland has been criticized for the failure to bring down prices or to achieve a credit-worthy coinage; but it should be remembered that he was faced with an unprecedented problem, and that even the most experienced financier could hardly have solved it without some dislocation.

The vagaries of the currency were accompanied by fluctuations in English trade. Overseas demand for English cloth increased in the mid-1540s, to reach a peak in 1549–50. There was then a sharp fall in the next two years. Part of the reason for the increase in trade was probably the decline in the exchange rate, which was itself responding, albeit slowly, to the debasement of the currency: the decline began in the autumn of 1546, proceeded steadily until late 1550, and then accelerated downwards to its lowest point in July 1551, after which the pound began to rise. The crisis in the export market in the years 1550–1 and 1551–2 cannot have been wholly caused by currency manipulation; but probably the uncertainties bred in those years hampered commerce. Whatever the reasons—and they were complicated—in 1551 and 1552 the country faced a period of high food prices, collapsing cloth markets, and mounting confusion. Not all of this was the government's fault: bad weather was certainly the principal enemy of the food supply; and Somerset's debasement was much more culpable than Northumberland's clumsy efforts to restore the currency. But social disaffection was widespread and some of the hostility was directed at Northumberland himself.

In foreign policy, Northumberland had only a narrow range of choices open to him. Somerset's Scottish plans had disintegrated in 1549, Boulogne was almost within the grasp of the French, and the Crown was hopelessly in debt. Negotiations were opened with the French in January 1550 and a treaty of peace was signed in March, under which Boulogne was returned to the French King at once for half the sum agreed in 1546. Under the terms of the treaty England agreed to end the war with Scotland and to withdraw her troops from the Scottish fortresses. Paget, one of the negotiators of the treaty, explained the position starkly to Northumberland: 'we have agreed upon a peace although not with so good conditions as we could have wished'; but the need to pull out of the war was paramount.[36]

Once peace had been achieved Northumberland began to explore the possibility of a closer alliance with France. Relations with Charles V were

[36] *Letters of William Paget*, 98.

deteriorating as the government put pressure on his cousin Mary to conform. She had previously been allowed to practise her Catholic rites in
private, but early in 1550 she became so alarmed at the Council's attitude
that plans were made for her to flee abroad. They came to nothing, but in
March 1551 she entered London at the head of a large retinue of knights
and gentlemen. While she may not have intended to be provocative, her
appearance was threatening to the government, which resorted to further
pressure upon her. Edward VI personally told her that her conduct had only
been tolerated in the expectation of her 'reconciliation' to the established
religion and that there now seemed no hope of that. In reply Charles V
threatened war if Mary was compelled to conform. The English government stuck to its position, ordered Mary's household officers to forbid
private masses, and imprisoned them when they failed to comply.
Thunderbolts from Charles were averted by the outbreak of war between
France and the Empire; and England's position was secured by the Treaty
of Angers with France, under which the planned marriage of Edward with
Mary Stewart was abandoned and an alternative match arranged between
the King and Elizabeth Valois. The demands on Mary Tudor now ceased.
She continued to hear Mass in private, her household officers were released
from prison, and her relations with Edward improved. The consequences of
these events were, however, serious. Mary blamed Northumberland for her
troubles and it became clear that he would not survive her accession to the
throne.

Northumberland has sometimes been criticized for following a weak
foreign policy and reducing England to the status of a second-rank pawn.
But she was never in a position to match the resources of the Habsburg
and the Valois. Peace was essential to England; Somerset's Scottish objectives were no longer attainable, if indeed they ever had been; and
the concessions made to France were not particularly damaging. While
Northumberland's diplomacy was uninspiring, it at least provided a respite
from war.

3. RELIGIOUS CHANGE

In the long run the most significant aspect of Northumberland's rule was
the continuation of religious change. If there had ever been any thought
among those who overthrew Somerset of returning the country to the old
ways it was soon extinguished. Rumours that the Roman Mass was to be
revived were explicitly denied in a proclamation of 30 October 1549. A
more emphatic statement, delivered on Christmas Day, ordered the destruction of all missals and other service books according to the Roman

use.[37] While it is unlikely that Northumberland ever intended to reverse Somerset's religious settlement, his commitment to the Protestant cause was strengthened by his reliance on Cranmer to win him favour with the King and by Edward's preference for the reformed religion. Early in the following year Northumberland was being eulogized by reformers as a zealous friend of the true faith.

The second Prayer Book of the reign was carried through Parliament in the early months of 1552 and came into effect in the following November. It was the model for the Elizabethan Book, which was itself only slightly modified in 1662; with a few changes and a brief interim under Mary, the liturgy established under Northumberland's aegis was followed by the Church of England for the next four centuries. The most significant differences between the First and Second Prayer Books of Edward VI are found in the communion service. It is impossible to list them all, but a few examples will show the general trend. The words for the administration of the sacrament in 1549 had been: 'The body of our Lord Jesus Christ which was given for thee, preserve thy body and soul unto everlasting life.' In 1552 any hint of transubstantiation—the change of the substance of the bread and the wine into the body and the blood of Christ—was removed and the emphasis was placed upon remembrance and spiritual nourishment: 'Take and eat this, in remembrance that Christ died for thee, and feed on him in thy heart by faith, with thanksgiving.' The prayer for the Church in 1549 had rendered praise and thanksgiving for the virtues of the Virgin Mary, the patriarchs, prophets, apostles, and martyrs: these words were omitted from the 1552 book. Vestments were now forbidden except the rochet for bishops and the surplice for priests; and music was reduced to a minimum.

However, the 1552 Book was by no means as radical as some reformers wished, and by comparison with the service devised by John Knox a few years later for his Genevan congregation, it was positively ritualistic. Knox proclaimed that the provision in the Book for kneeling before the bread and wine at the communion service was idolatrous; and when Cranmer insisted that the instructions on this matter be retained, a compromise was reached with the 'black rubric', which affirmed that kneeling implied no adoration of the sacrament, but rather a 'humble and grateful acknowledgment of the benefits of Christ'. The conclusion of the matter was probably more satisfying to Cranmer than it was to Knox. The conservatism of the Book appeared also in the words of the prayer of humble access, which, while omitting the phrase 'in these holy mysteries', asked God to 'grant us . . . so to eat the flesh of thy dear son Jesus Christ, and to drink his blood, that our

[37] *Proclamations*, i, nos. 352, 353.

sinful bodies may be made clean by his body and our souls washed through his most precious blood', strongly suggesting that the communion service was more than the mere act of commemoration which Knox and his allies would have it.[38]

The liturgical changes set out in the 1552 Prayer Book were completed by forty-two articles of faith drawn up by Cranmer and issued by the Council, without reference to Convocation, in 1553. Article XI affirmed the Protestant doctrine that 'justification by faith only in Jesus Christ . . . is the most certain and most wholesome doctrine for a Christian man'; article XVII that 'predestination unto life is the everlasting purpose of God, whereby . . . he hath constantly decreed by his counsel, secret unto us, to deliver from curse and damnation those whom he has chosen out of mankind'; article XXIX that 'transubstantiation . . . is repugnant to the plain words of scripture'; and article XXX that 'sacrifices of masses . . . were fables and dangerous deceits'. The reformed doctrines were thus unequivocally proclaimed, although it is significant that the articles denounced anabaptism as vigorously as they condemned popery.[39]

Who were responsible for these changes? What were their intentions and what doctrines did they hold? Why was a more radical settlement made after 1549? These questions have been debated with a great deal of theological passion and it is unlikely that any undisputed answers can be given, for little is known of the deliberations which produced the new Prayer Book. Probably its principal author was Archbishop Cranmer, as he was of its predecessor; but he was certainly influenced, aided—and perhaps hindered—by a flow of advice from continental reformers like Martin Bucer and Peter Martyr and from such English theologians as Nicholas Ridley and John Hooper. The young King himself, however, showed no apparent interest in the Book, in spite of his Protestant beliefs: there is no entry about it in his *Chronicle*. The bishops had met for revising the services as early as January 1551; there had been heated debate between Gardiner and Cranmer on the nature of the Eucharist; and Bucer had completed his *Censura*, commenting on the first Book, in the same year. The final liturgy was evidently the result of several months' debate and preparation.

Cranmer's eucharistic beliefs are difficult to define. Evidence can be found for the view that he denied any presence of Christ in the elements: 'he is not in it, neither spiritually, as he is in man, nor corporally, as he is in heaven, but only sacramentally'. Elsewhere he claimed that 'the sacramental bread and wine is not bare and naked figures, but so pithy and effectuous

---

[38] For a fuller discussion see G. J. Cuming, *A History of Anglican Liturgy* (London, 1969), ch. 5; on the black rubric see Jasper Ridley, *Thomas Cranmer* (Oxford, 1962), 336–7.

[39] G. Burnet, *History of the Reformation* (3 vols., London, 1679–1715), ii. 209–20.

that whoseover worthily eateth them, eateth spiritually Christ's flesh and blood'.[40] It is impossible to derive a wholly consistent view on the nature of the elements from Cranmer's writings, largely because they were mostly polemical and his formulation varied according to the opponent of the moment. But he does seem, after 1549, to have held a clear view on the 'effectuousness' of the Eucharist: it was no mere reminder of Christ's life, as Zwingli and Knox would have had it, but a means of spiritual nourishment for the believer not available in any other way. At the same time he was, even as early as 1548, firmly opposed to the doctrine of transubstantiation. His attitude towards the Eucharist informs the 1552 service and seems not very different from that held by him when the first Prayer Book was promulgated.

Bucer had thought that the 1549 Book was an interim measure which retained some ceremonies for a time in order to avoid opposition and to give opportunity for the people to be more fully instructed in new ways. If that is correct we have a large part of the explanation for the liturgical changes under Northumberland: they were already contemplated before Somerset's fall. Yet even if Cranmer and other divines had regarded the 1549 Book as a permanent solution, it very rapidly became clear that this could not be. The Book had pleased virtually no one and displeased many. Gardiner objected strongly to it, but was reluctantly prepared to use it under royal command, even indicating certain features that were acceptable to orthodox Catholics; and that alone was enough to condemn it in Protestant eyes. Many priests continued to use certain old ceremonies which were not specifically forbidden; and Bishop Ridley's visitation articles of 1551 even complained that some of them were still accustomed to 'counterfeit the popish Mass, as to kiss the Lord's Table'. Moderate Protestants were critical of the 1549 Book and radicals like John Hooper considered it to be 'very defective, and of doubtful construction, and, in some respects indeed, manifestly impious'.[41] Therefore, even if the 1549 Book represented the views of Cranmer at the time it was written, which is unlikely, it could not have survived unchanged, partly because conservatives used it in ways that were intolerable to reformers, partly because it was considered inadequate by most Protestant divines from the moment of its birth. To ask why Northumberland chose a more radical course than Somerset is to pose the question wrongly, for there was no choice other than a return to Roman orthodoxy. The promulgation of the second Book followed ineluctably upon the first; there was no change in direction, merely a continuation on

---

[40] *Writings and Disputations of Thomas Cranmer relative to the Sacrament of the Lord's Supper*, ed. John Edmund Cox, Parker Soc. (London, 1844), 238.

[41] Cuming, *Anglican Liturgy*, 97.

the same course. It is more relevant to ask why the reforms of 1552–3 were not more radical still. John Hooper, John Knox, and many of the foreign Protestant exiles from Europe expected a Church to be founded on the lines of Zwingli's at Zurich and were bitterly disappointed at what they conceived to be at best a half-measure. Their defeat stemmed partly from the stalwart opposition of Cranmer and Bishop Ridley of London, partly from Northumberland's realization that his protegé Hooper was a political liability.

The 1552 Prayer Book was the greatest single achievement of Edward's reign. But it was not the only notable ecclesiastical measure. A committee established in 1551 produced a massive proposal for the reform of ecclesiastical laws. The objectives were, to some Protestants, as important as the alterations in the liturgy, for the document proposed a strict system of ecclesiastical discipline, based upon the authority of elders and pastors in the parishes. Not surprisingly, this medicine seemed too harsh for the laity and the *Reformatio legum ecclesiasticorum* was blocked in the House of Lords. It remains an impressive monument to clerical aspirations and a reminder that, while Parliament might accept the liturgical decisions of bishops, it would resist any attempt to improve spiritual discipline.

Important changes were made in the leadership of the Church. Edmund Bonner, Bishop of London, had been deprived of his bishopric shortly before Somerset's fall, and he was followed by Bishops Gardiner, Day, Heath, Vesey, and Tunstall, all of whom were deprived in 1551 and 1552. Some notable Protestants were appointed to their sees: Nicholas Ridley moved from Rochester to London; John Ponet succeeded Gardiner at Winchester; John Hooper filled Heath's see of Worcester, combining it with Gloucester; Miles Coverdale succeeded Vesey at Exeter; and John Scory replaced Day at Chichester. Together with Cranmer at Canterbury, Holgate at York, and Goodrich at Ely, these men made up an imposing Protestant team; but there remained many bishops of whom the most that could be said was that they were uncommitted.

The effect of Northumberland's rule upon the property of the Church was savage. Most images of saints and the Virgin had already been destroyed during the Protectorate; and rumours that the government coveted communion plate, ecclesiastical ornament, jewels, and vestments prompted parish officers to hide or sell their valuables. The Privy Council riposted by ordering that inventories be compiled, first by bishops and then, when that proved ineffective, by sheriffs and Justices of the Peace. A further commission was issued during the parliamentary session of 1552, while the second Act of Uniformity was being carried; and expropriation was finally ordered in February 1553 after the issue of the second Prayer Book. By then it was too late for much to be done before Edward's death. The Crown seems to have profited little from the operation, largely because parish valuables had mostly been sold off for repairing churches and relieving the poor. The Protestant objective of stripping churches of their plate and ornaments was largely achieved before 1553, but not in the way that the Crown had intended.

More significant for the future was the government's expropriation of episcopal lands and revenues, from which the Crown and leading laymen were the beneficiaries. The most vulnerable of the bishops were those newly appointed or translated, on whom pressure could be applied before they entered their sees. The process had already begun under Somerset, when the income of the bishopric of Lincoln was reduced by £1,300 out of nearly £2,000, that of Bath and Wells by £1,450 out of £1,850. A lavish helping of this profit went directly to Somerset himself, who acquired four large manors and some smaller ones from Lincoln, seven manors from Bath and Wells, and the site where Somerset House was built in London upon the ruins of three episcopal palaces. No other politician seems to have been greatly enriched by Church lands between January 1547 and October 1549. Northumberland's policy was different in two respects. First, no single see suffered under his regime as had Lincoln and Bath and Wells under Somerset. But the overall losses were large. Under Edward VI the total income of English sees fell from about £30,000 per annum to about £22,500; and of this around £3,500 was taken during the Protectorate and £4,000 under Northumberland. In the latter period London, Winchester, Exeter, Durham, and Worcester suffered most. Secondly, Northumberland made much less personal gain than Somerset, dispersing most of the expropriated lands among his noble and courtly allies. The Winchester lands acquired after Gardiner's fall were divided between the Marquis of Winchester, the Earl of Pembroke, Andrew Dudley, Sir John Gates, Sir Philip Hoby, and three others. This dispersal of patronage was an important way of mobilizing and preserving lay support.[42] Paradoxically, Northumberland, who was less personally grasping than Somerset, attracted greater criticism from the bishops. By the end of the reign he was on bad terms with most of them, perhaps because he criticized them openly, while Somerset had been careful with his words as he stripped them of their property.

Can England be described as a Protestant nation at Edward's death? The liturgy was fully reformed and probably the second Prayer Book was being used in most churches. The forty-two Articles of Faith were unequivocally Protestant. The leading bishops were reformers and the most staunch

[42] For figures and details see Felicity Heal, *Of Prelates and Princes* (Cambridge, 1980), chs. 6, 8.

conservatives had been expelled from the episcopal bench. A great deal of plate, ornaments, and vestments had disappeared, in one way or another, from the parishes churches. The chantries had been dissolved. The practices and symbols of the old faith had been, for the most part, destroyed. But none of that made a Protestant people. Bucer told Edward VI in 1550 that the reforms had not been accompanied by preaching or discipline, but 'by means of ordinances which the majority obey very grudgingly, and by the removal of the instruments of the ancient superstition'.[43] It is unlikely that much progress had been achieved three years later. The government made no serious effort to provide the necessary structure of preaching: a scheme for appointing six itinerant preachers in Lancashire, Derbyshire, and Wales came to nothing. Two bishops, Ridley in London and Hooper in Worcester and Gloucester, were astonishingly vigorous in preaching and in disciplining; yet, while Ridley's efforts may have had some effect, the diocese of Gloucester was not effectively purged of conservative clergy until well into the reign of Elizabeth. The difficulties encountered by the Elizabethan authorities suggest that the Protestant faith had impinged only lightly on clergy and laity by 1553.[44] The religious complexion of the nation varied greatly from one area to another: in London and Kent the reformers were fairly successful; Sussex was conservative until well after 1558; and the north, especially Lancashire, was predominantly Catholic. The response of the clergy to their freedom to marry provides one indication of this variety, although a married clergyman was not necessarily a committed Protestant. In London nearly one-third of the clergy married, in Lincolnshire only 10 per cent, and in Lancashire only 4 per cent. In most sees the number of men coming forward for ordination had been falling since 1536, and it continued to be low under Edward. The general impression given by the Church in 1553 was that it contained some stalwart Catholics and Protestants, but that these men and women were in a minority. Most were confused and uncertain, acquiescent in any lead from above (Plates 1, 10).

4. IRELAND

Since the fourteenth century English authority over Ireland had been steadily declining, as the area controlled by the Dublin government was restricted and the revenue derived from the country diminished. The demands made upon English resources by the French wars reduced almost to nothing any support that might be given to Dublin by the Crown. In consequence, Ireland had long been left to govern itself, with occasional

---

[43] D. M. Loades, *The Oxford Martyrs* (London, 1970), 97.
[44] Below, Ch. 7 s. 1, Ch. 11 s. 1.

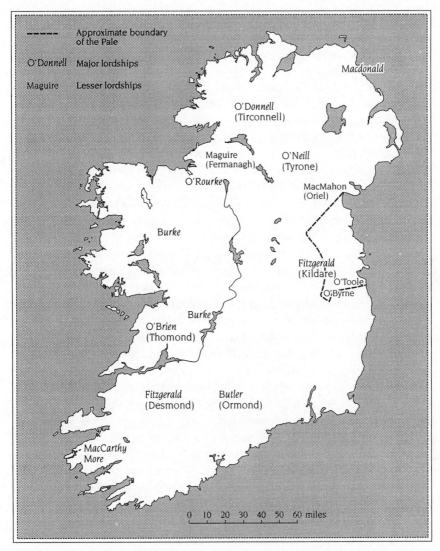

Approximate boundary of the Pale

O'Donnell Major lordships

Maguire Lesser lordships

Macdonald

O'Donnell
(Tirconnell)

Maguire
(Fermanagh)

O'Neill
(Tyrone)

O'Rourke

MacMahon
(Oriel)

Burke

Fitzgerald
(Kildare)

O'Toole

O'Byrne

Burke

O'Brien
(Thomond)

Fitzgerald
(Desmond)

Butler
(Ormond)

MacCarthy
More

0 10 20 30 40 50 60 miles

MAP 7. The lordships of Tudor Ireland

intervention from England. Although this policy worked just about adequately for most of the time, the standard of law and order was low, the dangers of political subversion were real, and pretenders like Simnel and Warbeck could exploit them.

The king ruled Ireland through an administration in Dublin modelled upon the institutions of Westminster and headed by a Lord Deputy appointed, in theory at least, by the Crown. In practice the Deputy was nearly always an Anglo-Irish nobleman, for most of the seventy-five years before 1534 one of the earls of Kildare. While the English government maintained a tenuous authority over the Dublin administration, the latter was the effective ruler only of the Pale, and not very effective even within that small area.[45] Beyond the Pale, in Leinster, most of Munster, Clare, and Galway the great Anglo-Irish feudal magnates ruled their lordships, owing formal allegiance to the Crown but exercising virtually complete independence from its commands. South-west Munster, northern Connacht, and Ulster were controlled by the Gaelic chieftains, who only partially accepted the authority of the English Crown and ruled by a separate system of law. In principle the Anglo-Irish and Gaelic societies were markedly different: the one based upon feudal tenure and primogeniture, the other upon clans or septs which collectively owned the land. In reality the social and cultural distinctions between the indigenous Gaelic society and the Anglo-Irish conquerors had become blurred over time. Lords and chieftains were concerned with local and dynastic conflicts; and they were bound together only by hostility to interference from Dublin or London. Their power derived from hired troops, either native Irish retainers or Scottish gallowglass, maintained by the unfortunate peasantry, who had to billet and feed them.[46]

Both Henry VII and Henry VIII made sporadic efforts to exert more effective control over Ireland; but the cost of sustained conquest was too great. In 1534, however, the first steps were taken towards a major change in the political relationship between the Crown and Ireland. Partly under the influence of Irish reformers, partly out of concern to establish royal authority on a stronger foundation at the time of the breach with Rome, Thomas Cromwell proposed the installation of an English Lord Deputy and reform of the Dublin administration. His plans were interrupted by the rebellion of the tenth Earl of Kildare, Silken Thomas. With the defeat of the Kildare revolt Cromwell continued with his plans, installing Sir William Skeffington as Deputy, appointing other Englishmen to key posts in Dublin and establishing a permanent English garrison in Ireland. The essence of the Cromwellian reforms was the subjection of Dublin to London: never again would a Kildare rule Ireland in the King's name. Yet this did little or nothing to establish effective royal government beyond the Pale. Sir Anthony St Leger, appointed Lord Deputy in 1540, attempted by a policy

---

[45] For the Pale, see Ch. 1 n. 32.

[46] See Map 7. Gallowglass, from *galloglaich*, meaning a Scottish mercenary employed by Irish chiefs, named after their type of axe. The gallowglass had settled in Ireland in earlier centuries; during the sixteenth century other Scottish fighters, the redshanks, came over as mercenaries but did not settle.

of conciliation to remedy that failing. His policy of surrender and regrant involved the surrender by the Gaelic chieftains of their lands, which they received back as a fief held from the Crown and passed to their heirs by primogeniture. In return for submission they gained security of title. St Leger also secured the Act for the kingly title in 1541, which made Henry King, rather than merely Lord, of Ireland, reformed the Irish Parliament by introducing representatives from the Gaelic regions, and brought two Gaelic chieftains, Tyrone and Thomond, onto the Irish Council.

However, most of the influential members of the Dublin administration were opposed to St Leger's policy of reconciliation and integration; and on his return to London in 1546 it came abruptly to an end when Sir William Brabazon, the vice-treasurer, provoked rebellion by the O'Connors in Leinster. St Leger's opponents in Dublin and London gained the ear of Protector Somerset and, although he returned for a time to Ireland, military command was entrusted to the bellicose Sir Edward Bellingham, who superseded him as Deputy in 1548. The English element in the Irish government accused St Leger of being 'more favourable to Irishmen than to the King's subjects'—in itself a revealing phrase.[47] After suppressing the rebellions, Bellingham embarked on a policy of protecting the Pale by fortification and colonization. Fort Governor and Fort Protector were built in the counties of Offaly and Leix and settlers placed on the lands of the rebels. Although St Leger again returned briefly to Ireland in 1550 after Bellingham's death, he had little support from Northumberland and the Council, and was forced to give way to a military expert, Sir James Croft. Northumberland's approach to Ireland was little different from Somerset's, except that his apparently more radical religious policy made firm action the more necessary. Croft was provided with 2,000 English soldiers and £24,000 a year to pay his army. With that force he was able to quieten the whole island and to complete the plantations in Leix and Offaly. He was, however, aware of the risks inherent in his policy and of the dangerous consequences of debasement of the currency. The country, he wrote to Cecil, was 'never liker to have turned to a revolt by mean of the money [sic] and decay of the cities and towns'.[48] His military power prevented that, but at a heavy cost: £250,000 was spent on Ireland during Edward's reign. At the very end of the reign the government once more turned to St Leger in the hope that he might rule Ireland more economically. But by then the trust that he had built between the Gaelic chiefs and the Crown had been destroyed.

[47] Dean G. White, 'The reign of Edward VI in Ireland: some political, economic and social aspects', *Irish Historical Studies*, 14 (1965), 201.
[48] Ibid. 207.

While the Edwardian Council's secular policy was destroying the chances—slender though they may have been—of creating an integrated government in Ireland, its religious changes bred further mistrust. The royal supremacy had been enacted by the Irish Parliament in 1536 without objection, although there was short-lived opposition to the dissolution of the monasteries. A state Church was established in Ireland, as in England, but it was less readily accepted there, even in Dublin. Under Edward, liturgical reform began slowly, partly because St Leger believed in caution and tact, partly because he had enough political trouble on his hands with the O'Connor revolt. Bellingham and Archbishop Browne of Dublin tried to force the pace of change, but the firm opposition of Archbishop Dowdall of Armagh provided a nucleus of resistance. When St Leger returned in 1550 he reverted to the conciliatory policy of gradual change, even providing a Latin version of the 1549 Prayer Book. But this was too feeble for St Leger's enemies, and on his recall Croft was encouraged to undertake more vigorous reform. Dowdall went into exile and the other bishops were lukewarm. The Protestant John Bale, appointed Bishop of Ossory, found that even in Waterford the 1549 Prayer Book was being used with all the ceremonies of a Roman Mass; prayers were being spoken for the dead; and at funerals there were 'prodigious howlings and patterings'. Yet the royal supremacy was generally accepted and liturgical reform made some progress, even if the radical Bale found it negligible. The Crown had gained control over the Church; St Leger's programme of reform by persuasion and teaching might have had some effect had it been given a chance. At the death of Edward Protestant worship had won only a little success; but it had not yet alienated the people of Ireland.

5. THE SUCCESSION CRISIS

Having committed himself unequivocally to the Protestant cause, Northumberland was dangerously dependent on the life and favour of Edward VI. In February 1553 it became evident that Edward's health was disintegrating; and the doctors warned that his life was in danger. With occasional remissions his terrible and painful illness rapidly worsened over the next four months. He was spitting blood; he was racked by a harsh and continuous cough; his body was dry and burning. The symptoms point to the final stages of acute pulmonary tuberculosis. The legal position over the succession was clear. Under the Succession Act of 1544 the Crown was to pass to Mary and then to Elizabeth if Edward died childless; Henry VIII was empowered to designate further provisions by his will. That will, having confirmed the position of Mary and Elizabeth, named as next in line the descendants of Henry's younger sister Mary—Lady Frances Grey and her daughters—rather than those of his elder sister Margaret, grandmother of Mary Stewart.[49] Northumberland, determined to avoid his own political eclipse, persuaded Edward to sign a 'Devise' for the succession which bequeathed the throne to the male heirs of Lady Frances Grey and her daughters and excluded Mary Tudor and Elizabeth. The document was plainly illegal since it flouted both the statute of 1544 and the will of Henry VIII. Furthermore it named non-existent persons as heirs, for Lady Frances had only daughters, who themselves had as yet no children. Northumberland married the eldest Grey daughter, Jane, to his son Guilford Dudley, and the second, Catherine, to Lord Herbert, son of the Earl of Pembroke. Reliable councillors were sent to guard key points in the realm. By the time of the marriages, in late May, it was clear, at least to the shrewd Jehan Scheyfve, that the Council intended to exclude Princess Mary from the throne. By the end of May the doctors reported that Edward had only two months to live: there was no possibility that a male heir could be born to any of the Grey family in time. Edward's 'Devise' was therefore changed to make Lady Jane herself the heir. The judges, summoned to cast this strange document into legal form, declared it unlawful, as it certainly was: 'we refused to make the said books for the danger of treason', declared Chief Justice Montague. First Northumberland and then Edward himself angrily insisted that they obey. Letters Patent were drawn up to exclude Mary and Elizabeth and to bequeath the throne to Lady Jane; privy councillors and other notables were forced to sign them, so that they would be fully committed to the scheme. Early in July the leading councillors arrived in London with their 'powers': Northumberland with 500 men in livery, Suffolk with 300, and others in proportion to their rank. On 6 July 1553 Edward died and, after his death had been kept secret for a few days, Lady Jane was proclaimed Queen.

Events then moved very fast. Two days before Edward died, Mary, warned of Northumberland's plans, left Hunsdon, twenty miles north of London, and moved her household through Hertfordshire, Cambridgeshire, and Norfolk, where she stopped briefly at Kenninghall, before proceeding to Framlingham Castle in Suffolk. As she went, support came to her from Norfolk and Suffolk: 'every day they flocked to their rightful queen, ready to lay out for her their wealth, their effort and life itself', wrote one of her supporters. At Framlingham, which she reached on 12 July, she formed a Council and issued orders as Queen. The Earls of Bath, Sussex, and Oxford, Lords Wentworth and Windsor, and several

---

[49] Above, Ch. 2 s. 1, for a description of Henry VIII's will.

important East Anglian landowners joined her with considerable forces. Sussex took charge of the army and prepared for battle, while in London Northumberland marshalled his troops against her.[50] After Lady Jane had begged that her father be excused from commanding them, Northumberland led them out of London on 13 July. A few days later the Privy Council heard that a naval squadron, sent to Great Yarmouth to arrest Mary if she tried to flee, had deserted to her. This damaged the morale of the councillors, and as other news came in of accessions of strength to Mary, they began to leave the Tower, where Lady Jane was lodged, proclaiming Mary as Queen in London on 19 July, only thirteen days after the death of her brother. By the following day the Earl of Arundel, Lord Paget, and Lord Rich had reached Framlingham and sworn fealty to Mary, reporting to her the glad news that London had accepted her. In the City itself 'great was the triumph . . . The Earl of Pembroke threw away his cap full of angelletes . . . The bonfires were without number . . .'.[51]

What had gone wrong with the plans of that skilful Alcibiades, Northumberland? His situation in the weeks before Edward's death had been agonizingly difficult, but even so his plans were ill-conceived.[52] To marry his son to Jane and then to have her declared heir to the throne was a blatant show of ambition; and his insistence upon an illegal settlement of the throne disturbed many of the councillors. Although he was politically in a strong position—controlling the machinery of government, occupying the capital, and commanding the royal troops—he made feeble use of his advantages. The navy was poorly manned; there was little money to pay sailors or soldiers. Above all, he failed to secure Mary's person at the outset, giving her the opportunity to make her courageous stand at Framlingham. However, the events of those thirteen days remain in many ways obscure. The idea of a nation rising in united protest to defend the legitimate rights of the Tudor dynasty is not convincing. Although the desertion of the naval squadron was thought at the time in London, and has often been taken since, to have been the consequence of popular pressure and mutiny among the crews, recently uncovered evidence suggests that the mutiny was unconnected with the politics of succession and that neither captains nor

[50] Dale Hoak, 'Two revolutions in Tudor government: the formation and organization of Mary I's Privy Council', in Christopher Coleman and David Starkey (eds.), *Revolution Reassessed* (Oxford, 1986), 87–115; Diarmaid MacCulloch (ed.), *The* Vita Mariae Angliae Reginae *of Robert Wingfield of Brantham*, Camden Soc., 4th ser. 29, Camden Miscellany 37 (London, 1984), 253.

[51] *Chronicle of Queen Jane*, 11. An 'angellet' or 'anglet' was a gold coin worth 3s. 9d.

[52] For another view, see Jordan, *Edward VI: The Threshold of Power*, ch. 14, where it is argued that the plans to alter the succession originated with Edward and were forced by the young King on a reluctant Northumberland.

crews were willing to commit themselves against Mary when she already had strong local support. Townsmen in East Anglia, like the sailors, were perplexed and undecided; borough councillors vacillated, waiting upon the outcome, swayed more by local faction than by national issues.[53] While there was probably some popular support for Mary among the common people, more important was the backing given to her by nobles and gentlemen, especially in East Anglia and the Thames Valley. Some of these men were Protestants, but most seem to have been Catholics, looking to Mary for a restoration of the true faith. The equivocation and ultimate desertion of the Council in London was critical. Northumberland himself had suspected treachery when he left London: 'if ye mean deceit . . . God will revenge the same', he warned them—to little effect.[54] Had Mary been captured, had there been no show of support for her, the Council might have stood by Northumberland. But the mobilization of her army at Framlingham meant that civil war was bound to follow if Jane's cause was maintained. Civil peace could best be preserved by the Marian succession, which was achieved during two weeks of confusion and bewilderment by a strong regional movement in her favour, led by nobles and gentlemen, and a shift of allegiance by uneasy councillors.

[53] J. D. Alsop, 'A regime at sea: the navy and the 1553 succession crisis', *Albion*, 24 (1992), 577–90; R. Tittler and S. L. Battley, 'The local community and the Crown in 1553', *BIHR* 57 (1984), 131–9.
[54] *Chronicle of Queen Jane*, 7.

CHAPTER 4

The Reign of Mary Tudor

1. THE INSTALLATION OF THE REGIME

The Queen proclaimed in July 1553 had lived for six years in almost total isolation from political life. True, she had often visited her brother's Court and had occasionally received English politicians and imperial envoys, but her household, an island of the true faith in a sea of heresy, had turned in on itself. Under pressure to abandon the Mass, Mary had been forced on to the defensive, into tearful scenes with her brother and ill-planned attempts at escape abroad. Her reaction has often been described as hysterical, yet she had few resources other than tears and flight: although her cousin, Charles V, uttered threats on her behalf, there was little he could do. When the moment for action came, at the death of Edward and again during Wyatt's revolt, she was courageous, decisive, and determined. But she had little experience of government or of politics, and not much inherent sense of manœuvre: as an imperial envoy put it, she was 'inexpert in worldly matters and a novice all round. I believe that if God does not preserve her she will be deceived and lost . . .'.[1] Her presence lacked the majesty of her father and her sister. The Venetian ambassador, Soranzo, described her as short, rather thin, with a red-and-white complexion and a poor dress-sense; he added that she suffered from headaches and heart pains.[2] An anonymous Spaniard in the retinue of Philip of Spain wrote that 'The Queen . . . is not at all beautiful: small and rather flabby than fat, she is of white complexion and fair and has no eyebrows. She is a perfect saint and dresses badly.'[3] Her portraits reveal a sad, pinched, rather plain woman, who wins our sympathy but does not command our respect. She worked hard at the business of government, was brave and resolute in the face of opposition, but lacked that quality of 'magnificence' which was an essential element of Renaissance monarchy (Plate 2a).

The men who had administered Mary's household when she was princess—Robert Rochester, Edward Waldegrave, Henry Jerningham, and

---

[1] *CSP Span.* xi. 227–9.   [2] *CSP Ven.* v. 934.   [3] *CSP Span.* xiii. 30–1.

others—were loyal, honest, and devoutly Catholic; but they also lacked the
political experience or the social weight to rule the country. Some others
who rallied early on to her support, like the Earl of Sussex, were men of
substance but, like the household group, had no knowledge of government.
Yet by 16 July 1553 twenty-one such men had been sworn as members of
Mary's Council. Had they continued as the ruling junta there would have
been a transformation in the leadership of the country. But it was not to be.
On 20 July the Earl of Arundel, Lord Paget, and Lord Rich reached Mary's
headquarters at Framlingham, and from that moment the career politicians
of the two previous reigns were brought back to the centre of power. During
the next twelve weeks those three men and twenty others were appointed
to the Privy Council, increasing it to forty-four members. Within that
unwieldy body nineteen were to be active in attendance and they were
predominantly career politicians: of Mary's household councillors only
Rochester was of great significance. Bishops Gardiner, Heath, Tunstall,
and Thirlby, who had been influential under Henry but thrust into the cold
under Edward, were now restored to the Council. More numerous were
the Edwardian survivors: Arundel, Paget, Pembroke, Bedford, Winchester,
Petre, and others. By November 1553 a small 'select council' of advisers,
an informed inner ring of the main Privy Council, had been formed. Its
members—Rochester, Gardiner, Thirlby, Arundel, Paget, Petre—were
drawn from each of the main groups; but the professional politicians,
whether clerics or laymen, outnumbered the household loyalists.[4]

One other figure held significant influence at Mary's Court. This was
Simon Renard, who had come to England in June 1553 as one of Charles
V's envoys and became in September the principal Imperial Ambassador.
Trained in the law, Renard had a subtle intelligence combined with high
ambition and sensitive vanity. He quickly won Mary's confidence and
operated for two years at the very centre of English affairs. Although he was
a persuasive diplomat, he was easily unnerved by exaggerated fears and
quickly resentful at imagined lack of recognition.

On 3 August Mary rode into London through streets 'so full of people
shouting and crying "Jesus save her Grace", with weeping tears for joy, that
the like was never seen before'.[5] Under the restraining influence of her
cousin Charles's ambassadors she was at first cautious and conciliatory. An
immediate problem, which could hardly wait long, was presented by the

[4] For names and details see Dale Hoak, 'Two revolutions in Tudor government: the
formation and organization of Mary I's Privy Council', in Christopher Coleman and David
Starkey (eds.), *Revolution Reassessed* (Oxford, 1986), 87–116.

[5] Charles Wriothesley, *A Chronicle of England*, ed. W. D. Hamilton, Camden Soc, NS 20
(London, 1877), ii. 95.

funeral of Edward VI. Should he be buried by Protestant or by Catholic rites? Mary would naturally have preferred the Catholic, but was wisely persuaded to allow the English service, although a Requiem Mass was sung in the chapel royal. Punishment for the attempted alteration of the succession was remarkably restrained. Only the Duke of Northumberland, Sir John Gates, and Sir Thomas Palmer were executed, Northumberland declaring his devotion to the Catholic faith. When Lady Jane Grey heard this news she cried 'woe worth him! He hath brought me and our stock in most miserable calamity . . . by his ambition.'[6] The imprisoned bishops—Gardiner, Bonner, Tunstall, and others—were released and restored to their sees. During August and September Cranmer, Latimer, Ridley, Hooper, and many other less prominent reformers took their places in prison. On 18 August a royal proclamation announced that for the time being the Queen, while hoping that her subjects would embrace her own religion, 'mindeth not to compel any her said subjects thereunto', commanding them 'to live together in quiet sort and Christian charity'.[7] This apparently tolerant and conciliatory measure was deceptive: to begin with, it was contrary to the law, since it permitted forms of worship forbidden by statute; and it gave concessions only to Catholics, for Protestants already had the right to worship according to their beliefs. Predictably, both sides ignored Mary's exhortation to seek concord and made open demonstration of their animosities. When the Catholic Dr Bourne preached at St Paul's Cross a dagger was thrown at him and some of the crowd cried 'kill him'. Yet a few days later the London chronicler, Wriothesley, reported that the Latin Mass was being sung in several parishes, 'not by commandment but of the people's devotion'.[8] On Sunday 27 August the Sarum use was performed in St Paul's and the stone altar there rebuilt. Early in September the imperial envoys reported that 'the cause of religion . . . is making very good progress in the kingdom'.[9]

The policy of apparent conciliation and equivocation could not long survive. Decisions had soon to be made about the Queen's marriage and about religion. Was Mary to marry, and if so whom? How far was the restoration of the Roman religion to proceed and how was it to be managed? The solution to the first question evolved in the last three months of 1553, although its political consequences were to dominate much of the following year. The second problem was keenly debated in the autumn Parliament and a partial but temporary settlement established.

At the end of July Charles V had proposed to his only legitimate son, Philip of Spain, that he marry Mary of England. Charles was concerned not

[6] *Chronicle of Queen Jane*, 25.   [7] *Proclamations*, ii. 390.
[8] Wriothesley, *Chronicle*, ii. 101.   [9] *CSP Span.* xi. 198.

only to win the support of England against France, but also to build up the strength of Philip, his heir in Spain and the Netherlands, against the Austrian branch of the Habsburgs, headed by his nephew Ferdinand, King of the Romans. Philip was unenthusiastic but obedient. Mary, who would never marry anyone without Charles's consent, nevertheless required some persuasion before she agreed. Her subjects, including some of her most influential advisers, were opposed to a foreign marriage and still more hostile to the prospect that England might be absorbed into the Habsburg empire. Led by Bishop Gardiner the opponents of the Spanish match proposed Edward Courtenay, Earl of Devon, a descendant of the Yorkists. His royal blood was Courtenay's only recommendation: he was not unfairly described by Renard as 'proud, poor, obstinate, inexperienced and vindic-tive'.[10] Unfortunately he was the only possible native candidate. After mak-ing tentative suggestions to Mary in August, Renard presented a formal but secret proposal of marriage on behalf of Philip early in October. At the same time he began to sound out the English councillors through Paget, who supported Philip's candidature, perhaps because he thought a foreign prince and a Habsburg alliance to be necessary for England's stability, perhaps because his chief rival, Gardiner, backed Courtenay. For a month the negotiations were carried on in secret, Renard and Paget lobbying selected councillors in favour of Philip, Gardiner pressing the claims of Courtenay. Mary was determined against Courtenay from the start, would indeed contemplate no one other than Philip, and at the end of October secretly promised herself to him. Once she had decided, she pretended to consult the Council, but this was little more than a formality. It is unlikely that her father had ever consulted his Council over his marriages and Mary was under no obligation to do so. Discussing the matter with Gardiner, she informed him that she had made up her mind, and when he told her that the people would not tolerate a foreigner, she retorted that he was disloyal if he preferred the wishes of her subjects to her own.[11]

However, that was not the end of the affair. Encouraged by the French Ambassador, Antoine de Noailles, several members of both Houses of Parliament petitioned the Queen to marry an Englishman, urging upon her the danger that England's independence would be threatened if her husband were a foreigner. The Speaker set out the arguments at such length that Mary was obliged to sit down to hear them. She then replied in person—not, as was normal, through the Chancellor—with a cutting rebuke: 'Parliament was not', she said, 'accustomed to use such language to the kings of England, nor was it suitable or respectful that it should

[10] Ibid. 323–4.   [11] Ibid. 337–43.

do so.'[12] The delegation withdrew, silent and defeated. Peaceful opposition in Parliament and Council was over; but there remained a smaller group hostile to the Spanish match which was shortly to carry antagonism into violent action.

The terms of the marriage treaty were remarkably favourable to England. Were a child to be born to Mary and Philip, he or she would inherit England and the Netherlands, while Don Carlos—Philip's son by an earlier marriage—would acquire Spain, her Italian possessions, and the New World. If there were no issue, neither Philip nor Don Carlos would have any claim on the English throne, which would pass to the next successor by right and law—though the identity of that person was carefully left vague because of Mary's strong objection to her half-sister Elizabeth. Philip would have no authority in England and would appoint no foreigners to office. These concessions were made in part because Charles V needed the marriage a great deal more than did the English, partly because Paget harped on the spectre of popular opposition in order to procure favourable terms. Philip, however, was distinctly less enthusiastic than his father and secretly declared that since the treaty had been agreed without his knowledge, he did not consider himself bound by it. Gardiner, to do him credit, had foreseen this possibility in November, telling his Queen that 'a foreigner will promise things he will not keep once the marriage is concluded'.[13] However, these impediments were not visible. Amid conflicting reports from Renard—that the marriage was highly unpopular, that the nobles were favourable but the people hostile, that all would be well if the business were handled tactfully—Charles's commissioners arrived two days after Christmas and concluded the treaty early in the New Year. On 14 January 1554 the Crown published the full terms of the treaty in a royal proclamation, a remarkable and unprecedented attempt to win over public opinion. So far Mary had been distinctly successful. At the urging of the Imperial Ambassador and with the advice of Paget she had made up her own mind about the marriage against the wishes of a substantial section of the Council and of Parliament. The real test, however, was yet to come; but before we deal with that we must return to the assembly of Parliament in October 1553.

The government was faced with a complicated set of ecclesiastical problems. The Queen herself wished to repeal all the religious changes made under her father and her brother, returning as soon as possible to orthodox

---

[12] Jennifer Loach, 'Opposition to the Crown in Parliament, 1553–1558' (unpublished D. Phil. thesis, University of Oxford, 1974), 77. I am grateful to Dr Loach for allowing me to quote from her thesis. See *CSP Span.* xi. 363–4.

[13] *CSP Span.* xi. 343.

doctrine and the authority of the Pope. The great danger, warned Renard, was that she would 'attempt to right matters at a stroke'.[14] She was persuaded that this must wait. Yet certain existing statutes made it difficult to separate matters of doctrine from questions of authority: under Henry VIII new treasons and new definitions of praemunire had been introduced—for instance it was held to be treason to deny the validity of Henry's marriage with Anne Boleyn, a law which impugned Mary's own legitimacy.[15] A bill for repealing such treasons aroused understandable suspicion that its real object was to undermine the royal supremacy over the Church; and although it passed into law, it set up tensions and anxieties at the very beginning of Mary's first Parliament. Holders of monastic and chantry lands, whatever their doctrinal beliefs, feared that a return to Rome would threaten their property.[16]

Return to doctrinal and liturgical orthodoxy was more easily achieved. The principal measure was a parliamentary bill repealing the Edwardian statutes that governed the Prayer Book, the abolition of images and the marriage of priests. The bill was discussed against the background of a long theological disputation in Convocation, contemptuously dismissed by Renard as 'scandalous wrangling'. These learned debates were indeed irrelevant to the outcome, for neither side was in the least likely to alter its opinion and the laity who attended them were simply confused. Control of religious politics was exercised by laymen in Council and in Parliament, not by theologians. Although the bill was debated with some vigour, it was carried by 270 votes to 80 in the Commons, the minority being in Renard's opinion 'not men of importance'. The size of the minority is often cited as evidence of the government's difficulties; but the width of the margin between the two votes is a more reliable witness to its authority in purely religious matters and to the indifference of the bulk of the laity to liturgical and doctrinal issues. The statute authorized services to be said as they had been at the death of Henry VIII and also made Protestant services and the marriage of priests illegal. The subsequent deprivation of married clergy was particularly pleasing to the orthodox: Robert Parkyn, a Yorkshire priest, wrote ecstatically that 'it was joy to hear and see how these carnal priests . . . did lower and look down, when they were commanded to leave

[14] Ibid. 307.

[15] The term 'praemunire' derives from statutes passed in the fourteenth century to protect the rights of the Crown against papal interference; the scope of praemunire was extended in 1393 to cover all invasions of royal jurisdiction; under Henry VIII it was used as a weapon against the king's opponents especially in ecclesiastical matters.

[16] The autumn Parliament of 1553 had two sessions: the first ran from 5 to 21 October, when the bill for repealing the 'new' treasons of Henry's reign was carried; the second from 24 October to 6 December when the Edwardian legislation was repealed.

and forsake the concubines and harlots'.[17] On the day of Parliament's dissolution a dog with a shaven crown and a halter round its neck was thrown
into the presence chamber at Court, with a threat that priests and bishops
should be hanged. Mary was indignant and warned Parliament that such
acts would move her to be less merciful. But the event, vivid in itself, was
an isolated gesture, a trivial reaction to the reversal of the entire religious
policy of the previous reign.

Once the legislation was carried the Crown and the ecclesiastical authorities began to implement it. In March 1554 comprehensive injunctions were
issued to every diocese: no heretics were to be appointed to benefices;
married priests should be deprived; 'laudable' ceremonies were to be observed; uniform and true doctrines must be promulgated in homilies.[18] For
the time being that was as far as the authorities could go, since the heresy
laws had been repealed under Edward and were not to be re-enacted until
the autumn Parliament of 1554. Throughout that year married priests were
deprived of their benefices. In the country as a whole some 20 per cent of
priests had married, and so serious a shortage of ministers was produced by
the deprivations that some men were reinstated in different parishes after
they had done penance and put aside their wives. Even so, the disruption
was considerable and the consequences for individual clerics and their
families were catastrophic. New and orthodox bishops were appointed and
a beginning was made in restoring the revenue of depleted sees. Protestant
fellows of Oxford and Cambridge colleges were deprived and replaced by
Catholics, Mary's regime having a much more serious impact upon the
universities than had the relatively tolerant policies of Somerset and
Northumberland. Leading Protestants in many parts of England, especially
from London and East Anglia, were imprisoned on charges of treason and
sedition, while others began to leave England for the refuge of Protestant
cities abroad, and the government wisely made no attempt to stop them.
Even before the main persecution began in 1555 the Protestant leadership
was weakened by imprisonment and emigration.[19]

2. WYATT'S REBELLION AND ITS AFTERMATH

On the political front the outlook was far more threatening to Mary's
government. Although the Council had accepted her decision to marry
Philip, popular feeling was hostile to Spaniards and to the match. Philip's
envoys were pelted with snowballs—lowering to their dignity, though not
otherwise damaging—and the proclamation of the marriage treaty was

[17] 'Robert Parkyn's Narrative', ed. A. G. Dickens, *EHR* 62 (1947), 82.
[18] *Proclamations*, ii, no. 407.   [19] Below, p. 113, for a discussion of the exiles.

badly received in London. More serious than popular grumbling was the conspiracy formed at the end of November 1553 by a group of well-to-do landowners, dismissed officials, and soldiers. Sir James Croft, head of an influential Marcher family, William Thomas, Clerk to the Privy Council under Edward, Sir Peter Carew, soldier and Devonshire landowner, and Sir Thomas Wyatt, a Kentish gentleman, were the most important leaders. They were later joined by the Duke of Suffolk, Lady Jane's father, while Edward Courtenay, Earl of Devon, hovered unreliably on their fringes. Their common purpose lay in opposition to the marriage; but their strategy was less clear. William Thomas proposed the assassination of Mary followed by the elevation of Elizabeth. This was too drastic for his colleagues, who later asserted in public that they wanted only to persuade Mary to change her mind about the marriage, not to dislodge her from the throne. However, they almost certainly realized that they would never be able to force so major a concession without depriving her of the Crown; and they probably intended to bring about the marriage of Elizabeth to Courtenay, followed by their joint succession to the throne. The conspirators planned four simultaneous risings for the following spring in the Welsh Marches, Devonshire, the midlands, and Kent, and they obtained assurances from Noailles that they would receive naval and financial aid from France. Unfortunately rumours of their plans began to leak out and were picked up by Renard's effective intelligence service. Renard informed the Council, Gardiner interrogated Courtenay, and enough was soon known for the government to act. In January the conspirators were forced into the open before their preparations were complete and at an unsuitable time of year: 'this cold damp weather is not usually selected by the English for insurrections', remarked Renard, as if he were discussing a garden party.[20] Nothing happened in the Welsh Marches: Sir James Croft failed to act at all. In the midlands the Duke of Suffolk gathered only a humiliatingly small body of support, was rebuffed by the town of Coventry, and was arrested hiding in a hollow tree. Sir Peter Carew, an able and adventurous soldier, frightened the government by his stirrings in the West Country, but rallied even less support than Suffolk: possibly memories of his role in suppressing the 1549 revolt made him unpopular; and Courtenay, who was influential in the region, obediently followed Gardiner's warnings to lie low. Carew sensibly fled abroad.

Only in Kent was there serious action. On 25 January Sir Thomas Wyatt issued a proclamation at Maidstone insisting that he and his followers intended no harm to the Queen, 'but better counsel and councillors'. He

[20] *CSP Span.* xii. 52.

then moved to Rochester, where some thirty Kentish gentlemen joined him with about 3,000 followers. A distinctly smaller number openly opposed him under Lord Abergavenny, the most powerful magnate in the county. The greater part of the Kentish gentry remained neutral. With such slender resources and the total collapse of the conspiracy in the rest of England, Wyatt's prospects seemed unpromising. But the government presented him with an unexpected bonus by sending against him the aged Duke of Norfolk in command of an army containing the London trained bands, the Whitecoats, whose loyalty was suspect. When Norfolk unwisely launched his attack at Rochester, the Whitecoats deserted to Wyatt, crying 'we are all Englishmen!'[21] The remnant of Norfolk's force returned home in ruined uniforms, without arrows, bowstrings, or swords; Wyatt's band, its morale heightened, marched towards London. On 31 January, in order to win time, Mary offered to discuss grievances over the marriage and pardon all those rebels who returned home at once. Wyatt refused the offer, partly perhaps because he suspected that it was not sincere and partly because it did not meet his real aims. Instead, he put forward his own demand that the Tower be surrendered to him and Mary handed over as a hostage. But Mary's offer had virtually forced him to admit that he would not negotiate with the present regime. Mary rejected Gardiner's advice that she leave London and made a brave and effective speech to the citizens at the Guildhall. The City's defences were prepared and troops mustered. Wyatt entered Southwark without meeting any resistance, but found London Bridge held against him. With Lord Abergavenny rallying men from eastern Kent in his rear he had no choice but to launch a direct assault on the capital, and he marched up river to cross the Thames at Kingston, advancing on London through Knightsbridge, where his men rested overnight. Early on the morning of Wednesday 7 February Wyatt led his army towards the City. However, he had lost the advantage of surprise, for by 10 a.m. Pembroke and Clinton, the royal commanders, had drawn up their forces around St James's and Charing Cross. An extraordinary scene followed, when Pembroke allowed the main body of rebels to pass through his lines, attacking only the rearguard. 'The Queen's whole battle of footmen standing still', Wyatt reached Charing Cross and proceeded along Fleet Street, where he and his company 'passed along by a great company of harnessed men, which stood on both sides, without any withstanding them'.[22] But at Ludgate Wyatt was halted: he demanded entrance to the City and was refused by Lord William Howard, whose organization of London's de-

[21] John Proctor, *The History of Wyat's Rebellion* (2nd edn., 1555), repr. in *Tudor Tracts, 1532–1588*, ed. A. F. Pollard (London, n.d.), 230.
[22] *Chronicle of Queen Jane*, 49–50.

fences may have been decisive. Wyatt turned back towards Charing Cross and gave himself up after some desultory skirmishing. Meanwhile, a small detachment of rebels had branched off down Whitehall to attack the Court. Here they caused panic and confusion, the Lord Chamberlain, who commanded the outer gate, falling in the mud in his hurry to retreat. Yet their threat was feeble and they soon surrendered. The assembly of several thousands of armed men at the very threshold of Court and City was dramatic and alarming. Allegedly, the cries of women and children at Charing Cross could be heard in the Tower of London; and the ladies of the Court fell into panic. However, the fighting was short-lived and half-hearted: only about forty men were killed in London and twenty or thirty in the earlier stages. Neither side had fire in their bellies and when the City held firm Wyatt's rebellion collapsed in a few hours.

Apart from Suffolk, who proved useless, no magnate supported the rebellion. Its leaders were knights and gentlemen, landowners, office-holders past and present, and soldiers. They were men of some substance but not of outstanding influence in Court or country. Although most of the rank and file came from parishes dominated by the rebel leaders, some were yeomen and husbandmen from other parts of Kent and some were independent townsmen. The revolt differed from the Pilgrimage of Grace, when magnate families played an important part and when there were also spontaneous rural risings, and from the revolts of 1549, when the gentry supplied very few leaders.

Wyatt's objectives and motives have long been debated by historians. He himself declared in public that he objected only to the Spanish marriage, not to Mary's religious changes. The government, concerned to tarnish Protestantism with the stigma of defeated rebellion, insisted that his objection to the marriage was merely a screen behind which he worked for the restoration of heresy. Probably, however, his proclaimed cause was the true one. Although intense English hatred for the Spanish was only brought to the boil under Elizabeth, there was a general hostility to foreigners and a real fear of the consequences of the Spanish match. A Norwich carpenter joined Wyatt's revolt in the belief that if the marriage went forward 'we should lie in swine sties in caves and the Spaniards should have our houses, and we should live like slaves'.[23] His outburst shows that the poor were not simply manipulated by the gentry and reveals the existence of hostility in a county where there was no uprising at all. In the upper reaches of society

[23] Walter Rye (ed.), *Depositions Taken before the Mayor and Aldermen of Norwich* (Norwich, 1905), 56. Proctor , *The History of Wyat's Rebellion*, 210, claims that Wyatt's real motive was religious; but Proctor was concerned to disseminate the government view and to discredit Protestants by associating them with rebellion.

the marriage brought fears that the best offices would be occupied by foreigners and that England would become a Habsburg dependency: harsh imperial rule in the Netherlands had earlier provoked a serious uprising at Ghent. But preventing the marriage in effect entailed the replacement of Mary by Elizabeth, for the Queen would never have renounced Philip; and such a course may well have been too extreme for most men.

Although the restoration of Protestantism was probably not the principal motive, several leaders had reforming views, the only planned rising to gather momentum was in a county where Protestantism was strong, and moreover it began in a particularly Protestant part of that county. Furthermore, although Wyatt and others had earlier supported Mary against Lady Jane, knowing that Mary was a Catholic, they may not have expected her to attempt more than the reversal of the Edwardian settlement. The Spanish match carried with it the danger that she would restore papal authority and perhaps the secularized church lands, a prospect much more alarming than the abolition of the Edwardian liturgy. Thus religious fears—specifically about Roman jurisdiction and ecclesiastical property—may have converted widespread dislike of the marriage into open revolt.

Although the revolt was a dangerous threat to the regime, most Englishmen were unresponsive and neutral. Croft, Carew, and Suffolk rallied virtually no support. The majority of Kentish landowners were uncommitted. Wyatt surrendered quickly to save lives. On the other side, Abergavenny, in spite of his great power in Kent, was unable to stop Wyatt's march on London. On the final day the royal commanders were slow to engage the rebels, and only London's firm resistance under Lord William Howard was decisive. A crucial episode in Tudor history was thus determined with most of the political nation standing aside and even the active participants behaving equivocally and hesitantly.

Although the rebellion failed, it marks a turning-point in English politics. Previous Tudor 'revolts' had sought a remedy for grievances, not power. Wyatt and his colleagues intended an alteration of the monarchy; and they fought not merely for dynastic purposes but for issues. The revolt was the forerunner of two further conspiracies against Mary and of successive plots against Elizabeth, all intending a change of regime, all proclaiming that they acted from religious or political principle.

The government was now confronted with the problem of punishing those rebels who had not, like Sir Peter Carew, escaped to France. Renard, reflecting a robust Habsburg attitude, urged severe retribution all round, and in particular the execution of both Elizabeth and Courtenay, whom he saw as the principal threats to Philip. Gardiner wanted the removal of Elizabeth to prevent the accession of a heretic, but hoped to save his protegé, Courtenay. Paget favoured a merciful policy, strongly opposing the execution of Elizabeth on the ground that this would alienate large sections of opinion. A few victims were quickly dispatched: Suffolk went to his death in February, preceded by his unfortunate daughter, Lady Jane, and her husband, who were under suspended sentence of death for their part in the 1553 conspiracy. Wyatt and other leaders of revolt were kept alive for some weeks in the hope that under interrogation they would incriminate Elizabeth. They did not do so. In April Wyatt himself and Sir Henry Isley of the Kentish leaders were executed, as was William Thomas, but several others escaped abroad or received pardons. Of the rank-and-file rebels 480 were convicted, but nearly 400 were pardoned, so that only about ninety suffered death. Only two conspirators who had not actually rebelled were brought to trial, Sir Nicholas Throckmorton and Sir James Croft. Throckmorton was acquitted by a London jury against the summing-up of the chief justice: the populace rejoiced and the government sent the jury to the Tower. Croft was found guilty, but only after the Crown had packed the jury with additional members. Debate over the fates of Elizabeth and Courtenay wound on until May. Renard passed from initial optimism to impatience at the delay and to fury at their ultimate release. On the whole the government had been remarkably lenient: large numbers of proven rebels were pardoned and probably many fewer suffered than in 1549. Certainly the death-roll from both battle and trial was much smaller: perhaps as many as 10,000 were killed on both sides in 1549, only about 200 in 1554. However, comparison with 1536 shows a similarity: after the Pilgrimage only 180 were executed out of a far larger body of rebels. The uncertainty and ultimate leniency of the government in 1554 have been attributed to faction-fighting and confusion in the Council; but such a conclusion is probably misleading. The evidence was far too weak to convict Elizabeth and Courtenay, when much stronger evidence against Throckmorton failed; and Paget was certainly right in arguing that the execution of Elizabeth would have been politically disastrous. The general leniency was fairly characteristic of Tudor responses to revolt, and so was the element of chance that decided who should die and who should survive. The aftermath of 1554 seems confused only because Renard, Gardiner, and possibly Mary herself pressed for politically unwise severity.

By the time Wyatt was executed, the second Parliament of the reign had assembled on 2 April 1554. It opened in an atmosphere of tension between Paget and Gardiner, and it closed after acrimonious debates during which Paget lost his favoured position in government. Gardiner was determined to press on more rapidly with the suppression of heresy and hoped to exclude Elizabeth from the throne. On both issues he was confronted with opposi-

tion from the Council, where the programme of legislation to be laid before
Parliament was a major subject of contention. All councillors supported a
bill confirming the royal marriage treaty and another extending the treason
laws so that they covered offences against Philip as well as against Mary.
However, Gardiner also proposed the revival of the statutes against
heresy—necessary for the trial of the Protestant bishops—forfeiture of
the lands of the rebels, and abandonment of the royal supremacy over
the Church. The marriage treaty was confirmed without difficulty; but
Gardiner's religious plans excited a lively suspicion that he intended 'establishing a form of Inquisition against the heretics, setting up again the power
of the bishops and dealing with the Pope's authority'.[24] Paget, Arundel,
Pembroke, and other nobles evidently thought that Gardiner was going
much further than had been agreed in Council and feared that his religious
measures might threaten property. Paget urged Renard to use his influence with Mary to get the Parliament dissolved: 'the weather is beginning to
be warm and men's tempers will wax warm too'.[25] In Paget's eyes Gardiner
was endangering the marriage and the political balance by driving ahead
with plans which had never been agreed in Council. Mary did not intervene
and Paget was forced to oppose and to defeat the heresy bill in the Lords.
His assessment that too rapid a religious reaction would arouse widespread
hostility, especially out of fear for property, was probably sound. But his
next move was extraordinarily ill-judged: he created such difficulties over
the bill applying the treason laws to Philip that it did not become law in
this Parliament. His first offence had been rash, the second unforgivable.
Paget was in dark disgrace with Mary, and Renard transferred his affection
to Gardiner, who now became the leading figure in government. Yet,
although Paget suffered a serious blow to his influence with Mary, he had
successfully hindered Gardiner's plans. Of all the main measures proposed
by the Crown only the confirmation of the marriage treaty had been secured. Mary's second Parliament, one of the most dramatic of the century,
showed that the Crown could achieve its objectives only if these were
accepted by the Council; a dissident group there could block measures in
the Lords.

3. THE SPANISH MARRIAGE AND THE RETURN TO ROME

Unsatisfactory as the Parliament had been, its dissolution was followed by
a slackening of tension as preparations for Philip's arrival were unfolded.
True, Renard was constantly reporting plots and rumours; but that was his

[24] *CSP Span.* xii. 216.   [25] Ibid. 220.

habit. Nobles and gentlemen had mostly accepted the marriage; and anti-Spanish feeling was expressed only at a popular and ineffective level. After several hesitations and postponements Philip, a reluctant bridegroom but a dutiful son, reached Southampton on 20 July 1554. Although eleven years younger than his wife, he had much wider experience of the world and of politics. He had already been married once and had begotten an heir, the unlucky Don Carlos. He had spent the first twenty years of his life in Spain, taking over effective government of his kingdoms there when he was 16, under the prudent supervision of his father. His education had been planned with the thoroughness characteristic of Charles V, and he was an assiduous reader, meticulous in his religious devotions, astonishingly industrious. Yet he had a lighter side, collecting animals for a zoo, planning gardens, playing cards, and dancing. From 1548 to 1551 he had travelled through the Habsburg dominions in Italy and the Netherlands. In Italy he seemed haughty and insolent, but by the time he reached the Netherlands he was prepared to ingratiate himself a little with the nobility. He struck observers in England as the image of a true king: 'of visage he is well favoured', wrote John Elder, 'with a broad forehead, and grey eyes, straight nosed and manly countenance . . . His pace is princely . . . [and] he is so well proportioned as nature cannot work a more perfect pattern . . . whose majesty I judge to be of a stout stomach, pregnant witted, and of most gentle nature.'[26] Before the marriage Charles V reminded him that he was marrying to produce heirs, not to enjoy himself; he should therefore avoid undue sexual exertion and visit his wife's bed only occasionally. Philip's cold, reserved nature was well fitted for this advice, and he was more often away from Mary than with her. Unfortunately perhaps for her, she was devoted to him from their first meeting, perhaps before that. His remoteness never wore down her affection, but it saddened the last years of her life.

The general reaction to his arrival was less favourable. Although Mary had established for him a full English household, he brought with him a complete Spanish entourage as well. The Spaniards disliked and despised the English, who resented and insulted the intruders. While relations between Spanish and English were never harmonious, Philip set about him to win the favour of the nobility, lavishly distributing pensions. By October these were having their expected effect and the leading English notables acquired a respect for Philip which they never lost. His presence gave a focus of authority to government, while Mary's supposed pregnancy, reported in September, held reassurance for the future. The regime could

---

[26] 'John Elder's Letter', in *Chronicle of Queen Jane*, 165–6.

now complete the process of reconstruction by returning the nation to the authority of Rome.

The man chosen by Pope Julius III for the reconciliation of England to Roman authority was Cardinal Reginald Pole, great-nephew of Edward IV.[27] Since 1532 he had lived in Italy, working unceasingly for the restoration of papal jurisdiction in England and achieving high standing in the Roman Church. Essentially a reformer, he had adopted a doctrine of salvation very little different from Luther's justification by faith alone; but, unlike Luther, he believed above all in the unity of the Church and the necessity of obedience. Therefore he avoided open proclamation of his beliefs and strove for the reconciliation of Protestants and Catholics. When the Council of Trent decreed a doctrine of salvation wholly contrary to his own Pole accepted it; but he was always thereafter under suspicion of heresy from the orthodox. In some ways a reserved and diffident man, who nevertheless nearly became pope without any marked ambition for the role, Pole had for many years been forced to conceal his views and temporize with authority. Yet there was never any question for him of compromise over restoring England to obedience to Rome. Unlike Gardiner, he refused to accept the need for caution and circumspection. From the moment of his appointment as papal legate in August 1553 he was impatient to return to England; all secular impediments must be swept aside in the urgent task of reuniting England and Rome. 'It is imprudent and sacriligious', he wrote in 1553, 'to say that matters of religion must be cleverly handled, and left until the throne is safely established. . . . What greater neglect can there be . . . than by setting aside the honour of God to attend to other things, leaving religion to the end?'[28] Even Mary had been persuaded for a time that such insistence might be disastrous; but with the consummation of her marriage achieved, there seemed no further obstacle to the full restoration of the true religion.

However, although Philip, Mary, and the Council agreed that the kingdom should now be reconciled to Rome, they differed over tactics. The determination of the lay holders of monastic and chantry lands to keep them was fundamental and unyielding. Renard told Charles V that 'the Catholics hold more church property than do the heretics'; Gardiner insisted that 'the Cardinal must come with ample powers to confirm the possessors of church property in their tenure, and with no thought whatever of recovering it for the Church'.[29] Julius III and Pole were prepared to issue dispensations, but insisted that these should be given only after the submission of England,

[27] His name was almost certainly pronounced 'Pool', a source of several bad jokes by his contemporaries.
[28] *CSP Span.* xi. 420–1.   [29] Ibid. xiii. 46, 22.

and awarded separately to individual landowners. The English Council, Philip, and Charles V recognized that this would be unacceptable to Parliament and insisted on a general dispensation. After the intervention of Charles himself Pope Julius reluctantly agreed: it would be better to 'abandon all church property rather than risk the shipwreck of this undertaking'.[30] Pole accepted his new instructions reluctantly.

At first all went well. Parliament assembled on 12 November 1554 and repealed Pole's attainder before he reached London. Pole preached to Parliament, promising that 'I come to reconcile, not to condemn. I come not to compel but to call again'.[31] Both Houses responded on 30 November with a petition for papal absolution and a return to Roman jurisdiction: there was only one dissident voice in the Commons. But obstacles then came into view. Parliament requested that the papal dispensation be included in the body of the statute repealing the Henrician legislation, thus giving it greater legal force, and that holders of church property be absolved in their consciences. Pole refused both demands: in no way would he admit that the property-owners had a morally valid title or make any concession which would make it seem that the submission to Rome had been purchased by a bargain. With reconciliation nearly achieved the entire negotiation seemed on the threshold of disaster. From 21 to 24 December long and bitter debates were held in the Privy Council, the councillors denying that any foreigner could have authority over English property, Pole insisting that civil rulers had no right to dispose of Church property. Pole threatened to return to Rome, Mary supported him, and even hinted that she would abdicate. However, ultimately a compromise was reached, by which the dispensation was included in the statute but no relief given to consciences. The great Act of Repeal, reuniting England to Rome, finally passed into law in January, 1555.[32] The continuing disagreements over Church property had hampered and threatened the reconciliation for months; and Pole's grudging acceptance of the ultimate compromise left some residue of anxiety and suspicion among the holders of Church property.[33]

Two bills which had been rejected by the Lords in April were now carried in this Parliament. The first revived the statutes against heresy originally devised against the Lollards and repealed under Edward VI.[34] Objection was raised in the Lords that the bill restored the jurisdiction of bishops and imposed excessive penalties; but otherwise it had an easy

---

[30] Ibid. 79–80. [31] *Chronicle of Queen Jane*, 159. [32] 1 & 2 Philip & Mary, c. 8.
[33] Jennifer Loach, *Parliament and the Crown in the Reign of Mary Tudor* (Oxford, 1986), 106–15; J. H. Crehan, 'The return to obedience', *The Month*, NS 14 (1955), 221–9; *CSP Span*. xiii. 124–5.
[34] 1 & 2 Philip & Mary, c. 6.

passage. The other, giving Philip the same protection from the treason laws as was due to Mary, provoked a more intense and complicated debate, some members evidently wanting to strengthen, others to weaken its provisions.[35] It too was finally carried, with an additional item that Philip should be guardian of any child born to the royal couple should Mary predecease him. In practice, of course, this clause never came into operation, but potentially it was highly significant. Philip would have liked one additional measure: his own coronation. Legally it would not have added to his powers, but Renard considered that he would derive great prestige from it since 'in England the coronation stands for a true and lawful confirmation of title, and means much more here than in other realms'.[36] In the end the government did not press the matter in Parliament, probably because this might have prejudiced the fate of other more urgent and important bills.

Mary's third Parliament, sitting from 12 December 1554 until 16 January 1555, had been a real, if mixed, success for the Crown. It carried twenty-one statutes, three of major importance. The kingdom was restored to Rome, the ultimate punishments could be inflicted on heretics, and Philip was protected by the treason laws. None of these measures had been achieved without debate, and the first of them had come near to being wrecked. It is not clear why the other two should have been passed now after they had failed in April: probably Paget had learned the risks in opposing the Queen, while landowners were largely, though not entirely, reassured about their holdings of Church property.

4. PERSECUTION AND WAR, 1555–1558

Mary had by this stage achieved her main purposes: the Habsburg marriage had been consummated; Philip had been installed as king; the Edwardian reforms in the Church had been annulled; and England had been reconciled to Rome. The Queen and her advisers could now concentrate upon implementing policy. Almost immediately after the dissolution of Parliament on 16 January 1555 Bishop Gardiner summoned to his house eighty imprisoned preachers and urged them to recant their Protestant beliefs. Only two complied. A week later the trials for heresy began in front of Gardiner and other specially appointed commissioners. On 4 February the first victim, John Rogers, a prebendary of St Paul's, was burned. 'He was the first proto-martyr of all the blessed company that suffered in Queen Mary's time, that gave the first adventure upon the fire.'[37] The persecution had two principal objectives: to remove the infection of heresy and to persuade the people of

[35] 1 & 2 Philip & Mary, c. 10.   [36] *CSP Span.* xiii. 102   [37] Foxe, vi. 612.

God's true way. Myles Huggarde, the most successful of the Catholic apologists, asserted that burnings made a stronger impression upon men's minds than preaching, for many would go to watch an execution who would stay away from a sermon.[38] In the early days there was always the hope that Protestants would recant rather than endure the fire and would thus provide telling witness to the truth.

We cannot be certain who initiated the burnings. Gardiner favoured them at the start; but, soon realizing that they were failing to intimidate the Protestants, he withdrew from an active role. Pole had opposed the rigidity of the Roman Inquisition when he was in Italy and argued that private expressions of doubt could be countered by 'the way of charity and mildness'; but open support for heresy must be suppressed to save the people from heretic 'wolves'.[39] Bishop Bonner was convinced that a clerical officer must act 'as a good surgeon [who] cutteth away a putrified and festered member, for the love he hath to the whole body'; but although he played a continuous and sometimes explosive role in examining prisoners, he acted under instruction and sometimes even under pressure from the Council. Indeed, he was once rebuked for being too lenient.[40] Renard was positively hostile to the burnings: 'the haste with which the bishops have proceeded in this matter may well cause a revolt', he complained.[41] Philip did not oppose the proceedings, but neither does he seem to have encouraged them. Mary herself undoubtedly believed persecution to be necessary, although she considered that it should be undertaken 'without rashness' and directed against learned men who might mislead others rather than against ordinary people. As so often with a discredited policy, it is impossible to be certain who originated it: most likely Mary initiated the burnings, supported at first by Gardiner and throughout, perhaps with reservations, by Pole and Bonner.

Once begun, the burnings could not be stopped without the government seeming to confess failure; and as the flames spread they engulfed men of humble life and little learning, whom Mary had not intended as victims. However, the first martyrs were Protestant clerics. Rogers was soon followed to the fire by Bishop Hooper, Laurence Saunders, preacher at Northampton, and Rowland Taylor, minister of Hadley in Suffolk, whose death provoked emotional scenes in his parish. The most celebrated victims were the three Oxford martyrs—all of them educated at Cambridge, but

[38] Myles Huggarde, *The Displaying of the Protestants* (1556), 40.
[39] Dermot Fenlon, *Heresy and Obedience in Tridentine Italy: Cardinal Pole and the Counter-Reformation* (Cambridge, 1972), 247.
[40] Gina Alexander, 'Bonner and the Marian Persecution', *History*, 60 (1975), 376.
[41] *CSP Span.* xiii. 138.

executed at the sister university. Ridley and Latimer were burned outside
Balliol College in October 1555, Latimer uttering the unforgettable words:
'be of good comfort, master Ridley, and play the man. We shall this day
light such a candle, by God's grace, in England, as I trust shall never be put
out.'[42] Cranmer, who watched their hideous sufferings, was kept alive for
a few more months, partly because of legal complexities, partly because
the government hoped, with some reason, that he might recant. Whereas
Latimer and Ridley, like most of the martyrs, were charged simply with
denying the Catholic doctrine of the Mass, Cranmer was indicted more
comprehensively on sixteen counts. The government hoped to use his trial
to undermine the royal supremacy and therefore concentrated upon his
rejection of papal authority, the front on which Cranmer was most vulnerable and had least carefully prepared his arguments. In consequence his
defence was weak and his resolution wavered. Left in isolation for weeks,
Cranmer finally yielded to persuasion and admitted that the obedience
which he owed to the monarch as supreme head must compel him to accept
that monarch's command for a return to papal jurisdiction: he was impaled
upon a logical fork. But at the end, when the Catholics expected him
publicly to abandon his heresies, Cranmer renounced his earlier recantation
and dramatically deprived his persecutors of their moment of triumph.
Mary, who had hoped for Cranmer's recantation *and* his death, might have
secured the first had she not insisted on the second as well.

Persecution was not confined to burnings. From the autumn of 1553
Protestants had been harried and from January 1555 the harassment grew
more intense. They were driven from their homes and thrown into prison.
Some, as we have seen, escaped to the continent, while others went into
hiding in England. Informers were especially active in London, denouncing
suspected heretics to the authorities, nourishing the growth of suspicion
and fear (Plates 11*a*, *b*).

Yet Pole had told Parliament that he came to reconcile, and he meant
what he said. The extirpation of heresy was necessary to that end, but it was
not the end itself; nor was it the only requirement. The clergy were poor,
ill-educated, and often indifferent; ordinations had been falling for two
decades; the wealth of episcopal sees had been eroded; cathedrals and
churches had been stripped of ornaments, images, communion plate, and
vestments; the tithe revenues of many parishes had been impropriated by
laymen when they bought monastic lands; the laity was ignorant and bewildered by the rapid changes of the previous generation.[43] In short, the

---

[42] Foxe, vii. 550.
[43] The term 'impropriation' refers to the annexation of tithes to an institution or individual. Before the Reformation it was generally used of tithes taken over by monastic houses;

Church had to be rebuilt, and Pole and Mary had the opportunity to provide it with more effective leadership: by the beginning of 1555 only seven of the twenty-two bishops in office at the death of Edward still held their sees, deprivation and martyrdom having cleared the way for new men. Those deprived of their bishoprics under Edward—Gardiner, Bonner, and others—were restored early in the reign. Able divines were appointed to the vacant sees and twelve new bishops had been consecrated by the end of 1555. The older of Mary's bishops, like Gardiner, Tunstall, Thirlby, and Heath, had been appointed to the bench under Henry VIII and had been servants of the state as well as of the Church. The newcomers were essentially concerned with theological endeavour and were mostly men of the Counter-Reformation.

Pole himself saw the problems of the Church mainly in pastoral terms. The clergy must be a disciplined body which would impose obedience upon the laity and provide them with spiritual care. Sermons were necessary, but an intensive campaign of preaching, before order had been restored, would only stir up controversy: hence, probably, Pole's rejection of Loyola's offer to send Jesuit preachers to England. The thrust of Pole's reforms stemmed from his legatine synod, which met at Lambeth and Westminster from November 1555 to February 1556.[44] Although it completed only one session, the synod set out a strategy for restoring and reconstructing the Church. The emphasis of its twelve decrees lay upon the obligation of bishops to reside in their sees, to preach, and to supervise the religious life of the parishes, and upon the necessity of obedience on the part of the parochial clergy. The most striking and original proposal was for the establishment of seminaries to be attached to cathedrals for training priests.[45]

However, by the autumn of 1555, before the synod met, the conditions for reconstruction in Church and in state had become discouraging. The Queen's protracted pregnancy was silently accepted by all, save perhaps herself, to be a sad illusion. The chances were now high that Elizabeth would succeed to the throne when Mary died. Philip wanted to return to the Netherlands in preparation for the abdication of his father and for his own assumption of power. He left in August, promising to return soon, but was in the event away for eighteen months and only stayed for four when he

---

after the dissolution of the monasteries it was applied to the tithes attached to properties acquired by lay persons.

[44] The best authority on the synod is J. P. Marmion, 'The London Synod of Reginald, Cardinal Pole, 1555-6' (MA thesis, University of Keele, 1974), *passim*. I am glad to acknowledge the help of this work.

[45] For a general assessment of the Marian Church, see below, pp. 113–19.

did come back. Although his interest in English government was intermit-
tent, he could and did intervene effectively when he roused himself; and the
Venetian ambassador reported that 'with the King's departure all business
will cease'.[46] This was an exaggeration, but Philip's presence did add some
leadership and cohesion to the administration: he was the one man, apart
from Renard and Pole, whom Mary could trust. After he left England, the
direction of affairs was entrusted to an informal inner ring of the Privy
Council, which could control major matters of government and keep Philip
himself informed. Its members were Gardiner, Thirlby, Paget, Arundel,
Pembroke, Winchester, Rochester, and Petre; Pole could attend when he
wished. In Philip's absence this group seems to have been, along with Mary
herself, the effective government of the country; and after Gardiner's death
in November it was largely dominated by Paget.

   To add to the Crown's problems, an attempted mediation between
France and the Emperor Charles by English commissioners broke down
and war between them continued. Although England was not yet involved,
it was increasingly difficult for her to remain neutral, and, as always, the
government's financial situation was precarious. Peacetime expenditure was
running at the annual rate of about £138,000, while non-parliamentary
revenue was only about £132,000. Heavy debts had been inherited from
Edward and more were incurred abroad in the first year of the reign: money
was now needed to redeem them. The harvest of 1555 failed and grain
prices for the ensuing year were to be 50 per cent higher than in the
previous twelve months; taxpayers were in no mood to be generous.

   The pressing need for money for both Church and Crown lay behind the
summons of Mary's fourth—and reputedly most difficult—Parliament in
October 1555, which largely coincided with Pole's legatine synod. The
Crown asked for a subsidy and three-fifteenths from Parliament; announced its intention of restoring First Fruits and Tenths to the Church;
proposed to confiscate and profit from the lands of exiles; and hoped, more
tentatively, to secure the coronation of Philip.[47] Demands for taxation were
met by complaints of poverty from the Commons following the exceptionally poor harvest. Even so, Mary secured a grant of £180,000 to be spread
over two years, which amounted to 40 per cent of royal revenue. The bill
restoring First Fruits, Tenths, and impropriated tithes to the Church raised

---

[46] *CSP Ven.* vi/1. 174.
[47] The subsidy was a parliamentary tax on property; the fifteenth was an earlier form of
tax, imposed on movable property, usually granted concurrently with the subsidy. First
Fruits and Tenths were ecclesiastical taxes, the former being a levy of the first year's income
of any new incumbent, the latter involving an annual payment of one-tenth of his income,
both payable to the papacy before the Reformation. The taxes were appropriated by the
Crown in 1534.

'great disputes and contentation' in the Commons. Significantly, the money surrendered by the Crown was not to go to the Pope, as it had done before 1534, but was to be distributed among the English sees to supplement poor livings and help poor scholars. The main objection lay against the Crown's depriving itself of revenue while demanding new taxes, but there were also fears that holders of Church property would be pressured into surrendering it. However, the bill passed into law by 193 votes to 126 after the doors of the chamber had been closed to prevent waverers from slipping away before the division. The third contentious bill ordered the return of all exiles within four months on pain of having their lands confiscated if they failed to comply. The Commons protested that no one ought to be deprived of his liberty to go and reside wherever he pleased. Again the doors of the House were shut, this time by the orders of Sir Anthony Kingston, one of the principal opponents of the bill; and this time the opponents won and the bill was defeated. The last of the Crown's objectives, the coronation of Philip, was never achieved, whether because the Crown, fearing defeat, decided not to bring the issue forward, or whether because the bill was proposed and lost it is impossible to tell from the fragmentary evidence. Either way, the Crown suffered a defeat.

This Parliament was described by the Venetian envoy, Giovanni Michieli, as 'more daring and licentious than former houses', being 'quite full of gentry and nobility (for the most part suspected in the matter of religion)'.[48] His comment has been taken by several historians to indicate that this Parliament marked a watershed in relations between Crown and Commons. But the composition of the Lower House was not much different from that of earlier Parliaments, and opposition was against demands for taxation, threats to property, and Philip's coronation, not against religious changes as such. However, the sessions were marked by unusually outspoken and dramatic scenes, perhaps in part due to the death of Gardiner in November, which removed the Crown's most effective manipulator of Parliaments. In short, while the 1555 Parliament was more turbulent than had been usual before, the controversies arose out of the demands made by the Crown and do not appear to mark any change in the composition of the Lower House or any novel attitude of opposition to the monarchy.

The months before this session opened had been punctuated by rumours and reports of conspiracies. None of them seems to have been very menacing, but as the Parliament drew to its close a much more dangerous plot was being concocted between English exiles in France and discontented gentle-

[48] *CSP Ven.* vi/1. 251.

men in England. Its principal architect was Henry Dudley, distant cousin to the late Duke of Northumberland and a talented soldier who had sunk into debt. Through the French Ambassador, Noailles, he made contact with Henry II of France, hoping to mobilize troops abroad with the King's aid and to launch an invasion which would coincide with a rising in the west country under Sir Anthony Kingston. The strategy depended upon finding a supply of money with which to buy arms and to pay mercenaries. Had the French King given financial backing, as the conspirators hoped, the rising might well have been dangerous; but Henry refused and they had to fall back on a risky plan to rob £50,000 from the Exchequer. Long before the rebels were able to act, the Exchequer plot was revealed to Pole and the leading figures in England were arrested. Gradually it became obvious that action was impossible and the conspiracy petered out. It is difficult to know how seriously it should be taken. The government suspected several prominent nobles and gentlemen of complicity. But, except for a few like Sir Anthony Kingston, there is no evidence to link any substantial number of notables with the plot. The active participants were mostly lesser gentry, younger sons, and professional soldiers, men down on their luck and prepared to take risks to restore their fortunes. They had no support from Protestant leaders, English or foreign, little influence of their own in England, and no real backing from Henry II. As events turned out, the conspiracy scarcely shook the security of the regime. The Crown found evidence to indict only thirty-six men, about half of whom were abroad: only thirteen in all were convicted.

The remaining years of Mary's reign were dominated by diplomacy and war. England was drawn by events into conflict not only with France but also with the Pope. In May 1555 Cardinal Carafa had been elected to the papal throne as Paul IV. His own hatred of the Habsburgs was reinforced by the political ambitions of his nephew, Carlo, who persuaded his uncle to enter an alliance with France against the Empire. Although France and the Empire had been briefly at peace from February 1556, Carlo Carafa provoked a Spanish invasion of the papal states in September, and by January of the following year Philip II and Henry II were again at war. In March 1557 Philip returned to his English kingdom, not out of any affection for his wife, but in order to persuade the Council to join the conflict with France. A month later Cardinal Pole's legatine commission was revoked and he was recalled to Rome: the man who had accomplished the reconciliation of England to the papacy was disowned by the Pope. Paul IV had long been hostile to Pole, whom he regarded as a heretic and protector of heretics; and neither the pleading of Mary nor of Pole himself secured his reinstatement.

The reconstruction of the Church in England was cruelly damaged by the breach and Pole himself was broken in spirit: 'the Cardinal is a dead man', reported Count Feria, the new Spanish Ambassador.[49]

Political debate centred on Philip's attempts to persuade the English Council to enter the war. Most members of the active Council, with the important exception of Paget, favoured peace, arguing that the common people were already 'pinched with famine' and, in some cases, 'miscontented for matters of religion', so that the demands of war might produce dangerous results.[50] At this point, however, Philip's arguments were assisted by a curious incident. Thomas Stafford, grandson of the last Duke of Buckingham, laid claim to the English throne from his exile in France and landed at Scarborough in April 1557 with a small troop of French and English followers. He captured Scarborough Castle, but five days later was himself captured by the Earl of Westmorland. It seems improbable that Henry II would have supported so foolish a venture and it is possible that Stafford was lured into revolt by *agents provocateurs* employed by Paget. Whatever the truth, Philip and Paget, by representing the expedition as a French attack, were able to persuade their colleagues into a declaration of war. Although many of the Council had been opposed to war and many others resented the prospect of paying more taxes, there was nevertheless considerable support for royal policy among the nobles. The Earls of Pembroke and Shrewsbury, appointed to command in France and on the northern border, mustered troops enthusiastically. Noblemen and gentlemen who had been out of favour joined the army to work their way back. The Earl of Bedford even returned from exile to lead West Country troops; the three sons of the Duke of Northumberland all served in France; Sir James Croft and Sir Peter Carew, both deeply involved in Wyatt's conspiracy, commanded troops. The English expeditionary force of about 7,000 men under the Earl of Pembroke was equipped with somewhat old-fashioned weapons and lacked experience in battle, though the navy was more effective. Twenty ships under Lord William Howard cleared the Channel for Spanish transport, and conveyed Pembroke's army to Calais.

At first the campaign prospered. English troops under Pembroke were present when St Quentin was captured from the French in August 1557. Then, on New Year's Day 1558, the Duc de Guise appeared before Calais with 27,000 men. An attack in winter was entirely unexpected and the garrison had been considerably reduced. The Council in London was unable to mobilize and dispatch reinforcements before Calais had fallen. Lord

[49] *CSP Span.* xiii. 366.
[50] D. M. Loades, *The Reign of Mary Tudor: Politics, Government and Religion in England, 1553–1558* (London, 1979), 242.

Wentworth, commander of the garrison, was later tried for treason. On that charge he was rightly acquitted; but he had almost certainly been negligent in failing to call earlier for help from England or from Philip. So, for that matter, had been the Council in allowing the garrison to be run down in the winter months. But the French had done the unexpected, taken a big gamble, and found luck on their side.

Reaction in England was mixed. The defeat was a severe blow to military morale. The Council refused to raise the troops requested by Philip for the recapture of Calais: they pleaded, with only some exaggeration, the poverty of the realm from famine and disease. When Parliament met in January 1558, shortly after the fall of Calais, it was surprisingly co-operative. The Queen asked for a double subsidy and two-fifteenths to be collected over two years. After debate the Commons offered a single subsidy and one-fifteenth to be levied in the forthcoming year. They were ready to give the Queen what she asked for one year but unwilling to commit themselves for two. Although this Parliament did not provide exactly what the Crown asked, it showed itself helpful; that Mary summoned the same Parliament for a second session in November shows its amenability. The fall of Calais, damaging as it was to prestige, did not destroy loyalty to the regime or begin its dissolution.[51] Most people were probably more deeply affected by the devastating epidemics of 1557 and 1558 than by political events. Two waves of virulent infection, most likely influenza, swept the country in those two years, following the harvest failures of the two previous summers. Wriothesley's *Chronicle* reported for 1557 that 'this summer reigned in England divers strange and new sicknesses, taking men and women in their heads, as strange agues and fevers, whereof many died'. The death toll was heavy, perhaps the worst in the century, and the population may well have fallen by 5 per cent or more in the second half of the 1550s.[52]

Politically the weakness of the regime lay less in the failures of government than in Mary's health and her inability to produce an heir. In 1557 she had again believed herself to be pregnant; but few others thought so. By the spring of 1558 the possibility had vanished, since Philip had left in the previous July. Throughout the summer she grew weaker and by October her death was considered imminent. All those involved, even Philip, recog-

---

[51] For a different view on Mary's last years see ibid., ch. 14.

[52] Wriothesley, *Chronicle*, ii. 139. I am grateful to Professor David Palliser and to Dr Ralph Houlbrooke for helpful discussion of this point. On mortality see P. A. Slack, 'Mortality crises and epidemic disease in England, 1485–1610', in Charles Webster (ed.), *Health, Medicine and Mortality in the Sixteenth Century* (Cambridge, 1979), 9–59; E. A. Wrigley and R. S. Schofield, *The Population History of England, 1541–1871: A Reconstruction* (London, 1981), 212 n. 28. For another view, D. M. Palliser, *The Age of Elizabeth: England under the Later Tudors, 1547–1603* (London, 1983), 33–6.

nized Elizabeth as the only possible successor, and finally Mary herself
agreed to this. Soon after, on 17 November 1558, she was dead. Elizabeth
was immediately proclaimed Queen and formally accepted as such by the
Spanish Ambassador.

5. MARIAN IRELAND

Ireland reverted to Catholic worship and papal authority immediately on
Mary's accession, without waiting for formal enactments. Bishop Bale reported miserably on the joy of the people of Kilkenny when they heard of
Mary's proclamation as Queen: copes, candlesticks, and censers were at
once brought out and displayed. The Protestant bishops were soon deprived and Catholics appointed in their places. Archbishop Dowdall, exiled
under Edward, was restored as Primate. Yet although the religious
measures of Edward were immediately reversed, there was less change in
secular policy. St Leger, already selected again as Lord Deputy before
Edward's death, was formally appointed in October 1553, with instructions
to reduce the garrison and to rule as economically as possible. For three
years he governed quietly, attempting to keep the various dynastic quarrels
of the Irish in check with a minimum of force. But in 1556 he was succeeded
as Lord Deputy by the Earl of Sussex, a man who had rallied to Mary very
quickly in July 1553. There seems to have been no significance in the
replacement of St Leger by Sussex: the one was weary of settling Irish
disputes, the other was a prominent nobleman trusted by the Queen. Yet
Sussex, supported by Sir Henry Sidney as Vice-Treasurer, immediately
adopted the aggressive policies of St Leger's predecessors. He was a vigorous, ambitious man who believed in firm policies and had little sympathy
for the Irish, of whom he later wrote 'I have often wished [them] to be
sunk in the sea'.[53] In the summer of 1556 he marched into Ulster, where
Shane O'Neill was beginning to challenge the right of his elder brother
Matthew to succeed their father. In the following year Sussex campaigned
westwards towards the Shannon against the O'Mores and O'Connors. He
stepped up the policy of plantation in Leix and Offaly, now renamed
Queen's County and King's County, pushing the O'Mores into a small part
of their original territory (Map 8). His solution to the problem of Ireland
was the creation of forts to the west and north of the Pale, the costs to be met
by settling the garrisons on the lands of expropriated Irish. After the
outbreak of war with France in 1557, Sussex and Sidney, who ruled for a
time as Lord Justice in his place, became increasingly alarmed at the danger

[53] Nicholas P. Canny, *The Elizabethan Conquest of Ireland: A Pattern Established, 1565–1576* (Hassocks, 1976), 30.

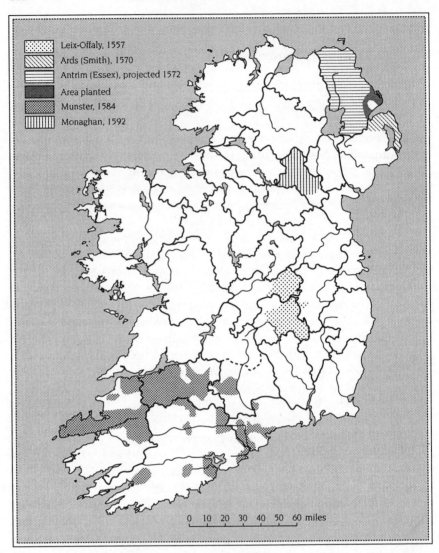

Leix-Offaly, 1557
Ards (Smith), 1570
Antrim (Essex), projected 1572
Area planted
Munster, 1584
Monaghan, 1592

0   10   20   30   40   50   60 miles

MAP 8. Tudor plantations in Ireland

of Irish intrigues with the French. The garrison was increased and the policy of force intensified.

The authoritarian, military government of Sussex won him few friends and many enemies. The Gaelic lords against whom he directed his attacks were naturally hostile. That great Anglo-Irish lord, the Earl of Desmond, insisted that it would be better to use 'fair means' than force. Ironically, the most severe critic of the Marian regime in Ireland was the restored Primate, Archbishop Dowdall, who presented a cogent attack upon Sussex: 'Considering that clemency and discretion is more meet in a governor than rigour or cruelness', he wrote, '. . . the deputy must behave himself accordingly to win the love and favour of all the country and specially of mere Irish.'[54] Winning such love and favour was what Sussex had conspicuously failed to achieve. He had indeed managed to unite magnates and churchmen, Gaelic chiefs, Anglo-Irish lords, and men of the Pale in hostility to English rule. In spite of the religious changes back and forth between 1547 and 1558 there is a sad unity in that period of Irish history: the English government then began the policy of repression and colonization that brought to birth a hatred which has lasted for more than four hundred years.

6. MARIAN RELIGION

For centuries Mary's reputation has suffered from a bombardment of hostile propaganda, its intensity determined from the beginning by John Foxe. In Protestant and Elizabethan tradition she is displayed as the arch opponent of true religion and as the friend of England's enemy, Spain. Her contribution to English history has been scorned as a legacy of hatred both for her faith and for the country of her husband. 'Sterility', in Pollard's cruel judgement, 'was the conclusive note of Mary's reign'.[55] However, within the last decade several historians have modified, even in some respects reversed, that verdict.

The restoration of the Catholic Church was Mary's supreme purpose and her rule must primarily be assessed in the light of that policy. Although there was much more to it than the destruction of Protestants, the persecution has loomed largest in the case against her and its effects must be considered first. From January 1554 onwards the imprisonment of ministers and the harrying of their congregations drove Protestants to find refuge in the cities of Germany and Switzerland. About 450 men and their families—some 700 persons in all—settled in Zurich, Strasbourg, Frankfurt, Geneva, and a few other towns. About a third of these exiles were gentlemen, a quarter students, one-seventh clergy, and one-tenth merchants; very few belonged to the artisan or labouring classes. A second stream of refu-

---

[54] Brendan Bradshaw, *The Irish Constitutional Revolution of the Sixteenth Century* (Cambridge, 1979), 271.

[55] A. F. Pollard, *The History of England from the Accession of Edward VI to the Death of Elizabeth* (London, 1910), 172. Contrast, for instance, Loades, *The Reign of Mary Tudor*, *passim*; Jennifer Loach and Robert Tittler (eds.), *The Mid-Tudor Polity*, c.*1540–1560* (London, 1980), *passim*.

gees left for France after the defeat of Wyatt's rebellion and subsequent conspiracies. They were fewer in number—about 100—and were mostly single men, often younger sons, sometimes adventurers driven by political ambition rather than religious principle. As a source of plots they caused the government some alarm, but their significance was short-lived. The German and Swiss groups, the religious exiles, were of much greater importance for the future. Although it is highly unlikely that the exodus was part of any planned campaign for the preservation and restoration of the true religion, the exiles maintained close contact with those Protestants who stayed behind, receiving money and reports of the persecution, sending back religious propaganda. It is common for exiled communities to quarrel among themselves and the English Protestants were no exception. The congregation at Frankfurt was divided between those who wished to preserve the 1552 Prayer Book and radicals who hoped to purify it. Pressure from moderates at Zurich and the arrival of Richard Cox led to the more extreme sects withdrawing to Geneva, where a congregation was established under John Knox. This did not resolve the disputes at Frankfurt, where the pastor in charge, Robert Horne, was accused of setting himself above the Church at large. These bitter differences were pregnant for the future. In Mary's reign the exiles sent to England more than eighty books and pamphlets on religion. The costs of production seem mainly to have been met by sales and it is therefore likely that, in spite of Mary's censorship, this literature was widely distributed in England. Most of the writers were concerned to sustain and comfort their fellow-Protestants in the time of persecution. Suffering was necessary for 'the confirmation of a Christian life', not a sign that God had abandoned them. Some pamphlets considered how godly rule could be restored; most of them urged peaceful action in Parliament by nobles and gentlemen, but a few—especially those by John Knox, Christopher Goodman, and John Ponet—advocated active resistance. This group, which has attracted the attention of historians by the originality of its views, was a very small minority, firmly rejected by most exiles and by Protestants in England. 'Let us avoid murmurations against the higher powers, for they are God's instruments', wrote an anonymous exile; while Mathew Parker in England remarked that 'if such principles be spread into men's heads . . . what master shall be sure in his bedchamber?'[56] Although the advocates of political change had little effect, it seems likely, to judge from the demand, that the more purely devotional works did help to support and inform Protestants in Marian England.

[56] Jennifer Loach, 'Pamphlets and Politics, 1553–58', *BIHR* 48 (1975), 39, 44.

Two other achievements of the exiles had their effect in the future. In Geneva, William Whittingham and his colleagues produced a translation of the New Testament. By contrast with the heavy, expensive black-letter folio of the Great Bible, this Geneva Bible was relatively cheap and compact. It became the main source of scriptural knowledge for devout Protestants in Elizabethan England. Meanwhile, in Frankfurt and then in Basle, John Foxe was collecting material for his *Book of Martyrs*, published in Latin in 1559, in English in 1563. Foxe did more than any other man to preserve and celebrate the story of the persecution, and his work is still our principal source for its history: five editions were produced under Elizabeth and many more since. The absorption of this book into popular mythology was later to inspire loyalty to the reformed Church and hatred for Spanish Catholicism.

The burning of Protestant heretics, which had begun in February 1555, continued until the last month of Mary's reign: 237 men and 52 women were burned at the stake, almost half of them in four cities (London (60), Canterbury (40), Colchester (23), Lewes (17)). Twenty-five were ministers of religion and eight were gentlemen; the rest were husbandmen, artisans, and women. In social composition they were thus completely different from the exiles. Many others were harassed and arrested, but escaped: some, like John Underhill, to live in hiding in England, others, like Thomas Mountayne, to flee to the Continent. Sometimes the burnings aroused popular sympathy for the victim. Rowland Taylor, the loved and respected rector of Hadley, Suffolk, was escorted to his death by a great crowd of men and women: 'with weeping eyes and lamentable voices they cried, saying one to another, "Ah, good Lord! there goeth our good shepherd from us . . ."'.[57] Occasionally, opinion was divided. When George Tankerfield was burned at St Albans a crowd gathered round, 'among the which multitude some were sorry to see so godly a man brought to be burned; others praised God for his constancy and perseverance in the truth. Contrariwise some there were which said, it was a pity he did stand in such opinions; and others, both old women and men, cried against him . . .'.[58] Overall, Foxe's account gives the impression that in London, and occasionally in East Anglia, the martyrs were supported by the onlookers. But elsewhere there is no evidence of strong reaction. Nor did the government encounter serious difficulty in securing the co-operation of laymen. The Earl of Derby in Lancashire, Sir John Tyrrell in Suffolk, Lord Darcy, Lord Rich, and Sir Anthony Browne in Essex, and Sir John Baker in Kent were active in hunting heretics. They were helped by lesser men, 'promoters' (informers),

---

[57] Foxe, vi. 697.   [58] Ibid. vii. 345.

who accused their own neighbours and created an atmosphere of tension and suspicion. More than three-quarters of the martyrs and two-fifths of the exiles came from East Anglia and the south-east. This suggests that, while Protestantism was certainly strongest there, persecution was carried out most zealously in that region, less rigorously elsewhere (Plates 11*a*, *b*).

Persecution did not eliminate heresy; and scattered congregations of Protestants met in many places. London was the safest haven for them in spite of the presence of central government, and reformers assembled there on board ship, in taverns, in the fields, in prisons, and in private houses like that of Anthony Hickman, merchant, and his wife Rose, where, according to the latter's 'recollections', 'we did table together in a chamber, keeping the doors close shut for fear of the promoters'.[59] But the Protestant clergy, the leaders of their Church, were either executed or exiled; the faithful in England were often led by laymen; and there seems to have been no missionary movement organized by the exiled Protestants, in sharp contrast to the missions despatched to England by exiled Catholics under Elizabeth.

While many Protestants showed heroic constancy under persecution, their numbers were gradually reduced. John Bradford, a leading Protestant preacher, wrote from his prison of the London people that 'not the tenth part abode in God's ways'; and the Catholic Dr Story wrote triumphantly in 1555 of London 'daily drawing partly for love, partly for fear, to conformity'. The effect of government pressure can be seen in the life of the Hickman family. After the government tightened its grip in March 1554, enjoining all subjects to receive the sacrament 'after the popish fashion', the Hickmans were afraid to keep Protestant preachers in their house any longer and sent them to Antwerp after supplying them with money. Hickman was imprisoned for this, and after his release went over to Antwerp himself with his wife and children. However, Rose Hickman's brother, Thomas Lock, unable to persuade his wife to depart, outwardly conformed and 'was so grieved in mind thereat, that he died shortly after with seven of his children'.[60] Although the Protestant faith survived in England, neither its organization nor the level of its support suggest that it could have made headway against the Catholic Church while Mary lived.

The constructive aspects of Marian Catholicism were less dramatic than the persecutions, but even so were not negligible. Mary and Pole were able,

---

[59] J. Shakespeare and M. Dowling, 'Religion and politics in mid-Tudor England: the recollections of Rose Hickman', *BIHR* 55 (1982), 99.

[60] Susan Brigden, *London and the Reformation* (Oxford, 1989), 573–4; Shakespeare and Dowling, 'Religion and politics', 99, 101.

as a result of deprivation and death, to appoint—or in some cases to re-store—to the episcopal bench men of unquestioned loyalty to the Catholic faith. Bishops like Thomas Goldwell of St Asaph had been trained in the climate of Counter-Reformation Catholicism; unlike the Henrician sur-vivors, such as Gardiner, they had been educated as theologians, not as lawyers, and were essentially pastors rather than politicians. All the Marian bishops who lived into the reign of Elizabeth refused to conform to her settlement of religion: the one exception, Kitchin of Llandaff, had been consecrated under Henry VIII. The leaders of the Marian Church were as well qualified to provide pastoral guidance and discipline as any bench of bishops in the century; and it was not necessarily a disadvantage to the Church that some of them—Gardiner, Heath, Thirlby, and Tunstall—were members of the Privy Council. Yet, able and devoted as they were, they lacked the calibre or the spirit to inspire a true rebuilding. Pole himself, once a committed reformer, had been defeated at the Council of Trent and now put his trust in ceremony and obedience. He was, besides, an old, sick man, whose last eighteen months were marred by his quarrel with Pope Paul IV. That conflict hindered the consecration of new bishops, so that on Mary's death seven sees were vacant.

Although historians have generally awarded greater praise to Protestant writings in Mary's reign than they have to Catholic, the latter were more significant than is generally believed. Bonner, best known for heresy trials, wrote and published an important work of catechesis, *A Profitable and Necessary Doctrine*; and new primers were issued, running to nearly forty editions. English Catholics produced sixty-four titles between 1554 and the end of the reign—fewer than the Protestant score of ninety-eight, but still considerable. Among these were major works of scholarship, such as the complete edition of the works of Thomas More, published in 1557.

As Chancellor of both Oxford and Cambridge universities Pole did what he could to convert them into nurseries for the priesthood. The new stat-utes that he issued at Oxford shortened the curriculum for the MA course with a view to producing priests more rapidly; but they had not come into effect by the time of Mary's death. However, two new colleges were founded at Oxford, Trinity and St John's, and one, Gonville and Caius, was refounded at Cambridge. The high point of Pole's work for the provision of a true Catholic clergy came with his London synod of 1555–6. Its rec-ommendation for the establishment of seminaries was original and impor-tant; but only one seminary was set up—at York—before the end of the reign, and the significance of this scheme was seen less in England than in the final session of the Council of Trent, where the idea was adopted as a formal decree.

Central to the restoration of the Catholic Church were priests, ceremonial equipment, and money. Visitations and episcopal records reveal great contrasts between different parts of the country. In Lancashire the long decline in ordinations was halted, and after 1553 men entered the priesthood in large numbers, while almost all parish churches in the county were equipped with service books and communion plate. In the diocese of Canterbury the picture was very different, and here restoration was slowest and least complete. The visitation of 1557 records that 32 out of 243 parishes had no resident priest, and that in many churches holy-water stoups, altars, and service-books were still missing. In London, according to Protestant witnesses, parishioners eagerly set up 'all manner of superstitious things again'; but while the restoration of roods, altar-cloths, ornaments, and service-books was complete in some City parishes, in others the churches were, according to Pole, in ruins.[61] It seems that throughout England the success of the Counter-Reformation depended very much on the commitment of parishioners. Apart from the diocese of Canterbury, most places saw a remarkably thorough restoration of altars, service-books, and church plate, but two elements of the Old Faith were seldom restored: the images and cults of saints, and prayers for departed souls in Purgatory. More seriously still, the Mass, which had, before the Reformation, been a symbol of reconciliation, had now become a source of bitterness and contention, especially in London.

The government took some steps to remedy the spoliation of Church wealth that had taken place under Henry and Edward. But it was not easy for the Crown to restore even those Church revenues that were in its own possession: First Fruits and Tenths had to be used mainly for the payment of monastic pensions, and only in the last year of the reign did the impropriated tithes restored by the Crown benefit parish churches. Administrative difficulties, especially confusion and uncertainty about Church revenues, delayed implementation. Surprisingly, Mary did not do much for the episcopal sees which had suffered under her predecessor: York and Canterbury received back considerable revenues, but others got only a little.

There can be little doubt that on Mary's death England was still largely Catholic. When Elizabeth succeeded, the returning Protestant exiles found it a country of popish darkness: at Oxford there were 'few gospellers . . . and many papists'. In many sees the new bishops had to struggle against the old faith: Bishop Horne described Winchester in 1562 as 'nursled in superstition and popery'. Undoubtedly religious attitudes

---

[61] Brigden, *London and the Reformation*, 586, 592.

varied dramatically from one region to another. Lancashire was loyal to Catholicism; Protestants were stronger in London, Essex, and Kent. Yet there was no easy distinction between a Catholic north and a Protestant south: the traditional loyalties of Sussex disprove any such simple contrast.

However, although the country was officially Catholic and likely to remain so as long as it was ruled by a Catholic monarch, the health of the Church could please neither active papists nor rigorous Protestants. Both groups identified some of the same weaknesses: the revenues of the Church had been despoiled and were too small to maintain episcopacy or parish clergy; many parishes had no incumbent; many priests were pluralists and were alarmingly ignorant of the central truths of Christianity, their parishioners still more so. Whatever they might disagree about, Catholics and Protestants could agree on that. While the reign of Edward VI had made matters worse, Mary's did only a little to improve them. Much of the explanation for that failure lies in lack of time and money, in the administrative problems confronting reformers, and in the reluctance of laymen to re-endow the Church. But was the direction of policy right? Did Mary and her bishops not devote excessive time and energy to persecution? Ought not Pole to have called in the Jesuits and launched an active preaching campaign? In short, would the Church have been substantially transformed if Mary had lived longer? Most historians would probably answer 'no' to that last question, and probably they would be right, not so much because Pole was using outdated or irrelevant methods, as because the task was, given the available resources, almost impossible.

7. MARIAN POLITICS

Simon Renard constantly and scathingly criticized Mary's Privy Council for being excessively large and in consequence both administratively inefficient and dangerously torn by factions. Until recently his assessment has been generally accepted by historians.[62] The Council was certainly large: it had more than forty members from October 1553 until the end of the reign. However, it quickly developed an inner caucus responsible for general policy and delegated much of its administrative work to committees. The membership of the inner group was fairly constant: in November 1553 it contained Arundel, Paget, Petre, Gardiner, Thirlby, and Rochester; in 1555 they were joined by Pembroke and Winchester, with Pole attending when he wished. The personal and political disagreements of Paget and Gardiner

[62] G. A. Lemasters, 'The Privy Council in the reign of Mary I' (Ph.D. thesis, University of Cambridge, 1971) contains the most substantial account of this subject and I gratefully acknowledge its help.

certainly caused friction, especially in the spring Parliament of 1554, but there is no good evidence, in spite of Renard's assertions, that either had a consistent following in the Council. Historians have perhaps been too ready to identify factions in sixteenth-century England. Leading politicians often fought for dominance and enticed others to support them; yet the lesser men usually tried to keep the lines open to both sides, supporting one leader on one issue, his opponent on another.

Much more damaging than faction, hypothetical or not, was the lack of any capable politician to whom Mary could give her trust. She relied upon Paget for the first nine months, but his conduct in the second Parliament destroyed her faith in his loyalty. Gardiner was more consistently in her favour, but she never seems to have been fully at ease with him, for he had betrayed her mother under Henry VIII and opposed her own marriage at the start of the reign; but even so, his death in November 1555 left a worrying gap. Pole was personally sympathetic, but remained detached from secular politics. The two men to whom she gave most of her confidence were foreigners, Simon Renard and her husband, Philip. Renard obviously could play no direct part in government and his influence with Mary was resented by many of her councillors. Philip had Mary's full trust and devotion, was liked by many English nobles, to whom he gave generous pensions, and had the ability to direct affairs effectively when he chose. Unfortunately he was in England for only two periods, one of thirteen months and the other of four; and during those times he was only intermittently concerned with the government of the country.

On the whole, the Council and the principal officers of state administered England with reasonable competence. Finance was the most testing area of government. Early in 1554 the Crown issued letters patent uniting the Courts of First Fruits and Augmentations to the Exchequer, a measure whose groundwork had been prepared under Edward. This endowed the Exchequer with more centralized control over finance, under the general supervision of the Privy Council. It was also intended to secure economies in administration, but like so many schemes to reduce the expenses of bureaucracy, then and now, it achieved little. At her accession Mary inherited a debt of £185,000. One of her first acts was to remit the final instalment of Edward's last subsidy, depriving herself of about £50,000, a popular move but not perhaps a wise one. During the first year of her reign she took up further loans, especially in Antwerp; but thereafter, until the outbreak of war in 1557, the Crown was able, thanks largely to the parliamentary subsidy of 1555, to repay much of its debt. The expenses of war were covered partly by borrowing, partly by direct taxation, and partly by an increase in customs duties. This last feature, achieved by issuing a new Book of Rates in May 1558, was less help to Mary than to her successor. In the first financial year of Elizabeth's reign the customs brought in an additional £50,000, a substantial sum when the whole ordinary revenue of the Crown had earlier been only about £132,000. Mary, having begun with debts of £185,000, passed to her successor liabilities of between £260,000 and £300,000, against which must be set the improvement in ordinary revenue. The record was not outstanding, but for a government at war it was at least adequate.[63]

Mary's reign coincided with a period of acute commercial and economic crisis. The export of cloth to Antwerp had fallen sharply in 1551–2, and although there was then some recovery, trade continued to look precarious. Harvest failures in 1555 and 1556 raised the price of grain to an unprecedented level. These short-term crises occurred when population was growing, prices rising, and many towns declining in the face of industrial competition from the countryside. There was not a great deal that could be done to remedy matters by regulation; but some attempts were made. Two parliamentary statutes forbade countrymen to sell by retail in the towns and limited the number of looms that could be operated by rural weavers.[64] Both were moves to protect urban economies against competition, and their origins are uncertain: they may have been born in the Commons rather than the Council. Even if, as is likely, they had no dramatic effect, they were a sign that Parliament was at least aware of the problem. Rather more significant was the Crown's intervention in overseas trade. Under Edward VI the privileges of the Hanseatic merchants, who paid low customs duties, had been revoked. Mary restored the privileges at the beginning of her reign, but in 1555 the English company of Merchant Adventurers persuaded her, not merely to revoke the Hanse privileges once more, but to prohibit Hanseatic merchants from almost all trade between England and the Netherlands. With the weakening of the Antwerp market, English traders got some further support from the Crown, in the form of royal charters to enable them to seek other commercial outlets. A company was formed for trading with the Guinea coast of Africa in 1553 and made five voyages before Mary's death: the life of the company was brief—it was wound up after Hawkins's calamity at San Juan de Ulúa in 1567—but it was the forerunner of the prosperous and odious transatlantic commerce in African slaves developed over the next two centuries. Moroccan trade also began to flourish in the 1550s, but without the creation of a formal company. The role of the Crown was more active in commerce with Russia: a royal charter

[63] Details of the royal finances are to be found in Loades, *Reign of Mary Tudor*, chs. 6, 9, 12.
[64] 1 & 2 Philip & Mary, c. 7; 2 & 3 Philip & Mary, c. 11.

established the Muscovy Company in 1555, and a letter from Philip and Mary helped it to acquire substantial trading rights from the Tsar. The reign of Mary was thus a significant stage in two major developments of the economy: the elimination of foreign merchants from English commerce and the extension of that commerce to new, more distant countries. The Crown played an important, though not a dominant, role in both.

Mary's government paid some attention to England's defences. New ships were built and administrative control of the navy improved. By February 1559 the Crown had thirty-one ships, the basis of the Elizabethan navy. Little attention had been paid to England's land forces during the peace, but after the fall of Calais two statutes were carried to improve the militia.[65] One imposed penalties on men who failed to appear at the annual musters, the other brought up to date the weapons which men of each social group were required to possess. Both statutes were conservative in their approach, but each did something to improve the militia and its equipment.

The general impression gained from the working documents of the Council is that the administration was thorough, careful, and, by the stand-ards of the day, fairly efficient. There were continual reports of plots and conspiracies; but these were no more frequent than they had been under Northumberland and not much more frequent than they were to be in the first five years of Elizabeth. The Council was sufficiently vigilant, after the crisis of Wyatt's revolt, to prevent any serious threat to the regime. Its principal members had served a long apprenticeship in government under Henry VIII and Edward VI; and men like Paget, Petre, and Winchester were, at the lowest estimate, very competent administrators. Continuity in government service operated in the middle and lower ranks as well as in the highest. Most of the Edwardian judges and law-officers continued in their posts after 1553; and in the counties there was little change in the ranks of Justices of the Peace, except for the intrusion of a few enthusiastic Catholics in East Anglia, Kent, and Sussex. The sharp reversal of religious policy under Mary was executed by the old guard of lay administrators. Only the leaders of the Church were changed, and they were changed utterly.

No one could pretend that the policies of Mary Tudor were popular. Her foreign marriage bred fears of Spanish domination and the return to Rome alarmed many, especially the holders of Church lands. Anxiety on both these scores was only partially allayed. Nevertheless Mary secured her main objectives: the restoration of the Mass, the return to Roman jurisdiction, the marriage to Philip, and entry into her husband's war with France. She was denied only the bill for confiscating the lands of exiles and authorization

---

[65] 4 & 5 Philip & Mary, cc. 2, 3.

for the coronation of Philip. Within the limits set upon government action at this time she was reasonably, even remarkably, successful. Her ability to secure objectives which were far from popular shows the strength of the mid-Tudor monarchy; the difficulties that she encountered in achieving and implementing legislation reflect the dependence of that monarchy upon landowners, lawyers, and merchants. But there was of course one great failure: the lack of a male heir. Mary's illness induced men to look to Elizabeth and weakened the enforcement of her policies. Time's winged chariot and her own barren womb did more to frustrate her desires in the long run than anything else.

Reviewing the period from 1547 to 1558—sometimes described as the mid-Tudor crisis—one is struck by the government's ultimate stability in the face of minority rule, succession crises, religious dissension, war, and famine. The reasons are complex and will emerge more fully in later chapters; but four aspects of the English polity are worth noticing now. First, there was great continuity among the secular rulers at the centre and in the shires. Secondly, few magnates wished to threaten the regime, and after the alarms of 1549 the landowning class was remarkably cohesive, most of its members profiting from Edward's reign and hoping to keep those profits under Mary. Thirdly, popular uprisings were limited in their aims and not very violent in their means. Finally, there was little of that vicious, sectarian religious hatred which was to tear apart the France of Catherine de Medici. Englishmen in all ranks of society were mostly compliant to the authority of government. Yet to men living at the time, these comforting aspects were less evident than they are to us. Harvest failure and plague had impoverished and killed many; the country was still at war; the treasury was empty; and the accession of Elizabeth foreshadowed further religious upheaval.

CHAPTER 5

The Structure of Government

I. THE ROYAL COURT

Under Henry VIII the royal Court had become the centre of the political, social, intellectual, and religious life of the nation. While influences from Burgundy and Italy had earlier helped to mould it, and while several of its features were already evident under the Yorkists and Henry VII, Henry VIII made it the focus of men's ambitions, the place where promotion, favour, rewards, and fame could be won. Its growing importance was partly the consequence of Henry's own personality, partly the result of institutional change, in particular the emergence of the Privy Chamber as the directing force at Court. Yet what was the Court? As well as being the focus of ambition for the political élite, it was also a place, an assemblage of buildings located mainly in royal palaces, especially and increasingly centred upon Whitehall, but to be found also in the private houses of the great when the king went on progress. Besides the monarch himself, its members included his consort and the officials who ran the royal household; but the great nobles, the major officers of state, and the royal favourites were very much a part of it, even if they did not hold any official position there. It is difficult to draw a precise boundary around this institution, but it had a clearly defined and highly organized central core, with an extensive periphery whose size and composition varied from time to time according to the needs of the moment and the wishes of the monarch. The institution thus formed under Henry VIII continued to be the centre of the nation's political life—and of much else—for the rest of the sixteenth and most of the seventeenth centuries.

Politically, the Court was a theatre of display for the monarch and attendant notables, a principal forum for the informal discussion of affairs and for the making of decisions, a market-place for the seekers and distributors of patronage, and a crucial link between the Crown and the regions.[1] Where the role of the Court ended and that of the more formal institution,

---

[1] See Ch. 10, *passim*, for discussion of the Court as a 'cultural centre'.

the Council, began is hard, often impossible, to say. Nor had the institutions of the Court ceased by 1547 to play a part in the purely administrative side of government. The definition of its boundaries, the firmness with which they were drawn, depended greatly upon the personality of the monarch and his or her closest advisers.

By the accession of Edward VI the Court's physical layout and formal organization were clearly established. It was divided into two sections: the *Domus Providencie*, or Household proper, supplied the physical needs of the Court—food, drink, clothing, transport, and so on; the *Domus Magnificencie*, or Chamber, was the front of the house where monarch and courtiers lived and presented themselves. The term Household can be ambiguous, for, while strictly speaking it applied only to the supply and housekeeping departments, it could also refer to the Court as a whole: context alone enables one to tell. Before 1540 the Household—in the strict sense—had been ruled by the Lord Steward, almost always a great noble. Reforms devised by Thomas Cromwell had established the post of Lord Great Master, who was intended to control both Household and Chamber. This arrangement continued until 1553, with Northumberland holding the post from 1550 until the death of Edward. After that the office of Lord Great Master was abolished and the Lord Steward was restored. Under Mary and Elizabeth a succession of nobles held the post: the Earls of Arundel, Pembroke, Lincoln, Leicester, Derby, and Nottingham. Men like this were not going to supervise royal housekeeping and the real work was done by the Treasurer of the Household, the Comptroller—both of them usually knights—and the Cofferer, a professional administrator who had risen in the service of the Household. Between them they formed the Board of Greencloth, a management committee and accounting agency which oversaw the work of the kitchens, larder, cellar, bakehouse, laundry, and so on. This department also looked after the Great Hall, once the centre of the life of the Court, now used only for occasions of high ceremony, and supervised the Knight Marshal, who was responsible for discipline within the Court and ran its prison, the Marshalsea.

The arrangement of the *Domus Magnificencie*, more usually called the Chamber in the second half of the sixteenth century, was basically the same in all royal palaces and in private houses visited by the monarch. Largest of its rooms was the Great or Presence Chamber, to which access was easily obtained by members of the upper gentry and where the monarch might usually be seen passing through to chapel or to meals. Beyond that lay the centre of Court life, the Privy Chamber, to which entry was much more tightly restricted, and beyond that again was the royal bedchamber, the most private part of the Court. This arrangement allowed the monarch to see and be seen by prominent subjects and foreign visitors, but carefully regulated the degree of access that was allowed. The Chamber was controlled by the Lord Chamberlain, who was subject to the Lord Great Master from 1540 to 1553, but whose office, unlike that of the Lord Steward, remained in being during that period. The Chamberlain, like the Steward, was usually a great noble—the Earl of Arundel held the post from 1546 to 1550. But in the later years of Edward's reign and under Mary men of lesser rank were appointed, like Sir Thomas Darcy, firm supporter of Northumberland, and Sir John Gage and Sir Edward Hastings, both devout Catholics. Elizabeth reverted to the aristocratic tradition, appointing Edward Lord Howard of Effingham in 1558, followed by the Earl of Sussex, Charles Lord Howard of Effingham, the first Lord Hunsdon, Lord Cobham, and the second Lord Hunsdon. The Chamberlain played a more active role than the Steward, for although he delegated the day-to-day running of his department to others, he was responsible for allocating accommodation within the Court, a task which exposed him to many ardent requests and frequent complaints, for rooms were often in short supply and he could easily find himself in the uncomfortable position of the manager of an over-booked hotel. His principal under-officers were the Vice-Chamberlain and the Treasurer of the Chamber, both usually of knightly rank and courtier background.

The principal attendants upon the monarch under Henry VIII and Edward VI were the eighteen Gentlemen of the Privy Chamber, to whom four principal gentlemen were added in 1549, together with six Lords of the Privy Chamber. Their leader was the Groom of the Stool, who had had the seemingly disagreeable but highly coveted task of emptying the royal chamber-pot, and came, as a consequence of this intimacy, to be Chief Gentleman. Under Edward the gentlemen looked after the Privy Chamber itself and the royal bedchamber, the stool-room (lavatory), and so on; key figures in his reign and that of his father, they became, for obvious reasons, less significant under Mary and Elizabeth, for whom ladies of the bedchamber performed these intimate roles.

The small military force of the Court also fell within the Chamber organization. The yeomen of the guard, one hundred strong and armed with pikes, had been formed under Henry VII; their numbers increased to 200, with a reserve of a further 200, in 1550, when Northumberland was shoring up his position at Court and in the country at large. Fifty gentlemen pensioners, known also as 'spears', had been established in 1539 and were reorganized by Northumberland with a strength of sixty. In February 1551 he had created a force of 850 gendarmes, or cavalry; but this had been discontinued in the following year when money ran short. The guard and the pensioners remained in being under both Mary and Elizabeth, but became courtly sinecures rather than effective military protectors of the monarch.

Beyond the Household proper and the Chamber were other departments on the periphery of Court life. The Great Wardrobe provided tents for progresses, props and costumes for revels. The stables, controlled by the Master of the Horse, and the kennels played important roles in a Court culture almost obsessed with the chase. On the other hand, the Office of Works, extremely busy under Henry VIII, was relatively inactive under his children, none of whom spent much time or money on building. The Chapel Royal was set somewhat apart in the organization of the Court: it was part of the Chamber but not controlled by the Lord Chamberlain. Mary's Catholic devotion and Elizabeth's liking for ceremony ensured the survival and indeed the flowering of English church music, under the direction of Thomas Tallis and William Byrd.

In an age of large households the royal Court was a substantial affair. The *Domus Providencie* numbered 250–300 persons, the *Domus Magnificencie* perhaps as many as 400, including its various offshoots. The stables, kennels, Great Wardrobe and Chapel Royal probably employed about 300 and the 'military' strength of the guard and the pensioners came to 260. This would produce a total of about 1,250 posts, of which about 200 at the beginning of the period and 175 at the end were suitable for a gentleman. This was far larger than the noble households of the time, which generally numbered 75 to 140, and was comparable to the Court of Henry IV of France, which had 1,500 officials, excluding his large military force. By comparison with the establishment of 10,000 at Versailles in the mid-eighteenth century the late Tudor court was a modest affair, but it probably equalled in size all the other departments of state added together.[2]

Under Edward VI and Mary the display function of the Court was relatively neglected. Although lavish festivities were held during the Christmas season of 1551–2 and a royal progress was arranged in the following summer, Edward's reign was too short and the monarch too young for a strong tradition of courtly magnificence to develop. Mary showed little enthusiasm for public display and the entry of Philip and herself into London in 1554 was the only occasion of any splendour during her reign. Elizabeth revived the theatrical aspects of the royal Court with her entry into London in January 1559, but regular displays did not become a feature of her rule until the 1570s, when the great tournaments of her

---

[2] On the organization of the Court, its officers and numbers, see David Loades, *The Tudor Court* (1986), esp. ch. 2 and appendices.

father's time were revived by Sir Henry Lee, the Queen's Champion, with special attention given to the celebration of Elizabeth's accession day, 17 November. Although these were essentially Court occasions, they were attended by members of the public—several thousands of them according to a German observer, von Wedel—who each paid 12*d.* for the privilege of watching from beyond the barriers.

This presentation of the Queen as the centre and head of a knightly and chivalric Court was reinforced by the progresses of the reign. In May 1575 Elizabeth left London for Burghley's house, Theobalds, Hertfordshire, and toured with her vast entourage through Northamptonshire, Warwickshire, Staffordshire, and Worcestershire, staying on the return journey for nineteen days at Kenilworth Castle near Warwick, the grandest residence of the Earl of Leicester. She was greeted by a Savage Man—a favourite figure on occasions of this sort—who told her that the castle had originally belonged to King Arthur and was being guarded by Leicester for Arthur's heir, herself. On the following day the 'lusty lads and bold bachelors' of the parish gathered to present a burlesque marriage before the Queen, and in the afternoon the citizens of Coventry came out to present their Hock Tuesday play commemorating the victory of the English over the Danes in 1002. Next the Queen was treated to a more formal masque held on the banks of the lake outside the castle walls. Triton appeared swimming on a mermaid, to tell Elizabeth that a cruel knight, Sir Bruce Sans Pity, lay in ambush for the lady of the lake. He begged Elizabeth to save the lady, which she duly did by putting Sir Bruce to flight. Naïve as all this may sound, it enabled the Queen to present herself to her people, combined popular and courtly entertainments, and built up a picture of the monarch as both heir to King Arthur, the possessor of magical power, and yet an accessible human being. Modern image-makers would find the process familiar; and it was one in which the Court played a central part.[3]

Semi-religious Court ceremonies inherited from their predecessors enabled the Tudor monarchs to emphasize the divine aspects of monarchy. From a very early date English kings had touched those afflicted with the king's evil, scrofula, had blessed metal cramp rings, used to cure epilepsy and cramp, and had washed the feet of poor persons on Maundy Thursday. These practices had been little used in the fifteenth century until they were revived by Henry VII. His son was less concerned with them, and there is no record of Edward VI touching. Mary revived the rituals and performed them with great devotion, combining the blessing of the cramp rings and the touching with creeping to the Cross on Good Friday. However, accord-

---

[3] See below, Ch. 10 s. 2 for further discussion of pageantry. The Kenilworth visit is described by Robert Laneham, in an account printed in *Captain Cox, his Ballads and Books; Or Robert Laneham's Letter*, ed. F. J. Furnivall (London, 1871), *passim*.

ing to the Venetian Ambassador, 'she chose to perform this act privately in a gallery where there were not above twenty persons'. Elizabeth did not continue the blessing of the cramp rings and soon abandoned creeping to the Cross; but she continued to touch and to wash, performing the acts with much more public ceremony than her sister had used. During the Kenilworth progress, according to Robert Laneham's account, 'by her highness' accustomed mercy and charity, [there were] nine cured of the painful and dangerous disease, called the king's evil'. By the end of the reign touching had become so accustomed a part of royal duties that James I was to be persuaded by his advisers, against his own inclinations, to continue it. The rituals were an important demonstration of sacred kingship, the more necessary for Mary and Elizabeth, perhaps, in view of their sex and of the religious uncertainties of the time.[4]

The Court's role as the market-place of patronage contrasted sharply with the theatre of display. Through the Court, its officials, and its hangers-on some 3,000 or more petitions were presented to the monarch each year for offices, leases, wardships, or other royal favours. Many were trivial, but in sum they were substantial; and a few of them involved very large amounts. The rewards provided by the Court were at their most lavish under Edward VI: looking back on that period towards the end of his life Burghley remarked that never had he been so generously rewarded. That reign saw the rise of such great dynasties as the Dudleys, the Russells, and the Herberts. Mary was more restrained: she restored a few old and discredited families, such as the Percies and the Howards, but built up no new ones. Elizabeth followed her example. Large numbers of men and women profited from royal patronage in a small way, but only a few were able to found great fortunes. Burghley was able to create two dynasties out of the rewards of service, one for his eldest son, Thomas, and another for his younger, Robert, later Earl of Salisbury. While no other great dynasty was founded under Elizabeth, Sir Christopher Hatton and Sir Walter Ralegh, among the courtiers, achieved great wealth from royal favour. The most famous of royal favourites, Leicester and Essex, were less fortunate: Leicester because he spent huge sums on the Netherlands expedition and died without heirs, Essex because of his disgrace and execution. But although great fortunes were only to be made by the fortunate few, the Court remained the centre of hope for the most aspiring of Elizabeth's subjects. Access to it, to the Council, and to the Queen herself was essential to success. Robert Laneham, keeper of the door of the Council chamber, described a typical scene in the Presence Chamber:

[4] Quoted in Carol Levin, ' "Would I could give you help and succour": Elizabeth I and the politics of touch', *Albion*, 21 (1989), 197, 200.

Now, sir, if the Council sit, I am at hand, wait at an inch, I warrant you. If any make babbling, 'peace' (say I), 'wot ye where ye are?' . . . But now they keep good order; they know me well enough. If 'a be a friend, I make him sit down beside me on a form or a chest: let the rest walk, 'a God's name.[5]

In 1594 the press of persons at Court was so great that special orders were drafted to control access: an usher and a waiter were to attend every day with two clerks to see everyone coming to Court; officials and nobles were to hand in lists of their servants. Other lords and gentry who came to Court without having lodging there were to give the porter their names. Masters of Requests were to have a room outside the gates with orders to interview all suitors and allow no one to enter without a licence. The confusion resulting from men pressing to put their suits produced a very different atmosphere from the stately picture presented on the outside. Yet that picture too had its truth. Paul Hentzner, a German traveller, received permission from the Lord Chamberlain to enter the Presence Chamber one day in 1598. He described the emergence of the Queen from her private apartments and her passage through the Presence Chamber to chapel, preceded by a procession of gentlemen, barons, earls, and knights of the garter, followed by ladies of the Court, and guarded by fifty gentlemen pensioners. As she went along 'in all this state and magnificence, she spoke very graciously, first to one, then to another, whether foreign ministers, or those who attended for different reasons, in English, French, and Italian'. While she was in the chapel, from which Hentzner heard excellent music, the company watched her dinner table being set out formally in the Presence Chamber. However, when she returned it was carried into an inner chamber where she dined with only a few attendants.[6] The scenes presented by Laneham and Hentzner are very different: confusion and competition in Laneham's, a delicate combination of formality and accessibility in Hentzner's. Both show real and important aspects of the Court's role in society: it created an image and it provided gifts.

While entry to the Presence Chamber was strongly contested by many, the key to real influence lay in access to the Privy Chamber and to the Queen herself. Essex, writing to Bacon after the latter had been excluded from the royal presence, told him that he was to be allowed 'access' but not 'near access', which was only allowed to those whom the Queen 'favours extraordinarily'.[7] The difference was crucial; and towards the end of Elizabeth's reign 'near access' became increasingly difficult. Bishop

[5] *Captain Cox*, ed. Furnivall, 58–9; 69 n. 2.

[6] P. Hentzner, *Travels in England*, trans. R. Bentley, ed. H. Walpole (London, 1889), 46–51.

[7] Birch, *Memoirs*, i. 120–1.

Goodman, writing in the reign of James I, commented that Elizabeth was 'ever hard of access and grew to be very covetous in her old days'.[8] In the final decade of the reign the inner group at Court was small and tightly knit: the Cecils; Essex until 1599; the Howards; Ralegh; Elizabeth's cousins, the Careys and the Knollyses; and the Stanhopes.

The hopes and frustrations of Court life naturally created ambivalent feelings. To its inhabitants it presented a double face. Edmund Spenser, while glorifying Elizabeth and her Court in *The Faerie Queene*, vented his rage against it in *Colin Clouts Come Home Again*. Those 'shepherds' who sought to come to Court must know that

> ... it is no sort of life,
> For shepheard fit to lead in that same place,
> Where each one seeks with malice and with strife,
> To thrust downe other into foule disgrace,
> Himselfe to raise: and he doth soonest rise
> That best can handle his deceitfull wit,
> In subtil shifts, and finest sleights devise.[9]

Dissimulation and deceit were the qualities that won success: the complaint is echoed again and again by critics of the Court. Yet they seldom followed the logic of their words and departed. Most of them stayed in the hope that their fortunes would look up. This double attitude was in no way new: Sir Thomas Wyatt had painted the evil and corruption of Henry VIII's Court in a series of bitter Epistolary Satires. But there is a difference. While Wyatt's poems reveal a deep and real fear, which was fully understandable in the light of Henrician politics, the poems of Spenser and his contemporaries seem by contrast conventional, for a poet was almost obliged to criticize this world even while he looked to it for advancement. The difference is important: the Henrician Court still belonged to the savage political era of the fifteenth century: a small mistake could easily cost a man his life or his freedom; and this was still true under Edward VI. By the reign of Elizabeth the Court had been tamed.

2. THE PRIVY COUNCIL

By the death of Henry VIII the Privy Council had been formally established for at least seven years as the select ruling board of the realm, advising the monarch on policy, executing decisions, carrying responsibility for general administration and public expenditure, co-ordinating the work of all

[8] Godfrey Goodman, *At the Court of King James the First* (2 vols., London, 1839), i. 96–7.
[9] Edmund Spenser, *Colin Clouts Come Home Againe*, ll. 688–94.

agencies of government, and exercising certain quasi-judicial functions. It had a small permanent staff, headed by the clerk of the Privy Council, and its formal decisions were recorded in a register. Under Henry's will sixteen men were appointed to act as privy councillors to his son: they included great officers of Church and state, such as the Archbishop of Canterbury, the Keeper of the Privy Seal, the Lord High Admiral, and the Chief Justice of the Court of Common Pleas; some prominent courtiers; and one of the two principal Secretaries of State, who acted as the key figure in conciliar government, providing information, drafting letters, and acting as a link-man between Council and monarch. A few great nobles of old creation had normally been members of Henry's Council, but there were none in this first Edwardian Council. However, they soon reappeared after 1547, al-though for the most part they rarely attended, and with a few exceptions, like the Earl of Arundel, exerted little influence.

Although the Henrician Council was perpetuated in his will and survived his death, it met serious challenges in the next ten years and underwent some changes over the subsequent half-century. The Duke of Somerset, having begun his rule as Protector with the authority and co-operation of the Council, began to abandon it from December 1547, relying upon the advice of Lord Paget and members of his own household. Meetings of the Council became infrequent and largely formal, Somerset himself taking the major decisions of state. However, faced with the risings of 1549, he needed its support, and after his fall later that year it was restored to its position as the central organ of state. Northumberland, having packed the Council with men favourable to himself, ruled through it much as Henry VIII had done. True, his Council was larger than Henry's, numbering about thirty as against the nineteen or twenty of the years 1540–7, but effective attendance was usually between ten and twelve. It contained all the major officers of state, two or three bishops, some great nobles, the principal officers of the Court, some soldier-courtiers and associates of Northumberland, and some judges. The King himself did not attend Council meetings, but had special conferences arranged to brief him. Not surprisingly under a boy King, the Council, working in close co-operation with the principal officers of the Court, wielded unprecedented power. But although it served the interests of Northumberland and his followers, it also operated effectively as a policy-making board and executive committee in a way that it had not done under Somerset.

On Edward's death the Council came near to being transformed. As Mary moved into East Anglia she began to form a council, first at Kenninghall and then at Framlingham. She appointed to it men from her own household, together with nobles and gentry who came in to support her in those early and anxious days. Most of them were Catholics and none had any experience of government. To the twenty-one men who swore the councillor's oath in mid-July 1553 she then added several more experienced politicians and administrators. Some of them were survivors from the Edwardian regime, like Paget, Pembroke, and Winchester, who quickly transferred their allegiance when it was clear that Northumberland's cause was defeated; others were Henrician politicians like Gardiner and Norfolk, who had been barred from power in the previous reign. Thanks to these additions the full Marian Council was much larger even than Northumberland's, running to forty or fifty names throughout the reign. It also contained a large number of Household officials, whose qualifications lay in their religion and in their personal devotion to Mary rather than any experience of government. But in practice the differences between the Edwardian and Marian Councils turned out to be slight. Apart from Gardiner, who died in 1555, the Henricians played only a minor role; and of the Household men only Sir Robert Rochester, the Comptroller, was active in the Council. Conciliar power lay with the Edwardian 'professionals', like Paget, Winchester, and Petre. Very quickly an informal inner group appeared, which met regularly and conducted the main business of the realm. In 1555 the Council was provided with its own seal, a further step in its development as a formal institution. However, there was one important difference between the Edwardian and Marian Councils: under Edward membership of Council and of Household had overlapped, while under Mary there was a clear distinction between the two bodies. In secular matters this probably made little difference, control of policy and administration remaining in the hands of the 'professionals' in the Council; but the Household men, including perhaps some of Philip's entourage, may possibly have played a larger role in the conduct of religious affairs.

Immediately on her accession Elizabeth reduced the Council to nineteen members; and by the 1590s it had come down to eleven. The Marian Household men were at once removed, and the Elizabethan Council consisted of experienced administrators, officers in her own Court, and a few great nobles. As the reign progressed, the aristocratic element was steadily reduced. Significantly, only one bishop, Whitgift, was made a councillor in the entire course of the reign. The Council was a thoroughly professional body, with a small enough membership to ensure the efficient conduct of business; it met three days a week in the early part of the reign and six days towards the end. Successive Secretaries of State—William Cecil, Francis Walsingham, and Robert Cecil—organized its affairs and supplied the vital links with the Queen and other departments of her government. The demarcation between Household and Council disappeared, since the most

important officers at Court—men like Sir Francis Knollys—were influential in the Council too; and the two most powerful figures in the first part of
the reign, Burghley and Leicester, were equally at home at Court and in the
Council Chamber.

The main functions of the Council were to discuss matters of state and to
present advice to the Queen, who seldom attended its meetings. Unfortunately, the Council's registers, which are largely in the form of a letter-
book, provide no information on its debates, which are known only from
casual gossip. The Council's official papers are filled with the business of
administration: the handling of relations between the Queen and her subjects, and the execution of policy already decided in consultation with the
monarch. Almost any matter of government business, however weighty or
however trivial, might come before the Council, whether it concerned
foreign policy, military strategy, the apprehension of burglars, the rebuilding of a town destroyed by fire, or the repair of the banks of a river. But
perhaps the most important of its functions, apart from the discussion of
policy, lay in its control of finance: the days when the monarch might
personally supervise accounts were over, and the authorization of expenditure came to be a matter for the Council, in conjunction with the Exchequer. On the whole the Elizabethan Council was a remarkably united
body, at least until it was fractured by the disputes between Essex and the
Cecils in the latter part of the reign. Some issues divided it, most notably
Elizabeth's proposed marriage to the Duke of Anjou; but more often it
found itself united in urging a course upon a reluctant Queen, as in the
1560s when it tried in vain to persuade her to marry.[10] As if the conduct of
high politics and the detailed administration of the realm were not business
enough, the Council also exercised a quasi-judicial role. Disputants in legal
cases constantly petitioned the Council, asking for justice against their
opponents. Sitting in Star Chamber, the councillors acted as a formal court
of law. Yet, although they seem sometimes to have forgotten whether they
were in Star Chamber or in Council, the demarcation between the two was
real. The Council did not itself hand down judgements. Sometimes it
delegated cases to arbitrators, a common and generally popular way of
dealing with disputes; sometimes it instructed the judges in one of the law
courts to hear the case. Its role was to supervise the working of the legal
'system', not to act as a court in the fullest sense.

The sixteenth century in Europe was an age of conciliar government. Yet
the English Privy Council differed significantly from its counterparts in

---

[10] Below, Ch. 7 s. 2; Ch. 8 s. 2.

France and Spain. The king's Council in France sometimes met in full session as the *conseil d'état*, but these occasions seem to have been largely formal. The real business was done in smaller, specialized councils: the *conseil des affaires*, which dealt with high politics; the *conseil des finances*; the *conseil des parties*, which heard disputes between private parties. The names of the various branches of the French royal Council were constantly changing, itself a testimony to the relative absence of a formal structure. In the Habsburg realms the formality was real enough, as one might expect; but the councils were of two types: regional and departmental. There were regional councils for Castile, Aragon, the Indies, and so on, departmental councils for war, finance, and the Inquisition. Above them all was the Council of State, which was usually dominated by great aristocrats and in consequence became more of a political battleground than an administrative board. By contrast with the conciliar structures in France and in the Habsburg territories the Tudor Privy Council exercised a unitary control which gave government valuable cohesion, but at the cost of unrelenting effort by its members.

3. PARLIAMENT

Of all the decision-making bodies in Tudor England, Parliament—meaning King-in-Parliament—had the highest authority through its enactment of statutes. Its medieval history had been complicated and views on its nature had varied; but by the 1560s contemporary opinions on Parliament had become settled and the writings of Sir Thomas Smith clearly described the institution. 'The most high and absolute power of the realm of England', he said, 'is in the Parliament. . . . There is the force and power of England.' In it nobles, knights, esquires, gentlemen, and commoners, together with bishops and clergy, 'consult and shew what is good and necessary for the common wealth.' 'That', he went on, 'is the Prince's and whole realm's deed.' Parliament abrogated old laws, made new ones, established forms of religion, defined doubtful rights, and set taxes. It 'representeth and hath the power of the whole realm both the head and the body. For every Englishman is intended to be there present, either in person or by procuration and attornies . . . from the Prince (be he King or Queen) to the lowest person of England.'[11] This doctrine that Parliament represented all and that the monarch was a part of it was relatively new in the sixteenth century; but by the accession of Edward VI it was clearly established. King and Parliament

---

[11] Sir Thomas Smith, *De republica Anglorum*, ed. Mary Dewar (Cambridge, 1982), 78–9.

were not separate entities, but a single body, of which the monarch was the senior partner and the Lords and the Commons the lesser, but still essential, members.[12]

The monarch alone could summon, prorogue, or dissolve Parliament; and no statute could become law without royal consent. Under Henry VIII, although immense changes were brought about through Parliament in both Church and state, statutes were still cast in the form of declaratory statements, definitions of the law as it was thought to stand. This was a polite and fairly obvious fiction, which was dropped in Edward's reign, when the Reformation statutes, such as the two Acts of Uniformity, explicitly enacted new laws: since there was no possible precedent for what they were doing, the change was unavoidable, and was in any case a change in form rather than in content. The Reformation Acts of Henry VIII and his son effectively removed any limitation upon the authority and scope of statute. Some judges might occasionally question the wording of a statute, and later in the century Richard Hooker revived the doctrine that natural law could override an unjust Act of Parliament. But in effect there was no area of national life on which Parliament could not make laws and no other form of law which could be pleaded against statute.

We have become accustomed to considering the Commons as the most important of the two Houses in the modern era. Yet in the sixteenth century the Lords certainly saw themselves as the superior House and had some reason for so doing. They met in the palace of Westminster itself, from which the Commons were excluded until the reign of Edward VI; their members were politically more powerful and had far greater social prestige. Their numbers in 1547 were smaller than they had been before 1536 when the abbots of the larger monasteries had sat there: in 1547 the temporal peerage numbered fifty-four and the bishops twenty-six. In practice some of the peers and bishops were prevented from attending—Norfolk for example was in prison under Edward VI—and the actual number of members under Edward VI and Mary fluctuated between sixty-five and eighty, of whom only about half attended at any given time. Preponderant among the active members were royal officials and the bishops. To the full members were added certain 'assistants': some of the judges, the Attorney-General, and the Solicitor-General, who were able to provide expert legal advice. Well staffed though the Lords were with royal servants, the House was not always subservient to the wishes of the monarch: divisions in Council in the spring Parliament of 1554 frustrated some of the legislation put forward by Mary and Gardiner, while in 1563 and 1566 the Council

[12] For comments on specific Parliaments see references in Index.

itself used the Lords—and the Commons—in an attempt to persuade Elizabeth to marry.

The Commons numbered 343 in 1547 and 462 in 1601. From 1549/50 they acquired a permanent home in St Stephen's Chapel in Westminster Palace, which not only brought them closer to the centre of affairs, but also allowed voting by division to take place, since the chapel had a vestibule to which one group of members could retire to be counted. Of the members, ninety represented county seats: two each for the English shires and one each for the Welsh. They were elected on a wide franchise which gave the vote to all males owning freehold land worth 40s. a year or more; but in practice the shire constituencies were a good deal less democratic than the voting system suggests, for elections were usually decided in advance by the major landowners, and contested elections were rare. The borough members were returned by a bewildering variety of franchises, some very broad, as at Shrewsbury, where all resident burgesses might vote, others confined to the owners of a few specific properties. Perhaps the most common electorate was the corporation—the mayor, aldermen, and common council of the borough, who generally, like the county landowners, avoided the uncertainty and inconvenience of contested elections.

The increase in the number of borough seats during the sixteenth century probably resulted from the desire of the Crown to find places for useful men in Parliament—councillors, other royal officials, and lawyers—not in order to pack the House with supporters, but to help in the complicated matter of managing the business of the Commons. Significantly, most of those who sat for newly created borough seats were servants of the Crown; equally significantly, the Crown seems after the middle of Elizabeth's reign to have become cautious about enfranchising further boroughs, perhaps because it had by then acquired enough managers and did not want to create new boroughs out of small or decayed towns. By the middle of the century the proportion of landowners in the House was high and rising. In theory the boroughs were supposed to be represented by men resident within the constituency; but theory had long ago ceased to bear much relation to practice. By 1601 about three-quarters of the borough seats—as well as all the shire seats—were occupied by gentlemen landowners, most of whom lived outside the towns.

The main business of Parliament was the making of statutes, or Acts. These were divided into two categories, public and private, which seems simple and straightforward. Unfortunately for historians trying to unravel parliamentary business this was far from being the case. To begin with, private Acts often involved matters of public concern: for instance, the statute of 1559 legitimizing Elizabeth. Then we find that public bills might end up as private Acts and vice versa. The only certain rules are that public Acts were those printed in the sessional statute of Parliament, while private Acts were left in manuscript record, and that fees were payable to the clerical officers of Parliament on private bills but not on public. However, while the intricacies of the subject are great, we can simplify the matter by saying that usually private Acts involved either individuals—conferring naturalization, for example—or specific localities such as towns, and were generally promoted by persons or groups with a vested interest. Public Acts were normally of general application, and were often, but certainly not always, initiated by the Crown or by leading statesmen acting on its behalf. It seems usually to be true that until the last two decades of the century legislation was initiated from outside Parliament and not generated from within.

By 1547 the procedures by which a bill was transformed into an Act were on the way to being established, although there was still some flexibility. Bills could be introduced into either House and usually—almost invariably from the middle of Elizabeth's reign—had three readings: at the first, the House was literally informed of the contents by a public reading of the text; at the second, debate took place upon the broad issue; there might then follow, and increasingly often did, a committee stage at which the details of the bill were examined and perhaps amended; any amendments were reported to the House and if carried were incorporated into the bill which was then 'engrossed' or written onto parchment; the engrossed bill was presented at a third reading and if successful was sent to the other House, where the same procedure was repeated. The final stage came at the end of each session, when the monarch gave or withheld assent to each bill. The veto was imposed thirty-four times by Elizabeth in the first seven sessions of her reign.

While rather more bills began life in the Commons, a fair number started in the Lords, and a rather higher proportion of the latter were ultimately successful. Partly because their numbers were smaller, partly because they were less encumbered with bills, the Lords generally dispatched business faster than did the Commons. The procedure of Parliament sounds cumbersome, but was effective in telling members the contents of a bill, allowing discussion on its general principles, and providing for examination of the detail. The frequency with which bills were amended, in both Houses, shows that they were given a thorough scrutiny before they passed into law. The procedure did not, however, prevent legislative log-jams; they were frequent and the main task of the Crown's parliamentary managers was to prevent them from holding up government business. This was not always successful.

Parliament had secured certain privileges and liberties to which it clung tenaciously. Of these the two most important were the privilege of freedom from arrest and liberty of speech. Freedom from arrest was a clearly defined legal right; but it was a good deal narrower than is often supposed. Its object was only to protect members against arrest in civil suits, principally those for debt, although the Commons claimed that it should also protect them from being arrested for words spoken in Parliament itself. After the sequestration of Strickland from the Commons in 1571, which aroused angry protests in the House, the Crown used its powers of arrest only for offences committed outside Parliament: Peter Wentworth was imprisoned in 1593 for writing tracts on the succession, not for speaking in Parliament. Otherwise the privilege gave no protection to members of either House against the Crown and was not intended to do so. It was not difficult for the government to find an excuse for incarcerating a troublesome member without invoking his activities in Parliament itself.

Liberty of speech had been granted explicitly in 1523 and was confirmed in all subsequent Parliaments: it was a firmly and clearly accepted right. But what did it mean? As the Crown's spokesmen reiterated, there was a boundary between liberty and licence; but there was no agreement on where that boundary lay. Elizabeth claimed that Parliament could only discuss such matters of state as were introduced by the Crown or explicity permitted by it. In this insistence she was going further than the historical precedents allowed and her prohibition was vigorously challenged, most famously by Peter Wentworth in his speech of 1576, which opened with the words 'sweet indeed is the name of liberty and the thing itself a value beyond all inestimable treasure'. Two things hindered liberty, he claimed: one was the rumour which sometimes ran round the House, 'take heed what you do, the Queen's Majesty liketh not of such a matter'; the other was the bringing in of messages 'either of commanding or inhibiting, very injurious unto freedom of speech and consultation'. 'I would to God, Mr Speaker', he urged, 'that these two were buried in Hell, I mean rumours and messages, for wicked they undoubtedly are: the reason is, the Devil was the first author of them, from whom proceedeth nothing but wickedness.'[13] Although some members shared his concern and frustration, such stuff was too strong for the Commons as a whole, which itself ordered Wentworth to the Tower. Elizabeth held to her views on the restraints that should be placed upon debates, but she was usually careful to allow some flexibility; the powers of inhibition and sequestration from the House were generally held in reserve.

[13] Hartley, *Proceedings*, i. 426–7.

Parliament was used by the Crown much more intensively under Edward and Mary than under Elizabeth. There were seven sessions in the six and a half years of Edward's reign, six in the five and a half years of Mary's. By contrast, in forty-four years, Elizabeth called Parliament to only thirteen sessions. Between 1547 and 1559 statutes transformed the religious complexion and life of the country; and under both Edward and Mary there was ambitious social and economic legislation. Once Elizabeth had secured the ecclesiastical settlement of 1559 she and her Council sought little legislative intervention. Their main concern with Parliament was to secure grants of money, and subsidy bills were carried, with little or no contention, in every one of the thirteen sessions, except that of 1572. While Elizabethan Parliaments carried a substantial body of legislation, apart from the Acts of Supremacy and Uniformity, only the Treason Acts, the Statute of Artificers of 1563, the Poor Laws of 1572, 1576, 1597, and 1601 could be regarded as both innovatory and important. Several Acts extended the scope of the law on treason and sedition to contain the Catholic threat, while the Council's initiative lay behind some, but not all, of the legislation on apprenticeship, vagrancy, poor relief, depopulation, maintenance of tillage, and the regulation of trade and manufacture. On the other hand, the debates that have been recorded in members' diaries reveal a House intensely concerned with the secular and religious issues of the day. There was no such thing as a 'Puritan opposition', as was once believed, but the debates reflect strongly held and often conflicting views about many issues. Yet, since members were concerned above all with the specific problems of their own constituencies, a great deal of legislative business involved local rather than national matters.

During the first two decades of Elizabeth's reign, the initiative in introducing bills lay generally with the Council. But in the 1580s and 1590s a change can be observed. In the mid-1580s Presbyterian members brought forward the Bill and the Book, which, if carried, would have radically changed both liturgy and Church government. In 1597 proposals for restricting enclosures, promoting tillage, and preventing depopulation were introduced by private members and Commons committees. The 1597 Poor Law and its successor of 1601 seem also to have been the work of private members rather than of the Council. Most important of all in revealing the independence of Parliament were the monopoly debates of the last two Elizabethan Parliaments: strongly felt grievances were voiced and this had some small effect upon the attitude of the Crown.

Obviously Parliament under the later Tudors had, on its own, a limited effectiveness. Most of the major statutes from 1547 onwards were the consequence of government initiative, and the two Houses had only slight political leverage unless they could count on the help of powerful councillors. Nevertheless, Tudor Parliaments were far from being rubber stamps. To get its way the Crown had to manage them, using privy councillors and individual members on whom it could rely. Usually this worked well, unless the Crown wished to introduce thoroughly unpopular legislation—such as the proposal for the coronation of Philip—or the Council itself was divided, as it was in the first Parliament of 1554. By comparison with the Parliaments of Henry IV, for instance, Tudor Parliaments were remarkably compliant, but the government could never rely upon that compliance: it had to be worked for, and the process of working for it varied from one Parliament to another.

4. THE EXECUTIVE MACHINE

By the beginning of the fifteenth century a complex system for issuing commands from king and Council had been established. Decisions were processed by three writing offices, each of which produced formal documents authorized by the application of a seal. The most recently established was the Signet Office, used by the king for his personal commands. Older and superior in the hierarchy was the Privy Seal Office, which received and transmitted orders from both king and Council. Finally there was the most ancient writing office, Chancery, which drew up the most formal documents, requiring full legal authorization by the Great Seal, which was in its custody. Usually Chancery only acted on receipt of a written and sealed command from one of the two lesser offices. Commands, land grants, warrants, and so on followed various paths according to their nature and purpose.

The Signet Office was headed by the Clerk of the Signet, whose office was taken over by the Secretary of State in the course of the sixteenth century. The Privy Seal Office was formally headed by the Lord Keeper of the Privy Seal, who had ceased by the end of the fifteenth century to be concerned with the actual running of the office and now occupied what was in effect a grandiose sinecure, possessed by one of the major statesmen of the time: Lord Paget, Lord Burghley, Francis Walsingham, and Robert Cecil all held it. Chancery was normally governed by the Lord Chancellor; if the monarch wished to reduce the prestige of the head of the office, he was entitled Lord Keeper of the Great Seal. Until the fall of Wolsey the post of Lord Chancellor had generally been occupied by an ecclesiastic, usually the dominant figure in the royal administration. Thereafter, with a brief intermission under Mary, when the post was held by Bishops Gardiner and Heath, it usually belonged to lawyers. The Chancellor had nothing to do with the routine side of Chancery business and became entirely associated with its judicial role, being in effect the senior member of the judiciary. Although the posts of Lord Chancellor and Lord Keeper preserved great standing, their holders no longer exercised the influence in government which had once been wielded by men like Morton and Wolsey.

While this complicated and formal structure of writing offices and seals remained in being after 1547, and indeed long after that, there was growing up beside it the far more flexible and adaptable system operated by the Privy Council in conjunction with the Secretary of State. As has already become apparent, the Council was not only the major policy-making body in the realm, but it also issued a constant barrage of letters, commands, enquiries, and warrants. Attached to it was a small staff, headed by the Clerks of the Council, usually four in number, two serving at any given time; but the key figure in guiding and indeed controlling the Privy Council was the Secretary of State. Originally very much the personal secretary of the monarch and still, at the end of the century, formally a member of the royal household, the Secretary had come, during Thomas Cromwell's tenure of the office, to be the servant—sometimes perhaps the master—of the Council and the monarch. None of Cromwell's immediate successors, except possibly Paget, wielded his power, and to some extent the importance of the office continued until the seventeenth century to depend much upon its holder. However, under Elizabeth the great succession of William Cecil, Francis Walsingham, and Robert Cecil gave the post of Secretary of State its central, permanent, and critical significance in government. The duties of the Secretary were so many, so various, so indiscriminate in their sequence that they are impossible to describe in full; but valuable insight can be gained from contemporary treatises on the office, particularly from one compiled in 1592 by Robert Beale, Clerk of the Council, for Sir Edward Wotton, then an aspirant for the post.[14] Beale begins with advice on the business of the Privy Council, to which the Secretary acted as chief-of-staff. As such he prepared the Council's agenda and presented to it matters for deliberation. 'Of such things as the Secretary is to proffer to the Council', advised Beale, 'let him first have in a several [i.e. separate] paper a memorial or docket of those which he mindeth to propound and have despatched at every sitting.'[15] At meetings of the Council he must 'have a care that the time be not spent in matters of small moment'—still good advice, seldom enough followed, for any chairman or committee secretary.[16] Besides managing the Council, the Secretary acted as the main liaison officer between it

---

[14] Beale's memorandum is printed in Read, *Walsingham*, i. 422–43.
[15] Ibid. 424.   [16] Ibid.

and the monarch, a task which demanded a good deal of circumspection: 'when there shalbe any unpleasant matter to be imparted to her Majesty from the Council or other matters to be done of great importance, let not the burden be laid on you alone but let the rest join with you', wrote Beale.[17] Again, this was good advice, but not always easily followed, as poor William Davison discovered over the execution of Mary Stewart. The Secretary was the monarch's servant as well as the Council's and had to prepare royal business as well: 'have in a little paper a note of such things as you are to propound to her Majesty, and divide it into the titles of public and private suits.' Tact was essential in dealing with Elizabeth and Beale advised the Secretary to 'learn before your access her Majesty's disposition by some in the Privy Chamber . . . for that will stand you in much stead'.[18] Of all the royal officers the Secretary had to be the best informed. He must have a special cabinet for his signets, cyphers, and 'secret intelligences'. He must have regular reports from officers of the Crown in the counties and from ambassadors and merchants abroad. These, according to Beale, must be 'digested' into ten or twelve books, on religion, the regional Councils, coastal fortresses, ordnance and armour, ships, musters, and so on. This counsel was probably never followed, but, even so, the various series of State Papers in the Public Record Office witness the staggering volume of information that came to the Secretary; and information, then as now, was power. Whatever else may be disputed about sixteenth-century government there is no doubt that it had far more information at its disposal than any of its predecessors. Not only did the Secretary receive this mass of incoming reports, but he was also the principal draughtsman of memoranda and instructions from both the Council and the monarch. However, a wise Secretary would, wrote Beale, avoid signing orders himself: he would read the draft first and then get the Council or the monarch to sign. The records of Elizabeth's great Secretaries suggest that this was their practice: they prepared agenda, provided information, drew up memoranda on the Council's deliberations, and drafted instructions. That gave them the greater share of power without exposing themselves to risk by signing documents as well.

This does not exhaust the business of the Secretary. He had a crucial role in the distribution of patronage; he had the power of making arrests; he controlled the business of the Signet Office; and he was the principal spokesman for the Crown in the Commons. All this had to be done with a very small permanent staff. The under-clerks of the Signet dealt with the affairs of that office, but these were largely formal. For the great bulk of his

[17] Ibid. 425. [18] Ibid. 437.

work the Secretary brought with him on appointment his own personal servants, who left the office when he did.

While most of the executive work of government went through the hands of Council and Secretary two specialized offices were established under Henry VIII to supply the needs of war. The Navy Board, under the Lord Admiral, supervised the building and equipping of royal ships; and Sir John Hawkins, as clerk of ships under Elizabeth, performed an important role in improving ship design and developing armaments. There was no corresponding body for land forces, since there was no standing army; but the Ordnance Office, also the creation of Henry VIII's reign, stored and maintained weapons, ammunition, and equipment, although it did little to develop them. Abroad, the second half of the sixteenth century saw the emergence of permanent embassies. There was as yet no foreign office—diplomatic work like everything else landed upon the desk of the Secretary of State—and there was no career diplomatic service. Nevertheless something of an ambassadorial network had been established by the end of the century, with professional and amateur agents to provide ambassadors and the home government with intelligence.

In response to the pressures of religious dissension, economic and social stress, and foreign rivalries, sixteenth-century governments, in other countries as in England, developed a style of administration which differed from that of the past without breaking from it. Many of the new procedures were established in England under Henry VIII; but they needed the continuity of Elizabeth's reign and the skill of her councillors and Secretaries for their full development. Two things in particular are characteristic of post-Reformation government in England: it operated with a flexibility that was impossible under the old system of Signet, Privy Seal, and Chancery; and it was much better informed.

5. FINANCIAL INSTITUTIONS

The medieval monarchy had developed a sophisticated machine, the two-tiered Exchequer, for dealing with the business of collecting, spending, and accounting for money. The Upper Exchequer was an accounting office which conducted audits in the style of a lawcourt. Anyone who received money on behalf of the king had to acquit himself before its officers, the Barons of the Exchequer, by proving what he had done with it and producing authorization for any expenditure. The Lower Exchequer, also called the Exchequer of Receipt, was the royal treasury: it took in revenue from royal officers and handed them receipts in the form of wooden notched sticks called tallies, which they then took to the Upper Exchequer; it also paid money out to the government's creditors. To this central treasury had been added, on the accession of Henry of Lancaster to the throne in 1399, the Court of the Duchy of Lancaster, whose lands, although part of the king's estate, were administered separately from the rest.

While the Exchequer effectively protected the king from fraud and embezzlement, by the second half of the fifteenth century it was failing to provide him with the stock of ready money that he needed for government. To meet this need the Yorkist kings and Henry VII used the institutions of the royal Court, in particular the Treasurer of the Chamber and the Keeper of the Jewel House, as their main 'banking facility', with a new audit board, the Office of General Surveyors, to check their accounts. To increase revenue from 'feudal dues'—the right of wardship over heirs in particular—Henry VII established an Office of Wards, later promoted to the status of the Court of Wards in 1540. In the 1530s immense new wealth accrued to the Crown from the Church and two new agencies were created by Thomas Cromwell for handling it: the Court of First Fruits and Tenths collected the levy on clerical incomes which had previously been paid to the pope and now went to the king; the Court of Augmentations was responsible for the revenues derived from the dissolved monastic houses. The role of the Treasurer of the Chamber as a national finance officer declined during this decade, but the *Privy* Chamber came to play as important a part in the handling of money as it did in politics. From 1540 there were two Privy Chamber accounts: the Privy Purse, which dealt with the king's personal expenses, and the Privy Coffers, which was responsible for 'secret affairs', in particular for the financing of war. Finally, from 1542 until 1551 the royal Mint was used to generate much-needed revenue by the process of debasing the coinage.

This recapitulation of developments before 1547 has been necessary in order to show how it had come about that on the accession of Edward VI there were as many as ten independent offices handling the king's revenue and expenditure: the Exchequer, the Court of the Duchy of Lancaster, the Chamber and the Jewel House in combination, the Court (originally the Office) of General Surveyors, the Court of Wards, the Court of First Fruits, the Court of Augmentations, the Privy Purse, the Privy Coffers, and the Mint. They had different tasks and each handled its own in a specific and fairly formalized manner. Some overlap in the personnel of the various offices enabled them to work harmoniously together, and there seems to have been little rivalry or competition between departments, although there was sometimes in-fighting within them. Even so, it was a diverse 'system', which had grown up piecemeal in response to particular needs over the previous seventy-five years or so. Between 1547 and 1558 a series of changes took place to simplify the arrangements. In January 1547, shortly before the death of Henry, the Courts of General Surveyors and of Augmentations were merged by royal letters patent, confirmed by statute under Edward, into a single new Court of Augmentations; and early in Mary's reign, following a commission of inquiry under her brother, Augmentations and First Fruits were absorbed into the Exchequer. By this time the Treasurer of the Chamber had ceased to exercise any financial role outside the Court, the Mint no longer generated revenue after debasement was brought to an end in 1551, and the operations of the Privy Coffers in national finance appear—though we cannot yet be certain of this—to have been brought to an end under Mary or Elizabeth. The various offices of the Court were thereafter spending agencies only. The business of collecting and accounting for revenue was confined after 1558 to the Court of Wards, the Court of the Duchy of Lancaster, and, above all, to the Exchequer, which had dealt with no more than one-third of revenue in 1547 but was handling three-quarters at least, probably more, under Elizabeth. Although these changes certainly produced a simplified, apparently more 'rational' system, they were not the result of any coherent long-term planning; they arose, like the changes of the 1530s, as pragmatic responses to immediate needs, in particular to the financial crisis produced by the imprudent rule of the Duke of Somerset.

The newly organized Exchequer of 1554 incorporated some new procedures taken over from the offices with which it merged—for instance, the use of arabic rather than roman numerals—but was not fundamentally changed from its earlier self. However, the financial machinery of the second half of the century was nevertheless different from that of the first. To begin with, financial matters were now handled by specifically financial departments, not by officers of the royal Court who had other functions. This was a change not merely from the procedures of the Yorkists and the first three Tudors, but also from those of the fourteenth and fifteenth centuries, when the king's Chamber and Wardrobe had been used for national, not merely for Court finances. Secondly, the Privy Council rather than the monarch exercised general supervision over finance, especially over the control of expenditure through the issue of warrants. Thirdly, the Lord Treasurer, for long a great noble proudly detached from any duties in the Exchequer, became, after Winchester's appointment in 1550, the active departmental head, assisted by the Chancellor of the Exchequer. Fourthly, the Exchequer was not the immutable and immobile animal of legend, but was constantly subjected to changes, if not always reforms, in its procedure: Burghley as Lord Treasurer and Mildmay as Chancellor tried hard to mend its ways.

Unfortunately these efforts were not very successful. Moves for change came sometimes from a genuine desire for reform, but at least as often from the ambitions of departmental officers determined to improve their status and income. The Exchequer became more deeply riven by internal rivalries and disputes than any other department of government—perhaps because more was financially at stake there. A major scandal erupted during the early years of Elizabeth, when five tellers in the Lower Exchequer defaulted at a total cost to the Crown of £44,000. The reforms introduced by Burghley and Mildmay were designed to prevent a recurrence of such disasters; but they did not last. There were constant debates within the Exchequer over its procedure: mostly they were the product of attempts by the officers to extend or defend their own administrative territory; and they were conducted, not in terms of the efficiency or effectiveness of the department, but almost entirely by the deployment and counter-deployment of historical precedents. By comparison with conciliar control over general administration, the working of the financial system appears less flexible and less responsive to the needs of government. The accounting system was not designed to produce any sort of budget and financial planning was virtually impossible. The local branches of the revenue machine, the customs and the estates officers, were subject to little control. The administration of the customs services oscillated between direct administration and farming out—an early version of what is now called 'privatization': neither was satisfactory and no effective reform in the service was introduced. The management of Crown lands seems to have lacked the dynamism and systematization which was becoming common on private estates from about 1570. The collection of revenue was particularly defective. Farming out the customs enabled the Crown to forecast what income it could expect, but at the cost of passing the profits of the operation to entrepreneurs and of allowing corruption to flourish. Parliamentary subsidies were assessed and levied by local gentlemen acting as commissioners, and they treated themselves and their fellow property-owners leniently.

The deficiencies of the system are apparent in the revenues of the Crown. Its total ordinary revenue amounted in 1547 to approximately £170,000; by 1603 this had risen to about £300,000, not enough to keep pace with inflation. Customs revenues, which had fallen to about £26,000 in 1547, were sharply increased by Mary's government and Elizabeth reaped the benefit with a return of £89,000 in 1558–9. But forty years later, when prices had risen considerably, the customs were only providing £91,000. The landed estates of the Crown could do no better. Partly as a result of land sales, partly as a consequence of cautious administration, rents rose slowly, from £86,000 in 1558–9 to only £111,000 in 1601–2, over a period when private landowners were reaping large gains in rental. Some compensation for these failures was provided by Parliament: direct taxation, in the form of parliamentary subsidies, yielded an average of £20,000 a year in times of peace, about £140,000 in the later years of war. However, the tax base of the subsidy was continuously eroded. Under Henry VIII the average assessment of a sample of landed estates for the subsidy was 68 per cent of the value of the same estates made by the feodary, an official of the Court of Wards; by the reign of Elizabeth the ratio had fallen to 38 per cent. More disturbingly still, the poorest taxpayers were more rigorously assessed than the richest. The tax assessments of men with goods valued at less than £10 on their deaths averaged 59 per cent of the probate valuations; those of men with goods rated at more than £100 averaged a diminutive 10 per cent of probate valuations.[19]

Some of the failure to expand revenue to match inflation resulted from political considerations, especially from the concern shared by the Queen and Burghley to avoid social disruption. Yet, deficient though the fiscal system was, it enabled the Crown to build up an accumulated surplus of nearly £300,000 by 1584; and the government made no great effort to increase its income in peacetime because it could manage without the extra money. The test came in wartime, when the limitations of the revenue system became uncomfortably apparent; but even then the Crown waged war for eighteen years without incurring an unmanageable debt. Provided that expenditure was stringently supervised and that military and naval ambitions were prudently limited, royal revenues were adequate. But they left little room for manœuvre in a crisis or for meeting new calls upon government.

6. THE LAWCOURTS

In early modern England government meant above all the execution of the law. The monarch was charged with many duties, but the most important of them was administering justice; and for most people their most likely contact with the processes of government was as litigants or as jurymen. The main administrative and financial departments already discussed were mostly described and organized as courts; and Sir Thomas Smith, surveying 'the manner of government or policy of the realm of England' in his *De republica Anglorum*, after talking of different types of rule and analysing

[19] The figures are drawn from Roger Schofield, 'Taxation and the political limits of the Tudor state', in Claire Cross et al. (eds.), *Law and Government under the Tudors* (Cambridge, 1988), 227–55, esp. p. 255.

social distinctions, devoted almost the whole of his discussion of institutions to the law and the lawcourts.[20]

The oldest common-law courts, sitting in Westminster Hall, were Common Pleas and King's Bench (properly called Queen's Bench when the
monarch was a woman, but referred to here as King's Bench throughout for
convenience). Common Pleas heard civil suits, especially over land and
debt. King's Bench originally dealt with criminal cases and possessed a
jurisdiction in error over other courts; by the end of the Middle Ages it had
come to exercise a civil jurisdiction as well. The third, and least important,
of the common-law courts was the Exchequer of Pleas, which heard matters
concerning the revenues and lands of the monarch. Alongside these courts
there had developed, mainly in the fifteenth and early sixteenth centuries, a
range of others, chiefly intended to provide simpler forms of justice. Of
these the most significant was the Court of Chancery. Chancery had originally been, and still was, the writing-office of the king; but it also developed
a jurisdiction designed to provide a more equitable procedure than that of
the common-law courts. Its documents were written in English and its
procedures less bound by formulas; it issued judgements based upon equity
rather than rigid rules, or, as a seventeenth-century Chancellor put it,
judgements designed 'to correct men's consciences'.[21] Such a court might
have led to conflicts with the older institutions, and under Wolsey it did.
But after his fall, except briefly under Mary, all Chancellors were trained in
the common law and disputes were short-lived and occasional. Another
court of equity developed in the Exchequer Chamber, whose jurisdiction
largely duplicated that of Chancery. (Confusingly, there was a second court
known as Exchequer Chamber, established by statute in 1585, which consisted of the judges of the common-law courts, giving judgements in disputed cases.)

Other courts developed out of the King's Council under the Yorkists and
early Tudors. The best-known and most important of these was Star
Chamber, which by 1547 had come to consist of the privy councillors,
assisted by judges, sitting as a formal court, separate from the Privy Council
itself. Originally Star Chamber was intended to hear cases of minor violence: riots, unlawful assembly, assault, and so on. By the middle of the
sixteenth century and increasingly thereafter it came to entertain suits of an
essentially civil kind, brought to it by litigants under the claim that some
form of violence had been committed. The later reputation of Star
Chamber as an instrument of despotism is not borne out by its activities in

[20] Smith, *De republica*, title-page.
[21] J. H. Baker, *An Introduction to English Legal History* (London, 1971; 2nd edn., 1979),
90.

this period, when it was largely used by private litigants, for whom it was a popular court. Its advantages for them were that its procedure, like that of Chancery, was simple: suits were brought by bills rather than technical writs, evidence was derived from interrogatories and answers, and the language used was English rather than Norman-French or Latin. Similar in its procedure and origins, as an offshoot of the Council, was the Court of Requests, which acted as a court for the poor. In the regions, two bodies, the Council in the North and the Council in the Marches of Wales, combined the functions of Chancery and Star Chamber. Apart from these there were some specialist courts in London, of which the most important were the Court of Admiralty, which dealt with cases arising on the high seas, and the Court of Wards, established to deal with issues arising out of 'feudal' tenures. Highest of all courts was Parliament; but in practice it did not act at all in a judicial capacity during this period.

These institutions formed the topmost layer of a great mass of courts in the counties, boroughs, and manors, which will be considered in the next section. Two points in particular need to be made about the working of the lawcourts of Tudor England. First, although procedure was designed to reach a legal judgement, there was always a strong preference in the Council and among judges for disputes to be settled by arbitration. Secondly, it is impossible to talk of a 'system' of lawcourts in this period. There was a complex network of interlocking and overlapping jurisdictions, but nothing resembling the more modern structure of lower courts with an appellate hierarchy above them. The Privy Council attempted to provide some degree of co-ordination by directing particular cases, but that was all.

Not only did the sixteenth century see the development of new courts, such as Star Chamber, but it also witnessed important changes in the law. The criminal law was given closer definition by statute and by judicial pronouncements. In civil cases, the use of procedure by 'actions on the case' gave a flexibility to the common-law courts which was impossible in their traditional system of actions by specific writs; and one particular form of such actions, *assumpsit*, was of great importance in the law of contract. King's Bench managed to extend its civil jurisdiction by the use of two fictitious devices known as the Bill of Middlesex and the writ of *latitat*. But these are technical matters and the main changes had been made in the earlier part of the sixteenth century, although they were not fully worked out until the seventeenth.

For the second half of the sixteenth century the most striking and significant development in litigation was its immensely increased volume. In 1490, 500 cases had reached an advanced stage of proceedings in King's

Bench, 1,600 in Common Pleas: a total of 2,100. By 1560–3, there were
annual averages of 781 in King's Bench and 4,497 in Common Pleas,
totalling 5,278; and by 1606, these figures had risen to 6,639, 16,508, and
23,147 respectively. Over the course of Elizabeth's reign litigation in King's
Bench had thus increased 8.5 times, in Common Pleas 3.6 times, and the
two together 4.4 times. The volume of business in other courts had also
increased: in Chancery it rose from about 1,000 cases a year at the end of
Mary's reign to 1,600 at the end of Elizabeth's. But the two common-law
courts were between them hearing nearly four times as many cases as all the
other courts combined. Some idea of the intensity of litigation in this period
can be gained by comparing the number of cases begun in all central courts
in 1606 with those for later times. In 1606, 1,351 cases were begun for every
100,000 head of population: the comparable figure for 1823–7 was an
average of 653 a year, and for 1975 it was 560. The reasons behind this
astonishing growth of litigation are complex. It does not seem to have arisen
either from the development of new courts, since the major part of the
growth came in the old ones, or from the use of such new procedures as
actions on the case, since the bulk of suits were for debt. Judging from the
huge number of these suits—16,260 in 1606—the main cause of growth
would seem to have lain in the increased commercial activity in most levels
of society above the wage-earning class. Important as the changes in the
legal forms and procedures were for the later history of English law, they do
not seem to have greatly influenced the effect of the law upon society in the
sixteenth century. However, it is worth noting that the conservatism of
lawyers in the common-law courts was reinforced by the lucrative flow of
business: they had no need to adopt the new methods of Chancery since
they made a comfortable living with the old.[22]

The increased business of the courts was, not surprisingly, reflected in
the growing number of barristers and lesser lawyers, mostly known as
attorneys. To take first the upper branch of the profession, the barristers: in
the decade 1510–19 only ten men were called to the bar; in 1560–9 this had
risen to eighty-five, in 1580–9 to 383, and in 1590–9 to 411. The expansion
of the lower branch was even more dramatic. In 1560 there were 200
attorneys practising in the two common-law courts; this had risen to 1,050
by 1606, when there was one attorney for every 4,000 people. Over the
second half of the sixteenth century a major new profession had come into
being, second only to the clergy in size and importance.[23]

[22] The figures in this paragraph are derived from C. W. Brooks, *Pettyfoggers and Vipers of
the Commonwealth: The 'Lower Branch' of the Legal Profession in Early Modern England*
(Cambridge, 1986), chs. 4, 5.
[23] Ibid., ch. 6. Cf. W. R. Prest, *The Rise of the Barristers* (Oxford, 1986), ch. 1.

The growth in litigation and in the number of lawyers was not matched by the number of judges or court officials. Throughout the later Tudor period Common Pleas and King's Bench were each headed by a Chief Justice and three puisne—or lesser—justices; the Exchequer was headed by the Chief Baron and three puisnes. So there were twelve judges in all to hear the mass of cases in the central courts and to travel on assize circuits twice a year. The number of court officers seems also to have remained static and low: there were only about thirty permanent officials in Common Pleas. But it is in practice difficult to distinguish between the officials of the courts and the attorneys, since many of the former also acted as advisers to clients. However, it is very far from clear how the small permanent staffs of the central courts, especially of Common Pleas and King's Bench, were able to deal with the huge and increasing volume of business.

7. LOCAL GOVERNMENT

Linking the localities to the centre were six assize circuits, each travelled twice a year by two professional judges, who sat for up to a week at a time in the county towns and tried both criminal and civil cases in each shire. Through the assizes the central government maintained contact with the regions and the Westminster courts controlled the local administration of the law. Within the counties themselves the oldest royal office was that of sheriff. By the sixteenth century, although they still collected certain revenues, held county and hundred courts, assisted in the mustering of military levies, executed judicial writs, and acted as returning officers in parliamentary elections for the shires, sheriffs had lost their earlier preeminence. The most important officers of county administration were by then the Justices of the Peace, firmly established as judicial and administrative authorities. In the previous century they had exercised an extensive jurisdiction over major crimes, such as murder and felony, and over lesser offences—known as misdemeanours—such as riot, unlawful assembly, and forcible entry. In the course of the sixteenth century the assizes seem often, though not always, to have come to monopolize jurisdiction over felonies, leaving the JPs to deal mainly with misdemeanours, with offences against economic and social regulations, and with general administration. The major business of the JPs was conducted at Quarter Sessions, held four times a year, usually in the county town; but individual justices, acting alone or in pairs, could examine suspects, bind men over to good behaviour, arrest rioters, and send vagabonds to gaol. By the end of the century, as the pressure of business increased, informal meetings of JPs—later to develop into petty sessions—were being held in several counties. Other county officials were the coroners, escheators, and feodaries. The coroner, whose office had originated in the twelfth century, was responsible for investigating every violent and suspicious death by an inquest or 'view upon the body', and for reporting the result to assizes. The escheator had in earlier times collected wardship and other feudal dues; but as an unpaid official, annually appointed, he consistently failed to extract payments from his neighbours, and although the office continued, its work came to be performed by the professional local agent of the Court of Wards, the feodary.

Below Quarter and petty sessions were various secular and ecclesiastical courts. There were two forms of manorial court: courts baron for civil disputes and courts leet for minor assaults and affrays. Judgements in these courts were normally given collectively by the tenants of the manor, although the lord's steward usually presided. The ecclesiastical courts exercised much jurisdiction that would today be undertaken by the civil arm. The archdeacon's court was probably the most often used, although the bishop's, or consistory, court, which ranked above it, also played a part in county government. These bodies heard not only cases concerning religion and the conduct of the clergy, but also tithe disputes, matrimonial and testamentary suits, charges of sexual misconduct, and accusations of defamation. The last two areas of jurisdiction gave them an important role in the social control of local communities.

At parish level there was a real, though limited, degree of self-government. The lowest executive officers of the shire were the constables: high constables were appointed for each major division of the county—hundred, wapentake, or rape according to the region—and were responsible for making presentments of all offences to Quarter Sessions, executing writs and orders sent down by the sheriff and the justices, arresting suspects, and acting as links between the county administration and the parishes. At the very bottom of the hierarchy were the parish, or petty, constables, ridiculed by Shakespeare in the persons of Dogberry and Dull, and by countless historians since then. The office of parish constable had originated in the early Middle Ages in the tithing man, responsible as representative of the vill for the maintenance of order. By the thirteenth century tithing men had been saddled by the Crown with the role of mustering armed villagers and had thus acquired the military title of constables. Over the centuries new duties and obligations were heaped upon them by statute and proclamation until they became the final links in the long chain of general administration. They were responsible for arresting suspects and vagrants, supervising alehouses, organizing the hue and cry, repairing highways, maintaining the village stock of weapons and armour, mustering the militia, pressing men for military service abroad, and collecting taxes. Usually elected by the parish for a year, constables were at one and the same time agents of the Crown, servants of the higher county officials, and representatives of the village community.

The county officials below the rank of assize judge were, apart from the feodary, unpaid, and for the most part untrained. However, some of them had professional assistants: the sheriff used an under-sheriff and bailiffs to carry out routine tasks; the clerk of assizes and the clerk of the peace at Quarter Sessions kept the records of their respective courts, drafted indictments and other legal documents, and provided administrative continuity. Yet although there was a professional element in county government, the amateurs prevailed. Sheriffs, JPs, high constables, and parish constables were all members of their own communities as well as officers of the Crown. The grand juries, who presented offenders at assizes and Quarter Sessions, and the trial juries who decided their fates were also drawn from their own neighbourhoods. Such a system had a strength which centralized professional bureaucracies lacked, for when it worked as intended, the officials provided essential contact between the Crown and the localities. But there was a price to be paid. Officers, often uncomfortably pressed by the conflicting demands of the central government and the interests of their own neighbours, could find their executive role difficult to perform.

This structure of courts and officials served for routine administration and jurisdiction within the counties. In the early and mid-Tudor periods, when the Crown needed other tasks to be performed, it used specially appointed commissioners for each occasion. If troops had to be levied for the suppression of disorder or for war, commissions of array and of muster were issued to assist the sheriffs. Protector Somerset issued special enclosure commissions to inquire into the decay of tillage. The dissolution of the chantries in the reign of Edward VI was undertaken by small county commissions, made up generally of the bishop of the see, one or two professional administrators from the Court of Augmentations, and a clutch of local gentlemen. Parliamentary subsidies were assessed and levied by county commissioners specifically appointed by Parliament on the occasion of each grant. These *ad hoc* commissions, together with the permanent institutions of assizes and Quarter Sessions, and such officials as circuit judges, sheriffs, and JPs, worked adequately enough during the first half of the sixteenth century.

However, increasing pressures of rising population, food shortages, endemic poverty, religious dissension, and war forced the Crown to establish a firmer, more complex, and more permanent structure of county government. This process was essentially piecemeal, a series of responses to immediate and pressing needs. It began under Edward VI with the appointment by the Duke of Northumberland of Lords Lieutenant in every county, 'for the levying of men and to fight against the King's enemies'.[24] This move was probably as much part of Northumberland's construction of a personal power base in the localities as a remodelling of county administration; and after his fall lieutenants were for some time used only sporadically. Under Elizabeth, however, they gradually became a permanent feature of government; and from 1585 Lords Lieutenant were regularly appointed in every shire, with a command structure of deputy lieutenants, captains, and professional muster-masters to assist them. Although the main task of the lieutenancy system lay in training the militia and levying troops for foreign campaigns, the Lord Lieutenant acquired responsibility for raising money, exercising surveillance over recusants, and generally acting as the focal point for the supervision of county affairs. Other permanent bodies that developed under Elizabeth included commissions for the restraint of the grain trade, for piracy, for fen drainage, for charity, and for debtors. Ecclesiastical and recusancy commissions played a vital part in the enforcement of the religious settlement. New paid officials appeared: provost-marshals for executing martial law upon rogues and vagabonds; overseers of the poor for providing relief to the destitute and for putting the unemployed to work.

Sixteenth-century towns were, in principle, self-governing. Their constitutions varied in detail and were often highly elaborate; but they usually conformed to the same basic structure. The highest authority was vested in two councils, a small council of aldermen and a larger of common-councillors. Between them these bodies regulated the affairs of the town through by-laws, administered corporate property, and carried out the commands of central government. Each body was self-perpetuating, nominating new members when a vacancy occurred. The principal executive officer was either the Mayor, or the Lord Mayor in large cities, or two bailiffs in the smaller boroughs. Either on their own or in conjunction with the aldermen, they acted as JPs and held Quarter Sessions. Below them was a host of lesser officials, from auditors to scavengers. All these officers were normally elected by the councils, occasionally by a rather wider constituency. Vestiges of representative systems survived in some boroughs, but for the most part they were dominated by the small and wealthy oligarchies of aldermen. In so far as the towns elected or appointed their own JPs and executive officers, they were more independent than were the counties, whose JPs were appointed by the Crown. However, in practice the contrast was probably not great. The Crown was limited in its choice of county JPs to

[24] Gladys Scott Thomson, *Lords Lieutenants in the Sixteenth Century* (London, 1923), 149–51.

members of the important landed families, while the towns, even London, showed little real independence of central government.[25]

8. THE ROYAL SERVANTS

What sort of men staffed these institutions of Court and government? On what tenure did they hold their posts? How were they rewarded? How were they appointed and how were they trained? How many were there? While no generalization will cover every case some broad conclusions may be stated. It is important to emphasize at the outset that we are dealing here with officers who were rewarded either by salary or by fee for the work that they did on behalf of the Crown. However, most of the government's business was performed by men who, officially at any rate, received no pecuniary reward: Justices of the Peace, sheriffs, constables, and the like.

Almost all the important posts in government were held by a grant of royal patent for life, though a few were formally hereditary. In several cases, and increasingly towards the end of the period, reversions were granted by the Crown: that is to say, a grant was made of the succession to an office after the death of the holder. By means of reversions many officers were able to convert life tenures into semi-hereditary ones. The security of tenure given to officers encouraged them to regard their posts as pieces of property as much as jobs to be done; and some of them delegated the work to deputies while enjoying a share of the rewards as a form of rent. One consequence of this was that the Crown had little control over its officials: the deputies were responsible to the office-holder, not to the Crown, and the office-holder could only with great difficulty and for exceptional reasons be removed. Nor was it easy for the Crown or a departmental head to carry out any reforms without meeting entrenched resistance from vested interests. Problems of this kind are not unknown in modern bureaucracies, but they were probably more firmly built into the Tudor system than into that of the twentieth century.

Salaries from the Crown were only a small part of the rewards of office. The greater part came in the form of fees paid by the Crown's subjects for each task performed on their behalf: for instance, a litigant would find himself paying officials of the lawcourt concerned for every stage of process. One effect of this system of reward by piece-rates was an endeavour by officials to extend their own 'empires', sometimes by encouraging an increase of business and sometimes by competition with colleagues. Rivalry between departments became a feature of Tudor bureaucracy and often

---

[25] Below, Ch. 6 ss. 2, 3, for more detailed discussion of urban government.

occupied more time than the performance of normal duties. A second effect was the introduction of gratuities. If individuals paid fees for work done, it was an easy step for extra amounts to be given to hasten the process; and since the government kept official fees largely static over a long period of inflation, taking gratuities was often the only way in which officials could maintain the real value of their incomes.

Most men gained their posts through patronage or family interest. There were no competitive examinations and, except for certain legal offices, no formal qualifications. In some instances the holder of an office would pass it to his heir by the use of a reversion; and by this method certain posts in Wards and Exchequer became family perquisites. More usually, it was necessary to secure the backing of someone with the ear of the monarch and make use of the system of Court patronage. In a few areas, notably in the middle ranks of Household offices, there was a rudimentary career ladder which enabled men to move from being Clerk of the Pastry to the Larder, the Scullery, the Woodyard, and so in sequence to the Kitchen; but such progression was rare. Officers of the lawcourts normally had a legal training. In financial departments, such as the Exchequer, the experts were usually trained in-house, often by family networks: whatever complaints there might be about the performance of Exchequer officials no one could accuse them of ignorance about the minute details of departmental procedure. Elsewhere, for instance in the upper reaches of the Chamber, connections were undoubtedly more necessary than qualifications. Overall, where specialized qualifications were needed, the officer concerned usually possessed them. Beyond that their quality is harder to assess. Debate has mostly been concerned, then and now, with the honesty of Tudor officials. The line between a legitimate gratuity and a bribe was difficult to draw and was probably often crossed. A recent study of early modern barristers has shown that they frequently acted as agents in the passing of gratuities or bribes between litigants and judges. Their conduct was sometimes excused on the ground that litigants were responsible for offering the bribes in the first place; but the defence is not very convincing and the evidence bears out many contemporary complaints of corruption in the legal profession.

The size of the bureaucracy can only roughly be estimated, for many offices were too menial to be counted, and some were often held by the same man. However, restricting the count to salaried and fee'd offices of the Crown, it seems that they numbered between 2,000 and 2,500 in this period. Of these about half carried the status or rewards necessary to attract gentlemen. Some 1,200 posts were attached to the royal Court and another 600 were concerned with the management of Crown lands: thus over two-thirds of the offices dealt with the business of the monarch rather than the commonwealth—though that distinction would hardly have been made at the time. The largest single department outside the Court and the estate administration of the Crown was the Exchequer, where there were about ninety posts. Approximately 100 men worked as officers of the principal lawcourts, servicing the litigation brought by more than 1,000 attorneys and perhaps 200 barristers at the end of the period. Almost all the paid officers of the Crown worked in London, except for a small number of customs officials who operated in the outports. The balance of officialdom could hardly have been more different from that of a modern state, and the small size of the bureaucracy contrasted with contemporary France, where there was one official for every 400 inhabitants. The comparable ratio in England was 1:2,000 if one counts all offices, or 1:4,000 if one restricts the number to the higher levels.[26] The dependence of the English state upon the 'amateur' services of untrained lay administrators and judges, especially in the provinces, is abundantly clear.[27]

Compared with the reigns of her Tudor predecessors, Elizabeth's saw only limited protest against government officers or the burdens laid by the Crown upon its subjects. Under Henry VII, Henry VIII, and Edward VI, there had been open protest against fiscal demands, of which the most significant was the 'taxpayers' strike' against the Amicable Grant in 1525. Elizabeth and Burghley were careful to avoid the possible consequences of imposing heavy taxes; and, at some cost to the treasury, they succeeded.

Nevertheless, while there was general acquiescence in the taxes voted by Parliament, criticism was directed against some specific impositions and the men who levied them. Purveyors, who bought supplies at low prices for the royal household, were a constant source of grievance inside and outside Parliament. More objectionable still were monopolists and patentees, the target of strong attack in the Parliaments of 1597 and 1601. The needs of war led the Crown to exploit more vigorously than before these 'prerogative' sources of money. War created other grievances: against local taxes, such as coat-and-conduct money, and against the levy of troops. Raising troops for service overseas was a fruitful source of corruption, when the better-off could bribe their way out of service; and some muster-masters and deputy-lieutenants took advantage of their position.

The 'law's delays' were inevitably a cause of general complaint; but there was virtually no criticism of such courts as Star Chamber and Chancery,

[26] I have revised these figures somewhat from those given in Penry Williams, *The Tudor Regime* (Oxford, 1979), 107–8.

[27] I have discussed the topics dealt with in this chapter at greater length in *The Tudor Regime*, chs. 1–4.

which were to be the subject of strong attacks under the early Stuarts. Attorneys, the lower branch of the legal profession, were vilified as the cause of the great multiplication of lawsuits; and were memorably described by Lord Keeper Egerton as the 'pettyfoggers and vipers of the commonwealth'.[28] Equally detested were informers, who made a living from bringing actions against those who had infringed penal statutes. In the absence of a police or prosecuting service, informers were necessary for the enforcement of the law, but the prospect of men profiting from infringements was not attractive.

Satires and squibs were of course launched against the great men of state by their factional rivals. Yet, on the whole, the leading servants of the Crown do not seem to have been the subjects of general criticism under Elizabeth, as they were to be under the Stuarts. Grievances were directed in the main against men of middle or lower rank: purveyors, patentees, attorneys, and informers.

[28] Brooks, *Pettyfoggers and Vipers of the Commonwealth*, 139.

CHAPTER 6

English Society

I. PRICES

Two prolonged and connected processes determined much of English history during the sixteenth century: the growth in population, discussed earlier, and the unprecedented rise in prices.[1] Each had begun before 1547 and each was to continue, though less rapidly, after 1603. Consequently the span of this chapter will not be rigidly confined by those dates.

Paradoxically, while the population of sixteenth-century England was steadily increasing, prices were rising as well and the real wages of the greater part of the population falling. The century-long rise in prices was in part the result of the increase in population, which exerted a gentle upwards pressure, and was probably combined in the second half of the century with a favourable balance of trade, which drew in bullion. However, the most dramatic inflationary pressures followed from the debasement of the coinage in the middle years of the century and from bad harvests, which produced severe food shortages in the late 1540s, 1550s, and 1590s, poor roads and inadequate means of storage making the supply of grain dangerously vulnerable to the weather.

In the last five years of the century flour prices in London were almost four times those of the late fifteenth century; and the price of meat had risen more than fivefold. A price index of the consumption of an artisan family suggests that for them prices rose overall by about 240 per cent over the century. However, this overall increase conceals some major fluctuations. Until the 1540s the rise in prices had been relatively gradual: only 22 per cent. There followed two decades of rapid increase. The first, during the 1540s, was probably in the main the result of coinage debasement under Henry VIII and Edward VI, which left prices 77 per cent higher than before. In the second period, the latter half of the 1550s, poor harvests in 1555 and 1556 pushed prices to their highest point so far, although relief followed in the next two years of better crops. The decade ended with prices

[1] Above, Ch. 1 s. 1.

TABLE 1. *Composite price indices for London, 1490–1609 (1457–71 = 100)*

Decade	Mean	Increase (%)
1490–9	98	—
1500–9	101	3.1
1510–19	108	6.9
1520–9	115	6.5
1530–9	122	6.1
1540–9	145	18.9
1550–9	212	46.2
1560–9	224	5.7
1570–9	241	7.6
1580–9	257	6.6
1590–9	316	23.0
1600–9	332	5.1

Note: The index is based upon a composite unit of consumables: flour, meat, poultry, fish, dairy, drink, fuel, marrowbone, suet; it reflects retail rather than wholesale prices for processed foods (e.g. flour rather than grain) in London.

Source: Steve Rappaport, *Worlds within Worlds: Structures of Life within Sixteenth-Century London* (Cambridge, 1989), table 5.2, p. 131.

about double their level at the end of the previous century. Overall, prices then remained fairly level throughout the next three decades, although there were sharp rises in individual years of bad harvest, particularly in 1585–6. The situation changed for the worse in the last decade of the century, when four successive years of dearth—1594, 1595, 1596, and 1597—produced the worst living conditions of the century. However, whereas the inflationary decade of the 1540s had kept prices at a permanently higher level than before, the harvests of the 1590s had a less prolonged effect.[2]

The rate of inflation over the whole century was, by modern standards, not high: only about 1 per cent per annum. Its effect upon the population,

[2] Figures on prices are taken from Steve Rappaport, *Worlds within Worlds: Structures of Life in Sixteenth-Century London* (Cambridge, 1989), ch. 5. These figures are derived from London evidence and may not be fully representative of other towns and regions. They are, however, based upon retail rather than wholesale prices, and upon larger samples than other price series, e.g. those produced by E. H. Phelps-Brown and Sheila Hopkins in *A Perspective of Wages and Prices* (London, 1981). See also Peter Bowden, 'Agricultural Prices', a statistical appendix in Joan Thirsk (ed.), *The Agrarian History of England and Wales*, iv: *1500–1640* (Cambridge, 1967), 593–648, 814–70. See Statistical Tables 1–3.

TABLE 2. *Prices of selected items in London, 1490–1609 (1457–71 = 100)*

Decade	Flour	Meat	Poultry	Dairy	Fish	Drink
1490–9	106	97	100	101	95	90
1500–9	112	100	107	100	94	91
1510–19	128	109	120	101	97	89
1520–9	143	119	131	120	90	88
1530–9	143	135	140	144	86	89
1540–9	167	176	189	186	104	90
1550–9	254	247	320	323	112	101
1560–9	253	272	347	344	118	100
1570–9	301	324	359	323	115	94
1580–9	286	389	369	353	137	106
1590–9	373	507	476	364	164	157
1600–9	359	563	458	391	192	175

Note: 'Flour' includes flour made from all grains. 'Meat' consists of mutton and rabbit. 'Poultry' includes chicken, goose, and eggs.

Source: Rappaport, *Worlds within Worlds*, table 5.4, pp. 140–1.

especially the poor, was the result more of short-term fluctuations than of the long-term trend. For instance, the price of flour almost tripled in London between 1594 and 1597, causing acute problems to families on the margin of subsistence. Nor could the poor always manage by switching to cheaper foods, for the price of oats and rye sometimes rose more rapidly than that of wheat. Fortunately, the cost of dairy products, an important part of the diet of the poor, rose less rapidly in general than did grain prices, since bad weather usually had a more damaging effect upon grain harvests than it did upon livestock. It should not, however, be supposed that bad harvests had unpleasant consequences for everyone. Substantial farmers sowing a large acreage of arable could grow a surplus for sale at high prices in times of bad harvest and reap the profit accordingly, whereas the small-holder might have difficulty in finding seed-corn for the following year.[3]

2. LONDON

In its size, social composition, and demographic history Tudor London was unique among English communities; and there were few cities on the continent to match it. While estimates of London's population can only be approximate, it is reasonable to say that from about 55,000–70,000 inhabitants in 1550, it rose to 86,000–100,000 in 1570, and to 130,000–152,000 in

[3] See below, pp. 172, 197–8, for a discussion of the social and economic consequences of the price-rise.

TABLE 3. *Annual price series, London, selected decades*
(1457–71 = 100)

Year	Composite prices	Flour
1540	116	95
1541	124	109
1542	125	143
1543	134	136
1544	162	286
1545	160	252
1546	176	273
1547	142	109
1548	139	95
1549	174	170
1550	194	239
1551	229	320
1552	224	314
1553	196	211
1554	206	286
1555	226	314
1556	231	300
1557	214	211
1558	196	143
1559	207	198
1560	235	320
1590	295	327
1591	271	266
1592	239	218
1593	260	225
1594	312	416
1595	332	429
1596	375	539
1597	388	600
1598	365	464
1599	320	245
1600	334	348

Source: Rappaport, *Worlds within Worlds*, table A.3.1, pp. 403–7.

1600. The population of ancient Rome in the age of the high empire had reached one million or more; but, between the fall of the Roman Empire and the early years of the Reformation, European cities were small. The great agglomerations of Asia—Baghdad, Delhi, and Peking—dwarfed even the largest cities of medieval Europe. By 1500 Rome probably had no more than 60,000 inhabitants, while Naples and Paris, the two largest European cities—not counting Constantinople, which was scarcely European—held between 150,000 and 200,000 apiece. However, in the early sixteenth century the major European cities began to revive. Naples, Paris, Milan, and Venice were in the vanguard of the advance; London was then in the middle rank, but came to outstrip its competitors by the middle of the seventeenth century. In 1500 there were probably nine European cities larger than London and fifteen of approximately the same size; by 1600 it had overtaken every European city apart from Paris and Naples. Other English towns were dwarfed by London: second place was occupied by Norwich, which had perhaps 12,000 inhabitants in 1520 and 15,000 in 1600; while Bristol came third with 10,000 and 12,000 respectively. Thus not only was London a giant among English cities but it was growing at a far greater rate. Most cities and towns grew more slowly than the English population as a whole, London much faster, increasing by 185 per cent during the second half of the sixteenth century compared with 35 per cent for England generally.[4]

While the national population grew slowly in a 'low-pressure' system, with a small but significant lead of births over deaths, Londoners inhabited a 'high-pressure' system, with a low age of marriage for London-born women, high fertility, and an even higher mortality. Expectation of life at birth in London during the middle years of Elizabeth's reign was only 25–30 years, compared with 37 years nationally; the death rate was about 40 per 1,000 and the birth rate 35, compared with national figures of 25 and 33 respectively. London's growth was achieved entirely by a high rate of migration into the city, averaging some 6,000 people each year. These migrants not only cancelled the unfavourable balance between deaths and births, but created the surplus of new inhabitants necessary for growth. The constant influx of people into London took up about half the national surplus of births over deaths needed to keep the population stable. London therefore grew by tapping the natural growth of the rest of England, attracting people, most of them male, by higher wages and the prospect of social and economic advancement.[5]

London was made up of two separate cities: the City of London proper, that famous and congested square mile within the walls; and the City of Westminster, stretching from Temple Bar on the east to the old Palace of Westminster on the west. Across the Thames lay the borough of Southwark, which fell within the jurisdiction of the City of London; and by the time that John Stow published the first edition of his *Survey of London*

---

[4] On problems of estimating London's population, Vanessa Harding, 'The population of London, 1550–1700: A review of published work', *London Journal*, 15 (1990), 111–28.
[5] On the demography of London generally, Rappaport, *Worlds within Worlds*, ch. 3.

in 1598, several suburbs had been built beyond the walls to the east and the north, to accommodate the influx of newcomers.[6]

The City of London itself was a dense conglomeration of halls, shops, churches, and houses, thrown together in no apparent order or plan within the walls, which ran from the Tower on the east, past Aldgate, Bishopsgate, Moorgate, Cripplegate, Aldersgate, Newgate, and Ludgate to Blackfriars steps on the west, near the present site of Blackfriars Bridge. An eighth gate stood on London Bridge itself; and there were several minor steps allowing access from the river. The main gates were imposing entrances through the walls, open but guarded at night, capable of being closed against intruders, as Wyatt found to his cost in 1554. Of the twenty-six wards into which the City was divided, three—Portsoken, Faringdon Without, and Bridge Ward Without, which covered most of Southwark—lay outside the walls; three— Bishopsgate, Cripplegate, and Aldersgate—lay partly within and partly outside the walls; the remainder were wholly within. Most of the old City was destroyed by the great fire of 1666; but its plan and appearance can be reconstructed from Stow's *Survey*, from the drawings and engravings of Wyngaerde, Hollar, and others, and from a series of maps, starting in the middle of the sixteenth century. London had no imposing centre like St Mark's Square in Venice or the piazza of Siena. Its few great buildings were scattered, tucked in among the narrow streets, separated one from another. The Tower stood out as a major landmark on the east; but this was the stronghold of the Crown, not of the City. The principal civic buildings were the Guildhall in Cheapward, built early in the fifteenth century, and the Royal Exchange, erected by Sir Thomas Gresham in 1566 on Cornhill. There were ninety-seven parish churches within the City walls, fourteen in the liberties north of the Thames and three in Southwark, with another nine in the suburbs. The monasteries and friaries had gone, their sites quickly bought for secular buildings. By Ludgate stood Old St Paul's, with its pulpit cross in the churchyard from which many famous sermons were delivered. In 1561 it was struck by lightning and fire consumed the steeple and roof. The roof was repaired, but the steeple was never rebuilt, and the tower had a curiously truncated appearance until the entire building was destroyed by the great fire of 1666. Outside the walls was Moorfields, the site today of Liverpool Street Station. This was the great open space of the city, where the citizens came to lay out laundry, practise archery, and milk their cattle. Beyond lay the countryside: Finsbury Fields, Wood Green, Hampstead. To the north and east suburbs were beginning to spring up

---

[6] The second edition of Stow's work, that of 1603, is available in *A Survey of London by John Stow*, ed. C. L. Kingsford (2 vols., Oxford, 1908).

beyond the outer wards of the City. From St Katherine's Hospital, next to the Tower, eastwards to Wapping was 'a continual street, or filthy straight passage, with alleys of small tenements or cottages builded, inhabited by sailors' victuallers', put up in the forty years before Stow wrote. Hog Lane, which ran from Whitechapel to Spitalfields, 'within these forty years', wrote Stow, 'had on both sides fair hedgerows of elm trees, with bridges and easy stiles to pass over into the pleasant fields, very commodious for citizens therein to walk, shoot, and otherwise to recreate and refresh their dulled spirits in the sweet and wholesome air'. Now it was 'a continual building throughout, of garden houses and small cottages'.[7] By and large the wealthier citizens lived in the central parts of the City, the poor along the waterfront and in the wards outside the walls; but even in the central parishes there was a social mixture, rich merchants occupying houses on the street, the poor living in hovels tucked away at the back.

East of Temple Bar, by Chancery Lane, began the City of Westminster. The Inns of Court lay immediately to the east of the City liberties, with Lincoln's Inn Fields and Covent Garden still, in 1603, free of housing. Between the Strand and the Thames were the houses of the great: Essex House, Somerset House, the Savoy Palace, Russell House, and William Cecil's 'large and stately house of brick and timber' at Ivy Bridge. From Charing Cross to Westminster Palace Yard stretched Whitehall Palace. Acquired by the Crown from the archbishopric of York, when Wolsey held the northern see, it had been fashioned by Henry VIII as the principal London residence of the monarch and the centre of executive government. Enclosed by two gates, the palace buildings were constructed around the 'privy garden', which stretched to the river. It was described by an Italian visitor of the seventeenth century as 'nothing more than an assembly of several houses, badly built at different times and for different purposes'. Much of it was destroyed by fire in 1698, and the gatehouses were demolished in the eighteenth century. Of the old palace only the magnificent Banqueting House, designed by Inigo Jones for James I, remains.

Up river from Whitehall stood the Old Palace of Westminster, built by the Norman kings as their principal residence. The vast monument of Westminster Hall had long been abandoned by the monarch and was converted into the principal seat of English justice. Here sat the courts of Common Pleas near the entrance on the right, King's Bench half-way up on the same side, and Chancery at the far end on the left. Within this huge open-plan building the major lawcourts of the realm conducted their business. In other parts of the hall were the Court of Exchequer, Star Chamber,

[7] The second edition of Stow's work, ii. 71, i. 127.

the Parliament House, where the Lords met, and St Stephen's Chapel, after 1550 the normal meeting-place of the House of Commons. To the west of Westminster Hall stood the Abbey, one of the very few buildings of Stow's London to be seen today. Rebuilt by Henry II and Richard II, it had more recently been embellished by the magnificent fan-vaulting of Henry VII's Chapel. The Abbey was the setting, as it still is, for the greatest state occasions: coronations, royal weddings, and the services before the opening of Parliament.

The main artery of Westminster and the City of London was the River Thames, 'a sure and most beautiful road for shipping'. Since the streets were pitted and dirty, many people preferred to travel by boat, whether they were crossing to Southwark or going from one part of the north bank to another. A series of 'gates', stairs, or jetties provided regular points for embarkation between Westminster Palace and the Tower. Stow estimated that there were 2,000 wherries plying for hire; and most contemporary drawings and engravings show the Thames as a crowded thoroughfare. It was also the setting for solemn processions. Henry Machyn's diary describes the Lord Mayor's pageant of 1553, when the Mayor's barge, decorated with streamers and banners, was accompanied by craft decked out by the livery companies. There were vessels with drummers, trumpeters, and flautists, savage men carrying clubs, and a devil. After dining at Westminster the procession returned to St Paul's, 'with all the trumpets and waits blowing', and then back to the Mayor's house.[8]

The manufacturing and commercial activities of medieval London had been organized into more than sixty craft and trading guilds. By the beginning of the sixteenth century twelve major guilds or companies had emerged to dominate the economic, social, and political life of the City: the Grocers, Mercers, Fishmongers, Drapers, Goldsmiths, Skinners, Vintners, Ironmongers, Merchant Taylors, Haberdashers, Salters, and Clothworkers. All these guilds had developed two elements: a wholesale trading section and a retail or manufacturing group. By 1500 the wholesale merchants included the richest and most influential members and had formed themselves, with some retailers and prosperous craftsmen, into an upper governing tier of each guild, known as the livery, with the humbler retailers and most of the craftsmen making up the more numerous body of yeomanry. Disputes between the livery and yeomanry of various guilds were common in the sixteenth century and generally ended with an extension of power for the livery.

[8] David Bergeron, *English Civic Pageantry, 1558–1642* (London, 1971), 125–6. *The Diary of Henry Machyn*, ed. J. G. Nichols, Camden Soc. 42 (London, 1848), 47.

The apparently clear demarcation of trades and crafts between the various guilds was, however, deceptive. By the custom of London no man could trade within the City by retail unless he was a member of a guild; but a merchant was not restricted to dealing in the goods handled by his own guild. Even in the fourteenth century, many great merchants dealt in several commodities; and by the sixteenth the most important and profitable branch of commerce was the export of cloth to the Netherlands, especially to Antwerp. This trade was monopolized by the Merchant Adventurers' Company. Unlike the City guilds—which were often called 'companies'—the Merchant Adventurers formed a national organization, run from London and from centres abroad. Theirs was a 'regulated' company, in which each man traded on his own account, as distinct from the joint-stock companies, which appeared after 1550 and became the normal type of trading organization in modern times. Although the Merchant Adventurers formed a national company, their members were drawn almost exclusively from London and nearly always belonged to one of the twelve senior livery 'companies'. The export of English cloth to Europe increased from an average of 55,000 cloths in the mid-fifteenth century to 130,000 in the mid-sixteenth, with London merchants dealing in 90 per cent of the trade. In the first half of the century English exports went almost entirely to Antwerp. However, from 1558, and more dramatically from 1572, Antwerp's position as a commercial centre was first eroded and then destroyed by civil dissension and war. The Merchant Adventurers sought new ports in northern Europe as centres for their trade and found them in Hamburg, Middleburg, and Stade. At the same time English clothiers recognized the need to diversify their product and their markets. The new draperies, a lighter form of cloth combining wool and worsted, were an attractive export to southern Europe. New trading companies were formed: the Muscovy Company, trading to Russia; the Barbary Company, trading with Morocco; the Levant Company, trading to the eastern Mediterranean; and finally the East India Company. The traditional cloth exports of London held up fairly well under Elizabeth at about 100,000 cloths a year, worth £750,000 per annum, a little below the average for the years 1545–54. The new draperies were bringing in £250,000 per annum by the end of the sixteenth century, so that London's exports exceeded £1 million. At the same time the trade of the outports revived, so that in the period 1606–14 their exports averaged £400,000 per annum, compared with £1,100,000 from London. Imports, apart from corn in years of dearth, were mainly luxury goods, such as spices, sugar, linen, and silks.

Five points about London's trade in the second half of the Tudor period stand out. First, although the boom of the first half of the century came to

an end in the 1550s, the introduction of the new draperies and the development of fresh markets allowed a modest, although not a dramatic, growth.
Second, while London remained the supreme outlet for English trade, the
outports had improved their position, both relatively and absolutely, by
1600, even if their plaintive cries hardly suggest this. Third, foreign merchants, particularly the Hansards, were gradually excluded from London
trade during the 1550s. Fourth, the glittering prizes of the City's trade were
not open to many: about a hundred rich Merchant Adventurers dominated
the export trade of London. Fifth, the export trade of the City gave little
employment or wealth to most inhabitants of London. Essentially London
was a funnel through which poured the woollen cloths of England, bringing
prosperity to wool-growers and weavers in the provinces, but not much
affecting the economy of London as a whole.

Most of London's inhabitants were still dependent for their livelihood
upon craft industries and domestic trade—a fact which has often been
obscured by the preoccupation of economic historians with statistics for
overseas commerce. Some of the traditional crafts, which had been subordinated in the past to commercial interests, were again beginning to reassert
themselves. The Feltmakers' Company secured independence from the
Haberdashers, the intensity of their struggle a testimony to the importance of their craft. New industries were being set up in the suburbs:
sugar-refining, glass-making, alum- and dye-working, copper and brass
milling, pin-making. The economic and social life of London reflected in
Elizabethan drama is more often concerned with master-craftsmen, small
traders, retailers, and apprentices than with the Merchant Adventurers.

The government of the City was firmly controlled by a small number of rich
merchants who made up the Court of Aldermen. Each of the twenty-six
wards was represented by its own alderman, who sat for life. In theory he
was chosen by the wardmote, the assembly of all householders in the ward;
in practice the Court itself, which could veto any nominee, seems to have
filled vacancies in its own membership. As the chief executive body for the
whole City it was both powerful and busy: it sat twice a week during the law
terms; it scrutinized ordinances carried by the 'legislative' assembly, the
Common Council; it made appointments to about 150 offices; it managed
the finances of the City; and it had special responsibility for the orphans'
fund. All citizens' children whose fathers died before they married or
reached the age of 21 became wards of the City, and administering the
affairs of orphans took up more than one-third of the Court's business,
becoming an important source of patronage. The senior aldermen, together
with the Recorder, had extensive judicial powers, holding commissions of

oyer and terminer (authorizing the hearing and judging of criminal cases), of gaol delivery, and of the peace.

The Common Council, 212 strong by the end of the sixteenth century, was annually elected by the wardmotes. In principle it controlled financial levies, supervised transactions concerning the City's property, and made by-laws. In practice most of the real work was done by the Court of Aldermen, which maintained a right of veto over legislation. The Common Council sat no more than six times a year, sometimes less; and it seems to have been important as a platform from which a man might further his career rather than as a body in its own right. Third of the governing institutions was Common Hall, or Congregation, the assembly of all livery-men, some 2,500 in number. This was an electoral body, which in theory chose the most important officers of the City. In reality the Lord Mayor, nominally elected by Common Hall, was selected by seniority. Of the two sheriffs the Mayor chose one and Common Hall, in principle, the other: in practice the second sheriff was the most junior alderman who had not yet held the post. Two of the four MPs were elected by the Court of Aldermen; the other two were chosen by Common Hall, which almost always chose aldermen or senior councillors.

Chief of the City's executive officers was the Lord Mayor, appointed annually by seniority, who acted as chief magistrate and presided over Courts and Councils. The two sheriffs had expensive offices with limited powers. Indeed, by the end of the sixteenth century the main function of their post seems to have been the raising of money by fining candidates who refused to serve. The Chamberlain was responsible for administering City finances, in particular the orphans' fund: he held office for life. The Re-corder was the chief legal adviser to the City, and was generally an MP. Then there were many lesser offices too numerous to describe: bridge-masters, hospital governors, and so on.

These were the formal institutions of City government. The elements of popular participation enshrined in Common Council and Common Hall had, however, become attenuated, for real control lay in the hands of the aldermen, of whom about a hundred held office long enough to be signifi-cant in the reign of Elizabeth. The authorities were buttressed by other agencies. At ward level the wardmote, summoned by the alderman respon-sible for the ward, appointed juries, elected officers, and licensed brewers, innkeepers, and so on. The twenty-six wards were divided into 242 pre-cincts, each with its own officers, with the constable at the head and the scavenger at the tail. Parallel with the structures of ward and precinct government were the parishes. The affairs of the parish were conducted almost entirely by laymen, the incumbent being the only cleric to have any

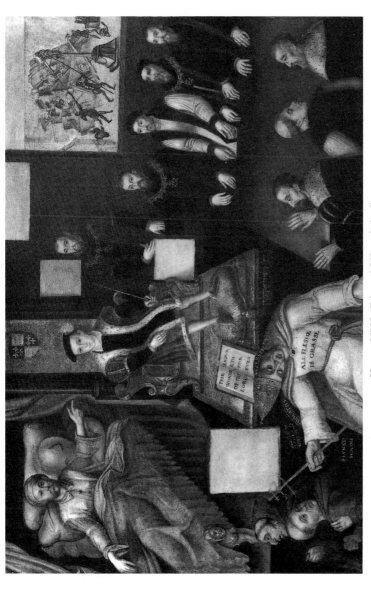

1. *Henry VIII, Edward VI and the Pope*

An Allegory of the Reformation, painted *c.* 1568 to promote the Protestant cause. Images are being destroyed top right, while at the bottom monks are fleeing to the left and the Pope's neck is broken. Henry VIII hands on the task of reformation to his son. See Margaret Aston, *The King's Bedpost: Reformation and Iconography in a Tudor Group Portrait* (Cambridge, 1993).

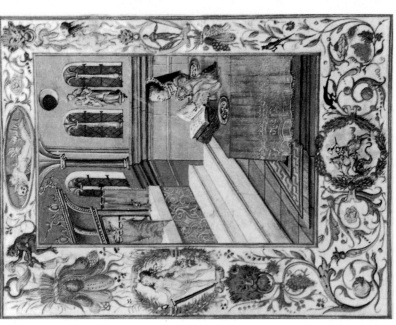

2a. Mary as Catholic Queen.

Mary is shown at her devotions in a contemporary manuscript book of prayers: a statue of the Virgin hangs on the wall. Elizabeth is portrayed presenting the Bible in English.

2b. Elizabeth I from The Bishops' Bible

7a. Raby Castle, Co. Durham

7b. Longleat, Wiltshire

Raby, home of the Earls of Westmorland, is typical of the inward-looking, fortified castles of the late middle ages. Longleat, built by Sir John Thynne in 1567, was the earliest Renaissance country house in England, in no way defensible.

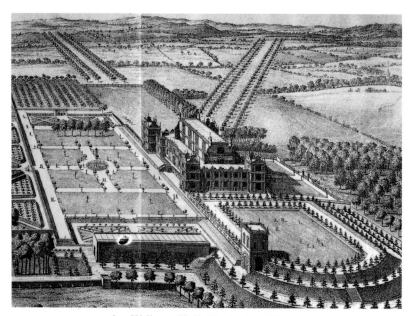

8a. Wollaton Hall, Nottinghamshire

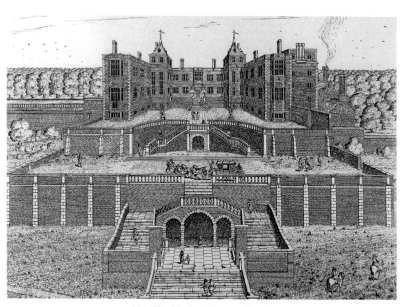

8b. Wimbledon House, Surrey

Wollaton, built for the Willoughby family by Robert Smythson, is a building of great originality: set on a hill, it combines mass with elaborate decoration. Wimbledon, built by Thomas Cecil, second Lord Burghley, in 1588, has a traditional open plan with a 'Renaissance' approach of terraces and steps. It has not survived.

voice. Each parish had two or three churchwardens, who kept accounts and collected church dues. They were responsible to the parish vestry, which was often limited to a small number of men who had held office in ward or precinct. The vestry drew up by-laws for the parish, collected parliamentary taxes, investigated reports of vagabondage and disorderly houses, and kept the church fabric in repair. The livery companies also played a part in the running of government, raising loans for the Crown when called upon, holding musters of the city militia, ensuring the supply of corn, looking after poor and sick members of their own guilds. Civic ceremonial was largely in their hands. Each company had its master, wardens, and court of assistants, who virtually monopolized control over its affairs; and within the multitude of companies the twelve great livery companies dominated the scene, providing the majority of officers, aldermen, and councillors.

Three paths led up to the pinnacle of power where the aldermen sat in dignified security: the ward, the parish, the livery company. These paths were by no means separate: they converged, intertwined, and overlapped. Successful dignitaries would almost always have held office in each of the three spheres; and some offices belonged to more than one—the constable was an officer of his parish as well as his ward. The typical man of influence would have acted as churchwarden, belonged to the parish vestry, held office in his livery company, and been a member of Common Council before entering the Court of Aldermen. He would almost certainly have belonged to one of the great trading companies: of twenty-eight aldermen in 1603, fifteen had been masters of their livery company and twenty-two had an interest in overseas trade; almost all Lords Mayor and over half the aldermen in Elizabeth's reign were Merchant Adventurers. The community of sixteenth-century London was held together by this interlocking pattern of courts, councils, wards, parishes, guilds, and trading companies. Only a very few men might reach the top of the pyramid, but many more played some part in maintaining its middle and lower levels. The upper tier of City government was oligarchic, and so, too, was the administration of wards, parishes, and companies; but the profusion of connected offices and committees provided many Londoners with a chance to participate and a hope of climbing the social ladder. In the upper levels at any rate London was sustained by a powerful civic pride, surprising in a community whose families had mostly been established there for only a short time. Stow summed it up: 'the estate of London for government is so agreeable a symphony with the rest, that there is no fear of popular discord to ensue thereby.'[9]

---

[9] *Survey of London*, ii. 207.

TABLE 4. *Nominal and real wages, London, 1490–1609 (1457–71 = 100)*

Decade	Nominal rates		Real rates	
	Skilled	Semi-skilled	Skilled	Semi-skilled
1490–9	100	100	102	102
1500–9	100	100	100	100
1510–19	100	100	93	93
1520–9	100	100	88	88
1530–9	100	100	82	82
1540–9	108	110	75	77
1550–9	148	159	70	75
1560–9	173	200	78	90
1570–9	189	200	79	84
1580–9	200	200	78	78
1590–9	209	222	67	71
1600–9	231	250	70	75

Source: Rappaport, *Worlds within Worlds*, tables 5.2, 5.3, pp. 147, 149.

Stow was, however, being somewhat optimistic. Although popular discord presented no major challenge until 1641, it was not wholly absent in the sixteenth century; and there were other tensions within the City. Apprentices rioted in 1590; there was a 'tumult' in Southwark two years later; and in 1595, a year of high, but not yet vertiginous, price levels, there was a succession of food riots, culminating in a demonstration against the Lord Mayor and the City fathers.

There is no doubt that many Londoners were in severe poverty at the end of the sixteenth century, even though their hardships may not have been quite as desperate as some historians have believed. While wages rose slowly over the century, they failed to keep pace with prices. The long-term decline in real wages from the last decade of the fifteenth century until 1610 seems to have been in the order of 30 per cent: large enough, but not in itself catastrophic.[10] However, there were periods, notably the 1540s and 1590s, when the fall was much sharper. Between 1542 and 1551 real wages declined by as much as 20 per cent; but fortunately this experience was followed by a rise after the epidemic disease of the late 1550s, which created a labour shortage. From the 1560s to the 1580s there was a gradual fall, of about 5 per cent overall, followed by a further rapid drop of 20 per cent between 1590–3 and 1596–8. For those on, near, or below subsistence level the threat was severe; and this was a substantial group. Probably about 7 per cent of households depended on regular poor relief for survival, even in

[10] Rappaport, *Worlds within Worlds*, 145 ff. See Statistical Table 4.

normal years, while a further 18 per cent needed help in crisis years. Between them, these vulnerable groups made up 14 per cent of London's inhabitants.[11]

How then did the City survive the terrible years of the 1590s, marked as they were by high food prices, falling real wages, and the demands of foreign war? Certainly the cohesive elements in London government at parish and ward level helped to reduce the strain: when a large number of men were able to participate in the administration of their local communities, there was less danger of social fissure. The corporation was conscious of the problem of poverty and its social policies were directed towards ensuring an adequate supply of food. A high proportion of male inhabitants, about 75 per cent, were full citizens, and were thus members of guilds: a man who served out his apprenticeship and did his time as a journeyman had a seven to one chance of owning his own shop or workplace. Such social mobility reduced the danger of conflict between masters and artisans.[12] However, this portrait of a largely harmonious society, its problems resolved by consensus rather than coercion, may be too simply drawn and too rosily coloured. To begin with, the City fathers expressed a good deal of alarm at the possibility of disorder, even at the start of the 1590s. Protesting against a proposal for a monopoly of sealing certain types of leather in 1592, the aldermen warned the Privy Council of possible trouble: 'What great mischiefs have risen of less beginnings your Lordships can consider & experience hath taught us in this City before, where popular multitudes being once incited and assembled together can hardly be suppressed and kept within obedience by any authority of magistrate whatsoever.'[13] The aldermen were of course making a political point; but fear of disturbance was shared by the Crown, for in 1595 the Master of the Revels, Sir Edmund Tilney, censored the play *Sir Thomas More*, instructing the authors to 'leave out the insurrection wholly and the cause thereof'.[14] Such fear was real enough, even if, looking back, we can see that it was exaggerated. The success of the City rulers in preventing disturbances did not, however,

---

[11] Ian W. Archer, *The Pursuit of Stability: Social Relations in Elizabethan London* (Cambridge, 1991), 150–4.

[12] For a relatively 'optimistic' view of the government of Elizabethan London see Rappaport, *Worlds within Worlds, passim*, and Valerie Pearl, 'Social policy in early modern London', in Hugh Lloyd-Jones, Valerie Pearl, and Blair Worden (eds.), *History and Imagination: Essays in Honour of H. R. Trevor-Roper* (London, 1981), 115–31.

[13] Archer, *Pursuit of Stability*, 8. See ibid., *passim*, for a less 'optimistic' view than that offered by Rappaport and Pearl; in general I have preferred Archer's interpretation to theirs.

[14] Laura Caroline Stevenson, *Praise and Paradox: Merchants and Craftsmen in Elizabethan Popular Literature* (Cambridge, 1984), 174–6. *More* was written by Munday, Dekker, Chettle, and Shakespeare.

depend entirely upon consensual relations with the mass of the population. Although participation in London government at the local level was widespread, the key institutions, particularly the parish vestries, were falling increasingly under the control of the élite. That élite, moreover, was united to an extent that it had not been in earlier centuries, when conflict had appeared. Harmony of economic interests and social attitudes prevented serious political divisions from developing at the top; while below that level the artisans were too often divided in their concerns to unite effectively against the rulers of companies. That is not to say that all ran smoothly between the livery and the yeomanry, or between merchants and artisans. In the Clothworkers' Company the small masters in the yeomanry resented the domination of their company by the rich merchants of the livery. However, in the long run, the artisans needed the protection of the livery against unfair competition from aliens and others, while the rulers of companies recognized the need to soften the hardships suffered by the poor. In general, the system of relief was sufficient to prevent the poor from starving or, except occasionally, from rioting; but it was directed predominantly to citizens and their families, and outsiders in consequence suffered.

The power of the London élite was assisted by the close co-operation of City and Crown. At the official level the City provided the Crown with loans raised from the livery companies, levied men, and supplied weapons for service overseas. Less formally, individual citizens sat on commissions, went on embassies, and performed a miscellany of governmental tasks. More important were the financial services provided by rich merchants and the rewards offered by the commercial system to favoured courtiers. Great financiers like Sir Thomas Gresham and Sir Horatio Palavicino acted as the Crown's brokers overseas. Groups of merchants lent money to the government and the City stood guarantor for the monarch's credit, while, in return, the merchants expected and received important financial concessions, especially in the leases of the customs.

A firm set of links between merchants and courtiers was forged by the system of export licences. In order to protect the dyeing and finishing branches of the cloth industry, Parliament had enacted statutes forbidding the export of undyed and unfinished cloth, unless it was cheap; an Act of 1542 set a price threshold above which unfinished cloth could not be exported.[15] However, inflation soon brought all cloth, by a kind of fiscal drag, within the prohibition. The Merchant Adventurers failed to secure the repeal of the Act, and a solution was found in the granting of licences by

[15] 33 Henry VIII c. 19.

the Crown to permit the export of unfinished cloths, notwithstanding the statute. These licences were generally granted to courtiers, who then sold them to merchants. The system proved useful to the Crown for rewarding its servants or favourites; they in turn profited from selling off the licences; and the Merchant Adventurers were able to circumvent the restrictions. The interests of merchants, courtiers, and Crown were thus mutually enmeshed, with rich prospects of gain and sharp practice.

The influence of the Crown was also useful in defending the City against the attacks of the 'outports', those provincial towns which were suffering from London's dominance over foreign trade. Their resentment came to the fore in the Parliament of 1604, but it had been stirring for some years before that. Hull had complained in 1575 that 'all the whole trade of merchandize is in a manner brought to the City of London'.[16] Although the Crown's policy had its shifts and turns, it was usually prepared to defend the charters of the great trading companies, which had after all been granted by the monarch as part of the royal prerogative.

Although outports and provincial towns were beginning an economic recovery in the final quarter of the sixteenth century, the extent of London's dominance over the financial and commercial life of the country can hardly be exaggerated. Not only was it the principal outlet for English exports, but the needs of its populace stimulated agrarian production in neighbouring counties. It was the site of national government, its principal citizens were closely linked to the royal Court. Westminster School, St Paul's School, Gresham College, and the Inns of Court made it a great centre of education. The printing-press was almost entirely established in London, with other presses only in Oxford and Cambridge: the contrast with most European countries, where many small towns had their presses, is marked. Above all, London was the home of English drama, the greatest cultural achievement of the Elizabethan age. The combination of the royal Court, great wealth, a large population, and spreading literacy made London the undisputed cultural master of England.[17]

3. PROVINCIAL TOWNS

London was separated in size from other English towns by a gulf already wide in 1520 and wider still by 1600. During the first two decades of the sixteenth century London's population was five times that of the next largest city, Norwich; by the death of Elizabeth it was nearly ten times as

---

[16] *TED* ii. 49. [17] Below, Ch. 10, *passim*, for more details.

MAP 9. England and Wales: principal cities and towns

big. The provincial towns ranged in a steady progression from Norwich, a small city of 12,000 inhabitants, to hundreds of market towns, many of them little different from large villages. If we limit the term 'towns' to urban centres of 5,000 inhabitants or more there were probably eighteen at most in 1603, excluding London.[18] From north to south they were: Newcastle, York, Chester, King's Lynn, Yarmouth, Norwich, Shrewsbury, Coventry, Worcester, Cambridge, Ipswich, Colchester, Oxford, Bristol, Canterbury, Salisbury, Exeter, Plymouth. Of these only the first three lay north of the Wash, and none was in Wales. Perhaps 8 per cent of the English population lived in towns by 1603, 135,000 in the provinces and 150,000 in London. If we extend our definition of 'town' to communities of 2,000 persons or more, then the total number of urban centres would increase by about eighty and the urban population would rise to about 500,000, approximately 12 per cent of the population. Half a century earlier the proportion would have been somewhat smaller.

At the apex of the hierarchy of provincial towns were five regional capitals, Newcastle, York, Norwich, Bristol, and Exeter. All played some part in long-distance trade, York through Hull, Norwich through Yarmouth, and the others in their own right; they were important centres of inland commerce: and they were the social centres of large areas. All, except perhaps Newcastle, had populations of 8,000 or more in 1520; and by 1603 they had risen to 9,000 for Newcastle and Exeter, and up to 15,000 for Norwich. Below this small group were one hundred or so substantial towns, some the capital centres of their shires, others at about the same level of prosperity. While they were not social centres in the sense that the regional capitals were, their complex structure of government aligned them with the upper group and distinguished them from the 500 to 600 market towns with populations ranging between 500 and 2,000.

Apart from London, most English towns were in sad decay at the death of Henry VIII. Leland said of Bridgwater that 'there hath fallen in ruin and decay above 200 houses . . . in time of remembrance'.[19] Foreign observers were contemptuous of all English towns except London; and the townsmen themselves complained incessantly of their poverty—though we must recall that these complaints were often voiced in order to lighten the burden of taxation. Some towns, large and small, had remained fairly prosperous throughout the later Middle Ages and the early sixteenth century; but of the regional capitals only Exeter seems to have escaped serious damage. Most of the towns that prospered were small clothing towns like Lavenham in Suffolk. For the great majority, the years 1500–50 had been a time of difficulty, sometimes of disaster. The population of Coventry had fallen from 8,000–9,000 in 1500 to only 6,000 in 1523; by that year 565 houses in

[18] See Map 9.
[19] Charles Phythian-Adams, 'Urban decay in late medieval England', in Philip Abrams and E. A. Wrigley (eds.), *Towns in Societies: Essays in Economic History and Historical Sociology* (Cambridge, 1978), 168.

the town were empty, representing 25 per cent of its housing stock. York, which had had perhaps 12,000 inhabitants in 1400, was down to 8,000 by 1548 and may have lost a further 2,000 in the epidemics of the late 1550s. Norwich, Bristol, Southampton, Ipswich, Canterbury, Leicester, and Gloucester were all growing poorer in the first six decades of the century: their experience seems to have been typical. The cloth industry was increasingly carried on in rural villages rather than in the traditional urban centres: the mayor of York complained of 'the lack of cloth making in the said city as was in old time accustomed', blaming competition from the large rural parishes of the West Riding.[20] Disease and mortality were especially rife in the towns. The competition of London sapped the trade of provincial ports. In cities like York and Canterbury, which had been important religious centres, the dissolution of monasteries and chantries, together with the ending of pilgrimages to shrines, removed an important source of wealth. The imposition of royal taxation and the heavy expenses of civic office and ceremonial were driving away the well-to-do. To a greater or lesser extent these damaging processes eroded the population, wealth, and morale of all but a few, exceptionally fortunate, English towns.

However, in the last quarter or so of the sixteenth century this gloomy depression seems to have lifted in all the provincial capitals, in some of the more substantial towns, and in many of the smaller ones. Each major city benefited from the more diversified commerce and industry of the late sixteenth century. York was helped by the opening up of the Baltic trade, Exeter and Bristol by the Atlantic; the introduction of the new draperies restored to health the textile industry of Norwich and the surrounding region; and coal shipments from Newcastle increased twelvefold between 1565 and 1625, bringing great riches to the small, closed group of Hostmen, who controlled the trade. Comparative freedom from major epidemics after 1558 allowed urban populations to rise, although they owed more to immigration from the countryside than to natural increase. While rising population was not invariably a sign of prosperity, the increase usually indicated some change for the better in urban societies.

The fortunes of the hundred or so substantial towns were more varied and, on the whole, less rosy. The success of the rural, or village, clothing industries of the West Riding, the south-west, and East Anglia had kept most urban textile manufacture depressed, and falling or stagnant population in the fifteenth century had reduced the traditional activity of the country markets. The heavy burdens of civic expenditure and government

[20] D. M. Palliser, *Tudor York* (Oxford, 1979), 208.

taxation had driven some of the more prosperous inhabitants from many towns, depriving those towns of the investment capital needed for recovery. Thus, the first three-quarters of the sixteenth century saw most medium-sized towns in decline, complaining often and loudly about their plight. However, special opportunities or resources enabled some towns to pre-serve their wealth during this period, while others began to thrive after 1550. Worcester, an old established centre of the textile industry, was protected from rural competition by a statute of 1533, which prohibited the manufacture of cloth in Worcestershire outside the city itself and four other market towns.[21] The population of Worcester grew from about 4,000 in 1540 to 8,000 a hundred years later; the textile manufacturers and mer-chants prospered in a modest but solid way. Shrewsbury benefited from the establishment by its Drapers' Company of a *de facto* monopoly of cheap Welsh cloths, known as 'cottons', which were bought by the drapers at Oswestry, 'finished' by the Shrewsbury shearmen, and then sold by the drapers at Blackwell Hall, London. The population of the town grew from about 4,000 in 1520 to a little over 7,000 in 1580; and the cloth trade brought work and riches. A little further south, Ludlow, which had grown on the foundation of the weaving industry, was becoming impoverished by rural competition. Its fortunes revived, partly as a consequence of the Reforma-tion, when the property of the rich Palmers' Guild was transferred to the town corporation, and partly because it became the permanent seat of the Council in the Marches of Wales. This regional law court, with a jurisdic-tion over the whole of Wales and the border counties, had a large staff of officials and attracted a growing body of litigants. The victualling traders and innkeepers of Ludlow acquired a modest prosperity, confirmed by the town's cries of anguish at proposals for the abolition of the Council. Hull was a town in decay during the early years of the sixteenth century, its once thriving wool trade collapsing into insignificance. However, from the middle of the century, especially from 1570, cheap Yorkshire cloth was being sent to northern Europe in return for flax and corn, and the coastal trade with London was growing. In 1560 the port had only six ships of more than 100 tons; by 1626 it had twenty. An industrious hinterland combined with ready access to the Baltic had restored the town's prosperity.

Some new towns, unincorporated and therefore unhindered by the bur-dens of civic ceremony and government, were developing as industrial centres. Leland had said of Birmingham that 'a great part of the town is maintained by smiths'; Camden found it 'echoing with forges, most of the

---

[21] 25 Henry VIII c. 13.

inhabitants being iron-manufacturers'; and William Smith wrote of the
'great store of knives' made there.[22] Manchester, too, was beginning its
spectacular rise to success in linen and textile manufacture. For both these
towns the seventeenth century was to witness still greater gains; but a
start had been made in the sixteenth. They were, however, exceptional in
their manufacturing activities, and so too, was Worcester, in being able to
preserve its traditional weaving industry. For the manufacture of textiles
had, by 1500, moved outside most towns to the countryside. Only with the
introduction in Elizabeth's reign of the new draperies did a few towns, like
Norwich, Ipswich, and Colchester, become substantial textile centres. Most
others, whether they were regional capitals or smaller boroughs, were
dominated by the small-scale crafts of tailoring, tanning, victualling, and
building.

Many medium-sized towns either stagnated or grew only slowly—which
probably seemed to their inhabitants very much like decline. The authorities of Gloucester complained in 1626 of 'the great fall of trade generally in
this city . . . chiefly occasioned by the decay of clothing'.[23] Almost certainly
they exaggerated their misfortunes; but equally, Gloucester was not prospering like Bristol, Worcester, or Shrewsbury. Leicester's population of
3,000 in 1509 climbed to about 3,500 in 1600, and probably the quickening
of agrarian activity in the region stimulated its market; but, as the capital
city of the shire, it was insignificant and economically backward. The same
could be said of several other county towns. Warwick had only about 2,000
inhabitants in 1550, rising to about 3,000 in 1600; it seems to have prospered in its modest way, but poor communications inhibited its trade. The
markets of Lincoln and Stafford did rather more business towards the end
of Elizabeth's reign; but they remained small, dependent on the trade
brought by Quarter Sessions and assizes for upholding the dignity and
ceremonies of a county town.

By contrast, the small market towns of fewer than 2,000 inhabitants
had many advantages in the late sixteenth century. They were free from
the heavy encumbrances of a large civic oligarchy and from expensive
ceremonials; their inhabitants could easily combine farming with commerce; and they could take advantage of quickening economic activity in the
countryside. Psychologically, their people were less likely than the citizens
of such towns as Gloucester or Lincoln to look back nostalgically to a more
prosperous age, preserved in the stone of their cathedrals, but lost in their

---

[22] Peter Clark and Paul Slack, *English Towns in Transition, 1500–1700* (Oxford, 1976), 38;
VCH, A History of Warwickshire (London, 1964), vii. 81. Leather was perhaps as important
in 16th-cent. Birmingham as metal-working.
[23] Clark and Slack, *English Towns*, 103.

market-places. However, there were fewer market towns overall in England during the sixteenth century than there had been before the Black Death, when there may have been well over 1,000. As population fell in the fourteenth and fifteenth centuries, many small markets collapsed and never revived: in Norfolk, for instance, there had once been 130, but in the sixteenth century there were only thirty-one. However, towards the end of that century some markets were reviving and new ones were appearing. While some of these towns were very small, a good number had between 500 and 2,000 inhabitants, each county containing perhaps six or more of this size. Their prosperity, while not dramatic, probably matched the increase in their number and was reflected in the growing revenue from tolls and in the competition to levy them.[24] No market town was typical. The site, the lines of communication, and the products of the region determined their layout and the pattern of their trade. Some markets were all-purpose, some—the more important—specialized in particular products, though not to the exclusion of others. Specialized corn-markets were characteristic of East Anglia; livestock markets of the Midlands; wool and cloth markets of the west.

The Cotswold town of Burford today preserves many features of an early modern market town—thanks to its decline in the nineteenth century, when both the main road from Oxford to Cheltenham and then the railway passed it by. In 1600 it had a population of about 800, in 1963 of 855. Poverty has embalmed it for tourists and antique shops; but in the sixteenth century its weekly market in wool, cloth, and corn, with its two annual fairs, made it the third richest town in Oxfordshire, next to Oxford itself and Henley. The medieval layout of the town is still apparent, built along the backbone of the High Street, which runs straight uphill from the valley bottom of the River Windrush to the top of the ridge. The Market Cross stood about half-way up and the houses were closely packed on each side of the street. Enough medieval features survive in the houses to show that the town was well established before the Tudor period; but the stone fronts in 'Cotswold' style were built in the late sixteenth and seventeenth centuries, testimony to its increasing prosperity.

The social structure of the major and middling towns showed a marked stratification in wealth. At the top of the pyramid were a few families owning the bulk of property: in 1525 2 per cent of the taxpayers of Norwich owned 40 per cent of the wealth; 6 per cent in all owned 60 per cent; 11 per

---

[24] On market towns see Alan Everitt, 'The marketing of agricultural produce', in Thirsk (ed.), *Agrarian History*, iv. 466–592.

cent in all owned 75 per cent; and the remaining 89 per cent owned only 25 per cent. A similar pattern is revealed elsewhere. By comparison with the great London merchants the provincial traders were men of modest means: Exeter merchants averaged £2,000 in money and goods at death, Londoners £7,800; yet, even so, the city fathers of provincial England could cut a handsome figure. In most provincial towns some 60 per cent of the male inhabitants were wage-earners, about half of them taxpayers whose incomes provided their families with food, fuel, housing, and clothes of the most modest kind; the others, 30 per cent of the total population, paid no taxes at all and might be supposed to be nearly destitute. However, tax returns are not always reliable, and evidence from Coventry suggests that several of those who paid no taxes had living-in servants. A very rough estimate indicates that about 10 per cent of townspeople were well off; that the next 70 per cent occupied the middle ground, able to support themselves tolerably well in good times and to survive adequately without poor relief even in bad; that about 15 per cent maintained a bare subsistence in favourable years but needed relief in periods of crisis; and that some 5 per cent were in deep poverty, permanently dependent on the support of others.[25]

The political 'constitutions' of sixteenth-century towns were, given their small size, remarkably elaborate. Mostly they were modelled on the same basic pattern, with some variations. Ludlow, to take a medium-sized town first, was ruled by two councils: the Twelve, consisting of aldermen; and the Twenty-five, who were common-councillors. The chief executive officers were the two bailiffs, one chosen from and by the Twelve, the other from and by the Twenty-five. They acted as JPs and were given legal advice by the Recorder, usually a prominent, non-resident lawyer. A crowd of lesser officials assisted them: serjeants, constables, auditors, inspectors of cloth, and so on. The two councils elected the town's MPs and filled vacancies in their own numbers; aldermen and councillors served until voluntary retirement or death. The councils acted as agents of central government in collecting taxes and raising troops; they administered the town's property, saw to the repair of its buildings, regulated trade, and promulgated by-laws. The officers were responsible for holding various borough courts: Quarter Sessions, courts leet, and so on. In Shrewsbury matters were a little different. Again, there were two bailiffs, twelve aldermen, and twenty-four councillors, each body co-opting new members when a vacancy occurred. But

[25] Cf. Charles Phythian-Adams, *The Fabric of the Traditional Community* (Milton Keynes, 1977), 34–5; Paul Slack, *Poverty and Policy in Tudor and Stuart England* (London, 1988), ch. 3.

the choice of officials was more 'democratic' and in practice more complicated. The outgoing bailiffs nominated two councillors, who chose twenty-five burgesses, who in turn elected the new bailiffs, the common serjeant, six auditors, and various other officers. The proceedings were at times contentious, and in 1565 it took twenty-six hours to complete the elections. At York, a provincial capital, the mayor and twelve aldermen were assisted by a second council of Twenty-four. These two bodies conducted the day-to-day business of the city, mayor and aldermen acting as JPs. There was also a common council of forty-one members, indirectly representing the different crafts and electing various officers. Aldermen served for life and vacancies were filled by election by the common council; the mayor, aldermen, and common council elected members of the Twenty-four. The common council chose three candidates annually for the office of mayor, from whom the aldermen chose one. York was divided into wards, which were in turn subdivided into parishes; and much routine business was conducted at these levels. Although the composition of the ruling bodies of different towns varied a good deal, it can fairly be said that the main control over affairs was in the hands of small, self-perpetuating oligarchies, mostly drawn from the richer members of the community. A remarkable illustration of this is supplied by the parliamentary elections of 1597: 6,000 voters met in York to elect the Knights of the Shire, 61 to elect the representatives of the city. The voice of the people was occasionally heard in some towns, in others never.

Not surprisingly, the steeply tapering pyramids of urban wealth, the large numbers of distressingly poor families, the fluctuations in the prosperity of many towns, and the concentration of power in small cliques provoked discontent and protest. There were occasional food riots in various towns, especially in the 1590s, and the populace sometimes used what voice it had too loudly and coarsely for the taste of the élite. In Shrewsbury a claque of 'bawling fellows' was said to be so rumbustious that the 'better sort' stayed away from elections. Occasionally there were concerted campaigns for reform. In Ludlow, for instance, John Bradford and John Sutton had in 1593 'breeden great disobedience', according to the council, persuading the 'meaner and simpler sort' that they 'would overthrow the said ancient government and bring all in common'. They were later accused of trying to bring government 'into a popularity'. The main complaint of Bradford and his followers was that the aldermen and councillors were giving themselves leases of corporation lands on very favourable terms, their principal demand that vacancies in the two councils should be filled by an election in which all free burgesses should have a vote. The matter was brought before the Privy Council and the Court of Exchequer. The upshot was total victory for the oligarchy, whose power was unequivocally upheld.[26]

The incident at Ludlow, in itself of no great moment, and the histories of many other boroughs, suggest certain conclusions about the exercise of authority in Tudor towns. First, there was in the second half of the sixteenth century very little serious disruption of urban government: the opposition at Ludlow quickly petered out. Stability was more apparent than turbulence. Second, dissension was more likely to break out among the middle group of citizens than among the very poor, who were preoccupied with keeping alive. The main issue at Ludlow was the leasing of corporation lands, hardly a matter which would have roused men and women whose main concern was buying their daily bread. Third, the Crown was concerned to preserve the established order within the towns. It tried to protect them against rural competition, sometimes with a degree of success, as at Worcester, more often fruitlessly. Its support for rule by small groups of well-to-do townsmen was consistently expressed in the charters which it issued during the sixteenth century.

The limits of discontent and the desire of the Crown for firm government are only part of the explanation for the stability shown by English urban communities in the strained conditions of the later sixteenth century. The most important paths to understanding lie in the nature of urban society. To begin with, it was bound together by very close and interlocking ties of kinship and guilds. The men who counted in any town were members of craft or trade guilds, whose elaborate structures of hierarchy provided marks of status, united their members, and formed the rungs of a ladder to positions in borough government. The crafts played the major role in the ceremonials, feasts, and processions which punctuated the year, and which, after the Reformation, became increasingly secular and more concerned than before with the dignity of the mayor and his fellows. Society in a sixteenth-century town was closely controlled and tightly meshed; yet, although the ultimate control of borough government rested in a few hands, many men held some sort of office and participated from time to time. There were few oligarchic dynasties and the councils were open to new members. Such openness, especially characteristic of York, was a feature, if less marked, of many other towns and cities. Able, determined, financially successful men always had a good chance of entering the oligarchy.

[26] Penry Williams, 'Government and Politics in Ludlow, 1590–1642', *Transactions of the Shropshire Archaeological Society*, 56/3 (1960), 282–94.

By comparison with English boroughs of the Middle Ages or with Continental cities of the sixteenth century, Tudor towns contributed little to the artistic, social, or intellectual life of the country. Centres like Winchester, York, Canterbury, and Chester had once produced magnificent cathedrals and sculptures, sumptuously illuminated manuscripts, and great mystery plays. Across the Channel a city like Nuremberg, with not more than 20,000 inhabitants, still had its characteristic urban culture: Dürer would have been an exceptional man at any time, but he was far from being the only artist in the city; the Meistersingers were not invented by Wagner; geographers like Martin Behaim were known all over Europe; and Nuremberg's printing-press produced the splendid town *Chronicle*. No English town of similar size in the sixteenth century could match even one of these achievements. The building of cathedrals and churches came to an end with the Reformation; the mystery plays were suppressed by the government of Elizabeth. Large towns were admittedly important centres for the diffusion of religious opinion; their clusters of parish churches and the lectureships established by their corporations provided a base from which preachers could instruct clerics and laymen from the surrounding countryside; and in time many towns became celebrated as nurseries of the reformed religion.[27] Some of them, like Shrewsbury, Winchester, Bedford, and Windsor, had famous schools. But that was the limit of urban culture.[28]

The regional capitals, however, played an important role in bringing together the county nobility and gentry—a role that was to become still more important in the seventeenth and eighteenth centuries. York and Ludlow were the headquarters of regional councils; the county towns were the seats of Quarter Sessions and assizes, where the notables of the shire assembled to deliberate on local affairs and where the circuit judges brought the commands of central government to the localities. But the social centre at Ludlow was the castle, seat of the Lord President, and the entertainments provided there reflected the ceremony of a great country house rather than a town corporation. The socially prestigious events of a county town—cock-fighting and horse-racing, for instance—were activities of the gentry imported into an urban setting. One can of course carry this line of thought too far, for there was no great social barrier fixed between the gentry and the borough notables. But the values and activities most admired were those of landowners, not of burgesses. The towns themselves looked inwards, welcoming the custom and prestige brought by visiting gentlemen, yet anxious to preserve their own independence from the outside world. However, the local oligarchs, determined to remain in control, depended to some extent

[27] Below, Ch. 11 ss. 4, 5.   [28] Below, Ch. 10 ss. 1, 2.

on the support of the Crown and of the county notables. In securing their
own authority within the town, they sacrificed their independence and
accepted a passive role in national politics. London was of course the great
exception. Its dynamic role in government, commerce, finance, and drama
can hardly be exaggerated. For that reason alone it would be absurd to talk
of the 'de-urbanization' of English life; and in the late sixteenth century
many provincial towns played important roles in the economic life of their
regions and in some cases of the nation. Not all sacrificed their independence: the coal-owners of Newcastle, for instance, began to colonize the
rural hinterland. Yet by 1600 the process was beginning by which most
were becoming subordinate communities within their shires. During the
seventeenth century the intellectual, cultural, and political leadership of
England was taken over by the Court at Whitehall, the City of London, and
the great country houses.

4. RURAL SOCIETY

The twin pressures of population growth and price rise upon rural England
naturally varied from one farming region to another.[29] The 'champion' areas
of open-field arable and the infertile pastoral uplands were probably most
affected; in the fens, marshlands, and woodland-pasture districts the inhabitants were protected to some degree by having space in which to expand
and by developing alternative ways of making their living. Population and
prices were not the only agents of change. New farming techniques and
crops, the development of rural crafts and industries, the demand for food
from growing towns, and improvements in transport helped to lift the
standards of living for some. On the other hand, the pressure exerted by
landlords for a higher return from their property threatened the poorer
husbandmen. The legal relationship between lords and tenants was complicated and changing, so that security of tenure could in practice be difficult to gauge. But broadly and generally the second half of the sixteenth
century was part of a long continuity, lasting from about 1450 to 1800,
during which English rural society was transformed from being a world of
small or middling tenant occupiers to one composed mainly of large tenant
farmers and landless or nearly landless labourers. The process was accompanied by the engrossment, or amalgamation, of farms; by the consolidation
of holdings; and by enclosures, or the extinction of common rights. Sometimes these changes occurred simultaneously; sometimes they took place at
long intervals. In the nation as a whole the change was long drawn out; in

---

[29] See Maps 1, 2; Ch. 1 for topographical description of farming regions.

particular villages or regions it might happen very suddenly. To understand the complexity of the process we shall first consider some case-studies, to illustrate the variety of responses to change, before moving to a more general analysis.

Chippenham, Cambridgeshire, was an open-field village, the economy of which depended upon sheep and corn, the sheep mostly belonging to the lord of the manor, who pastured them on the arable fields after harvest and during the fallow years; in this way the land was manured.[30] There were 1,286 acres of arable land and some 600 acres of heath. In 1544 all the arable land was held by copyhold; eleven men held more than 50 acres each, fourteen between 12 and 50, eighteen less than 12.[31] By 1636 the number of substantial tenants had not greatly changed; ten men held more than 50 acres, some of it copyhold, some leasehold. But where there had previously been only two holdings of more than 100 acres—one of 111 and one of 101—there were now four, two of them over 200 acres. More remarkable, only three men had holdings between 12 and 50 acres, only ten less than 12 acres. The total population of the village (300 to 360 people) had not greatly changed, and the disappearance of the middling group of tenants seems to have been the result of a transformation in the structure of landholding rather than of emigration.[32] The landlord had been able to convert more than 500 acres from copyhold to leasehold, and these holdings had been leased by the more substantial farmers. It is likely that copyholders were forced out by economic pressure, falling into debt in periods of bad harvest and being compelled to sell their landed interest in order to pay their creditors. Their secure legal tenure was no protection against economic pressures. The landlord gained from charging higher rents to the new leaseholders, while they in turn profited from selling the produce of their larger holdings at rising prices. Significantly, the open fields remained: there was engrossing but no enclosure.

At Cotesbach, Leicestershire, 80 per cent of the original arable land was in open fields at the end of the sixteenth century; the rest, about 200 acres, was old demesne land, which had been enclosed for grazing at the beginning of the century. Of the unenclosed demesne 660 acres was let to thirteen tenants, on renewable leases; three freeholders held 152 acres between

[30] Margaret Spufford, *A Cambridgeshire Community: Chippenham from Settlement to Enclosure* (Leicester, 1968), *passim*; and id., *Contrasting Communities: English Villagers in the Sixteenth and Seventeenth Centuries* (Cambridge, 1974), ch. 3.

[31] Copyhold tenants held their land 'by copy of court roll': that is to say their tenures were subject to the custom of the particular manor. These customs varied greatly.

[32] It is, however, possible that some of the larger tenants sublet parts of their holdings. Where this happened, there would have been a concealed group of smaller tenant farmers surviving.

them; and 22 acres belonged to the rectorial glebe. The tenants were mixed farmers producing corn, cattle, and sheep. The manor was sold in the 1590s to a London merchant, John Quarles, who took possession in 1601. In the following year the leases of the tenants fell in and Quarles demanded greatly increased rents. When the tenants refused to meet his terms he decided to enclose the common fields. He had first to buy out the freeholders: one sold his property of 60 acres for £750, having originally paid £520 for it; the second agreed to take enclosed land in exchange for his existing strips; and the third, who held only 2 acres, was ignored. The rector accepted 22 acres of enclosed land in return for his glebe. Quarles then employed surveyors to draw up a plan for enclosing the manor and petitioned James I for a licence to exempt him from the provisions of the tillage acts. In spite of a protest from the leaseholders he secured the licence, which enabled him to enclose 950 acres, converting 530 to pasture; the second freeholder was allowed to enclose 130 acres and convert 90. The leaseholders were then offered new tenancies at higher rents than those they had earlier refused. After the enclosure and conversion had been carried out Quarles and the rector were charged in Star Chamber with depopulating sixteen houses of husbandry. Quarles denied this, claiming that only seven tenants had left. Whatever the truth of the matter—and it is not easy to judge between competing versions—it seems likely that the number of tenant farmers was halved. As at Chippenham the smallholders lost out; but the means here were different. The legal insecurity of the majority of tenants had enabled an 'improving' landlord, with the co-operation of two freeholders and the rector, to enclose the land and convert much of it to pasture. Not only was the structure of landholding altered, but the system of agriculture and the use of the land were drastically changed. The value of the manor rose from £250 per annum in 1589 to £500 per annum after enclosure, which cost a capital sum of £500. It may be some consolation to know that Quarles, who deprived several men of their livelihood, himself went bankrupt. It is not surprising that Cotesbach became the epicentre of the agrarian rising in the Midlands in 1607: 'there assembled of men, women and children to the number of full five thousand' to destroy the hedges.[33]

Terling, Essex, differed from both Chippenham and Cotesbach in having been enclosed at an early date. The land was of good quality and farmers concentrated on the production of corn. The parish contained four different manors and about 2,800 acres of arable, meadow, and pasture. About 450 acres were freehold, 250 copyhold, and the remainder demesne land

[33] L. A. Parker, 'The agrarian revolution at Cotesbach, 1601–1612', in W. G. Hoskins (ed.), *Studies in Leicestershire Agrarian History* (*Transactions of Leicestershire Archaeological Society*, 24, 1948), 41–76.

which had been leased out. In the subsidy assessment of 1524–5 there were thirty-seven gentlemen or substantial farmers, eighteen husbandmen, and eighteen labourers. The hearth-tax returns of 1671 show thirty-nine in the first category, twenty-one in the second, and a remarkable increase to sixty-two in the third. The proportion of landless labourers had thus risen from 27 to 50 per cent while the population had increased from 76 to 120 households, or from about 330 to 580 people. The prosperous farmers held their lands by leasehold and paid the market rent, which still allowed them to live very comfortably; the freehold land was mostly held in medium-sized units of 40 to 60 acres; the copyhold tenements were very small. Thus the least secure form of tenure, leasehold, was the foundation of the most prosperous farms, and the most secure, copyhold, was the status of men whose holdings produced only a bare subsistence. The general structure of landholding in Terling would seem to have remained largely unchanged from the middle of the sixteenth century until the end of the seventeenth, although the evidence is not conclusive. The major change lay in the rise in population, which brought with it a substantial increase in the number and proportion of landless labourers.[34]

A rather similar pattern emerges in five parishes within the Forest of Arden: Solihull, Yardley, Sheldon, Bickenhill, and Elmdon. By contrast with Chippenham, Cotesbach, and Terling, this was woodland-pasture country, lying on heavy clay, mainly used for the raising and feeding of cattle. The land had long been enclosed into small fields, and settlements were mostly scattered in hamlets and isolated farms. The land had evidently been fairly evenly divided in the Middle Ages, but by 1524–5 8 per cent of the tenants paid 25 per cent of the subsidy. In the period 1530–69 thirty-four men occupied holdings above average, thirty-one between average and half the average, fourteen between half and a quarter, and none below a quarter. By the middle of the seventeenth century the number of smallhold-ings had fallen from forty-five to thirty-five, and the number of virtually landless poor had greatly increased, while prosperous farmers had become very much better off. Between 1570 and 1650 the population had risen from 2,250 to 3,400, partly as a result of the high birth rate and partly as a result of immigration. In the Forest of Arden substantial farmers became richer, smallholders became fewer, and a large class of landless wage-earners was formed from migrants and from the sons of the poorer farmers. However, the region contained a good deal of common pasture and it is possible that the 'landless' were able to improve their condition by keeping pigs and

[34] Keith Wrightson and David Levine, *Poverty and Piety in an English Village: Terling, 1525–1700* (London, 1979), *passim*.

cows. Migration into the area suggests that it offered at least the possibility of a livelihood, even if a meagre one. Life in the Forest of Arden had few of the attractions advertised in *As You Like It*; but after a period of severe hardship in the early seventeenth century the region was evidently able to support a growing population.[35]

So far the case-studies have revealed a somewhat gloomy picture of growing poverty among lesser farmers and of increasing numbers of landless labourers. But this pattern was not universal. Willingham was a village on the edge of the Cambridgeshire fens, containing at most 1,200 acres of arable, divided into three open fields, the remaining 3,300 acres being fenland or mere. An estate survey of 1575 shows that of eighty-three tenants, five held more than 25 acres of arable, twenty-eight held between 16 and 25 acres, twenty-nine held below 16 acres, and twenty-one were landless cottagers. By 1603 the number holding more than 25 acres had risen to nine; the second group had fallen to nineteen; the third remained as before; and the number of landless cottagers had risen to thirty-one. In 1575 a high proportion of tenants (60 per cent) had holdings too small to support a family, and this proportion had increased by 1603. However, the impression of vulnerability given by these figures takes no account of the benefits of the fenland. Until the middle of the seventeenth century villagers could pasture cattle on the fenland without stint, and, according to the indignant protests of the lord of the manor, they made lavish use of this privilege: they 'do common there with such a multitude of cows, horses, sheep and other cattle' that the lord 'is debarred of mowing . . . and feeding'. The gathering of reeds and willows, fowling, and fishing all supplemented incomes. In consequence a man could live comfortably with a very small holding of arable, or even with none at all. This security depended entirely upon their rights within the fenland. Sir Miles Sandys, the lord of the manor, tried to enclose the fenland commons in the late sixteenth and early seventeenth centuries. He was confronted by the united and effective opposition of the tenants, who 'raised and collected great sums of money amongst themselves by rate or tax' to defeat him; and in this they were successful. Elsewhere in the Fens smallholders were unable to prevent the reduction of their rights by drainage schemes; and there the result was impoverishment and violent resistance.[36]

The major changes in the layout and allocation of landholdings occurred in the periods *c*.1400–*c*.1550 and again after 1590. In the fifteenth century the

[35] Victor Skipp, 'Economic and social change in the Forest of Arden, 1530–1649', in Joan Thirsk (ed.), *Land, Church and People* (Reading, 1970), 84–111; id., *Crisis and Development: An Ecological Case Study of the Forest of Arden, 1570–1674* (Cambridge, 1978), *passim*.
[36] Spufford, *Contrasting Communities*, ch. 5.

continuing fall in population had made it difficult for landlords to find tenants and they had often converted open arable fields to pasture, enclosing great sheep-walks for their own use. In this way the Spencers had been able to buy up grazing in Northamptonshire and Warwickshire which carried 13,000 sheep and lambs by the middle years of Elizabeth's reign. The later Middle Ages had been the time when the worst depopulation took place and when some villages totally disappeared: the Leicestershire village of Whatborough, already reduced to four or five houses, had been enclosed by the priory of Launde in 1494–5; and by 1586 there was only one inhabitant, the shepherd, and the great pasture of 408 acres had been divided into smaller fields. In the decades before the uprisings of 1549 more serious threats to tenant farmers had come from landlords encroaching upon and enclosing the common pastures. From 1550 until the repeal of the tillage acts in 1593 enclosure does not seem to have been the most serious agrarian problem; and after 1590 it came increasingly to be recognized as beneficial. Sir Walter Ralegh opposed the laws compelling men to keep land in tillage with commonsense practical arguments: 'I know land which if it had been unploughed (which it now is because of the statutes of tillage) would have been good pasture for beasts.'[37] Yet although enclosure had ceased to be a widespread threat and was even becoming morally respectable, it still at times brought deprivation, suffering, and protest. Quarles's activities at Cotesbach do not stand alone. John Isham, another London merchant, bought the manor of Lamport, Northamptonshire, in 1560 and began to 'improve' it ten years later. In return for enclosing some of his own strips in the common arable—and thus depriving the villagers of grazing—he reduced the size of his flocks on the common waste. By 1583 he had enclosed and converted to pasture enough land to keep more than 1,000 sheep. Quarles and Isham both enclosed land in 'champion', open-field country. Sir Robert Cecil bought two parks at Brigstock in Rockingham Forest, one of 775, the other of 1,460 acres. Each was well stocked with deer and provided pasture, fuel, and opportunities for poaching to the inhabitants. Cecil proposed to concentrate all the deer into the smaller park and to enclose the larger for grazing cattle. The villagers protested angrily and 'a troop of lewd women of Brigstock', led by two local gentlemen, obstructed Cecil's workmen. His agents pacified the rioters and the process of enclosure was eventually completed, but with the rights of the cottagers apparently preserved.

Although enclosures were a less emotive issue than they once had been, they could still arouse strong feelings and violent actions. But the enclosure

[37] M. W. Beresford, 'Habitation versus improvement', in F. J. Fisher (ed.), *Essays in the Economic and Social History of Tudor and Stuart England* (Cambridge, 1961), 45.

riots of the sixteenth and early seventeenth centuries were not always simple struggles of oppressed tenants against improving landlords. The protests at Brigstock were fuelled by various elements, including the un-popularity of Sir Thomas Tresham, to whom Cecil proposed to lease the smaller park. Tresham was a notorious recusant, described by Cecil's agent as 'most odious in this country' because of 'his hard and extreme usage of his tenants and countrymen'; and some of his opponents were called 'puri-tans' by the local vicar. The two gentlemen who led the protests were evidently his personal enemies. Thus local feuds and religious animosity, as well as economic grievances, formed part of the background to the rioting. But while disputes over enclosure were not always as simple as they ap-peared at first, they could and did involve issues of supreme importance for village communities. In their struggle to preserve common rights in the fenlands against Sir Miles Sandys, his tenants at Willingham forcibly en-tered his enclosures, 'being all armed with swords, staves, daggers, pitch-forks . . . and other weapons', and pastured their own beasts upon them, assaulting Sandys's bailiff when he tried to impound the animals.[38]

However, very often enclosure was carried out by agreement between tenants or between tenants and their lord, to the benefit of many—though perhaps not all—and the improvement of the land. John Norden, the surveyor, reckoned that enclosed land was worth one and a half times the value of unenclosed. Sometimes the lands of a village might be enclosed piecemeal over a long period, sometimes in a single operation. Much more damaging to the interest of the small farmer was 'engrossing', the amalga-mation of two or more farms into a single unit, with the consequent decay of some farmhouses, leading to depopulation. This process might be ac-companied and assisted by enclosure, but it could well be brought about independently, as it was at Chippenham, Cambridgeshire.[39] The pressure upon smallholders came from manorial lords and from richer tenants; and it was generally accompanied by a change in tenure from copyhold to leasehold. Legally, the copyholder was protected from dispossession after the middle of Elizabeth's reign by the action of ejectment; before that he was less secure. But the legal position seems less important than the econ-omic. Where a copyholder held insufficient land to provide for his family in times of dearth he was likely to fall into debt and might ultimately have to sell his interest. If that happened there were prosperous farmers prepared to pay a higher rent for leaseholds than the smallholder could afford. Thus many lesser men were gradually being dispossessed, to become landless labourers or to move elsewhere. At the same time the rise in population was

[38] Spufford, *Contrasting Communities*, 123–5.   [39] Above, p. 187.

ensuring that there were more men available than there was land to occupy and cultivate.

Fortunately the inhabitants of rural England were not entirely dependent for their livelihood upon rearing stock and growing corn. Although many crafts were carried on within the towns, a great deal of industry was located in the countryside. Mining was, almost inevitably, conducted outside urban centres. Although the tin-mines of Cornwall were the oldest extractive industry, they were surpassed in the sixteenth century by other operations. Of these coal-mining was probably the most important and the most rapidly growing. There were coalfields in the Tyne and Wear valleys, with Newcastle as the port for its shipment to London and elsewhere; others lay in the midlands and in South Wales. Most of the coal was used for domestic purposes, especially in London, but some was employed in industry. The lead-mines of Derbyshire and the Mendips increased their output from 600 tons per annum in 1500 to 12,000 in 1600, most of the growth coming in the last quarter of the century. The extraction and smelting of iron ore in the Weald also developed, about 3,000 tons being produced in 1500 and nearly 12,000 a hundred years later. The production of salt from sea-water and from brine pits in Cheshire, Worcestershire, and Northumberland was stimulated during Elizabeth's reign by the interruption of imports from France and the Netherlands, as a result of war.

These new or newly developing industries grew considerably in size, providing useful employment for the larger population of labourers. In the mining regions some men combined this work with farming, while others became professional, full-time miners. The lead-mines of the Mendips were mainly worked by independent or hired professionals, who generally flourished by comparison with those who attempted to combine two occupations, since the professionals maintained high productivity in a period when the price of lead was rising. In Derbyshire the reverse was true: productivity was low and the peasant miners were numerous and poor.[40] But not all the new industries developed in the countryside. Some, especially those catering for the well to do or producing high-quality goods, were generally established in the towns; it is as fallacious to conceive sixteenth-century industry as being largely rural as it would be to imagine it as similar to its modern—and urban—counterpart. The best knives were made in Sheffield, inferior ones in surrounding villages; superior stockings were knitted in Norwich, the cheapest in the northern shires. In the seventeenth century stockings, lace, pins, pottery, and knives came to fill shops

---

[40] See Ian Blanchard, 'Labour productivity and work psychology in the English mining industry, 1400–1600', *EcHR* 21 (1978), 1–24.

and the packs of travelling salesmen. However, during the reign of
Elizabeth, England was only in the early stages of this boom in the manufacture of consumer goods.

Manufacturing was dominated by the making of textiles. Although cloth
was still woven in some towns, such as Worcester, and the finishing industry was located in others, like London and Shrewsbury, the bulk of textile
manufacture seems to have been established, before the fifteenth century, in
the villages and hamlets of Gloucestershire and Wiltshire, East Anglia, the
West Riding of Yorkshire, and south-east Lancashire. Mostly it was organized on the domestic 'putting-out' system by which an entrepreneur, the
'clothier', supplied looms and raw wool to cottagers, whose children and
wives carded and spun while the men worked the looms. In some places
fully independent craftsmen survived, but they were a minority. English
textile output had greatly increased in the first half of the sixteenth century,
suffered a severe contraction in the early 1550s, and then recovered to
something near the level of the boom years of the 1540s. The introduction
of the new draperies into East Anglia and Kent by Flemish refugees led
to increased output, but otherwise textile manufacture, England's largest
single industry, remained fairly stable in the second half of the sixteenth
century.[41] Yet, although its progress after 1558 or so was much less exciting
than that of coal, iron, or lead, it was certainly more important to the
economy than any of these, both in the volume of its exports and in the
numbers employed.

The growing population was thus provided—in some areas—with occupation and additional income by the spread of rural industry. But it had still
to be fed. In years of dearth grain was often imported from the Baltic; but
since a bad harvest in England frequently coincided with the failure of crops
elsewhere, this was a partial and unreliable solution. The only effective
response was the improvement of agriculture and the extension of the
cultivated area. Writers, landowners, and farmers recognized, before the
sixteenth century was over, that the land could be made to yield more
produce and that there was a ready market for it, especially in the towns. A
note of optimism and expansiveness was struck by John Norden: 'there is
not a place so rude and unlikely, but diligence and discretion may convert
it to some profitable end.'[42]

Several new crops were introduced towards the end of the sixteenth
century. Woad, for dyeing cloth, was extensively planted in southern
England. By 1586 some 5,000 acres were sown with it and 20,000 people

[41] Above, p. 168, for the new draperies.
[42] Joan Thirsk and John Cooper (eds.), *Seventeenth-Century Economic Documents* (Oxford,
1972), 110.

employed for part of the year in its cultivation. It was profitable for the farmer and required intensive labour in harvesting. Tobacco was first sown in 1571 and grew well in the Vale of Evesham. Probably more important than either of these was rape, or coleseed, valuable as manure, as fodder for sheep, and as a source of oil. In the Home Counties fruit and vegetables were grown in orchards and market gardens for the London market. New varieties of fruit were introduced during the sixteenth century: pippin, apricots, and gooseberries, for instance, under Henry VIII. William Lambarde extolled the produce of Kent: 'as for orchards of apples, and gardens of cherries, and those of the most delicious and exquisite kinds that can be, no part of the realm (that I know) hath them, either in such quantity, . . . or with such art and industry, set and planted.'[43] Carrots—'a beneficial fruit' in Norden's words—were being grown in fields as early as 1597, turnips and cabbages in market gardens.

Pastures were improved by the 'floating' or flooding of water-meadows. Fitzherbert had recommended the practice in 1535: 'another manner of mending of meadows is, if there by [?be] any running water or land flood, that may be set or brought to run over the meadows . . . they will be much the better.'[44] The most scientific techniques for the purpose were developed later, towards the end of the century, by Rowland Vaughan in the Golden Valley of Herefordshire. The river was dammed and the meadows flooded in winter through trenches and gutters; the water then spread nutritious sediment over the grass and protected it from frost. 'He that doth drown is a good husband' became a common saying in Herefordshire, and Vaughan reckoned that his land increased seven or eight times in value.[45]

Much land, especially the coastal marshlands and the inland fens, was underused in the middle of the sixteenth century. The building of sea-walls and the reclamation of marshland began before 1550 and continued into the seventeenth century. While the most dramatic enterprise was the reclamation of the Fens by Vermuyden from the 1620s onwards, smaller operations had begun from the middle of Elizabeth's reign. Drainage schemes met with serious opposition, as at Willingham, from the fen-dwellers, and dykes were often thrown down. The cost of the schemes was large and it is unlikely that many of them repaid the investment. Drainage of the Fens in the sixteenth and seventeenth centuries seems to have been more impressive than rewarding.

[43] William Lambarde, *A Perambulation of Kent* (1st edn. 1576; quoted from edn. of 1826), 4.
[44] Eric Kerridge, *The Agricultural Revolution* (London, 1967), 251–2.
[45] Rowland Vaughan, *Most Approved, and Long Experienced Water-Workes* (London, 1610) reports on experiments made several years earlier than the date of publication.

In the long run the most important and productive innovation in English agriculture during the centuries before the Industrial Revolution was the introduction of up-and-down husbandry—sometimes called 'convertible' husbandry or ley farming. This involved the ploughing of pasture and the laying of arable down to grass for a number of years, in place of the traditional practice whereby grassland remained grassland and the arable was tilled in a strict rotation. Like many other advanced practices it had been recommended by Fitzherbert in 1535, and it was gradually adopted in the next 150 years. The use of up-and-down husbandry improved both the grass and the grain crops. Ploughing of pastures aerated the soil, cleared moss, and drained the ground, thus protecting sheep from foot-rot. Corn was better for the quantity of manure bestowed on the ground and for the improved soil texture produced by the turf. Farmers who used convertible husbandry generally kept one-quarter of their land as permanent pasture and the rest alternated between grass and tillage in the proportion of two-thirds grass and one-third tillage. Therefore at any one time about three-quarters of the land was under grass and one-quarter under crops. In the common-field system about half was under grass and half under crops. In convertible husbandry the land produced about the same amount of grain as before, from a smaller acreage, and a higher yield of milk, meat, and wool.

It is impossible to say how far these advances in agriculture had travelled by the end of the Tudor period; it is, however, certain that in the second half of the following century England generally exported corn, while supporting a population nearly double that of 1540. While most of the technological changes which made this possible originated in the sixteenth century, their main effect was delayed until the seventeenth; and for every efficient cultivator of the soil, there was perhaps at least one other firmly harnessed to the old and unproductive ways. Increased output from the land in the sixteenth century was probably due more to the extension of the cultivated area than to the improved productivity of labour or technical development.

Growing population, rising prices, new farming methods, and changing structures of landholding produced great and varied effects upon the different groups in rural society. Although the response differed from one individual, one group, one region to another, some general trends are apparent. Farm workers lay at the bottom of the economic heap. They were of two types; between one-third and one-half of hired farm workers were 'servants in husbandry', young unmarried men and women who lived in the household of their employer; the others were day-labourers, married heads of families living in their own households. The servants were essentially a transient group, in more ways than one. They usually left home at about 14, rather later in the case of girls, to live in the family of their master, eating at his table and receiving a small money wage. They seldom stayed long with the same master, binding themselves to him by oral contract, usually for the space of a year, and then moving on to another farm. By their early twenties they had generally saved a little money and were able to marry. Their material conditions of life were probably tolerable, since they ate at the farmer's table; but living permanently under the eye and authority of their employer, as part of his family, cannot have been easy and, to judge from the frequent movement of servants, was often distasteful. Yet passage through a period of service was a regular phase in the lives of some 80 per cent of men and 50 per cent of women, whether they were farm servants, domestic maids, or, in the towns, apprentices; in accepting the status of 'servant' they were not committing themselves to permanent dependence and humiliation. By the age of 25 most of them had moved on, to farm on their own account or to work as married day-labourers.[46]

The other part of the rural work-force was paid at a higher daily rate than servants, but employed only when they were needed. In the second half of the sixteenth century and for most of the seventeenth their numbers were increasing and their living standards falling. By a statute of 1589, all cottages were to be allocated at least 4 acres of land, which should have enabled labourers to supplement their wages with their own produce.[47] But out of a broad sample of labourers' holdings in the sixteenth and seventeenth centuries, only 7 per cent had the statutory holding and 41 per cent had no more than a cottage and garden.[48] Common rights were vital to the livelihood of labourers and their deprivation threatened ruin, provoking the kind of resistance seen at Willingham.[49] Most labourers had some livestock, usually one or two milking cows and often a few sheep; but between 1500 and 1640 the proportion leaving wills who possessed no beasts whatever rose from 5 to 13 per cent; and many poorer men left no will at all.

The worst-paid labourers received 4*d*. or 5*d*. a day in 1540–9, 8*d*. or 9*d*. in 1570–9, 8*d*. to 10*d*. in 1590–9. The increase in wages was less rapid than that in prices, and by the end of the century the living standards of labourers had fallen to unprecedented depths. Assuming that a labourer earning 9*d*. a day worked for 312 days in the year during the 1590s, his annual wage would come to £11. 14*s*. 0*d*., scarcely more than the bare level of subsistence

---

[46] Ann Kussmaul, *Servants in Husbandry in Early Modern England* (Cambridge, 1981), *passim*.

[47] 31 Elizabeth c. 7.

[48] Alan Everitt, 'Labourers', in Thirsk (ed.), *Agrarian History*, iv, ch. 7, esp. 401.

[49] Above, pp. 190, 192.

TABLE 5. *Agricultural wage rates, Southern England, 1490–1609* (1450–99 = 100)

Decade	Average daily rate (pence)	Wages index	Prices index	Real wages
1490–9	4.00	101	97	104
1500–9	4.00	101	104	97
1510–19	4.00	101	114	89
1520–9	4.17	106	133	80
1530–9	4.33	110	138	80
1540–9	4.66	118	167	71
1550–9	6.33	160	271	59
1560–9	7.00	177	269	66
1570–9	8.17	207	298	69
1580–9	8.00	203	354	57
1590–9	8.66	219	443	49
1600–9	8.66	219	439	50

Note: As well as being based on rural rather than urban wage rates, this table uses different data for prices from those used in Tables 1–4. These figures may exaggerate the fall in real wages.

Source: P. J. Bowden, 'Statistical Appendix', in Joan Thirsk (ed.), *Agrarian History of England and Wales*, iv: *1500–1640* (Cambridge, 1967), tables xv, xvi, pp. 864–5.

(Statistical Table 5). Skilled occupations on the farm were more remunerative. When normal labouring earned 1s. a day, ploughing brought in 1s. 2d., reaping 1s. 6d., hedging 1s. 9d. Although such work was seasonal, some labourers were able to maintain a decent living standard and perhaps to raise their status by keeping stock, cultivating smallholdings, and following a part-time craft. Ellis Hanmer of Myddle, Shropshire, for instance, was prosecuted in 1581 'for erecting one bay of a house upon the lord's waste ground in Myddle wood'; he was evidently a squatter who, by paying a fine and an annual rent of 1s., became a permanent resident. His son John improved the property, and his rent rose to 10s., but he was still described, like his father, as a labourer. John's eldest son Thomas, born in 1596, was 'brought up to be a good English scholar', worked as a ploughboy, but was dismissed after quarrelling with his fellow labourers, and set up as a schoolmaster. His son went to Oxford and became a minister. John's second son left the parish to work at Sandbach forge, while the third, Abraham, 'a litigious person among his neighbours', was a labourer all his days but seems even so to have been comfortably off: he adopted the bastard son of his brother Thomas and his family continued to live at Myddle until the eighteenth century.[50]

[50] David G. Hey, *An English Rural Community: Myddle under the Tudors and Stuarts* (Leicester, 1974), 178–9.

However, the lives of other labourers present a stark contrast to the sparse comfort of the Hanmers. The most wretched were migrants who moved from parish to parish, living on the edge of subsistence. At Terling 80 per cent of the men who married and baptized a child in the period 1580–1619 had themselves been baptized elsewhere; conversely, only half the fathers whose children were baptized in Terling were themselves buried in the parish. Not all these migrants were labourers, but labourers were probably more mobile than most. Rural communities both attracted immigrants with the prospect of a livelihood and drove them away when hopes were disappointed. The labouring population was constantly exposed to the menace of desperate hunger. Margaret Peplo, a labourer's wife in Myddle, was found dead on the highway, 'and by the judgement of men and women was starved to death'.[51] Even the grand jury of Essex, respectable men of property, reported in 1604–5 that labourers were 'like to suffer great want and penury'.[52] In the countryside, as in the towns, some 5 per cent of the population consisted of the impotent poor—the elderly, the infirm, and orphaned children—who were unable to work and were wholly dependent upon charity or the poor rate. Labourers and their families made up a further 15–20 per cent who might well fall into destitution in times of dearth or through misfortune.

Was there widespread starvation in Tudor England? Between 1547 and 1603, three harvests were poor enough to be classified as times of dearth—1555, 1556, 1596—and four others—1550, 1585, 1597, and 1600—were very bad.[53] However, in most of England disease was a much more dangerous killer than starvation, although the effects of malnutrition probably weakened resistance to infection. The worst years of mortality in the centuries between 1541 and 1871 were those of 1557–8 and 1558–9.[54] Both came after, but not immediately after, harvests classified as dearths, 1555 and 1556; the times of high mortality themselves came in harvest years that were good and average respectively, two severe epidemics of influenza bringing death to thousands. By contrast, the terrible harvests of 1596 and 1597 were accompanied by periods of high, but not appalling, mortality, with death rates of 30.11 and 31.41 per 1,000 respectively. This suggests that, while there were serious local shortages in the mid-1590s, especially in the northern border counties, but also even in some southern towns, English grain

---

[51] Ibid. 50.   [52] Wrightson and Levine, *Poverty and Piety*, 42.

[53] The classification of harvests as 'dearth', 'bad', and so on was not used in the 16th cent. but has been devised by modern historians. For the criteria used see D. M. Palliser, *The Age of Elizabeth: England under the Later Tudors, 1547–1603* (London, 1983), 189–90, 385–7.

[54] E. A. Wrigley and R. S. Schofield, *The Population History of England 1541–1871: A Reconstruction* (London, 1981), 333, table 8.

production was sufficient in the second half of the century to feed the growing population, except in times of really bad harvests.[55]

Apart from an adequate, or nearly adequate, level of grain production, England may have avoided mass starvation because the population, compared with its level in 1300, was still relatively small, no very dramatic increase in cereal production being required to feed it. For the population as a whole the middle years of Elizabeth's reign were, indeed, a time of surprisingly low mortality: in no quinquennium between 1566 and 1596 did the death rate exceed an average of 26.85 per 1,000 and the expectation of life at birth was 38.6 years. Yet this generally optimistic view should not be allowed to hide the real suffering that occurred. Although England did not encounter a Malthusian crisis of rising population leading to famine, disease, and savage mortality, the landless section of the population did get larger and almost certainly poorer, while in some areas people did starve. The mortality crises of early modern England were real enough.[56] In the towns and in the densely populated region of the south-east they were mainly the consequence of disease: bubonic plague, typhus, and influenza. But in the sparsely populated uplands of the north and west harvest failure could be disastrous, given the poverty of the arable land and the inaccessibility of markets. In the north, the west, and the south-west, men, women, and children did starve: the north-west suffered famine or near-famine in 1587–8, 1597–8 and 1623–4. However, such crises were localized, usually confined to small parishes or thinly populated regions, and lasted only a short time. Epidemic diseases struck richer and more populous communities, especially towns, often lasted longer, and had a more drastic effect upon the population; in London the death rate in the worst plague years was 200 per thousand. The highest mortality came when, as between 1557 and 1559, widespread disease followed closely upon bad harvests.

Consideration of poverty and dearth in the labouring classes has led away from our survey of the various groups in English rural society. Above the labourer was the smallholder or husbandman, occupying and farming land which provided his main livelihood at, or a little above, subsistence level.[57] The husbandman generally occupied from about fifteen to thirty acres. A smaller holding could not have maintained a family without a large supple-

[55] Palliser, *Age of Elizabeth*, 189–201.

[56] For a statistical definition of 'mortality crisis', see Wrigley and Schofield, *Population History*, 647.

[57] Contemporary documents sometimes use the term 'cottager' to describe husbandmen and smallholders; but since the word is also applied to labourers it can lead to confusion and has been avoided here.

ment from wages; a larger farm would have raised him into the status of 'yeoman'. However, the size of a typical smallholding naturally varied according to the quality of the soil, the type of farming practised, and the opportunities for exploiting common rights. The husbandman might hold his land by one of various different tenures: freehold would give him complete legal security; copyhold of inheritance was almost as secure after the middle of Elizabeth's reign;[58] the tenant-at-will, as the name implies, had little protection and was generally the holder of a very small plot; the leaseholder held for a finite term, either for a specified number of lives, generally three, or for a number of years, commonly twenty-one. The copyholder had to pay a fine on entry to his landlord, and on many manors these fines were described as 'arbitrary': in practice, however, even arbitrary fines could not be raised by the lord to an impossible sum, for they had to be 'reasonable' and agreed as such by the jury of the manorial court. A good deal of confusion has arisen from the use of the term 'freehold'. Strictly speaking it meant any tenure which was not copyhold or leasehold. But, as Sir Edward Coke pointed out, 'a freehold is taken in a double sense', for it could be used for anyone who had an estate in his land for life or longer.[59] Therefore a copyholder was often in practice described as a 'freeholder' and many 'freeholders' were in fact copyholders for life or for inheritance.

These legal distinctions have to be explained, for they could affect the condition and fate of a peasant farmer. However, most often the economic pressures of prices, rents, wages, markets, and weather weighed more heavily upon him than legal status. The evidence of Chippenham has shown that smallholding husbandmen were forced off the land between 1560 and 1636, most rapidly after 1598. The tenants were copyholders and their legal position fairly secure. Yet they went under. Similarly, at Cotesbach, Quarles was able to force the leaseholders into paying higher rents or departing; and several departed. Various pressures helped to eject these smallholders. Landlords were anxious to secure a market rent and thus to protect themselves against inflation as well as to grow richer. More prosperous peasants were ready to enlarge their holdings so that they produced a bigger surplus for market in a period of rising prices. The husbandmen themselves endangered their holdings from the best of motives by dividing them in their wills to provide for younger sons; and subdivision produced plots too small for subsistence, leading to the ultimate surrender of tenements. That is one possible pattern of events; but there were others, and much still remains to be discovered by intensive local studies. However, it

[58] Eric Kerridge, *Agrarian Problems in the Sixteenth Century and after* (London, 1969), ch. 3.
[59] Ibid. 33.

seems indisputable that in many Midland villages there was an active
market in land during the late sixteenth and early seventeenth centuries,
and while many smallholdings might survive, several individual husbandmen were selling up and migrating. On arable manors the critical size of
holding seems to have been about 30 acres. In a year of adequate harvest,
around the turn of the sixteenth century, a peasant with such a farm might
hope to achieve a net profit, in money and kind, of £14 to £15, about 25 per
cent more than the annual wage of a poor labourer.[60] But in a period of really
bad harvest, even though the price of his corn would be higher, he would be
unable to pay his rent and other farm expenses. He might be able to survive
for a year or two by borrowing, but a series of bad harvests must bring ruin.

However, husbandmen were not everywhere the passive victims of
weather and circumstance. In woodland regions immigrants were squat-
ting on common land and carving out encroachments for themselves. The
verderers of Rockingham Forest complained that 'of late years by evil
permission and sufferance divers and many poor people are crept into forest
towns [i.e. villages]'.[61] These incomers were generally regarded with suspicion by the propertied classes, John Norden remarking that 'the people
bred amongst woods are naturally more stubborn and uncivil than in the
champion counties'.[62] Yet the husbandmen of woodland parishes were not
all disorderly squatters: at Myddle, for instance, they formed a respectable
and remarkably stable group.

At the summit of farming society were the yeomen. The strict legal
definition of a yeoman was, according to Coke, 'a freeholder that may
dispend forty shillings per annum'.[63] However, this definition was useless,
since inflation had long ago made 40s. wholly inadequate for a livelihood
and the term freeholder was ambiguous. Men described as freeholders
were, as we have seen, often copyholders or leaseholders.[64] The status of
yeoman was never precise: some men were alternatively called 'yeoman' and
'gentleman', others 'yeoman' and 'husbandman'. In general the yeoman was
a working farmer, economically above the level of the husbandman, normally employing farm labourers and domestic servants, but without the
social pretensions of the gentleman, though often enough a yeoman's son
entered the ranks of the gentry. The extent of his lands varied greatly in

---

[60] From calculations by Peter Bowden, in Thirsk (ed.), *Agrarian History*, iv. 652–63.
[61] P. A. J. Pettit, *The Royal Forests of Northamptonshire*, Northants Records Soc. 33
(Gateshead, 1968), 143.
[62] Thirsk (ed.), *Agrarian History of England*, iv. 411.
[63] Mildred Campbell, *The English Yeoman under Elizabeth and the Early Stuarts* (1st edn.
Yale, 1942; 2nd edn. London, 1960), 23.
[64] Above, p. 201.

different counties. In Kent a yeoman could be well established on 25 acres, though most had more. They lived frugally and carefully, devoting themselves to the management of their farms. Using improved techniques, taking advantage of rising market prices, they were generally able to prosper. Some of them, as in every social group, might be unlucky or spendthrift; but, for most, economic circumstances were on their side. At Chippenham the richer farmers were steadily 'engrossing' holdings, adding acre to acre. In 1544 the average size of the six largest farms was 84 acres, in 1560 it had risen to 110, and in 1636 to 142. In the latter year one man, Thomas Dillamore, leased land that had once been occupied by fifteen smallholders. Sometimes one can see the rise of a family up the social ladder. William Bennett was a mere 'husbandman' in Glamorgan in 1546; his son John had become a 'yeoman' by 1587; and his grandson was a 'gentleman' by 1638. The legal tenure of their land was usually a matter of indifference. Whether they were freeholders, in the strict sense, copyholders, or leaseholders, they were able to meet any obligations to the lord of the manor. Conversion of land from copyhold to leasehold probably suited them: farming larger holdings, they produced a bigger surplus for market than did the husbandmen, could afford higher rents, and could thus engross farms when the less fortunate smallholder had to sell. Sooner or later yeoman families were unable to resist the temptation of higher social status and they provided a steady flow of recruits into the gentry.

The families at the top of the social and economic hierarchy were affected by more varied and complex economic circumstances than those below them. They derived their incomes from a greater number of sources, were often involved in politics, and were more exposed than lesser men to the temptation of conspicuous consumption. Writing in 1601 Thomas Wilson grouped the gentlemen into three sections: knights, whose revenues were between £1,000 and £2,000 per annum; esquires, with incomes between £500 and £1,000; and lesser gentry, with under £500. However, he admitted that in the Home Counties a gentleman would need £666 to £1,000 per annum to be of any account, while in the north country he could cut a considerable figure with £300. Like everyone else in the sixteenth century the nobles and gentlemen were exposed to the pressures of inflation. At the same time, rising prices, especially of food, presented an opportunity to those who would take it. Landowners with fixed incomes would inevitably become poorer in real terms unless they took action to improve their estates. Since most of them depended heavily upon rents, which were often determined by custom, the adjustment could be difficult. Landlords had to wait until leases fell in and consequently there was a time-lag between the first onset of inflation and the successful response of the gentry.

Revenues from landed estates could be improved in various other ways. Arable land might be enclosed, converted to pasture, and farmed by the landowner himself as grazier. The common pasture could be stocked more heavily than before with the landlord's flocks and might in some cases be enclosed. Farms might be engrossed and let out in larger units, which would generally command a higher rental per acre. Copyhold tenures might be converted to leasehold so that a 'rack-rent', or market rent, might be charged instead of the old customary sums. Manors might be enclosed to allow more efficient and profitable use of the land. Farming techniques could be improved by introducing convertible husbandry, the flooding of water-meadows, the use of marling, and the introduction of new crops. New land might be brought into cultivation by drainage. Finally, some landlords might exploit natural resources to develop rural industries. Examples of all these methods come readily to hand.

The Spencers of Althorp, Northamptonshire, bought land which had already been laid down to pasture and converted other properties to grazing. Their special skill lay in the selection of suitable land for purchase. By the middle of Elizabeth's reign they kept a flock of 14,000 sheep and lambs, farmed both for wool and for mutton. In 1545 the lambs of John Spencer were valued at £455 per annum, admittedly an underestimate. In the early seventeenth century the family income was reckoned to be between £6,500 and £8,000. The increase resulted from ploughing back profits into judicious purchase of new land and from skilled management of enormous sheep flocks.[65] Landowners elsewhere also farmed directly as large-scale graziers. The Southwells in East Anglia, for instance, had a flock of nearly 18,000 in 1561, heavily overstocking the common pastures. However, the direct exploitation of land on such a large scale was unusual, and after 1630 the Spencers ran down their flocks and leased out their estates. John Quarles at Cotesbach demonstrated the advantages of engrossing and enclosure.[66] Many landlords succeeded in converting copyhold tenures into leases for twenty-one years or for three lives. The rental of the Seymour estates in Wiltshire rose from £475. 12s. 5½d. in 1575–6 to £1,429. 11s. 0d. in 1639–40. In Glamorgan the Herberts increased their rental from £450 per annum in 1570 to £1,169 in 1631; the Mansels made an even more spectacular gain from £215 per annum in 1559 to £1,498 in 1642. The most general rise seems to have come after about 1570 as old leases began to fall in. Some landlords seem to have been practising up-and-down, or convertible, husbandry before 1600, although this was much more generally

[65] Mary Finch, *Five Northamptonshire Families, 1540–1640*, Northants Record Soc. 19 (Oxford, 1956), ch. 3.
[66] Above, p. 187.

practised in the seventeenth century. Fen drainage began in the second half of the sixteenth century, although it, too, was carried out on a much larger scale in the seventeenth. Woad for dyeing cloth had been grown in England since the Middle Ages, but it was more extensively cultivated after 1540. Iron-founding, coal-mining, copper-smelting, and glass-making all presented opportunities: the Sidney family developed iron and steel manufacture in both Sussex and Glamorgan.

Given even moderately efficient management and the avoidance of excessive expenditure, a landed estate was a solid foundation for prosperity. Yet the profits of land were not always easily won, nor were they the only element in family fortunes. Families at the top of the social tree were tempted to enter the competition for profit and prestige at Court. The prizes were high, since successful politicians and courtiers could found magnificent dynasties. Pre-eminent among them was the Cecil family, whose great palaces and spreading estates were founded upon the political triumphs of William Cecil and his son Robert. Most of the great fortunes of the Elizabethan period were made from royal favour, trade, or the law. Land provided a safe and profitable investment, but by itself could hardly raise a family into the topmost ranks of society. However, courtly life was a gamble: a large outlay was required and expenses were heavy. George, third Earl of Cumberland, nearly ruined his family by high living at Court, then tried to recoup his fortunes by privateering, and ended more heavily in debt than ever. His successors in the earldom, by withdrawing from Court and managing their estates carefully, were able to restore the family's riches.

Some prominent landowners were hit by the misfortune or profligacy of having too many daughters. Marrying a daughter was an expensive operation and large capital sums could be required. The Treshams of Northamptonshire demonstrated that even sound estate management could be nullified by personal extravagance or religious obstinacy. Sir Thomas Tresham began to improve his landed revenues from 1575, raising rents and extending his sheep flocks. An estate worth £666 in rents in 1580 had a rental of £1,000 ten years later, in addition to £1,500 per annum from sheep and £1,000 from other miscellaneous sources. But this substantial income was insufficient for the weight of expenditure placed upon it. Sir Thomas's Catholicism forced him to pay £8,000 in fines between 1581 and 1605; his generous provision for his young sons and daughters, his lavish hospitality, and his extensive building programme made matters worse. By 1605 he was £11,000 in debt.

Most county studies suggest that landowners were prospering between 1550 and 1640, especially after 1570. They controlled the scarce resource of land in time of rising population. Yet success was not guaranteed. Revenues

had to be raised to meet inflation and this might be difficult for landlords
with estates largely held by copyholders. By and large the adjustment seems
to have been hardest for the lesser gentry, who lacked the reserves to meet
periods of crisis, and the risks greatest for the Court nobility, who might be
tempted into extravagance. In Yorkshire the number of gentlemen rose
from 557 in 1558 to 679 in 1642; but in the interval 181 families had died out
in the male line, 64 had left the county—many of them in difficulties—30
had disappeared, and 9 had been promoted to the peerage. Several families
were in financial difficulty at some point during this period, but the majority weathered the storm, produced male heirs, and survived, while about
400 families entered the gentry, mostly from the ranks of yeomen farmers.
The prosperity of the gentry as a group was thus accompanied by and owed
much to the success of the yeomen, many of whose sons rose into the higher
class.

5.   DOMESTIC HOUSES AND PALACES

According to William Harrison, whose *Description of England* was first
published in 1577, old men in Essex remarked that three notable changes
had occurred within their lifetimes in houses and their contents: 'the multitude of chimneys lately erected'; 'the great (although not general) amendment of lodging'—that is to say, the use of mattresses, pillows, and so on;
and 'the exchange . . . of treen [wooden] platters into pewter, and wooden
spoons into silver or tin'.[67] His testimony to greater domestic comfort is
confirmed by the evidence of wills, surveys, and buildings. But this improvement was not as sudden as Harrison's witnesses suggested; nor did it
occur at the same time over the whole country. The transformation of rural
housing—and here we are discussing the homes of yeomen and husbandmen—had begun in south-east England during the fourteenth century,
while in the midlands, the north, and the west the period known as the
'Great Rebuilding' arrived later, when those regions caught up. The most
important change in rural dwellings had begun in the south-east and East
Anglia during the later Middle Ages, when the better-off yeomen and
husbandmen began for the first time to build permanent houses intended to
last for more than a generation or so. The 'typical' improved home of such
families in those regions then had a central hall open to the roof, with a fire
in the middle whose smoke disappeared, if at all, through a hole above. At
one end was a cross-passage, with service rooms beyond and chambers over
them, at the other, beyond the 'high table', there was often another wing

---

[67] William Harrison, *The Description of England*, ed. Georges Edelen (Ithaca, NY, 1968),
201.

containing a parlour with chambers above it. The structure consisted of a wooden frame filled in with plaster. This so-called 'Wealden house' began its history in Kent, but spread later into most of lowland England.

In the first half of the sixteenth century Kentish and East Anglian yeomen began to insert a ceiling into the hall with a chamber above it and added more rooms to the basic plan: service and store rooms, sleeping accommodation for living-in servants. Once the hall was roofed over, a separate fireplace and chimney were built, with a staircase often constructed around the chimney-stack. Substantial farmhouses of twelve or so rooms had become the standard homes of south-eastern yeomen by the mid-sixteenth century. In the next hundred years the midlands and lowland Yorkshire began to catch up with the south and east. The far north, Wales, and the south-west took longer to develop substantial farmhouses of this type; but eventually they were constructed in those regions too, albeit on a less lavish scale. The belief that houses in the highland zone of England and Wales were fundamentally different from those of the lowlands is an illusion. Welsh houses were essentially similar to English and utterly different from their grim Celtic counterparts in Ireland, Scotland, and the counties of the northern border.

Poorer husbandmen lived in houses much more primitive than their yeoman neighbours. Richard Carew, writing towards the end of Elizabeth's reign, commented that within living memory the dwellings of the poor in Cornwall had 'walls of earth, low thatched roofs, few partitions, no . . . glass windows, and scarcely any chimneys other than a hole in the wall to let out the smoke'. But he boasted that in his own day 'most of these fashions are universally banished, and the Cornish husbandman conformeth himself with a better supplied civility to the eastern pattern'.[68] As the labouring population grew, so their cottages multiplied over the whole of England. Most were probably very small, of one bay only, but built of stone or timber, with a fire and a chimney.

The houses of the lesser gentry were not greatly different from those of rich yeomen; and there is a smooth progression upwards from small manor-houses to the massive prodigy-houses of Elizabethan and Jacobean England. The houses of the gentry were being substantially remodelled and in many instances built afresh between 1500 and 1640. Like the yeomen, gentlemen were adding rooms, putting a ceiling over the hall, building chimneys and fireplaces. The emphasis was on greater comfort and privacy. No longer was the hall the centre of the life of the household. The master

---

[68] Richard Carew of Antony, *The Survey of Cornwall*, ed. F. E. Halliday (London, 1953), 138. M. W. Barley, *The English Farmhouse and Cottage* (London, 1961), 113.

and his lady usually ate apart from their servants, for whom separate sleeping quarters were created. The commonest plan was a hall range with two projecting wings in the shape either of an H or a U. The front of the house generally presented a symmetrical face to the world. Stone and brick were much more commonly used than before, since timber was less durable and becoming more expensive. Although timber-framed houses were still being built in the south-east and along the Welsh border, brick was replacing timber in East Anglia, the Home Counties, and Yorkshire, while in the great limestone belt running across central England from the Wash to the Severn estuary, stone was increasingly used for remodelling old houses and for building new ones. Monastic buildings and granges often provided the starting-point for successful conversions. In Glamorgan, Sir Edward Carne transformed Ewenni priory into a comfortable manor-house with a hall, dining-room, three parlours, study, gallery, sixteen bedrooms, a cockloft, and eight service rooms.

A few really large houses had been built in the early part of the sixteenth century to take the place of the magnates' castles of the Middle Ages. However, the most prolific builder of great houses before 1547 had been Henry VIII, who remodelled Hampton Court and Whitehall, and whose greatest creation was Nonsuch Palace, Surrey, a turreted Renaissance château. By the time of his death the Crown was well provided with palaces and none was built by his children. Beginning with Protector Somerset's house in the Strand and continuing long after the death of Elizabeth, English noblemen and courtiers devised the huge prodigy-houses, different in style and scale from anything seen before in England. The medieval dwellings of the great had had three principal characteristics: they were usually built around a courtyard, turned inwards on themselves rather than looking towards the outside world; decoration was mostly reserved for the inner walls; and the exterior was generally austere and unsymmetrical. Raby Castle, home of the earls of Westmorland in County Durham, illustrates this (Plate 7a). So do several university colleges, where this tradition of building survived into the seventeenth century: it can be seen, for example, at Wadham College, Oxford, although there the front is symmetrical. The great medieval houses were generally fortified, but not very strongly. They could seldom have withstood a siege, but were useful for housing armed retainers: they were barracks rather than strongholds. The households contained in these bleak edifices were predominantly masculine. Apart from the lord's own immediate family there would probably be no more than four or five women among a hundred or more officials, retainers, and servants.

Various changes killed off the fortified houses and brought to birth the prodigy-houses of the late sixteenth century: stronger government and more peaceful ways; a growing desire for privacy; the presence of greater numbers of women; the intrusion of Renaissance fashions; and the arrival of the 'man of taste'.[69] Somerset House, London, and Longleat in Wiltshire proclaim the arrival of Renaissance architecture in England. Both were probably conceived by the same man, Sir John Thynne, Somerset's steward. Somerset House, long ago demolished, presented to the Strand a splendid classical front, French Renaissance in style. Longleat still stands, built by Thynne in the early years of Elizabeth, the sole truly Renaissance building that survives from sixteenth-century England. Influenced by Italianate ideas on architecture brought into England by John Shute, it was built on a courtyard pattern. But unlike the courtyard houses of an earlier period it looked outwards, presenting its impressively decorated front to the world. The magnificent entrance to the hall lies, not within the courtyard, but in the middle of the symmetrical and classical façade (Plate 7b).

However, Longleat did not set the pattern for the prodigy-houses that followed. Intended above all to proclaim the grandeur and taste of their owners, to display subtle and elaborate architectural conceits, and to provide accommodation for the monarch and the Court, they were mostly designed on an H or half-H plan with a long central range and two wings at either end. Households remained large and the buildings had to accommodate huge numbers, while providing privacy for the lord and his immediate entourage. The largely classical style of Longleat was abandoned for a strange amalgam of exuberant pinnacles and turrets, native Gothic mullioned windows, and Renaissance decoration. Some prodigy-houses were built in a style unique to themselves, like Hardwick, with its compact medieval design, abundant frontage of glass, and symbolic plan of two linked Greek crosses.

The great chamber was the ceremonial centre of these houses, as it had already been developing before 1500, the hall being reserved for the most formal occasions. The lord and his lady ate in the chamber, received visitors, watched the performance of masques, and lay there in state after death. It was richly furnished and decorated with tapestries, plasterwork, and heraldic glass. A new feature of the prodigy-house was the long gallery, used for exercise and displays of pictures. The finest of these—at Hardwick, Hatfield, the Vyne, and Broughton Castle, for instance—form some of the most beautiful of all sixteenth-century interiors. Apart from these great public rooms, there now appeared 'withdrawing chambers' where the lord and his family could find the privacy they desired. Thus the

[69] Kenilworth, fortified by the Earl of Leicester under Elizabeth, was an exception. See below, Ch. 10 s. 2.

prodigy-houses fulfilled two functions: they were the setting for great ceremonial occasions, culminating in a state visit from the monarch, and they allowed the owner to live part of his life in some privacy.

Elizabethan society from the highest ranks to the lowest was fairly mobile, socially as well as geographically. Just as people moved from place to place so they climbed up and down the ladder of social status. Landowning families might be extinguished or lose their position. Younger sons often fell several rungs on the ladder, as one of them, Thomas Wilson, bitterly wrote in 1601: the elder brother 'must have all, and all the rest that which the cat left on the maltheap, perhaps some small annuity'. Lawyers and yeomen—but fewer merchants—moved into the ranks of the gentry. Lesser husbandmen often lost their small tenements and became dependent labourers.[70]

The great social distinction within this society was drawn between the gentry and the rest. William Harrison distinguished four 'sorts' of men within the population: gentlemen, citizens or burgesses, yeomen, and artificers or labourers. His 'gentlemen' included peers of the realm, knights, esquires, and 'simple gentlemen'.[71] Below the gentry social status was derived mainly from wealth and occupation; but the terms 'noble' and 'gentleman' carried more complex and deeper meanings. The quality of 'nobility' and 'gentility' had been profusely debated since the fifteenth century. For some authors it rested upon birth alone, and only long lineage could make a gentleman; for others, especially such humanist writers as Thomas More, virtue alone constituted true nobility. Some devised a compromise: Thomas Elyot, in *The Boke Named the Governour* (1531), while admitting that nobility was greatly enhanced by birth, insisted that it was error and folly to suppose that 'nobility may in no wise be but only where men can avaunt them of ancient lineage'.[72] The debate continued throughout the sixteenth century. Could gentility be acquired, or was it restricted to those of high birth? Were virtue, military prowess, or learning essential components of gentility? Was trade compatible with it? Different answers to these questions were provided by lawyers, heralds, preachers, and statesmen. Edward VI was hostile to changes of status and protested at the claims of graziers and merchants to be gentlemen. In the most persuasive account of the matter written in the Elizabethan period, William Harrison argued that the

[70] *The State of England, 1600: By Sir Thomas Wilson*, ed. F. J. Fisher, Camden Soc., 3rd ser 52, Camden Miscellany 16 (London, 1936), 24.

[71] Harrison, *Description of England*, 94, 120.

[72] Thomas Elyot, *The Book Named the Governour*, ed. S. E. Lehmberg (London, Everyman edn., 1962), 104.

monarch could reward virtue where he found it, gentlemen 'being made so good cheap' in England. Lawyers, university graduates, and all who 'can live idly and without manual labour, and . . . will bear the port, charge and countenance of a gentleman' will, he wrote, be taken for one.[73] This, in his view, was no disadvantage to prince or society. His defence of social mobility was criticized by many of his contemporaries, especially among the heralds. However, these men, professional defenders of the bastions of traditional gentility, earned their livings by granting coats of arms and respectable genealogies to new families. Not surprisingly, their writings are ambiguous. Sir John Ferne's *Blazon of Gentrie* (1586) scorned Harrison's views, yet admitted that 'virtue hath power to exalt the ungentle to nobility'.[74] However subtly the line might be drawn between gentlemen and their inferiors, the boundary was there and men agreed in general where it should be placed; yet in spite of the objections to making new gentlemen, it could in practice be crossed without undue difficulty by the rising yeoman or the successful lawyer.

6. DIFFICULTIES IN GOVERNING TOWN AND COUNTRY

Three spectres threatened the security of local communities and haunted the minds of their rulers: crime, poverty, and plague. The concept of crime is slippery, for legal definitions do not always coincide with public attitudes: today, for instance, motoring offences, punishable by the courts, are seldom regarded as 'real' crimes. In the sixteenth century such offences as fornication and the bearing of bastards were indictable at law, whereas in the twentieth they cannot be prosecuted in the United Kingdom by anyone, though some people might regard them as sins. Sir Thomas Smith, the leading Elizabethan authority on the government of England, included in the category 'causes criminal' felonies, which were punishable by death, as well as riots and unlawful games, but implicitly excluded ecclesiastical offences. Some twentieth-century historians deny altogether the validity of the term 'crime' for the sixteenth century, pointing out that contemporaries distinguished sharply between felonies and lesser matters.[75] However, it

[73] Harrison, *Description of England*, 114. See also Sir Thomas Smith, *De republica Anglorum*, ed. Mary Dewar (Cambridge, 1982), 71–3. Probably Smith was copying these remarks from a manuscript version of Harrison's *Description of England*: see Smith, *De republica Anglorum*, app. iii; Palliser, *Age of Elizabeth*, 390–1.

[74] J. P. Cooper, *Land, Men and Beliefs: Studies in Early Modern History*, ed. G. E. Aylmer and John Morrill (London, 1983), 67. Compare the account of Ferne given in Mervyn James, *English Politics and the Concept of Honour* (*Past and Present*, suppl. 3, 1978), 64–5.

[75] Thomas Smith, *De republica Anglorum*, 103–7. For that notion of crime see G. R. Elton, in J. S. Cockburn (ed.), *Crime in England, 1550–1800* (London, 1977), 2–3.

seems reasonable to treat as 'crimes' all actions which might lead to prosecution in the secular or ecclesiastical courts, while recognizing that felonies—treason, murder, and grand larceny—were set apart, by carrying the
death penalty, from such lesser offences as assault, riot, unlawful assembly,
sexual misconduct, the procreation of bastards, defamation, recusancy,
drunkenness, and vagrancy.

Throughout the sixteenth century, and especially towards its close, the
attitudes of rulers hardened towards those accused of crime. William
Lambarde, antiquarian and Kent JP, complained that 'sin of all sorts
swarmeth', that the last age of the world had come, when sin and wickedness would abound.[76] Edward Hext, a Somerset magistrate, told Burghley
that thieves had 'grown so exceeding cunning by their being often in the
gaol as the most part are never taken'.[77] His logic is not very strong, but its
very weakness illustrates the unthinking alarm of the ruling élite. Their
fears are reflected in the legislation of the sixteenth century. Under the first
two Tudors, several offences had become felonies by statute, punishable
by death: hunting at night, abduction of women, buggery with man or
beast, theft by servants from their masters, and witchcraft. Some of the
relevant statutes were repealed under Edward, but they were revived under
Elizabeth. Laws were introduced to limit benefit of clergy and to deny it
entirely to those convicted of certain offences. Measures were brought in
to facilitate prosecution: under Mary JPs were charged with the duty of
examining suspects and taking evidence from those who accused them.[78]
Juries were made liable to increasingly heavy penalties for bringing in false
verdicts. Punishments were harsh: traitors were hanged, cut down while
still alive, and disembowelled; felons, who might in law have done no more
than steal goods worth 12*d*., were hanged by slow strangulation; lesser
offenders were branded, mutilated, whipped, or sent to the galleys. The
more fortunate were fined or imprisoned in houses of correction.

What do the records of the lawcourts tell us about sixteenth-century
crime? Was Tudor England a violent and crime-ridden society? What sort
of people became criminals? How effective was the government in preserving law and order? Answers do not come easily. Survival of the records has
been scanty and uneven; their interpretation is uncertain; and more can be
said about the operation of the law than about the nature and incidence of
crime itself.

It is easiest to consider first the trial of felonies, since they were clearly
defined in law and were mostly tried at assizes—though sometimes at

[76] J. S. Cockburn, 'Nature and incidence of crime in England, 1559–1625', in Cockburn
(ed.), *Crime in England*, 49.   [77] *TED* ii. 340–1.
[78] 1 & 2 Philip and Mary, c. 13; 2 & 3 Philip and Mary, c. 10.

Quarter Sessions—so that we are not faced with the problem of conflating the records of several courts. The vast majority of trials at assizes were for theft of one form or another. In the Essex assizes between 1559 and 1603 there were 3,129 prosecutions in all, of which 1,860 (60 per cent) were for larceny, 320 (10 per cent) for burglary, 110 (3.5 per cent) for highway robbery, 157 (5 per cent) for homicide, and 172 (5.5 per cent) for witch-craft.[79] Although offenders were supposed to be brought to trial by JPs and constables, it usually fell to the victims of theft or violence to report and investigate cases and to carry forward the prosecution. Not surprisingly many cases went unreported or unprosecuted. Edward Hext complained that 'the simple countryman and woman ... would not procure a man's death for all the goods in the world'.[80] Yet, in spite of the difficulties involved in bringing cases to trial in the absence of a police force, the number of prosecutions rose dramatically. In Kent, for instance, arraign-ments rose from 33 per annum in 1571–5 to 54 per annum in 1586–90, and to 70 per annum in 1596–1600. A similar trend is seen in the other shires on the Home Circuit—Essex, Hertfordshire, Surrey, and Sussex—and it con-tinued until the 1620s.[81]

Once the accused had been brought to assizes and the indictment drawn, his case came before the Grand Jury, which consisted mostly of minor gentlemen or yeomen, and whose task was to decide whether or not there was sufficient evidence for the matter to come to trial.[82] If they decided that there was, they returned a verdict of *billa vera*; if not, they endorsed the indictment *ignoramus* and it was then torn in pieces. In consequence we know little about the cases which they rejected; but it is evident that the proceedings of the Grand Jury were no mere formality. However, the fate of the accused hung mainly upon the trial jury, composed of men of somewhat lower rank. The inconvenience of serving on juries was con-siderable and brought no rewards. As a result sheriffs found it difficult to impanel sufficient juries to deal with the growing number of prisoners, rising from an average of 4.5 for each jury on the Home Circuit at the beginning of Elizabeth's reign to 8.1 between 1584 and 1588. The prisoners were brought before the jury in succession; the evidence for the Crown was rehearsed orally; and, when the jury had heard all the cases allocated to it, it retired to reach its verdicts. Plainly, proceedings were hurried and the jury cannot have been able to weigh the evidence accurately after hearing

[79] Figures derived from Cockburn, 'Nature and Incidence of Crime', 55.
[80] *TED* ii. 341.
[81] Figures derived from J. S. Cockburn (ed.), *Calendar of Assize Records: Introduction* (London, 1985), 128. Only the Home Circuit records have survived for this period.
[82] Below, p. 218, on prosecutions.

seven or eight cases in succession, perhaps involving as many as eighteen prisoners. According to Sir Thomas Smith, writing in the 1560s, juries complained if they were charged with more than two or three cases, saying to the judge, 'my Lord, we pray you charge us with no more, it is enough for our memory'.[83]

The speed with which felonies were tried does not nourish faith in the assize system, which had been devised for a much lighter case-load. The prisoner had no counsel and could call defence witnesses only at the judge's discretion. Much then depended upon the judge; but this did not mean that the prisoner was doomed. About 40 per cent of those arraigned for felony were found not guilty; of those convicted only 20 per cent were sentenced to death, many of the rest successfully pleading benefit of clergy; and of those sentenced 10 per cent or so may have been reprieved or pardoned. Thus only about 10 per cent of those originally arraigned were ultimately hanged. When one remembers that in all likelihood a minority of serious crimes was brought before the courts, it is apparent that criminals had a good chance of survival. The victims of the crime, parish constables, and JPs were all involved in the complex and time-consuming actions which led to a prosecution, and this made the process highly selective.[84] Juries seem to have convicted or acquitted as much by reason of the nature of the offence and the character of the accused as from consideration of the evidence, for which they were given little time. Men charged with burglary or the theft of horses were more likely to hang than those accused of grand larceny; and outsiders had a poorer chance of survival than had members of the community where the offence had been committed. Judges often softened the severity of the criminal law, and it was taken as an axiom that 'life is greatly favoured and preferred in law'.[85] Confronted by the mounting pressure of cases upon the resources of the courts, judges seem in the latter years of the century to have adopted an informal system of 'plea bargaining', inducing the accused to plead guilty in return for a reduction in the charge from felony to petty larceny.

When we turn from assizes to the lesser courts we enter a confusing and uncertain world. Quarter Sessions, borough courts, manorial leets, and the disciplinary courts of archdeacons heard a far wider range of offences than did assizes, and their jurisdictions often overlapped. In analysing felonies we can be reasonably certain that the assize records, incomplete as they are, cover almost all the cases brought to trial in the counties for which records have survived, except for a few which went to Quarter Sessions. But misdemeanours might be tried in several courts, and the same case could even be

---

[83] Thomas Smith, *De republica Anglorum*, 114.   [84] Below, p. 218, on prosecutions.
[85] J. H. Baker (ed.), *The Reports of Sir John Spelman* (London, 1978), ii. 300.

heard in more than one. Unless we have examined them all we can reach only tentative conclusions about the nature and incidence of crime. Even so, there is abundant evidence of the offences brought before these courts, and records of Quarter Sessions survive for a much larger number of counties than do the records of assizes. Many of the cases involved offences against persons or their property: petty theft, forcible entry, assault, defamation, destruction of hedges, blocking of highways, witchcraft. A small number concerned failure to carry out public duties: the repair of roads and bridges, the performance of the office of constable. A larger group involved infringements of order: keeping illicit alehouses, drunkenness, sexual misconduct, the bearing of bastards, absence from church, illegal begging, and vagrancy. The division of the mass of miscellaneous offences into these three categories is somewhat arbitrary. However, although the boundaries are blurred, there is a broad difference between actions which directly affected individuals—stealing their property or harming their persons—and those which were considered a threat to the good order or moral well-being of the community. Cases in each of these two categories seem to have outnumbered those in the middle group—failure to perform obligations—and evidence from Terling, Essex, suggests that offences against public order rose rapidly after 1600 and outstripped personal offences; but we need more studies of single communities before we can be confident that this was a general trend.

There is, however, reasonable ground for saying that, like prosecutions for felony, prosecutions for these lesser crimes were increasing towards the end of the century, and that there was growing concern about disorderly and immoral conduct. Such concern was by no means new, but it seems to have become more intense after about 1580, reaching its peak in the reign of James I. William Lambarde's charges to juries express it vividly. In 1582 he charged the jury at a special session of the peace in Maidstone to rid the gaol and the 'country' of 'a many [sic] of mighty, idle and runagate beggars, wherewith we are much pestered'. 'We are', he remonstrated, 'touched in sorrow for the horrible uncleanness and other mischiefs that they commit amongst us.' Eleven years later he upbraided the county's grand jury for their neglect of 'three special things': first, allowing the religious peace of the Church to be endangered by 'a sort of elvish and obstinate recusants'; second, enduring for so long 'so many wretched oppressions by means of the purveyors'; and third, 'seeing our country to be overspread not only with unpunished swarms of idle rogues and counterfeit soldiers but also with numbers of poor and weak but unpitied servitors'.[86]

---

[86] Conyers Read (ed.), *William Lambarde and Local Government* (Ithaca, NY, 1962), 168–9, 114.

Three offences against public order particularly concerned the government and local officials: the keeping of illicit alehouses; sexual misconduct and the bearing of bastard children; and vagrancy. Alehouses were distinguished from inns, which provided good-quality wine, food, and accommodation for the prosperous, and from taverns, which sold inferior wine and offered limited accommodation for the moderately well-to-do. Essentially they were drinking-places selling ale, beer, and cider to the poor: husbandmen, artisans, labourers, and servants. To the alarm of the respectable classes the number of alehouses rapidly increased in the late sixteenth and seventeenth centuries. A government survey estimated that there were 15,000 alehouses in 1577 (roughly one for every 140 inhabitants); and by the 1630s this number had more than doubled. To most of the propertied classes—though some were more tolerant—alehouses were centres of crime and prostitution, enemies of family life and morality, competitors with the parish church, and consumers of scarce grain in the process of brewing.[87] A statute of 1552 required that all alehouse-keepers be licensed; but it was loosely drawn and authorities in town and country often supplemented it with their own regulations.[88] Presentments of disorderly alehouses were particularly common in Hertfordshire during the 1590s. In 1596–7 alehouse-keepers in that county were bound over to keep specific regulations: they must declare the names of new arrivals if a robbery had been committed, prohibit unlawful games, and close their houses to customers after 9 p.m. in summer and 8 p.m. in winter. However, in many places, for instance in Terling, the drive against alehouses only got fully under way in the seventeenth century, and the principal decrees of Parliament and Privy Council were issued under James I and Charles I.

The birth of illegitimate children was initially feared for its economic consequences: bastards might become a charge on the parish. The years between 1590 and 1610 seem to have witnessed a peak in illegitimacy rates and it is not surprising that the respectable classes should have become alarmed. The mothers—and the fathers if known—were prosecuted efficiently and punished harshly. Seventy-one illegitimate births are known to have occurred in Terling between 1570 and 1640, of which sixty-one (80 per cent) were brought before the courts. The parents, if convicted, were whipped and put in the stocks, though the father often escaped punishment. Abigail Sherwood was ordered by the Kent justices to be whipped for bearing a bastard, while the identity of the father was left to the ecclesiastical courts to discover, since she admitted that she was carnally known of many men. However, the disapproval of the authorities was not confined to

<hr>

[87] Below, Ch. 12. s. 6.   [88] 5 & 6 Edward VI c. 25.

illegitimate births, since fornicators and adulterers were prosecuted in the archdeacons' courts and also at the Council in the Marches of Wales.[89]

Bastards were relatively few in number and posed only an economic and moral threat. Vagrants produced more intense anxiety. The masterless roving poor were regarded in the sixteenth century as a new, or at any rate much magnified, problem: no longer were beggars to be pitied and given succour. The pressures of rising population, unemployment, and poverty certainly increased the number of migrants. Lambarde complained in the 1590s that, not only were they more numerous, but also there was a new sort of poor: disbanded soldiers and sailors.[90] Pamphleteers described their misdeeds in vivid detail. In a society where every person was supposed to have his or her fixed place the existence of the migrant and the masterless in itself seemed shocking, and a series of statutes was passed through Parliament ordering their punishment: whipping, galley-service, ear-boring, branding, and, for repeated offences, hanging. The reality of the migrant poor was, however, very different from the picture conveyed in statutes, proclamations, sermons, and pamphlets. The huge and threatening bands of sturdy beggars were largely mythical, for most migrants travelled in pathetic groups of three or four, committing petty thefts perhaps, but hardly capable of terrorizing others. However, groups of disbanded soldiers and sailors were a different matter; and especially in the late 1580s and 1590s they caused real alarm in the southern counties and in London.

The authorities were, however, thorough in their repressive measures. Only the licensed poor were allowed to beg; the rest could be, and were, punished. Regular watches were carried out. In Shrewsbury eleven bands of 'watchers' were formed in 1569 to search out vagrants. Provost-Marshals were appointed in London and Middlesex to round them up. JPs and constables had the power of executing summary justice and sentencing vagrants to branding and whipping. In the latter part of the century they could be sent to houses of correction, or bridewells, which were intended to reform the vagrants by providing work, but in practice became places of punishment and imprisonment. Whether or not the state and its officials succeeded in controlling or diminishing vagrancy no one can tell; but they certainly punished large numbers of migrants after only the most perfunctory of trials.

The crime of witchcraft had become a felony under Henry VIII, and although the relevant statute was repealed in 1547 it again became a capital offence in 1563. It has recently attracted a great deal of attention from

---

[89] Below, Ch. 12 s. 2, for further details on illegitimacy rate and bastardy.
[90] *William Lambarde and Local Government*, 181.

historians and the study of witchcraft prosecutions throws some light upon the enforcement of the law. Although it has many of the characteristics of an offence against public order, prosecutions were nearly always brought by the supposed victims: accusations of witchcraft were generally the result of local tensions and quarrels. For instance, Margery Stanton of Wimbish, Essex, was charged in 1578 with bewitching a gelding; found guilty at Quarter Sessions, she was acquitted at assizes. Yet the formal prosecution represented only the culmination of a series of misfortunes inflicted by Margery: she tormented a man, killed chickens, caused a woman to swell so that she looked pregnant, and made cattle give 'gore stinking blood' instead of milk.[91] Witchcraft both involved personal damage to the victim and induced fear and disapproval in the community. Like the other offences just discussed, the number of prosecutions seems to have increased under Elizabeth, and some historians have concluded that this is a sign of rising social tension.[92] That there was tension cannot be denied; but it is well to remember that witchcraft prosecutions formed a very small proportion of indictments in most of those counties for which records survive: only in Essex did they amount to as much as 4 per cent. It was a localized offence, and much less prominent in England than elsewhere. There were, for instance, many more witchcraft prosecutions in Scotland than there were in England. North of the border accusations of diabolism played a greater role than in the English counties and the state was far more prominent in bringing prosecutions. In England there were many more cases of witchcraft recorded than there were actual prosecutions, and the emphasis in indictments lies more heavily on the status of the accused than on the harm inflicted. Trials for witchcraft appear to be most convincingly explained as part of that general wave of moral and social anxiety which inflicted the penalties of the law upon alehouse-keepers, drunkards, bearers of bastards, and vagrants. While there were evidently more witchcraft prosecutions in Elizabethan England than there had been before 1558, the country was free from the great witch-hunts which were conducted by state and Church in contemporary Scotland and in continental Europe.

It is evident that the process of bringing a prosecution in English lawcourts was selective. Compared with the legal systems of other countries, which were, for example in Scotland, inquisitorial and centralized, English procedures were localized and pragmatic. The decision to prosecute involved a complex interplay between the reputation of the offender,

[91] The case is described by A. D. J. Macfarlane, 'Witchcraft in Tudor and Stuart Essex', in Cockburn (ed.), *Crime in England*, 77.

[92] Ibid., *passim*.

the attitude of the victim where theft or bodily harm was involved, the pressures of local opinion, the energy or inertia of constables and JPs, and their personal relations with the alleged criminal and his accusers. Against the desire of victims or officials to prosecute—by no means conspicuous in every case—there was often communal pressure for resort to conciliation or arbitration. When the tithingman, or constable, of a Wiltshire village, helped by neighbours, searched the house of Thomas Morris and found there a sack of stolen corn, Morris begged the 'searchers to be good unto him and his children or else he should be utterly undone'.[93] The tithingman, 'moved with pity, sought his neighbours that this business might be concealed'. When a charge of felony was brought against John Day in Staffordshire, a local gentleman wrote to the Quarter Sessions to say that the accuser was more likely to have intended malice than the accused and that the prosecution was malicious and brought by a 'Machiavellian'.[94]

Often those finally arraigned were men or women of notoriously bad character and persistent misconduct. Hugh Smith, indicted before Staffordshire Quarter Sessions for selling unwholesome ales and victuals, was also accused of turning his house into a brothel, while his wife was alleged to be a strumpet whose behaviour with other men caused trouble with their wives. This case probably arose from a communal feud, since other inhabitants of the village certified that Smith was well behaved. There is less doubt about the character of George Pannell of Rugeley, who was accused of keeping a disorderly house, assaulting various persons, including his own father, playing cards for money, and inciting quarrels as a result.[95] Probably the marginal groups in society were the most vulnerable to prosecution: vagrants were more often suspected of theft than settled people; young, unmarried servants were more likely than others to be accused of sexual immorality or, in the case of girls, of bearing bastards. The operation of the law, which often protected the occasional and 'respectable' offender, bore harshly upon the destitute, the transient, and the defenceless.

Since the processes of the law were so selective, we can say little with certainty about the incidence of crime in general or the nature of criminals. Besides that, there is a large but unmeasurable 'dark area' of lost prosecutions and unsolved crimes. We can, however, be reasonably sure that, among the felonies, larceny predominated in the sixteenth century as it had

[93] M. J. Ingram, 'Communities and courts', in Cockburn (ed.), *Crime in England*, 128.

[94] S. A. H. Burne (ed.), *Staffordshire Quarter Sessions Rolls*, ii: *1590–1593* (Stafford, 1930), 43–5.

[95] Ibid. 49; iii. 289.

in the fourteenth and was to continue to do so in the seventeenth and eighteenth.

We know, too, that much of the business of sixteenth-century courts, from the courts leet at the bottom of the hierarchy to Star Chamber at the top, was taken up with personal violence. 'Bloods and frays' were a regular feature of the lesser courts, riot and unlawful assembly of Quarter Sessions and Star Chamber. Men normally went about armed with dagger or staff; farm implements could easily be turned into weapons; tempers quickly exploded into anger. The leaders of society often broke the peace that they were expected to keep. In 1600 Sir Edmund Baynham of Boxley, Kent, and his friends made an affray at the Mermaid tavern in London, threw off their cloaks, drew rapiers and swords, and attacked the watch. They were eventually fined and imprisoned by the Star Chamber. The retainers of noblemen and gentlemen were particularly apt to get involved in brawls. Disbanded soldiers and sailors wandered unpaid in London and terrified the citizens. Yet by the end of the century the courts do appear to have begun the process of bringing upper-class violence under control. While 'bloods and frays' continued, they seem seldom to have led to death or serious injury. However, homicide did occur, and since it was a relatively precise offence—unlike, say, assault—and was more difficult to conceal than most, its incidence can be measured and used as a crude and imperfect temperature-gauge for the intensity of violence in society. Unfortunately the assize records, available only for the Home Counties circuit in this period, are represented solely by the indictment files, which are open to widely different interpretations. However, the annual homicide rate for Kent between 1560 and 1601 has been calculated as ranging between 3.3 and 6.0 per 100,000 inhabitants, averaging out at 4.6; it rose significantly in the last twenty years of the sixteenth century, from 3.5 in 1561–81 to 5.6 in the next two decades. These figures compare with 12 per 100,000 for the thirteenth century, 1.85 for the last four decades of the eighteenth, and 0.4 for the years 1941–81. On this evidence, which is admittedly subject to wide margins of error, the incidence of homicide in Elizabethan Kent was high but not excessively alarming.

A high rate of killing seems to be associated with the habit of carrying weapons and, in particular, with the introduction of rapiers and the intensified fashion for duelling in the final decades of the sixteenth century. It is often said that domestic homicides are much more common today than they were in the sixteenth century, when most killings took place outside the home, as a result of quarrels between neighbours or strangers, rather than between kith and kin. But, if infanticide is included among domestic homicides, then the proportion of family killings to the whole was as high as 31 per cent, identical with the figure for the years 1920–59, although lower than that for 1985 (45 per cent).[96]

Criminals did not all belong to the poorer classes: gentlemen participated in disorderly brawls, and their retinues were notoriously quarrelsome. Although the upper classes may have become more peaceable from about 1580, they still committed murder and fathered bastards. However, the gangs of outlaws and robbers led by gentlemen seem to have become a thing of the past, their place taken by the privateers and pirates who preyed on shipping. Nor is there much hard evidence of organized crime, even in London, although writers like Thomas Harman, in his *Caveat for Common Cursitors* (1566), gave elaborate descriptions of confederacies of pickpockets and rogues. A school for cutpurses seems to have existed in London, run by a gentleman fallen on hard times; but most criminals, even professionals, worked on their own. Prostitution was, however, an exception, being fairly highly organized in the capital by pimps and the owners of brothels. In general, while society was, of course, in some ways violent, men and women could usually travel the highways in safety and villages were not terrorized by bandits.

If we remain largely in the dark about the dimensions and physiognomy of crime itself, we can have no doubt that prosecutions for most offences were rising from the middle of Elizabeth's reign and continued to do so until the 1620s. At present we can only guess at the reasons. Pressure from the central government may account for some of this. Parliamentary statutes tightened the criminal law and reflected a growing concern; but the failure of the government to expand the machinery of assizes to deal with the heavier case-load suggests that this cannot alone have been responsible. A more conscientious approach to their duties by JPs and constables may possibly have played a part, in spite of the criticisms launched against these local officers; but on the whole the evidence suggests that JPs seldom fulfilled their obligation to collect and present evidence before the courts. So here again we have only a partial explanation. The concern of the more 'respectable' about the pressures of population and the growth of the migrant element almost certainly promoted accusations of vagrancy, bastardy, sexual offences, and the keeping of disorderly alehouses. Such concern may also have helped to swell the prosecutions for theft, and the spread of Protestant piety may possibly have led some members of the official classes

[96] J. S. Cockburn, 'Patterns of Violence in English Society: homicide in Kent, 1560–1985', *Past and Present*, 130 (1991), 70–106. Also, Lawrence Stone, 'Interpersonal Violence', *Past and Present*, 101 (1983); J. A. Sharpe, 'History of Violence', *Past and Present*, 108 (1985); Stone, 'A Rejoinder', *Past and Present*, 108 (1985). Note that the homicide rate almost doubled between 1967 and 1985.

and the village élites to enforce a more acceptable moral order. Finally, there may, especially in the 1590s, have been a real increase in the number of thefts: bad harvests were usually followed, after a time-lag of one or two years, by a rise in cases. While none of these factors by themselves explains the increase in prosecutions for crime, taken in conjunction they probably go some way to doing so.

The spectre of poverty imposed increasing burdens upon the local authorities of town and country. Wandering groups of homeless migrants, orphaned children, the elderly and infirm, families ruined by sudden catastrophe, all demanded a response from society. One reaction was the imposition of more stringent laws against vagrants.[97] But both urban authorities and the central government recognized the growing need of positive relief for those poor who could not help themselves. At the death of Henry VIII poor relief was still governed by a statute of 1531, a more ambitious Act of 1536 having lapsed.[98] The 1531 Act, having ordered that able-bodied and unemployed vagrants be whipped, allowed the 'impotent' poor to beg under licences issued by JPs: the role of the state was thus confined to authorizing the licensed poor to beg for assistance. In 1552, under the regime of Northumberland—not a man usually thought to be sympathetic to the poor—Parliament ordered that collectors be appointed in all parishes and that they 'gently ask' for alms and distribute them; anyone refusing to give would be admonished by the parson and then, if need be, by the bishop.[99] In the second Parliament of Elizabeth's reign, in 1563, alms-giving was made compulsory, continued refusal being punished by imprisonment.[100] However, only in 1572, following the alarming revelations of a survey of vagabonds made in the previous year and perhaps with the urging of towns like Norwich, was a national poor rate instituted under the supervision of JPs, who were to appoint overseers in each parish.[101] Four years later, Parliament carried a statute ordering the provision of raw materials on which the able-bodied could work.[102] The two major and better-known statutes of 1597 and 1601 built upon these foundations and added specific details.[103] By the end of the sixteenth century the Crown had accepted that it and local officials bore reponsibility for at least the minimum subsistence of the poor. The Crown also tried to ensure that food, particularly corn, was available at a reasonable price. The export of grain was forbidden and its import encouraged in times of dearth; local gentry were appointed to county commissions for the restraint of the grain trade;

[97] Above, p. 217.   [98] 22 Henry VIII c. 12; 27 Henry VIII c. 25.
[99] 5 & 6 Edward VI c. 2.   [100] 5 Elizabeth c. 3.   [101] 14 Elizabeth c. 5.
[102] 18 Elizabeth c. 3.   [103] 39 Elizabeth c. 3; 43 Elizabeth c. 2.

and in 1586–7 a Book of Orders was issued to JPs for ensuring a fair distribution of corn at the markets.

The impetus for this large and increasing body of regulation for the relief of the poor seems to have come in part from the Crown itself, which in 1536 had proposed measures too radical for the propertied classes, and in part from the localities, especially from certain towns, which from mid-century onwards were putting into operation their own schemes for maintaining the poor, before the national legislation was enacted. In Norwich, for instance, a census of the poor was made in 1570, revealing that 504 men, 831 women, and 1,007 children—nearly a quarter of all the inhabitants—were destitute. Indiscriminate begging was forbidden in the town and a compulsory tax levied, which produced £530. 9s. 9d. per annum. Private charity was also crucial: in Ipswich the Foundation of the rich merchant Henry Tooley provided almshouses and a hospital, as well as giving outdoor relief to the poor in their own homes.

London was a special case, in its rapid overall growth and in the special fear of the authorities, central and metropolitan, that it attracted a high proportion of destitute migrants. Five hospitals were established there: Bridewell for vagrants; Bethlehem, or Bedlam, for the insane; Christ's for orphans; St Bartholomew's and St Thomas's for the 'impotent' poor and the sick. Private charity contributed substantially to poor relief in London as well as in the provinces, providing some £4,375 per annum in the 1590s, compared with £3,500 from the Crown's endowment to the hospitals and £2,250 from the City's poor rate. The total sum available for poor relief rose from c. £7,000 per annum in the early 1570s to c. £11,700 in the mid-1590s. Impressive as this looks, it was not enough to match inflation and the rising number of poor. A typical pension from parish funds covered only about one-third of the needs of a non-working widow in the mid-1590s, or three-quarters of the needs of a working widow with one child. It is not at all clear how, or even whether, these gaps were filled. By pressing the well-to-do to contribute generously to collections for the poor and by taking measures to ensure an adequate supply of grain, the aldermen of London managed to stave off serious disorders. They were not, it seems, able to eliminate desperate poverty or to keep beggars off the streets.[104]

It is difficult to know how much was done for the poor in country parishes, where the problem of poverty was often as acute as in the towns. However, the laws certainly had some effect. Wiltshire JPs fined people for failing to contribute to the poor chest. Essex records show poor rates being collected in some parishes from 1563 onwards: at Wivenhoe widows re-

---

[104] Archer, *The Pursuit of Stability*, ch. 5.

ceived 3*d*. or 4*d*. every Sunday, and 2*s*.–3*s*. were provided weekly for the board and lodging of orphans. At Shorne, Kent, eleven poor people were supported out of a rate that provided for the annual disbursement of £7. 0*s*. 8*d*. This cannot by itself have been sufficient, and was probably supplemented by the casual alms-giving that the Elizabethan statutes were supposed to replace. Probably the native poor of any particular town or parish were kept alive, although at a miserable level. The greatest sufferings were inflicted upon migrants, whom no community wished to accept. A motherless child, Daniel Brooker, was born at Yalding, Kent, but nursed at Brasted, where his father died; the local JP ordered his return to Yalding, where the parishioners refused him succour. An 'impotent woman' with a child was whipped for vagrancy in Oxfordshire; one Catherine Boland, whose birthplace was uncertain, was moved backwards and forwards between a Northamptonshire parish and the city of Leicester. Neither parish would accept responsibility for the orphan, but they were eventually ordered by the justices to share the burden. The story illustrates both the callousness of villagers towards outsiders and the capacity of the 'system' to provide a basic maintenance. At least in southern England the combined efforts of national legislation, urban charities, and private alms-giving seem to have been enough to prevent starvation and to check serious disorder; but that should not allow us to forget that a large part of the population, perhaps 20 per cent, lived under the constant threat of destitution.

The increasing concern of central and local authorities for the condition of the poor was paralleled in the sixteenth century by growing alarm at the horrifying effect of plague and by some effort to relieve its victims. Bubonic plague had been endemic in England since the fourteenth century, but it was not until the sixteenth that the English government took steps to contain it. The speed at which plague spread, the ghastly nature of its symptoms, and the very high rate of fatality combined to arouse a special horror at its approach which set it apart from other diseases. Its heavier incidence among the poor, especially in towns, produced social tensions between the affluent and their less fortunate neighbours. Although a proclamation had been issued by Wolsey in 1518 to control contagion by marking infected houses and their inmates, only tentative steps were taken in English towns over the next sixty years to prevent the spread of the disease. In 1578 the Privy Council issued plague regulations under which JPs were to meet every three weeks during epidemics to receive reports and 'devise and make a general taxation' for the relief of the sick; infected houses were to be shut up with their inhabitants inside them and watchmen were appointed to enforce the order; the clothes and bedding of victims should be burned. Whereas the legislation on poor relief seems to have been inspired at least in part by local opinion, the strict rules against plague were devised and imposed by the Privy Council; not until 1604 did they receive statutory form. Town authorities and their populations resented the order to shut up the infected and the healthy in the same house; and they were probably right in thinking that this did little to prevent the spread of contagion. More effective was the erection of pesthouses in which the victims could be isolated outside a town, and the Privy Council urged their erection from 1580 onwards. But, except in London, few, if any, seem to have been built before the middle of the following century. Confining the infected and their families to their houses was expensive, since they could be kept there only if they were provided with food. Generally a bargain was struck: the JPs would levy a rate and provide relief on condition that the victims kept themselves isolated.

The principal concern of governors at the centre and in the localities seems to have been the preservation of order. Plague was regarded by them as a disease that emanated from the poor: some Oxford citizens complained in 1603 that the onset of the disease was due to 'the most lewd and dissolute behaviour of some base and unruly inhabitants'. The mayor of York told his colleagues in the following year that unless they took great care in governing the city and relieving the sick, 'the poorer sort will not be ruled'.[105] Isolation must be imposed upon the poor, but they must in return be given the means of subsistence. The response of the governing classes to the horror of plague combines two features which have already become apparent in our analysis of crime and of poor relief: alarm at the threat to good order posed by the conduct of the poor and a humanitarian concern to provide them with a basic subsistence. Confronted with plague the authorities seem to have been rather more active in imposing order than providing relief. Yet the willingness of some magistrates to stay at their posts and their activity in levying poor rates shows that they were not insensitive to human needs. Whatever their motives—and these obviously varied—the magistrates in town and country did succeed in enforcing the regulations about isolation and in preventing the collapse of local administration.

Assessing the quality of local government in Tudor England is a precarious operation. Control was exercised by a host of officials, ranging from the grandees who were appointed as Lords Lieutenant to the humbler men elected as constables; and they faced pressures and problems that varied

---

[105] Paul Slack, *The Impact of Plague in Tudor and Stuart England* (London, 1985), 304–5. These paragraphs are largely based on Slack's book.

from time to time and from place to place. But they nearly all had one thing in common: they were untrained amateurs who were members of their communities, rather than professional administrators appointed from outside. As such they represented their localities as well as the Crown and generally responded to local feeling. Lacking anything other than, at best, a minimal permanent staff, they depended heavily upon the help of their neighbours in prosecuting crime, levying troops, and collecting taxes. Government was a process of informal co-operation and consent. Its success depended, obviously and inevitably, on individual officials and their relations with those above and below them in the hierarchy; and there was no uniform response from the localities. Yet some estimate can be made of the system's success by comparison with earlier and later periods in British history and with events overseas.

At the bottom of the hierarchy those often maligned and mocked creatures, the constables, exhibited greater efficiency than might have been expected from the holders of so thankless an office. They were mostly literate and were drawn from the more respectable elements of village society. They were conscientious and tolerably effective in collecting taxes, mustering the militia, and levying men for military service. True, they were often inert in the pursuit of crime, leaving investigation and prosecution to the victims; and their frequent reports of *omnia bene* suggest undue complacency. Yet surprisingly few cases of flagrant abuse of office have been recorded for the Elizabethan period. Under the severe pressures of war, plague, and food shortage in the 1590s, they mostly continued to carry out the government's orders in a modestly co-operative way. The contrast exhibited in the late 1630s is instructive. The government's demands were then heavier and far less popular, and the Crown met widespread resistance to taxation and the levy of troops. By then the overburdened constables were becoming noticeably less co-operative.

JPs, like constables, have at the time and since been the targets of derision. As Dogberry and Verges have represented the constable in literature, so the image of the justice has been supplied by Robert Shallow. The Elizabethan JPs were certainly selective in their concern with their duties and many of them were casual in attending Quarter Sessions. They do not, for instance, seem actively to have carried out the tasks assigned them by the Marian statutes in prosecuting crime.[106] Probably the main burden of county government was carried by a few devoted and conscientious men: model officials or tiresome busybodies depending on one's point of view. Since they were usually chosen for their status in the counties rather than

[106] Above, p. 212.

their capacity for business, their quality was inevitably uneven. But the fact that they did broadly represent the 'county communities' ensured some degree of local co-operation. County studies have not so far shown many scandalous abuses among JPs; and those that did step over the boundaries of propriety were usually checked by the judges of assize or by Star Chamber. The history of Tudor Wales provides a rough standard by which the office of JP can be assessed. It was introduced there by the Acts of Union under Henry VIII, against the advice of the Lord President of the Council in the Marches, Bishop Rowland Lee. Yet the history of Welsh government shows conclusively that whatever the deficiencies of Welsh JPs may have been, they were a great deal fewer than those of the officials in Marcher lordships who had preceded them.

In England, as distinct from Wales, JPs were an old-established institution. The new departure of the later sixteenth century was the creation of Lords Lieutenant and Deputy Lieutenants. Appointed only occasionally in the first twenty-five years of Elizabeth's reign, they became a regular feature of county government from 1585. Their defects—and their protests against the burdens of military levies—were regularly noted at the time and have been emphasized by historians since. Yet it must be remembered that during the 1590s, in the early days of the lieutenancy system, they were coming under very heavy pressure from the Crown and having to contend with growing resistance from the shires as the war dragged on. Compared with the previous, random, and *ad hoc* system of muster commissioners, the lieutenancy achieved a good deal: trained bands were formed and exercised, the militia was mustered and certificates returned to the Privy Council, local armouries were established and maintained. The charges of incompetence and corruption were mainly levelled at the provision of levies for overseas service, and here there were certainly abuses and worse. But the Deputy Lieutenants had to operate a system—if it can be called that—of selective conscription which was inevitably open to bribery, evasion, and injustice. Much depended upon the personalities of the Lords Lieutenant and their deputies. Some, like Sir Christopher Hatton in Northamptonshire, had a strong position in the Council and worked well with two energetic and efficient deputies, Knightley and Montagu. Others, like the Earl of Hertford in Wiltshire, were in perpetual dispute with their deputies and were consequently ineffective. Yet, overall, the lieutenants were able to keep the armies in France, the Low Countries, and Ireland supplied with large numbers of recruits over a long period. By contrast, the levies raised by Charles I to meet the Scots in 1639 and 1640 produced only disaster.

Even more than the countryside, Elizabethan towns were exposed to severe pressures from food shortages, high prices, vagrancy, and plague, especially during the 1590s. In many towns there were disorders: apprentices demonstrated against foreigners; the poor rioted for food; disbanded soldiers committed 'outrages'. Yet, given the harsh conditions, the structure of urban society was surprisingly little shaken. London was probably threatened with greater dangers than any other town; and its rulers certainly lived in constant fear of vagrants, food riots, criminal bands, and general disorder. These fears were probably exaggerated; but the social problems and tensions that lay behind them were not. The aldermen of London were unable to eliminate poverty or even, in bad times, effectively to alleviate it; but they could and did contain the tensions that it generated. They did this partly by coercive measures, disciplining offenders in Bridewell, tightening up regulations against alehouses, and closing brothels; but they also attended to social needs by provisioning London with food and persuading the wealthy to give to the poor. Thus they preserved some degree of social cohesion in the City. Elsewhere, urban magistrates showed a similar concern and, at times, remarkable devotion to their townsfolk. When plague threatened Exeter, Ignatius Jordan, a prominent magistrate and puritan, refused to flee the town, insisting that although 'he would not causelessly expose himself to danger, yet being in the discharge of his duty he feared not the plague'.[107]

Comparing the government of English shires and towns with the scene across the Channel it is easy to seem complacent. English government was, by and large, more successful than its Spanish and French counterparts. The large-scale banditry that terrorized many regions of Spain was almost unknown. The virtual collapse of government in many French towns during the last years of the Valois monarchy and the peasant revolts of France in the early seventeenth century were avoided. The credit for England's good fortune must go largely to the country's freedom from wars fought on her own soil, rather than to any special virtues in the system of government or the men who operated it. Yet it remains true that by the standards of that unhappy century England was relatively well governed.

[107] Slack, *Impact of Plague*, 262.

CHAPTER 7

The Establishment of Elizabethan Rule
1558–1572

1. ACCESSION AND SETTLEMENT, 1558–1563

'I should not have seen England weaker in strength, men, money and riches. . . . As much affectionate as you note me to be to my country and my countrymen, I assure you I was then ashamed of both.'[1] So wrote Sir Thomas Smith of the state of England under Mary. Armigal Waad, clerk to the Privy Council under Edward VI, summed up 'The Distresses of the Commonwealth' at the beginning of Elizabeth's reign: 'The Queen poor. The realm exhausted. The nobility poor and decayed. Want of good captains and soldiers. The people out of order. Justice not executed. All things dear. The French King bestriding the realm.'[2] Both were writing to a purpose—Smith to prevent Elizabeth from marrying a foreigner, Waad to urge caution in the settlement of religion—and both darkened the picture to suit their arguments; yet even when allowance is made for their bias, we can see that the government faced urgent problems. England's armies had been defeated in the field and their morale was low, while she was still at war with France, whose Dauphin was married to the young Mary Stewart. At home, Elizabeth's advisers were preoccupied by the problems of the royal marriage, the succession, and the Church. In spite of Mary's financial reforms, the Crown was in debt to the tune of £260,000–300,000. Society was shaken by the experience of bad harvests and epidemics: prices were high, labour short, and the currency still corrupted. In Ireland the Gaelic chiefs and the lords of the Pale had been alienated by aggressive policies under both Edward and Mary.[3]

Looking back from the perspective of the twentieth century the contrast between the dead Queen and her successor is striking: the elder sister brave

---

[1] John Strype, *Life of Sir Thomas Smith* (Oxford, 1820), 249. Smith had been Secretary of State under Somerset and was to hold the office again from 1572 until his death in 1577.

[2] Henry Gee, *The Elizabethan Prayer-Book* (London, 1902), 211.

[3] For a definition of the Pale see Ch. 1 n. 32.

and tenacious, yet lacking the presence to dominate or inspire her subjects, qualities so abundantly developed in the younger. The contrast is not only the product of hindsight, for the Spanish Ambassador, Feria, commented after an early interview with Elizabeth that 'she seems to me incomparably more feared than her sister and gives her orders and has her way as absolutely as her father did'. He added perceptively: 'she is a woman of extreme vanity, but acute.'[4] Her education had been entrusted to eminent scholars, Roger Ascham perhaps the most important, and her academic intelligence was high. Ascham said of her with more than a touch of male condescension: 'her mind has no womanly weakness, her perseverance is equal to that of a man, and her memory long keeps what it quickly picks up.'[5] She had an excellent knowledge of Latin, Greek, French, and Italian: she was even capable of losing her temper in Latin during an audience with the Ambassador of Poland. Yet she had had little or no training in the business of government, for her political education had been in the arts of survival. She had been wooed as a girl by Thomas Seymour, the Protector's brother, and had come dangerously near to being involved in his fall. Under Mary she had, as she herself later recalled, come to know the traps set around an heir apparent. Imprisoned in the Tower after Wyatt's rebellion, she had subsequently withdrawn from Court and waited upon events at Hatfield. The popular acclaim at her accession and her acceptance as Queen by Philip were a tribute to her capacity for manœuvre. The lessons she had learned from distinguished scholars and from adversity were invaluable, giving her the confidence to hold her own in debate and implanting a well-developed sense of political caution. Two other qualities were born within her and were apparent very early in her reign: the ability to choose first-rate advisers and a remarkable gift for winning the devotion of the public (Plate 2b).

Immediately she came to the throne Elizabeth made swift and sweeping changes among the leading ministers and courtiers. She had probably decided upon some of the most important appointments before her sister died and by January the rearrangements were complete. At the end of Mary's reign there had been thirty-nine councillors; Elizabeth reduced the number to nineteen, of whom only ten had served her sister. Seven great nobles were continued as councillors: the Marquis of Winchester, the Earls of Arundel, Derby, Pembroke, and Shrewsbury, Lord Clinton, and Lord Howard of Effingham, of whom only two had held administrative posts— Winchester as Lord Treasurer and Clinton as Lord Admiral. The earls

[4] *CSP Span.*, *Elizabeth*, i: *1558–1567*, 7; P. F. Tytler, *England under the Reigns of Edward VI and Mary* (London, 1839), ii. 498.
[5] J. E. Neale, *Queen Elizabeth* (London, 1934), 26.

were men of a stature that almost compelled their inclusion; Winchester had had long experience and had shown useful talents at the Exchequer; Howard was a kinsman to Elizabeth. Two administrators, Sir John Mason and Sir William Petre, were kept on, both of whom had served Henry VIII and Edward VI as well as Mary. Committed Catholics were, predictably, excluded. More surprising was the removal of that notable survivor Lord Paget, who expected to wield influence and was mortified at his exclusion. The new councillors were mostly Protestants. William Cecil, Elizabeth's first Secretary of State, was from the very start the man in whom she placed the greatest trust. Having risen swiftly to power in Somerset's entourage, he fell with his master in 1549, dexterously recovered to become Secretary in the following year, and withdrew from royal service at the accession of Mary. Even before Elizabeth's death, Feria had predicted that Cecil would become Secretary: 'he has the character of a prudent and virtuous man, although a heretic.'[6] Like many of Feria's comments it was a shrewd judgement. Cecil's brother-in-law Nicholas Bacon, now Lord Keeper of the Great Seal, was probably the most influential of the other councillors. He had served Mary in a middle-ranking post, but was certainly more at home under the Protestant Elizabeth. He was essentially a man for the middle way. In one of his poems he wrote:

> The surest state and best degree
> Is to possess mediocritye.

Of the rest, Sir Francis Knollys had gone into exile in Germany and was a zealous adherent of the reformed religion; Sir Edward Rogers had been involved in the conspiracy of Sir Thomas Wyatt; William Parr, Marquis of Northampton, had supported Lady Jane Grey; and Francis Russell, Earl of Bedford, was widely regarded as the aristocratic leader of the more ardent Protestants. One man, Sir Thomas Parry, who had been steward of the Princess Elizabeth's household and stayed close to her after her accession, was something of an enigma: his early death in 1560 ensured that he remained so.[7]

Elizabeth also made changes in the upper ranks of the royal Household. Devout Catholic courtiers like Edward, Lord Hastings, Sir Henry Jerningham, and Sir Edward Waldegrave were removed; and Sir Thomas Cheney, Treasurer of the Household, helpfully cleared the board by dying

---

[6] James Anthony Froude, *History of England from the Fall of Wolsey to the Defeat of the Spanish Armada* (London, 1898), vi. 118 n. 1.

[7] For a list of councillors, Penry Williams, *The Tudor Regime* (Oxford, 1979), 453; and for comments Wallace T. MacCaffrey, *The Shaping of the Elizabethan Regime* (London, 1969), ch. 2. The quotation from Bacon is in Patrick Collinson, *Godly People: Essays in English Protestantism* (London, 1983), 41.

in December 1558. By January the new high command of the Court was in post: Sir Thomas Parry was Treasurer of the Household; Sir Edward Rogers was Comptroller and Master of the Horse; Lord Howard of Effingham was Vice-Chamberlain. Only Sir John Mason, Treasurer of the Chamber, survived the purge of Marian officials. Mary's Catholic ladies-in-waiting were also dismissed, their places filled by relatives of the new Queen and of her councillors. The men and women newly promoted to places of trust in the Privy Council and at Court were predominantly opposed to the Marian regime and were inclined—in some cases more than inclined—to favour the Protestant cause. The Edwardian politicians had come back into harbour after five years on the open sea.

Elizabeth moved quickly to ensure public support. The date for her coronation was fixed, after consultation with the distinguished mathematician and astrologer John Dee, for Sunday, 15 January 1559; and a formal progress through the City of London was arranged for the previous day. There was not much time to prepare: scaffolds had to be erected for the City pageants; verses composed; robes and costumes created. The customs officers were instructed to impound any crimson silk entering the ports; sixteen yards of velvet were found for each of the thirty-nine attendant ladies; for the Queen herself a mantle was concocted out of twenty-three yards of gold and silver tissue. An enormous sum, £16,000—8 per cent of the annual royal income—was allocated to the expenses of the coronation ceremony, with further budgets for the ten-hour banquet that followed. On the Saturday the Queen passed through the City in formal procession from the Tower to Westminster. London was transformed into 'a stage wherein was shewed the wonderful spectacle of a noble-hearted Princess towards her most loving people'. Five separate 'pageants', or tableaux, were constructed on scaffolds along the route, to celebrate the accession of a worthy and Protestant ruler. The religious message was pronounced at the final stage, in Fleet Street, where Elizabeth was welcomed as Deborah, 'the judge and restorer of Israel'. Elizabeth herself, learning that she was to be presented with the Bible in English, thanked the City for their gift and demanded that she be given it at once. Making public her religious allegiance, she did not forget the personal touch. She responded graciously to every presentation, showing 'perpetual attentiveness in her face' when the endless verses were recited; she smiled at the mention of her father's name; she kept in her carriage, until she reached Westminster, a sprig of rosemary given by a poor woman.[8]

On the following day she was crowned in Westminster Abbey. Her

---

[8] *The Passage of our Most Dread Sovereign Lady, Queen Elizabeth* (1st pub. 1559 by R. Tothill), repr. in A. F. Pollard (ed.), *Tudor Tracts, 1532–1588* (London, n.d.), 365–95.

coronation service was the last to be performed in Latin rather than English; but the form of the service remains uncertain. It was once supposed that the Catholic Bishop Oglethorpe celebrated Mass, while Elizabeth withdrew into a separate closet to avoid the embarrassment earlier caused on Christmas Day when he had elevated the Host in her presence and she had at once left. However, more probably Oglethorpe performed the coronation ceremony itself, while George Carew, Dean of the Chapel Royal, celebrated Mass without elevating the Host. The incident illustrates the obscurity of religious events during these early months, an obscurity that continued until decisions were made on the government of the Church and on its liturgy. Once the coronation was over the Queen and her Council gave their main attention to this problem.

The principal lines of the settlement of religion in 1559 were laid down in four statutes carried during Elizabeth's first Parliament. In the Act of Supremacy papal authority was once more rejected and the monarch acquired the title of Supreme Governor of the Church, not, as Henry VIII had been acclaimed, Supreme Head. The difference was important: devout Protestants believed that only Christ could be Head of the Church, and that the Queen exercised power in his name. The Act of Uniformity ordered that services be conducted according to the rites of the second Edwardian Prayer Book of 1552, with various minor and three major alterations.[9] The holding of services by any other rites was forbidden, on pain of imprisonment, and absence from divine service was punishable by a fine of 1s. a week. The first significant amendment to the Edwardian Book was the omission of the 'black rubric' concerning kneeling.[10] The second ordered that the ornaments and vestments used in 1549, rather than 1552, should be retained for the time being 'until other order shall be therein taken'. The third was the addition of two sentences from the 1549 Book to those used in 1552 for the administration of the bread and wine in the communion service. This softened the 'Zwinglian' or commemorative tenor of the 1552 Book by implying that Christ was present, at least in some spiritual sense, in the elements.[11]

The other two statutes concerned Church property. One reversed Marian policy and restored the revenue derived from First Fruits and Tenths to the Crown.[12] The other, significantly debated at great length in Parliament since it involved questions of property, allowed the Crown, during the vacancy of episcopal sees, to hand over to the bishoprics the

---

[9] 1 Elizabeth cc. 1, 2. Below, Ch. 11 s. 1.
[10] For the black rubric see above, Ch. 3 s. 3.
[11] For details on the Prayer Book, below, Ch. 11 s. 1.   [12] 1 Elizabeth c. 4.

spiritual revenues it had temporarily acquired—tithes and so on—in exchange for their temporal revenues. It also prohibited bishops from leasing out their lands for more than twenty-one years—a sensible precaution in times of rising prices—except when the Crown was the lessee.[13] The Crown took less direct advantage of the opportunities for exchange than it might have done; but courtiers often secured long leases of Church lands through the agency of the Crown, which sublet to them. The threat of expropriation, foreseen by some foreign observers, never materialized; but the bishops were dangerously exposed to encroachment on their possessions by the monarch and her Court.

The manœuvres leading to the settlement of religion were complicated and obscure. A brief timetable of the proceedings in Parliament may help to present the scenario. Parliament met on 25 January 1559, and the supremacy bill, introduced by the Crown, was given its first reading on 9 February. Between 15 and 21 February it was amended in committee and sent to the Lords as a second supremacy bill. The Lords removed most or all of these amendments and returned the truncated version to the Commons, who passed it on 22 March. Meanwhile the Commons had carried a bill allowing worship to be conducted according to the 1552 Prayer Book: this bill, however, disappeared in the Lords. Elizabeth intended to prorogue or dissolve Parliament on 24 March, assenting to the supremacy bill as passed by the Commons; but either on the previous night or early that morning she adjourned it until after Easter, which fell on 26 March: no bills received royal assent at that point. While Parliament was in recess a public disputation was held at Westminster between Protestant and Catholic divines; not surprisingly it was inconclusive. After Parliament reassembled on 3 April the bill of supremacy and a new bill of uniformity, authorizing the modified version of the 1552 Prayer Book, passed the Commons easily and the Lords narrowly, following vigorous debate. Both bills received the royal assent on 8 May.

What interpretation is to be put on the amendments made to the various bills in both Commons and Lords, and on Elizabeth's change of mind on 23 and 24 March? Was the final settlement planned by the Crown or forced upon it by political and religious pressures? The traditional interpretation of events was based on the near-contemporary account of William Camden. He described the settlement as the successful outcome of royal policy, formed before Parliament assembled and set out in a document known as 'The Device for the Alteration of Religion'. This account was challenged in 1950 by the argument that Elizabeth wanted a liturgy based on the first

---

[13] 1 Elizabeth c. 19.

rather than the second Edwardian Prayer Book; that she intended to introduce only a supremacy bill in her first Parliament, leaving liturgical and doctrinal changes until later; and that this plan was frustrated by radical Protestant pressure-groups inside and outside the Commons, who forced her into an earlier and more 'advanced' settlement than she wished. If the settlement was a compromise, then it was not between Elizabeth and the Catholics, but between Elizabeth and the reformers, with most of the success going to the latter.[14] This analysis has been challenged in its turn.[15] Its critics argue that the main obstacles to Elizabeth's plans came from the House of Lords, in particular from the bishops, rather than from any radical group in the House of Commons; and they conclude that Elizabeth surmounted these obstacles to achieve a settlement broadly in accordance with her own plans and predilections.

Neither of these interpretations is wholly acceptable. The first exaggerates the role of radicals in the Commons and underestimates the influence of the Lords, while its critics fail to convince us that Elizabeth found the settlement altogether agreeable: her dispute with the Protestant bishops over her wish to retain the crucifix in the Royal Chapel is clear indication of that. The arguments are too complex for a full discussion here, and in any case the available evidence is slender and uncertain. Nevertheless, some conclusions seem at least plausible. First, Elizabeth intended from the beginning to restore royal authority over the Church and probably wished to introduce a Protestant service of some kind, though of what kind remains unclear. She had, after all, chosen Protestant advisers like Cecil and had publicly withdrawn from the Mass on Christmas Day when Bishop Oglethorpe elevated the Host. Secondly, Protestants were dominant in the Commons. The amendments made to the first supremacy bill transformed it into a measure for liturgical reform. But the House was not led by returned exiles, few of whom were back before the end of February; and it is significant that the committee which drafted the crucial amendments was headed by Sir Francis Knollys and Sir Anthony Coke, both of whom were connected to the regime. Thirdly, the Lords vigorously contested both the royal supremacy and the proposed liturgical changes, reluctantly accepting the former before Easter, but passing the latter only after two Marian bishops had been sent to the Tower. The delays in carrying the legislation

[14] J. E. Neale, 'The Elizabethan Acts of Supremacy and Uniformity', *EHR* 65 (1950), 304–32.
[15] W. S. Hudson, *The Cambridge Connection and the Elizabethan Settlement of Religion, 1559* (Durham, NC., 1980), *passim*; Norman L. Jones, *Faith by Statute: Parliament and the Settlement of Religion, 1559* (London, 1982), *passim*. Both authors, working independently, reach similar conclusions.

resulted more from the opposition of the Lords than from coolness on the part of the Queen. Yet several uncertainties remain about Elizabeth's attitude and the role of her leading advisers; and it is impossible to know exactly what plans were in the minds of government before Parliament met. The Queen was the key figure: she proposed the original measures and without her consent the final settlement could never have been reached. But others played a significant role. The dominant group in the Commons, directed probably by men close to the Court like Knollys and Coke, pressed for an unequivocal Protestantism. The Marian bishops and the conservative peers obstructed proposals for change and compelled Elizabeth to look for support to the Protestants in the Commons and to ministers returning from exile. She could hardly consent to the supremacy bill as amended by the Lords without antagonizing Protestants and she would not gain Catholic support by such a compromise. Hence, probably, her change of policy on 24 March, when she adjourned Parliament without giving assent to any bills. From that moment she was committed to a Protestant solution, not because she was forced to it by a pressure-group from the Commons, but because she needed Commons support against the Lords. Such an account, necessarily hypothetical, omits one important element: the privy councillors and courtiers. The most influential among them were committed Protestants: some, like Cecil, moderate but definite in their faith; others, like Knollys, zealous and unyielding. Such men operated within the walls of the Court and virtually nothing can be known of their manœuvres. Yet it is impossible to believe that they did not use their influence in support of the Protestant cause; and that influence may have been more important than any other in deciding Elizabeth's actions.

Although we cannot know all that we should wish about these events, collectively some of the most important in English history, their complexity does reveal something about Tudor politics. The Queen could not press through her policies without a good deal of difficulty and may well have had to modify her original intentions; yet there was no real confrontation between Crown and Commons. There was, however, confrontation between Crown and Lords, and between Lords and Commons. The settlement was the outcome of manœuvring, consultation, compromise, and adjustment, in which the Queen played the leading role, but in which the support of substantial groups in Court, Council, Parliament, and the clergy was necessary for a successful, that is to say an acceptable and lasting, outcome.

From May 1559 the Church had a Governor and a Prayer Book, but lacked bishops. With the notorious exception of Kitchen of Llandaff, the Marian bishops refused to accept the royal supremacy and were removed during the summer and autumn of 1559; Elizabeth evidently hoped that some at least would conform and postponed the final stage of deprivation in a few cases. However, her persuasions were in vain: Tunstall was the last to be deprived in September. The appointment of their successors was gradually achieved during 1559. Matthew Parker was nominated to Canterbury in July: a man of moderate views, he had been Master of Corpus Christi College, Cambridge, until the accession of Mary drove him into hiding, but not, significantly, into exile. He was a married man, a firm but temperate Protestant, a good scholar and administrator. Elizabeth chose five other bishops at the same time, most notably Richard Cox for Ely, Edmund Grindal for London, and John Jewel for Salisbury: all had been in exile under Mary. In the course of the following two years most of the remaining sees were gradually filled, although three were still vacant at the end of 1561. Fourteen of the bishops in the 1563 Convocation had gone into exile under Mary and six had lived in retirement; only five had continued to serve as priests during the Catholic regime. Yet the new bishops were not consecrated until December 1559 at the earliest—four Edwardian bishops, deprived under Mary, performing the ceremony—so that for nine months after the parliamentary statutes were carried Elizabeth ruled the Church directly. Injunctions for its government were issued during the summer. For the most part these followed the Edwardian Injunctions of 1547, commanding strict performance of duties by the clergy, the destruction of 'monuments of . . . idolatry', and the avoidance of contention and strife.[16] Reluctantly Elizabeth permitted the clergy to marry, pointing out that many had previously been indiscreet in their choice of wives. At the same time she appointed royal visitors to secure the subscription of the clergy to the royal supremacy. Only the visitation records for the northern province have survived: they indicate a fairly low proportion of refusals, about 90 out of 1,000, but a higher number of absentees. Outright refusal was rare among parish priests, commoner in cathedral chapters and the universities. The large numbers who avoided committing themselves suggest that the Elizabethan Church was a long way from winning firm support. But by the beginning of 1560 the foundation of that Church had been laid and Elizabeth was able to delegate the task of administering it to her bishops.[17]

While the religious bills were moving back and forth in Parliament, negotiations were proceeding to end the French war. Discussions between Spain, England, and France had begun in September 1558, had been adjourned at the death of Mary, and were reopened in February 1559. The

---

[16] Above, Ch. 2 s. 4; *Proclamations*, ii. 460.   [17] Below, Ch. 11 ss. 1, 2.

French and Spanish monarchies were virtually bankrupt. England had neither the arms, the men, nor the money to continue fighting: 'our state can no longer bear these wars', wrote Sir John Mason.[18] Although all parties desperately needed peace, the negotiations were not simple. Elizabeth was determined to secure the return of Calais but found the Spanish unwilling to help her unless England provided at least half the force required for its recovery. She also needed to conclude peace with the Scottish Queen, for 'the greatest burden of these our wars resteth upon Scotland'. In the end, fearing that the Spanish might themselves conclude a separate treaty, she conceded the matter of Calais. In April the Treaty of Câteau-Cambrésis was signed, bringing peace between Spain, France, England, and Scotland. The French were to keep Calais, but after eight years either to restore it or to pay an indemnity of 500,000 crowns. In the short term the treaty provided an essential respite for England; but it carried with it the alarming prospect that, once at peace, Spain and France might unite to restore Catholicism by force in their own dominions and in other countries. Although in reality this threat was remote, since Philip was unlikely to tolerate the accession of Mary Stewart and consequent French hegemony in England, the fear of a great Catholic alliance was to haunt English Protestants and to influence English policy for decades. More immediately menacing was the danger that the French, released from the pressure of war in Europe, might intervene more forcefully than before in Scotland.

For some years Mary of Guise, mother of Mary Stewart, had been acting as Regent of Scotland, where the Protestant cause had been making steady advances under the leadership of Lord James Stewart, Mary's half-brother, the Earl of Argyll, and other magnates. In 1557 they signed the Band of the Lords of the Congregation, promising to maintain the Protestant religion and to drive out the Catholics. Four further bands, or covenants, were made in the course of the next five years. To begin with, the Regent tolerated the Protestants, whose political support she needed; but the accession of Elizabeth altered the pattern of politics. The Regent could not risk the prospect of an alliance between Scottish Protestants and the English Queen, and she acted to suppress the movement. Against the threat and then the reality of persecution the Lords of the Congregation declared in May 1559 that they would take up arms unless 'this cruelty' ceased. Under their leadership and the self-proclaimed inspiration of John Knox, a broad attack was launched upon the Catholic Church. The death of Henry II in July brought Mary Stewart's husband Francis to the French throne and the Guise family to power in France. French policy turned more directly than before to achiev-

---

[18] MacCaffrey, *Shaping of Elizabethan Regime*, 42.

ing dominance in Scotland and to pressing the claims of the new Queen, Mary, to the English throne. In August French contingents landed at Leith and by the end of the year were beginning to establish themselves.

These events presented both a danger and an opportunity for England. The danger stemmed from the threat of French control over Scotland— 'the postern-gate of England'—and from Mary Stewart's claim to the English throne. The opportunity lay in an alliance with the Lords of the Congregation, which might permanently secure England's northern border. From the beginning, that usually cautious figure William Cecil urged intervention. He told Sir James Croft, the Governor of Berwick, to 'kindle the fire, for if it be quenched the opportunity will not come again in our lifetime'.[19] At first he advocated only moral support for the Protestant lords, but in August, following the French landings, he presented a long memorandum to Elizabeth. In it he avoided the striking phrases he had used to Croft and drew up a comprehensive list of arguments for and against more tangible aid. Although he seemed to be setting out both sides of the case in a balanced and objective manner, his conclusion cautiously favoured limited intervention. To begin with, money, but nothing else, was sent secretly to the Protestants. By December it was evident that this was not enough and that their position was critical. The whole issue was debated in the Privy Council, Cecil arguing that the French must be removed from Scotland to prevent them attacking England across the border. On the other side, his brother-in-law, Lord Keeper Bacon, contended that the English forces were too weak and Englishmen themselves too sharply divided over religion to risk war against France. By Christmas Eve Bacon and all his supporters, except the Earl of Arundel, had been won over to Cecil's policy. An address was presented to Elizabeth advocating the dispatch of a squadron of ships and the preparation of an expeditionary force on land of 5,000 men. The naval force, under William Winter, had in fact already left with instructions from the Council to say that they had been blown accidentally into the Firth of Forth. But Elizabeth rejected her Council's advice, endorsed by Cecil with the words 'not allowed by the Queen'. Cecil then made his biggest gamble. In conciliatory and deferential words he told Elizabeth that he could not continue to serve her if his advice was rejected. The threat of resignation is a card that can be played only seldom in politics. Cecil timed it well and the Queen gave way.

Winter's fleet reached the Firth of Forth in January 1560, cut off the Regent in Leith from the main French forces in Fifeshire, and blocked their supply lines. The Scots began at once to rally to the Protestant cause, and

[19] Read, *Cecil*, 142.

in March English troops entered Scotland under Lord Grey. Although the operations on land were disastrous and Grey's attack on Leith met with humiliating defeat, Winter's appearance had given the Scots heart and French resistance weakened. The Regent died in June as religious tumults were beginning to break out in France, and Cecil was sent north to conclude an agreement. At the Treaty of Edinburgh, signed on 6 July 1560, the French and English agreed to withdraw their forces and assurances were given on behalf of Mary Stewart that she would recognize Elizabeth's title as Queen of England and would allow liberty of worship to Scottish Protestants. The Reformed Church was established by the Scottish Parliament in August. Although the problem of the northern border had not been permanently resolved, an important step forward had been made. The decision to intervene illustrates once again the complexity of English politics, for policy was made, not by the Queen alone, but by debate and manœuvre among a small group of people. In that group Elizabeth had the most important voice; yet the decision had not been to her liking.

Mary Stewart returned to Scotland in August 1561 after the death of her husband, Francis II of France, in the previous December. The Franco-Scottish alliance was by then considerably looser than it had been. Mary herself was at this stage very different from the Papist *dévote* of later years. She heard Mass privately but was content to accept the Reformation; and she made no attempt to reimpose Catholicism. Her main concern lay outside Scotland altogether: she wished above all to secure the succession to the throne of England. Elizabeth insisted that before any concession be made Mary must cease to style herself 'Queen of England'. Mary would not give up her current title without an assurance for the future; and Elizabeth would not commit herself to that. A meeting between the two queens, agreed in July 1562, was indefinitely postponed, Elizabeth remarking that 'in assuring her [Mary] of the succession we might put our present state in doubt'.[20] Mary then refused to ratify the Treaty of Edinburgh. However, for the moment these disagreements were no great threat, since Mary left Scottish government largely to the Protestant party, in particular to her illegitimate half-brother Lord James Stewart, now Earl of Moray, and to William Maitland of Lethington, the 'Scottish Cecil'. The disagreements did of course complicate the whole question of the English succession, but Anglo-Scottish relations were relatively calm until Mary's marriage to Darnley in 1565.

That could not be said of Anglo-French relations. Since the death of

[20] Mortimer Levine, *The Early Elizabethan Succession Question, 1558–1568* (Stanford, Calif., 1966), 35.

Henry II in 1559 civil tension had been steadily mounting in France in spite of the efforts of the Queen Dowager, Catherine de Medici, to bring the Catholic Guise party to an accommodation with the Huguenots under the Prince de Condé and Admiral Coligny. In April 1562 civil war broke out and Elizabeth's ambassador at Paris, the outspokenly Protestant Sir Nicholas Throckmorton, urged support for the Huguenot cause: 'you must', he wrote to Cecil, 'animate and solicit the Princes Protestant with speed by all means you can, not to suffer the Protestants to be in this realm suppressed.'[21] Cecil supported his plea, arguing strongly that the victory of the Guise faction would bring France into close alliance with Spain, imperilling Protestants generally and the realm of England in particular. Lord Robert Dudley, Cecil's rival, had already been in contact with the Huguenot leaders and warmly supported the proposal, so that Elizabeth was faced with a united front of advisers. This in itself would not necessarily have persuaded her; but she hoped to extract some benefit to herself from the French wars and insisted that English troops occupy Le Havre in the Protestant interest, exchanging it for Calais when the war was over. She concluded a treaty with the Huguenots along those lines in August and English troops under the command of Lord Ambrose Dudley, Robert's brother, entered Le Havre and Dieppe. A combined force of English and Huguenots failed to relieve the siege of Rouen, and Dieppe soon fell to the Catholics. In March 1563 the Huguenots and Catholics made peace, leaving Warwick's forces trapped in Le Havre under savage attack from the plague. Elizabeth's demands for Calais alienated all sections of French opinion and no help was forthcoming. In July Warwick's demoralized and depleted army returned home. The war was in effect over, although the Treaty of Troyes was not signed until the following year. Unlike the intervention in Scotland, the expedition to France had been a humiliating failure, costly above all in lives carried off by plague. Elizabeth became more reluctant than ever to engage in foreign campaigns and Cecil's approach became more cautious.

The security of the realm depended ultimately upon the succession to the throne, and practical politics dictated that Elizabeth should marry. The most favoured foreign suitor was the Archduke Charles, third son of the Holy Roman Emperor and first cousin to Philip II of Spain. If Philip were not to marry Elizabeth himself, he preferred that she marry into the Austrian branch of the Habsburgs. From 1560 until almost the end of the decade the Archduke was dangled before Elizabeth: the wooing was pro-

---

[21] Read, *Cecil*, 244.

longed, tepid, and ultimately ineffective. Emotionally more serious was
the Queen's affair with Lord Robert Dudley, younger son of the Duke of
Northumberland. Dudley was no mere adventurer, reliant on his handsome
looks and courtly manners, although he exploited these in full measure. He
was the leader of a powerful political following, inherited from the days of
his father's dominance and including his brother Ambrose, Earl of Warwick, the Earl of Bedford, and Sir Henry Sidney. Almost exactly the same
age as Elizabeth, he had known her well from her childhood and shared the
same tutor, Roger Ascham. From the beginning of her reign he had been
active in obtaining patronage for laymen and clerics; and early in 1560 there
were rumours that he was planning a divorce from his wife Amy Robsart
in order to marry the Queen. There is little doubt that Elizabeth was
strongly attracted and that Dudley was hoping to marry her. Nicholas
Throckmorton, ambassador to the French Court, insisted that Cecil 'do
all your endeavour to hinder that marriage', for if it took place 'God and
religion will be out of estimation; the Queen discredited, condemned and
neglected'.[22] Cecil himself, in a remarkable conversation with the Spanish
Ambassador, Bishop de Quadra, talked of resigning his office and retiring
into the country. It is unlikely that he intended anything of the sort, more
probable that he hoped to use de Quadra's offices to convince Elizabeth
that the marriage would be unwise. However, Dudley's path seemed to
be cleared in September by the mysterious death of his wife, found at
the bottom of a staircase with her neck broken. It is improbable that she
was murdered, more likely that she was weak and ill. But the scandal
made Elizabeth draw back, and although Dudley continued to press his
suit, himself now using de Quadra as go-between, the affair was dead. Its
significance is not easily assessed. Foreign ambassadors sent highly
coloured reports to their masters; and Throckmorton, writing from
France, was shrill in opposition. There is little doubt that Cecil, Norfolk,
Throckmorton, and many privy councillors saw Dudley's pretensions as a
dangerous threat and did their successful best to prevent the marriage by
convincing Elizabeth of its unpopularity. But it does not follow that Cecil
wished to oust Dudley from the political scene. Dudley's following was too
influential for that to be achieved; and, once the danger of marriage had
receded, Cecil was reconciled to him, earning Dudley's thanks for his help.
The two men remained rivals for power and influence, and they differed
over certain aspects of policy; but for the most part their rivalry was friendly
and contained. The comparative harmony of Elizabethan Court politics was
enhanced in 1561, when de Quadra opened intrigues with Catholic noble-

[22] MacCaffrey, *Shaping of Elizabethan Regime*, 75.

men to secure the admission of the papal nuncio to England. Although Dudley seems to have manœuvred on the fringes of this affair, the main actors were ex-councillors of Queen Mary. Cecil intercepted the chaplain to one of them, Sir Edward Waldegrave, who implicated his master and other Catholics. The discovery discredited the remnants of the Marian faction, killed the plan for bringing over the nuncio, and confirmed Cecil's authority.

Unfortunately, as long as Elizabeth remained unmarried, the political sky was clouded by the question of the succession. Among various possible claimants, only two were serious contenders: Mary Stewart and Lady Catherine Grey, sister of Lady Jane. As a Catholic, Mary was unacceptable to the dominant Protestant group at Court and had ruled herself out in Elizabeth's eyes by refusing to give up her title of 'Queen of England'.[23] Lady Catherine was the least unacceptable Protestant candidate, but late in 1560 she secretly married the young Earl of Hertford, son of the Duke of Somerset, and was found in August 1561 to be 'big with child'. A commission of inquiry, headed by the Archbishop of Canterbury, found the marriage to be invalid, as Elizabeth had probably intended that they should, and the couple were sent to the Tower. However, although Catherine Grey and her illegitimate progeny were damned in the eyes of the Queen, the Protestant lobby continued to support her. The play *Gorboduc*, performed in January 1562, portrayed the dangers of a Scottish succession and advocated the claims of the English line. In October of that year Elizabeth fell critically ill of smallpox and the menace of a disputed succession came alarmingly close. John Hales, Somerset's tactless adviser, wrote a tract in favour of Lady Catherine and joined her in the Tower. The House of Commons petitioned Elizabeth in 1563 to name a successor and warned her against the threat from Mary Stewart; but the Queen refused their request. At the end of that year the issues of marriage and succession were still undecided, as they remained until Elizabeth's death.

Wretched harvests, mortal epidemics of influenza in 1557 and 1558, and heavy expenditure on war had combined to present the government with social, military, and financial problems at least as pressing as religious dissensions. There were many signs that the conjunction of dearth and epidemic had inflicted alarming wounds upon society. The population, which rose steadily through most of the sixteenth century, fell in the last two years of Mary's reign.[24] Labourers were said to be 'out of obedience',

---

[23] Above, p. 240; Genealogical Tables 1, 2.   [24] Above, Ch. 4 s. 4.

deserting their masters and demanding excessive wages; apprentices were becoming undisciplined; vagabonds and thieves abounded. Contemporary comment probably exaggerated the problems: the previous abundance of labour had temporarily disappeared and the poor were momentarily in a better position to make their own terms. Yet for landowners and employers this was a threat of anarchy or, at least, a warning sign of the 'looseness of the times'.

Several bills were introduced into the Parliament of 1559 to deal with these problems, but none passed into law. During the next four years both central government and local authorities tried to establish some order. The Council in the North rebuked the corporations of Hull and York for their failure to enforce the laws. In particular, it told them to ensure that 'none to take more wages than hereafter is declared', enclosing the schedule of wage rates for 1514, by now deeply eroded by inflation.[25] Rather surprisingly, there was some response to this: at York assizes in January 1562, 113 labourers were indicted for taking unlawfully high wages; and in Northamptonshire, Buckinghamshire, Worcester, and elsewhere local orders were issued laying down the appropriate wages and compelling all to work at their trades when required. The culmination of these tentative and sometimes contradictory efforts by national and local rulers came with the celebrated 'Statute of Artificers' in 1563.[26] This Act sanctioned compulsory labour, especially in harvest time; imposed a minimum period of one year for the hire of workmen, during which they could not leave their masters or be dismissed without good cause; forbade anyone to practise a craft without having first served an apprenticeship of seven years; and ordered JPs in every shire to fix maximum rates for wages. None of this interference by government with 'labour relations' was unprecedented; but the statute brought together, within the confines of a single Act, regulations governing employment, apprenticeship, and wages. Furthermore, it abandoned the principle enshrined in a statute of 1389, which laid down national maximum wages but also allowed local justices freedom of action.[27] The origins and nature of the Statute of Artificers have been much debated. Its principal measures seem to have been prepared by the Council, although clauses were undoubtedly added, revised, and possibly abandoned as the bill proceeded through Parliament. While it is hard to be certain about the extent of parliamentary amendments, we can be sure that the Crown's advisers, as well as local justices and town corporations, were deeply concerned that the shortage of labour following the recent famine and pestilence should not allow workers to push up wages, abandon their em-

---

[25] Donald Woodward, 'The background to the Statute of Artificers', *EcHR* 33 (1980), 37.
[26] 5 Elizabeth c. 4.   [27] 13 Richard II c. 8.

ployers, leave the fields unharvested, or enter crafts for which they were not trained.[28]

While the government was grappling with the problems of the labour market it also set itself the task of restoring the currency. Northumberland's attempted reforms had been incomplete, leaving a great deal of debased coinage circulating alongside the sounder coins struck since 1551, and plans formulated under Mary for a further reform had been postponed. A few months after Elizabeth's accession a new commission was appointed to devise a scheme, and in 1560 a proclamation was issued to reduce the value of debased coins by 25 per cent or more. The base testons, once worth 1s., reduced to 6d. by Northumberland, were now 'called down' yet again to 4½ d., and some of the most heavily adulterated coins to even less than that. Holders of debased coinage were encouraged to bring it into the mint where they would be recompensed with new good coins, according of course to the reduced face value of their money. The reduction in value was justified by the argument, at least partly sound, that the debased coins caused prices to 'grow daily excessive to the lamentable and manifest hurt of the state', especially of pensioners, soldiers, and wage-earners.[29] The Queen insisted that she would 'sustain the burden' of the operation; but this, as the government must have known, was the opposite of the truth. The total amount of currency in circulation before the reforms was about £1,700,000, of which about £1 million was debased. This debased coin was bought by the government below its true value and converted into £670,000 of new fine currency. The government made a profit of £50,000 on the process of reminting, the loss being borne by those unlucky enough to hold debased currency. However, it can at least be said that the Crown did not again resort to debasement in the sixteenth century, and for the rest of Elizabeth's reign the country benefited from a sound and stable currency.

Fiscal problems darkened the accession of Elizabeth, as they had done in 1547 and 1553. With an ordinary revenue of about £200,000 per annum the Crown could pay its way satisfactorily in times of peace, Mary's reform of the customs duties having raised that source of revenue from about £30,000 to £80,000. In the long run the situation was reasonably favourable; but Mary's wars had left a debt of almost £300,000, about two-thirds of it to

[28] See S. T. Bindoff, 'The making of the Statute of Artificers', in S. T. Bindoff et al. (eds.), *Elizabethan Government and Society: Essays Presented to Sir John Neale* (London, 1961), 56–94; review of above by Penry Williams, in *EcHR* 14 (1961), 141–4; Woodward, 'Background to the Statute of Artificers'; G. R. Elton, *The Parliament of England, 1559–1581* (Cambridge, 1986), 263–5.

[29] *TED* ii. 195–9.

English creditors. In the first two years of her reign Elizabeth paid off about £130,000 of the domestic debt, but this operation, combined with some heavy purchases of armaments abroad, raised the debt on the Antwerp bourse to £280,000 by the early months of 1560. Serious as this might be, the problem of debt was not uncontrollable; and effective management combined with parliamentary subsidies had probably placed government finances on a reasonably firm foundation by about 1563.

By the end of that year the immediate threats which had faced Elizabeth at her accession had been removed or at least diminished. She had established her own political control, exercised through privy councillors and household officers entirely loyal to her and to her religious policy. The danger of religious dissension had been removed by a settlement which, if not welcomed by all, was tolerated by most. Elizabeth's withdrawal from the Dudley marriage had smoothed relations between the leading politicians at Court, although the major question of the succession to the throne and its accompanying problem of the royal marriage remained. The French had been expelled from Scotland and relations with Spain were improving. True, England was still technically at war with France, but the Treaty of Troyes was to bring peace in 1564. In Scotland Mary was ruling in an apparently moderate style and seemed anxious to negotiate with Elizabeth. Although the rebellion of Shane O'Neill was disrupting Ireland, this was not a serious danger to English security as long as relations with France and Spain remained tolerably harmonious.[30] For the moment the political situation of Queen and kingdom seemed reasonably settled, although relations between England and the Habsburg government in the Netherlands were deteriorating to the point at which, in the last months of 1563, the Spanish Regent imposed an embargo on English exports.

2. THE YEARS OF PEACE, 1564–1568

Compared with the risings in the Netherlands and the intensified religious struggles in France, events in England between 1564 and 1568 were relatively undramatic. There was, it is true, manœuvre, dispute, and debate between the Queen and her councillors over the linked questions of Elizabeth's marriage and the succession to the throne. If the first could be solved, then, with luck, the second would be settled in the course of nature. But as long as Elizabeth held back from marriage the question of her successor lay wide and dangerously open. Most of her advisers hoped that Elizabeth would marry—though Dudley may have envisaged only himself as bride-

[30] Below, s. 4.

groom. Cecil pressed continuously for a marriage, even though it would probably have weakened his own influence. Unfortunately the available candidates were few and unsatisfactory. Dudley, created Earl of Leicester in 1564, was no longer a realistic competitor; and Elizabeth was to offer him to Mary. The most serious foreign contender was, as before, the Archduke Charles, whose suit was revived, somewhat tentatively in 1563, and with increasing enthusiasm on the part of most privy councillors in the following three years. However, negotiations proved abortive in 1567, when the Earl of Sussex was sent to the Imperial Court. The Habsburgs insisted that Charles should be allowed to practise his own religion in private. The English Council was divided in its response: Cecil, Norfolk, and their allies would accept the terms as a basis for negotiation; Leicester, Northampton, Knollys, and others were for immediate rejection. Elizabeth refused to allow her husband the right to worship separately and the matter was ended. It is improbable that Elizabeth's religious feelings really decided the matter; more likely she did not seriously intend to marry at all at this stage. The only other, half-serious, candidate proposed for her was Charles IX of France. Leicester and his new adviser Sir Nicholas Throckmorton seem to have been the promoters of this scheme, probably as a blocking tactic to stop the Austrian marriage. It was certainly not a serious proposition, for Elizabeth was twice the age of the 15-year-old French King and the problems created by a match between two reigning monarchs, of different religions, would have been insoluble.

With marriage a distant prospect, the question of the succession had to be decided. Catherine Grey's standing with Elizabeth was low, and her sister Lady Mary put herself out of the running by marrying the Serjeant Porter of the Court. The Earl of Huntingdon had a remote claim through his descent from the Duke of Clarence, and was pushed forward by some Protestant courtiers; but he had no ambition for the throne and could not be considered a serious candidate. Support for Catherine Grey survived, although her chances, given Elizabeth's hostility, were slim; and the most likely candidate was Mary Stewart. Although her religion made her objectionable to fervent Protestants, she had accepted the Protestant settlement in Scotland, while maintaining her own right to Catholic worship. Given a satisfactory Protestant husband she did not seem an impossible sovereign for England; and this would appear to have been Elizabeth's view, although she still held out against recognizing Mary as her heir. The crucial question was Mary's own marriage. She herself considered various suitors: Charles IX of France, Don Carlos of Spain, the Archduke Charles—much the same team as had competed unsuccessfully for Elizabeth. Diplomatic pressures of various kinds ruled out each of them; and then, in 1564, Elizabeth

proposed her own domestic ex-suitor, Robert Dudley. The proposal, surprising as it may seem, made political sense for England, since Mary would
be tied to a Protestant and English consort. But psychologically it could not
be taken seriously, for Mary had no intention of allying herself to a commoner, more particularly to her cousin's rejected suitor. The Scots regarded it as a manœuvre by Elizabeth to hamper Mary's other plans and
tried to use it as a ploy for securing Elizabeth's recognition of Mary as heir
to her throne. Such recognition Elizabeth adamantly refused. In 1565 Mary
broke off the dilatory negotiations by marrying another cousin, Henry
Darnley, thus uniting two claims to the English throne. The marriage was
disastrous for Mary's position in Scotland, while for Elizabeth it marked the
end of her attempts to control Mary through a husband.[31] In seriously
diminishing Mary's qualifications as Elizabeth's successor the marriage had
momentous consequences in English politics.

This was the situation when Parliament met in 1566, shortly after the
birth of an heir, later to be James VI and I, to Mary. Parliament had been
summoned to provide money for easing the Crown's serious financial difficulties, but its members took the opportunity to raise publicly the issue of
the royal marriage and succession. The discussions and debates that ensued
in the Privy Council and in Parliament highlighted the central problems of
Elizabeth and her advisers at this juncture, summed up by Cecil in a
memorandum for the Council.[32]

To require both marriage and the establishment of the succession is the uttermost
that can be desired.
    To deny both is the uttermost that can be denied.
    To require marriage is most natural, most easy, most plausible to the Queen.
    To require certainty of succession is most plausible to all people.
    To require the succession is hardest to be obtained, both for the difficulty to
discuss the right and for the loathsomeness in the Queen's Majesty to consent
thereto.

At the Council, with Elizabeth herself present, the Duke of Norfolk,
supported by the rest of the board, urged Elizabeth to allow Parliament to
discuss both marriage and succession. She would have none of it and left the
Council Chamber. In Parliament speaker after speaker urged upon her the
need for her to marry and to secure the succession. She replied in a formal
speech to delegates from both Houses that she had already promised to

---

[31] Below, p. 252. Darnley was descended through his mother from Margaret Tudor, the
elder sister of Henry VIII, by her second husband, the Earl of Angus; he was first cousin to
both Mary Stewart and Elizabeth I, Henry VII having been great-grandfather to Mary and
Darnley, grandfather to Elizabeth. See Genealogical Table 2.
[32] Read, *Cecil*, 357.

marry, which should be enough for them, and that her own experience as heir to the throne, as 'second person', convinced her of the dangers of naming a successor. 'At present it is not convenient [to do so], nor never shall be without some peril unto you and certain danger unto me.' She ended with a rebuke to the members for daring to advise her on such matters: 'it is monstrous that the feet should direct the head.'[33] In the end, after a protest in the Commons, Elizabeth withdrew her veto on debate and remitted one-third of the subsidy requested—no great concession, for the original demand had been 50 per cent bigger than was usual. However, her tactics worked, for no further pressure was exerted by the Commons.

Late in the session six bills on religion were introduced into the Commons. Labelled by the Clerk of the House with the letters A to F, they became known as the 'alphabetical bills' and have often been regarded as part of a concerted puritan drive to reform the Church. Although Elizabeth disapproved of them, they were not specifically puritan, having the general approval of the bishops. Bill A was designed to give statutory authority to the Thirty-nine Articles, which had been approved by Convocation in 1563; bill B enforced episcopal control over preaching; and the remainder attempted to purge the clergy of such abuses as absenteeism, simony, and so on. These were all moderate reforming measures which won the support of the Church hierarchy, William Cecil, and many other councillors. The Commons concentrated on bill A, allowing the others to remain in suspension after each had had a first reading. Having been carried in the Commons, bill A was sent up to the Lords, where Elizabeth ordered its progress to be halted. After a protest from the bishops, the Upper House complied: and no more was heard of any of the bills until 1571, when they were again brought forward.[34] Once again Elizabeth had frustrated the expectations of a sizeable body of her servants, including Cecil, who commented gloomily on the session as a whole in a 'Memorial to the Queen at the end of Parliament': 'The succession not answered. The marriage not followed. A subsidy to be levied [the one bright note from his point of view]. The oppression of informers not amended. . . . The bill of religion stayed, to the comfort of the adversaries.' He went on to enumerate the 'dangers ensuing', which included 'general discontentations' and 'danger of sedition'.[35]

[33] Hartley, *Proceedings*, 148.

[34] The 'alphabetical bills' were described as a 'planned drive' in Neale, *Parliaments*, i. 165–9. A contrary and more convincing view is given in Elton, *The Parliament of England*, 205–7. Below, p. 260, for the session of 1571.

[35] Neale, *Parliaments*, i. 170.

The political leaders of the country had been united in demanding of Elizabeth that she marry and name a successor. However, they were disunited in proposing candidates for either role; and in that disagreement lay her ability to frustrate them. Sussex, Norfolk, and Cecil supported the Austrian match; Leicester opposed it; some urged Mary Stewart as successor; others feared her religion. Disputes over policy were inflamed by personal antagonism. Leicester and Norfolk had quarrelled in the tennis-court: while the occasion was trivial—Norfolk resented Leicester's borrowing the Queen's napkin to wipe his brow—its very triviality suggested deeper resentments. Leicester and Sussex disagreed about Ireland, where Sussex had been Governor, and their tempers ran so high that Sussex claimed his life was in danger. But Cecil did not regard these rivalries as dangerous. Men no longer thought that Elizabeth would marry Leicester, yet he had sufficient favour for 'his good satisfaction'; Norfolk 'loveth my Lord of Sussex earnestly, and so all that stock of the Howards seem to join in friendship together, and yet in my opinion without cause to be misliked'; and as for himself, Cecil insisted that 'I have no affection to be of a party'. In this he was probably speaking the truth, for although he was much more favourably inclined to Norfolk—'a father and a stay to this country'— he tried, with some success, to keep on good terms with all the major courtiers.[36] Although there were strong friendships and animosities, it would be wrong to see the Court divided between factions: unity of aim and purpose generally overrode personal discord.

The dangers to Elizabeth and to England in these years came from without. Anglo-Habsburg dissension had already appeared in 1563 when Philip II's Regent in the Netherlands, Margaret of Parma, imposed an embargo upon the English cloth trade to Antwerp. Her action arose partly from disputes between her government in Brussels and the Privy Council in London over the activities of English pirates in the Channel, partly from Habsburg resentment at the reception given to Dutch refugees in England, and, most important perhaps, from the hope of her principal adviser, Cardinal Granvelle, that the cessation of trade would disrupt the English economy and polity to the advantage of Philip II. Granvelle's hopes were vain: although the embargo caused unsold cloths to pile up in England and brought some hardship to Antwerp, the English government found an alternative mart at Emden. This, although not entirely satisfactory, enabled the export of English cloth to be resumed and demonstrated that the trade was not dependent upon Antwerp, a considerable source of strength to Elizabeth's negotiations. The embargo was lifted in January 1565 and the

[36] Read, *Cecil*, 331–2. For Ireland, below, s. 4.

Merchant Adventurers returned to Antwerp. The episode was in itself a minor interruption to commerce, but it foreshadowed greater events.[37]

In 1566 economic grievances and Protestant discontent combined to produce massive rioting in Antwerp and other cities of the Low Countries. Margaret temporized and issued a general pardon to the offenders, which she was at once forced by Philip to revoke. The Duke of Alba was dispatched to the Netherlands in 1567 with a large army and instructions to destroy all opposition. His brutal treatment of the populace rekindled the revolt, gave it a unity which it had previously lacked, and provided a leader in William of Orange. To all these events English merchants had been merely passive spectators, but, as Alba won military control, England became involved. The importance of the Antwerp trade and the presence of Dutch exiles, the Sea Beggars, in English ports, made it impossible for Elizabeth to remain aloof for long. Alba's march to the Netherlands at the head of Spanish troops sounded the alarm to European Protestants, who saw in this the opening move to restore Catholic dominance in Western Europe: fears that had been provoked by a meeting between Alba and Catherine de Medici at Bayonne in 1565 were now intensified. Suspicions of an impending alliance between Spain and France for the destruction of the 'true religion' were certainly false, but they linked the French and Dutch revolts in the pattern of European politics, and drew England slowly into the contest.

Most immediately threatening were events in Scotland. With the expulsion of the French in 1560 the Scottish Parliament had abolished the Mass, broken with papal jurisdiction, and ratified the Confession of Faith, which affirmed Protestant doctrine and worship. Yet the Reformation in Scotland remained incomplete. The population was still very largely Catholic; the Catholic clergy continued to receive their revenues; the monasteries remained in being; and the secular-minded Parliament refused to ratify the Book of Discipline which would have established the Calvinist clergy in power. Mary Stewart, therefore, inherited a volatile and uncertain situation when she returned to Scotland from France in 1561. Yet she made no attempt to exploit it in favour of her co-religionists. Concerned mainly with the succession to the English throne, she was content to leave the government of Scotland to the largely Protestant Council. She also accepted legislation passed by the Parliament of 1563 to strengthen the Protestant Church; and she supported the Protestant Moray in his feud with the Catholic Earl of Huntly, whose title and possessions were forfeited to the Crown.

[37] Below, s. 3, for the events of 1569–72.

This uneasy situation, in which Protestants effectively ruled on behalf of a Catholic Queen, ended with Mary's marriage, by Catholic rites, to Henry, Lord Darnley, in July 1565.[38] Moray, supported by a section of the Protestant nobility, left the Council and went into rebellion against the Queen. He was easily defeated and fled to England in October. Other Protestants, such as Maitland, remained loyal to Mary, although she was now looking for support to their rivals and encouraging a Catholic revival. Darnley almost at once turned out to be unsatisfactory both as a husband—except in his fathering of James VI—and also as a king. Drunken, idle, and arrogant, he neglected government business, antagonized the nobles, and alienated his wife. Mary came to rely for advice and support upon foreigners in her largely Catholic Household, principally upon her secretary David Rizzio. Her relations with him caused a scandal that led to an alliance between Darnley, who was jealous of Rizzio, and the Protestant lords, now once more united, this time against Mary's foreign and Catholic favourite. The murder of Rizzio in Holyrood Palace, almost in the Queen's presence, followed in March 1566; and, after an interlude during which Mary seemed momentarily to have control, the Protestants under Moray regained power.

In June Mary gave birth to her son, a personal triumph for her, but one which was to be short-lived. To free herself from Darnley, Mary looked to the men responsible for the murder of Rizzio, in particular to the Protestant Earl of Morton, and to James Hepburn, Earl of Bothwell, soon to be her lover. In February 1567 the Edinburgh house in which Darnley was staying, Kirk o'Field, was blown up and his dead body was discovered in the garden. He had died from suffocation, probably by one of Morton's adherents. There followed Bothwell's capture of Mary, her alleged rape, and their marriage by Protestant rites. Mary had scandalized her subjects and tied herself to a Protestant noble who was hated by his co-religionists and by the Catholics. A new bond was signed, for 'rescuing' Mary from her husband; and the army of its signatories, the 'confederate lords', met Mary's forces at Carberry Hill. Her troops failed to fight; and she herself was captured and compelled to abdicate. Moray, of whom it had earlier been prophesied that he would 'look through his fingers thereto, and behold our doings, saying nothing to the same', returned to Scotland and to power as Regent.[39] It seemed that he and the Protestants had finally defeated their Queen. But in the following May, 1568, Mary escaped from imprisonment and won considerable support from men who had earlier opposed her but

[38] Above, n. 31.
[39] The phrase was Maitland's, quoted in Jenny Wormald, *Mary Queen of Scots: A Study in Failure* (London, 1988), 160.

now condemned her deposition. She failed to capitalize on this success and her troops were defeated at Langside, near Glasgow. Mary fled south and reached England, abandoning her supporters and presenting the English government with the apparently intractable problem of dealing with a dangerous royal prisoner.

3. THE CRISIS YEARS, 1568–1572

During 1568 the clouds which had been gathering in Scotland and across the Channel darkened the English sky. In the spring the English envoy at Madrid, John Man, was refused access to the Spanish Court. Man, a Protestant cleric, had been a strange appointment in the first place, and was foolish enough to abuse the Pope and the Catholic religion. Although Cecil protested, he was recalled and no successor was appointed. At almost the same time Guzman de Silva, the Spanish Ambassador in London, who had maintained friendly personal relations with Elizabeth's advisers, was replaced by the blustering Guerau de Spes. England and Spain were therefore less well represented than before at a time when serious problems were affecting their relations. One source of tension arose from English incursions into the West Indies, where the Spanish Crown had imposed a strict embargo on foreign trade. Since Spanish merchants were unable to supply the needs of the colonists, especially in slaves, a flourishing but illicit commerce was developing between English traders and the Caribbean. The most successful entrepreneur was John Hawkins of Plymouth, who made his first, and highly profitable, slaving voyage in 1562, followed by a second in 1564. Three years later Elizabeth authorized a third voyage, in spite of Spanish protests. In September 1568, after selling his slaves, Hawkins put in at the port of San Juan de Ulúa, on the mainland of the Gulf of Mexico, where the Spanish attacked him, capturing one of his three ships. The incident was not, in itself, more than an irritant in Anglo-Spanish relations, but it came at a time when irritants were best avoided, and was a forerunner of later, more dramatic, English incursions into the Spanish Empire.

News of the so-called 'massacre' of San Juan reached England at almost the same moment as four ships from Spain were driven by storms and Huguenot privateers into various harbours along the southern coast of England. They carried money, amounting to about £85,000, which was being loaned by Genoese bankers to Philip II for the payment of his troops in the Netherlands. Technically this money still belonged to the Genoese and might therefore be borrowed from them by the English Crown. While some at Court and in the Council favoured this course, mercantile opinion was largely opposed to it, in view of the possible reprisals. But the bullion could hardly stay safely on board the ships, where it was vulnerable to the Huguenots, and Cecil ordered that it be landed, to which the Spanish captain somewhat reluctantly agreed. In London, Philip's Ambassador, de Spes, took a different view: assuming, on very little evidence, that Cecil intended to seize the treasure he urged Alba to arrest all English merchants in the Netherlands and to impound all English shipping and cloth. With considerable misgivings Alba complied, and Elizabeth responded by imprisoning Spanish traders and ordering the bullion to be taken to the Tower. The embargo episode of 1563 was now replayed, with much more serious consequences.[40] While Cecil and Elizabeth had perhaps aroused the suspicions of de Spes by concealing their own intentions, and while he had been understandably alarmed at the anti-Spanish feeling in London provoked by the news of San Juan, his own rash and premature demand to Alba was largely responsible for the subsequent events, which brought about precisely what he had intended to avoid—the loss of the bullion.

Unfortunately, this rupture in Anglo-Spanish relations occurred at the moment when the English government was trying to solve the problem of Mary Stewart. Since her arrival in May 1568 the Scottish Queen had appealed insistently to Elizabeth for help in securing her restoration. Elizabeth, although determined to avoid any meeting with her cousin, was not entirely averse to helping her; but her mind, as so often, oscillated between different policies. Sometimes she favoured giving a hearing to the case put forward by the Regent, Moray, and his allies, sometimes she proposed that Mary be restored to power. The Council was adamantly opposed to any restoration and got its way. What then was to be done with Mary? As Cecil unhappily commented, if she were sent to France she would find support for her claim to the English Crown; if she were restored to the throne of Scotland the friends of England would be 'abased'; and if she were kept in England she would conspire with her friends, 'for no man can think but [that] such a sweet bait would make concord betwixt them all'.[41] He recommended that if Moray wished Elizabeth to hear the charges against Mary then Elizabeth should consent. The English Council urged Moray to make the strongest possible case against Mary in order to weaken her position, and Moray responded by producing the celebrated 'casket letters', allegedly (and probably) written by Mary to Bothwell, implicating her in the plot to murder Darnley. Mary refused to answer the charges, except with a general denial and an assertion of 'the word of a princess'. The hearing could go no further: the Regent returned to Scotland and Mary was held prisoner in

[40] Above, p. 250. I have followed the account of this episode in G. D. Ramsay, *The Queen's Merchants and the Revolt of the Netherlands* (Manchester, 1986), chs. 5–8.
[41] *CSP Scot.* ii: *1563–1569*, 418–19.

England at the Earl of Shrewsbury's castle at Tutbury. A decision had been taken, leaving the problem unsolved, but for the present contained.

Early in 1569 Cecil wrote, probably for the Queen, 'A Short Memorial of the State of the Realm', summarizing clearly and at length the dangers that confronted the kingdom.[42] 'The perils are many, great and imminent', he sombrely began; the 'recovery of the tyranny of Rome' was supported by the great monarchies of France and Spain, where the Huguenots and the Dutch rebels were near to defeat. This danger was heightened by 'the pretence and earnest desire to have the Queen of Scots possess this Crown of England'. Against this combined menace of France, Spain, the Pope, and Mary Stewart, Elizabeth's resources were slender. Undoubtedly Cecil exaggerated the strength and coherence of the Catholic alliance: Spain and the Pope, for instance, were in sharp disagreement. Yet his analysis reflected the fears of many English Protestants, who viewed international politics in essentially religious terms. Cecil did not advocate open intervention abroad against these perils, for he had no desire to repeat the disastrous expedition to France, but proposed instead alliances with foreign Protestant princes, support for Moray in Scotland, repression of Catholics at home, and rebuilding of the English militia and navy.

The international dangers and the threat from Mary inevitably became linked with manœuvres at Elizabeth's Court. The French Ambassador, Fénélon, reported that a conspiracy against Cecil was being engineered by a group of nobles headed by Norfolk. His evidence is not wholly reliable, since foreign ambassadors tended to accept reports of faction-fighting and disruption at face value; but it has some support from the dispatches of de Spes, written at the same time, and from the later account of William Camden. While the events are obscure, it seems probable that Norfolk and Arundel, alarmed by Cecil's provocative attitude towards Spain, tried, along with Leicester and others, to curb Cecil's influence with Elizabeth and, perhaps, to remove him from office. The Queen quickly demonstrated her support for Cecil, and the conspiracy, if there was one, disintegrated. By June 1569 Cecil felt himself secure and wrote to a friend that he believed 'all my lords from the greatest to the meanest think my actions honest and painful [i.e. painstaking] and do profess inwardly to bear me as much good will as ever they did heretofore'.[43]

The problem posed by Mary Stewart was more acute. Even Cecil had to recognize, however much he might dislike it, that her claim to the succession was strong, resting as it did upon 'the universal opinion of the world for the justice of her title, as coming of the ancient line'.[44] Several Protestant

[42] Printed in Haynes, *State Papers*, 579-93.   [43] Read, *Cecil*, 444.
[44] Haynes, *State Papers*, 580.

courtiers, including Leicester, concerned both to protect their own position should Elizabeth die and to safeguard religion in the event of Mary's succession, saw their best hope in the marriage of Mary to an English nobleman who would be able to control her. She could then be restored to Scotland, where she would be isolated from English events, though not from English influence. They chose the Duke of Norfolk. While not entirely convincing as the husband to restrain Mary's Catholic urges, he was at that stage a Protestant, was generally respected, and was not so powerful as to be feared. In a desperate situation the plan to marry Mary to Norfolk had something, if not very much, to commend it. There were three drawbacks. First, English Catholic nobles were drawn into the plan through the suspect medium of the Florentine banker Roberto Ridolfi; and this seriously undermined the original Protestant intention. Secondly, a Scottish convention of nobles, bishops, and commissioners from the towns refused to accept Mary's return. Thirdly, Elizabeth was known to be hostile to any action which might further the recognition of Mary as her heir. By September Elizabeth learned of the marriage proposal and made her disapproval starkly clear, at which Norfolk's Protestant allies dropped away, leaving him only with Catholic support. He departed from Court for East Anglia, uttering vague words of resistance; but when summoned back by the Queen he obeyed her command and within a week was lodged inside the Tower. Three of his principal friends at Court—Pembroke, Arundel, and Lumley—were put in detention for a time, but were soon released. Norfolk's fate, however, was uncertain and he stayed in prison. The Court 'conspiracy' in favour of Mary had been dissolved, although dangers still threatened from the north.

The northern counties were by 1569 no longer as heavily dominated as they had once been by the great magnate families of Percy, Neville, Clifford, and Dacre. The Percy earldom of Northumberland had been in abeyance between 1537 and 1557, the family lands taken over by the Crown, and the continuity of tradition broken: and the seventh Earl, restored to the title by Mary, had been subsequently weakened by Elizabeth's appointment of southern lords and lesser northerners to the wardenships of the northern marches. Even so, the ties of kindred and allegiance were still strong; and the principal earls, of Northumberland and Westmorland, were discontented by the intrusion of others into offices that they considered to be their own by right; and both were surrounded by Catholic advisers. Westmorland was married to Norfolk's sister and, although neither earl seems to have had high regard for Norfolk, they had been drawn into his marriage plans. On the Duke's imprisonment the northern earls began to mobilize retainers for their own protection. Rumours spread in the north that the Norfolk–Mary marriage had taken place, that a Catholic rising had begun. Both earls protested their loyalty to the Queen and have in consequence been damned by romantic historians as vacillating and feeble. They were not, admittedly, strong or decisive men, but they were sensible enough to recognize that a successful northern rebellion could no longer be mounted. Westmorland, urged by his Catholic officers to rise for religion, replied: 'No . . . ; those that seem to take that quarrel in other countries, are accounted as rebels; and therefore I will never blot my house, which hath been this long preserved without staining.'[45] But he had not reckoned with Elizabeth. Against the advice of Sussex, Lord President of the North, then in York, the Queen insisted that the two earls come to Court. Sussex vainly protested that this would drive them into revolt from fear and urged Elizabeth either to desist or to send enough troops to compel them. She refused to do either. Lady Westmorland, Norfolk's sister, rallied the earls and their followers with bitter words: 'we and our country were shamed for ever, that now in the end we should seek holes to creep into.'[46] Two concepts were at war in the northern camp: Westmorland's belief in loyalty and his wife's in resistance for the sake of religion. The Countess won.

By November the earls were in open revolt, claiming to march for true religion and the deposition of false councillors. They entered Durham, where they destroyed English bibles, set up stone altars and holy-water vats, and had the Mass sung in Latin. With the object of getting Mary married to a Catholic and recognized as heir to the throne they marched south to secure her person. Their force was small: about 4,000 foot-soldiers and 1,800 horsemen. The tenurial bonds between the lords and their men were weaker than fifty years before, especially after the long interregnum on the Percy estates; and the earls had not the money to pay many foot-soldiers. Nevertheless their armed horsemen were a serious threat to the government, which could only muster 400 horse in the north. By 23 November they had reached Selby, 14 miles south of York; but their inability to pay wages was depleting their force, and the government had quickly moved Mary southwards. A week later the earls were back in County Durham. Sussex then emerged from York and began the pursuit, driving them into Scotland just before Christmas.

Meanwhile a massive army of 12,000 men had been mobilized in the south under the Earl of Warwick and Lord Clinton. It arrived too late for any military action, but in time to expect the pickings of victory: 'others

[45] Cuthbert Sharp (ed.), *Memorials of the Rebellion of 1569* (1840), repr. ed. Robert Wood (Shotton, 1975), 196.
[46] Ibid. 199.

beat the bush and they have had the birds,' remarked Lord Hunsdon sourly.[47] Punishment of the rebels was, at Elizabeth's command, severe even by Tudor standards. The poor were executed by martial law; but since this did not bring lands to the Queen the better off were tried by jury. Although local officers seem to have mitigated her harsh orders for revenge, about 450 men were executed—a heavy toll compared with 178 after the Pilgrimage of Grace and 90 after Wyatt's rebellion.

The consequences of the rising for northern England were drastic. Although the Percies soon recovered their title, to which the seventh Earl's brother succeeded, they became in effect a southern family, forbidden to reside in the north and robbed of all power there. The Dacres, involved in a small rising the following year, were similarly broken, and Westmorland's estates were confiscated. Of the four great northern affinities only that of the Cliffords, Earls of Cumberland, remained. Southern nobles, like Lord William Howard, picked up many of the forfeited estates.

By the beginning of 1570 Elizabeth could momentarily feel more secure. The north was cowed; support for Mary at Court and elsewhere had disintegrated; the Spanish monarch was confronted with the Ottoman invasion of Cyprus and the capture of Tunis. However, the relief was short-lived. On 23 January the Scottish Regent, Moray, was assassinated, and Mary's party, led by the Hamiltons, claimed the right to rule. On Corpus Christi Day, 2 June, the papal bull *Regnans in excelsis*, deposing Elizabeth by order of Pius V, was nailed to the Bishop of London's palace. Fears and rumours of invasion were rife. The government had now to solve the problems of Mary Stewart, secure the northern border, search for alliances abroad, and counter the threats from Catholics within the kingdom.

In September 1570 William Cecil and Walter Mildmay, Chancellor of the Exchequer, were sent to negotiate with Mary Stewart, then a prisoner at Chatsworth. Neither man was sympathetic to her and the terms offered were severe: in return for her restoration to Scotland, Mary must confirm the Treaty of Edinburgh, surrender all claims to the English throne during Elizabeth's lifetime, and send James to reside in England. Although Mary accepted almost all the English demands in order to secure her freedom, matters moved slowly. Commissioners from the dominant 'King's party' in Scotland, headed by the Earl of Morton, arrived in England determined to impede Mary's restoration, which would, they believed, destroy them. Cecil was reluctant to see Mary freed and happily collaborated in procrastination: in March 1571 Elizabeth suspended the talks. That killed the negotiations and kept Mary a prisoner.

[47] *CSP Dom. Add., 1566–1579*, 195.

Using the presence of the English rebels north of the border as her excuse, Elizabeth had already ordered Sussex to invade Scotland in the spring of 1570, capture the rebels, and punish those who were protecting them. This powerful English intervention had been directed against the Marian party and had enabled the Protestants to regain control. Although Elizabeth herself had soon become anxious about the extent of English involvement, Sussex had been able to reassure her and to ensure that the Protestant Earl of Lennox was elected Regent. Lennox survived in this position for only a year before he was killed in September 1571, and his successor, the Earl of Mar, died in October 1572; but by then Mary's supporters were in retreat. The rising of the northern earls had provoked Elizabeth into positive action in Scotland and had brought home to the Marians the danger of opposing her. After Morton became Regent in 1572 the Catholic nobles gradually deserted Mary's cause, and in February 1573 most of them accepted the 'Pacification of Perth', recognizing James as King and Morton as Regent. Only a small party held out for Mary in Edinburgh Castle. Pressed hard by Morton, Elizabeth now agreed to send a force to take part in its siege. By contrast with Sussex's army this one was puny—so poorly equipped that its soldiers had to scavenge for cannon-balls round the castle walls; but eventually pressure of numbers, bombardment by English guns, and shortage of water forced the defenders to surrender. For the next five years Scotland was dominated by the Protestant and pro-English Morton; and the north was secure, thanks in part to Elizabeth's military interventions, especially Sussex's campaigns, and to the recognition by the Marian party that they were vulnerable to English action.

In April 1571 Parliament assembled, summoned by Elizabeth to provide for the costs of suppressing the northern rebellion. It was a productive session in which forty-six bills were enacted, twenty-nine of them public, the rest private. While various grievances over the administration of royal finances and of the law were remedied, at least on paper, the most important business lay in the security of Queen and realm, and in the reformation of religion. A treason bill, drafted by government lawyers, was introduced to make mere words against Elizabeth treasonous, thus restoring to the statute-book the Act of 1534, which had been repealed in 1547. This was insufficient for many MPs, possibly for some councillors. Thomas Norton, one of the government's men-of-business in the Commons, added a proviso that anyone claiming the throne during Elizabeth's lifetime should be debarred from the succession. Since his addition was retroactive, it would have had the effect, obviously intended by him, of depriving Mary of her rights. In the event this retroactive element was removed, but the rest of Norton's proviso stood, important testimony to the effectiveness of a private member who had the backing, off-stage, of privy councillors. In addition to the treason Act bills were passed making it an offence to bring in papal bulls or to leave the realm without royal licence.[48]

Norton and his allies were less successful in their religious proposals, which revived the 'alphabetical bills' of 1566 and added others. Some of the measures put forward could reasonably be described as 'puritan' and were distasteful to bishops and councillors as well as to the Queen; but for the most part they were intended to strengthen the Church against the Catholic threat. One such bill was for making attendance at the communion service compulsory; another revived the *Reformatio legum*, first put forward in 1552 for tightening ecclesiastical discipline;[49] others aimed at improving the quality of the clergy, eliminating non-residence, and so on. Only one, proposed by William Strickland, for amending the Prayer Book by abolishing surplices, kneeling at communion, and other rites, could be described as 'puritan' in the sense that it aimed at an alteration of the settlement. Predictably it won little support. The proposal to enact the *Reformatio legum* was dropped. Most of the bills for improving the quality of the clergy made small progress; the bill for compulsory communion was carried but vetoed by the Queen; a short measure against simony (the buying or selling of benefices) was enacted. Only one important religious bill became law, and that after some contention: its original form, supported by the bishops, made subscription to the Thirty-nine Articles compulsory for all clergy; but some members demanded that only the doctrinal articles be insisted upon, and that others, such as the article on homilies, should be omitted from the bill. Somewhat surprisingly, this group—presumably of mildly 'puritan' inclination—got its way and the amended bill was enacted, although the bishops in practice insisted upon subscription to all the articles.[50]

Before Parliament was dissolved in May 1571 the government had caught the scent of a dangerous conspiracy. Roberto Ridolfi, the Florentine banker, imprisoned in 1569, had gone abroad in the spring of 1571 after his release. Once overseas he sent letters to John Leslie, Bishop of Ross, Mary Stewart's Ambassador to Elizabeth, outlining plans for an invasion of England by the Duke of Alba with papal backing. Mary herself was wholly involved in the plot; Norfolk resisted for some time but fatally allowed himself to be committed to the scheme. Alba responded with much less enthusiasm; he had enough on his hands in the Netherlands and formed a realistic estimate of the chances of success. Unfortunately for him Philip II was, in his own words, 'so convinced that God our Saviour must embrace

---

[48] 13 Elizabeth cc. 1, 2, 3.   [49] Above, Ch. 3 s. 3.   [50] 13 Elizabeth c. 12.

[the plan] as his own cause, that I cannot be dissuaded from putting it into operation'.[51]

Ross broke under interrogation, confessing that he himself, Mary, Norfolk, and Guerau de Spes, the Spanish Ambassador, were all involved in the plot. De Spes was at once ordered to leave, and in January 1572 Norfolk was brought to trial before his peers. Although there was some sympathy for him among nobles and gentry his condemnation for treason was inevitable. However, Elizabeth hesitated before bringing her cousin to the scaffold: twice she signed his death-warrant, twice she recalled it.

Parliament was summoned in March 1572 to devise laws for the safety of the Queen. Two matters dominated the session: the lesser was the execution of Norfolk; the other, 'the great matter', was the fate of Mary Stewart, not yet brought to trial. Lord Keeper Bacon opened Parliament by declaring that 'God of his merciful providence had detected great treasons and notable conspiracies very perilous to her Majesty's person and to the whole state of the realm.' 'Some present remedy' was urgently needed.[52] The members took their cue from Bacon, who almost certainly spoke for a majority of the Council. Thomas Norton, Thomas Digges, and others urged the execution of Norfolk: mercy might be desirable in a monarch, but 'mercy without her Majesty's safety causeth misery'. He was supported by Sir Francis Knollys, Treasurer of the Household: 'and surely to the Duke, he would wish him dead though he were his brother'.[53] Towards the end of May the Commons resolved, with only one dissentient voice, that Norfolk must die. Five days later, on 2 June, he was executed.

The problem of Mary was much less easily resolved. Two bills were drawn up: the first for the attainder of Mary as a traitor; the second, possibly favoured by the privy councillors, for debarring her from the succession. Elizabeth insisted that only the second be considered. Both Houses responded with a petition that Mary be brought to trial. Nicholas St Leger complained that the Queen, 'lulled in sleep and wrapped in the mantle of her own safety', was unwilling that Parliament should deal with 'the monstrous and huge dragon, and mass of the earth, the Queen of Scots'.[54] Finally, Parliament, with the misgivings of many, agreed to the second, less drastic, bill. To their surprise the Queen refused her assent, explaining unconvincingly that she was not vetoing the bill but merely postponing it until the prorogued Parliament met in November. In the event it did not assemble again until 1576.

From this time onwards the danger posed by Mary Stewart gradually subsided. Support for her cause from English Protestant nobles had col-

---

[51] Geoffrey Parker, *The Dutch Revolt* (London, 1977), 124.
[52] Hartley, *Proceedings*, 336.   [53] Ibid. 325, 377.   [54] Ibid. 312.

lapsed in 1569, and after the execution of Norfolk Catholics were hesitant to commit themselves. Even exiles like Parsons and Allen were lukewarm. Mary herself became more interested in securing release from imprisonment than in overthrowing Elizabeth; and while she was certainly involved in assassination plots, she did little to secure serious backing for them. The plotters were mostly men of little substance, and while even the most hare-brained of schemes could by chance have succeeded, the threat was remote. Its principal function was to provide a bogy which Burghley, Walsingham, and their parliamentary allies could use to drum up support for security measures.

Only one statute of significance emerged from this Parliament, the Poor Law Act, which instituted a national scheme of taxation for the relief of poverty and at the same time inflicted the most savage measures of the reign upon vagabonds, who were to be whipped and bored through their ears at the first offence, and hanged for felony at the second unless they were taken into service for two years.[55] The Act derived from an unsuccessful bill that had been proposed in 1571. This time it had the backing of the Privy Council, which had perhaps been alarmed by reports coming in from JPs, whose searches after the rising of 1569 had revealed disconcertingly large numbers of vagabonds. The bill encountered opposition: some members objected to a national tax, others thought that the poor were being too generously treated; but with government support it was carried and marked an important stage in the provision of relief for the poor. With that exception, the session was a disappointment. Cecil, created Lord Burghley in 1571, commented sadly: 'all that we laboured for and had with full consent brought to fashion, I mean a law to make the Scottish Queen unable and unworthy to wear the crown, was by her Majesty neither assented to nor rejected.'[56]

While little had been done at home to strengthen national security, negotiations with the French Crown were slightly more promising. The third civil war in France had ended in August 1570 with the Treaty of Saint-Germain, which left the Huguenot party stronger than before. The French Protestants and the Queen Mother, Catherine de Medici, favoured a marriage alliance between Elizabeth and Henry, Duke of Anjou, Catherine's third son, the heir to the throne, in the hope of detaching him from the Catholic Guise party. Burghley supported the marriage as a solution to the succession problem and a defence against both Mary Stewart and Spain. Even Elizabeth was prepared, with the usual reservations, to enter into discussion. The new Ambassador to the French Court, Francis

---

[55] 14 Elizabeth c. 5.   [56] Read, *Burghley*, 50.

Walsingham, reported in guardedly favourable terms upon Anjou: 'in complexion somewhat sallow, his body of very good shape, his leg long and small, but reasonably well proportioned. What helps he had to supply any defects of nature I know not.'[57] The crucial barrier to the marriage was religion. Anjou insisted that he be allowed to worship by Catholic rites; Elizabeth refused to make any public concession on the point. In retrospect it seems almost impossible that the match should have been made: neither of the principals was enthusiastic, and Anjou was most of the time distinctly hostile. Nevertheless Burghley and Catherine pressed for it strongly, while it suited Elizabeth's book to keep the prospect open. Throughout 1571 there were continuous negotiations without any progress being made: when Anjou seemed slightly less cold, Elizabeth drew back; when Elizabeth appeared to come forward Anjou resumed his hostility. But late in the year the necessity for some form of Anglo-French alliance became more pressing. The dangers revealed by the Ridolfi plot, Philip II's victory over the Turks at Lepanto in October, and the growing strength of the French Catholics were highly alarming. Unsettling in a different way was the plan concocted by the French King, Charles IX, and the Huguenot leader, Admiral Coligny, for intervening in the Netherlands in support of the Dutch rebels: such an invasion might end with French troops replacing Spanish in the Low Countries, an unattractive prospect for England. In December 1571 Sir Thomas Smith, an experienced statesman, newly appointed to the Privy Council, was sent to France to take charge of negotiations in concert with Walsingham. Although Burghley still hoped for a royal marriage, most of Elizabeth's advisers had come to realize its impossibility and to urge instead a straightforward alliance. The prospects for the marriage were killed at Smith's first audience with the Queen Mother. When Catherine insisted that her son must be allowed openly to practise the Catholic religion, Smith replied, with remarkable rudeness: 'Why, Madame, then he may require also the four orders of friars, monks, canons, pilgrimages, pardons, oil and cream, relics and all such trumperies.'[58] Smith and Walsingham suggested that Elizabeth might instead marry Anjou's younger brother, the Duke of Alençon. Walsingham admitted that the main impediment to this proposal was 'the contentment of the eye': for, he went on, 'the gentleman sure is void of any good favour, besides the blemish of smallpox'.[59] But to balance these disadvantages he was said to be more flexible in religion. Even so, Walsingham was not enthusiastic about the marriage and preferred to concentrate on a diplomatic tie, which was finally

[57] Read, *Walsingham*, i. 110. [58] Read, *Burghley*, 64.
[59] Read, *Walsingham*, i. 256.

achieved in April 1572 with the Treaty of Blois, a defensive alliance in which each country promised to come to the aid of the other if attacked. It was not much, but at least it began the process of building foreign support for England against the Spanish.

Meanwhile Elizabeth's relations with Spain were becoming even more complex than usual. A few years previously the Dutch Sea Beggars, nobles exiled after the revolt of 1566, had been allowed to shelter with their ships in Dover harbour. At first they had made their living and advanced their cause by preying upon Spanish shipping, but by 1571 they were getting out of hand and attacking English vessels as well. After many attempts to discipline them, Elizabeth finally, on 1 March 1572, ordered them to leave Dover at once. Their expulsion set off momentous events, for within a month the Sea Beggars had captured the Dutch port of Brille and had begun to take over the northern provinces of the Netherlands from the Spanish. Nineteenth-century historians believed that Elizabeth had conspired with their leader, the Count de la Marck, and that the expulsion was merely a blind. This seems unlikely.[60] The Dutch pirates had long been a nuisance and their removal was probably the culmination of many attempts to control them rather than a cunningly disguised strike against the Spanish. However, once the Sea Beggars had established themselves in Brille and Flushing, Elizabeth allowed first Flemings and then English volunteers to cross the Channel in their support. There was no harm in keeping Alba's troops pinned down, provided that the English government was not directly committed.

During July it looked as though England would be drawn into a closer alliance with France as the Huguenot leaders, backed by Charles IX, urged intervention in the Netherlands in support of William of Orange; and the disastrous defeat of Orangist and Huguenot troops by the Spanish at Mons made English co-operation even more necessary to the Huguenot faction, which momentarily dominated the French Court. However, the alliance between Charles IX and the Huguenots was suddenly broken. An attempt upon the life of Admiral Coligny, the principal Huguenot leader, provoked Catherine de Medici, afraid of Huguenot retaliation, into joining forces with the Guises. There followed the infamous Massacres of St Bartholomew's Day, 24 August, in which Coligny himself, many other Huguenot leaders, and thousands of their followers lost their lives. Catherine and Charles proclaimed that the killings were justified; English Protestants were horrified; and although the defensive treaty was retained,

---

[60] The evidence is rehearsed in J. B. Black, 'Queen Elizabeth, the sea beggars and the capture of Brill, 1572', *EHR* 46 (1931), 30–47; and in N. M. Sutherland, *Princes, Politics and Religion, 1547–1589* (London, 1984), ch. 9.

there was now no question of proceeding with the Alençon marriage or of strengthening the alliance.

It was time for England to mend her fences with Spain. The embargo on English trade with the Netherlands, imposed by Alba, was ruining Dutch prosperity and, more to the point, reducing the Spanish government's revenue. Alba was therefore anxious to come to terms. The English volunteers were withdrawn from Flushing in November 1572, and in April of the following year a two-year treaty was signed in which commercial relations were restored.

4. IRELAND, 1558–1572

Elizabeth's government inherited an alarming situation in Ireland. The administration in Dublin had virtually no control over the lands outside the boundaries of the Pale, for in most of Ireland Anglo-Irish feudal lords or Gaelic chiefs, supported by armed retainers and Scottish mercenaries, ruled the country and oppressed the peasantry. The conciliatory policy of surrender and regrant, developed by St Leger in the final years of Henry VIII, had been effectively abandoned by 1556.[61] St Leger's successor, Thomas Radcliffe, Earl of Sussex, Lord Deputy 1556–60 and Lord Lieutenant 1560–4, then laid the foundations for a new and more aggressive policy. He warned Elizabeth of the danger of a French invasion of Ireland, 'aided by civil faction, so easy to be compassed, and the resisting thereof so difficult', and urged immediate defensive action, 'not so much for the care I have of Ireland, which I have often wished to be sunk in the sea', but because France would then possess an entrée into Scotland and be able to 'utterly take from England all kind of peaceable traffic by sea'.[62] To prevent this he proposed that the Earl of Kildare be removed from Ireland and given lands in England as compensation; that Shane O'Neill be expelled from Ulster, where he had usurped all the rights of the Crown; that military presidencies be established in Ulster, Connacht, and Munster; and that plantations, or colonies of Englishmen, be extended in Leinster to protect the Pale. His programme over-simplified the problems of Ireland, ignored the obstacles created by faction rivalry there and at Court, and underestimated the cost. Political and financial constraints prevented it from being executed wholeheartedly or consistently. But for the first fifteen years or so of Elizabeth's reign Sussex's ideas, taken up and developed by his successor, Sir Henry Sidney, coloured English policy and alienated the Irish.

[61] Above, Ch. 4 s. 5.
[62] J. S. Brewer and W. Bullen (eds.), *Calendar of the Carew Manuscripts, 1515–1574* (London, 1867), no. 227; see also no. 236 for Sussex's proposals.

The most urgent problem was set by Shane O'Neill, who had rebelled in 1558 against the Marian government's decision to confer the earldom of Tyrone upon his illegitimate half-brother Matthew, Baron Dungannon. Having had Matthew murdered—shortly before the accession of Elizabeth—Shane proclaimed himself Earl of Tyrone and launched raids into the Pale. By 1561 he had won control of Tirconnell. When Sussex marched north into Ulster, Shane, as many of Elizabeth's commanders were to find, simply retreated into his country. Then, while Sussex led his armies through the north, Elizabeth invited Shane to Court in 1561, to the fury of her Lieutenant, who expostulated that 'if Shane be overthrown, all is settled, if Shane is settled all is overthrown'.[63] His anger reflects the frustration of most Elizabethan viceroys in Ireland, as Court faction diminished their authority and the Queen alternated between half-hearted conciliation and inadequate military response. In this instance his forebodings were fully justified, for Shane, having sworn to keep Ulster at peace, almost at once resumed his raids upon his neighbours. After one dreary campaign had followed another, a treaty was finally arranged in 1563, giving Shane effective supremacy in Ulster. Sussex left Ireland thankfully in the next year, and for a brief period the fragile settlement survived under the conciliatory rule of Sir Nicholas Arnold, who held the temporary post of Lord Justice.

By the beginning of 1565 the weakness of government was shown up by the feud between Gerald Fitzgerald, Earl of Desmond, and Thomas Butler, Earl of Ormond: their retinues fought at Affane in February 1565 and Desmond was taken prisoner. With Ulster still dominated by the unruly O'Neill, Elizabeth reverted to sterner measures and a stronger governor. Sir Henry Sidney, who had seen previous service in Ireland and was now Lord President of the Council in the Marches of Wales, was appointed Lord Deputy in 1565. Although the politics of faction were muted in England at this time, in Ireland the intense rivalries of the great Anglo-Irish families, especially of the Geraldines and the Butlers, led each of the protagonists to seek support at Elizabeth's Court: the Geraldines had tied their cause to Dudley, the Butlers to Sussex and the Howards. Irish governors had to contend not only with the bitter feuds of the Gaelic chieftains, the feudal lords, and the Palesmen, but also with the manœuvres conducted behind their backs at Court.

As Leicester's brother-in-law, Sidney was aligned with Desmond and distanced from Sussex, but he took up and developed the policy of the latter. He proposed the gradual destruction of Gaelic rule in Leinster, the

---

[63] Nicholas P. Canny, *The Elizabethan Conquest of Ireland* (Hassocks, 1976), 40.

absorption of that province into the Pale, the military overthrow of Shane O'Neill, the expulsion of Scottish settlers from Ulster, and the establishment in Munster and Connacht of regional presidencies modelled upon the Welsh pattern, but with greater military backing. This ambitious strategy for extending English control was beset with problems: it would require large sums of money, either from the Queen or from taxes levied in Ireland; it was likely to alienate the Anglo-Irish magnates and to provoke them into exploiting factional rivalries against it; and it depended upon a consistency of purpose in Elizabeth herself—never a dependable commodity. Trouble began almost at once in Munster, where a project to establish a Council had been fully agreed before Sidney left England, Sir Warham St Leger, son of the earlier Lord Deputy, having been appointed President. The plan at once aroused the hostility of Ormond, who considered the Council to be a threat to his own power and St Leger an enemy to his family. Elizabeth ordered Sidney to favour Ormond against Desmond: he was to 'make some difference twixt tried, just and false friend'.[64] The influence of the Howards and of Sussex was evidently working in favour of the Butlers, and the immediate consequence was the failure of Sidney's plan. Elizabeth told Sidney that she did not consider St Leger a suitable appointment: 'we do much muse who hath thus blinded you in appointing him to such office,' she wrote to Sidney.[65] She also insisted that the expenses of the Council were to be borne by local taxation rather than money from England. As the Queen placed one obstacle after another in the way of the Munster Council Sidney wrote despairingly to Cecil that 'nought it is and worse it wilbe unless means to minister justice be provided, and provided, maintained in credit'.[66] However, although he revoked the appointment of St Leger, nothing was done in return to help him and the proposed Council lapsed.

Sidney's handling of the dispute between Ormond and Desmond was equally frustrated. It had been made clear to him that Desmond was to be treated as an enemy, and his attempts to provide impartial justice met with harsh criticism from Elizabeth. Both earls were bound over in sums of £20,000 each to keep the peace, and in 1567 Sidney, probably under pressure from the Queen, ordered Desmond's arrest and the forfeiture of his bond. Elizabeth signified her approval, but the action led to the progressive alienation of Desmond, whose financial needs were driving him to regain his power. Sidney's policy in Munster was therefore an almost total failure.

[64] Collins, *Letters*, i. 7; Queen to Sidney, 6 Jan. 1566.
[65] Trinity Coll., Dublin, MS 745, no. 19: Queen to Sidney, 14 May 1566. Cf. PRO, State Papers, Ireland (SP 63), vol. 17 no. 49.
[66] PRO, State Papers, Ireland (SP 63), vol. 19 no. 51: Sidney to Cecil, 18 Nov. 1566.

Elizabeth had once sympathized with him for being 'entered into that realm as a large field or world overrun with brambles and replenished with ravening beasts';[67] but she had done nothing to make his path through the Irish political jungle any easier.

Fortunately for Sidney he had the compensation of a resounding victory in Ulster. Shane O'Neill was known to be negotiating with both Charles IX of France and Mary of Scotland for military support. Action against him was imperative and Elizabeth told Sidney to consider 'how such a cankered rebel may be utterly extirped'.[68] Sidney needed no urging and marched against Shane in the winter of 1566-7. His strategy was based upon a naval landing at Lough Foyle to establish a permanent garrison there, combined with an overland march under his own command into Ulster. The two-pronged attack—to be used unsuccessfully by Essex in 1599 and triumphantly by Mountjoy in 1600-2 went favourably: a fortress was built at Derry and Sidney marched almost unopposed through Ulster, displaying royal power to the Gaelic chiefs and restoring Shane's rivals, the O'Donnells, to power in Tirconnell.[69] Unluckily, the fort at Derry, which had survived an attack by Shane, was accidentally destroyed by fire in the spring of 1567. However, this was outweighed by a greater piece of fortune that summer, when Shane attacked the O'Donnells, was heavily defeated by them, and was ultimately murdered by Scots settlers, the Macdonalds, in Antrim. His head was sent to Dublin 'pickled in a pipkin'.[70] Although his end came at the hands of his Gaelic and Scottish enemies, credit for his defeat belongs to Sidney, whose campaign had convinced the O'Donnells and Macdonalds that royal power was greater than Shane's. Turlough Luineach O'Neill, Shane's tanist, succeeded him in Tyrone, and the ground was now ready for a more permanent settlement of the province.[71] Sidney returned to England for consultations in the autumn but was back in Ireland the following year with extended plans.

Sidney came back to Ireland with proposals for using the Dublin Parliament to enact political and social reforms, for establishing presidencies again in Munster and Connacht, and for encouraging colonization by private individuals. In the Parliament which met in 1569 he encountered widespread resistance to his plans from Palesmen and from borough representatives: little was achieved. The first steps in colonization were taken with grants to Sir Peter Carew and Sir Warham St Leger in Munster; but

[67] Trinity Coll., Dublin, MS 745, no. 14: Queen to Sidney, 8 Mar. 1566. Cf. PRO, State Papers, Ireland, vol. 16 no. 69.
[68] Trinity Coll., Dublin, MS 745, no 14; PRO State Papers, Ireland, vol. 16 no. 69.
[69] Below, Ch. 9 s. 5.   [70] Canny, *Elizabethan Conquest*, 59.
[71] The 'tanist' was the successor-designate of a chief.

plans to set up colonies in Ulster, kept carefully secret, came to nothing for
the time being. The immediate effect of the Munster grants was to stir
revolt among the Fitzgeralds and the Butlers, and Sidney's plans for presidencies were frustrated by the Queen's insistence on economy. Sir Edward
Fitton was appointed President of Connacht in 1569, but Sidney's choice
for Munster, Sir John Pollard, turned down the post because the financial
provision was inadequate. Sidney commented in discouraging terms to
Cecil that he had economized as far as he could to solve 'your dutiful and
natural perplexity between the sparing of the Queen's treasure and advancing this country's common wealth'.[72] He summed up admirably the contradiction at the heart of English policy.

With the Munster presidency vacant, the Earl of Desmond in prison, and
tension provoked by the colonizing activities of Carew and St Leger, it is
not surprising that revolt broke out in the south. It was led by James
Fitzmaurice Fitzgerald, a cousin of the Earl, who, having got himself
elected captain of the Desmond territory, joined forces with the dissident
brothers of the Earl of Ormond, attacked a garrison near Cork in July 1569,
and spoiled the country round Waterford, killing or stripping naked the
English settlers. He proclaimed the Roman Catholic religion and asked
for help from Spain; but this was not forthcoming. Fitzmaurice was an
ineffective leader and his revolt lacked sustained support; but coming as it
did when relations between England and Spain were deteriorating, it gave
the government cause for anxiety, the more so as the Earl of Thomond
rebelled at the same time. Countermeasures were quickly taken. Ormond
was sent back to Ireland, where he persuaded his brothers to desert
Fitzmaurice and went on to receive the surrender of Thomond in
Connacht. Sidney appointed Humphrey Gilbert as colonel in Munster and
a brutal campaign of suppression, backed by martial law, was waged.
Fitzmaurice was defeated in the field, though he managed to escape;
twenty-three rebel strongholds were taken, all who resisted—men, women,
and children—being slaughtered. By the end of 1569 the real danger was
over and government victory was symbolized by the knighting of Gilbert on
New Year's Day 1570. Fitzmaurice remained at large for another three
years with steadily decreasing support. Unlike some of his unlucky followers he was treated mercifully by the Queen and was later able to escape to
France. In 1571 Sir John Perrott, a strong-minded, quarrelsome knight
from Pembrokeshire, was appointed President of Munster. He continued
Gilbert's repression, executed 800 rebels, and made it clear that while 'a
man may easily shew gentleness when he will, . . . whiles I have dealings

here, my meaning is not to rule by entreaty, for that (in my judgement) hath of long time hurt this nation'.[73] The savagery that marked Irish wars for the future had begun.

Sidney left Ireland in 1571, with Sir William Fitzwilliam—a lesser figure—appointed to succeed him; and two years later Perrott departed from Munster. During the years 1558–71 Ireland had been ruled by two strong governors, Sussex and Sidney. While their policies differed in detail, they had a common purpose of extending royal authority into the whole of Ireland, setting up military presidencies in Munster and Connacht, expelling Shane O'Neill, and establishing English settlers in parts of Leinster and Ulster. Shortage of money, the vacillations of Elizabeth, and the obstructions of Court faction frustrated their aims. Although Sidney met with some success in Ulster, the regional councils were abandoned, military forces reduced, and economies ordered by the Queen. But his deputyship saw the beginnings of private colonization and the progressive alienation of Gaelic and Anglo-Irish lords.[74]

By the summer of 1573 England could feel reasonably secure after the turbulence of the previous five years. The rising of the earls had been easily put down and the powers of the great northern magnates and of the Howards had been severely curtailed. The Catholics seemed to be quiescent and loyal: missionaries were yet to arrive from overseas, and although many priests survived in England from Mary's reign, they did not present a serious threat to the established Church. Regent Morton and his Protestant allies were in control in Edinburgh, while the Geraldine rebellion had been crushed in Ireland. The Treaty of Blois ensured tolerable relations with France and the endemic disorders there prevented any real danger from that quarter. Finally, trade had been resumed with the Habsburg domains and political relations with Philip II had become calmer.

[73] Canny, *Elizabethan Conquest*, 103.
[74] Below, Ch. 8 s. 3.

CHAPTER 8

The Road To War
1573–1588

1. FRANCE AND THE NETHERLANDS, 1573–1578

Although the outlook for England was indeed more hopeful in 1573 than it had been in the previous five years, the crises in France and the Low Countries continued to threaten. In France the death of Charles IX in 1574 brought to the throne his brother, Henry III, until then King of Poland. Unlike Charles, the new King was a determined enemy of the Huguenots and an ally of the Catholic Guises. Hostility between him and his younger brother, Francis, now Duke of Anjou,[1] set off a further bout of civil war, as Anjou joined the Protestant princes, Condé and Navarre, in a coalition against the King and the Guises. At the same time the Spanish were fighting the Dutch Protestants, who had occupied several towns in the northern provinces of the Netherlands. These dissensions brought both opportunities and dangers for England. There were attractions in stoking the fires of civil war in order to prevent the French from interfering in Scotland and to keep the Spanish tied down in the Low Countries; yet there was a real possibility that the Guises might triumph in France or Philip II in the Netherlands, endangering both England and the Protestant cause. There was, too, the prospect that Henry III might solve the problem of his younger brother, Anjou, by encouraging him to support the rebel cause in the Netherlands: the establishment of French power in that region would be as unwelcome to England as the triumph of Spain. Anjou became, for the next ten years or so, until his death in 1584, one of the key figures in European politics. Relatively insignificant in personality and markedly incompetent as a leader, his status as a prince of the blood and as heir presumptive to Henry III made him an attractive ally for both the op-

---

[1] On Henry's accession his previous title of Duke of Anjou passed to his younger brother Francis, until then Duke of Alençon. Some historians continue to refer to the latter as Alençon, but I have chosen to use his correct title of Anjou, by which he was known to contemporaries.

ponents of the Guises in France and for the Dutch rebels, who sought a
royal figurehead and French assistance. For Elizabeth, Anjou was a tool to
be used against her enemies and a potential threat to be countered: to entice
him into serving her own purposes, she held out the baits of military
alliance and marriage with herself.

One other new figure appeared in the political arena at this point. Francis
Walsingham had been English ambassador in France since 1570 and was
appointed Secretary of State in 1573. Dynamic, determined, and able, he
was yet an intensely private man, who revealed little of himself in his
correspondence except an overwhelming zeal for the Protestant religion.
Serious and almost obsessionally methodical, he instructed a nephew about
to travel in Europe that he must set aside a time each day for prayer, let
no day pass 'without translating somewhat', learn history, languages, and
mathematics, and 'take heed of lewd youths of wanton, dissolute dispositions'.[2] He was, too, a knowledgeable gardener and an enthusiastic
patron of letters, eulogized by Spenser as 'the great Maecaenas of this age'.
Politically he was described by Camden as 'a most subtle searcher of hidden
secrets' and by Sir Robert Naunton as 'one of the great allies of the austerian
embracement'.[3] Fortunately for the historian he had a gift for writing sharp,
energetic prose—a relief from the ponderous memoranda of Burghley.

As Henry III was travelling from the kingdom of Poland to his recently
acquired throne in France, Walsingham urged the Queen to give speedy
help to Anjou and his Huguenot allies. Even Burghley believed that some
action must be taken 'to counterpoise the tyrant that shall come from
Poland';[4] but he was at this juncture more concerned with his own health
than with France. While Elizabeth was characteristically reluctant to commit herself, she did, however, respond with mild favour to renewed proposals that she should marry Anjou. However, this was not enough for
Walsingham, who feared for Anjou and Navarre, both of whom were by
now imprisoned at the French Court: 'we seek neither to conserve friends
nor to provide for withstanding our enemies', he lamented to Burghley. To
Elizabeth he wrote in urgent terms: 'for the love of God, madam, let not the
cure of your diseased state hang any longer on deliberation. Diseased states
are no more cured by consultation . . . than unsound and diseased bodies by
only conference with physicians, without receiving the remedies by them
prescribed.'[5] Finally Elizabeth was persuaded into a very limited response,
sending an agent to Elector Casimir of the Palatinate—the most active

[2] Read, *Walsingham*, i. 18–20.
[3] David Kynaston, *The Secretary of State* (Lavenham, 1978), 43. By 'austerian' Naunton
meant 'puritan'.
[4] Read, *Burghley*, 153.   [5] Read, *Walsingham*, i. 286, 289.

Protestant mercenary general—with the offer of a loan of £15,000 to finance a military force. Agreement of a kind was reached, although Casimir made plain to Elizabeth that the sum was far too small, and German troops entered France in support of the Anjou–Huguenot alliance. Faced with formidable opposition, Henry III capitulated and signed a treaty—the Peace of Monsieur—which gave the Huguenots most of what they wanted—or would have done had the King and his Guisan allies intended to keep to its terms. Elizabeth reacted fiercely against the treaty and reprimanded Navarre for making peace; but he had little alternative, since Elizabeth could not be relied on for consistent support.

The Queen seems to have been equally reluctant, during these middle years of the decade, to shape a consistent policy in the Netherlands. Her advisers were divided. Walsingham urged open support for the Dutch, whose cause was godly and just, against the Spanish, who threatened both England and Protestantism. Burghley was more concerned to prevent the French from occupying the Netherlands ports, and to that end was even ready to assist Alba, provided that the Spanish restored the ancient liberties of the Low Countries; but he was not opposed to unofficial aid to the Dutch and was generally regarded as the protector of English volunteers. Elizabeth herself was much more hostile than her advisers to William of Orange, and more inclined to rebuild her links with the Spanish; by 1573 she was actively mediating between the protagonists in the Netherlands struggle. Although pacification seemed hopeless at that time, within a year Spanish authority in the Netherlands collapsed. Desperate shortage of money led to violent and terrifying mutinies by the Habsburg army during the summer of 1576, culminating in the 'Spanish Fury' at Antwerp in November, when 8,000 people died. The Estates General took over authority, and in the Pacification of Ghent the Catholic provinces joined Holland and Zeeland against Spanish policies. The new governor, Don John of Austria, was forced to subscribe to its terms and to order the withdrawal of Spanish troops early in 1577; and for a few months it seemed that a satisfactory solution had been secured without any effort by England. But the situation was highly unstable. Disagreements and jealousies between Orange and the other magnates of the Netherlands made it unlikely that the new unity of the provinces would survive. Don John seized the citadel of Namur, made an attempt on Antwerp, and in January 1578 defeated the army of the Estates General at Gembloux. Hope for the rebels was transformed to danger.

For a year Elizabeth had been contemplating aid to the Dutch, partly in order to prevent a return of Spanish troops, partly to inhibit them from approaching Anjou. Half-promises had been followed by equivocation: she offered money and troops in September 1577, and withdrew the offer in

MAP 10. The Netherlands

December. In the middle of this decade Elizabeth seemed to flounder in a state of indecision unusual even for her. Missions were sent to the Huguenots and the Dutch; offers were tentatively made and frequently withdrawn. The view of one historian that by 1578 the 'carefully defined neutrality' of earlier years had been abandoned in favour of a new, more committed strategy is unconvincing.[6] While neutrality was probably impossible in the changed circumstances after Gembloux, this was not the result of any coherent shaping of policy in England. One obstacle to such shaping was the frequent absence of Burghley from the centre of affairs.

[6] Wallace T. MacCaffrey, *Queen Elizabeth and the Making of Policy, 1572–1588* (Princeton, NJ, 1981), ch. 8, esp. 240–2.

Generally regarded as standing continually at the shoulder of his monarch, he was in fact often away from Court in these years, sick with gout, at home in Theobalds, or taking the cure at Buxton. Sir Thomas Smith, Secretary of State in partnership with Walsingham, wrote to Burghley: 'we have great want of you here for dispatching of matters.' The Queen was, he said, 'at all times uncertain and ready to stays and revocation . . . This irresolution doth weary and kill her ministers, destroy her actions and overcome all good designs and counsels . . .'.[7] Walsingham, while he did not always see matters in the same light as Burghley, also wanted him at hand. In these years there was no real division between the councillors: although some, like Walsingham, were more inclined to intervention than was Burghley, they all wanted decisions to be made and maintained, and they favoured giving some assistance to the Dutch. Yet Elizabeth's irresolution is easily understood. The groups of French and Dutch nobles who begged for her aid were unreliable: the alliances between Anjou and the Huguenots, and between Orange and the grandees of the Southern Netherlands were brittle.[8] Nor would a firmer commitment by Elizabeth have made much difference at that point either in France or in the Netherlands.

There was, however, one English initiative overseas which betrayed none of the indecision and irresolution of Elizabeth's diplomacy. On 13 December 1577 Sir Francis Drake sailed from Plymouth harbour with a fleet of five ships on a three-year voyage which was to carry him round the world. The achievements and consequences of that enterprise will be discussed later; but the origins of the voyage were closely linked to the diplomatic manœuvres of the mid-1570s. After the disaster of San Juan de Ulúa in 1568,[9] Drake had made three expeditions to the Caribbean, none of them conspicuously successful. His new voyage was backed by the Earl of Lincoln, who was Lord Admiral, and by the Earl of Leicester, Walsingham, Hatton, and others; it also had the support of the Queen. Its objectives have been debated at length, and it is impossible to be certain about them. Most probably Drake's intentions were to sail through the Straits of Magellan, and then explore northwards along the coast of Chile in the hope of securing gold and possible sites for settlement: circumnavigation of the globe was not originally envisaged. Implicit in the scheme, though not its main purpose, was the plunder of Spanish ships and ports to secure a profit; and for that reason the plans were kept secret from Burghley. In its inception Drake's voyage was certainly provocative, but not nearly so aggressive as its success

[7] Read, *Burghley*, 144–5.

[8] The Walloons, southern French-speaking Netherlanders, were temporarily in alliance with Orange at this point.

[9] Above, Ch. 7 s. 3.

ultimately made it. He sailed when Spain's position in Europe was weak after Don John's capitulation, and when Elizabeth could reasonably hope to exploit the New World for her own profit. At the very moment that she was withdrawing her support from the Dutch Estates she allowed Drake to sail into Spanish waters; and this contrast well illustrates the kind of short-term calculations upon which her decisions were often based.[10]

English security was threatened by dangers at home as well as abroad. Sir Francis Knollys, elder statesman of the royal household, neatly analysed the problems confronting government: 'The avoiding of her Majesty's danger doth consist in the preventing of the conquest of the Low Countries betimes; secondly, in the preventing of the revolt of Scotland from her Majesty's devotion . . . ; and, thirdly, in the timely preventing of contemptuous growing of the disobedient papists here in England.'[11] During the first half of the decade the bishops reported a disturbing increase in the number of Catholic recusants and non-communicants. In 1574 the first seminarist missionaries reached England from Douai and two years later there were rumours that an 'Enterprise of England' was being planned. In 1575 the Privy Council sent a general letter to the bishops instructing them to investigate recusants, and in August and succeeding months suspect gentlemen were summoned to London. Next year the Lord Keeper was told to remove certain men from commissions of the peace; and a census of recusants was ordered in all dioceses, the universities, and the inns of court. Priests were arrested and the executions began: the first victim was Cuthbert Mayne, condemned for treason at Launceston in 1577 on dubious legal grounds.

The 'hotter sort of Protestants' presented a more complex problem, since although the Presbyterians caused the government anxiety, it needed support from confirmed reformers in the fight against popery. However, alarmed by radical propaganda and by the activity of Presbyterians in London,[12] the Council had issued a proclamation in 1572 condemning the 'insolent and inordinate contempt of such as refuse to come to common prayer'—a double-barrelled blast against both Catholic and Presbyterian recusants.[13] Suspect ministers were ordered to subscribe to articles on controversial issues; the assize judges were told to examine Presbyterian nonconformity; and several ministers, most of them in London, were deprived of their livings and imprisoned. The Presbyterian leader, Thomas Cartwright, fled to Heidelberg; but by 1574 the tension was relaxing and the

[10] Below, p. 288 for the story of this expedition.
[11] Patrick Collinson, *Archbishop Grindal, 1519–1583: The Struggle for a Reformed Church* (London, 1979), 57.
[12] Above, Ch. 7 s. 3, and below, Ch. 11 s. 4.   [13] *Proclamations*, ii. nos. 597, 599.

suppression of the more extreme radicals seemed successful. However, the Church under Archbishop Parker lacked the dynamic leadership needed to combat popery, for Parker, at odds with the leading councillors and almost morbidly suspicious of them, had turned for solace to antiquarian studies. His death in May 1575 made room for the appointment of a man who could bring together active Protestants in a movement to revitalize the Church. The man was at hand in the person of the Archbishop of York, Edmund Grindal, an active, evangelizing cleric, who was sympathetic to moderate puritans and to preaching, but hostile to Presbyterianism, and had the support both of Burghley and of the more zealous Walsingham. Shortly after his translation to Canterbury, Parliament met in February 1576. Its main purpose was to provide money; and significantly it voted a subsidy, not for war, but as preparation for possible future trouble, 'as wise mariners in calm weather do then most diligently prepare their tackle and provide to withstand a tempest', in the words of Sir Walter Mildmay.[14] The House of Commons also presented a moderate petition for ecclesiastical reform, supported by several privy councillors. They asked for the removal of unlearned ministers, the prevention of pluralism, and the suppresion of papists: all of them unobjectionable, though probably unattainable, ends. The stage seemed set for a revival of godliness.[15]

In the next eighteen months, these hopes were killed, for in the summer of 1576 reports were sent to Grindal of 'disorders' at prophesyings in the midlands. Prophesyings were conferences principally of local clergy at which sermons were given and discussions held on the points raised. Although laymen were sometimes admitted to hear the preaching, the main purpose was the education of parish priests. For the most part, these prophesyings were conducted with the approval of the bishops and according to well-established rules; but occasionally radical voices were heard and dissension stirred. Partly for this reason and partly from a general suspicion of preaching, some of the more conservative bishops and, more important, Elizabeth herself looked on them with disapproval. The Queen ordered Grindal to suppress the prophesyings and 'abridge' the number of preachers. In a letter of considerable length Grindal expounded his reasons for refusing. 'I cannot', he told Elizabeth, 'with safe conscience and without the offence of the majesty of God give my assent to the suppressing of the said exercises . . . Bear with me, I beseech you, Madam, if I choose rather to offend your earthly majesty, than to offend the heavenly majesty of God . . .'. 'Remember, Madam', he reminded her, 'that you are a mortal creature.'[16] His astonishingly rash language and his total refusal to compro-

[14] Hartley, *Proceedings*, i. 442.   [15] Ibid. 445-7.
[16] Collinson, *Grindal*, chs. 13, 14.

mise robbed him of support from such sympathetic councillors as Burghley, Mildmay, and Leicester. In the summer of 1577 Elizabeth ordered that Grindal be suspended from the exercise of his office and proposed that he be deprived of it. The deprivation of an archbishop involved complex and doubtful points of law, and in the end the affair was left unresolved: Grindal's suspension was not lifted but he was never dismissed. Until he died in 1583 the Church had no active head.

The political intrigues behind Grindal's fall are tantalizingly obscure. It was rumoured at the time that Leicester had betrayed him, though this seems improbable; and that the Court physician, Dr Julio, had a grudge against Grindal and may have worked on the Queen, which seems more likely. Whatever the truth, Grindal's fate was lamented by both Burghley and Walsingham: 'these proceedings', wrote Burghley, 'cannot but irritate our merciful God'.[17] Yet none of the Court politicians could save Grindal once he had taken up a wholly intransigent stance. Support for the godly was one thing; support for outright disobedience would endanger any politician's standing with the Queen. These events marked a significant turning-point in the religious history of the reign. After Grindal's suspension the men appointed to the episcopal bench were predominantly hostile to the reforming tradition for which he, Burghley, Walsingham, and Leicester all, in different ways, stood.[18]

2. THE ANJOU MATCH AND THE NETHERLANDS, 1578-1582

Throughout 1578 and 1579, as the Spanish undermined the position of the Estates General in the Netherlands, England was in real danger. Don John's victory at Gembloux in January 1578 began the Spanish recovery; and although his death in October seemed at first to be a setback for the Habsburg cause, he was succeeded by Alexander Farnese, Duke of Parma, a leader with political and military skills of the highest order. Torn by religious dissension and by provincial and personal rivalries, which were exploited by Parma, the Estates General fell apart into two separate Unions of Utrecht and Arras, while the Spanish consolidated their military position. In Scotland the Protestant and pro-English rule of Regent Morton began to decline in 1578, when James started to take decisions for himself; rebellion broke out in Ireland in 1579 and raged for four years; and at home the mission of Campion and Parsons posed the threat of a dissident Catholic movement against the regime.

---

[17] Collinson, *Grindal*, 252.   [18] Below, Ch. 11 s. 4, for further discussion.

Alarming as the situation might be in Scotland, Ireland, and England itself, the centre of the storm lay in the Netherlands. Here the fundamental character of the English government's problem had not changed: the Spanish must be prevented from imposing absolute rule and the French must be kept out. However, an urgent decision was now demanded, for no longer could Elizabeth dangle promises of support before the Estates General and then withdraw them. In March 1578 she offered to advance £40,000 to finance the hire of a force under the inevitable Casimir of the Palatinate. Her offer was accepted, but it was insufficient to meet the military needs of the Estates, who now turned to Anjou with definite proposals to buy his aid. Frightened by the prospect of French intervention in the Netherlands, Elizabeth threatened to cancel the proposed loan and consulted her Council. She received three conflicting opinions. Lord Keeper Bacon regarded Anjou's activities calmly and advised allowing the Estates to continue their negotiations with him: the involvement of France in the Netherlands would, in his view, embroil her with Spain, and the consequent struggle must be to the advantage of England. Burghley considered the French danger to be greater than any other. He proposed that Elizabeth send ambassadors of high standing to the Estates and warn them that, unless they broke off their negotiations with Anjou, she would be forced to ally with Don John, but that if they complied with her wishes she would send them men and money in their fight against Spain. Walsingham was much more gloomy than the other two. He was highly suspicious of Anjou's motives and urged Elizabeth to bear in mind the Massacres of St Bartholomew's Day, which he had witnessed only six years before: 'I am greatly in doubt', he wrote, 'that those that were authors in that banquet have their hand in the pie in this new intended matter.'[19] He was firmly in agreement with Burghley that Anjou posed a dangerous threat, but seems to have been for the moment uncertain how it should be met.

Burghley's advice that an embassy be sent to the Netherlands was accepted, and Walsingham was appointed to it in conjunction with Lord Cobham. Walsingham had rich diplomatic experience, Cobham none; but, as Lord Warden of the Cinque Ports, Cobham provided the mission with social prestige. Their instructions were to mediate between Don John and the Estates General in an attempt to bring about peace. If that failed they were to investigate the needs and resources of the Estates and attempt to dissuade the Dutch from committing themselves to Anjou; if their inquiries showed that the Estates could not defend themselves against Don John they were to promise direct aid from England in return for the cession of some

---

[19] Read, *Walsingham*, i. 377.

towns as security. At the same time Elizabeth sent Sir Edward Stafford to France with indications that she was ready to resume negotiations for marriage with Anjou. She was trying to keep open as many roads as possible; a mediated peace was desirable above all, but should it fail she would contemplate assistance to the rebels and alliance with Anjou. She had not committed herself—she seldom did—but she had come nearer to doing so than before.

Walsingham and Cobham travelled to the Netherlands in June 1578 with an imposing retinue of 120 men. This was a full-scale embassy, far greater in size and prestige than the missions of lesser agents sent in previous years; but it achieved little more success. Within a fortnight of their arrival they realized that the terms offered by the Estates to Don John would never be accepted; and they reported that the Estates were capable of withstanding Don John, but must have money if they were to succeed in that and in avoiding dependence upon the French. Elizabeth had promised to provide bonds of £100,000 on which the Estates could borrow, and her ambassadors urged that these be sent at once: delay would be fatal, for without money the Dutch must let in the French. Within weeks the danger grew worse when Anjou entered the province of Hainault and occupied Mons. In spite of this, Elizabeth refused either to lend any more money or to provide the bonds which could be used as security for borrowing. Burghley told Elizabeth that if she dealt so harshly with the Dutch, 'they will, yea, they must, give themselves over to the French . . . She shall lose not only her money already lent but also all her good will shall be buried and unkindness be raised up in the place.'[20] But although her principal advisers—Burghley, Leicester, and Walsingham—all urged action upon her, she stubbornly refused to move and let them know her displeasure. Walsingham wrote to Hatton in despair: 'it is an intolerable grief to me to receive so hard measure at her Majesty's hands, as if I were some notorious offender.' Yet he managed to maintain a bitter humour in spite of everything: 'it is given out . . .', he wrote to a cousin, 'that we shall be hanged at our return . . . The worst is, I hope, we shall enjoy our ordinary trial, my Lord to be tried by his peers and myself by a jury of Middlesex.'[21] The Queen relented to the point of instructing her ambassadors to offer money and a thousand or so men, but insisted that the proposal come as a suggestion from them rather than a promise from her. Although she seemed to have accepted her councillors' arguments, Burghley warned that nothing could be certain. By that time, in any case, the Dutch had given up hope of support from England, and in spite of protests from the English ambassadors had signed a treaty with Anjou,

[20] Read, *Burghley*, 195.   [21] Read, *Walsingham*, i. 394–5.

under which he was recognized as Defender of the Belgic Liberties in return for supplying an army of 2,000 horse and 16,000 foot for three months.

Elizabeth's delays and prevarications have been condemned by one historian as responsible for the Dutch failure to exploit Don John's weakness in the summer of 1578 and thus for losing a major opportunity of keeping out the Spaniards.[22] In her defence it has been argued that the intervention urged by Walsingham would have been ineffective in stopping Don John and dangerous in alienating the Spaniards.[23] Neither judgement seems entirely correct. The first exaggerates both the chances of a decisive Dutch victory and the effectiveness of English aid. On the other hand, Elizabeth was thoroughly inconsistent in the execution of policy. While agreeing with her advisers on the general lines of strategy, she failed to deliver what she promised. The consequence was 'the alienation of this country people's [i.e. Dutch] hearts from her Majesty'—to quote Walsingham—and the entrance of Anjou into the affairs of the Netherlands.[24] Her persistent disregard of advice left Walsingham in despair: 'the only remedy left unto us is prayer, where consultation will take no place.'[25]

Early in 1579 another aspect of policy became dominant. Elizabeth already seemed to view favourably the prospect of marriage with Anjou; and after his campaigns in the Netherlands had failed in 1579, the Duke reopened negotiations. There followed a year of intensive courtship. Respectable political arguments could be, and were, presented for this marriage. Burghley wrote two long memoranda, presenting both the objections to the match and the answers to them. Against hypothetical objections over the Queen's age and a general repugnance to her marriage with a French prince, he insisted that Elizabeth could still bear children, that her marriage was necessary for the safety of the kingdom, and that if Anjou were refused he might marry a Habsburg princess and present England with a dangerous combination. If there were no marriage, Burghley implied, it would be urgently necessary to muster troops, mobilize the navy, fortify the coast, and secure alliances with Protestant princes. All this would be expensive, whereas marriage would provide security with less peril and cost. On the other side Walsingham and Leicester were vehemently opposed. Among the many reasons advanced by them two stood out: Anjou's religion and the uncertainty of his motives. A Catholic marriage would bring down on England the wrath of God and divide her people.

[22] Charles Wilson, *Queen Elizabeth and the Revolt of the Netherlands* (London, 1970), 66–70.

[23] R. B. Wernham, *The Making of Elizabethan Foreign Policy, 1558–1603* (Berkeley, Calif., 1980), 49–55.

[24] Read, *Walsingham*, i. 416.   [25] Ibid. 418n.

Throughout 1579 Elizabeth seemed to everyone set on the marriage, and many observers regarded it as almost a *fait accompli*. In January Anjou's envoy, Jean de Simier, 'a most choice courtier, exquisitely skilled in love toys, pleasant conceits and Court-dalliances', arrived at Court.[26] Elizabeth was delighted with him, nicknaming him her 'ape'. She did everything to convince him that she was determined on marriage and pressed for Anjou to come over. In the middle of August he came, and was given the nickname of 'frog'. Pock-marked and ill-formed, he did not make an attractive prospect; but Elizabeth was not put off, entertaining him lavishly, albeit secretly, during his fortnight's stay.

However the proposed marriage stirred dissensions in the country. Philip Sidney quarrelled over the match with the Earl of Oxford, a supporter, and later wrote an open letter to Elizabeth in which he described Anjou as 'the son of that Jezebel of our age'.[27] Sermons were preached against the marriage in London, and in September was published the most important polemic against it, John Stubbs's *The Discovery of a Gaping Gulf*. Stubbs attacked the House of Valois as 'a principal prop of the tottering house of Antichrist', objected to Elizabeth's marriage with a foreigner, and urged that England defend herself by the 'bridling bands of the sea' rather than rely upon French 'cormorants'.[28] he was condemned for seditious libel and sentenced to have his right hand cut off. After the public amputation he held up the bloodied stump to the crowd and called 'God save Queen Elizabeth'. His defence counsel, who had objected to the legal grounds of the prosecution, was imprisoned.

In October Elizabeth referred the matter to her Privy Council, which debated the marriage proposals continuously for five days. Differences had by now hardened, with Burghley and Sussex apparently alone in supporting the marriage, the rest in opposition. Burghley urged the need to provide for the succession; the other side, realizing that Elizabeth wanted a favourable opinion, declined to press their view; and the Council informed the Queen, to her fury, that they would give no recommendation until they knew her own mind. After some deliberation and a good deal of recrimination, Elizabeth told them that she was determined to marry, and Simier was sent back to France with Elizabeth's terms: they included a proviso that she would

[26] William Camden, *Annals or the Historie of the . . . Princess Elizabeth* (London, 1635), 200.

[27] Philip Sidney, 'A discourse of Sir Philip S. to the Queenes Majesty touching hir marriage with Monsieur', in *The Complete Works of Sir Philip Sidney*, ed. Albert Feuillerat (Cambridge, 1923), iii. 51–60, esp. 52.

[28] John Stubbs, *The Discoverie of a Gaping Gulf whereinto England is like to be swallowed by an other French marriage* (London, 1579; STC no. 23400), sig. B. 3.

not marry without the consent of her subjects and that the treaty must be delayed for two months so that she could win them over. By the early weeks of 1580 she was prevaricating further and Burghley recognized with regret that she had turned her back on the marriage.

The whole episode is in many ways strange. How strongly was Elizabeth committed to the Anjou match? What were her motives? And why did she abandon it? These questions can never be answered with certainty. One historian has asserted that although there were sound political grounds for the marriage, the Queen was moved principally by strong personal attraction for matrimony, that she herself was responsible for initiating the negotiations, and that she abandoned them because her Council and many of her principal subjects were hostile to the policy. In his words the events reveal that 'new energies [were] at work within the English political order'.[29] It is impossible to gauge Elizabeth's motives. Certainly she enjoyed the business of courtship and indulged energetically in its pleasures; and probably she, rather than any councillor, took the lead in promoting the marriage; but the impression remains strong, as on other occasions in her life, that flirtation and courtship attracted her more than marriage itself. There was no overriding political reason for her to draw back when she did, and while political opposition played its part in her decision—or indecision—so too did reluctance to take the step into marriage itself. It would be unwise to infer from these events that there was a new force operating in English politics. Mary, too, had met opposition from councillors, notables, and parliamentarians; but she overrode it because she was whole-heartedly determined to marry Philip. Elizabeth was seldom decisive or determined about any positive step, especially when matrimony was involved.

From the beginning of 1580 England's position weakened as the Habsburg and Catholic forces revived in Europe. In January the aged Cardinal-King Henry of Portugal died, and by the autumn of 1581 Philip had succeeded him, establishing full control over Portugal. In the long run the conquest had its drawbacks for Spain, since the extensive Atlantic coastline was vulnerable to attack; but the immediate effect was an increase in Philip's naval resources. In France, as the endless civil wars dragged on, the Catholic Guise party gained strength and drew closer to Philip. The rebellion in Ireland gathered momentum and attracted foreign support.[30] The gradual erosion of Regent Morton's authority in Scotland finally led to his fall on the last day of 1580.[31] In the Netherlands the power of the Estates

---

[29] Wallace T. MacCaffrey, 'The Anjou Match and the making of Elizabethan foreign policy', in Peter Clark *et al.* (eds.), *The English Commonwealth, 1547–1640* (Leicester, 1979), ch. 5; and id., *Queen Elizabeth and the Making of Policy*, ch. 11.

[30] Below, s. 3.   [31] Below, p. 286.

General was rapidly dissolving: Parma was winning allies in the south; and the northern provinces were in desperation turning again for help to Anjou. At home the government was alarmed by the arrival in June 1580 of the two most celebrated Jesuit envoys, Edmund Campion and Robert Parsons: by now the number of Catholic missionaries in England had risen above one hundred. The only gleam of success shone out when Francis Drake sailed into Plymouth on 26 September; and triumphant as his great voyage had been, it only intensified the hostility between England and Spain.[32]

Anjou remained the key to English diplomacy in spite of Elizabeth's abandonment of the marriage negotiations. In January 1580 Orange proposed that Anjou be offered the sovereignty of the Netherlands in place of Philip II. After several months of difficult bargaining agreement was reached between the Estates and Anjou in September, followed by the abjuration from Philip II almost a year later. But the elevation of Anjou provided only nominal authority over those provinces in revolt; the Estates neither wanted the sovereignty nor had the unity to exercise it; and Orange, who could have led the Dutch, was not offered the power to do so. The English government reacted very slowly to Anjou's rise. A Council meeting in July 1580 was presented with a characteristic memorandum from Burghley. The alternatives, stated in elliptical terms, were direct assistance to the Dutch or a reversion to the marriage negotiations with Anjou; but Burghley enumerated so many objections to both courses that the Council made no recommendation.

However, by the end of the year negotiations with the French were resumed, and in April 1581 commissioners arrived from France to negotiate a marriage treaty. When Elizabeth insisted that she wished to suspend consideration of the marriage and discuss only terms for an Anglo-French alliance, the French commissioners replied that they were not empowered to treat of an alliance without the marriage. The impasse was complete. Elizabeth did not, however, wish to abandon the possibility of gaining support from Anjou or Henry III, and in July she sent Walsingham on a mission to the French court. Her choice of the ablest diplomat in England is strong evidence that she took the negotiations seriously; but the instructions given him, while strong on rhetoric, did not reflect a clear policy. Walsingham was to tell the French 'how necessary it is for the Crown of France as well as for ours, yea, for all Christendom, that the King of Spain's greatness should be impeached'. It would, said Elizabeth, be a grave mistake 'to leave the King of Spain to increase to such greatness as hereafter neither the force of France nor England nor any that may be confederate with them

---

[32] Below, p. 288.

shall be able to withstand any thing that the King of Spain shall attempt'.[33] This seemed unequivocal enough. But the details of Walsingham's instructions were a great deal more ambiguous, and he found his efforts constantly undermined from home: 'I would to God', he wrote to Burghley, 'her Majesty would resolve one way or the other touching the marriage . . . When her Majesty is pressed to marry then she seemeth to affect a league and when a league is yielded to, then she liketh better of a marriage . . . This sparing and unprovident course' would make any councillor prefer to live 'in the farthest part of Ethiopia rather than enjoy the fairest palace in England.'[34] Elizabeth's caution is perfectly understandable; but when one contrasts the lofty tone of her instructions with her hesitant direction of diplomacy one can only doubt whether she had any clear conception of policy.[35]

At all events Walsingham's embassy produced no agreement with the French Court. When he had his final meeting with Henry III on 10 September 1581 the French King made it clear that the Anjou marriage was an essential condition for an alliance, and that was effectively the death of Walsingham's negotiations. However, it was not the end of relations with the French, for Anjou now announced that he intended to come to England again himself. He may still have had marriage in view, although it is unlikely that he had much hope in that direction; more probably his main objective was to secure money from Elizabeth, and even before he left France he had secured from her a loan of £30,000 for paying his troops at Cambrai. He landed in England at the end of October and overstayed his welcome until February 1582. On this visit he was entertained much more publicly than before, in itself perhaps a sign that Elizabeth was no longer serious about marriage, if she ever had been. She did, however, encourage him with a notorious piece of 'courtship' in which, according to the Spanish ambassador, she kissed him on the mouth and gave him a ring from her finger. The practical negotiations surrounding Anjou's visit lay not in these flirtations—which were probably intended only to impress Henry III and Philip II—but in financial bargaining. Before he left England Anjou had secured the loan of a further £10,000 down, with the promise of another £50,000, of which £30,000 was actually paid. In all Elizabeth lent her suitor £70,000, a fairly considerable sum, far larger than that advanced by his brother, the King of France. But it represented the limit of her commitment. There was no alliance, no promise of troops. Elizabeth, through intermediaries, simply acted as Anjou's banker. Her involvement in the

---

[33] MacCaffrey, *Elizabeth and the Making of Policy*, 289.
[34] Read, *Walsingham*, ii. 75, 88.
[35] For a different view see MacCaffrey, *Elizabeth and the Making of Policy*, 288–9.

affairs of the Netherlands was strictly contained and indirect, for all her fine words about the necessity of bridling the King of Spain.

Since the establishment of the Earl of Morton as Regent of Scotland in 1572 England's northern border had been secure against the dangers that had threatened it during the first fourteen years of Elizabeth's reign. But towards the end of the 1570s Morton's power came under challenge: first, in March 1578, from the Earls of Athol and Argyll; and then in the autumn of 1579, much more dangerously, from Esmé Stewart, Sieur d'Aubigny, kinsman to the Earl of Lennox. D'Aubigny reached Scotland from France in September 1579, having set out with the encouragement of the Guise family. Although he travelled under the auspices of the Guises, he was not a committed Catholic, not indeed committed to anything beyond the advancement of his own career. But he was prepared to use French support and to appeal to Scottish Catholics in that cause. However, his principal strength lay in the personal hold which he quickly established over the young King James, now aged 13 and beginning to resent the authority of Morton. In alliance with James Stewart, a soldier of fortune who had become Captain of the King's Guard, d'Aubigny rapidly built up his own influence at Court, gathering around him Morton's personal enemies, like the Earls of Athol and Argyll, as well as the Catholic party.

By April 1580 Burghley and Walsingham were thoroughly alarmed at the prospect of a Scotland dominated once again by a Catholic faction in alliance with either France or Spain. Robert Bowes, treasurer of the garrison at Berwick, was sent with £500 to Scotland to win support for Morton. At the same time he was ordered not to offend d'Aubigny, now Duke of Lennox, since Elizabeth was still negotiating with the French. Bowes found Morton's situation almost desperate and urged that any delay in helping him would lead him to distrust Elizabeth; but the Queen refused either to send more money or to use force. By the end of the year Morton's support had declined far enough for his opponents to strike, and on 31 December he was arrested, charged by James Stewart with complicity in the murder of Darnley. Elizabeth apparently reacted to this with more energy than before and mustered troops on the northern border; yet when Walsingham advocated military action to unseat Lennox, she refused. In June Morton was executed and Lennox took over power, supported by James Stewart, now created Earl of Arran. The Scots Protestants feared, with reason, that a Catholic regime might be re-established. Although Lennox had no religious commitments, he was linked with the Guises; and the arrival of a Jesuit mission in Scotland was disquieting. Both France and Spain were manœuvering to set up Scotland as a client state, and for this reason,

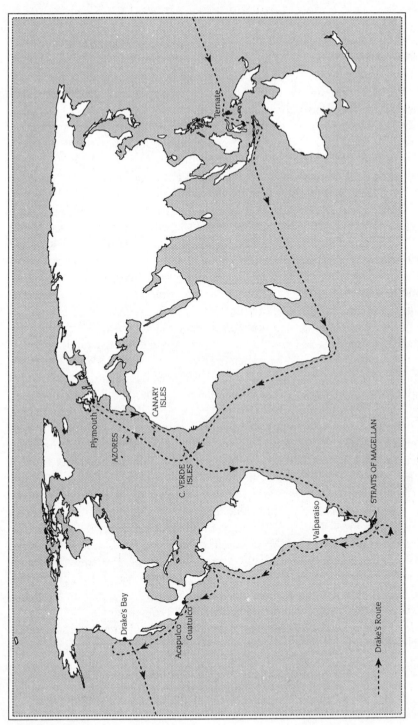

Plymouth

AZORES

CANARY
ISLES

C. VERDE
ISLES

Ternate

Drake's Bay

Acapulco
Guatulco

Valparaiso

STRAITS OF MAGELLAN

Drake's Route

Map II. Drake's voyage, 1577–1580

among others, the matter of James's marriage became an urgent question. Walsingham hoped to get him safely espoused to a Danish princess 'before he was out of his shell'. But Elizabeth would do nothing to help; nor would she spend any money on supporting Lennox's opponents. 'All remedies are rejected', wrote Walsingham despondently.[36]

In July 1582 the Earl of Angus, exiled leader of the 'English' party in Scotland, asked Elizabeth for financial support in his bid to topple Lennox. The Queen was sympathetic and encouraging, but would give no more than promises. However, the opposition went ahead and in August John Ruthven, Earl of Gowrie, seized James in the Ruthven Raid and imprisoned Arran. Lennox tried briefly to recover his position but retreated to France at the end of the year; for the time being the threat to England was lifted. Yet Elizabeth did nothing positive to support the new regime of Ruthven and Angus, while the French and James Stewart busily tried to undermine it. The whole conduct of English policy towards Scotland in these years contrasts bleakly with the decisive intervention at the beginning of the reign. Scotland was secure, but only temporarily so.[37]

In contrast to those demoralizing events the return of Drake in 1580 brought an element of triumph and colour. He had left Plymouth in 1577, with a lavishly equipped fleet of five ships, led by the *Golden Hind*.[38] He himself dined formally each day off silver dishes to the music of trumpets and clarions, while spiritual needs were met by a chaplain, Francis Fletcher, and some services were conducted by Drake himself. The fleet sailed down the African coast, taking various Spanish and Portuguese ships as prizes on the way, and then crossed the Atlantic to the coast of South America. Here occurred the first of several traumatic events. Thomas Doughty, one of the gentlemen accompanying the fleet, was brought to trial for treason and executed. Neither the precise charge nor the cause of the dispute is entirely clear, but it seems likely that Drake feared some challenge to his authority and struck first. The incident may have reflected discord between the gentlemen on board and the sailors, for after Doughty's execution Drake spoke of 'such controversy betwixt the sailors and the gentlemen, and such stomaching between the gentlemen and the sailors, that it doth even make me mad to hear it'. 'I must', he insisted, 'have the gentleman to hand and draw with the mariner, and the mariner with the gentleman.'[39]

In August 1578 the fleet, by now consisting of three ships, passed through the Straits of Magellan and entered the Pacific. Drake appointed a

[36] Read, *Walsingham*, ii. 178.
[37] Below, s. 4.   [38] Originally named *The Pelican*.
[39] K. R. Andrews, *Drake's Voyages: A Re-assessment of their Place in Elizabethan Maritime Expansion* (London, 1967), 81.

rendezvous on the coast of Chile but before he reached it his ships were scattered by three weeks of battering storms: one vessel sank, a second returned to England, and Drake sailed on in the *Golden Hind*. Off Peru he took several Spanish prizes and even entered the harbour of Lima, where he learned of the recent departure of a rich treasure-ship, the *Cacafuego*, which he captured on 1 March 1579. Well stocked with booty he now made a leisurely voyage home, first sailing northwards along the coast of California, probably in search of the north-west passage—the supposed Strait of Anian—as a return route. Perhaps because he concluded that this journey would be too difficult, he sailed instead across the Pacific, calling at Ternate off the Moluccas and making a safe voyage home to arrive in Plymouth nine months later.

After some hesitation Elizabeth welcomed Drake, who was knighted on board the *Golden Hind* in April 1581. The prize money was considerable: Drake kept £10,000 and the same amount was distributed among his crew. He himself became a popular hero, 'the people swarming daily in the streets to behold him'.[40] But his voyage had much more than personal significance. His journal and paintings supplied valuable information about the Pacific coast of America and about south-east Asia. His contact with the Sultan of Ternate marked the beginning of English trade with Asia, although the East India Company was not formed for twenty years. More immediately important, Drake had shown the vulnerability of Spain. While the great colonial empires of the sixteenth and seventeenth centuries were rich in resources, the possessing states lacked the naval power to protect them from intruders. Hence the history of the New World and Asia is marked by the continuous activity of pirates and privateers. These were no chance phenomena, but an inevitable consequence of wealthy empires inadequately protected. Drake was not the first to exploit the opportunities; but his resounding success inspired several others to follow his lead. Before his return, Humphrey Gilbert and Richard Hakluyt were planning the establishment of English bases in America; and after 1580 Drake himself, Hawkins, Ralegh, and others planned and executed voyages for settlement and privateering. None of this helped England's relations with the Spanish, who protested energetically at the depredations; but at a time when the King of Spain seemed to be advancing his case on every other front, Drake raised English morale by his success.

At home the government concentrated in these years upon the destruction of papist missionaries and the repression of English Catholics. The arrival of the first Jesuits, Campion and Parsons, in June 1580, following the

[40] Ibid. 98, citing J. Stow, *Annals* (London, 1615 edn.), 807.

rebellion in Ireland, thoroughly alarmed the government, which issued a proclamation against the spreading of rumours that invasion by the Pope and Philip II was imminent.[41] The Parliament, which had first met in 1572, was now summoned for its third session in January 1581. The purposes of the Crown were vigorously stated in the speech of Sir Walter Mildmay, Chancellor of the Exchequer, who spoke of the 'implacable malice of the Pope and his confederates', of their belief that 'England is th'only sovereign monarchy that most doth maintain and countenance religion', of Elizabeth's constancy in the face of these threats, and of the necessity to take steps for the security of the Queen, the realm and religion.[42] These measures amounted to stricter laws against the Catholics and a subsidy. The latter was quickly granted. The former were enshrined in a statute which raised the fine for recusancy to the enormous sum of £20 a month—hardly ever in practice exacted—and brought down the penalties of treason on anyone claiming authority to absolve subjects from their allegiance to the Queen or acting with the intention of withdrawing them from their obedience. In the event the second part of this statute was seldom used, since it was exceedingly difficult to prove intent, and the government issued a proclamation in the following year making it treason for Jesuits or seminary priests to remain in the country and misprision of treason for anyone to succour or conceal them.[43] This remarkable extension of the law, which made it treasonous merely to belong to a particular order, was not given statutory confirmation until 1585. The parliament of 1581 also produced a set of articles for improving the ministry of the church and sharpening the instrument of excommunication. The articles were probably devised with the help, and almost certainly the support, of Mildmay and Walsingham; and like other so-called 'puritan' articles they were mainly designed to strengthen the Church against its papist enemies. The Queen promised to remove the disorders of which the Commons complained, and Mildmay presented the articles to her again after the end of the session; but Whitgift, by now dominant in ecclesiastical matters, was obviously opposed to these reforms and nothing came of the petition.[44]

In the summer of 1581 Edmund Campion, best known of the Elizabethan Jesuits, was captured in Berkshire. His *Decem rationes*, written to draw men from the Protestant faith, had been printed in the spring and copies were laid on the benches of St Mary's church in Oxford to surprise the congregation at the commencement ceremony. Campion's personal appeal, high scholarship, and total integrity had made him a prime target for the govern-

[41] *Proclamations*, ii, no. 650.   [42] Hartley, *Proceedings*, i. 502–8.
[43] *Proclamations*, ii, no. 660.   [44] Hartley, *Proceedings*, i. 510–21.

ment, and after confining him to the Tower, councillors tried to win him
over by persuasion, with no success. They then resorted, equally unsuccessfully, to torture and to a public debate with the Deans of St Paul's and
Westminster. Campion and his colleagues were brought to trial in November and quickly condemned under the old treason law. Asked by his judges
what he had to say, he replied: 'in condemning us you condemn all your
own ancestors' a thrust not easily parried.[45] After Campion's execution
Burghley wrote and published a substantial work of propaganda, *The Execution of Justice in England* (1583), to justify the proceedings against priests.
The central thrust of his argument was that the papal bull of excommunication amounted to a declaration of war and lay behind all the rebellions
against Elizabeth; those who supported the Pope were therefore guilty of
treason. It was not a strong legal argument, but it made abundantly clear the
government's insistence that the executions were made on political, not
religious, grounds.

3. IRELAND, 1573–1588: COLONIZATION AND REBELLION

As England became increasingly drawn into the Netherlands conflict, her
government was confronted by major troubles in Ireland. When Sir Henry
Sidney left Ireland in 1571 the Fitzmaurice rebellion had been put down
and Elizabeth had determined upon a more economical policy, handing the
extension of English control over the island to private enterprise, and
reviving the policy tentatively but abortively conceived in 1569.[46] The first
entrepreneur was Sir Thomas Smith, classical scholar, man of affairs, and
privy councillor, whose interest in the Roman Empire may well have inspired his ambition to set up a colony in Ireland. In November 1571 he and
his son, also Thomas, were granted letters patent to establish a 'plantation'
in the Ards peninsula, east of Belfast. The enterprise was financed as a
joint-stock company, subscriptions to which were encouraged by a pamphlet outlining the rosy prospects and setting out the principal objective as
the founding of a colony 'of natural Englishmen born . . . at their own
charges and perils'.[47] The capital seems to have been adequately subscribed,
by gentlemen rather than by merchants, and 800 or so men assembled at
Liverpool for embarkation. Unfortunately for the project, Smith senior was
sent on a diplomatic mission to France and had to hand over control to his
less than competent son.[48] Only 100 men reached Ulster in the end, to be
met by strong resistance from the leading chieftain of the region, Sir Brian

[45] *DNB* iii. 854.   [46] Above, Ch. 7 s. 4; Maps 7, 8.
[47] Nicholas P. Canny, *The Elizabethan Conquest of Ireland*, 85.
[48] Above, Ch. 7 s. 4.

McPhelim O'Neill; and the enterprise ended in disaster when the younger Smith was killed 'by the revolting of certain Irishmen of his own household, to whom he overmuch trusted'.[49]

By this time a more powerful figure had stepped into the Irish arena. This was Walter Devereux, first Earl of Essex, a nobleman with modest estates and high ambitions. With strong connections at Court—he had married the daughter of Sir Francis Knollys—he was better placed than Smith for raising the necessary support. Having been granted the territory of Clandeboy, roughly equivalent to Co. Antrim, he raised a mortgage of £10,000 on his English and Welsh estates, and recruited a distinguished following of noblemen and gentlemen, including Lord Rich, Sir Peter Carew, and Francis Drake. His army was, however, too small to overcome the combined resistance of Brian McPhelim, Turlough Luineach, head of the O'Neills, and their Scottish mercenaries. Fitzwilliam, the Lord Deputy, gave him no effective support and he was soon hard pressed by financial burdens, Irish armies, and the diseases that spread among his men. Having lured McPhelim, his wife, and followers to a Christmas feast of reconciliation in 1574, Essex had the chief and his lady taken prisoner, their men slaughtered. A worse atrocity was committed in the following year when Francis Drake and Captain John Norris, later to be Lord General in Ireland,[50] assaulted the Scots settlement on Rathlin Island, killing all its inhabitants—men, women, and children. This was an act of desperation, prelude to Essex's admission of failure: 'Why', he wrote to the Queen, 'should I wear out my youth in an obscure place without assurance of your good opinion?'[51] The problem now lay in finding a means to extricate Essex without inflicting dishonour upon him: he solved that by dying of dysentery in September 1576.

His failure marked the end of private colonization, for it was by now apparent that only government enterprise and intervention could achieve success. As Burghley commented, 'how hard it were to reduce any province to conformity without the special charges and countenance of her Majesty'.[52] The colonizing ventures of the 1570s had introduced a new spirit into English relations with the Irish. Hitherto plantations had involved the dispossession of the native chiefs, but not of their subjects. The experience of Smith and Essex convinced many, including perhaps Elizabeth, that brutal measures against all the Irish would be needed. Essex

[49] Richard Bagwell, *Ireland under the Tudors* (3 vols., London, 1885–90), ii. 247.
[50] Norris was one of four brothers, all of whom distinguished themselves, sometimes brutally, in Elizabeth's wars.
[51] Bagwell, *Ireland under the Tudors*, ii. 324.
[52] Canny, *Elizabethan Conquest*, 91.

actually welcomed an alleged breach of faith by Brian McPhelim because the Irish had thus 'given me just cause to govern such as shall inhabit with us in the most severe manner, which I would not without evil opinions have offered if their revolt had not been manifest'.[52] Extreme severity, to the point of atrocity, became acceptable to many English colonizers, soldiers, and officials. To Sir Henry Sidney the Irish were not even Christians: 'I cannot find that they make any conscience of sin'.[54] Against such predispositions the inhabitants of Ireland, whether Old English of the Pale, Anglo-Irish families of the south and west, or Gaelic lords of the north, reacted with growing hostility.

During the rule of Lord Deputy Fitzwilliam (1571–5) the government's policy was tough but economical. Fitzwilliam considered the regional presidents and councils to be a useless extravagance, and when Lord President Perrott left Munster in 1573 he was not replaced. Fitzwilliam also believed that the Irish must be subdued by the sword before they could be ruled by the law: they have lived too long, he wrote, 'in beastly liberty and sensual immunity'.[55] Although Elizabeth wished to know as little about Irish events as possible and to avoid discussion of policy, the return of Sidney to Ireland as Lord Deputy in 1575 revived active and forward government. He succeeded in persuading the Queen to allow the re-establishment of presidencies, to which she was hostile on grounds of expense, while he believed them to be an essential means of reducing the power of the great magnates, who not unnaturally regarded them with suspicion. His second governorship began auspiciously. He toured through Ulster, Munster, and Connacht in the winter of 1575–6 and secured the appointment of Sir William Drury in Munster. A minor revolt by John and Ulicke Burke, sons of the Earl of Clanricarde, delayed an appointment in Connacht; but Colonel Nicholas Malby suppressed the revolt—'I spared neither old nor young', he commented with satisfaction—and was rewarded with the presidency.[56]

So far Sidney's policy had gone smoothly, but it broke upon the rocks of money and taxes. Sidney had promised, before his appointment, that he would make the government of Ireland financially self-sufficient and would ensure that the presidencies paid for themselves. The main plank of his scheme lay in a series of proposed 'compositions', whereby the rights of government and of lords to traditional payments should be commuted into fixed rents or taxes. In the Pale this involved the commutation into a cash rent of the imposition known as cess. Like purveyance in England, cess had been instituted as a means of supplying the monarch's representative in

[53] Ibid. 121.   [54] Ibid. 124.

[55] PRO State Papers Ireland (SP 63), 37/60: Fitzwilliam to Burghley, 25 Sept. 1572.

[56] Bagwell, *Ireland under the Tudors*, ii. 329.

Ireland with transport, food, and drink, either free or at a low cost; but by the reign of Elizabeth it was being used to supply English troops and had in consequence become a heavy burden and a major source of grievance, especially in the Pale. Disputes over this levy were to be a central feature of Irish politics in the 1570s and 1580s. In response to complaints, Sidney offered to take a composition rent of £5 per ploughland in return for surrendering the royal right to cess, which the Palesmen estimated as a burden of £8 per ploughland.[57] To this the gentlemen of the Pale replied that cess could not be levied without parliamentary consent and that the rate now charged was far higher than ever before. The Privy Council received this contention coldly and imprisoned three envoys from the Pale, while Sidney arrested the principal noblemen of the region. In the end, however, an agreement was reached, thanks partly to Elizabeth's growing disapproval of the cost of Sidney's rule. Although compositions were more easily se-cured in Munster and Connacht, his time had run out, for in 1578 he was again recalled, complaining bitterly and with some justice that he had been maligned by his enemies in Ireland and at Court. Drury was appointed Lord Justice to govern in his place, with instructions to rule more economi-cally, concentrating his attention upon the Pale. Once again the Queen had abandoned the forward policy urged by Sidney.

However, the retreat into a more conciliatory attitude came too late. In July 1579 James Fitzmaurice, who had been collecting support on the continent for the previous four years, landed at Smerwick on the Dingle peninsula with a force of Italian and Spanish soldiers under the auspices of Pope Gregory XIII. He was accompanied by Dr Nicholas Sanders, a Cath-olic scholar in exile, who brought to the rising the spirit of a religious crusader. At first it seemed that the revolt would be over almost before it had begun, since James Fitzmaurice was killed in a skirmish a few weeks after the landing and his kinsman, the Earl of Desmond, protested his loyalty to the Queen. However, Desmond was gradually drawn, against his will, into rebellion. Although he was the greatest hereditary lord in Mun-ster, his hold on the province had been weakened during the past decade. Heavily in debt to the Crown from fines imposed for his misconduct during the 1560s, he found his finances further eroded when his tenants refused to pay him his dues. With Sidney's help Desmond seemed to have solved his problems by a 'composition', under which he commuted his feudal rights, such as 'coign and livery', into a substantial rent.[58] However, this solution,

[57] A 'ploughland' was a very rough measure of approximately 120 Irish acres.

[58] 'Coign and livery' were general terms for Irish exactions derived from the lord's right to billet followers on the country. They were equivalent in the private sphere to cess in the governmental.

satisfactory as it was for the Earl, reduced the status and influence of his immediate kinsmen and followers, who accused him of betraying them and withheld their rents from him. At the same time Sidney's departure from Ireland deprived him of his principal supporter in government and exposed him to the enmity of rival Irish factions, especially the Butlers.

Soon after Fitzmaurice's death, the Earl's brother, Sir John of Desmond, killed a government envoy and assumed command of the revolt. He put himself at the head of 2,000 men, against a government force in Munster of only 500, commanded by Drury, who was dying. At this point Colonel Malby took command and defeated the rebels in a minor battle at Monasternenagh. An old enemy of Desmond, Malby seemed a major threat to the Geraldine clan, the more so when he demanded the Earl's total surrender. Up to that point Desmond had been loyal, but now he hesitated, and when Lord Justice Pelham proclaimed him a traitor, he had little choice but to join his own kinsmen in revolt. He publicized his decision by sacking the town of Youghal. A rebellion which might have been crushed at the start, like many of the minor risings of the 1570s, had gathered momentum partly as a result of the vulnerability of Desmond and his lack of control over his followers, partly through the impetuous and provocative conduct of Malby and Pelham. Unlike its predecessors, this revolt acquired a European dimension, proclaimed by Sanders as a religious crusade. Sir Humphrey Gilbert described—and exaggerated—the danger of the situation: 'this spark of rebellion is attended with bellows, both French, Spanish, Portingals, Italians, and of all sorts of papists throughout Christendom . . . I think this is an universal conspiracy.'[59] He was wrong about the conspiracy, but he reflected the mood of English settlers and soldiers in Ireland.

Having allowed earlier opportunities to slip, the government now acted firmly and expeditiously. The Earl of Ormond was appointed General in Munster; and he and Pelham marched against the rebels. Pelham burned Desmond's castles and devastated his lands, with the object of driving him into Kerry and depriving him of victuals. By the summer of 1580 matters seemed to be under control, but once again affairs went wrong for the Crown. Resentment had been stirring in the Pale since Sidney's attempt to levy the cess, and now a young Catholic peer from the Pale, Lord Baltinglass, joined his Wicklow neighbours, the Byrnes, in revolt under the papal banner, declaring it to be 'great want of knowledge and more of grace, to think and believe that a woman uncapax of all holy orders, should be

---

[59] J. Hogan and N. McNeill O'Farrell (eds.), *The Walsingham Letter-Book or Register of Ireland, May 1578 to December 1579* (Dublin, 1959), 121.

supreme governor of Christ's Church'.[60] This was the year in which Parsons and Campion landed in England, an ominous conjunction. Baltinglass was no great military leader, but he was fortunate that the new Lord Deputy, Arthur, Lord Grey of Wilton, who had landed with Walter Ralegh and Edmund Spenser among others, played into his hands. Grey attacked the rebels in the wooded valley of Glenmalure and was humiliatingly beaten back. The English losses were not heavy, but the moral impact of the defeat encouraged others to stir, including Turlough Luineach in the north. A few weeks later the temporary withdrawal of the English ships patrolling the Irish coast enabled 600 Italian and Spanish troops to land at Smerwick. Grey marched at once to the fort and, when its garrison surrendered, massacred them to a man. Whether or not he had promised them their lives was and still is disputed; but even if he had not, the incident reveals the increasing brutality of the war.

In the following year (1581) Grey began to establish control. Dr Sanders died in April, depriving the rebels of their propagandist. The Lord Deputy dealt harshly with the Pale, imprisoning several nobles, including Kildare, and executing others. A savage policy of devastation was unleashed in Ireland, its grim results described by Spenser: from woods and glens people came 'creeping forth upon their hands, for their legs could not bear them. They looked like anatomies of death, they spake like ghosts crying out of their graves, they did eat of the dead carrions . . . In short space there were none almost left and a most populous and plentiful country suddenly left void of man or beast . . .'.[61] In July 1582 Baltinglass fled abroad and the revolt of the Pale was finished, leaving the Old English discontented. Although Munster was still in rebellion its pacification was now only a matter of time. After Grey was recalled to England, Ormond was restored to the post of General in Munster, from which he had been dismissed a year earlier, and gradually Desmond's followers died or deserted, until in November 1583 he was taken near Tralee and killed by his captors.

The military conquest of the rebels in Munster and the Pale provided the opportunity for which advocates of a forward policy had long been asking. The new Lord Deputy, appointed in 1584, was Sir John Perrott, who had earlier been Lord President of Munster. He had a good knowledge of Munster and was friendly with Ormond; unfortunately he had an overweening temperament which won him a wide range of enemies. Sir John Norris was appointed Lord President in Munster and Sir Richard Bingham in Connacht, both of them able and experienced soldiers. Perrott returned

---

[60] Bagwell, *Ireland under the Tudors*, iii. 51.

[61] Edmund Spenser, *A View of the Present State of Ireland*, ed. W. L. Renwick (Oxford, 1970), 104.

to the problems of finance and composition, intending, unlike Sidney, to solve them with parliamentary consent. When Parliament met, three major measures were put before it: the attainder of Desmond and his fellow rebels; Perrott's proposals for fiscal reform, which included composition for cess, the creation of a uniform basis for assessments, and the commutation of 'coign and livery'; and the enactment in Ireland of various English statutes, including the savage penal laws of 1581 against Catholics. For this programme to be achieved, the suspension of Poynings' law would be necessary in order to circumvent its cumbersome procedures. From the start Perrott was faced with opposition on two fronts. One was formed by a group of landowners in the Pale, who called themselves 'commonwealth men'. They disliked his proposals for cess, feared the imposition of penal laws, and obstructed his proposals for the suspension of Poynings' law. The other was led by the Lord Chancellor, Archbishop Loftus, and composed of government officials, who suspected the Lord Deputy of being too conciliatory to the Irish. The first session of Parliament was a disaster and Perrott prorogued it with the words: 'Well, my lords and masters, you have hitherto spent some time and charged your country to little purpose.'[62]

His hope that they would do better in the second session was vain. Heavy commitment by the English government to the Dutch war ensured that any extra money went to the Netherlands rather than to Ireland, while at the same time poor harvests in 1585 and 1586 made any increase in the tax burden dangerous.[63] The Queen told Perrott that in view of the 'general mislike' of the statutes on religion he should 'take order for the stay thereof': she did not want 'discontentment to grow to disobedience', and wrote that 'I marvel you lack so much discretion in these dangerous days to touch that point of religion'.[64] Opposed by the 'commonwealth men' and by the government's own officials, Perrott retreated—too late for his own political security.[65] His high expectations had been dashed: 'when I might have pulled down mountains', he wrote to a friend, 'I shall be driven, sith they will have it so, to sit down upon a molehill.'[66] Some fiscal reforms were put through by a Great Council after the dissolution of Parliament, but the major proposals were abandoned. The Lord Deputy was not the only loser: the failure of the Irish Parliament to provide for the needs of government led to its neglect by successive Lord Deputies and by the

[62] Victor Treadwell, 'Sir John Perrott and the Irish Parliament of 1585–6', *Proceedings of the Royal Irish Academy*, 85 C, no. 10 (1985), 287.
[63] Below, s. 5.   [64] Treadwell, 'Sir John Perrott', 292.
[65] Perrott was charged with treason on his return and sent to the Tower in 1591.
[66] Treadwell, 'Sir John Perrott', 305.

Irish opposition. Only two Irish Parliaments met in the course of the next fifty years.

Perrott's other objectives were to settle Connacht by 'composition' and Munster by plantation. His policy was reasonably successful in Connacht, where, in a series of agreements between the Lord Deputy and the major landowners, he surveyed the lands, fixed annual rents, and abolished Gaelic jurisdictions and captaincies. The rent paid to the Lord President enabled Bingham to govern without depending on outside support; in return Bingham ruled harshly, and by ruthlessly crushing revolts established a firm military base, which was bolstered by the loyalty of the two earls, Clanricarde and Thomond.

In Munster the lands of the Earl of Desmond and 135 other rebels were confiscated by Act of Attainder: significantly, almost all the attainted rebels were already dead, while living rebels kept their lands. Lord Justice Pelham had announced in 1580 that he hoped to see Munster 'like well tempered wax, apt to take such form and point as her Majesty will put upon it'.[67] The impress to be made upon Munster was colonization by English settlers. On this privy councillors and their advisers were agreed, but there was some dispute about the composition of the settlers: should they be 'natural' Englishmen—that is to say, from England? Should they be a mixture of 'mere' Englishmen and English from the Pale? Or should some of the rebels be allowed to repossess their lands? In practice the second solution was adopted. The land was surveyed in 1584 and its extent estimated at half a million acres—an exaggeration, since the actual extent was 300,000. It was valued at £10,000 per annum, £7,000 of which was thought to be derived from Desmond's lands. Unlike earlier ventures this one was to involve the introduction of English cultivators as well as landlords; given the severe depopulation brought about by starvation and disease, there was room for new settlers, indeed they were essential to restore agriculture.

The plan devised, largely by Burghley, involved the division of the cultivated land into twenty-five seignories of 12,000 acres each.[68] Every seignory was to be settled by a grantee, known as an undertaker, and ninety other households headed by men of English birth. Grants were issued in the end to thirty-five undertakers, each of whom paid an annual rent for his seignory. Most of the original undertakers were soldiers or country gentlemen from western England, Ralegh and Hatton being the most prominent. For them the attractions of extensive lands were considerable and by 1588

[67] Michael MacCarthy-Morrogh, *The Munster Plantation* (Oxford, 1986), 19.
[68] Ibid., *passim*, on the actual process of devising the division and allocation of land, which was a great deal more complicated than this brief account allows.

all the seignories had been taken up. But from this point difficulties arose. The surveyors worked slowly, acreages were overestimated, and endless litigation ensued between the original inhabitants and the settlers. Above all, it proved difficult to attract tenants, for prospective settlers found that leases were short and rents high. Consequently the influx of farmers from England was not nearly so rapid as the government had hoped. In theory there should have been about 15,000 settlers, but in the event there were about 3,000 in 1592 and 4,000 in 1598. Instead of becoming an English colony the plantation came to be inhabited by a mixture of English and Irish. The investment demanded had been rather too high and the attractions of Munster insufficient. Nevertheless, the colony was not a total failure, for although the English settlers were driven out by the rebellion of 1598, plantation was resumed with some success under James I.[69]

4. ASSASSINATION PLOTS AND THE SPANISH THREAT, 1583–1585

From 1582 England's prospects grew even darker than before. Anjou proved utterly inept as sovereign of the Netherlands, returning home for good in 1583 after ignominious defeats, while Parma continued his inexorable reconquest of the south. Anjou's death in 1584 was no great loss, but the assassination of Orange almost immediately afterwards left the Dutch leaderless. In France the Catholic forces tightened their links with Spain, formally allying with Philip II in December 1584; and in the following July Henry III was forced to join them, abandoning previous edicts of pacification with the Huguenots. In the summer of 1583 James VI of Scotland escaped the control of Ruthven and the 'English party', reinstating Arran and thwarting that recovery of English influence which had begun with the Ruthven Raid. At home, assassination plots against Elizabeth frightened Privy Council and Parliament into further measures against Catholics, while the unity of English Protestants seemed to be endangered both by the activity of radical Presbyterians and by the harsh disciplinary measures of Archbishop Whitgift.

In August 1583 Sir Francis Walsingham, against his will, was sent on an embassy to Scotland in the hope of restoring English influence. His hostility to Arran and his overbearing attitude to James were hardly likely to make his mission a success. As he himself saw it, the object was to persuade James to accept English guidance, and his methods were to discredit Arran, whom he wrongly suspected of popery, and to lecture James. Walsingham's first

[69] Below, Ch. 9 ss. 3, 4.

meeting with the boy King was not propitious: the King, he wrote, fell 'into some kind of a distemperature and did with a kind of jollity say that he was an absolute King'.[70] James's reasonable assertions of independence were taken by Walsingham as indications of 'pride and contempt' towards Elizabeth. The King's self-esteem can hardly have been soothed by the long discourse on politics which Walsingham insisted on delivering, tactlessly pointing out the errors in his government.[71] Eventually the Secretary concluded that James was so far 'alienated' from the Queen that further persuasion was useless. By September Arran was in complete control. However, there was little serious danger that he would restore French influence, and Elizabeth sensibly refused to intervene. The 'English party' attempted a *coup* in the following year and was badly mauled, its leaders retiring into exile in England.

English diplomacy now fell into confusion. Some of Elizabeth's advisers, notably Lord Hunsdon, favoured an accommodation with Arran; Walsingham urged forcible support for the exiled lords; others suggested co-operation with Mary against her son. Eventually, in 1585, James accepted in principle the notion of a league with England in return for a pension, and in November of that year Elizabeth allowed the exiled lords to return to Scotland. Within a few days they had toppled Arran, with little or no assistance from England, and after further and protracted negotiations James agreed to enter into a league with England, securing in return a pension of £4,000 a year. The northern border was again secure.

The Scottish situation had had its repercussions in England. Various minor plots centred around Mary Stewart had been uncovered during the 1570s. In 1582 Walsingham began to get hints of a more serious conspiracy, involving two Scottish Jesuits, Creighton and Holt, the Spanish ambassador, Mendoza, the French ambassador, Mauvissière, and Mary herself. The link between Mary and Mendoza was Francis Throckmorton, a member of a Warwickshire Catholic family, who had been in Madrid and Paris, and had returned to England early in 1583. For six months Throckmorton was watched by Walsingham's agents until he was arrested in November. After torture he confessed, revealing a plan by which the Duke of Guise would invade England, with the backing of the Pope and of Philip II, to release Mary and install her by force upon the throne. The principal actor in this drama was Mendoza, who was expelled, protesting indignantly, in January 1584; Throckmorton was executed in the following summer.

---

[70] Read, *Walsingham*, ii. 213.   [71] Ibid. 216-19.

The so-called 'Throckmorton plot'—it would be better named the 'Mendoza plot'—had serious consequences. Mary Stewart was in due course removed from the lax vigilance of the Earl of Shrewsbury to closer confinement at Chartley, Staffordshire, where Sir Amias Paulet, a severe puritan, became her guardian: she could now be more effectively watched. Relations with Spain grew more tense after the expulsion of the ambassador, and Elizabeth's ministers became deeply alarmed at the prospect of her assassination and of invasion from across the Channel. To meet these dangers Burghley and Walsingham proposed more stringent measures against Jesuits and other Catholics, together with a Bond of Association. The Bond, circulated in October 1584, bound its signatories by oath to pursue to the death anyone attempting to gain the throne by harming the Queen, and debarred from the succession any person who made such attempts or, most important, on whose behalf they were made. The target was obvious. The oath was taken rapidly and enthusiastically in solemn ceremonies across the country by noblemen, gentlemen, and office-holders.

Another part of Burghley's plan was the strengthening of the Protestant faith within the Church. This proved a great deal more contentious, partly because the radical Presbyterian movement was beginning, though as yet very slowly and hesitantly, to take shape; partly because Archbishop Grindal, who died in July 1583, was succeeded at Canterbury by John Whitgift, a man obstinately committed to the persecution of puritans. In October Whitgift issued three articles, to which all ministers of religion were compelled to subscribe. The second of these stated that the Prayer Book contained nothing contrary to the word of God, a proposition from which many ministers, even very moderate puritans, recoiled. They won the support of several privy councillors, including Sir Francis Knollys, who protested that 'the most diligent barkers against the popish wolf' were being treated as enemies to Queen and state.[72] Whitgift was undeterred, and during the last two months of the year subscription was demanded of all clergy in the province of Canterbury. Protests were made to Whitgift himself and then to the Privy Council, where the threatened ministers won considerable support. Burghley complained, in well-known words, that 'this kind of proceeding is too much savouring of the Romish inquisition'.[73] Under pressure from councillors and county notables Whitgift retreated a step and allowed ministers to swear merely that they would use the Prayer Book. In consequence all except the most radical were able to accept the

[72] Patrick Collinson, *The Elizabethan Puritan Movement* (London, 1967), 247. Below, Ch. 11 s. 4.

[73] Read, *Burghley*, 295.

articles and Whitgift's opponents were divided; but the damage was done. The radical clergy turned to the Presbyterian movement; while more moderate men, both clerical and lay, regarded Whitgift with suspicion and hostility. This was not a favourable climate for the defence of the Church against popery.

In this time of fear, suspicion, and acrimony Elizabeth summoned her fifth Parliament. It met in November 1584, was adjourned for Christmas, reassembled early in February 1585, and was dissolved in March. At the opening, Sir Walter Mildmay described at great length and with high rhetoric the menace of the Pope and his allies, who planned to invade and devastate the country. Two specific measures were proposed to strengthen the security of the realm: one was intended to ensure the safety of the Queen, the other to rid the country of Jesuits and other missionaries. The first of these, based upon the Bond of Association, was designed in effect, though not in so many words, to debar Mary from the succession and to provide for an interim government if Elizabeth were assassinated. This bill ran into various difficulties with the Queen in December and progress on it was halted when Parliament adjourned for Christmas. During the recess Burghley drafted a remarkable set of proposals for carrying on government in the event of Elizabeth's murder. All officers of state should continue in post, a Great Council should be created to assume the powers of the Crown, and Parliament should be summoned to take over supreme authority and choose a successor to the throne. Not surprisingly, Elizabeth rejected this scheme, which may have been personally objectionable to her and certainly had radical implications for the monarchy. When Parliament reassembled it resumed debate upon the original measure for the Queen's safety. A new bill was brought in to deal with the difficulties which had held up proceedings before Christmas. The principal obstacle lay in the position of James VI, who was exempted in the bill from penalties that might be imposed upon his mother, although this contradicted the Bond of Association, sworn to by most members, in which the sanctions extended beyond the immediate conspirator, in effect Mary, to her heir. The problem was clumsily solved by a proviso stating that the Bond should be interpreted as being consonant with the new statute. While James's right of succession was not established by this measure, his claim remained valid; but the difficulty of debarring Mary without injuring the position of her son was not really overcome. Nor was the matter of providing for the government of the realm after the sudden death of the sovereign, for Burghley's scheme had been rejected without anything being put in its place.

The second measure, finally enacted, laid down that any Jesuit or seminarist priest who failed to leave the country within forty days should suffer the penalties of treason, and that anyone who aided them should suffer the penalties for felony. In effect this gave statutory confirmation to the proclamation of 1582.[74] Its passage was marked by an astonishing intervention by Dr William Parry, who denounced the bill as 'full of blood, danger, despair, and terror or dread to the English subjects of this realm'.[75] Parry's words stimulated predictable outrage among the members and he was instantly removed from the House, only being allowed back on making a full submission. That was not, however, the end of Dr Parry's story, for in the following February he was charged with plotting Elizabeth's murder and confessed to the conspiracy. His career is puzzling. For some years he had acted as a government agent in the company of Catholic plotters; and it may be that, like many double agents, he had developed confused loyalties to both sides; it is possible, too, that he expected his service to the Crown to save him from the ultimate penalty. In that he was mistaken, for he was hanged in March. However, his plot, uncovered shortly after Parliament reassembled in February, gave urgency to the bill for the Queen's safety and helped to speed its course. Was he perhaps the victim of a plot himself? We shall probably never know, but the revelation of his treachery was very convenient for the government managers in Parliament.

The government's programme for national security took up only part of Parliament's time. Vigorous pressure was brought to bear for strengthening the Church by the removal of abuses. Some of this pressure emanated from the Presbyterian leaders, who were developing an impressive propaganda campaign and who urged that 'some of the best credit' should go to London 'to solicit the cause of the Church'.[76] But radical Presbyterianism made only a small showing in this Parliament. Shortly before the Christmas recess Dr Peter Turner introduced 'a bill and book . . . digested and framed by certain godly and learned ministers . . .'. The 'bill' was designed to introduce government of the Church by pastors and elders on the Presbyterian model, the 'book' was the Genevan Prayer Book.[77] Turner was instantly opposed by Sir Francis Knollys, a man intensely concerned for moderate reform of the Church, and by Sir Christopher Hatton. No more was heard of Presbyterian measures in this Parliament: their day was to come, briefly, in the next.[78] Proposals for moderate reform received far greater support,

[74] Above, s. 2.
[75] Simonds D'Ewes, *The Journals of all the Parliaments during the Reign of Queen Elizabeth* (London, 1682), 340. Parry was MP for Queenborough, Kent. He ran through his wife's fortune in the 1570s and entered Burghley's service, spying on Catholics abroad; by 1582/3 he had apparently gone over to their cause.
[76] Collinson, *Puritan Movement*, 279.   [77] D'Ewes, *Journals*, 339.
[78] Below, s. 5.

although they too failed, in the face of opposition from Elizabeth and Whitgift, to achieve anything. The principal measures were presented in a petition from the Commons that unsatisfactory ministers be removed, that there be 'the better assurance that none creep into the charge and cures being men of corrupt life', that no oaths or subscriptions be demanded except those provided by statute, that the radical ministers suspended by Whitgift be restored, that exercises and conferences be allowed, and that absenteeism and pluralism be abolished.[79] The petition was presented by Knollys and Mildmay to a committee of the Lords, where it was subjected to an unrestrained denunciation by Whitgift, who complained that one article 'savoured of popularity'. Following the rejection of this petition several bills were presented for securing similarly moderate reforms: they were either suffocated in the Lords or vetoed by the Queen. Elizabeth announced that 'she will receive no motion of innovation, not alter or change any law whereby the religion or Church of England standeth established at this day'.[80] Although she allowed some debate on religious matters, Elizabeth made it clear that she was Supreme Governor and would not 'tolerate new-fangledness' or allow private men to question her rule.[81]

Events in the Parliament of 1584-5 were overshadowed by the foreign crisis. Now, as for the past decade, the principal centre of concern lay in the Netherlands. With the deaths of both Anjou and Orange in the summer of 1584 the northern provinces lacked a constitutional head and had lost their greatest war leader, while Elizabeth's policy of using Anjou to protect the Dutch and stave off direct French intervention was ruined. Meanwhile Parma pushed his siege trains forward to recapture one city after another. By September he had occupied all Flanders, except Ostend, and most of Brabant: Bruges, Dendermonde, and Ghent had fallen during the summer, and Antwerp was directly threatened. In France the alliance of the Guises with Philip II threatened Henry III and reduced the possibility of his providing aid to the Dutch; at the same time any intervention in the Netherlands by Henry must be viewed by the English government with caution, for they could not control him as Elizabeth had attempted to control Anjou.

Late in the summer Walsingham drew up at the Queen's command a series of questions to be debated by the Privy Council. Could the Dutch hold out on their own? Would the King of Spain 'attempt somewhat against her Majesty' if he reconquered the Netherlands? Would it therefore be advisable to prevent him from repossessing those provinces? Should the

---

[79] D'Ewes, *Journals*, 357-9.   [80] Collinson, *Puritan Movement*, 285.
[81] Ibid. 286.

King of France be called upon for assistance? If he refused, should the Queen 'proceed therein alone'? Would this not 'draw on a war'? How much would that cost and how would the expense be met? 'What way there may be devised to annoy the King of Spain?'[82] For the next year or so the Privy Council was to wrestle with these problems. On one point Elizabeth was firmly decided: when the Dutch offered her the sovereignty of their provinces she refused it, believing that by accepting she would be drawn more deeply into the contest than she wished. Otherwise there was disagreement and uncertainty. At a meeting of the Privy Council Burghley stated the case both for and against intervention in a characteristic piece, with the arguments on each side carefully balanced. But his own view seems to emerge: that intervention would be expensive and dangerous. Camden, who probably derived his own account of this debate from Burghley, wrote that those against giving direct aid to the Dutch—of whom Burghley was probably one—believed that England must fortify herself and become impregnable. Others, especially Leicester and Walsingham, criticized them as 'degenerate and faint-hearted cowards'.[83] The conclusion of the Council's debate was that England should assist the Dutch sooner rather than later, if possible with the aid of the King of France. Accordingly, William Davison, a senior and experienced diplomat, was sent to the Netherlands to open negotiations. At this point divergent views among the councillors again hindered decisions. Burghley seems to have urged reliance upon France, Walsingham to have doubted the wisdom of this; and relations between the two became strained, Walsingham blaming the Treasurer for the Queen's irresolution. However, by the spring of 1585 Elizabeth was coming to accept direct intervention. Walsingham instructed Davison to tell some of the Dutch in confidence that the Queen, 'rather than that they should perish, will be content to take them into her protection'.[84] Yet the commitment was still vague, and just at this point Burghley seems to have been turning once more against intervention: the Dutch were a rebellious and divided people, he complained, not to be trusted as allies. News of the alliance between the Catholic League and Spain now reached England and again Elizabeth began to hold off from the Dutch. However, this was balanced by Philip II's seizure of English ships in Spanish harbours, which disposed the Queen once more to action. Finally, in June, the Dutch envoys arrived in England. Their offer of sovereignty to Elizabeth having been at once refused, negotiation began over the amount and timing of English aid, and over the security to be given by the Dutch. The envoys wanted im-

---

[82] Read, *Walsingham*, iii. 73–5.   [83] Camden, *Annals*, 282; Read, *Burghley*, 307–9.
[84] Read, *Walsingham*, iii. 93.

mediate help for Antwerp, which was dangerously threatened, and greater assistance for the long term. Early in August a subsidiary treaty was signed by which the Queen would send 4,000 troops to relieve Antwerp and supply them for three months. About ten days later, at the Treaty of Nonsuch, Elizabeth committed herself to providing £126,000 a year, until the end of the war, for maintaining an English force of 6,400 foot-soldiers and 1,000 cavalry. In return the Dutch would give up Flushing, Rammekens, and Brille as security for the repayment of the Queen's expenses when peace was signed. The agreement came too late to save Antwerp but committed England to war with Spain.

The uncertainty and hesitation of the English have been blamed for the loss of Antwerp; and there were those in the Netherlands at the time who thought the city could have been saved. Yet even if English troops had got there earlier, it seems improbable, given the tight grip of the Spanish upon the supply-routes, that they could have done more than postpone disaster. And the Dutch themselves must share part of the blame. They were often dilatory in responding to advances and in sending envoys; and the citizens of Antwerp did much to impede the arrangements for its defence.

English diplomacy between 1572 and 1585 had shown a gradual and erratic movement from amicable relations with Spain to open, though limited, war. The reasons are many: Mendoza's plotting alarmed and antagonized the English; the exploits of Drake and other seamen angered the Spanish. Yet, in the end, the Low Countries produced the decisive arguments, for the English government could not allow Philip II to establish an absolute regime and a powerful army in the Netherlands. On that point Elizabeth and her councillors were, most of the time, agreed. Disagreement arose over the means of opposing Spain. It is unrealistic to conceive of the Privy Council as divided between two factions, one for war and one for peace, since the questions were too blurred and the alignments too shifting for that. Over at least two issues, however, there was sharp division. One was the Anjou marriage; the other was the decision to provide direct aid to the Dutch. On both occasions Burghley was found in opposition to Leicester and Walsingham; and in general he favoured an altogether more cautious approach to foreign affairs than they. Walsingham in particular emphasized in his letters and memoranda the overriding need to protect the true faith and urged a more interventionist policy in Europe. But such differences of approach do not amount to a division between clearly defined factions: Leicester and Walsingham seem neither to have enjoyed close personal relations nor to have operated a single patronage network.

The process by which decisions were reached is often obscure. Elizabeth has been called 'the architect of policy'; and without a doubt no major decision could be taken unless she gave her consent.[85] But that hardly makes her the 'architect'. Sometimes, over the Anjou marriage for instance, she does seem to have taken the initiative. More usually her councillors were left to define the questions, set out the options, and assess the advantages and disadvantages of each step. At that point several men might bring their influence to bear, although the most prominent voice, unless he was ill, belonged to Burghley. Elizabeth's role, which must not be underestimated, lay in choosing, or often in refusing to choose, between policies drawn up and supported by councillors and others. Looking at the events of 1584–5 one point seems to emerge: whereas the protagonists of intervention were determined and consistent in their advocacy, the prophets of caution, like Burghley, were hesitant and equivocal.

5. WAR AND THE ARMADA, 1585–1588

By August 1585 England was committed to fighting Spain, although there had been no declaration of war and various sets of peace negotiations were being conducted through different channels right up to the sailing of the Armada. Against the apparently overwhelming might of Philip II, England had slender resources for fighting on land but much more encouraging potential at sea. Thanks to the work of Lord Howard of Effingham, the Lord Admiral, and John Hawkins, Treasurer of the Navy, the Queen had thirty-four ships of her own, nineteen of them major fighting vessels of 200 tons or more, equipped with a considerable armoury of guns and many of them, the culverins, capable of firing at long range. In addition the Queen could call upon the services of armed merchantmen and privateers, which together made up the bulk of all the naval expeditions dispatched in the next eighteen years. By the mid-1580s there were some forty privateering vessels of more than 100 tons. Although the voyages of Drake and others had trained a substantial body of officers and seamen, experienced in fighting at sea, and a tolerably efficient administration had been established in the Navy Board, there was no permanent corps of naval officers or sailors. The royal ships and the auxiliary merchantmen were commanded and manned by freelance captains and their crews,who temporarily took the Queen's pay.

The land forces looked less promising. During the 1570s the organization of the county militias had been greatly improved, so that a permanent command structure of Lords Lieutenant, deputy lieutenants, captains of companies, and muster-masters had begun to emerge by 1585. Armouries

---

[85] MacCaffrey, *Queen Elizabeth and the Making of Policy*, 346.

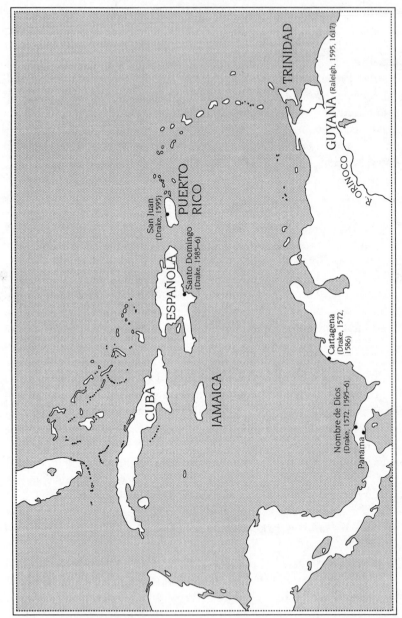

MAP 12. The Caribbean

had been set up in each county and beacons built to warn of invasion. Men, usually the better-off, were selected for training: paid a daily rate during training periods, they were provided with arms and given some instruction in their use. These men constituted the trained bands, available for home defence; and they were about 26,000 strong in 1588. In addition, there were some 200,000 militia men from whom the levies for overseas service could be drawn. These levies were the least satisfactory element in England's military strength: chosen generally from the poorest social classes, they were ill-nourished, poorly equipped, and largely untrained. Fortunately the effectiveness of expeditionary forces was bolstered by paid volunteers and unpaid gentlemen, who at least showed greater enthusiasm for war. The cavalry was almost entirely drawn from the followers and tenants of individual landowners: socially it was more presentable than the foot, although militarily not particularly useful. In the force of about 7,000 taken by Leicester to the Netherlands almost all the 1,000 cavalry and a similar number of foot-soldiers were volunteers, the remainder conscripted levies. While there was no shortage of noblemen and gentlemen anxious to serve as officers, very few of them had any experience of war and their training had been in the chivalric ceremonies of jousting, which were entirely inappropriate for the hard grind of siege warfare in the Netherlands.

The first thrust against the Spanish was made at sea. In September Drake left Plymouth for the West Indies with a fleet of more than twenty ships, two of which belonged to the Queen and the rest to private individuals. The real,though not the official, objective was to seize as much Spanish treasure as possible, sack some Caribbean ports, and, if possible, establish a base for further raids. The plunder was intended as a contribution to England's force in the Netherlands. Drake first assaulted Santo Domingo, on Española, which was easily captured and savagely treated; but the booty was small. His next target was Cartagena, east of Panama; this port, too, was easily taken, but was less easily held; and Drake gave up his plan for attacking Panama itself. In April 1586 he left Cartagena on the voyage home, landing first at Roanoke in Virginia, where Ralegh and Grenville had already established a small colony. The settlers, short of food, abandoned Roanoke and accepted a passage home in Drake's ships. By July Drake was back in Plymouth: he had shown the weakness of Spanish defences, but had secured little booty and established no base.

The expeditionary force to the Netherlands began to muster soon after the completion of the Treaty of Nonsuch in August 1585. Under pressure from the Dutch, Elizabeth named Leicester as commander-in-chief with a clear injunction that he was to assume no higher authority than that. The vanguard of his force left England in August, but Leicester himself did not sail until December. He was accompanied by a magnificent following: apart from ninety-nine officers and servants in his household, seventy lords, knights, and gentlemen made up his retinue, which was an assembly of the great names of English society, headed by that prince of chivalry, Sir Philip Sidney, appointed Governor of Flushing. The Dutch, or many of them, had for years looked to Leicester as the Protestant hope, and they greeted him with lavish receptions as he made his progress to the Hague. Although the Orangist party was anxious to limit his authority, a strong pressure-group in the Estates manœuvred to appoint him Governor-General, partly at least in order to commit Elizabeth more firmly to the war.

Within a few weeks of his landing he was offered 'the absolute government of the whole provinces', and after a few days of formal hesitation he accepted without consulting or even informing Elizabeth.[86] Not surprisingly, the Queen was furious when she eventually heard the news: 'We could never have imagined', she wrote to Leicester, 'had we not seen it fall out in experience, that a man raised up by ourself . . . would have in so contemptible a sort broken our commandment'.[87] Eventually, persuaded by Burghley and Walsingham, who acted together in Leicester's interest, she quietened her rage and referred the matter to the Dutch Council of State. By June a compromise had been agreed that Leicester should hold the post of Governor-General under the Estates and not under Elizabeth: it was hardly a satisfactory solution, but it at least absolved the Queen from direct implication in the government of the Netherlands.

Leicester managed not only to antagonize Elizabeth, but also embroiled himself in quarrels with his own officers and with the predominant party among the Dutch. Sir John Norris, the ablest of the English commanders in the Netherlands, was continually criticized by Leicester; and Thomas Cecil, Governor of the Brille, wrote to his father that 'if the enemy were as strong as we are factious and irresolute, we should make shipwreck of the cause this summer'.[88] The ruling element in the Netherlands, led by Count Maurice of Nassau and Johan van Oldenbarnevelt, were moderate in religion, inclined to toleration, and materially well endowed. Leicester, who had long played the role of Protestant leader, frustrated by the Estates, turned for support to an alliance of strict Calvinist exiles from the south, supported by 'democrats' in the large cities. Paul Buys, former Advocate of Holland and one of Leicester's earliest supporters, now became his principal scapegoat: 'he is a devil, an atheist, and the only bolsterer of all papists

---

[86] Leicester's own words in a letter to Burghley of 14 Jan. 1586, in *Correspondence of Robert Dudley, Earl of Leycester, during his Government of the Low Countries*, ed. John Bruce, Camden Soc., 27 (London, 1844), 57.

[87] Ibid. 110.   [88] Wilson, *Queen Elizabeth and the Revolt of the Netherlands*, 95.

over, if possible, to the anti-Spanish cause. After first promising money to Casimir, Elizabeth promptly changed her mind. Even Burghley was in despair: 'thus you see', he wrote to Walsingham, 'how her Majesty can find means at small holes to stop her own light. And so must I tell her today.'[91] Her hesitancy ended any hope that Henry III might be detached from his alliance with the Catholics; in May 1588 the Guises took Paris at the Day of Barricades; and two months later Henry III entered into a new union with the League. As the Armada approached, England was faced with the prospect of a pro-Spanish France.

At home the political scene was increasingly focused on the events leading to the execution of Mary Stewart. By 1586, after she had been moved to Chartley, Walsingham had discovered the tracks of a conspiracy involving Mary and the French ambassador, Chateauneuf, a supporter of the Catholic League. Arrangements were made for Mary to smuggle her letters in and out of Chartley in a beer-barrel, which was then searched by government agents. In the summer of 1586 the trap was sprung when letters were found from a young Catholic, Antony Babington, offering to assassinate Elizabeth, together with a reply from Mary which implicitly approved the plan. Babington was arrested in August and his confession was supported by the statements of Mary's own secretaries. Mary's letter was almost certainly genuine and her complicity constituted treason under the statute of 1585.[92]

In September she was sent to Fotheringay Castle, Northamptonshire, and a commission of forty, including all privy councillors, was appointed for her trial. Mary denied having written the letters, but a separate document, agreeing to transfer her right of succession to Philip II, was used to discredit her with James VI, the French Court, and the English Catholics. After hearing Mary's evidence at Fotheringay, the commission adjourned to meet again at the end of October. Although they quickly reached a verdict of guilty, the proclamation announcing this was held back until after the meeting of Parliament, which was at that moment assembling.

Parliament opened on 29 October, when the Lord Chancellor's speech emphasized that the Queen's main purpose in calling it was to receive advice concerning Mary's conspiracy. He was warmly supported in the Commons by two privy councillors, Sir Christopher Hatton and Sir Walter Mildmay. After Hatton had related the 'horrible and wicked practices and attempts caused and procured by the Queen of Scots so called', other members joined the attack.[93] Most eloquent of all was Job Throckmorton, member for Warwick, who termed Mary 'the daughter of sedition, the

---

[91] Read, *Burghley*, 386.　　[92] Above, pp. 302–3.　　[93] D'Ewes, *Journals*, 393.

mother of rebellion, the nurse of impiety, the handmaid of iniquity, the sister of unshamefastness'.[94] Both Houses petitioned Elizabeth that she proceed to the execution of Mary in accordance with the verdict. Elizabeth replied that she could give no speedy answer: 'We Princes', she replied, 'are set on stages, in the sight and view of all the world duly observed. The eyes of many behold our actions; a spot is soon spied in our garments, a blemish quickly noted in our doings.' Parliament had laid upon her a hard duty—'that I must give direction for her death, which cannot be but most grievous, and an irksome burden to me.'[95] On receiving this answer the Commons resolved that Mary must die and sent a delegation to Elizabeth at Richmond. To this second petition she returned, at considerable length, her 'answer-answerless'. Against the united persuasions of both Houses of Parliament and of her Privy Council, Elizabeth remained stubbornly undecided. But she did allow the public proclamation of the sentence against Mary on 4 December, two days after Parliament was adjourned for the Christmas recess. It was heard with general rejoicing.

That was not the end of the matter, since the warrant for Mary's death still required Elizabeth's signature and the imposition of the Great Seal. After weeks of hesitation Elizabeth signed the warrant on 1 February and gave it to William Davison, the junior Secretary of State. According to Davison she told him to have it sealed immediately, after which he took it to Burghley and they both agreed to have the warrant sealed. Next day Elizabeth asked Davison why he was in so much hurry. Davison consulted Hatton and Burghley, and the three men took the matter before the whole Privy Council, which authorized immediate dispatch of the warrant to Fotheringay. Elizabeth's story was different: after signing the warrant she had told Davison to keep it secret and on hearing that it had been sealed told him to take no action without direct order from herself. It is impossible to be absolutely certain of the truth, but it seems unlikely that Davison would have disobeyed an explicit instruction from his Queen. Just possibly she put the matter, as she often did, elliptically and Davison interpreted her meaning to fit his own desires. At all events, Elizabeth was certainly hoping for another way out. She told Davison to write to Sir Amias Paulet, ordering him to have Mary murdered so that she would be free of responsibility. Under protest Davison complied, but Paulet refused to obey. He wrote that while his life and property were at the disposal of the Queen, 'God forbid that I should make so foul a shipwreck of my conscience or leave so great a

---

[94] Neale, *Parliaments*, ii. 110. Job Throckmorton of Haseley, Warwickshire, was the nephew of Nicholas Throckmorton and cousin to Francis Throckmorton.
[95] Ibid. 119.

blot to my poor posterity to shed blood without law or warrant.'[96] On 8 February Mary went, with great dignity, to her death. The Queen who had begun her rule in Scotland as a pleasure-loving *politique* was seen by many Catholics as a martyr.

Elizabeth was furious and apparently grief-stricken. Davison was sent at once to the Tower, although he was allowed to keep the Secretary's emoluments and was released eighteen months later. The rest of the Privy Council was in disgrace. According to Burghley, Elizabeth even asked one of her judges whether she had the power by prerogative to order Davison to be hanged and the other councillors to be 'so convicted as we shall require pardon'.[97] At last, in June, she relented and made it up with Burghley by going to stay at his house at Theobalds. She had also to deal with foreign reactions, in particular the protests of James VI at his mother's death. James instantly stopped all communication with England and was reported to be plotting with the French. Walsingham wrote a long letter to James's secretary, urging him to persuade his master to return to friendship with England: James, he pointed out, was unlikely to win effective support from foreign princes, whereas his conduct would so alienate the English as to lose him the throne of England. James quickly saw where his personal interest lay.

Elizabeth's own part in the affair of Mary Stewart has long been debated. Was she genuinely afflicted by the death of a fellow-queen? Or were her vacillation and her rage designed to shift blame onto others? No simple answer can be given. While there was probably an element of calculation at times, particularly in the treatment of Davison, it is unlikely that her rage and grief were merely a performance staged to impress James and other monarchs. Burghley, who knew her well, was deeply frightened by her anger. In the end she had been forced by her councillors, her Parliament, and by public opinion into taking an action which repelled her; but probably she knew that there was no alternative to Mary's death, however it might be brought about.

The execution of Mary did not bring the Parliament to an end. Elizabeth needed money to finance her intervention in the Netherlands and to prepare against threatened invasion. When Parliament reassembled on 22 February 1587, two weeks after Mary's death, Hatton spoke of the dangers facing the realm: 'the Catholics abroad, the Pope, the King of Spain, the Princes of the League, the Papists at home and their ministers'. He reviewed the conspiracies and leagues of the Catholics and warned the members of Philip II's

[96] *The Letter-Books of Sir Amias Poulet*, ed. John Morris (London, 1874), 359–62. Read, *Burghley*, 367.

[97] Read, *Burghley*, 373.

preparations for invasion. The people of the Netherlands had been oppressed by the Inquisition, torture, taxes, and executions: they must be helped to prevent the King of Spain from establishing 'a monarchical seat' there.[98] Job Throckmorton, who had been active in the first session, was eloquent again, urging Elizabeth to accept the offer of sovereignty from the Netherlands, an offer which was 'an evident sign that the Lord hath yet once more vowed himself to be English'. Sweeping widely across Europe in his condemnation of Elizabeth's fellow-monarchs he warned against trusting 'the young imp of Scotland': only the people of the Netherlands could be trusted.[99] Throckmorton was sent to the Tower for his rash words; but although other speakers were more cautious, there was such support for Elizabeth to accept the sovereignty of the Netherlands that the Commons offered a yearly benevolence if she would do so. Elizabeth refused the offer and made it clear, once again, that she would not accept the sovereignty. In the end she secured the normal grant of a single subsidy.

While the Commons were pressing advice on the Queen about the conduct of foreign policy, the Presbyterians in the House, more numerous than in the previous Parliament, were urging their scheme for reform of the Church. After the failure of Turner's Bill and Book in 1585, their leaders prepared the campaign more thoroughly. They were now ready with a Book of Discipline, which laid down a scheme of Church government by elders and pastors at the parochial level, with conferences or *classes* at the intermediate stage, and synods at the top. The Genevan Prayer Book was to replace the existing liturgy. This proposal was dramatic and radical, utterly different in its objectives from the moderate proposals for reform put forward in previous Parliaments. It was supported only by a small group of MPs: Job Throckmorton, Peter Wentworth, Anthony Cope, and a few others. The 'bill and book' was introduced on 27 February but was not read after objections were made that to do so would bring down the Queen's wrath on the House. Elizabeth sent for the 'bill and book' and ordered five of the radical leaders to be sent to the Tower, where they stayed until after the dissolution. With the leaders out of the way, the Council's spokesmen were able to demolish the radical proposals. Defending the Prayer Book, Hatton asked the House: 'Will you take the book from us which we have been persuaded to think both good and godly?' He pointed to the danger that rights of patronage and even perhaps abbey lands would be taken from the gentry: it 'toucheth us all in our inheritances'. Mildmay, who followed, spoke of the menace of a 'mere popular' election of ministers. 'We live here', he added, 'under a Christian Princess, in a Church that professeth [the] true

[98] D'Ewes, *Journals*, 408-9.   [99] Neale, *Parliaments*, ii. 169-74.

religion of the Gospel.'[100] The radical proposals were quietly put to sleep. These events demonstrate clearly the contrast between the strong support in Parliament and Privy Council for a limited reform of the clergy and the general opposition to radical changes in the government and liturgy of the Church.

The Parliament of 1586–7 achieved relatively little. It added its voice to the chorus of vituperation against Mary Stewart; and that may have helped to bring about her execution. Its advice on foreign policy was rejected, but it is significant that such specific advice should have been given: MPs were taking upon themselves the role of councillors. The proposals for Church reform were killed. Only two statutes of any significance were carried: one for closing loopholes in the treason laws and the Act against recusants.

When this Parliament met for its second session Philip II was beginning to prepare his great enterprise against England. The time was auspicious for him: England's relations with Scotland were strained after the execution of Mary; suspicion and tension were mounting between the Dutch and their English allies in the Netherlands; nothing had been done to help the French Huguenots; and the position of Henry of Navarre was alarmingly weak. A crisis in the export market for English cloth coincided with bad harvests in 1585 and 1586, which pushed up grain prices to a record level: in some places the price of wheat doubled in the twelve months following the spring of 1586. Unemployment in the cloth-making districts led the Privy Council to order merchants to buy their usual quantities of cloth at the normal prices; but there is no evidence that it was obeyed. The times were not easy for merchants, wool-growers, or cloth-workers; and the government had to reckon with the possibility of social discontent and resistance to taxation at a moment when the dangers from abroad seemed greatest.

As before, the heart of the diplomatic and military encounters between England and Spain lay in the Low Countries. Leicester had left the Anglo-Dutch alliance in disarray at the end of 1586; and the surrender of Deventer and Zutphen fort in January 1587 had intensified the resentment of the Dutch. The Earl himself was on bad terms not only with the Dutch leader, Oldenbarnevelt, but also with Sir John Norris, whom he had left behind as military commander, and with Thomas Wilkes, the senior English representative on the Dutch Council of State. However, as the campaigning season approached, Leicester joined with the Dutch and the leading privy councillors in urging Elizabeth to reinforce the English army in the Netherlands, which had dwindled through disease and desertion to about 3,000 foot and 500 horse, about half its original size. Lord Buckhurst, a new

[100] Ibid. 158–61.

member of the Privy Council, was sent over in March to report on the situation. He recommended that Leicester be returned to the Netherlands with 1,000–2,000 more troops and a loan of £50,000 for the Dutch. Although Walsingham, Hatton, and even Burghley supported his proposal, Elizabeth was reluctant to incur any more expenditure. By now she was optimistic about the peace negotiations which had been conducted spasmodically since 1585. At least five parallel sets of negotiations had been opened, of which the most promising were conducted with Parma through Andrea de Loo, a Flemish merchant in London, and Carlo Lanfranchi, an Italian merchant in Antwerp. By the spring of 1587 the discontent of English merchants at the interruption of trade combined with the Queen's own inclinations to revive these overtures. Apart from Sir James Croft, the Comptroller of the Household, none of Elizabeth's advisers—not even Burghley—was enthusiastic for peace at this stage; but they could not afford to ignore the wishes of Elizabeth entirely. Unfortunately the prospect of peace weakened her resolution to prosecute the war and heightened Dutch suspicion.

However, when Parma besieged Sluys in June, Elizabeth accepted the need for action. Although Sluys was not in itself a good deep-water harbour, its capture would endanger Flushing, which would make an excellent base for the invasion of England. Accordingly Elizabeth at last agreed that Leicester should return to the Netherlands with 5,000 men and £30,000. Before he arrived Norris and Wilkes came home, the former to be forbidden the Queen's presence, the latter to be imprisoned in the Fleet. Buckhurst, who stayed overseas until Leicester's arrival, was likewise disgraced and put under house arrest. Such were the rewards of loyal service by men whose frank advice had incurred Leicester's displeasure. It is remarkable that, after his record as Governor-General, Elizabeth still favoured her 'sweet Robin' against his rivals: probably his care to avoid complicity in the execution of Mary paid dividends when other senior councillors were in disgrace.

Leicester's second tour of duty was no more successful than his first. Sluys fell to Parma in July—though that was hardly Leicester's fault; the conflict between the Earl and the Estates General grew worse; Elizabeth began to lose confidence in him; and Walsingham listened sympathetically to Leicester's critics. By now Elizabeth was vigorously pursuing the peace negotiations with Parma's agents. Walsingham wrote to Leicester in August that 'the loss of Sluys has wrought in her Majesty some alteration of her favour towards your Lordship and also towards the cause itself, in such sort as she seemed bent and resolved to abandon those countries'.[101]

[101] Read, *Walsingham*, iii. 263.

CHAPTER 9

The Final Years
1588–1603

1. DRAMATIS PERSONAE

Most of the men who had controlled the government of England from the beginning of the reign died soon after the Armada. The Earl of Leicester went in September 1588, Sir Walter Mildmay in 1589, Sir Francis Walsingham, tireless executor of diplomacy and intelligence, in 1590, and Sir Christopher Hatton, Lord Chancellor and royal favourite, in 1591. Their departures left Burghley as almost the only survivor from the first generation of Elizabethan courtiers and statesmen. He was now old, arthritic, tortured by the stone, rather melancholy. He found it difficult to extend his friendship to younger men, and only with his own family was he personally at ease. Thomas Cecil, his elder son by his first marriage, extravagant and neglectful in youth, had now reformed into a competent and dutiful member of the landowning class; but he was not of the calibre to succeed his father. That role was to fall to the younger son, Robert, child of Burghley's second marriage to Mildred Cooke. Hunchbacked and so short that Elizabeth called him her 'pygmy', he is shown in his portraits with a narrow, high-domed forehead and finely shaped, penetrating eyes. He had done all the right things in his youth: a grand tour of Europe, attendance at the Sorbonne, a minor role in a mission to the Netherlands; and he had made a good marriage to Elizabeth Brooke, daughter of Lord Cobham, Warden of the Cinque Ports. Yet, admirably suited as he was to take over from his father, he was in some respects a very different person. The sanctimonious side of Burghley is absent in Robert Cecil; his letters are light in touch and tone; but he was an intensely serious politician, willing to spend every waking hour upon the business of government, determined to climb the winding stair of advancement, and prepared, where his father was not, to contemplate radical changes.

On Leicester's death, the rising man at Court was his stepson Robert Devereux, second Earl of Essex. At the age of 19, he had gone to the Netherlands with Leicester as 'general of the horse'. Returning to Court, he was promoted to his stepfather's post of Master of the Horse, a major appointment. Already he was an acknowledged favourite of Elizabeth: 'when she is abroad, nobody near her but my L. of Essex; and, at night, my L. is at cards, or one game or another with her, that he cometh not to his own lodging till birds sing in the morning.'[1] No one could have presented a more brilliant contrast to the tireless administrator Robert Cecil. The poet George Peele described Essex at tournament:

> Young Essex, that thrice-honourable Earl;
> Y-clad in mighty arms of mourner's dye,
> And plumes as black as is a raven's wing,
> That from his armour borrow'd such a light
> As boughs of yew receive from shady stream:
> . . .
> And all his company in funeral black;
> As if he mourn'd to think of him he miss'd,
> Sweet Sidney, fairest shepherd of our green.[2]

Political heir to Leicester, spiritual heir to Philip Sidney, Essex seemed the epitome of the courtly hero: handsome, adventurous, ambitious, a brave soldier, and a fair poet.

His rival for the favour of Elizabeth was Sir Walter Ralegh, an older man, 36 in the Armada year, by then already established at Court. He had fought for the Huguenots in France at the age of 17; had sailed on a voyage with Humfrey Gilbert ten years later; had campaigned in Ireland, ruthlessly killing Spanish prisoners at Smerwick; and had organized expeditions—albeit unsuccessfully—to colonize Virginia. His looks were equal to those of Essex; his intellectual gifts altogether greater. He was a fine poet and a considerable historian; a man 'with a bold and plausible tongue'.[3] But for all his talents he never moved into the inner chambers of power, although he profited materially and abundantly from royal favour. In 1588 he and Essex were the principal rivals for courtly success; and Essex had the popular voice. When Essex was playing cards with Elizabeth throughout the night, Ralegh was described as 'the hated man of the world, in Court, city and country'. When the Queen slighted Essex's sister, Essex blamed it on 'that knave Ralegh, for whose sake I saw she would both grieve me and my love, and disgrace me in the eye of the world'.[4]

Fortunately for the stability of the political world, there were others, though not many, to balance the triangle of forces set up by Essex, Ralegh, and the Cecils. Lord Charles Howard of Effingham, Lord Admiral and

[1] Devereux, *Letters*, i. 185–6.
[2] George Peele, *Polyhymnia*, quoted in John Buxton, *Philip Sidney and the English Renaissance* (London, 1954; 2nd edn., 1964), 206.
[3] *DNB* xvi. 632.   [4] Devereux, *Letters*, i. 185–7.

conqueror of the Armada, was firmly established at Court and in the Privy Council. He benefited from membership of the Howard clan without the reputation for corruption and intrigue that hung round his kinsmen. Sir Francis Knollys, Treasurer of the Chamber since 1566, was a senior courtier who had married the Queen's first cousin and was grandfather to Essex. A lifelong supporter of the moderate puritan clergy, Knollys was by now a respected rather than a powerful figure; but his influence was strong enough to secure the succession to his office for his son, and the Knollys clan was well placed at Court. The Vice-Chamberlain, Thomas Heneage, had been an early favourite of Elizabeth and had once seemed to rival even Leicester: he was now a useful spokesman for the Crown in Parliament, but he never belonged to the top circle of politicians. Sir John Fortescue, second cousin to the Queen, succeeded Mildmay as Chancellor of the Exchequer in 1589, entering the Privy Council at the same time. As an administrator, he occupied a central place, and he successfully accumulated offices and lands; and if he lacked the weight of the Cecils, Essex, and Howard, he was nevertheless a figure to be counted. More influential was Thomas Sackville, created Lord Buckhurst in 1567. A privy councillor since 1585, he had been sent on important diplomatic missions, in particular to the Netherlands in 1587 with the task of settling the confusion created by Leicester. His eventual reward was the succession to Burghley as Lord Treasurer in 1599. Immensely influential in religious affairs was John Whitgift, Archbishop of Canterbury, the only one of Elizabeth's primates to enter her Privy Council. As the persecutor of puritans, he was hated by many and at odds with Burghley and with Essex; but he never lost the trust of the Queen. Other men were to rise to power and influence in the next fifteen years: the brothers Antony and Francis Bacon; Sir Edward Coke; Lord Henry Howard; Lord Mountjoy. But in 1588 their day was yet to come.

Finally, there was Elizabeth, dominating the political scene. Men and women were made and unmade by her will; no decision could be taken without her consent. The myth of Gloriana was still maintained, but with growing difficulty as she grew older. Paul Hentzner, a German traveller, described her appearance in a procession at Court in 1598: 'next came the Queen, in the 65th year of her age (as we were told), very majestic, her face oblong, fair but wrinkled; her eyes small, yet black and pleasant; her nose a little hooked, her lips narrow, and her teeth black . . . she had in her ears two pearls with very rich drops; her hair was of an auburn colour, but false.'[5] One portrait survives from this period, a pattern for miniatures by

[5] Paul Hentzner, *Travels in England during the Reign of Queen Elizabeth*, ed. H. Walpole, trans. R. Bentley (London, 1889), 47–8.

Isaac Oliver, that tallies—to some extent—with this account (plate 3*b*). But Oliver's version was, unsurprisingly, disliked by Elizabeth and her later portraits were executed by the reliable and flattering Hillyard, who tactfully smoothed over the disfigurements of age. However, it would be wrong to suggest that there was any simple contrast between image and 'reality'. Another German traveller, Thomas Platter, wrote of her in the same year as being 'most gorgeously apparelled, and although she was already seventy-four [actually sixty-five], she was very youthful still in appearance, seeming no more than twenty years of age'. There was probably some traveller's licence in this, but, unlike English courtiers, Platter had no reason to flatter. A similar account had been given, a few years earlier, by Liupold von Wedel: 'the Queen sitting all alone in her splendid coach appeared like a goddess such as painters are wont to depict.' Nature seems to have been imitating art; and at least from a distance Elizabeth's physical appearance, aided by her dresses and jewels, may well have matched her representation in portraits. Even so, there was some anxiety about her age and approaching death. According to Hentzner, Wolsey's unfinished tomb in St George's Chapel, Windsor, was already reserved for Elizabeth, whose funeral expenses were estimated at £60,000. Her subjects prayed that she be immortal, but increasingly seem to have admitted that her immortality would only be achieved in art. Spenser expressed this clearly in *The Teares of the Muses*:

> Live she for ever, and her royall P'laces
> Be fild with praises of divinest wits,
> That her eternize with their heavenlie writs.[6]

2. CONTINENTAL WAR AND DOMESTIC FACTION, 1588–1595

During the middle years of Elizabeth's reign, the terms of debate over policy had been set by a group of men strongly committed to the Protestant cause in Europe. Leicester was their leader, Philip Sidney their symbolic hero, Walsingham their intellectual and political manager. By 1590, all three were dead, and few, if any, of their successors at Court had their commitments. Essex saw himself, and others saw him too, as the political

[6] For this paragraph I am much indebted to Dr Helen Cobb's thesis 'Representations of Elizabeth I: three sites of ambiguity and contradiction' (D.Phil., University of Oxford, 1989), and am grateful to her both for allowing me to read and quote from it, and for illuminating discussions. The sources of the quotations, taken from part iii, s. 1, of the thesis, are: *Thomas Platter's Travels in England, 1599*, trans. Clare Williams (London, 1937), 192; V. von Klarwill (ed.), *Queen Elizabeth and Some Foreigners*, trans. T. H. Nash (London, 1928), 329; Edmund Spenser, *The Teares of the Muses*, in *Poetical Works*, ed. J. C. Smith and E. de Selincourt (Oxford, 1970), 486, ll. 580–2.

heir to Leicester. Yet although he sometimes favoured puritans, his ideology, whatever it may have been, was not religious, even in the rather ambiguous sense that Leicester's had been. In Europe, as the centre of action shifted from the Low Countries to France, the force of the Protestant ideal diminished. While Henry IV remained a Protestant until 1593, his conversion always seemed probable and no one could regard him as a religious leader. The arguments about English policy came to be formulated less and less in religious terms, increasingly in the language of national security against Spain and of material profit to be won from war. The points of debate involved the size of the English commitment, the type of warfare—whether on land or at sea—and the relative importance of different theatres of operation. How strictly should the Crown limit expenses? Should England concentrate on the defence of France or on war at sea? If on France, should the government give priority to Normandy or Brittany? If on the sea, then should the Queen launch invasions of the Iberian mainland, expeditions to the Azores for capturing the Spanish silver fleet, or raids into the New World? Burghley and Robert Cecil favoured a limited commitment, mainly directed to the defence of the Netherlands and of France. Presented with a proposal that troops be withdrawn from the Netherlands to participate in the 1589 expedition to Portugal, Burghley wrote to Walsingham: 'I doubt [=fear], whilst we attempt an uncertainty, we shall lose a certainty, and so seek for a bird in a bush and lose what we have in a cage.'[7] Burghley was not opposing the expedition as such, but was anxious that it should not jeopardize the security of the Netherlands. Or so he said; but we can never be quite sure with Burghley, for his arguments were obliquely framed and he would seldom come out unequivocally in opposition to anything. However, he held to certain fundamentals. The Netherlands must be kept secure, although they were in less danger now than before. The French king must be supported against his enemies, whether he was the Catholic Henry III, or the equivocating Henry IV, because victory for Spain and the Catholic League would be disastrous for England's security. Within France, the crucial theatre, in Burghley's opinion, lay in Brittany: 'I had rather both Paris and Rouen were left unrecovered, than have Brittany lost', he wrote in 1592, for a Spanish military base in Brittany could threaten England's position in Ireland.[8] Given this set of priorities, Burghley and his son responded to events, meeting threats as they occurred and taking opportunities as they developed.

Other leaders by contrast wanted to take initiatives and shape events. Ralegh and Hawkins believed that the war should be prosecuted with

[7] Read, *Burghley*, 438.   [8] Ibid. 481.

vigour, not 'by halves and by petty invasions' as it was under Elizabeth.[9] For them the key to victory—and profit—lay in the capture of the Spanish treasure fleet off the Azores or in the Caribbean. Ralegh thought deeply about the use of sea-power, insisting that navies had greater mobility as a striking force than land forces and studying minutely the design of ships. Essex, too, supported a forward policy but gave no impression of having a coherent strategy or a set of priorities. Any action appealed to him, whether in Portugal, at Rouen, at Cadiz, off the Azores, or even in Ireland, provided that it offered the chance of military glory.

No action, however minor, could be taken without the consent of Elizabeth, and that consent was generally given with great reluctance after long delay. The Queen did not appear to have any conception of priorities. She saw the risks inherent in most courses of action and gave greater weight to them than to the dangers of passivity. She wanted to conserve her revenue and to avoid unnecessary loss of life—praiseworthy objectives and often far more sensible than the rash courses proposed by men like Essex. But her hesitations and caution exposed her to constant petitioning from courtiers, generals, and sea-dogs who sought her backing for their enterprises; and sometimes she gave way to their importunities. Just occasionally she acted out of character and proposed schemes of her own.

Because of these conflicting views and the need to move a reluctant Queen, English policy and strategy in the last fifteen years of the reign were complex, changeable, and often obscure. Action was limited, not only by the clash of opinions, but also by the scarcity of resources. The ordinary peacetime revenue of the Crown was not large—perhaps £300,000 per annum—and while Parliament would usually grant the extra taxes that were asked, the government had to pitch its demands low and make its requests circumspectly. The Queen had few ships in her navy and had always to depend upon merchantmen and privateers in any major enterprise. Troops had mostly to be raised from the county levies, although there were usually some volunteers available, and manpower was scarce: if any expedition was sent to Brittany or Spain, soldiers probably had to be withdrawn from another theatre. To add to these problems, the English government had to reconcile its own interests with those of its allies. The Dutch, often on bad terms with England's representatives and at odds among themselves, were understandably reluctant to see troops diverted from the defence of the Low Countries. Henry III and Henry IV of France constantly demanded a commitment from Elizabeth, while failing, in her eyes, to give due weight to saving Brittany and the Channel ports from the Spanish.

[9] R. B. Wernham, 'Elizabethan war aims and strategy', in S. T. Bindoff et al., *Elizabethan Government and Society* (London, 1961), 340.

Although the defeat of the Spanish Armada was assured by the end of August 1588, there could be no relaxation of England's defences. The Spanish might, almost certainly would, rebuild their fleet and strike again; Parma was still advancing in the Netherlands; and the French Catholic League threatened the Channel ports. Elizabeth's first impulse, on hearing of the disasters that had befallen the Spanish navy, was to send a fleet to intercept the American treasure ships. But Lord Admiral Howard crisply pointed out that the condition of the English ships was too poor to enable an expedition to be launched in time: a voyage to the Azores 'is not as if a man should send but over to the coast of France, I do assure you'.[10] A more carefully considered plan was then developed to destroy the remnant of the Armada—thought to be sheltering in Lisbon and Seville—to take Lisbon itself if possible, and to capture the Azores as a base for seizing the treasure fleet. The sailing date was fixed for February 1589, with Sir John Norris, one of the ablest of the English commanders in the Netherlands, and Sir Francis Drake appointed to mobilize troops and to take command. To meet the heavy costs of this expedition and other war expenses Elizabeth needed at least £170,000. A 'privy seal' loan—a type of forced loan—produced £76,000, but only Parliament could make up the difference, and a session had therefore to be fitted in before the fleet could sail.

Parliament assembled on 4 February and was dissolved on 29 March. In a moving oration, Lord Chancellor Hatton impressed upon its members the grave dangers from the country's enemies and the Queen's need for supply: 'Our enemies make great preparation to assail us by sea: our navy must be made fit to encounter them. They have great strength to invade us by land: a correspondency of force must be had to withstand them . . . Our duties towards God, Her Majesty, and our country doth require all this at your hands.' His colleague, Sir Walter Mildmay, Chancellor of the Exchequer, followed with an unprecedented demand for a double subsidy, estimated to bring in £320,000. One member, Henry Jackman, a London merchant, made a brave protest in his first Parliament: 'our country', he protested, 'is at this present in no such desperate or dangerous case . . . the teeth and jaws of our mightiest and most malicious enemy having been so lately broken.'[11] However, his was a lone voice and was overruled; the House voted the double subsidy requested, its payment to be spread over four years. In return, the Commons asked for the remedy of grievances, in particular for preventing abuses in the levy of purveyance—the Crown's right to purchase supplies at below the market price—and in the operations of the Court of Exchequer. Burghley claimed that both touched the royal preroga-

[10] R. B. Wernham, *After the Armada: Elizabethan England and the Struggle for Western Europe, 1588–1595* (Oxford, 1984), 2.
[11] Neale, *Parliaments*, ii. 201, 206.

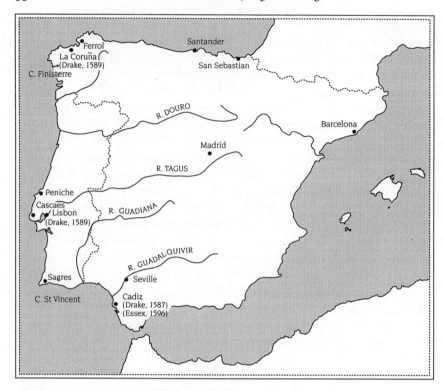

MAP 13. The Iberian Peninsula

tive and should not be debated; Elizabeth promised that she would herself reform matters and asked the Commons to appoint four men as members of a proposed committee. The issues were thus effectively shelved for the time being. Compared with the spirited and radical demands for religious reform in the previous Parliament, ecclesiastical matters were discussed in a low key. A bill was put forward to restrict the holding of livings in plurality: it got no further in the Lords than a first reading. Protests were made against the persecution of puritans, but had little effect upon the campaign being led by Whitgift. On the Sunday after Parliament opened, Richard Bancroft, a protégé of Christopher Hatton, later to become Bishop of London and then Whitgift's successor at Canterbury, preached at St Paul's Cross, denouncing the puritans as 'false prophets' and coming near to claiming *jus divinum* for the bishops. He was on the threshold of his relentless destruction of the Presbyterian movement.[12]

Provided with a substantial grant of taxation, the government was able to

[12] Below, Ch. 11 s. 4.

proceed with its plans for the great counter-stroke against Spain. If the throw were to be made, it had to be done without further delay, for across the Channel Philip's strength was growing. In early April Parma took the town of Geertruidenberg on the Maas, opening a gap in the southern defences of the Dutch. At the same time, Henry III, increasingly nervous about the progress of the Catholic League, pressed Elizabeth for money. However, in spite of these diversions, the great fleet sailed in April. The first ship to get away was the *Swiftsure*, with the Earl of Essex aboard in spite of the Queen's strict, indeed angry, prohibition on his taking part in the expedition. The full fleet sailed two weeks later. Seven royal ships, seventy private vessels, many of them armed merchantmen, and sixty Dutch transports carried 19,000 men. The total cost was little short of £100,000, of which the Queen had contributed £46,000. By comparison with Drake's Cadiz fleet of 1587, only twenty-three ships strong, this was an enormous force. Since the original proposals for the expedition in the previous autumn, the tactical position had changed: the battered and defenceless survivors of the Armada had found shelter, not in Lisbon, but in Santander and San Sebastian, ports on the northern coast of Spain, tucked well into the Bay of Biscay. Not only did this make them slightly more difficult to approach, but the opportunities for plunder were much less. Nor could an attack on Santander and San Sebastian be combined, as Essex, Drake, and Norris hoped, with the liberation of Portugal under the leadership of Don Antonio, pretender to the throne. Elizabeth's instructions were, however, unambiguous: Norris and Drake must 'first distress the ships of war in Guipuzcoa, Biscay, Galicia'; they were then allowed to attack ships in the Tagus and discover how much support Don Antonio might expect. If, and only if, this was substantial, might they 'make descent there'.[13] The commanders had different ideas: they hoped for the booty which Lisbon might yield and they planned the reconquest of Portugal, having a promise from Don Antonio that he would pay their army once it landed (Map 13).

The expedition sailed first to La Coruña, where five Spanish ships were discovered and destroyed. In May, the leaders set course, not for Santander or San Sebastian, but for Lisbon, in complete defiance of the Queen's orders. Their plan of operations was for 6,000 troops to land at Peniche, 45 miles north of Lisbon, under the command of Essex, Norris, and Sir Roger Williams, a veteran of the Netherlands, while the fleet, commanded by Drake, sailed on to Lisbon. After six days' march—slow progress which destroyed any hope of surprise—the army reached Lisbon, but by then Don

[13] Wernham, *After the Armada*, 97–8.

Antonio's plans had been betrayed and the leaders of his party in the city had 'disappeared'. Understandably, the native resistance movement failed to rise. Lacking artillery or help from within the city, the English had no hope of storming Lisbon, and after three days they marched off to Cascaes at the mouth of the Tagus, where Drake had halted the fleet. After a further week's delay, the expedition sailed westwards to try its luck at the Azores, but a southerly wind intervened to drive the ships back to England. By the end of June, all but a few had returned. The casualties had been high: possibly as many as 11,000 men had been killed or had died of disease; very little booty had been taken to cover the investment of £100,000; and none of the objectives had been achieved. Yet the opportunity to destroy the Spanish fighting fleet had been there. As one observer wrote from France, 'if Sir Francis had gone to Santander as he went to the Groyne [La Coruña], he had done such a service as never subject had done. For with 12 sail of his ships, he might have destroyed all the forces which the Spaniards had there, which was the whole strength of the country by sea.'[14] What went wrong? Most important, the Queen never had effective control of the expedition, for she supplied only half the cost and a smaller fraction of the ships. The merchant investors were out for profit, which was not to be found in the Bay of Biscay. As Elizabeth herself remarked, 'they went to places more for profit than for service'.[15] But the difference of interest between investors and the Queen was not the only handicap. Essex, Drake, and Norris, while keen on profit themselves, hoped also to achieve a major coup by putting Don Antonio on the Portuguese throne in place of Philip. Elizabeth, rightly as it turned out, was sceptical of any such plan. There was thus a strategic dispute as well as a conflict of interest: Elizabeth and Burghley thought in terms of a limited operation to destroy the Spanish fleet, while Essex and others had wider aspirations. For the time being, however, the failure of the Portugal expedition doomed any proposal for another such adventure. Sir Martin Frobisher was sent with four ships in September 1589 to intercept the silver fleet; but although he captured some prizes, he took no bullion.

By the time Norris and Drake had returned to England, Elizabeth and her councillors had reason for alarm at events across the Channel. Relations with the Dutch were deteriorating, partly through disputes about the dispatch of English troops from the Netherlands to the Portugal expedition, and partly because of alleged interference by the Queen's envoys in the domestic politics of the Low Countries. By the spring of 1589, Parma once again presented a dangerous threat. 'The state of these Provinces is weaker

[14] Wernham, *After the Armada*, 130.
[15] K. R. Andrews, *Drake's Voyages: A Reassessment of their Place in Elizabethan Maritime Expansion* (London, 1967), 167. See PRO, SP 12 (State Papers Domestic, Elizabeth), 254/50.

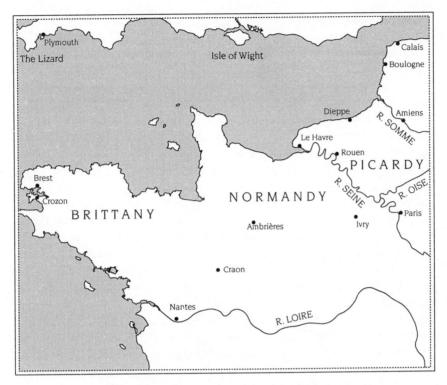

MAP 14. Northern France and the Channel

than it hath been these many years,' wrote Thomas Bodley, English representative on the Dutch Council of State; without help from Elizabeth, he added, 'there is little appearance that they can hold out long'.[16] Parma's capture of Geertruidenberg seemed to confirm these pessimistic warnings, although luckily he fell ill in April and a mutiny of Spanish troops in August held up operations. At the same time, Anglo-Dutch relations improved with the resignation of Leicester's successor, Lord Willoughby, a capable warrior but an impetuous politician. His successor, Sir Francis Vere, formally appointed in August, was not only an excellent soldier but a man of tact and sense, who quickly established good relations with Maurice of Nassau. As the momentum of the Spanish attack slowed down, the rifts in the north were healed. By the following year, Parma's forces were being diverted to France and the Netherlands were no longer under threat.

Diplomatic and military attention now focused on France, where England was forced into a position in which she could do little more than

[16] Charles Wilson, *Queen Elizabeth and the Revolt of the Netherlands* (London, 1970), 108.

respond to the initiatives of others. In April 1589 Henry III became officially reconciled to Henry of Navarre and together they forced the Catholic League onto the defensive. To exploit his advantage and to counter the
League's recruitment of German mercenaries, the French King asked
Elizabeth for £80,000 in order to hire German troops himself. After the
usual bargaining, hesitation, agreement, and withdrawal, Elizabeth provided him with £20,000 and underwrote a loan for the remainder—a generous offer considering the losses she had suffered from the Portugal
expedition. Her councillors were unanimous that Henry III must be supported, and Burghley drew up 'Instructions for a League with France' that
proposed an offensive and defensive alliance with France and with all other
nations opposed to Spain. However, the hope of a grand alliance and the
progress of the royalist party in France were destroyed by the assassination
of Henry III at the end of July. Navarre took the title of King, as Henry IV,
and the League put up Cardinal Bourbon as Charles X. With a Protestant
king, the royalist forces were weakened and the League revived. The dilemma of Henry IV was plain: to win the support of moderate Catholics, he
must make some promise that he would contemplate conversion; but any
suggestion of apostasy would alienate his Huguenot supporters. In September the leading English councillors agreed that Henry must have immediate
support, and Elizabeth lent him a further £20,000, agreeing at the same
time to levy 4,000 men under Willoughby in order to raise the siege of
Dieppe and support Henry's campaign in Normandy. Thus began
England's military involvement in France (Map 14).

Willoughby's force was well commanded and made up in part of men
from trained bands in the southern counties. It was intended to stay only for
a month in order to give Henry immediate help in saving Dieppe; but by the
time it landed, at the end of September, Dieppe had been relieved. However, Willoughby was too ambitious a commander to come straight home
and Henry agreed to pay the troops himself for a second month; in the event
they stayed a third. Surprisingly, Elizabeth accepted his action and even
loaned Henry a further £15,000. Probably she and her councillors realized
that the Channel ports were still under threat from the League and hoped
to keep Henry in northern France to save them. When Henry's aim of an
assault on Paris proved too ambitious, he made instead a sweep round
western Normandy which brought him substantial control of the region
between the Seine and the Loire. Willoughby's force of 4,000 men was an
important contribution to an army which was usually only 10,000 strong;
moreover, the English troops fought well and won commendation from
the French and gratitude even from Elizabeth, who wrote to Willoughby:
'My good Peregrine, I bless God that your old prosperous success fol-

loweth your valiant acts and joy not a little that safety accompanieth your luck.'[17]

The following year, 1590, was relatively quiet for England: her only troops stationed across the Channel were the auxiliary and garrison companies permanently stationed in the Netherlands. Yet, while military activity was low, diplomatic negotiation with the Dutch and the French was intense. It was made more burdensome for Elizabeth's councillors by the death in April of Sir Francis Walsingham, which threw the weight of foreign business onto Burghley and Robert Cecil. In the Netherlands, Maurice had gone quickly onto the offensive, exploiting the weakness of Parma's army after the mutinies of the previous autumn. After capturing Breda in February and thus cutting off Spain's fortresses on the Maas, Maurice switched his attack to the eastern front, where, with the help of Vere and the English troops, he launched a major offensive. Elizabeth took this opportunity to attempt to reduce her commitments in the Netherlands and to bring better order into the government of the United Provinces. Her agent, Thomas Wilkes, reported that the authority of the Estates was now much more effective than it had been and that Elizabeth would be advised to leave well alone. This she did, agreeing also to maintain her garrisons.

Henry IV's campaigns in France were a great deal more dramatic. His destruction of the League's field army in March opened his way to Paris, and by the end of July its fall was near. Only the arrival of Parma saved it— at the cost of weakening the Spanish forces in the Netherlands. Against Parma's protests and occasional obstruction, the direct military intervention of Spain in France had begun. It was to dominate military affairs in Europe for the next eight years. Henry could have overcome the League if it had had no external aid, but the support given to it by Philip meant that he must have foreign help. The appearance of Parma's troops in France also offered a direct threat to England and the landing of Spanish troops in Brittany in October 1590 brought home the point: their presence created a rallying-ground for the League and provided a base for the invasion of England or Ireland. As that experienced veteran Sir Roger Williams remarked: 'Then must we at least keep garrisons in all our ports and send our ships royal in good numbers always to convoy our merchants.'[18] England's situation would be worse still if Parma's army was able to march through Normandy and link up with the force in Brittany. Thus, although Henry IV had a glorious year of victory in 1590, the outlook for England was grim. Elizabeth's first response was to propose a major alliance between England, France, and the Protestant German princes. Turenne and Sir Horatio

---

[17] Wernham, *After the Armada*, 171.   [18] Ibid. 190.

Palavicino were sent to Germany to arrange the matter; but unfortunately Elizabeth was unwilling to promise enough support or to provide what she had promised. Palavicino found himself caught between the anger of his Queen when he seemed to be committing her too deeply and accusations of bad faith from the Germans. As he himself told the Queen, she should either support the raising of a proper army in Germany or do nothing at all.

At sea, England did little more against Spain than she did on land, for the futility of the Portugal expedition did not encourage any further large-scale attempts. Two small fleets of about six ships each were sent out under Frobisher and Hawkins, Frobisher to lie off the Azores for the silver convoy, Hawkins to wait off Finisterre for the assembling of a second Armada. Frobisher missed the bullion ships and Hawkins deserted his post, allowing the Spanish to land in Brittany. Once again the weakness of the Queen's control over her sailors was demonstrated. Much of the damage to Spanish shipping was done by privateering vessels, ninety-five of which were operating in the Atlantic in 1590; but these were mostly small ships, capable of capturing only small merchantmen. They could harass but they could not inflict real damage.

By contrast with the relative quiet of 1590, the two succeeding years saw English involvement in the Continental war at its height; and once again the Netherlands was the most successful front. By now the Dutch armies under Maurice were effectively organized and were co-operating well with the English troops under Vere, while Parma was constantly distracted by orders from Madrid to march into France. Early in 1591, Maurice assembled a field army of 12,000 men which included an English contingent of 2,000. He opened a vigorous offensive on the eastern front, capturing Zutphen and Deventer, then switched to the south and took Nijmegen. This kept Parma tied down in the Netherlands and unable to give aid to the League in France until the summer. In the following year, Maurice took two forts in the north-east, cutting off the Spanish troops in the far northern province of Groningen. To all this, the English made a useful, possibly vital, contribution, Elizabeth providing about a quarter of the money—in the form of a loan—and about one-sixth of the troops. This was not massive assistance, but Maurice might well have been less successful without that margin of superiority.

While the Netherlands could be regarded as safe, provided Elizabeth maintained her contributions at the agreed level, all was uncertainty in France. Elizabeth's councillors, even Burghley, were agreed that Henry IV must be supported, that his destruction would be disastrous for England; but Elizabeth herself was less than convinced and had constantly to be persuaded. She did, however, agree at the beginning of 1591 to an ambitious strategy for aiding Henry and protecting English interests. A combined naval and land force was to be sent to Brittany in order to strike a quick and decisive blow at the Spanish troops there. At the same time, the army supposedly being raised by Turenne and Palavicino in Germany would march through the Netherlands to trap Parma between its own advance and the forces of the French King. The difficulties were formidable. Without a mobile reserve army the Queen had to find the troops for these enterprises either by transferring men from the Netherlands, which involved obtaining the agreement of the Dutch, or by raising mercenaries in Germany, which she was not willing to pay for, or by levying men from the English militia, which took time and often produced only untrained, ill-equipped troops.

The original intention had been to send 6,000 men to Brittany under that capable and quarrelsome soldier Sir John Norris; but the Dutch would not release more than half the numbers requested and the force amounted only to 3,000. This ruled out the short, sharp shock that was meant for the Spanish and led to a long campaign. Little was achieved in 1591 after Norris had landed in May, and by the spring of the following year disease and desertion had reduced his force to about 1,000 men: the scale and swiftness of this reduction shows the general difficulty of keeping an army in the field abroad for any length of time. Against the army of the League, Norris and his royalist allies were almost helpless, and in May 1592 they were crushingly defeated at Craon. In view of the importance of Brittany to England, Elizabeth agreed to bring her strength there up to 4,000 on condition that Henry undertake to make no separate peace with Spain and deliver to her a port of security. Under duress, he accepted these terms, but unfortunately the reinforcements did not arrive until after a further defeat had been inflicted on the English and their allies at Ambrières in September. Norris then remained in Brittany until 1595; but not until the summer of 1594 was there any effective action in that province.[19]

Important as it was to English security, Brittany became something of a forgotten front in 1591–2 as attention focused upon the siege of Rouen by those heroic figures Henry of Navarre and Robert, Earl of Essex. Henry was not interested in Elizabeth's plan to trap Parma between the German army and his own, concentrating for the first months of 1591 upon besieging Chartres. However, having taken that city, he agreed to co-operate with an English force in besieging Rouen. Elizabeth was being importuned by Essex, who saw himself as the commander of this campaign; and in June she agreed to levy 4,000 men under his control for the attack on Rouen. This was Essex's first independent command and he took care to nominate many

[19] Below, p. 348.

of the captains himself: it was very much his own army, but by no means as badly led as some of his critics later claimed. At the end of July he landed at Dieppe and joined the small force under Roger Williams that was already operating in Normandy. Impatient to begin the assault on Rouen, Essex found that Henry IV, still 75 miles away at Noyon, was in no hurry to begin operations. Henry's principal concern at this stage was to draw Parma to battle and inflict a decisive defeat: Rouen was simply a means to the end. With such divided purposes, the campaign got off to a bad start. Essex made a quick dash across country to talk to Henry and was sharply reprimanded by Elizabeth, who was by now furious with Henry for his inactivity and with Essex for his rashness in courting danger. Recalled to England and termed a fool by his Queen, Essex fell into a melancholic fit; Elizabeth's letter 'put his honour in such an extreme agony and passion that he sounded often and did so swell that, casting himself upon his bed, all his buttons of his doublet broke away'.[20] His frustration was understandable; its wild manifestation typical of many later scenes. Eventually Elizabeth relented, Henry arrived with his army, and the siege of Rouen began on 31 October, three months after Essex had landed in Normandy. To begin with, it was conducted with gestures of chivalry reminiscent of the tiltyard, Essex issuing a challenge to personal combat to the garrison commander, who had the sense to refuse. But in April 1592 Parma's relieving army was reported to be at hand and Rouen was saved. Having achieved his objective, Parma retreated to the Netherlands, not wishing to face the superior forces now mobilized by Henry. The long campaign had been fruitless: Rouen remained in Catholic hands, Parma had not been brought to battle, and Elizabeth had become even more reluctant than before to hazard English men and money in support of Henry. Probably the failure was due in the main to the differing aims of the two allies. Henry was never fully committed to the siege and the English contingent was too small to ensure the success of a direct assault.

The naval plans for capturing the treasure fleet were even less successful than the campaigns on land. Lord Thomas Howard was sent to the Azores in the summer of 1591 with six royal ships. Ultimately he was promised a much larger fleet composed of fifteen royal ships and twenty-seven armed merchantmen. But by the end of August his reinforcements were yet to come, and at that moment he was caught at Flores by the main Spanish fleet sailing out from Ferrol to protect the silver convoy. Entirely outnumbered, Howard ordered his ships to weigh anchor and flee. All, except one, escaped. But the *Revenge*, under Sir Richard Grenville, bringing up the rear,

<hr>

[20] H. A. Lloyd, *The Rouen Campaign, 1590–1592* (Oxford, 1973), 114.

was caught by the Spanish and becalmed under the vast hull of the *San Felipe*. Throughout the evening and the whole of the night, the *Revenge*, bombarded from every side, fought off her attackers until her powder had run out and forty of her crew of one hundred were dead. Grenville, mortally wounded, ordered that the ship be scuttled, but his crew refused, and the Spaniards accepted an honourable surrender. A few days later, tempests sank thirty of the silver fleet and about six naval vessels: that year the weather did more damage to Spain than did the English ships. As so often, defeats are enshrined in English historical legends more gloriously than victory. The gallant fight of the *Revenge* became immortal; but the expedition was, for all that, a failure and Elizabeth took the point. No plans were made for large-scale naval expeditions for some years: the limited offensive at sea was mainly left to privateers.

However, Elizabeth agreed to take part in a private expedition organized by Ralegh and Howard in 1592: two royal ships accompanied ten privateers in a fleet commanded by Frobisher. Joining forces in the Azores with four ships belonging to the Earl of Cumberland and with three under other privateers, part of this fleet, under Sir John Burgh, captured the greatest prize of the war, the Portuguese carrack *Madre de Dios*, carrying spices, silks, and jewels from the East. The operation was not easy, for the carrack fought hard against ten English ships. Even in the declining days of the Portuguese 'empire', its great carracks did not offer a soft target, and only two others were captured between 1585 and 1603. Given the difficulty of taking Portuguese carracks, it is not surprising that the English failed to capture the much more heavily defended silver convoys from Spanish America. The value of the *Madre de Dios* was huge, amounting to about a quarter of a million pounds, not far off the annual peacetime revenues of the Crown. Of this cargo, about £100,000 worth 'disappeared' on the voyage back to England, but £140,000 was still available for distribution, of which the Queen took £80,000, roughly equivalent to a year's income from the customs.

During the three years that followed the defeat of the Armada, the political ground had been shifting inside England, with the deaths of Leicester, Mildmay, Walsingham, and Hatton. Their clients and followers had to find other patrons in a competitive world. As early as August 1589, one observer remarked that 'there was never in Court such emulation, such envy, such back-biting as is now at this time'.[21] The atmosphere was not to improve until the end of the reign. Burghley was left in growing isolation, relying more and more upon his son Robert, determined to secure and to

---

[21] Birch, *Memoirs*, i. 57.

pass on his near-monopoly of power. His immediate objective, brought very much into the foreground after Walsingham's death, was to secure for Robert Cecil the post of Secretary. Increasingly he insisted that he alone guarded the gates to royal favour and advancement. Sir Thomas Lake, a clerk of the signet and an acute commentator, advised Robert Sidney that, if he wanted office or assistance, he must keep in with Burghley: 'Old *Saturnus* is a melancholy and wayward planet, but yet predominant here, and if you have turn thus to do, it must be done that way; and whatsoever hope you have of any other, believe it or not.'[22] As Burghley grew older and more arthritic, he turned to his son to take on the burden of government which Walsingham's death had laid upon him: one of Walsingham's agents wrote of Robert Cecil that when his father was sick, 'the whole management of the secretary's place is in his hands'.[23] Almost incredibly, the office of Secretary, the hub of administration, was left vacant for six years after Walsingham's death; but the work was done by Robert Cecil, who laboured with desperate and tireless zeal: 'Sir Robert Cecil', wrote one of Essex's men, 'goeth and cometh very often between London and the Court, so that he comes out with his hands full of papers, and head full of matter, and so occupied passeth thro' the presence [chamber] like a blind man, not looking upon any.'[24] In August 1591, just after Essex sailed for France, Robert Cecil became a member of the Privy Council: Essex had to wait another eighteen months.

Essex was not content to watch the tightening of Cecil's power. Determined to succeed his stepfather Leicester as a great courtier, soldier, and politician, he courted the Queen and pressed forward his own men. In 1589 he tried unsuccessfully to get William Davison reinstated as Secretary. Three years later, the return to England of Antony Bacon, son of the Lord Keeper and brother of the more celebrated Francis, gave Essex the chance to build up an alternative intelligence network. Bacon had expected to secure advancement through his uncle, Burghley, but found the old man cool: he got 'no offer or hopeful assurance of real kindness' from him and turned instead to Essex, claiming disingenuously that he never expected Burghley to resent this.[25] Francis Bacon, by his own account, was also devoted to Essex: 'therefore', he wrote later, 'I applied myself wholly to him in a manner which I think happeneth rarely among men.'[26] By the end of 1593 Antony Bacon had taken up residence in Essex House and was controlling an informal intelligence system whose principal agents were Anthony Standen, an English Catholic recently returned from many years

---

[22] Collins, *Letters*, i. 331. [23] *CSP Dom. 1591–1594*, 97 (239/159).
[24] Birch, *Memoirs*, i. 155. [25] Ibid. 72–3. [26] Ibid. 73.

abroad, and Antonio Perez, once Secretary to Philip II and now exiled in England. Gathering around him skilled intriguers, soldiers, and intelligence agents, Essex built up a faction with which to challenge the Cecils and to rise from courtier to statesman.

At the end of 1592 rumours of impending Spanish invasion circulated with renewed intensity. Already alarmed by the possibility of English Catholics plotting with Spanish or Jesuit agents, the government became seriously disturbed at the discovery, in December, of the so-called 'Spanish Blanks' on a Scottish ship. These were blank letters signed by three Scottish Catholic earls: the ship's captain confessed under torture that they were part of a conspiracy to support a Spanish invasion. Elizabeth, accepting the need for French support in the face of this threat, agreed, under pressure from Henry's envoys and from Roger Williams, that she should send English troops once more to Normandy; and, in the early months of 1593, 1,200 men were levied from the southern counties and embarked for Dieppe. This further commitment led to the summons of the eighth Parliament of the reign, which assembled on 16 February 1593.

The 1593 Parliament met at the culmination of Whitgift's campaign against the puritans, launched by Bancroft's sermon at St Paul's Cross during the previous session.[27] Their secular protection weakened by the deaths of Leicester, Mildmay, and Walsingham, their spiritual leadership damaged by the death of John Field in 1588, the radical puritans were beginning to lose unity and direction. Some separated from the Church of England and formed independent congregations, while others produced brilliantly vituperative attacks upon the bishops in the anonymous Marprelate Tracts. For modern readers, 'Martin Marprelate' is a welcome relief from the solemnities of sixteenth-century theological controversy, but most contemporaries, even Presbyterians like Thomas Cartwright, were shocked at his excesses. The tracts provided an excellent excuse—if one were needed—for Whitgift and Bancroft to intensify their persecution. Search was made for Martin himself and, although his press was discovered, his identity has remained a matter of debate. Several preachers were harassed and interrogated, and in 1590 nine ministers, headed by Cartwright, were brought before the Court of High Commission. When they refused to take the oath, their trial was blocked: High Commission could and did deprive them of their benefices—except for Cartwright—but it could proceed no further with their trial. They were then brought before Star Chamber in May 1591, charged with refusing the oath and with seeking to introduce the Book of Discipline and thereby seditiously denying

[27] Above, p. 332.

the royal supremacy. The defendants consistently denied that they had acted or written contrary to royal authority, while Bancroft and his agents heaped up sheaves of depositions against them. By December, the prosecution had still to produce evidence of seditious acts, and gradually, during 1592, the accused ministers were released from imprisonment. However, the trial was never brought to an end, for the accused men were neither found guilty nor discharged. They did, however, promise not to hold formal conferences, and this marked the end, until the accession of James, of the active, organized Presbyterian movement.[28]

Yet this outcome was not satisfactory to Whitgift and Bancroft, who moved onto the attack in Parliament. The 1593 Parliament had been summoned principally to grant further subsidies, the final payment of the 1589 subsidies being due in February. But the government hoped also to tighten the laws against religious dissidents, both Catholic and puritan, and two bills were introduced to that end. One, brought first into the Lords, was a straightforward measure to restrict the movement of Catholic recusants, who were ordered to remain within 5 miles of their homes; a further clause imposed penalties of imprisonment upon any man suspected of being a Catholic priest who refused to answer to questioning.[29] The other bill was brought into the Commons in the form, at first, of a measure increasing the penalties against Catholic recusants, upon whom fines were now to be levied in proportion to their wealth, at a crippling rate. There was some criticism of the bill in the Commons, on the ground that it was too harsh, and also that it could be applied to Protestant recusants as well as to Catholics; it was allowed to sleep and a separate bill was then introduced into the Lords. This was directly aimed at Protestant sectaries: the Act of 1581 making it treason to withdraw men from their allegiance was now applied to them. Strong protests were made in the Commons by Sir Walter Ralegh and others. Ralegh cogently asked 'what danger may grow to ourselves, if this law pass, it were fit we considered. It is to be feared that men not guilty might be included in it.'[30] His fears were widely shared and the bill was heavily amended. By that time the government was forced to accept what it could get and the amended bill was enacted: attendance at unlawful assemblies and conventicles was placed on a par with popery and subjected to the penalty of imprisonment.[31] While these proceedings show that the Crown could not always count on the acquiescence of the Commons in its repressive measures, it is a remarkable sign of the change in the political climate since 1588 that such harsh legislation against Protestants should have been carried at all.

[28] Below, Ch. 11 s. 4, for a fuller discussion of the puritan movement.
[29] 35 Elizabeth c. 2.   [30] Neale, *Parliaments*, ii. 288.   [31] 35 Elizabeth c. 1.

The second objective of the Crown in this Parliament, as in most, was money. Robert Cecil opened for the government, stressing the dangers of invasion by Spain and referring to the 'Spanish Blanks'. At this stage, no specific number of subsidies was requested; but a few days later, Burghley, in the Lords, requested a conference between the two Houses, and when that met, he stated that the double subsidy of 1589 had brought in only £280,000, while the Queen had spent more than £1 million on the war. The Lords, he claimed, were insisting that three subsidies be granted, one to be paid in each year instead of at the normal rate of a half-subsidy per annum. In the Commons debate after the conference, two issues came to the fore, both raised by Francis Bacon. Accepting the grant of three subsidies, he objected to the matter being initiated in the Lords and to the doubling of the normal rate of payment. 'In histories', he claimed, 'it is to be observed that the English care not to be subject, base and taxable.'[32] Bacon's use of comparative history in debate is intellectually interesting, but it won him little support. The privy councillors, backed by Ralegh, opposed his arguments and urged the liberality of Elizabeth and the dangers of invasion. The Commons agreed to three subsidies, the first two of which were each to be paid in a single year, the third to be spread over two years—a slight concession to the taxpayer. For Bacon, the consequences were serious: his speech was reported to Elizabeth, who forbade him to enter the Court.

Francis Bacon's fall into disfavour could not have come at a worse moment for himself or for his patron, Essex. In the summer of 1593, not long after the dissolution of Parliament, Essex began to press for Bacon's promotion to the post of Attorney-General, left vacant when its holder, Sir Thomas Egerton, was promoted to be Master of the Rolls. Robert Cecil had already warned Bacon that he would be unable to help him and advised an approach to the Queen through Essex: possibly Cecil hoped to embroil both his rivals in a quest which would anger Elizabeth, though it is only fair to say that he also advised Bacon against any precipitate action. In October Essex pleaded Bacon's cause directly to Elizabeth, who, he reported, 'condemned my judgement in thinking him fittest to be attorney', even Bacon's uncle, Burghley, putting him in second place below Sir Edward Coke.[33] Essex took this disappointment as a personal slight upon himself, blaming the Cecils for his humiliation; and in February 1594, when he was travelling in a coach with Robert Cecil, his anger erupted. Cecil began the conversation by remarking that he wondered when the Queen would choose her new Attorney: 'I pray your Lordship let me know whom you will favour,' he disingenuously asked—for he knew the answer very well. Essex replied that he stood for Bacon. 'Good Lord', answered Sir Robert, 'I wonder your

[32] Neale, *Parliaments*, ii. 310.   [33] Birch, *Memoirs*, i. 125–6.

Lordship should go about to spend your strength in so unlikely a matter.' After Cecil had gone on to say that Bacon was too young for such a post, Essex replied that an even younger man, meaning Cecil himself, was aiming at a higher post—the office of Secretary. After defending his own claims as the pupil of his father, Cecil turned the conversation back to Bacon, suggesting him for the lesser office of Solicitor-General, which 'might be of easier digestion to her Majesty'. Essex then lost his temper: 'Digest me no digestions', he cried, 'for the attorneyship for Francis is that I must have; and in that will I spend my power, might, authority, and amity, and with tooth and nail defend and procure the same for him against whomsoever.'[34] The incident, relatively unimportant in itself, reveals the unrestrained commitment of Essex to his protégé and the growing intensity of his rivalry with the Cecils.

For the time being, relations got no worse. By March 1594 it was generally accepted that Coke would become Attorney, and Bacon's friends joined in recommending him to the Queen as Solicitor. Robert Cecil wrote to Egerton on Bacon's behalf: evidently the dividing lines of faction were not yet so sharply drawn that Cecil was averse to making things up with his cousin. Essex spoke directly to the Queen and was crossly told to go to bed, at which he went off saying that he would stay away until he was more graciously heard. Two days later, he reported that Elizabeth was 'out of quiet; and her passionate humour is nourished by some foolish women'.[35] For all the urging of both Essex and Robert Cecil, the Queen remained stubbornly opposed to the promotion of Bacon, and the post of Solicitor was left vacant for almost two years, going in the end to a mediocrity. Even when rival courtiers united, Elizabeth preserved her independence: she disliked being bullied and Essex had thrown everything into the cause. There is some truth in the bitter remark of old Lady Bacon, Francis's mother, that 'the Earl marred all with violent courses'.[36] The Cecils showed the wisdom that Essex lacked: they were prepared to help but only for the lesser post and then circumspectly. Such moderation was impossible for Essex and the whole affair foreshadows later political conflicts in which his excesses brought about his own failure.

However, shortly after he had failed to gain the Attorneyship for Bacon, Essex met with success in a different field. In the autumn of 1593, some servants of the pretender to the Portuguese throne, Don Antonio, were found to be selling information to the Spanish. Essex was entrusted with their interrogation and found—or claimed to have found—that the Queen's Portuguese doctor, Roderigo Lopez, was involved. When Robert Cecil told

---

[34] Birch, *Memoirs*, 152–3.   [35] Ibid. 166–7.   [36] Ibid. 270–1.

Elizabeth that there was no evidence against Lopez, she reacted angrily against Essex, calling him a 'rash and temerarious youth' for prosecuting a poor man of whose innocence she was certain.[37] After sulking in his room for two days, Essex pressed on with the inquiry and uncovered a plot in which Lopez had undertaken to murder the Queen. The unfortunate doctor was then examined in the Tower, confessed his guilt, and was quickly tried, convicted, and put to death. Even the Cecils accepted that he was guilty, and Burghley tried to gain some of the credit for the discovery by publishing an account of conspiracies against Elizabeth; but it was generally agreed that, in this affair, Essex 'won the spurs and saddle also'.[38] The truth of the matter was less important to competing politicians than the advantage to be won from it; but it seems likely from recently discovered evidence that Lopez was indeed guilty of offering to assassinate the Queen.[39]

By the spring of 1593, it was evident that Henry IV could no longer withstand the combined onslaughts of the Catholics and their Spanish allies unless he received far more substantial foreign aid than had yet been sent to him. Yet it was inconceivable that Elizabeth would send the 5,000–7,000 men he asked for. There was only one alternative for him: he could accept the Roman faith and in doing so win over many loyal Catholics from the League to the royalist cause. In May, he announced his intention to receive instruction; in June, the Parlement of Paris responded by ruling that no foreigner and no woman could wear the crown of France, thus eliminating the Spanish Infanta; and in July, Henry was received into the Roman Catholic Church. Elizabeth rebuked him indignantly when she heard the news: 'Ah! quelles douleurs, oh! quels regrets, oh! quels gémissements je sentais en mon âme par le son de telles nouvelles.'[40] But it is difficult to believe that she was surprised; nor can one take seriously the protests of a Queen who had so obstinately refrained from allowing religion to guide her own foreign policy. For some weeks, she vacillated even more than usual: she decided to recall Norris from Brittany and to send a further 1,500 men to Normandy; then she countermanded the levy for Normandy and ordered Williams to bring home those already there. In October, a Spanish threat to Ostend led to the Normandy contingent being sent to the Netherlands, leaving only Norris's Brittany force in France. She would have liked them to be withdrawn too, but, as Burghley told Norris, 'her mind is rather disposed to have you come away than to tarry, and yet she saith she yieldeth unto your tarrying because she findeth us that be of her Council to be of that mind'.[41] Elizabeth's enthusiasm for the Brittany commitment was not, it

---

[37] Ibid. 150.   [38] Ibid. 160.
[39] I am grateful to Professor David Katz for information on this point.
[40] Wernham, *After the Armada*, 497.   [41] Ibid. 508.

can be seen, very strong; but Norris's force stayed there until February 1595.

In most parts of France the year 1594 saw a triumphant run of successes by Henry IV as Leaguer grandees and cities came over to him. In March he occupied Paris, and Robert Sidney was writing to Burghley that by the end of the year Henry, if he lived, would have 'no other enemy in France but upon the frontiers and in Brittany'.[42] Conversion to the Catholic faith had done its work. But Brittany was a different matter, and it was a matter which deeply concerned the English government, given its potential as a base for invasion. The Spanish had maintained a force there since the autumn of 1590, Norris being able to do little or nothing against them; and in March 1594 they began to build a fort at Crozon, opposite Brest on the estuary, with the object of cutting off the city from the sea. Norris warned Elizabeth of the danger in the most urgent terms: 'I think there never happened a more dangerous enterprise for the state of your Majesty's country than this of the Spanish to possess Brittany.' It would, he added, be as 'prejudicial' as if they held Ireland—nearly a prophetic comparison.[43] The Queen perceived the danger and promised to send English troops. In July she ordered 3,000 men to be levied from the shires, reducing the number ten days later to 2,000: a characteristic change of mind. The force embarked with some difficulty, after mutinies at Portsmouth, but by September was in a position to besiege the Spanish in Crozon, aided by a small naval force under Frobisher. Two months later Crozon fell to the combined English and royalist force, and the threat to Brest was lifted. The English troops were withdrawn from Brittany—2,000 of the unfortunates being sent without warning to Ireland—and thereafter no English forces were left in France. By the spring of 1595 England's two principal allies seemed well placed. The Dutch had captured Groningen and thus secured the north-eastern Netherlands, while holding the Rhine–Maas line to the south. Henry IV had received the surrender of all but a rump of Leaguer nobles; but although internal dissensions were settled in France, he had still to face the armies of Spain, on whom he had now declared open war. The year 1596 was to tell a different story.

The pause between the ending of the civil strife in France and the beginning of the next phase of hostilities—the Spanish invasion of Picardy, the rebellion in Ireland, and the naval expeditions to Cadiz and the Azores—allows us to assess the cost and the achievement of England's military endeavours since the Armada. The levies of money and men had been heavy. Since the beginning of 1589 Elizabeth had spent roughly

---

[42] Wernham, *After the Armada*, 519.   [43] Ibid. 528.

£200,000 per annum on the war for slightly more than five years, bringing the total expenditure to £1,100,000. Of this, about £300,000 had been spent in France and £750,000 in the Netherlands. About 48,000 men had been dispatched overseas since the Armada, 19,000 to Portugal, 20,000 to France, plus the reinforcements to the garrison of 7,000 in the Netherlands. The equipment and weapons of the levies were a continuous drain upon the resources of the shires and their collection was a source of discontent and irritation. The county levies almost always fell short of their quotas and nearly 20 per cent of the men were usually deficient in arms or equipment. Nevertheless, the subsidies were voted; a high proportion of the required men was levied; and mutinies were few. Up to the middle of 1595, there is not much sign of serious hostility towards the Crown either from the counties or from Parliament. The willingness to pay and to round up levies over five years remains remarkable; but more testing times for the government and the counties were to come in the second half of the decade.[44]

3. THE LAST YEARS OF LORD BURGHLEY, 1595–1598

Towards the end of 1595, the military situation was, in most theatres, as threatening as ever. Only the Dutch seemed relatively secure behind their powerful defences. In France, although Henry IV had won the initiative against the Catholic League, the Spanish were advancing into Picardy, where they took Cambrai. English authority in Ireland, apparently growing more secure from 1588 to 1593, was now slipping back, and in May 1595, Hugh O'Neill, Earl of Tyrone, began the most serious revolt of the century against English rule.[45] At sea, the Spanish fleet had been rebuilt and Philip II was again capable of launching an Armada.

Rather surprisingly, Elizabeth allowed her resources to be used in 1595, not against any of these dangers, but in a major raid on the Caribbean. The last major naval enterprise having ended disastrously at the Azores in 1591, Drake and Hawkins now planned a highly ambitious project for the capture of Panama. They sailed in August after hearing that a rudderless galleon was stranded in the harbour of San Juan de Puerto Rico. The English fleet was powerful—six first-line ships and twenty-one armed merchantmen, with 2,500 men—but poorly provisioned and badly led. Drake and Hawkins shared the command and their disagreements led to uncertainty and delay: by the time they reached San Juan, where Hawkins died, the Spanish

[44] I have drawn most of my figures from Wernham, *After the Armada*, 415–19, 466–8, 564–8; but my assessment of the country's reaction to the burdens of war is less pessimistic than his.

[45] Below, pp. 356–9.

defences had been substantially reinforced. Frustrated at San Juan, Drake sailed on to Panama, where again the Spanish authorities had had ample time to mobilize troops. Drake's plan was to land 6,000–7,000 men at Nombre de Dios, who should then march overland to Panama, which he would attack by sea. The overland force was heavily defeated and Drake retired without making any attack. A few weeks later he was dead from dysentery and his fleet returned in late April. His end was a sad one, but has not much diminished the glamour of his name. He was neither a great strategist nor a successful commander of campaigns; but he was a superb navigator and a brilliant privateer. In the words of Thomas Maynarde, who sailed on this final voyage, Drake was 'better able to conduct forces and discreetly to govern in conducting them to places where service was to be done, than to command in the execution thereof'.[46] He was not alone in this failing. Elizabethan England produced many great sailors and dynamic leaders; but the planning and execution of a major combined operation was beyond their ability and the resources of the time (Map 12).

Weeks before the return of the Caribbean fleet, the government, prompted especially by Howard of Effingham and Essex, was planning a pre-emptive strike on the Spanish fleet at Cadiz. However, before that could depart, the Queen had to confront the more immediate threat pre-sented by the Spanish forces in France. The loss of Cambrai had produced urgent requests from the French for aid during the autumn of 1595, and when they were refused, Henry IV began to hint that he would make a separate peace with Spain. In response, Elizabeth sent Sir Henry Unton, an able and experienced diplomat, to the French King to dissuade him from making peace and to convey her goodwill. However, Unton carried secret, unofficial instructions from his patron, Essex: he was to advise Henry to keep up his threats of making peace with Spain so that the Queen would listen to her more aggressive advisers; otherwise, wrote Essex, 'such coun-cillors in England as have given credit to the French advertisements [i.e. Essex himself], and persuaded the Queen to satisfy the French King are utterly discredited'.[47] This remarkable attempt to conduct a double system of diplomacy, using foreign negotiations to promote a faction, had little effect. Henry would have used the gambit of a separate peace without any prompting from Unton, and the embassy had little consequence for English domestic politics. Unton had nothing to offer to the French and could only report his conviction—which was soundly based—that Henry was moving towards a treaty with Spain. However, Unton fell critically ill and told Henry on his deathbed that he believed that Elizabeth genuinely intended

---

[46] Andrews, *Drake's Voyages*, 205.   [47] Birch, *Memoirs*, i. 353.

to give help. Whether Henry was moved by this or not, he decided to send an envoy to England.

At the very moment of this decision, the end of March 1596, the Spanish army reached Calais and besieged it. The danger to England could not be ignored. Troops and ships for the Cadiz expedition were already being assembled and could be turned to the relief of Calais. Even Burghley was convinced that the Spanish must be prevented from taking it; and Essex wrote urgently that 'It is time for Her Majesty to draw her sword, for our doing nothing and the enemies being so undertaking, strikes a terror in the people of those parts [i.e. Kent], and I fear me as much in other quarters of the realm.'[48] Yet Elizabeth, determined to gain an advantage from the situation, harped once again on the English claim to Calais, a theme that had obsessed her in the past. The French envoy was told that help would be sent if Calais were, at least for the time being, restored to England; but while Elizabeth bargained, ordering levies to assemble and then countermanding the instructions, Calais fell. On 16 April, the day after its surrender, the Huguenot leader Turenne arrived in England to negotiate a fresh alliance.[49] In May Elizabeth and Turenne agreed to the Treaty of Greenwich, under whose public provisions England was to supply 4,000 men for six months, the expense being met by the Queen in the first place and repaid by Henry later. This agreement was for public and international consumption: a secret clause, demanded presumably because of Elizabeth's needs in Ireland, reduced the number of troops to 2,000 and stipulated that they be used only for garrison duty. In the autumn Turenne went to the Hague to negotiate a complementary treaty with the Dutch, and on the first day of 1597 this was finally ratified, bringing into being a Triple Alliance between England, France, and the Netherlands, committing the Dutch to making war alongside the French in Picardy. Strangely, this offensive and defensive league was created several years after the three powers had been separately allied. Its life was short.

During these protracted negotiations, the great English expedition to Cadiz had been launched and had returned. Under the dual command of Howard of Effingham and Essex, who financed it jointly with the Queen, the fleet consisted of eighteen royal ships, eighteen Dutch men-of-war, ten large London merchantmen, and about 100 smaller vessels, with nearly 10,000 soldiers. The four English squadrons were led by Howard of Effingham, Essex, Lord Thomas Howard, and Walter Ralegh. Its objectives were to attack and destroy Spanish ships in their harbours, to take and

[48] *CSP Dom. 1595–1597*, 199 (257/10).
[49] He was by now Duc de Bouillon, but is better remembered as Turenne.

destroy towns on the coast of Spain, and to capture booty. After many delays, some due to the siege of Calais, others to the diminishing enthusiasm of the Queen for the whole enterprise, the fleet sailed in June. Three weeks later, having proceeded with a dispatch notably lacking in the Drake–Hawkins voyage to the Caribbean, it appeared off Cadiz, surprising the Spanish, who had been deceived by skilfully planted information into thinking that the expedition was sailing to the Caribbean or to Brittany. Inside Cadiz harbour were four great men-of-war, twenty galleys, and at least forty merchantmen laden with cargoes for the West Indies. After an attempt to storm the town by landing troops on the shore had nearly led to disaster, the commanders were persuaded by Ralegh to withdraw from the beaches and make a naval assault into the harbour. Two of the Spanish galleys had been involved in the fight with Sir Richard Grenville in 1591 and Ralegh, leading the attack, had 'resolved to be revenged for the Revenge'. He succeeded brilliantly: the four Spanish men-of-war ran aground, two were burned by the Spaniards, the other two captured. Ralegh himself has left an account of the burning of the *St Philip* that ranks among the most vivid and compelling descriptions of war:

The spectacle was very lamentable on their side; for many drowned themselves; many, half burnt, leapt into the water, very many hanging by the ropes' end by the ship's side under the water, even to their lips; many swimming with grievous wounds stricken under water, and put out of their pain; and withal, so huge a fire, and such a tearing of the ordnance, in the great Philip and the rest, when the fire came to 'em, as if any man had a desire to see Hell itself, it was there most lively figured.[50]

Essex then seized the opportunity for an assault upon the town, which was quickly taken. He and Howard ensured that the civilian population was allowed to leave unharmed and unmolested, and Essex gained from this a reputation in Spain for chivalry and honour. Unfortunately, the attack upon the town diverted English attention from the merchant ships in the harbour, which were set on fire by the order of the Duke of Medina Sidonia, once commander of the Armada; while the Spanish lost the ships and their cargoes, they had the satisfaction of keeping them out of the hands of the English. Even so, there was plenty of booty to be had, and the army stayed in Cadiz for two weeks, looting and bargaining for ransoms. Essex and Sir Francis Vere, veteran commander from the Netherlands, argued strongly for keeping a force permanently in the town, which could become a base for naval operations against the Spanish coast and the treasure fleets. But their colleagues were understandably afraid to adopt so bold a policy without

[50] Printed in Walter Oakeshott, *The Queen and the Poet* (London, 1960), 210–16.

authority from the Queen. Before the army left Cadiz, thirty-three men were knighted by Essex, twenty-seven by Howard: the Cadiz knights included some of Essex's most loyal followers in subsequent years and became the object of Elizabeth's fury.

The expedition had produced a resounding victory over Spain. Yet, as Essex himself admitted, great opportunities had been missed. The merchantmen could have been captured and would then have augmented the profits of the voyage; Cadiz could have been retained for a time and used as a base; the treasure fleet from the Indies might have been intercepted; and other Spanish harbours might have been attacked and their warships destroyed. The failure to capture the merchantmen was largely due to Essex's own impetuous assault upon Cadiz; the other omissions followed from the caution of his fellow-commanders.

One immediate consequence of the Cadiz expedition was the determination of Philip II on a counter-stroke. Rumours of Spanish plans for an invasion had been circulating for two or three years and it now became a reality. In the summer, Philip II had sent encouraging messages and a military mission to the Irish rebels, and he now planned an expedition to Ireland. The English government grew alarmed: troops were sent to reinforce the Irish garrison and the militia in the southern counties was put into a posture of defence. In October ninety-eight ships sailed from the Tagus only to be struck by heavy storms off Finisterre. Thirty-two vessels sank with at least 2,000 men, and the remainder struggled back to port. The invasion was postponed for a further year.

By the time that Essex returned from Cadiz, his rivals had tightened their control of affairs at home. Robert Cecil was appointed Secretary of State in July, having performed most of the duties of the office for six years without any official position. He now had formal authority and the various candidates backed by Essex—Antony Bacon, William Davison, Thomas Bodley—were left in the cold. The triumph and adulation surrounding Essex's return soon died down as the victors quarrelled over the distribution of the spoils, of which the Queen was trying to secure a large share for herself. Robert Cecil, charged with making an inventory of the plunder, ran foul of Essex, who wrote to Antony Bacon that 'this day I was more braved by your little cousin than ever I was by any man in my life'.[51] However, Burghley and his son, having achieved their main objective, were anxious to conciliate the Earl and defended his right to a share of the spoils. This did Burghley little good, for the Queen called him 'a miscreant and a coward',

[51] Devereux, *Letters*, i. 380-1.

accusing him of favouring Essex. He wrote submissively to the Earl, who replied with generous condescension: 'I have ever desired, and so do, that your lordship were well edified of me.'[52] One at least of Essex's followers was distinctly less beneficent: Antony Bacon commented that Essex's success 'hath made the Old Fox to crouch and whine, and to insinuate himself by a very submissive letter to my Lord of Essex'.[53] By the end of the year, a surface calm had been imposed, although the deeper tensions remained. As Thomas Lake commented: 'the factions [are] never more malicious yet well smoothed outward'; the Queen, he went on, was balancing the weights rather than drawing all to 'one assize'.[54] This was a common cliché about Elizabeth's policy, but hardly fits the case, for although the Queen might look as if she were balancing the factions, in practice the real advantages were going to the Cecils. Francis Bacon told Essex frankly of the dangers of his situation and policy.[55] He had, he wrote, already told Essex to 'win the Queen'. 'But how is it now?', he went on: 'A man of a nature not to be ruled . . . of an estate not grounded to his greatness; of a popular reputation; of a military dependence . . .' Could there be 'a more dangerous image than this represented to any monarch living, much more to a lady, and of her Majesty's apprehension?' Bacon's advice was that Essex should show himself pliable, as Leicester and Hatton had done, avoid actions of war and aim for civil offices, speak out against popular causes, and mend his estate by dismissing some of his officers. It was sound counsel, and three years later Bacon was to give complementary advice to Elizabeth on her treatment of Essex, then in Ireland. She should keep him at Court, 'with a white staff in his hand' as Leicester had had, so that he would be removed from military power and made contented. 'To discontent him as you do', Bacon insisted with astonishing frankness, 'and yet to put arms and power into his hands, may be a kind of temptation to make him prove cumbersome and unruly.'[56] With Machiavellian realism, Bacon had perceived potent sources of trouble: poverty, ambition, and military ardour were a dangerous combination in a royal favourite. A decade or so of war had bred changes among the political élite. There were now many active soldiers among the nobility and gentry, experienced in war and hungry for reward, and with a potential leader like Essex, and jealous guardians of peace like the Cecils, they were an explosive force.

Early in 1597, the final illness and eventual death of old Lord Cobham plunged the Court into a hunt for offices. Since he was Lord Chamberlain,

[52] Birch, *Memoirs*, ii. 146-7.   [53] Ibid. 153.
[54] HMC, *Calendar of the MSS of Lord De L'Isle and Dudley at Penshurst Place* (3 vols., London, 1925-36), ii. 227.
[55] Spedding, *Bacon*, ii. 40-5.   [56] Birch, *Memoirs*, ii. 432.

Warden of the Cinque Ports, and Lord Lieutenant of Kent, the spoil was tempting. Cobham, dying, asked Elizabeth to allow him to pass all his posts to his son Henry Brooke. She refused him. On 6 March he was dead and the chase was on: 'the Court', wrote Rowland White to Robert Sidney, 'now is full of who shall have this and that office'.[57] Essex threw his weight behind Robert Sidney in the competition for the Cinque Ports, and, when Elizabeth expressed doubts, announced that he would secure the post for himself and then resign in favour of Sidney. It did no good. Sidney was passed over and the new Lord Cobham succeeded his father as Warden of the Cinque Ports and Lord Lieutenant of Kent; Lord Hunsdon was appointed Lord Chamberlain, and Robert Cecil picked up the office of Chancellor of the Duchy of Lancaster, for which he had long been angling. Essex became Master of the Ordnance: he could secure a useful office for himself but nothing for a loyal—and able—follower like Sidney. His secretary, Edward Reynolds, commented that he 'scorned the practices and dissembling courses' of the Court.[58]

Disenchanted with the Court and ignoring Bacon's advice, Essex decided on military endeavour, and drew up a strategic plan for attacking Spain.[59] Rejecting previous schemes for blockading the Baltic trade or attempting to intercept the treasure fleets in the Azores, he argued for the capture of Lisbon or Cadiz, either of which could be used as a base for destroying the Spanish fleet and cutting Spain's lifelines with the Baltic and the Indies. A small, well-trained force of about 3,000 men would, he considered, be better for the task than the large, unwieldy armies sent with previous expeditions. In spite of opposition from Burghley, who doubted the merits of the scheme, Essex was put in command of a further expedition in June 1597. Because Philip was again assembling an invasion force at Ferrol and La Coruña in north-west Spain, he was instructed first to destroy the fleet at Ferrol and then to proceed with his own plan. His fleet contained seventeen Queen's warships, forty-three smaller men-of-war, ten Dutch vessels, and fifty or so smaller ships, with 6,000 troops. The four squadrons were commanded by Essex, Lord Thomas Howard, Ralegh, and a Dutch admiral. Although smaller than the force sent to Cadiz the previous year, it was still a formidable expedition. The plan was intelligent; there was a single overall commander of high reputation; and the fleet was well organized. The prospects for success were good and everything went wrong. In July the expedition sailed only to be driven back by storms. Some weeks

---

[57] HMC, De L'Isle and Dudley, ii. 243; Collins, Letters, ii. 25.

[58] Devereux, Letters, i. 410.

[59] See L. W. Henry, 'The Earl of Essex as strategist and military organizer, 1596–97', EHR 68 (1953), 363–93.

were spent in refitting the ships and then infection struck the army. The shortage of supplies and the reduction of the fighting force compelled Essex to disband all but 1,000 soldiers. The plan for occupying Cadiz had to be abandoned. When the fleet sailed a second time, it was dispersed by further storms off Finisterre. Ralegh's squadron became separated from the rest and Essex decided to abandon the attack on Ferrol. After hovering for a time off the coast of Spain, the squadrons reunited in the Azores. A dispute between Essex and Ralegh, general indecision, and some misfortune frustrated success: Ralegh captured the island of Fayal, but to little purpose; the treasure fleet, with 10 million pesos on board, was sighted by an English captain but escaped; and in October Essex decided to sail for home. None of the original objectives had been achieved and there was little booty. It is ironical that an expedition designed to avoid the previous fruitless cruising off the Azores in the hope of intercepting the Spanish silver convoy should have become known as the Islands Voyage. It was the last of the major Elizabethan naval expeditions, the last in fact until Buckingham's fiasco at Cadiz in 1626. Luckily for England, the Spanish riposte, like its predecessor of 1596, was again frustrated: a large fleet of 136 ships and 12,600 men left La Coruña in October and was driven back by storms when it had come within sight of England. This was not the last Spanish Armada: another was actually to land at Kinsale, in Ireland, in 1601.[60]

On his return from the Azores, Essex was sourly welcomed by the Queen and returned her sourness with sulks. Apart from his failure to secure anything of profit for his followers, he was particularly angered by the promotion of Lord Howard of Effingham to be Earl of Nottingham. Essex reacted by challenging the new Earl or one of his sons to a duel, and then withdrew from Court in a rage. Hunsdon remonstrated with him, writing that Elizabeth considered—understandably—that 'a prince was not to be contested withal by a subject'.[61] An anonymous friend insisted that absence from Court would never secure contentment: 'let nothing draw thee from the Court; sit in every Council . . . Dissemble thou like a courtier.'[62] Eventually, his path smoothed by his being made Earl Marshal, with precedence over the Earl of Nottingham, Essex returned to Court and ostensibly friendly relations—expressed in high-flown terms—were resumed between him and the Cecils.

The sulks and furies of Essex at Court, productive as they were of gossip, were relatively minor problems for the government in the autumn of 1597. Ireland had been slipping over the past four years into its worst turmoil of

---

[60] Below, s. 5.   [61] Devereux, *Letters*, i. 467.
[62] *CSP Dom. 1595–1597*, 265/10 (pp. 532–3).

the reign, discontent in Ulster breaking into open revolt in 1595. At the beginning of the decade, Ireland had seemed to be under English authority; Connacht was firmly ruled by its president; Munster had, to all appearances, been 'planted' with English settlers; power in Ulster had been effectively divided between Turlough Luineach O'Neill, chief of the clan, Hugh O'Neill, Baron Dungannon, created Earl of Tyrone in 1585, and Hugh O'Donnell in Tirconnell.[63] However, under Perrott's successor as Lord Deputy, Sir William Fitzwilliam, the Dublin government encroached on the rights of the Gaelic lords in Ulster, partly as a matter of policy to bring the province under better control, and partly to satisfy the ambitions of English settlers like Sir Nicholas Bagenal, marshal of the army, and his son Henry. The chief of the MacMahons was executed in 1590 and his lordship of Oriel, recently shired as Co. Monaghan, was divided between subordinate lords and freeholders, who were now tenants of the Crown. The action was seen by the government as a precedent for future policy, by the Gaelic lords, especially Tyrone, who was MacMahon's overlord, as a threat to their authority. Ill-feeling between Tyrone and the English was exacerbated by hostility between himself and Sir Henry Bagenal; and their political rivalry was intensified by personal animosity when Tyrone carried off and married Sir Henry's sister Mabel without his consent.

The situation in Ulster was made particularly dangerous to the English by the alliance between Tyrone and Hugh Roe O'Donnell, son of Hugh O'Donnell, the reigning lord of Tirconnell. For decades the O'Donnells had been the enemies of their O'Neill neighbours and therefore the natural allies of the government in Dublin. However, during the latter part of the 1580s, the situation began to change when Hugh Roe married Rose O'Neill, Tyrone's daughter, a marriage that was useful to Hugh Roe in his struggles to establish his succession to the lordship of Tirconnell against dynastic rivals. The Dublin government kidnapped and imprisoned him in 1587 on a doubtful charge, but he made a dramatic escape from Dublin Castle four years later and secured his title to the lordship. The government was then in the position of having backed the defeated contender and alienated the successful. This mistake would have been less serious had it not been for English encroachment into the Maguire lordship of Fermanagh in 1593, which raised again the fear of a general attack upon Gaelic authority.

Subsequent events were, even by the standards of Tudor Ireland, confusing, largely due to the covert policy pursued by Tyrone. Claiming that

[63] On the outbreak of the Tyrone revolt see Hiram Morgan, *Tyrone's Rebellion: The Outbreak of the Nine Years War in Tudor Ireland* (Woodbridge, 1993), *passim*.

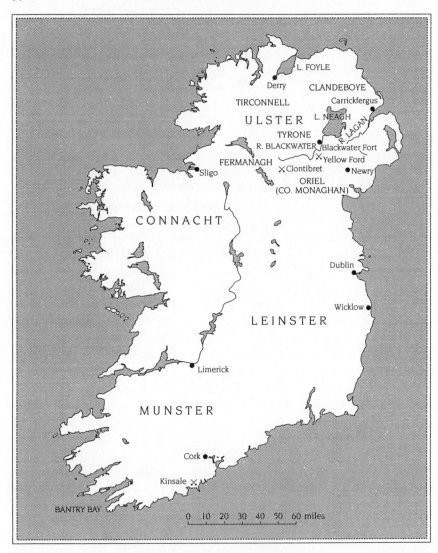

MAP 15. Ireland: Tyrone's rebellion, 1595–1603

he was unable to control his dependants, he co-operated for a time with the government against the Maguires, who had gone into revolt. Most probably this was an excuse to disguise his real policy of drawing together a confederacy of Gaelic lords with the object of regaining authority over their territories. Elizabeth, faced with the choice between making peace with the Ulster lords or waging full-scale war against them, did neither. She refused to pardon Tyrone, claiming that it would be detrimental to her honour, and in 1595 he was proclaimed a traitor. He moved into open rebellion, encouraged his brother to attack the Blackwater Fort, which controlled one of the main entries to Ulster, and then defeated Sir Henry Bagenal at Clontibret, south of the Blackwater River. Although the London government transferred troops from Brittany to Ireland, they did not arrive until March 1596 and were then one-third below their nominal strength of 2,000.

With the death of Turlough Luineach shortly after the battle of Clontibret, Tyrone became chief of the O'Neills. He commanded a force of 1,000 cavalry, 1,000 pikemen, and 4,000 musketeers, trained to fight in the English manner, well armed and well disciplined, maintained by a prosperous lordship. Already negotiating for support from the Pope and from Philip II, he posed a greater threat to the English presence in Ireland than any Irish lord of the century. To meet this threat the English could muster a force of about 3,000 men, some of them trained in the French wars but unenthusiastic about the Irish struggle, others raw recruits. For the next seven years, the confederacy led by Tyrone was to dominate the government's military policy.

The Crown's immediate response was to pardon Tyrone and to seek a truce, which was agreed in May 1596. At that time, Elizabeth was too heavily preoccupied with the danger of a Spanish armada and with Essex's pre-emptive strike at Cadiz to devote resources to Ireland. Yet, under cover of the truce, Tyrone was able to provoke rebellion against the settlers in Munster, while O'Donnell occupied part of Connacht. In 1597, a new deputy, Lord Burgh, arrived in Ireland and launched an ambitious two-pronged expedition into Ulster. However, he soon found that Tyrone's force was superior to his own and contented himself with rebuilding Blackwater Fort. As soon as it was complete, Burgh died and the garrison became a hostage to fortune, besieged by Tyrone. With the army outnumbered and Ireland without a governor, the Crown had no choice but to make yet another truce with Tyrone.

As the government made increasing demands upon its subjects for money and for men to maintain its overseas campaigns, the great majority of the people found themselves more and more pinched by want, hit either by taxes or by high prices.[64] Yet up to 1597, although the Exchequer was put under strain, there is no evidence that the government's fiscal demands produced more than persistent grumbling, occasional refusal to pay special levies, such as ship-money, and resentment at burdens like purveyance and monopolies. Continuous requisitioning of troops was certainly unpopular and commanders reported low morale, frequent desertion, and occasional

[64] Above, pp. 348–9.

petty mutinies; more seriously, the counties often failed to supply their levies with uniforms and weapons. But in general the money for the war was raised and troops were dispatched in something near to the required numbers.

The effects of serious harvest failures were far more alarming. Four successive harvests—1594, 1595, 1596, and 1597—ranged from bad to disastrous, with 1596 possibly the worst in the century. Wheat prices, which had averaged 19.9 shillings a quarter in 1590–2, rose to 23.00 shillings in 1593–4, 34.87 in 1594–5, 37.09 in 1595–6, 50.07 in 1596–7, and 46.18 in 1597–8, before falling back to 28.03 in 1598–9. The prices of cheaper grains rose even more steeply as the poor traded down-market to barley and rye. At harvest-time in 1596 a correspondent told Burghley that 'I greatly fear that this year will be the hardest year for the poor people that hath happened in any man's memory.'[65] He was unhappily correct. Urban officials complained of the shortage of corn and the misery of the poor, who were drifting into the towns in search of food. The Privy Council responded as best it could with admonition and instruction. Hoarders of corn, 'liker to wolves or cormorants than to natural men', were blamed for much of the trouble. The export of grain and the feeding of peas to cattle were forbidden. In the north and the south-west there was real starvation: it was reported from Newcastle upon Tyne that there were 'sundry starving and dying in our streets and in the fields for lack of bread'.[66] Elsewhere there was widespread hardship and high mortality, especially in pastoral districts and smaller towns. The death rate rose as the food shortage worsened, increasing by over 50 per cent between 1595 and 1597, the worst year. Terrible as the suffering of the poor undoubtedly was, the mortality was not as severe nationally as one might expect from the succession of disastrous harvests: the consequences were seemingly far worse in France, the southern Netherlands, and parts of Germany. For this there are many reasons: some of the poor switched their diet from wheat to less palatable grains; the larger town corporations bought up supplies of corn and provided effective relief; and England was free from the direct impact of war. Although catastrophe was avoided, central and local authorities were frightened by the apparition of mass starvation and the disorders which accompanied the dearth. A food riot was reported from Kent in 1595, and there was sporadic unrest in many towns over the next three years. London was the scene of mounting disorder from 1590: the worst disturbances came in 1595, when apprentices rioted against fishwives, butter-sellers, and alien merchants, culminating in

[65] John Walter, 'A rising of the people?', *Past and Present*, 107 (1985), 91.
[66] A. B. Appleby, 'Disease or famine?', *EcHR* 26 (1973), 419.

assaults on corporation officials upon Tower Hill. In November of the following year came the so-called Oxfordshire Rising, a protest against enclosures and the high price of corn. Three ringleaders tried to raise men to pull down enclosures, seize the weapons of the gentry, and march on London to join the discontented apprentices. In the event, only four men turned up at the rendezvous and the 'rising' never took place. But the Privy Council was profoundly disturbed: suspects were interrogated and tortured, and the offence was treated as treason. Considering the hardships suffered by the rural poor in these years, it is surprising that their response was so passive and that the riots of 1549 were not repeated in the 1590s. Probably the reason is that the 'better sort', who had led the East Anglian movements earlier, held back from action since they were by now economically secure, even—or perhaps especially—in years of dearth. The conspirators in Oxfordshire were young men, without family ties, who carried little weight in the countryside.[67]

When Parliament met in October 1597, postponed at Essex's request until his return from the Islands Voyage,[68] it was faced with urgent demands for money from the Crown to finance the war against Spain and the defence of Ireland, with, in the background, the threat of famine and the prospect of growing discontent at the government's demands for levies and the burden of high prices and enclosures. Lord Keeper Egerton put the emphasis of his opening speech upon the Queen's defence of her dominions by the expenditure of 'a mass of treasure . . . for maintenance of her armies by sea and land', with small help from her subjects.[69] When the Commons came to discuss the grant of subsidies, Francis Bacon, who had angered the Queen by obstructing her proposals in 1593,[70] reminded the House that four new dangers threatened since they had last met: the conversion of the French King to Rome, the Spanish capture of Calais, the breaking of the 'ulcer of Ireland', and the threatened retaliation of Philip II for the two expeditions sent against him. The House accepted his arguments and the persuasions of the Chancellor of the Exchequer: three subsidies were voted, to be levied in successive years. The only demur was over the rate of collection: the third payment was not, as on the last occasion, to be spread over two years. Otherwise the Commons demonstrated full support for the war and a readiness to finance it.

By contrast, the debates on social issues showed less harmony and some confusion. On the first day of full parliamentary business, Francis Bacon introduced two bills, one to preserve land in tillage, the other to prevent

---

[67] Above, Ch. 6 ss. 1, 4.
[68] He actually landed at Plymouth two days after the opening of the session.
[69] D'Ewes, *Journal*, 525.   [70] Above, s. 2.

depopulation and the destruction of farms. Not generally remembered as a defender of the poor, Bacon presented a bleak picture of English villages since the enclosure laws had been repealed in 1593: 'instead of a whole town full of people, nought but green fields, a shepherd and his dog.'[71] The Crown gave temperate support to what was essentially an unofficial initiative, and the bills were sent to committee. Both provoked major debates on their second readings. The tillage bill was supported by an anonymous member who echoed Thomas More by asking rhetorically whether England should be known as 'a . . . brutish land, where sheep shall devour men'.[72] His opponent, Henry Jackman, produced the more modern argument that market forces would provide the solution: as grain prices rose, farmers would turn back to tillage. However, the 'interventionist' cause carried the day and the Tillage Act became law,[73] declaring, that except in certain pastoral shires, land converted for pasture since 1588 should be turned back to arable. The measure against depopulation met with broad agreement in principle, dissent revolving around the strictness of its provisions. Eventually, a compromise seems to have been achieved, with an Act ordering that landlords who had allowed 'houses of husbandry' to decay within the past seven years should rebuild them with an allocation of 40 acres of land, if available, to each.[74] At the same time, the House, came to consider the plight of the poor and the problem of vagrancy. Henry Finch, showing 'horrible abuses of idle and vagrant persons . . . and . . . the miserable estate of the godly and honest sort of the poor subjects of this realm', moved for the appointment of a committee.[75] After proceedings of great obscurity and complexity two considerable measures emerged. One was relatively uncontentious, drawing together earlier measures on poor relief into a comprehensive statute, and ordering the appointment of overseers to levy parish rates for providing raw material on which the able-bodied poor could work and for maintaining the 'lame, impotent, old, blind and such other among them being poor and not able to work'.[76] The vagrancy bill provoked more debate—although the arguments have not survived. It ordered that vagabonds, a very broadly defined category, should be whipped until bloody and returned to their place of origin. If they offended again, they were to be imprisoned and might ultimately be committed to the galleys or to banishment. Since the Act was neither more nor less severe than previous

[71] A. F. Pollard and M. Blatcher, 'Hayward Townshend's Journals', *BIHR* 12 (1934), 10.
[72] Neale, *Parliaments*, ii. 339–43.   [73] 39 Elizabeth c. 2.
[74] 39 Elizabeth c. 1.   [75] Neale, *Parliaments*, ii. 338–9.
[76] 39 Elizabeth c. 3. There was also a statute, 39 Elizabeth c. 5, for 'erecting of hospitals . . . and working houses for the poor'.

measures about vagabonds, it is hard to see why there should have been controversy.[77]

Strong protests were made by the Commons of 1597 against monopolies and patents—grants of exclusive rights to particular trades or manufactures. The issue seems to have been raised on several occasions during the session by prominent unofficial members as the Crown fought a defensive, delaying action. Eventually the House was persuaded to present a moderately worded petition, thanking the Queen for ordering reformation, but complaining that abuses remained. In reply, Lord Keeper Egerton promised that the obnoxious patents would be tried by law, but insisted that the Queen would guard her prerogative, 'the chiefest flower in her garland'.[78] Apart from this set-back over monopolies, the Parliament of 1597 has an impressive record of achievement. Four major Acts of social legislation were carried, and, if none of them was particularly original, they demonstrate collectively the concern of the House and the initiative of unofficial members. The proceedings also show that the House and its committees engaged in real debates and in careful, even minute, scrutiny of legislation.

Before Parliament's dissolution the English government had become locked in a diplomatic entanglement with its French ally. Henry IV, having recaptured Amiens in September 1597, was in a position to negotiate with the Spanish from strength. Having received an encouraging response from the Spanish government in the Netherlands, he dispatched an envoy to London to sound out Elizabeth on his proposal for joint negotiations with Spain by the French, the Dutch, and the English. The Dutch were adamantly opposed to any form of treaty, and, rather surprisingly, the English Council was cool. Not that either Elizabeth or Burghley was enthusiastic about prolonging the war: they were, however, alarmed at the haste with which Henry wished to proceed, given the complexity of the issues. To discover Henry's intentions, Elizabeth sent a special embassy to France headed by Robert Cecil. Henry's immediate objective was to divide his two allies and he complained to Cecil that, for the sake of the Dutch, they must all 'be still miserable in perpetuity'. Cecil replied that it would be disastrous for both their countries if the King of Spain were to become 'by conquest or contract, owner absolutely of seventeen provinces'.[79] At this point, the English were presented with a piece of good fortune from the sea, when a fisherman drew from his net a packet of letters from the Cardinal-Archduke

[77] 39 Elizabeth c. 4.
[78] Pollard and Blatcher, 'Hayward Townshend's Journals', 25.
[79] Thomas Birch, *An Historical View of the Negotiations between the Courts of England, France, and Brussels* (London, 1749), 117–18.

of Austria (the Spanish Regent in the Netherlands). These made it perfectly clear that Henry was negotiating a separate peace without consideration for his allies. After trying to bluster his way out of the embarrassment, Henry told Cecil that he would break off negotiations with the Spanish if Elizabeth sent him more troops. This was out of the question and Cecil returned home in May, taking with him the Dutch envoys, and writing to Elizabeth that 'France will be France, and leave his best friends, though to his own future ruin'.[80] While he showed little understanding of the urgent need for peace in France, Cecil was right in judging that Henry would not be deterred from making a separate treaty. The King himself remarked that he did not intend to ruin his own affairs out of regard to the English, and soon after Cecil left France Henry had made peace with the Spanish at Vervins.

Robert Cecil arrived back in England to find his father dying, although the old man survived miserably until August 1598. The problems posed by the Treaty of Vervins and by the imminent death of Burghley relit the antagonism between Essex and his rivals, as each side manœuvred for advantage. Debate over the fundamental issue of peace and war, for long stilled by military necessity, broke out in Council. Burghley argued that it was essential now to come to terms with Spain. The war was draining England of wealth while the Dutch prospered, the common people were 'forward to sedition', and there was 'inbred malice in the vulgar against the nobility'.[81] Essex, at the Council board and in a letter to Antony Bacon, urged the opportunities for a profitable war in America and the absolute necessity of supporting the Dutch, for whom peace was at this juncture impossible.[82] Since the King of Spain was weak, no time was better than the present, he argued, for making war; a treaty would enable Philip to grow strong again while England became 'bewitched with the delights of peace'. Philip's present policy was simply to make a show of negotiating in order to prepare a Trojan Horse. Essex insisted that, while 'peace is to be preferred before war', a safe peace could not always be had. To the accusation that he loved men of war, he confessed that 'I love them for their affections; for self-loving men love ease, pleasure and profit; but they that love pains, danger and fame, show that they love public profit more than themselves.'[83] Burghley's reply, turning the pages of his bible in the Council chamber, was to point to the psalmist's warning: 'Men of blood shall not live out half their

---

[80] Thomas Birch, *An Historical View*, 152.

[81] William Camden, *Annals* (London, 1675 edn.), 492. See also J. Strype, *Annals of the Reformation* (4 vols., London, 1824), iv. 451–64.

[82] Subsequently printed as *An Apologie of the Earle of Essex* (London, 1603).

[83] Quoted from the *Apologie*, which is unpaginated.

days.'[84] Having urged the Dutch envoys, who had reached England in May, to make peace, Burghley advised Elizabeth to negotiate with Spain in an attempt to secure satisfactory terms for the Netherlands, which would ensure their security—and England's. If the Spanish refused to guarantee the Dutch free practice of their religion, their ancient liberty, and their present government, then the alliance must stand in spite of Henry's defection. And so the matter concluded: England continued to provide limited military assistance to the Netherlands, but at the expense of the Dutch. This was far less than Essex had wanted, and seems to have been close to the policy advocated by Burghley.

By now, Irish affairs had strained relations between Essex and the Queen. Francis Bacon had advised the Earl to take on himself the care of Irish affairs during Robert Cecil's absence in France. When Elizabeth proposed the appointment of Sir William Knollys, one of Essex's own followers, to the post of Lord Deputy, the Earl countered with the proposal that a Cecilian, Sir George Carew, should be sent, presumably to remove him from Court. When Elizabeth demurred, Essex turned his back on her, at which she slapped him on the face and he laid his hand on his sword. The Earl of Nottingham intervened to restrain him and Essex withdrew from the presence in a rage, swearing that he would not have taken such an insult even from Henry VIII. To entreaties from Lord Keeper Egerton that he submit, he replied; '[how] to serve as a servant and a slave I know not.'[85]

As Essex's ambition rose, Burghley sank into his grave. He had been declining since the beginning of the year, rallying when he went to his country palace at Theobalds, Hertfordshire, relapsing when he returned to Court. By the last days of July, he could no longer sit up in bed, his throat so swollen that he could hardly speak or swallow. On 3 August, he summoned his children and blessed them. His chaplain prayed with him until midnight, when he cried out, 'Oh what a heart is this that will not let me die!'[86] At eight o'clock in the morning of 4 August 1598 he died.

For forty years, Burghley had dominated English political life, more powerful than anyone except the Queen herself. He had largely fulfilled her estimate of him at the beginning of the reign.[87] Cautious in his approach, meticulous in his knowledge of affairs and his handling of detail, he, together with his royal mistress, supplied the continuity which was an essential feature of the reign. The stability was bought at a high price, for his financial conservatism allowed the Crown's revenues to be eroded by infla-

---

[84] Camden, *Annals*, 493; Ps. 55: 23.   [85] Camden, *Annals*, 496.
[86] Francis Peck, *Desiderata curiosa* (London, 1732), i. 55.   [87] Above, Ch. 7 s. 1.

tion; and his determination to maintain his power and transmit it to his son Robert was at least partly responsible for the severe faction-fighting of the final years of the century.

4. THE ESSEX RISING, 1598–1601

Burghley's death left the political field wide open. As Lord Treasurer he controlled the finances of the realm, as Master of the Court of Wards he wielded great patronage, as the Queen's closest adviser he largely determined the country's policy. In the void created by his death, courtiers and officials were hurled one against the other as they struggled for his political inheritance.

Ten days after his death, the Irish scene was transformed. Following the ending of the truce there in June,[88] Tyrone besieged the Blackwater Fort, whose garrison bravely held out. A relieving force under Sir Henry Bagenal marched north in August; but its commander foolishly and fatally allowed it to straggle on the march, so that Bagenal was humiliatingly defeated by Tyrone: he himself was killed and only half his force of 5,000 men returned to base at Armagh. The Crown was now powerless to prevent O'Donnell from gaining most of Connacht and the Munster rebels from driving out the English settlers, who mostly fled, leaving their possessions, to the dubious safety of the towns. By the autumn, all Ireland was lost to the Queen except Leinster, which Ormond was able to defend with the help of 6,000 troops from England. Ireland was now the supreme priority for the Crown: any plan that might have been hatched for combined operations against Spain had to be abandoned. Tyrone's strength lay in the wealth of Ulster and the large army it could support. The core of his force consisted of 4,000–6,000 'bonaghts', or native mercenaries, well armed and trained by ex-captains from the Queen's own armies, reinforced by Scots mercenaries. Tyrone had built an effective fighting force with solid organization and good supply-lines. It could probably confront the English in a set battle, although he generally preferred the traditional Irish tactics of ambush.

The struggles for Ireland and for Burghley's political inheritance now became almost inextricably enmeshed. In August, Essex had retired, in disfavour with Elizabeth and in bad humour, to his house at Wanstead, although he returned to Court in September seeking offices. By now, the competition for posts was rising to a pitch of near frenzy; rumours passed round the Court naming this man or that for the principal offices. But no one was appointed. Essex's mood was black: in October, he complained to

---

[88] Above, p. 359.

Lord Keeper Egerton that he found his enemies 'absolute' at Court, preventing him from securing any favours for his own friends. The Queen was cold towards him, although, he asserted, the fault was in no way his: 'what', he wrote in an extraordinary outburst, 'cannot princes err? Cannot subjects receive wrong? Is an earthly power or authority infinite?'[89] He could bear this treatment no longer and would live as a hermit. Yet of course he did nothing of the sort. By November, rumours were circulating that he was to be made Lord Lieutenant of Ireland; then it was reported that, after all, he was not to go. Essex himself was uncertain what to do. Earlier in the year he had been given wise advice by Francis Bacon, who encouraged him to deal in the affairs of Ireland, the most important 'of all the actions of state on foot at this time'.[90] However, Bacon proposed that Essex should nominate the principal commanders and confer with the Queen's leading officers there, not that he should go himself. Others thought differently and Essex was soon surrounded by a throng of nobles, courtiers, and soldiers hoping to be given commands in his army. He himself ruled out the appointment of Lord Mountjoy—ultimately to be the conqueror of Ireland—on the ground that he was too much given to 'bookishness'. In doing so, he was pointing the finger at himself, and at last, in January 1599, his appointment was confirmed. Again, Bacon was ready with advice. The service, he wrote, was one of great merit and of great risk. Victory would be a great honour, but, he cautioned, desire for fame and glory might lead Essex rather to seek 'the fruition of that honour than the perfection of the work in hand'. His warning was uncomfortably accurate. So was the comment of an anonymous soldier in Essex's army: 'observe the man who commandeth; and yet is commanded himself: he goeth not forth to serve the Queen's realm, but to humour his own revenge.'[91]

Essex realized the dangers: 'too ill success will be dangerous . . . too good will be envious.' Absence from Court would give opportunity to his enemies. Yet although 'the Court is the centre . . . methinks it is the fairer choice to command armies than honours'.[92] Having been granted an army of 16,000 men by the Queen—the largest ever sent to Ireland—he left London in March, accompanied by the earls of Rutland and Southampton, several barons, and a great flock of courtiers, gallants, and swordsmen. Elizabeth forbade her own household servants to go, but many slipped away. It is hard to know what attracted them to a war in the woods and

---

[89] Devereux, *Letters*, i. 499–502.   [90] Spedding, *Bacon*, ii. 95.

[91] Ibid. 132. Sir John Harington, *Nugae antiquae*, ed. Thomas Park (2 vols., London, 1804), i. 240–1.

[92] HMC, *Calendar of the MSS of the Marquess of Salisbury at Hatfield House* (24 vols., London, 1883–1976), ix. 9–11:

bogs of Ireland, for there could be little chance of booty. Perhaps they hoped for reflected glory from Essex, perhaps for a grant of the lands which he would conquer.

Essex was certainly right to think that, in leaving the Court, he was leaving the centre of affairs. Once he was off the stage, the Queen filled the vacant posts. The most important of all, the office of Lord Treasurer, went to Thomas Sackville, Lord Buckhurst. A writer and playwright in his youth—he wrote the Induction to the *Mirror for Magistrates* and was co-author of the play *Gorbuduc*—Buckhurst had long been a privy councillor and had performed useful diplomatic service. He was allied to neither Essex nor Cecil and stood somewhat aloof from Court politics; his role in government remains obscure, overshadowed by the power of Robert Cecil, who now obtained for himself, his family, and his allies the other key offices. Robert Cecil himself was made Master of the Court of Wards, an office which Essex had hoped to secure and which opened the way to valuable patronage. His elder brother Thomas, now Lord Burghley, became President of the Council in the North, a crucial post when the question of Elizabeth's successor was becoming urgent. His brother-in-law, Lord Cobham, was already Warden of the Cinque Ports. Sir Walter Ralegh, no great friend to Cecil but a great enemy to Essex, was made Governor of Jersey. Cecil himself controlled the major activities of government. It was said that 'the whole weight of the state rests upon him'; that the Queen was 'wholly directed by Mr Secretary, who now rules all as his father did'; that only Nottingham had equal influence with her and that he 'will do nothing but what stands with Mr Secretary's liking'.[93]

Essex reached Ireland in full confidence, announcing that 'By God, I will beat Tyrone in the field!'[94] A sensible plan had been devised for a two-pronged attack on Ulster, with a landing from the sea at Lough Foyle and a frontal attack by Essex marching north from Dublin. For this to succeed, ships and carriage-horses were essential, but Essex had neither. He decided to occupy the time until they arrived in subduing Munster and Limerick, where he spent two months and achieved virtually nothing. While he was engaged on this diversion, a small force of English troops was massacred in Wicklow and Sir Conyers Clifford, Governor of Connacht, was killed at Sligo. The first was a blow to morale but little more; the second was a catastrophic loss. When he got back to Dublin in July, Essex encountered the first blasts of Elizabeth's anger. She was thoroughly displeased that 'a

---

[93] HMC, *De L'Lisle and Dudley*, ii. 427, 389–90.
[94] Harington, *Nugae antiquae*, ii. 246.

base bush kern'—her name for Tyrone—should be accounted 'so famous a rebel'; Essex had given commands to inexperienced young men, notably the Earl of Southampton, appointed Master of the Horse, who must be dismissed; the 'unseasonable' journey into Munster had eaten up money and time; and Essex was to march against Tyrone at once.[95] The Council in Dublin and the colonels of the army unanimously advised against a northerly expedition; but Essex, having been dispatched with so large a force and such glittering hopes, could hardly refuse his Queen's command to act. In August he marched north from Dublin with 4,000 men. This was a feeble enterprise compared with the original strategy: there was to be no landing at Lough Foyle and Essex's force was too small to be effective, a larger part of his army being scattered in garrisons over southern Ireland. When he reached the River Lagan, on the northern border of the Pale, he was confronted by a far bigger force under Tyrone. Battle was out of the question; but Essex made the foolish mistake of meeting Tyrone alone without witnesses. While probably nothing sinister came of this conversation, it allowed his enemies to discredit him; and it was followed by a formal parley at which a truce was arranged, for successive periods of six weeks, with the rebels holding their conquests. Elizabeth's letters forbidding any such truce arrived after it had been agreed.

Essex's conduct of the campaign has been generally condemned. Yet the original plan was good, as Mountjoy was later to prove; and Essex was not to be blamed that the Privy Council failed to provide him with the necessary transport. But the Munster expedition was an unnecessary expense which depleted his force and delayed any direct attack upon Tyrone. By the time he reluctantly moved north, his army was too small, and he had little alternative but to make the truce: after all, there had been a regular succession of such truces ever since Tyrone rebelled. Although Essex made many mistakes in the execution of his plan, he was not given adequate backing from England, and the constant rebukes of Elizabeth, who grossly underestimated the strength of Tyrone, sapped the morale of the Lord Lieutenant and his officers. The English government at the time—and many English historians since—failed to understand that Tyrone's position in Ireland was incomparably stronger than that of any previous Irish leader.

Essex's triumphant return home had been prematurely celebrated by Shakespeare in *Henry V*, first performed in the summer or early autumn of 1599. At the beginning of the final act, in the only indisputable reference anywhere in his plays to a contemporary event, Shakespeare has the Chorus

---

[95] *CSP Ire. 1599–1600*, 205/113, 121 (pp. 98–101, 105–7).

compare Henry's return from France to Essex's expected return from
Ireland:[96]

> but now behold,
> In the quick forge and working-house of thought,
> How London doth pour out her citizens.
> The mayor and all his brethren in best sort,
> Like to the senators of th' antique Rome,
> With the plebeians swarming at their heels,
> Go forth and fetch their conqu'ring Caesar in:
> As, by a lower but high-loving likelihood,
> Were now the general of our gracious empress,—
> As in good time he may,—from Ireland coming,
> Bringing rebellion broached on his sword,
> How many would the peaceful city quit
> To welcome him? much more, and much more cause,
> Did they this Harry.

Essex might be accorded a lesser welcome than Henry V, but nevertheless
London would pour out her citizens to welcome him when he came back
after putting down Tyrone's rebellion. The reality was very different, both
in September 1599 and some eighteen months later when Essex tried unsuccessfully to rouse the citizens of London in support of his own rebellion.
Significantly, the choruses, including this one, were omitted from the
quarto version of the play published in 1600, when comparison of Essex to
Henry V would have been risky: they were reinstated in the folio edition of
1623.

Elizabeth had expressly forbidden Essex to abandon his command, but
on 24 September he left Dublin, reaching the Court at Nonsuch four days
later. He immediately ran to the Privy Chamber, where he found the Queen
'newly up, her hair about her face'.[97] He knelt before her, had some private
speech, and left her presence apparently content. By the afternoon,
Elizabeth's mood had changed to anger, and next day she referred his
conduct to a full meeting of the Privy Council. Essex attended before the
councillors and heard Cecil read out Elizabeth's charges against him, which
he answered calmly. After the Council had reported to the Queen, who
announced that 'she would pause and consider of his answers', the courtiers
hived off into factions and two separate groups went in to dinner: Cecil was
accompanied by Lord Grey, enemy to Southampton and no friend to Essex,
Lord Cobham (Cecil's brother-in-law), the Earl of Nottingham (a staunch

---

[96] *Henry V*, v, chorus, ll. 22–35; Annabel Patterson, *Shakespeare and the Popular Voice* (Oxford, 1989), ch. 4.
[97] HMC, *De L'Isle and Dudley*, ii. 395–7; Collins, *Letters* ii. 127–9.

supporter of Cecil against Essex), Sir Walter Ralegh, who hated his rival favourite, and various others. With Essex walked the Earl of Worcester, the Earl of Rutland, who had been with him in Ireland, Lord Mountjoy, who was to succeed him there, Lord Rich, married to Essex's sister Penelope, Lord Henry Howard, held by many to be politically 'a neuter', Sir William Knollys, Comptroller of the Household, and, more alarmingly, many knights.[98] While the Court seemed evenly divided between the enemies and the friends of Essex, London was filled with his followers—adventurous knights and unruly soldiers. The time was uneasy and Elizabeth was wise to be cautious. But on 1 October she made up her mind and committed Essex to house arrest at the residence of Lord Keeper Egerton. This was decisive, and within ten days Essex's servants were 'afraid to meet in any place to make merry', and of all the courtiers only Lady Scrope stood up for him, for which 'she endures much at the Queen's hands'.[99] Cecil had won his battle at Court, but there were still stirrings of popular support for the Earl outside it. According to rumour, the Council, a little later, urged Elizabeth to release Essex and only her anger and determination prevented this; but it is hard to know how much trust to put in such reports. At the end of November she decided to use the normal assembly of JPs at the close of the law-term, when they were harangued by the Lord Keeper, for a public defence of her treatment of Essex. That she should have felt it necessary to explain her actions is testimony to the continuing tension and to her recognition that she depended upon the willing support of nobles and gentry. The Lord Keeper's opening words show how unusual was such a step: 'though princes are not bound to give account of their actions, yet to stop such discourses, I will recount what the Queen has done for Ireland.'[100] The main burden of the government's case was left to Robert Cecil. In a long and eloquent speech, he defended the Queen and her ministers against 'libellous railers, sons of devils, who have not spared to tax her Majesty's self'; such men resembled 'some Jack Cade or Jack Straw'. Cecil was always acutely sensitive to the danger of popular disturbance and attributed most opposition to political agitators among the common people.[101] More to the point, he addressed himself to the soldiers, Essex's chief supporters. It had been reported, he told them, that those ministers who wanted peace with Spain 'persuade her Majesty to make small account of martial men'. This was, he proclaimed, totally untrue: 'her Majesty has a special care of such as be soldiers in deed'—an evident hit at Essex's failure to do battle with Tyrone. Having set the Irish revolt in the general context of European diplomacy

[98] Collins, *Letters*, ii. 129.   [99] HMC, *De L'Isle and Dudley*, ii. 400.
[100] *CSP Dom. 1598–1601*, 273/35–7 (pp. 347–54), esp. p. 347.
[101] Ibid., esp. p. 352.

and the need for peace, Cecil defended Elizabeth's policy in Ireland and criticized the Earl's failure to crush Tyrone. The speech skilfully avoided any personal animus against Essex, while convincingly justifying his dismissal and confinement.[102]

Cecil seems to have done his best in the next few months to achieve a reconciliation with Essex. That this was genuine, so far as it went, is confirmed by the advice given to Cecil by Ralegh, who thought that he was being far too lenient to the fallen favourite: 'if you take it for a good council to relent towards this tyrant, you will repent it when it shall be too late. His malice is fixed, and will not evaporate by any your mild courses.'[103] When Elizabeth, angered at the continuing sympathy shown for Essex in London, determined early in 1600 to bring him before Star Chamber, Cecil persuaded the Earl to submit himself to the Queen. When Elizabeth announced that she would degrade the men whom Essex had knighted in Ireland, Cecil and Nottingham dissuaded her. Throughout the first half of 1600 matters remained at a deadlock. Mountjoy, one of Essex's principal supporters, was appointed to govern Ireland in January and thus removed from the Court; Essex himself remained in confinement, albeit in his own house. In the face of criticism from the Earl's supporters that he was being condemned unheard, Elizabeth decided to bring him to trial at York House in June. He was charged with 'great and high contempts and points of misgovernance' in Ireland—in particular, the progress into Munster, the treaty with Tyrone, and his desertion of his post—and with 'divers notorious errors and neglects of duty'.[104] While he was expressly cleared of any accusation of disloyalty, he was found guilty of the contempts and was sentenced to forbear from taking the style of councillor or of Earl Marshal, to be suspended from executing the office of Master of the Ordnance, and to remain a prisoner during the Queen's pleasure. Essex was utterly cast down by this and was convinced that he could now live only a private life. When Antony Bacon urged him to take heart and seek Elizabeth's favour, he replied that his enemies would 'never suffer me to have interest in her favour'; 'the false glass of others' information' would alter the disposition of the Queen.[105] However, although Essex may have felt himself condemned to a life of retirement, he could not afford complete withdrawal from the affairs of the Court. On Michaelmas Day 1600 his lease of the customs revenues from imported sweet wines fell in and it became essential to him

---

[102] CSP Dom. 1598–1601, esp. p. 352.

[103] Edward Edwards, The Life of Ralegh (2 vols., London, 1868), ii. 222–3.

[104] Spedding, Bacon, ix. 179.

[105] HMC, MSS of the Marquess of Bath at Longleat (5 vols., London, 1904–80), v. 266–9, wrongly dated: it is after the York House hearing of June 1600.

to secure its renewal. But his requests were in vain and the Queen granted the lease to another. Essex could no longer hold off his creditors and began to lose all sense of political balance. He 'shifteth from sorrow and repentance to rage and rebellion so suddenly', wrote Sir John Harington, 'as well proveth him devoid of good reason as of like mind'.[106]

Essex had contemplated the forcible expulsion of his enemies for some time. In Ireland, during the summer of 1599, he had proposed taking an army over to England to rid himself of them, but had been dissuaded by the Earl of Southampton and Sir Christopher Blount. In the following summer, when he was under house arrest, he had sent his impetuous secretary Henry Cuffe to meet another of his followers, Sir Charles Danvers, at Oxford, where they had concocted a proposal for Mountjoy to send trusted captains from Ireland to the Court, in order to seize it on Essex's behalf. Nothing had come of the matter, and by Christmas 1600 Essex was desperate. He had lost his farm of the duty on sweet wines; his more responsible or calculating followers—the Earl of Worcester, Sir William Knollys, Francis Bacon, and others—had fallen away from him; and he was shut up in Essex House with an assortment of rash, inexperienced, and generally wild noblemen and soldiers. He wrote to James VI of Scotland, urging to him to co-operate in removing their common enemies Ralegh and Cecil, to which James responded cautiously, dispatching two ambassadors to make contact with Essex. Early in February, Essex and his bolder followers decided on action. The Earl drew up a general plan for seizing the Court, the City of London, and the Tower, and sent it to an inner circle of five close adherents, who met at Drury House on Tuesday, 3 February. Their leader was the young Earl of Southampton, who had served with Essex in Ireland and had been removed from his post of Master of the Horse on the order of the Queen. A man of quarrelsome disposition—he had challenged Northumberland, Essex's brother-in-law, to a duel and was involved in a bitter feud with Lord Grey—Southampton had made pregnant Elizabeth Vernon, a maid of honour at Court, and married her without permission, thus blackening his reputation with Elizabeth. Of the other planners, Sir John Davies had fought in the Netherlands, in Portugal, at Cadiz, and in the Azores: an experienced soldier, he seems to have produced the most realistic of the various plans. Sir Charles Danvers, earlier exiled for some years for killing a neighbouring gentleman, was a close friend of Southampton and had fought in the Netherlands and in Ireland. Sir Ferdinando Gorges had fought in the Netherlands under Leicester, gone to Portugal in 1589, and been knighted by Essex at Rouen. His wish to go with Essex to Ireland had

---

[106] Devereux, *Letters*, ii. 130.

been frustrated by the Queen, who wanted to keep him at Court. The only member of the Drury House group who had not seen military service was Sir John Lyttelton, another quarrelsome gentleman, whose original connection with Essex is obscure. Well within the inner circle, but not it seems at the main Drury House meeting, were three others: Sir Christopher Blount had served in the Netherlands under Leicester, and at Cadiz, in the Azores, and in Ireland under Essex, whose mother he had married; Sir Gelli Meyrick, steward of Essex's Welsh lands, had fought with the Earl in every one of his campaigns, and marshalled support for him in Wales; finally, Henry Cuffe, the Earl's secretary, had long been active in plotting the destruction of Essex's enemies. Of these eight men, six were experienced and probably disappointed soldiers; and three—Danvers, Blount, and Lyttelton—were Roman Catholics.

Davies presented a methodical plan for taking the Court. He, Danvers, Blount, and Gorges were to station themselves, with supporters, at critical points in Whitehall Palace. At a given signal, they would seize control, opening the way for Essex to approach the Queen. But Gorges, according to his own later testimony, refused to co-operate, and Southampton irritably dissolved the meeting, complaining that they would never agree on anything, for it was three months since these matters had been first mooted. A further meeting was fixed for the following Saturday. Before it took place, Meyrick and various others arranged for the Lord Chamberlain's Men to put on a performance of *Richard II*, including the prohibited deposition scene, at the Globe. This was presumably intended to present Essex as Bolingbroke, saving his country from misrule, an injudicious piece of casting. Before the play started, there was a meeting of the Earl's men at Essex House, interrupted by the appearance of Secretary Herbert,[107] who was sent by the Council—now alerted to the dangers—to order Essex and his principal followers to attend and explain their conduct. Essex had no alternatives but submission or revolt. He chose the latter.

Early on the following day, Sunday, 8 February, four principal councillors, Lord Keeper Egerton, the Earl of Worcester, Sir William Knollys, and Lord Chief Justice Popham, were sent with a message from the Queen ordering Essex to dissolve his company and come at once to Court. It was a skilfully chosen quartet, since all but Popham had once been friends and confidants of the Earl; but it made no difference. Essex took them to an inner room where they were kept as prisoners in the charge of Gelli Meyrick. It was by now obvious that any attempt to take the Court by

---

[107] Sir John Herbert had been made Secretary of State in 1600: he was very much Cecil's subordinate and was known as 'Mr Secondary Herbert'.

surprise was hopeless and Essex turned for support to the City. He had with him about 140 followers, many of them men of high rank: apart from the inner circle, there were the Earl of Rutland, the Lords Cromwell, Monteagle, and Sandys, and a battery of knights. Expecting that his popularity would win abundant support among the Londoners, Essex marched to the house of Sheriff Smythe in Fenchurch Street. Rumours that Ralegh and Cobham intended to murder the Earl brought a few men to his side, but most prudently held back. The carefully conceived scheme of Sir John Davies had been replaced by an unpremeditated and ill-organized escapade. The rest was tragedy played out as farce. While Essex spent three hours in Smythe's house after the sheriff had gone off to find the Lord Mayor, Robert Cecil organized the defence of Whitehall and barred the exit from the City at Ludgate. The Earl, unable to fight his way through, returned by boat with a few friends to Essex House. There he found that the privy councillors had been released by Gorges, who hoped by this to save his own skin—successfully as it turned out. With Essex House besieged, there was no serious prospect of resistance and the Earl surrendered at nine o'clock that night.

The rebels were treated with remarkable lenity. The only men to die were Essex himself, Danvers, Blount, Meyrick, Cuffe, and Sir Thomas Lea, who made a futile attempt to secure Essex's release after the original revolt by intruding on Elizabeth's apartments in Whitehall. It was noteworthy that two of these men, Danvers and Blount, were Catholics, and that the last three were of relatively humble origins. The rest were either condemned to death and then reprieved, or sentenced only to fine and imprisonment. Even Southampton, reprieved from death by Elizabeth, was released from prison by James two years later.

It is tempting to see the Essex rising as simply the desperate throw of an unbalanced and disappointed royal favourite; and there is little doubt that, by the end of 1600, Essex was on the edge of emotional breakdown. But his followers were not all fools or madmen. Southampton later showed himself to be a shrewd politician and Davies had concocted an intelligent scheme for taking the Court. They were, however, men who had temporarily or permanently lost touch with political reality and had disastrously exaggerated Essex's popular support. Had they carried through Davies's plan, they might just, but only just, have succeeded in gaining access to Elizabeth. They could hardly have achieved more than that; and once they hesitated and thus lost the advantage of surprise, they were doomed. Everything depended upon Essex's immediate followers in the great houses along the Strand and upon his alleged popularity in London. Certainly, he had support in the country: some gentlemen were on their way from Wales to help him when they heard the news of his surrender and turned back. But his regional strength was too scattered to provide a power base, and in any case he could not wait for his Welsh followers to arrive. He was essentially a courtier, dependent on the favour of the Queen, and a military leader who derived his strength, not from personal retainers, but from the captains of the royal army as well as from some discontented civilians. His role was perhaps unique in English history. Earlier aristocratic rebels had relied upon regional support, upon the tenants and retainers of their own houses and of their allies. Essex is a product of a particular stage in military history, when the 'bastard feudal' army had disappeared and the national army had not fully emerged. His counterparts are to be found overseas, in men like Condé and Turenne, commanders of royal armies who used the Crown's own forces against it during the Fronde.

Only a small band of marginal men followed Essex into revolt; and very few of those were made privy to his plans. Most of his original friends, like Francis Bacon and Robert Sidney, had already deserted him. But the rebels were the visible tip of a larger range of discontent. Many soldiers, courtiers, and country gentlemen resented the domination of Robert Cecil and the small inner group at the centre of power; but they were too disparate and disorganized to form a serious threat to the Cecilian regime. Once Essex was dead, his faction virtually ceased to exist. Some of the Catholic rebels were later involved in the Gunpowder Plot; others, like the Earl of Southampton and Ferdinando Gorges, promoted colonial settlement in the New World. Southampton indeed became a major political figure in the next reign; but his style then was very different from that of the Essex revolt: military confrontation gave way to parliamentary manœuvre.[108]

5. THE END OF THE REIGN, 1601–1603

The last two years of Elizabeth's reign, following the execution of Essex, were dominated by three great matters of state: the Parliament of 1601, military campaigns in the Low Countries and in Ireland, and the question of the succession to the throne. By the beginning of 1601 the government's need for money had become pressing, for the final instalment of the 1597 subsidies had been paid in the previous autumn and further taxes were essential for the war in Ireland. In view of the repercussions of the Essex revolt, the government delayed summoning Parliament until October. In

[108] I have been much helped by the unpublished thesis of Ms Gwyneth Hutson, 'The military following of Robert Devereux, Second Earl of Essex, and the rising of 1601' (M.Litt., University of Oxford, 1987), and I am grateful to her for allowing me to draw upon it.

one or two constituencies, for instance in Denbighshire, there were electoral contests between adherents of Essex and their rivals; but the battle between the Devereux and the Cecils was almost everywhere dead, even in the Earl's home county of Staffordshire. Where elections were disputed, the contests were over local issues or personalities.

On the assembly of Parliament, the Lord Keeper addressed both Houses. On the Queen's behalf, he granted the customary request for freedom of speech, while warning the members 'that the matter be not spent in idle and vain matters, pointing out the same with froth and volubility of words'. He passed on the royal command that they were 'not to make new and idle laws, and trouble the House with them'.[109] Possibly the legislative initiatives taken by members in 1597 had worried the Queen and her councillors; but if they hoped, by these warnings, to secure a peaceful session, they were to be disillusioned. Members who had been unable to gain access to the Upper House for the Lord Keeper's speech demanded that they be told its contents. Robert Cecil reported the gist of his own words and unwisely embroidered them with some further remarks. The urgent need, he asserted, was money for the wars, particularly for Ireland, where 4,000 Spanish soldiers had recently landed.[110] Three subsidies were proposed and a fourth added. The Council had no difficulty in getting agreement to these. But various members, including Francis Bacon and Walter Ralegh, proposed that the burden on the poorer taxpayers should be lightened, either by taxing them at a lesser rate or by raising the threshold. Ralegh, implicitly criticizing remarks by Cecil about the poor selling their pots and pans to pay subsidies, pointed out that the rich were too lightly assessed: it was unjust that the poor man should be taxed on a sum little less than his income when the estates of the rich, as shown in the subsidy books, 'are not the hundredth part of our wealth'.[111] He was certainly correct in saying that the subsidy assessments of the prosperous classes were absurdly light; but nothing was done to make them more realistic.

Measures about religion produced some mild debate. A bill introduced for the stricter enforcement of church attendance on Sundays ran into trouble when some members objected that JPs, who were to be entrusted with its enforcement, had too much authority already. The bill was lost. Another, abolishing pluralities in benefices, was frustrated by Whitgift, who told Elizabeth that it would encroach upon her prerogative and put an end to learning by depriving scholars and others of additional livings. The bill was either defeated in the Commons or halted by them. By contrast, the

---

[109] Hayward Townshend, *Historical Collections; or, An Exact Account of the Proceedings of the Four Last Parliaments of Q. Elizabeth* (London, 1680), 177–8.
[110] Below, p. 381.   [111] Townshend, *Historical Collections*, 204.

Poor Law Act, which re-enacted the statute of 1597 with some emendations and formed the basis of laws on the matter until the nineteenth century, was carried with no apparent dispute or debate.

The great contention in this Parliament arose over monopolies. Although some patents had been rescinded after the protests of 1597, new grants had also been made and discontent was much stronger than before.[112] The principal debate was opened on 20 November when Sir Francis Hastings, an experienced parliamentarian who sat for Bridgwater, proposed a bill to deal with the matter. Francis Bacon opposed the passing of a bill, which, he argued, would be seen as infringing the royal prerogative, and proposed, as a more diplomatic course, that they petition the Queen to remedy grievances. No one denied that monopolies were often attended by abuses, and the issue came to lie between the supporters of a bill and those who favoured a petition. Bacon, working his passage back to royal favour, summed it up: 'we ought not to deal or meddle with, or judge of Her Majesty's prerogative'.[113] Others, less cautious, argued that a petition would do little to remedy so pressing an evil, while a bill could not be regarded as an infringement of the royal authority. For the next ten days, the matter took up most of the Commons' time, with three debates in committee and two more in the full House. The bill was sent to committee on 21 November, to the fury of Bacon, who described it as 'very injurious and ridiculous'. However, the opponents of monopolies were equally vehement. Sir Robert Wroth told the Solicitor-General that, although there had been plenty of time since the last Parliament for remedy to be made, 'these patentees are worse than ever they were'. He proceeded to list the patents granted since 1597, at which Mr Hackwell of Lincoln's Inn jumped up and cried sarcastically 'Is not Bread there? . . . If order be not taken for these, bread will be there before the next Parliament.'[114] Two days later, the critics had begun to lobby members with a paper showing how specific monopolies had raised prices and lowered quality, and in the afternoon a list of patents and their holders was produced. In spite of Cecil's rebuke that the conduct of members was 'more fit for a grammar school than a Parliament', the organization of protest was orderly and effective—though obviously not to the liking of the councillors.[115] Elizabeth evidently decided that the moment had come for concessions and she summoned the Speaker, who reported her words to the House. She had, he told them, graciously consented to take immediate action, revoking some patents and suspending others. Cecil then again rebuked the House. Speeches, he claimed, had been leaked to the public:[116]

[112] Above, p. 363.   [113] Townshend, *Historical Collections*, 232.
[114] Ibid.   [115] Ibid. 246.   [116] Ibid. 251.

we are not secret amongst ourselves ... why, Parliament matters are ordinarly talked of in the streets. I have heard myself, being in my coach, these words spoken aloud: '*God prosper those that further the overthrow of these* monopolies! *God send the prerogative touch not our* liberty ... The time was never more apt to disorder, or make ill interpretations of good meanings. I think these persons would be glad that all sovereignty were converted into popularity.

Having uttered these rather wild accusations, Cecil recovered himself and made a half-hearted apology for having compared the House to a grammar school. On 28 November a proclamation was duly issued making void the most obnoxious monopolies—for the manufacture of salt, vinegar, starch, etc.—and referring grievances concerning the rest to the courts of common law. Finally, the Queen gave audience to the Commons and delivered what was to be called her 'golden speech'. 'There is no Prince that loveth his subjects better. There is no jewel, be it of never so rich a price, which I set before this jewel: I mean your love.'[117] The text as it has come down to us was carefully doctored by the Queen, but even so the occasion was impressive. The wounds were healed, but the angry debates had shown that the Commons could act as an effective channel for grievances and that the royal councillors were running scared.

The Parliament had been summoned to supply the needs of war. Although the main theatre of fighting for the English now lay in Ireland, Elizabeth's troops were also heavily engaged in the Netherlands during the final years of her reign. In 1600 the Dutch had sent an invasion force south of the Rhine delta with the object of recapturing Flanders. At the great battle of Nieuwpoort, 1,650 English soldiers under Sir Francis Vere fought alongside the Dutch and defeated the Spanish, who retaliated by attacking Ostend, still held by the Estates General. Ostend lay under siege from 1601 until 1604, when it finally surrendered to the Habsburg forces under Spinola. Vere had been made governor of the town in 1601, and more than 3,000 English troops—a very substantial number—were sent to support him. Two thousand of these were levied from London, where it was reported that the business was 'so disorderly performed by taking and, as it were, sweeping away serving men, country folks, and termers of all sorts and carrying them violently to the ships, that it is a general grievance and scandal at home, and a great dishonour to be heard of abroad'.[118] Allegedly there were 8,000 English troops in the Low Countries in 1602, 'the greatest number of disciplined men of our nation that hath been seen together in our age', according to Chamberlain, a prolific writer of gossip and news.[119] He

---

[117] Ibid. 263.
[118] N. E. McClure (ed.), *The Letters of John Chamberlain* (Philadelphia, 1939), i. 143.
[119] Ibid. 153.

may have exaggerated, but even so the defence of Ostend depended heavily upon Vere's skill as commander, until he left the town in 1602 to take up a post in the field, and upon the endurance of the English soldiers, who remained there until the port surrendered.

The support given to the Dutch imposed a considerable strain upon English resources at a time when the government was faced with the most dangerous Irish rebellion of the Tudor era. In February 1600 Charles Blount, Lord Mountjoy, friend and supporter of Essex, landed in Dublin Bay as Lord Deputy of Ireland, accompanied by Sir George Carew, the new Lord President of Munster. These two headed a formidable team of commanders. Mountjoy himself had earlier been described by Essex as 'too much drowned in book-learning' for the post, and he did not seem obviously fitted for military command.[120] Mildly hypochondriac, he was fastidious about dress, food, and drink, took a regular afternoon sleep, and smoked heavily; yet he proved to be the most effective Elizabethan ruler of Ireland. He was fortunate in his subordinates. Carew, although on uneasy terms with Mountjoy, was an experienced soldier and a skilful operator in the treacherous ground of Irish politics. Sir Arthur Chichester, governor of the fort at Carrickfergus, and Sir Henry Docwra, who commanded the force at Lough Foyle, were tough and experienced soldiers. Mountjoy's army of 14,000 foot and 1,200 horse was roughly equal to that of Essex: with similar resources, he had to succeed where his predecessor had ignominiously failed. His strategy followed that of Essex. Docwra was sent to establish a foothold at Lough Foyle, while Chichester from the east and Mountjoy himself from the south invaded Ulster. Meanwhile, Carew was sent with 3,000 men to subjugate Munster. By contrast with Essex's leisurely campaign, Mountjoy acted with dispatch and determination. Docwra established himself at Derry and won over two important Ulster chiefs, Art O'Neill, son of Turlough Luineach, and Neill Garve O'Donnell, brother-in-law to Hugh Roe O'Donnell, Tyrone's principal ally.[121] Chichester occupied much of Clandeboye, destroying as he went: 'we have', he wrote, 'killed, burnt and spoiled all along the lough [Lough Neagh] . . . We spare none of what quality or sex soever, and it hath bred much terror in the people.'[122] The war of intimidation and starvation had begun. Mountjoy himself moved cautiously, but was finally able, after some reverses, to force a crossing of the Blackwater in the summer of 1601. In Munster, Carew succeeded as much by policy as by force. Since his army of 3,000 was

[120] Richard Bagwell, *Ireland under the Tudors* (3 vols., London, 1885–90), iii. 315.
[121] Above, p. 357, for Turlough Luineach.
[122] Cyril Falls, *Elizabeth's Irish Wars* (London, 1950), 277.

severely reduced by sickness, he concentrated upon seducing the Munster chieftains: Florence MacCarthy More came over in October 1600 and others followed. In May of the following year the Sugane Earl of Desmond, James Fitzthomas, was captured.[123] By then, the rebellion in the south-west was almost crushed.

Only Spanish support could now save Tyrone and he was desperate to secure it. Although Philip III, who had succeeded his father in 1598, favoured a general disengagement from war, he believed that he could use an invasion of Ireland to extract better terms from Elizabeth. In April 1600, he sent one of his captains, Martín de la Cerdá, to O'Neill with a small shipment of arms. Cerdá contacted O'Neill and urged Philip to support him, arguing that the consequent diversion of English resources to Ireland would relieve Spain of the need to defend her shipping and that the capture of Ireland would so impress Elizabeth that she would withdraw aid from the Dutch. Philip was converted by these arguments, although his Council remained doubtful, and the disagreement ensured delay. Eventually the Council accepted the proposal, but by then the season was too late for an invasion, which was postponed until 1601. O'Neill advised the Spanish that if their force was large—6,000 men or more—it should land at Waterford or Cork; if it was between 3,000 and 4,000, it should aim for Limerick; and if it was smaller, it should go to the north. His sound advice was disregarded. The invasion force finally consisted of 4,400 men under the command of Don Juan del Águila, a competent and experienced soldier, who had fought the Dutch, the Turks, and the French. Águila favoured a landing in Donegal Bay, where the rebels could easily join him, but he was overruled by Fray Mateo de Oviedo, Catholic Archbishop of Dublin, the principal Spanish link with O'Neill.

Águila landed in October 1601 at Kinsale, west of Cork, with a depleted force of only 3,400 men. This was too small to attract the Munster chieftains to join it or to hold out on its own against Mountjoy; and O'Neill and O'Donnell were consequently forced to leave the security of Ulster in order to aid the Spanish. By the time they reached the southern coast, Mountjoy had besieged Kinsale with an army of 10,000 foot and 1,000 horse. Águila's force was reduced to 2,500 by November, but O'Neill brought 6,000 foot and 800 horse to his help. While the initial odds were in Mountjoy's favour, his troops were being swiftly cut down by disease; lodged between the Spaniards and the Irish, he had to fight on two fronts. Fortunately for him, the Irish attack, when it came, was half-hearted and ill-

---

[123] 'Sugane' was a Gaelic word for straw rope, hence in this context 'man of straw'.

organized; and Águila failed to come to its support. By superior deployment of his cavalry, Mountjoy routed the Irish and compelled Águila's surrender early in January 1602. The Spanish invasion force had been too small; it had landed in the wrong place; its commanders were divided among themselves; and it got poor support from Madrid. Its defeat was a disaster for the Irish cause.

The next twelve months saw the dissolution of the Tyrone rebellion. Carew overcame the last Munster leader, O'Sullivan Bere, at Dunboy Castle in Bantry Bay, killing those who survived the assault. In June Mountjoy again crossed the Blackwater River into O'Neill's territory and joined Docwra and Chichester. One by one, the northern chiefs made peace, until finally, on 30 March 1603, Tyrone submitted to the Queen, not knowing that she had died six days before. The terms preserved for him the ownership of the lordship of Tyrone. This was little less than he had demanded in 1594; but although he had nominally achieved his objectives in defeat, his power had been fatally weakened by the revolt.[124]

The wars, especially the Irish wars, imposed a heavy burden on English society, greater in the second half of the 1590s than in the first. Over the whole period of war from 1588 to 1603 some 105,800 men were sent overseas, about 48,000 in the period up to 1594, and 55,000 thereafter; and their arms, munitions, food, and wages had to be paid for. The total cost of war to the Exchequer, including the cost of defeating the Armada, came to £4,500,000, of which nearly £2,000,000 were spent on Ireland. Rather under half the total sum was raised from parliamentary taxes, the rest coming from the surplus on the ordinary revenue, sales of land, borrowing, and running down Exchequer balances which had been accumulated in times of peace. In 1584 these balances amounted to £299,000; by 1593 they had fallen to only £28,000. They then rose over the next two years to £131,000, before falling to their lowest level, £9,000, in 1599.[125] In the last years of the reign the Crown was hard pressed to pay its bills.

For most people, the burden of direct taxation was relatively light compared with the heavy charges upon taxpayers in France and Spain, although it bit more sharply at humbler men than at the well-to-do. Resentment was voiced more bitterly at the local taxes for coastal defence, ship-money, purchase of weapons, and coat-and-conduct money, than at parliamentary subsidies. Until the Armada year these local demands were relatively light, but they then rose fast. The most hated of these levies was probably ship-money: opposition to it was so strong in London in 1596 that the govern-

[124] Below, Ch. 13 s. 1, for the state of Ireland in 1603.

[125] R. B. Outhwaite, 'Dearth, the English Crown and the "Crisis of the 1590s"', in Peter Clark (ed.), *The European Crisis of the 1590s* (London, 1985), 27.

ment was forced to drop its demand; and in Suffolk the JPs were so recalcitrant about collecting it that the Privy Council accused them of 'dissuading the same by perilous arguments, meeter to move the people to discontentments than to concur in Her Majesty's service'.[126]

Continuous requests for men as well as money drained the patience of local officials and nourished the resentment of the Queen's subjects. By 1601 shires and towns were appealing for relief from these levies, while officers commanding troops destined for service overseas were gloomy about the quality of their men. The Bristol commissioners reported that 'there was never man beheld such strange creatures brought to any muster. . . . They are most of them either old, diseased, boys, or common rogues.' There was a great mutiny of Gloucester levies in May 1602, and in July a soldier stabbed his officer.[127] Complaints from the localities to the Council and reprimands from the Council to local officers became increasingly common during the 1590s until they were almost common form. It was the constant repetition of government demands, year after year, that made them irksome, rather than the weight of any particular levy, although service in Ireland, which drew the greatest proportion of men in the last years of the reign, was especially unpopular. However, serious trouble was averted and peace came in time for the Exchequer and the country. The Council had managed, just, to finance the war and supply the armies for eighteen years.

The problem of Elizabeth's successor was perhaps the most long-running issue of the reign. After the death of Mary Stewart in 1587, the field of possible candidates was large. As Thomas Wilson remarked, 'this crown is not like to fall to the ground for want of heads that claim to wear it, but upon whose head it will fall is by many doubted'.[128] The legal situation was complicated. Under the Succession Act of 1544, Henry VIII had been empowered to nominate heirs should his own children fail to produce offspring—as they did. In his will, he laid down that the crown should pass, after Edward, Mary, and Elizabeth, first to Lady Frances Grey and her heirs, second to Lady Eleanor Clifford, younger sister to Lady Frances, and her heirs, and third to the 'next rightful heirs'—a vague phrase indeed.[129] This gave low priority to the Stewart line. However, the protagonists of the

[126] *APC* xxvi. 553–4.
[127] HMC, *Salisbury MSS*, xi. 481–2; xii. 169, 208–9. Cf Shakespeare, *1 Henry IV*. iv. ii. 12–48.
[128] Joel Hurstfield, 'The succession struggle in late Elizabethan England', in S. T. Bindoff *et al.* (eds.), *Elizabethan Government and Society* (London, 1961), 373.
[129] See Genealogical Table 1: The Tudors.

Stewart succession, who were many and influential after the execution of Mary, held that Henry's will was invalid, having been signed with a stamp, not with his own hand. If this were accepted, then the best hereditary claim lay with James VI of Scotland. But there were two obstacles to his succession: his mother had been condemned for treason and he himself was a foreigner. Both could be held legally to debar him. Apart from James, there were four other serious candidates: Arabella Stewart, his first cousin, great-great-granddaughter of Henry VIII, who was English by birth; Lord Beauchamp, son of Catherine Grey by a doubtful marriage; the Earl of Derby, who was descended from Eleanor Clifford; and the Infanta Isabella, daughter of Philip II of Spain, who was descended, somewhat remotely, from John of Gaunt. James was the best available Protestant candidate; Arabella Stewart was thought to lean towards Rome and won some support from moderate Catholics; the Infanta was the hope of the Jesuits; and Lord Beauchamp, who had the best claim under Henry's will, had no serious backing at all.

In retrospect, the succession of James seems a foregone conclusion. He was an experienced, successful ruler and a Protestant who was thought by Catholics to be sympathetic to their claims. Yet no one could feel certain. The legal position was obscure and Elizabeth volatile. How would a successor be established if she failed to name one? What would happen if, perversely, she nominated someone unacceptable to the political nation? She was constantly urged to name her heir and as constantly refused, forbidding discussion of the issue; and as a result, debates were mostly conducted in secret or by men of unusually bold disposition. One of these, Peter Wentworth, wrote *A Pithie Exhortation to her Majestie for Establishing her Successor to the Crowne*,[130] in which he urged that the matter be settled by Parliament and prophesied civil war if it were not. Wisely, he refrained from publishing his work, and instead had it presented to the Queen through an intermediary. However, copies were distributed and the author imprisoned; released from prison, he lobbied for support in the Parliament of 1593, with the sole result that he was imprisoned again, this time in the Tower, where he remained until his death.[131] At the opposite end of the religious spectrum, Father Robert Parsons wrote and published, under the pseudonym of R. Doleman, *A Conference about the Next Succession to the Crowne of Ingland*, in which he asserted the right of peoples to depose their monarchs, and urged the claim of the Infanta Isabella.[132] His advocacy did not win total support from English Catholics, many of whom resented

---

[130] STC no. 25245.   [131] Neale, *Parliaments*, ii. 251–64.
[132] Probably printed at Antwerp, 1594. STC no. 19398.

Jesuit interference and hoped to win a measure of toleration from the government by accepting a Protestant monarch. The most balanced contribution to the debate was written, probably in 1602, by Queen Elizabeth's godson, Sir John Harington of Kelston, who wisely left his work in manuscript. In it, he urged James's succession on puritans, papists, and 'Protestants', arguing that he was more likely than any other candidate to unite the realm in religion, since he had no personal reason for persecuting any of the three main groups.[133]

James himself was uneasy during the 1590s. His pension from Elizabeth was not paid regularly and he suspected the Cecils of obstructing his cause. In Scotland, he had to manœuvre delicately between the factions and he wanted an assurance that he would succeed Elizabeth in order to strengthen his hand at home. However, since the Catholic party there was still strong, he could not declare unequivocal support for the Protestant cause. In this situation, he turned to Essex and Mountjoy. Late in 1599, the latter proposed to James that he raise troops in Scotland and demand recognition by Elizabeth as her successor: Mountjoy in Ireland and Essex in London would support him. James warily avoided committing himself and, in the following summer, Mountjoy, now making headway in Ireland, dropped the plan. Essex, however, continued to see James as a potential saviour, and on Christmas Day, 1600, wrote a long, unbalanced letter attacking Robert Cecil and his friends, 'this reigning faction', and accusing them of favouring the Infanta Isabella. Once more James was cautious in his response, but he did send two envoys, Mar and Kinloss, to keep in touch with Essex. By the time they reached London, the Earl was dead and they turned instead to Cecil.

The Secretary's position was now much easier. There is no doubt that he favoured the succession of James. Stories that he supported the Infanta derive from approaches which he made to the moderate Catholics in England with the object of dividing them from Parsons and the Jesuits. In the end, he won over only thirteen Catholic priests with a vague offer of concessions; but the contacts were undoubtedly made on behalf of James. Cecil could not publicly espouse James's cause or openly correspond with him; secretly, however, he developed contacts, himself writing a few letters to James, but handing over the main business of negotiation to Lord Henry Howard, a sinister figure of intrigue whose letters were aptly described by James as 'ample, asiatic and endless volumes'.[134] Cecil was also determined

[133] It was published eventually as *A Tract on the Succession to the Crown (A.D. 1602)*, ed. C. R. Markham (London, for the Roxburghe Club, 1880).

[134] This group of letters was published by Sir David Dalrymple, Lord Hailes, as *The Secret Correspondence of Sir Robert Cecil with James VI of Scotland* (Edinburgh, 1776).

to ensure his own political survival and frustrate potential rivals, in particular Ralegh, Cobham, and Northumberland. He advised James to rely upon a few well-chosen men—meaning in particular himself—and avoid a broad public appeal: 'you will find it in your case, that a choice election of a few in the present, will be of more use than any general acclamation of many.' Anyone, he went on, who persuaded James 'to prepare the vulgar beforehand, little understands the state of this question'.[135] James heartily agreed, saying that he well knew what a 'rotten reed *mobile vulgus*' would be to lean upon.[136] Howard's letters were designed to provide James with full intelligence of events in England and, above all, to blacken Ralegh, Cobham, and Northumberland in his eyes. Of the first two he wrote: 'Hell did never spew up such a couple.'[137] Ralegh was presented as an ambitious atheist who was secretly working against James's interests. There is no evidence that any one of these three was hostile to James; but the repeated doses of poison sent by Howard seem to have convinced James that they were unreliable. By the beginning of 1603, he was sure that Cecil was 'in effect King in England'.

Late in February of that year, Elizabeth fell ill, and by mid-March it was obvious that death was approaching. For some months she had been declining into melancholy. Sir John Harington told a friend in October 1602 that 'she walks much in her Privy Chamber, and stamps with her feet at ill news, and thrusts her rusty sword at times into the arras in great rage'.[138] When her younger cousin Robert Carey visited her in March she answered his enquiry after her health with the words, 'No, Robin, I am not well.'[139] Preparations were now being made for her death: nobles were summoned to Court, rogues and vagabonds were conscripted for service in the Netherlands to prevent disorder, watch and ward was carefully observed in London; Robert Carey held himself ready to ride with the news of her death to Scotland.

Accounts of her deathbed are conflicting. According to a pamphlet issued, probably by the Privy Council, shortly after the event, when asked by leading councillors who should succeed her, she replied, 'who should succeed me but a King?' And when Cecil enquired what she meant, she answered 'who should that be but our Cousin of Scotland?'[140] Since she had, according to other accounts, already lost the power of speech, this utter-

---

[135] John Bruce (ed.), *Correspondence of King James VI of Scotland with Sir Robert Cecil and Others in England during the Reign of Queen Elizabeth*, Camden Soc. 78 (London, 1861), 7–8.

[136] Ibid. 10.   [137] Dalrymple, *Secret Correspondence*, letter no. 10.

[138] Harington, *Nugae antiquae*, i. 318.

[139] *The Memoirs of Robert Carey, Earl of Monmouth*, ed. H. G. Powell (London, 1905), 71.

[140] Anon., *The Queen's Last Sickness and Death* (1603).

ance—all too convenient for the ruling clique at Court—is improbable. Carey's story that she put her hand to her head at the mention of James's name is a little more plausible. Whatever she may have said or done, the accession of James depended upon the decision of the Privy Council, which in turn relied upon an unspoken consensus among the political nation. After her death in the early hours of 24 March, Robert Carey galloped to Edinburgh without waiting for the Council's approval and brought the news to James, who began his leisurely progress southwards. There could have been no greater contrast than that between the accession of the first of the Stuarts and that of the first of the Tudors, 118 years before. Henry VII, with an equally dubious hereditary claim, had won the Crown on the battlefield with the support of a few noble families: everything had depended upon the chance outcome of his military gamble. James, dissuaded from military intervention, succeeded without question or dispute; and the group of courtiers which had directed his steps remained in power. It was an effective demonstration that power lay with the men who controlled the Court, not with the armies of magnates. Cecil's enemies were quickly removed: Cobham was ensnared in his brother's conspiracy with the Catholics known as the Bye Plot; Ralegh, already dismissed from the Captaincy of the Guard, was accused with him of involvement in the related intrigue of the Main Plot. Both were imprisoned in the Tower.

Elizabeth's reputation suffered some decline in her last years. In Book V of *The Faerie Queene*, Spenser implicitly criticized her procrastination over Mary Stewart. Portraying her as Mercilla, he tells us that

> at her feet her sword was likewise layde,
> Whose long rest rusted the bright steely brand.

In 1597 the French ambassador wrote that 'if by chance she should die, it is certain that the English would never again submit to the rule of a woman'. Her godson, Sir John Harington, described her in 1602 as 'a lady shut up in a chamber from her subjects and most of her servants, and seldom seen but on holy days'. Bishop Goodman, looking back on the reign some years after her death, said that 'the Court was very much neglected, and in effect the people were very generally weary of an old woman's government'.[141]

There were many reasons for dissatisfaction with her rule. In refusing to name her heir, she took enormous risks for her kingdom. All possible solutions to that problem carried with them dangers, but her course was the

---

[141] Cobb, 'Representations of Elizabeth I', 304–15; Edmund Spenser, *The Faerie Queene*, v. ix. 30; André Hurault, Sieur de Maisse, *Journal*, ed. and trans. G. B. Harrison and R. A. Jones (London, 1931), 11–12; Harington, *A Tract on the Succession to the Crown*, 51; Godfrey Goodman, *At the Court of King James the First* (2 vols., London, 1839), i. 96–7.

most dangerous of all, and only good fortune saved the country from a disputed succession. She procrastinated over matters of foreign policy and military strategy. She did little to strengthen her Church and a good deal to weaken it.[142] She allowed royal revenues to be eroded by inflation and she sold off the lands of the Crown. She let the Cecil group take over the Court, antagonizing Essex and many other of the younger nobles.

However, there is more to be said on the other side. Elizabeth had the great gift of choosing able ministers and of standing by them, giving her realm the stable regime that it had lacked under her father, her brother, and her sister. She had a skill in public display which made her deeply admired and, until her later years, loved by her subjects: she was perhaps the only really popular English monarch between Henry V and Queen Victoria. She was fortunate—and so was her kingdom—that she lived long, so that her Church and its liturgy became the accustomed religion of the majority. She was a relatively inactive ruler, who disliked innovation at home and intervention abroad. The recipe was successful, even if her kingdom did not much resemble the Elizabethan England of later myth. Thanks in part to her caution, the realm was preserved from the dissensions and calamities that beset Europe and the Crown was saved from the disasters that befell it under those two interventionist monarchs Charles I and James II.

Her reputation soon revived after the accession of James, who has been much less favourably treated by posterity. Goodman, having described the dissatisfaction of her later years, wrote that:[143]

After a few years, when we had experience of the Scottish government, then—in disparagement of the Scots and in hate and detestation of them—the Queen did seem to revive. Then was her memory much magnified—such ringing of bells, such public joy and sermons in commemoration of her, the picture of her tomb painted in many churches; and in effect, more solemnity and joy in memory of her coronation than was for the coming in of King James.

For her epitaph, the words of John Harington serve as well as any:

When she smiled, it was a pure sunshine, that everyone did choose to bask in, if they could; but anon came a storm from a sudden gathering of clouds, and the thunder fell in wondrous manner on all alike.[144]

---

[142] Below, Ch. 11, *passim.*   [143] Goodman, *Court of King James*, i. 98.
[144] *The Letters and Epigrams of Sir John Harington*, ed. Norman Egbert McClure (Philadelphia, 1930), 125.

CHAPTER 10

Art, Power, and the Social Order

The great flowering of English drama and poetry in the last quarter of the sixteenth century, together with the lesser, but still significant, developments in house-building, religious music, and portrait miniatures, cannot be understood in isolation. For the art of the time—and the phrase stands for literature and music as well as for painting and building—was not so much a reflection of the social and political order as a part of it. A portrait of the Queen was a political statement much more than it was a reflection of her appearance; the prodigy houses did not just display the wealth and prestige of their owners but were themselves integral to that wealth and prestige; and history plays, watched and heard by thousands, were part of the political discourse of the age. Given the close involvement of writers and their audiences, or of portrait painters and their sitters, with the great men and women of the time, it would be surprising if visual and literary images did not reflect the world of power and social ranking of which they were themselves a part. The purpose of this chapter is to explore some of the forms in which political and social values were given 'public signification'[1] in art and literature, and to investigate the ways in which different aspects of the social order interacted.

1. THE SOCIAL CONTEXT

The sixteenth century brought major changes in schools and universities, with important consequences for the education of boys and men in many levels of society. While a broad groundswell of educational change had begun in the fifteenth century, when laymen started to play a great part in running schools and members of the landed classes grew more literate, the major boom in the foundation of schools came in the middle and latter parts of the sixteenth century. In Kent, for example, most small towns had three

---

[1] Stephen Greenblatt, *Renaissance Self-Fashioning from More to Shakespeare* (Chicago, 1980), 5: 'social actions are themselves always embedded in systems of public signification, always grasped, even by their makers, in acts of interpretation'.

or four schools each in the reign of Elizabeth, while Canterbury had as many as ten in 1600. One-fifth of Cambridgeshire villages had a resident schoolmaster continuously during the period 1570–1620, while many more had occasional, temporary teachers. In these counties and others like them, most children lived within walking distance of a school of some sort; although of course not all parents could afford to send their children to one. The situation was less favourable away from southern, south-eastern, and midland England; in the north schools were harder to find, although even there they were becoming more numerous.

Broadly speaking, there were four different types of school. Petty schools, which were entered by boys at the age of 5 or 6 in towns, 7 or 8 in the countryside, taught only reading and writing. 'English' schools taught English grammar as well; boys entered them at the same age as in petty schools, but stayed on longer. Public grammar schools added Latin, and sometimes Greek, to the syllabus, were permanent and endowed, providing education for poor as well as rich until the end of the century. Private secondary schools taught the same syllabus, were not endowed, charged fees, and drew upon the well-to-do for their pupils; in Kent, and perhaps elsewhere, they were the fastest growing sector.

The task of the petty and 'English' schools was principally to turn out literate pupils. Unfortunately, it is difficult to estimate their success, for only one crude and imperfect measure of literacy is available: the ability of men and women to sign their names. The ability to sign does not necessarily indicate a capacity to do more than that, while inability to do so is not always a sign of illiteracy—a man making his will on his deathbed might not have the strength to sign. However, since the practice in schools was to teach reading before writing, it is reasonable to infer that anyone who could sign his name was, in some sense, literate: he, or less often she, could probably read to some extent. Yet, because the measure is essentially one of ability to sign, it is more accurate to talk of it as a measure of illiteracy than of literacy: those who could not sign were, except for a few special cases, illiterate. On this reckoning there was some fall in illiteracy, albeit a slow one, throughout the sixteenth century. It declined sharply during the 1530s, then remained on a statistical plateau during the next two decades, and fell rapidly again in the early years of Elizabeth. In 1550 just over 80 per cent of men and about 98 per cent of women were unable to sign; by 1600 the figures were 72 per cent and 92 per cent respectively.

However, these general figures conceal some wide variations between different areas, social classes, and dates. In 1530 almost all gentlemen and clergy in the midlands, the east, and the south could sign their names; yet in Co. Durham, 41 per cent of gentlemen were unable to do so even as late as the decade 1560–9, and there the advance came in the next thirty years, for by the first decade of the seventeenth century the proportion had fallen to 17 per cent. While yeomen and merchants were generally much less literate than gentlemen in 1550, the gap had considerably narrowed by 1600; but by contrast, husbandmen and labourers were largely illiterate in the middle of the century and had only slightly improved their position by the end. Not surprisingly, the extent of literacy varied from place to place, although by the seventeenth century the overall difference between northern and southern counties was less than might be expected. In 1641–4 about 75 per cent of men from the northern shires were unable to sign their names, while illiteracy in the midland and eastern shires ranged from a low 45 per cent in Suffolk to 74 per cent in neighbouring Hertfordshire. These county figures conceal remarkable variations between parishes, for which no explanation is yet forthcoming: while the overall figure for illiteracy in Essex was 63 per cent, its parishes ranged from an abnormally high 82 per cent in Hadleigh to a mere 45 per cent in Little Baddow.

If there was an advance in literacy in the sixteenth century, it directly benefited only certain favoured groups: the gentry of the north, yeomen, and merchants in most regions, and tradesmen and craftsmen in London. More schools and better teaching were becoming available, but the sons of the poor could seldom benefit for long since their labour was needed from an early age to supplement the family income; and except in the higher social groups, women hardly benefited at all. However, even a few literate husbandmen or labourers in a village could bring their neighbours into contact with the printed word, for while this was still in part an oral culture, chap-books and ballads were widely sold, as was the Bible: the printed and spoken words could supplement and complement each other. In the latter years of the century women readers appeared as an identifiable group for whom books were being written and published, in every case by men. Some were practical handbooks, but others were popular and chivalric romances like George Pettie's *A Pettite Pallace of Pettie his Pleasure* (1575).[2]

The sixteenth-century growth in literacy, achieved by the petty and 'English' schools, was matched by the increasing popularity of grammar school and university education. The number of grammar schools and

[2] The statistics and most of the material in the last three paragraphs are derived from David Cressy, *Literacy and the Social Order: Reading and Writing in Tudor and Stuart England* (Cambridge, 1980), *passim*. On popular literacy see also below, s. 8; Ch. 11 s. 5; Margaret Spufford, *Small Books and Pleasant Histories: Popular Ficton and its Readership in Seventeenth-Century England* (Cambridge, 1981), ch. 2; and Caroline Lucas, *Writing for Women: The Example of Woman as Reader in Elizabethan Romance* (Milton Keynes, 1989), *passim*. For a contemporary reference to sale of ballads, William Shakespeare, *The Winter's Tale*, IV, iii, iv; V. ii.

schoolmasters increased considerably in southern England during the second half of the century, although the development was delayed in the north:
overall 136 new grammar schools are known to have been founded between
1558 and 1603. After 1560 more schoolmasters than before were university
graduates, and in the best schools at least, teaching methods were influenced by the writings of Erasmus and other humanists. Erasmus recommended that after they had learned the elementary rules of Latin
grammar, pupils should be set to reading and imitating the best authors. His
own *De copia* became the standard text in English as well as in European
grammar schools: the first part provided an extended vocabulary, or thesau-
rus, while the second gave examples of figures of speech. Roger Ascham,
Queen Elizabeth's tutor, recommended a system of double translation, by
which the pupil took the English translation of a Latin original and turned
it back into the Latin, extending his knowledge of classical authors and his
skill at manipulating the language. Shakespeare's knowledge of the classics
is abundant evidence of the education provided by the grammar schools.
His use of classical allusions, phrases, and rhetorical devices could only have
been produced by someone thoroughly grounded in Latin literature: he
knew, for instance, all fifteen books of Ovid's *Metamorphoses* in the Latin;
but he probably read Greek plays in translation.[3]

Substantial growth in university education accompanied the development of the grammar schools. Student numbers at Oxford rose from about
1,150 in 1550 to 1,750 in 1566 and then more haltingly to about 2,000 by the
end of the century; and there was a similar increase at Cambridge. At both
universities slightly under half the students were sons of the gentry or
above, just over half were described as 'plebeian', a very broad category.
Unfortunately, limitations in the evidence prevent us from refining the
figures much further. It is not true that, as some contemporaries asserted,
the sons of the rich were driving out the poor; on the other hand, the thirst
of noble and gentry families for education was in part responsible for the
rising student population. It was probably not difficult for the able son of a
merchant to get to university, rather harder for the son of a yeoman, and
very difficult indeed for the son of a craftsman or labourer.

The old university curriculum still remained firmly in place, and some of
the sons of nobles and gentlemen followed it. However, as the colleges came
to exercise a more important role than before in the life of the universities,
teaching became sufficiently flexible to allow variations in the course of
study. Sir Henry Wotton, who matriculated from New College in 1584,

---

[3] For supporting evidence given in great detail, see T. W. Baldwin, *Small Latine and Lesse
Greeke* (2 vols., Urbana, Ill., 1944), *passim*; and Emrys Jones, *The Origins of Shakespeare*
(Oxford, 1977), ch. 1 and *passim*.

followed the normal curriculum, with the addition of Italian and medical science, and took his BA; on the other hand, Robert Townshend, from the same college, followed a much more relaxed course, studying music, some geography and French, and probably never took his degree. Diaries, inventories of books, and student notebooks combine to give the impression that the old curriculum survived alongside a more eclectic range of studies, itself shifting towards a more 'humanist' programme. While Aristotle remained the dominant figure, emphasis was now laid less on medieval commentaries, more on Greek texts and the art of rhetoric. The culture of the universities was, like that of the grammar schools, literary and rhetorical.[4]

For many of the gentry the Inns of Court in London provided a further extension of their education. By contrast with the custom overseas, where practising lawyers were trained in the universities, in England the academic branches of the law—Roman, canon, and civil law—were taught at Oxford and Cambridge, while the common law was expounded at the Inns in London. During the sixteenth century the number of students at the Inns increased, partly because the opportunities for professional lawyers greatly expanded, and partly because the sons of noblemen and gentlemen enrolled at the Inns in order to acquire a basic knowledge of the law and the social polish of London society. The established methods of teaching—public readings and discussions of hypothetical cases, known as 'moots'—declined, as serious students found that they could gain more benefit from books. Yet while the Inns decayed as training centres, they flourished from the beginning of Elizabeth's reign as societies, as dining-clubs, and as venues for plays and masques, in some ways like colleges at Oxford and Cambridge in the nineteenth and twentieth centuries. Their students, well-to-do, educated, and leisured, made up a large and influential section of the audience for the professional theatre.

What lay behind the remarkable increase in literacy and the growing numbers at schools, universities, and the Inns? There can be no single or simple answer to this question. Protestant reformers—and Catholic ones too for that matter—urged the importance of learning for the laity as well as the clergy; humanists emphasized the necessity of sound education for the service of the state; fashionable books on the upbringing of a gentleman—like Elyot's *The Boke Named the Governour* and Castiglione's *The Courtier*—insisted that he should be skilled in learning, especially in rhetoric, as well as in fighting and hunting; and yeomen and merchants believed that good schooling opened the paths to profit.

---

[4] On universities, James McConica (ed.), *The History of the University of Oxford*, iii: *The Collegiate University* (Oxford, 1986), chs. 1, 4, 5–7, 10.

Although the emphasis of school and university education was placed directly upon the classics, the English language developed during the sixteenth century as never before or since. In the early sixteenth century English was widely, almost universally, considered to be inferior to Latin, for, while it might have practical uses, it lacked an adequate vocabulary: there were, wrote Ralph Lever as late as 1563, 'more things, than there are words to express things by'.[5] Above all, English was thought incapable of the eloquence or elegance of the classical languages. Yet throughout Europe vernacular tongues were acquiring greater value and prestige, as Protestant reformers insisted upon the use of the native language for the scriptures and for worship: for example, Tyndale's translation of the Bible, brought into England from Germany in 1526, gave English a new force and stature. Law reformers urged that statutes be translated into English, the printer John Rastell demanding that 'in reason every law whereto any people should be bounden, ought and should be written in such manner and so openly published and declared, that the people might soon, without great difficulty, have the knowledge of the said laws'.[6] Educators emphasized the necessity of plain, clear English in order to teach the unlearned, Roger Ascham complaining that too many English writers, 'using strange words as Latin, French, and Italian, do make all things dark and hard'. The value of English for practical affairs and for teaching was increasingly recognized, grammars and dictionaries began to appear, and the vocabulary grew: 'we have more words than notions', wrote Selden in the next century, 'half a dozen words for the same thing'.[7]

Yet, even in the 1570s English was still not considered a literary language; and then, quite suddenly, its status rose in response to the conscious efforts of a group of poets led by Sidney and Spenser. Michael Drayton praised Sidney's achievement: he

> . . . throughly pac'd our language as to show
> That plenteous *English* hand in hand might goe
> With Greeke and Latine, and did first reduce
> Our tongue from Lillies writing then in use.

Samuel Daniel looked forward, accurately as it turned out, to the spread of English into the wider world:

---

[5] Ralph Lever, *The Arte of Reason* (1573), quoted in Richard Foster Jones, *The Triumph of the English Language* (Stanford, Calif., 1953; repr. 1966), 69.

[6] John Rastell's *Proheme* to his abridgement of the statutes (1519), quoted in Howard Jay Graham, ' "Our tong maternall maruellously amendyd and augmentyd" ', *UCLA Law Review*, 13 (1965), 97.

[7] *Table Talk of John Selden*, ed. Sir Frederick Pollock (1927), 67–8, quoted in Jones, *Triumph*, 246.

9a. Snape Castle, Yorkshire

9b. The Fettiplace tombs at Swinbrook, Oxfordshire

Snape, built by Thomas Cecil in about 1577, is an early example of the Gothic revival. The tombs, erected in the early seventeenth century for sixteenth-century members of the Fettiplace family, also reflect chivalric and military values.

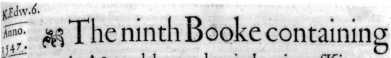

The ninth Booke containing
the Actes and thynges done in the raigne of King
Edward the sixt.

10. Things done in the reign of Edward VI

The frontispiece to Book 9 of John Foxe's *Acts and Monuments* (*The Book of Martyrs*) records the Protestant achievements of the reign of Edward: images are burned, churches are purged of popish 'trinkets', and the communion table replaces the altar.

11a. The martyrdom of Dr Rowland Taylor

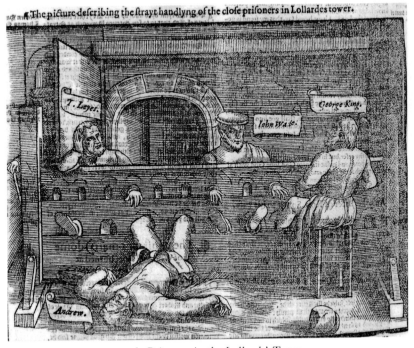

11b. Prisoners in the Lollards' Tower

Foxe records the sufferings of the Protestants under Mary. Taylor was a well-loved minister in Essex.

12. The Dance of Death

The Dance of Death of 1568–9 is a secularized version of a medieval
theme: there are no angels or demons, no day of judgement. A popular
song is printed below the picture.

13. Isaac Oliver, Lamentation over the Dead Christ

Oliver, renowned as a miniaturist and portraitist, also produced some of
the few religious pictures of Elizabeth's reign. He found few patrons
interested in this genre.

The moſt Rare and excellent Hiſtory,
Of the Dutcheſs of Suffolks Calamity,

To the Tune of, Queen Dido.

When God had taken for our ſin,
  that prudent Prince K. Edward away,
Then bloody Bonner did begin
  his raging malice to bewray:
All thoſe that did Gods Word profeſs,
He perſecuted more or leſs.

Thus whilſt the Lord on us did lowre,
  many in Priſon he did throw,
Tormenting them in Lollards Tower,
  whereby they might the truth forego:
Then Cranmer, Ridley, and the reſt,
Were burning in the fire, that Chriſt profeſt.

Smithfield was then with Faggots fill'd,
  and many places more beſide,
At Coventry was Saunders kill'd,
  at Worſter eke good Hooper dy'd:
And to eſcape this bloody day,
Beyond Sea many fled away.

Amongſt the reſt that ſought relief,
  and for their Faith in danger ſtood,
Lady Elizabeth was chief,
  King Henries Daughter of Royal blood;
Which in the Tower did Priſoner lye,
Looking each day when ſhe ſhould dye.

The Dutcheſs of Suffolk ſeeing this,
  whoſe Life likewiſe the Tyrant ſought:
Who in the hopes of heavenly bliſs,
  within Gods word her comfort wrought:
For fear of Death was fain to flye,
And leave her houſe moſt ſecretly.

That for the love of God alone,
  her Land and Goods ſhe left behind:
Seeking ſtill for that precious Stone,
  the Word and Truth ſo rare to find:
She with her Nurſe, Husband, and Child,
In poor array their ſighs beguil'd.

Thus through London they paſſed along,
  each one did take a ſeveral ſtreet,
Thus all along eſcaping wrong,
  at Billingſgate they all did meet,
Like people poor in Graveſend-Barge,
They ſimply went with all their charge.

And all along from Graveſend-Town,
  with Journeys ſhort on foot they went,
Unto the Sea-coaſt came they down,
  to paſs the Seas was their intent:
And God provided ſo that day,
That they took Ship and ſail'd away.

And with a proſperous gale of wind,
  in Flanders they did ſafe arrive,
This was to their great eaſe of mind,
  and from their heavy hearts much woe did
And ſo with thanks to God on high, (drive;
They took their way to Germany.

Thus as they travel'd ſtill diſguiſ'd,
  upon the high-way ſuddenly,
By cruel Thieves they were ſurpriz'd,
  aſſayling their ſmall company:
And all their treaſures and their ſtore
They took away and beat them ſore.

The Nurſe in midſt of their fight,
  laid down the Child upon the ground,
She ran away out of their ſight,
  and never after that was found:
Then did the Dutcheſs make great moan
With her good Husband all alone.

The Thieves had there their Horſes kill'd,
  and all their money quite had took,
The pritty Baby almoſt ſpoil'd,
  was by the Nurſe likewiſe forſook:
And they far from their friends did ſtand,
and ſuccourleſs in a ſtrange Land.

The Sky likewiſe began to ſcowl,
  it hail'd and Rain'd in piteous ſort,
The way was long and wondrous faul,
  then may I now full well report,
Their grief and ſorrow was not ſmall,
When this unhappy chance did fall.

14. The exile of the Duchess of Suffolk

A popular ballad of 1602, in the tradition of Foxe, tells of the exile of the
Duchess, a staunch Protestant, under Mary.

A spice spectator sic me docuere parentes
Me quoque maiores omnes, virtute carentes.

A Now when into their fenced holdes, the knaues are entred in,
To smite and knocke the cattell downe, the hangmen doe beginne.
One plucketh off the Oxes cote, which he euen now did weare:
Another lacking pannes, to boyle the flesh, his hide prepare.
C These theeues attend vpon the fire, for seruing vp the feast:
B And Fryer smelfeast sneaking in, doth preace amongst the best.

3 Who play thin Romish toyes the Ape, by counterfeiting Paull:
For which they doe award him then, the highest roome of all.
Who being set, because the cheere, is deemed little worth:
Except the same be intermixt, and lac'de with Irish myrth.
Both Barde, and Harper, is prepard, which by their cunning art,
D Doe strike and cheare vp all the gestes, with comfort at the hart.

15. The MacSwynes at dinner

In a woodcut from John Derricke, *The Image of Irelande*, the MacSwyne family from Co. Donegal is seen dining in the open air, with friar, bard, and harper. Men are publicly relieving themselves on the right. Derricke's intention was to stress the barbarity of the Irish.

16. The submission of Turlough Luineach to Sir Henry Sidney

Turlough was lord of Ulster and head of the O'Neills. Derricke urges that the Irish be tamed by strong military action.

17a. The arrival of the English in Virginia

17b. The Indians of Virginia making boats

Engravings by Theodore de Bry, after drawings by John White, published in de Bry's edition of Thomas Hariot's *Brief and True Report*. The authors picture Virginia as a fruitful land inhabited by primitive but industrious people; the intention is to stimulate peaceful colonization. Derricke's images of the Irish are, by contrast, meant to stimulate military conquest.

And who in time knowes whither we may vent
The treasure of our tongue, to what strange shores
This gaine of our best glorie shal be sent,
T'enrich unknowing Nations with our stores?
What worlds in th'yet unformed Occident
May come refin'd with th'accents that are ours?

Richard Mulcaster, the schoolmaster, epitomized the new pride in the English language: 'I love *Rome*, but *London* better, I favour *Italie*, but *England* more, I honour the *Latin*, but I worship the *English*.'[8] The growing sophistication and status of the language was both a necessary condition of the flowering of imaginative literature and also in part a creation of the Elizabethan poets.

This development of English fitted it, in the eyes of contemporaries, as a vehicle of rhetoric. Leonard Cox's *Arte or Crafte of Rhetoryke* had appeared in *c.*1529 , and Thomas Wilson's better-known *Arte of Rhetorique* was published in 1553. In the last quarter of the century several English hand-books on rhetoric came out, Henry Peacham's *Garden of Eloquence* probably the most significant of them. English was now important for the spoken word, particularly the public word, as well as for the written.

The increasing importance of the vernacular helped the growth of print-ing by encouraging the production of books in English, and was in turn itself helped by the press, which standardized the language and assisted its success, preserved texts, and made possible the clearer design of books. Spelling, however, remained unstandardized, which also helped printers by making it easier to 'justify' a page. Moreover, printing assisted Welsh as well as English, especially through the publication of the Welsh Bible. By 1500 printing had become established all over Europe, more widely in Germany, France, and Italy than in England. While literacy and the habit of reading had been growing before the invention of movable type, they were certainly encouraged by it. Just as the press both helped the growth of the vernacular and was helped by it, so literacy and education assisted the development of printing and were in turn stimulated by it.

The production of books from English presses increased rapidly in the first part of the sixteenth century from approximately 800 per decade in 1520–9 to 1,800 per decade in the first twenty years of Elizabeth and to nearly 3,000 in the last decade of the century.[9] Print runs averaged 1,200

---

[8] The quotations from Drayton, Daniel, and Mulcaster are drawn from Jones, *Triumph*, 179, 184, 193. The reference to 'Lillies writing' is probably to William Lily, author of the most widely used Latin syntax of the time, rather than to his grandson, John Lyly, author of *Euphues*.

[9] Figures taken from statistics derived from the *Short-Title Catalogue* and produced by

copies, though obviously there were wide variations between titles. By comparison with other countries in Europe England had a small printing industry, with only twenty to thirty printers at any one time, most of whom had no more than two or three presses, five at most, whereas Plantin had twenty-five. Yet, by the reign of Elizabeth, the presses were responding to demand, printing not only books of devotion and high literature, but also a wide range of popular works from ballads, folk-plays, and almanacs to chap-books.[10] The influence of the press can be roughly gauged from the evidence of inventories to wills. In Canterbury only 8 per cent of inventories recorded books in the 1560s, compared with as many as 45 per cent in the 1620s, while in Leicestershire, with a larger and less educated rural sample, hardly any men left books in the first fifteen years of Elizabeth's reign, whereas 7.8 per cent left some in the years 1600–24.[11]

Other evidence of the influence of the printing press is to be found in the appearance of private libraries. Until the middle of the sixteenth century, major collections of books were to be found only in monasteries, cathedrals, and university colleges; but after the Henrician and Edwardian Reformations, monastic libraries were dispersed. Nor were they the only ones to suffer: Duke Humphrey's library at Oxford was sold in 1557, with other parts of the university collection. John Dee, astrologer, magus, scientist, geographer, and antiquarian, set about repairing the damage by building a private library. So successful was he that Queen Elizabeth and the Privy Council came to Mortlake in 1575 to visit his library, which contained about 3,000 printed books and some 500 manuscripts. Although his was the largest library of the English Renaissance, Dee was not alone in his achievement: Archbishop Parker formed a great library of early medieval texts, now housed in Corpus Christi College, Cambridge; and the library of Lord Lumley contained some 3,000 works.[12]

the Institute of Bibliography, University of Leeds, as part of the project for *The History of the Book in Britain*. I am most grateful to the Institute and to Professor John Barnard for permission to use them. See Maureen Bell and John Barnard, 'Provisional count of *STC* Titles, 1475–1640', *Publishing History*, 31 (1992), 48–64; my thanks to Professor Barnard for this reference.

[10] Chap-books were small, easily transported books sold by travelling salesmen known as chapmen.

[11] Figures from Laura Caroline Stevenson, *Praise and Paradox: Merchants and Craftsmen in Elizabethan Popular Literature* (Cambridge, 1984), 68–70.

[12] Peter French, *John Dee: The World of an Elizabethan Magus* (London, 1972), ch. 3; Julian Roberts and Andrew Watson (eds.), *John Dee's Library Catalogue* (London, 1990), *passim*. The study of sixteenth-century libraries is poised to develop, thanks to R. J. Fehrenbach and E. S. Leedham-Green (eds.), *Private Libraries in Renaissance England* (Marlborough, 1992–), a project of which two volumes have so far appeared. I am grateful to Mr Julian Roberts for drawing my attention to this work.

However, it is important not to exaggerate the role of printing in the history of sixteenth-century literature. Playwrights were not interested in the printing of their works until the seventeenth century; Shakespeare was apparently unconcerned about the printing of his plays, but keenly interested in the publication of *Venus and Adonis* and *The Rape of Lucrece*. Sidney strictly but unsuccessfully forbade the printing of *Arcadia*, though this may have been for moral reasons, given the content of the *Old Arcadia*. John Donne considered—or pretended to—that the printing of poems was unbecoming to a gentleman: he wrote to Sir Henry Goodyer, asking for the return of some verses, since 'the going about to pay debts, hastens importunity . . . I am brought to a necessity of printing my Poems, and addressing them to my L[ord] Chamberlain . . . I apprehend some incongruities in the resolution.'[13] It is a mistake to regard printing as the only form of publication, for plays reached audiences through performance rather than reading, and the works of Sidney, Donne, and others circulated quite widely in manuscript.

Two major centres of literary and artistic achievement developed in the sixteenth century: London and the royal Court. The great size, rapid growth, and impressive wealth of London have already been described: it dwarfed every other town in England.[14] Like other large towns, it housed financiers, merchants, retailers, artisans, apprentices, whores, and crooks; but they were more numerous there than elsewhere. Furthermore, although the London season was not fully developed until the late seventeenth century, noblemen and gentlemen were attracted there in increasing numbers. This varied and mostly prosperous population made up a large potential audience for plays and a readership for books, as well as providing a rich set of characters upon whom authors could draw as models. Although the ethos of City government was hostile to the theatre, it was unable to curb the enthusiasm of Londoners for plays, and the official support for pageants and processions helped to build a tradition of public performance as well as supplying an additional livelihood for playwrights.[15]

London was the most literate—or least illiterate—community in England: 72 per cent of London tradesmen could sign their names in the 1580s, 83 per cent by 1603; in the suburbs the rise was even more striking, for while only 23 per cent of Middlesex tradesmen could sign in the 1580s, 69 per cent could do so in the first decade of the next century. Boys appren-

---

[13] Quoted in Guy Fitch Lytle and Stephen Orgel (eds.), *Patronage in the Renaissance* (Princeton, NJ, 1981), 232.

[14] Above, Ch. 6 s. 2 for population and social structure of London.

[15] See below, p. 408, for a discussion of theatre audiences.

ticed in London and Middlesex were expected to be able to read and write, and 82 per cent of them could do so; even among male servants 69 per cent could sign compared with only 24 per cent elsewhere.[16]

The printing industry and the Inns of Court were concentrated in London, and the only legitimate printers outside London were those in Oxford and Cambridge, whose contribution was not large. The Inns of Court attracted hundreds of students, many of whom had plenty of time for activities outside their studies. London was the site of two major schools, Westminster and St Paul's, and of many smaller ones; it housed a major cathedral, St Paul's, more than a hundred churches, and the principal residence of the Archbishop of Canterbury at Lambeth Palace. The only major 'cultural' institutions housed outside London were the universities, and perhaps for that reason they had only a limited influence upon the intellectual life of the nation.

Lastly, the royal Court was linked closely with the City of London, although physically separate from it.[17] Since the beginning of the sixteenth century or earlier it had attracted nobles and gentlemen from most parts of the country and had established a tradition of entertainments, public and private. The display functions of the Court were central to the art and literature of the time; its social ambience—dominantly masculine beneath a woman ruler, and highly competitive—helped to determine the artistic climate; and above all it was the fount of patronage.

2. PATRONAGE

Advancement, rewards, and reputation depended upon the support of patrons, and the status of patrons themselves was enhanced by the protection and help that they could give to those beneath them. Before the Reformation the Church had been the most important patron of learning, building, music, pictorial illumination, and literature; but following the Breach with Rome and the dissolution of the monasteries, the clergy had neither the resources nor, it would seem, the desire to emulate men like Cardinal Wolsey or Archbishop Warham. The Crown and the nobility, already active in patronage before this, now expanded their roles to take the place of the Church. Henry VIII acted as the great patron of artists, like Holbein, of builders, like those who designed his palaces, and, to a lesser extent, of poets. Much of the actual direction of patronage was undertaken by his servants, such as Thomas Cromwell, who first brought Holbein into the royal service; but essentially it was Crown patronage that mattered,

[16] The figures are taken from Stevenson, *Praise and Paradox*, 61–4.
[17] Above Ch. 5 s. 1, for the structure and functions of the Court.

whether exercised by the monarch directly or by his officers. Others, however, played important supporting roles: Henry's Queens—Catherine of Aragon, Anne Boleyn, Catherine Parr; Cardinal Morton, patron of the young Thomas More; Lord Mountjoy, friend of Erasmus. Under Edward VI the tradition of Court patronage was carried on for a short time by Protector Somerset, most notably in his great Renaissance building in the Strand, Somerset House; but after his fall it largely lapsed, to recover only under Elizabeth. She, however, provided little direct patronage; only in the production of tournaments and pageants, the employment of musicians and composers, and the commissioning of portraits was Elizabeth herself active. Adequately provided with palaces, she built none, and she was economical in her literary patronage. Her courtiers were, fortunately, more generous; and through their patronage and their own poems in praise of the Queen, the art and literature of the time remained, in many respects, part of a Court culture.

The town and country houses of nobles and rich gentlemen were the great architectural monuments of the Elizabethan era. Apart from Gresham's Exchange (1566?), there was little public building in London in the second half of the century. Neither cathedrals nor parish churches were built or much beautified after 1558; and while Oxford and Cambridge colleges had seen extensive building under Henry VIII, the new colleges founded under Mary and Elizabeth were mostly content to take over the buildings of dissolved monastic foundations or to absorb medieval halls. The field was open to the great magnates and courtiers. For the most part they had little interest in architectural theory of the kind that underlay the major works of Renaissance Italy: John Shute's *The First and Chief Groundes of Architecture* (1563) was the only book on the subject published under Elizabeth, and it had slight apparent influence.[18] The profession of architect, already well established and highly honoured in Italy, did not yet exist in England, at any rate in its modern sense, and Inigo Jones was the first Englishman who could properly be given that title. The largest building organization in the country, the Royal Works, was headed by its Surveyor, usually a man who had risen from one of the building crafts. Similar men filled some of the roles later occupied by architects, but they were not the authors of their buildings in the way that Inigo Jones, Christopher Wren, and John Vanbrugh later came to be; having begun life as artificers they could not aspire to the social status of 'gentleman' which was necessary for the full creation of buildings; and the word 'architect', in common use

---

[18] John Dee's preface to Euclid's *The Elements of Geometrie* (1570) had some remarks on the subject.

under the Stuarts, was rare in the sixteenth century. Large buildings were
mostly designed in outline by their owners, many of whom were enthusiastic, even obsessive, amateurs like Sir John Thynne, Sir Thomas Smith,
Lord Burghley, Sir Robert Cecil, and Elizabeth Talbot, better known as
Bess of Hardwick; the detailed execution was then carried out by a team of
artificers headed by the surveyor.

Two men, however, came near to filling the role of architect in the
sixteenth century: John Thorpe and Robert Smythson. Thorpe was originally a mason in the Royal Works, who left that office in 1601 to become a
land surveyor. He made many plans of buildings, some of which had been
designed by others, some of which were never erected; and he seems to have
been more important in influencing others than in the buildings which he
himself put up. Robert Smythson's achievements have been more fully
analysed and seem—perhaps for that reason—to be more impressive.[19] He
first appears in about 1568 at Longleat, Wiltshire, where he was described
as a mason; and he was soon engaged in Sir John Thynne's ambitious plans
to erect a new façade around the house, replacing an earlier one destroyed
by fire in 1567; this had been completed by about 1570, and it still stands
today. Thynne evidently directed many of the building operations himself,
while Smythson acted as one of two leading mason-designers, the other
being a French sculptor, Alan Maynard (Plate 7b). From Longleat
Smythson moved to Wollaton, near Nottingham, where he was employed as
surveyor to Sir Francis Willoughby until he died in 1614. Willoughby was
beginning an enormous, fantastical creation, financed in part from the
profits of his coalfields; and here Smythson's role as the main designer of
the house is much more evident than at Longleat. On his tombstone he was
described as the 'Architector and Surveyor unto the most worthy house of
Wollaton with divers others of great account'.[20] His epitaph and his role in
this and other houses illustrates his emergence as someone near to the
seventeenth-century idea of the architect, but still remaining part artificer,
part surveyor as well. Wollaton, built on a hill and visible from every
approach, is an impressive testimony to the status of its owner, and in its
mixture of styles—Italian and French Renaissance, Flemish and English
Gothic—was a major influence on the prodigy houses of the time (Plate 8a).
From his base at Wollaton, Smythson worked on the designs of many other
houses in the North Midlands, achieving his greatest creation at Hardwick,
Derbyshire; height, compactness and the bold arrangement of masses are
the principal features of his work. His style differs markedly from that of

---

[19] For Smythson see Mark Girouard, *Robert Smythson and the Elizabethan Country House*
(New Haven, Conn., 1983), *passim*.
[20] Ibid. 83; on the houses of gentry and yeomen, above Ch. 6 s. 5.

the designers of such courtyard houses as Wimbledon, built for Burghley's son Thomas (Plate 8*b*); and it is significant that none of his clients can properly be described as courtiers, rich, grand, and powerful though they might be. The designers of the great courtier houses—Holdenby, Burghley, Theobalds, and so on—are unknown to us: no more than Smythson can they truly be described as architects.

Fortunately the creators of Elizabethan music are not so obscure, for composers signed their works and we do not have to engage in complicated detection in order to discover their names or the identities of their patrons. Church patronage of music was in sad decline: as Thomas Whythorne, the madrigalist, wrote, 'in time past music was chiefly maintained by cathedral churches, abbeys, colleges, parish churches, chantries, guilds, fraternities, &c. But when the abbeys and colleges without the universities, with guilds and fraternities, &c., were suppressed, then music went to decay.'[21] There were, however, secular patrons willing to fill the gap, and the first of these was Elizabeth herself. In her Chapel Royal and in her company of the Queen's Musick she directly employed some sixty musicians, many greatly distinguished. Inheriting from her father a high tradition and some major performers and composers, like Thomas Tallis, she continued that tradition with the appointment of Thomas Morley, William Byrd, and others in the Chapel Royal.

Royal patronage was, moreover, supplemented by private. John Wilbye, the madrigalist, was the resident musician and music teacher of the Kytson family at Hengrave Hall in Suffolk; and John Dowland, composer of the earliest book of lute songs, came under the patronage of Robert Sidney. Networks of patrons developed around the country: the Kytsons, Petres, Cornwallises, Bacons, and Pastons in East Anglia; the Talbots and Cavendishes in the north; the Seymours and Thynnes in the west; and the Manners, Berties, and Willoughbys in the midlands. It is significant that some of these families—Thynnes, Talbots, Cavendishes, Willoughbys—were also notable patrons of builders. Many of the most active and devoted patrons of music were Catholics, like the Petres, as were some of the most important musicians, such as Byrd and, for a time, Morley and Dowland. Yet there were Protestant patrons as well—the Earl of Leicester, Christopher Hatton, and Lord Burghley—and both Catholic and Protestant patrons encouraged secular as well as sacred music, although the taste of the Catholics ran naturally to music for the Latin rite. In general the eclecticism and tolerance of both sets of patrons was remarkable,

---

[21] *The Autobiography of Thomas Whythorne*, ed. James M. Osborn (Modern spelling edn., London, 1962), 203.

typified by the Queen's own willingness to employ the Catholic Byrd in the Chapel Royal; and it indicates something of the religious temper of the times.[22]

Like surveyors, musicians were anxious about their status, and perhaps because their aspirations were higher, they were often disappointed. Whythorne's autobiography tells a depressing story of travelling from one tutor's post to another, and when he published a volume of songs, he found sales moving slowly; like many authors, he blamed his printer. Sadly he compared the situation of musicians in England with that of their colleagues in Italy. Italian gentlemen were accounted 'rudely and basely brought up who had no knowledge in music', and in consequence there was great demand there for new songs: 'and for that the printers would have every day new songs to print, they do fee the best musicians that they can retain'. In England musicians who served in private houses were regarded as mere minstrels, and minstrels were considered by beggars and rogues 'to be their companions and fellows'. Whythorne was certainly unjust to the many enlightened patrons of his day, and his own experiences may have been unfortunate. Even so, the cult of the amateur and gentlemanly musicmakers and the tendency to regard professional musicians as higher household servants, probably did inhibit their claims to status. Perhaps it was only at Court that they received the recognition that they believed to be their due.[23]

Sculpture and painting in sixteenth-century England were almost entirely confined to portraiture. There was little sculpture beyond funerary monuments in English cathedrals and parish churches: paid for by the families of the departed, they symbolized the landed and mercantile dynasties of England by depicting the lineage, qualities, and, to some extent, the likeness of the deceased. Earlier monuments, from the Middle Ages into Elizabethan times, had usually been free-standing altar tombs, but gradually, in order to save space, wall monuments came into vogue, and they were no less effective witnesses to the importance of the local family. Effigies could be placed in tiers, facing the viewer and impressing him with the importance of the dynasty, as with the Fettiplace tomb at Swinbrook, Oxfordshire (Plate 9*b*). Like the great buildings of the time, these tombs were mostly the work of local masons, with the social standing of artificers. Some of them, like John Gildon of Herefordshire, were highly skilled artists; but they were still socially subordinate. One, however, Epiphanius Evesham, also from Herefordshire, a county with a long and fine tradition

---

[22] See David C. Price, *Patrons and Musicians of the English Renaissance* (Cambridge, 1981), *passim*.

[23] Whythorne, *Autobiography*, 203–6.

of church sculpture, was a gentleman born, with a more independent approach to his work than that of the masons. Yet, although he achieved work of considerable distinction, his name was virtually lost to history until he was rediscovered in the twentieth century.

While English painting in the Tudor period was confined almost entirely to portraiture, a few noblemen collected other works from abroad. Lord Lumley owned many foreign pictures, mostly portraits, but a few of them religious in subject-matter; the Earl of Leicester was more eclectic, having a very large collection (about 220 pictures), 130 of them portraits, the others on religious, mythical, or historical subjects. Yet until the emergence in the seventeenth century of the earliest English connoisseurs, such as Sir Henry Wotton and the Earl of Arundel, no English nobleman or gentleman seems to have shown the same educated knowledge of painting as they did of architecture or music.

Portraits were commissioned by the monarch, courtiers, nobles, gentlemen, and Oxford and Cambridge colleges; the Church commissioned very few, beyond mediocre pictures of bishops. The most impressive and important of the large-scale portraits were by foreign artists—Holbein, Zuccaro, Eworth, Gheeraerts, and others; and most late Tudor portraits by native artists, including those of Queen Elizabeth, were inferior works painted by journeyman painters. To raise the standard of their work, the Privy Council ordered that no portrait of the Queen be allowed until 'some special person that shall be by her allowed, shall have first finished a portraiture thereof', after which others might 'at their pleasures follow the said patron [i.e. pattern] or first portraiture'.[24] From about 1570 a continuous stream of royal portraits was produced, mostly commissioned by Elizabeth's subjects rather than herself, and based upon a few authorized and well-known patterns. These pictures enhanced the status of the owner and symbolized the authority of the monarch (Plates 2b, 3a & b, 4a & b).

English-born artists showed distinction only in painting miniatures—or in 'limning' as it was sometimes called. Although some miniatures, especially those presenting their subjects in chivalric postures, were more like public portraits on a small scale, most were intimate works, serving as personal gifts or mementoes. Sir James Melville, Scottish ambassador to Elizabeth in 1564, described how the English Queen

took me to her bed-chamber and opened a little cabinet, wherein were divers little pictures wrapt within paper, and their names written with her own hand upon the papers. Upon the first that she took up was written, 'My Lord's picture'. I held the candle, and pressed to see that picture so named. She appeared loath to let me see

[24] Roy Strong, *Portraits of Queen Elizabeth I* (Oxford, 1963), 5.

it; yet my importunity prevailed for a sight thereof, and found it to be the Earl of Leicester's picture.[25] (Plate 5*b*)

The sense of a secrecy that can be penetrated—both the bedchamber and the little cabinet—indicates the attraction of miniatures. The art of painting them first came into England under Henry VIII, with the arrival of the Hornebolte family from Europe; and it was raised to a magnificently higher scale by Holbein, who perhaps painted them because he did not get enough commissions for full-scale portraits. After Holbein's departure, the tradition of miniature-painting continued, but at a lower level of both quality and quantity. The revival began in the 1570s, with the appearance on the scene of Nicholas Hilliard, who, together with Zuccaro, provided the standard image of Elizabeth. He was the first great English miniaturist, practitioner of the only visual art at which Englishmen of the sixteenth century really shone. Yet, in spite of the freshness and charm of his pictures he was, by the European standards of the day, backward and unsophisticated, with a remarkably erratic control of perspective. Isaac Oliver, to some extent his rival, was both more sophisticated and technically more accomplished. Trained overseas, he showed the influence of both the French and Flemish schools. His religious drawings—for instance, his *Lamentation over the Dead Christ* (1586)—are powerful works in the Mannerist tradition. Yet they met with little response from the English and he won few patrons, although the Earl of Essex and, later, Prince Henry appreciated his work. Unfortunately for him, his studio pattern for a miniature of Elizabeth was firmly rejected by her—not altogether surprisingly since it has a realism which the Hilliard images of perpetual youth tactfully lack. The history of miniature-painting, splendid as it is, shows the conservatism, caution, and cultural isolation of English patrons, and consequently of their portraits (Plates 3*b*, 13).

Processions, pageants, and tournaments were as much an 'art-form' for sixteenth-century men and women as were architecture, music, painting, poetry, or plays; and they were often as dramatic as performances in the theatre. While the monarch provided some of the money and equipment, the greater burden of payment and organization was borne by cities, towns, universities, and courtiers. The first of these great open-air events was Elizabeth's coronation procession in 1559.[26] Intended to celebrate and also to guide the new Queen, the shows in the procession were designed and

[25] Patricia Fumerton, ' "Secret" arts: Elizabethan miniatures and sonnets', in Stephen Greenblatt (ed.), *Representing the English Renaissance* (Berkeley, Calif., 1988), 93. For the history of sixteenth-century miniatures see Roy Strong, *The English Renaissance Miniature* (London, 1983), *passim*.

[26] Above, Ch. 7 s. 1 for the coronation procession.

paid for by Londoners, in particular by the guilds. Visits to the universities followed, to Cambridge in 1564 and to Oxford in 1566 (when Christ Church, a royal foundation, paid for the occasion and then complained about it).[27] The major cities of southern and midland England were visited in subsequent decades: it cost Bristol £1,000 to entertain the Queen in 1574, with a royal entry, mock battles, and an allegorical contest between War and Peace. Great courtiers entertained her on progress as well, as Leicester did for ten expensive days at Kenilworth in 1575. These were occasional events, but from about 1570 the Queen's Accession Day, 17 November, was celebrated annually with tilts at Court.[28] The Office of Revels provided the costumes and scenery for these mixtures of tournament and masque, but except in 1579 and 1582, when specially elaborate shows were put on for the Duke of Anjou, the competitors paid for the rest: it cost Sir Robert Carey, who was far from rich, £400 to take part in the tilts of 1593.

The patronage of literature was more complex than that of the other arts, partly because literary forms were more varied, partly because literature was more tightly attached to social and political life, and partly because the patronage of plays was very different from that of other works. The authors of non-dramatic works—a term embracing poetry, prose fiction, religious treatises, political tracts, works of history, advice on education and deportment, and so on—sought patrons for many reasons. Monetary reward was probably the least important of these: Spenser received £50 after the publication of *The Faerie Queene* and Jonson was granted an annuity of 100 marks (£66. 13s. 4d.) under the early Stuarts. However, such direct payments by patrons, whether royal or noble, were rare, and financial rewards came, if they came at all, from sales of books. Protection against censorship or against personal enemies could be useful, yet was hardly crucial. More significant was the hope of personal advancement in office: Spenser became secretary to Lord Grey, Lord Deputy of Ireland; on Grey's departure he was made secretary to the Council in Munster; and he later received a grant of 3,000 acres in south-west Ireland. (The grant did Spenser little good in the long run, for his house was burned by rebels in 1598; but it is unlikely that he actually died of starvation, as Jonson later claimed.) Noble households could offer to aspiring authors posts carrying a small monetary reward together with board and lodging: for example, Michael Drayton was a tutor at Wilton, Wiltshire, and Gervase Babington

[27] Christ Church paid £112 at first, but was later reimbursed with £37. 6s. 8d.
[28] See Ch. 5 s. 1 for a fuller account of progresses and tilts.

was chaplain there. Clerical writers could hope for livings and perhaps for promotion in the Church.

Writers usually sought patronage at Court, since, while little was to be expected from Queen Elizabeth herself, men of influence and discernment congregated there at the chief source of offices and other political rewards. Care and application were needed to secure a patron. The first step was usually the composition of a dedication or panegyric to a potential patron, in the hope of attracting attention. This was an uncertain business, but played with skill it could bring success; however, too great a significance should not be attached to dedications, which are not necessarily any indication of a real link between author and dedicatee. Patrons mostly wanted the prestige, the praise, and, with good luck, the posthumous fame that a successful writer might bring them; but they were seldom willing to pay much for the honour. Generally they were less interested in the content of works than in the credit conferred upon them; and authors usually wrote first and sought patronage through dedications later. Literary works—by contrast with portraits, funerary monuments, and buildings—were rarely commissioned by patrons.

The career of John Donne illustrates some of the hopes, disappointments, and ultimate rewards of patronage. After attending Lincoln's Inn and serving on Essex's expedition to Cadiz in 1596, Donne was appointed secretary to Lord Keeper Egerton, a promising beginning, through which he was able to maintain a detached and cynical attitude towards the Court. Then everything went wrong: Donne married Lady Egerton's young niece against the wishes of her father and was dismissed. He was now forced to approach the Court and search for patrons; and in 1608 he wrote in desperation to his friend, Sir Henry Goodyer: 'I would fain do something . . . to be no part of any body is to be nothing. [I] needed an occupation and a course which I thought I entered well into, when I submitted my self to such a service, as I thought might employ those poor advantages, which I had. And there I stumbled too, yet I would try again: for to this hour I am nothing . . .'.[29] Eventually, in 1615, Donne took the only remaining possible step and was ordained into the Church. This brought him success, for he was appointed a royal chaplain and embarked on a glittering career as a Court divine, ending as Dean of St Paul's.

Sometimes there was more to patronage than the mutual search for personal advancement and prestige. The Earl of Leicester was a thoroughly eclectic patron of puritans and proto-Arminians, lawyers, and poets, and at

---

[29] Arthur F. Marotti, 'John Donne and the rewards of patronage' in Lytle and Orgel, *Patronage in the Renaissance*, 207–34, quotation on pp. 228–9.

Leicester House in the Strand he gathered together a remarkable set of writers: his nephew Philip Sidney, Gabriel Harvey, and Edmund Spenser were the foremost of them. This was not, as Harvey jokingly called it, an academy or Areopagus, for it was an informal collection of men, attached to a single patron, whose purpose they served and who would, they hoped, serve theirs. However, in 1579 Leicester concentrated their minds and his own on opposition to the marriage of Elizabeth with the Duke of Anjou.[30] The Earl wanted to frustrate Anjou's marriage plans but use the latter's power in support of the Dutch rebels; and he hoped also to emulate Anjou's achievements as a patron of the arts and literature. John Stubbs was encouraged to write *The Gaping Gulf* (1579), attacking the proposed marriage, while Sidney wrote privately to the Queen advising her against matrimony.

Leicester had the wealth and political stature to be the greatest patron in England. His nephew Sidney was much less wealthy and influential, but had the literary talent and personal charm to attract writers. Together with his sister, Mary, Countess of Pembroke, he turned her house, Wilton, into a retreat for writers. It was, wrote Nicholas Breton, 'a kind of little Court'; and John Aubrey spoke of it as 'like a College, there were so many learned and ingenious persons'.[31] No more than at Leicester House was there a formal academy; but Sidney and his sister entertained men like Fulke Greville and Edward Dyer, with whom they hoped to raise English poetry from the trough into which, in their eyes, it had fallen since the days of Chaucer. With the publication in the 1590s of *The New Arcadia* and of the first three books of *The Faerie Queene*, they raised the status of English poetry, whose 'golden age' was the consequence of a deliberate campaign to emulate the French Pleiades and the Italian epic poets—in Spenser's words, 'to overgo Ariosto'. Yet that 'golden age' did not emerge unheralded: Wyatt and Surrey were its forerunners; the potent influence of Erasmus on the teaching of classical languages in schools made it possible; and it built upon a substantial body of mid-Tudor literature, of which Cranmer's Prayer Books, to name no other works, achieved lasting grandeur.

Courtly patrons were essential to the acting companies, for whom they provided protection against the law and against the enemies of the theatre in Elizabethan London. The 'Act for the punishment of vagabonds' of 1572 laid down that all 'fencers, bearwards, common players in interludes & minstrels, not belonging to any baron of this

---

[30] Above, Ch. 8 s. 2 for the Anjou marriage negotiations.
[31] John Buxton, *Sir Philip Sidney and the English Renaissance* (2nd edn., London, 1964), 234, 95.

realm or towards any other honourable personage of greater degree
... shall be taken adjudged and deemed rogues, vagabonds and sturdy
beggars'.[32] James Burbage wrote to the Earl of Leicester seeking protection
on behalf of his newly formed company, and specifically petitioning him
'that (as you have been always our good lord and master) you will now
vouchsafe to retain us at this present as your household servants and daily
waiters'. He prudently added: 'not that we mean to crave any further
stipend or benefit at your lordship's hands'. Two years later the company
received letters patent from the Queen authorizing them, as servants of the
Earl, 'to use, exercise, and occupy the art and faculty of playing comedies,
tragedies, interludes, stage plays, and such other like as they have already
used and studied'.[33] From then until the closure of the theatres in 1642 the
player companies operated under the patronage and protection of members
of the royal family or of great Court nobles. To Leicester's company was
added the Lord Chamberlain's, and then the Queen's, the Lord Admiral's,
Pembroke's, and Worcester's.[34] The Revels Office, made permanent in
1579, took charge of arrangements for presenting the plays at Court, enabling the grandees to compete with one another for presenting plays to the
Queen, especially over Christmas, and to use their companies to entertain
her when she visited them on progress.

Yet, important as the grandees might be in providing protection, the
risks and profits were taken, not by them, but by impresarios like Burbage
and Philip Henslowe, and by actor-shareholders like Shakespeare. The
rewards of success were very great: Alleyn died a rich man and Shakespeare
rose to the status of a gentleman. Most actors, however, died poor, for a
share in one of the companies was essential to material success. The real
patrons of the drama were not the noblemen, but the playgoers who paid for
their places and crowded the London theatres. The commonest type of
theatre in Elizabethan London was the open-air 'amphitheatre', based on
galleried inn-yards or animal baiting rings. Of these the earliest was the Red
Lion built in Whitechapel by John Brayne, Burbage's brother-in-law, in
1567; it was replaced in 1576 by Burbage's Theatre and in 1577 by his
Curtain, both in Shoreditch; and Henslowe and Alleyn followed with the
Rose in 1587. In these playhouses the less well-to-do stood in the yard with
no shelter, while the better-off occupied galleries, which, like the stage
itself, were covered from the weather. The audience paid a single fee,

[32] 14 Elizabeth c. 5.

[33] Andrew Gurr, *The Shakespearean Stage* (2nd edn., Cambridge, 1982), 30–1.

[34] The Lords Chamberlain were the Earl of Sussex (up to 1583), and then the 1st and 2nd
Barons Hunsdon. The Lord Admiral was Lord Howard of Effingham, created Earl of
Nottingham in 1597.

usually one penny, for entrance to the theatre and then paid extra to go into the galleries; admission to the Globe (1598) and the Fortune (1601) was simplified so that more galleries were built and their occupants entered by a separate door from those standing in the yard. The capacity of these later playhouses was considerable: the Globe, for instance, could hold 800 people in its yard and 2,000 in its galleries.

Hall playhouses, by contrast, were entirely covered and, inevitably, much smaller, holding at most 750–1,000 persons. The earliest of these were the Paul's theatre, used by the St Paul's boys from 1575 to 1590, and the first Blackfriars theatre, used by the Chapel Children from 1576 to 1583/4. A second Blackfriars theatre was built in 1596 for Burbage's adult company, though they were unable to use it until 1608. Prices here were very much higher than in the 'amphitheatres': sixpence for mere entrance to the theatre, and more for the better seats. Most of the cheaper theatres were built in the suburbs, outside the jurisdiction of the hostile City authorities, lying either to the north and east of the City—like the Red Lion, Theatre, Curtain, and Fortune—or—like the Globe, Rose, and Swan—in Southwark. The hall playhouses were either in a City precinct, like Blackfriars, or at the Cockpit, near Whitehall.[35]

The differences between the two types of theatre become important when we turn to the composition of Elizabethan audiences, a topic clouded by controversy. Some literary historians claim that Shakespeare wrote popular plays for the merchant and artisan audiences at the 'amphitheatre' houses, while 'coterie' playwrights wrote for élite playgoers at the halls; others argue that there was no distinction between the two types of audience and that both were made up of the 'privileged'.[36] Neither view is convincing, for although the playgoers at Blackfriars were certainly richer than those at 'amphitheatre' houses, they would have included merchants and their wives as well as courtiers and gentlemen. The Theatre, the Rose, the Swan, and the Globe certainly attracted a more plebeian audience of artisans and apprentices, but they brought in the élite as well. It does not follow that the plays presented were markedly different.[37]

---

[35] For details of the playhouses, see Andrew Gurr, *Playgoing in Shakespeare's London* (Cambridge, 1987), ch. 2. Terminology presents difficulties: 'public' is sometimes used for the 'amphitheatre' houses, and 'private' for the halls, but this is misleading in its implications. 'Amphitheatre' is not wholly satisfactory, but seems the best term available.

[36] Alfred Harbage, in *Shakespeare's Audience* (New York, 1941), and id., *Shakespeare and the Rival Traditions* (New York, 1952) presents the first view, Ann Jennalie Cook, in *The Privileged Playgoers of Shakespeare's London, 1576–1642* (Princeton, NJ, 1981) the second. Gurr, *Playgoing*, 3–4 gives a useful summary.

[37] I have followed the accounts of Gurr, *Shakespearean Stage*, ch. 6, and id., *Playgoing*, ch. 3, together with Martin Butler, *Theatre and Crisis* (Cambrdge, 1984), appendix ii.

The audiences for Elizabethan plays were astonishingly large. One historian estimates that 15,000 men and women visited the theatre each week in 1595, when there were only two theatres open, and that the figure approached 25,000 twenty-five years later when there were six. Perhaps as many as 20 per cent of the population of London and Southwark were accustomed to attending plays, providing a highly varied audience, many of whom, though perhaps not all, would have been able to read, and some of whom would have been informed and sophisticated.[38] While the reign of Elizabeth witnessed a remarkable transformation in English drama, the new phenomenon did not come out of a void, for there had been a long tradition of mystery plays, moralities, and interludes. Yet the change, when it came, was rapid and total. The old craft mystery plays of London and provincial towns died after 1558, and in their place impresarios, grandees, playwrights, actors, and London playgoers created a metropolitan and professional theatre.[39] The companies of players had fixed venues in the capital, which provided them with large audiences and a high income; and purpose-built, permanent theatres enabled them to put on more complicated plays, with larger casts. However, the pressures upon managers, playwrights, and actors were heavy: the public needed more and more plays, so that Henslowe's company was producing thirty-five new ones in a year. The playwrights met the challenge, and by the late 1580s the Elizabethan theatre had come of age. Kyd's *Spanish Tragedy* and the first part of Marlowe's *Tamburlaine* were produced in *c*.1587, Shakespeare's three *Henry VI* plays in *c*.1590.

Two general reflections may conclude this section. First, while patronage was obviously not the only element in the formation of Elizabethan culture, its different manifestations helped to shape artistic responses. For example, without the protection of patrons and the support of the London public, the achievements of the Elizabethan theatre would have been impossible; and without Elizabeth's patronage the music of Byrd would have been silenced. Secondly, while poetry, drama, and music rose to great heights, architecture, sculpture, and painting were much less successful. To some extent this may be the consequence of different relations between patron and client. Painters, sculptors, and surveyors were still regarded as artisans and lacked the social standing which had already been won by their contemporaries in Italy, and to some extent in France. True, playwrights and actors were held in low esteem in the early part of the reign, but the enthusiastic response of a wide public to their plays enabled them to rise socially and respond to the demands of their audience.

---

[38] Gurr, *Shakespearean Stage*, 196.   [39] See below, p. 413.

3. CENSORSHIP

Rudimentary machinery of censorship had been established under Henry VIII against the influx of heretical literature and was maintained well beyond the end of the Tudor dynasty. A statute of 1542/3 laid its foundations: claiming that heretical books and ballads had introduced false opinions and stirred up religious dissension, it ordered them to be purged from the realm and forbade their publication in future.[40] Under Somerset this statute was repealed and for a short time relatively free printing was allowed; but the disturbances of 1549 alarmed the government and restrictions were again imposed. In 1554, as the restored Catholic Church faced hostile propaganda from across the Channel, restrictions became still more severe, the statute on sedition (re-enacted by Elizabeth) authorizing the Crown to punish writings against King or Queen by severing the right hand of the author;[41] and in 1557 the Stationers' Company received a charter from the Crown, providing it with a monopoly of printing and making it the executive agent of censorship. Under Elizabeth enforcement was fairly relaxed until the 1580s, when the arrival of Catholic missionaries persuaded the government to take more rigorous steps: an Act of 1581 ordained capital punishment for the authors of seditious books and mutilation for those who spread seditious rumours.[42] In 1586 a decree was issued in Star Chamber tightening up the rules and procedures for licensing books. Anyone setting up a printing-press was to notify the Warden of the Stationers' Company; no presses were to be allowed outside London, except for one in each of the university towns; no book was to be printed unless it had first been perused and licensed by an archbishop or bishop; the Warden of the Company or his deputies were authorized to search all workshops and seize illegal books.

From about 1588 censorship was fairly effective within a limited field. Puritan and Catholic presses were firmly suppressed, and after the destruction of Thomas Cartwright's equipment in 1572, only two secret presses survived for more than a few weeks: Campion's in the early 1580s and the press responsible for the *Marprelate Tracts* in the 1590s. Under Elizabeth, apart from the occasional puritan tract which crossed the indistinct boundary between the legal and the illegal, there was little directly 'political' writing published in England that did not accept the doctrine of absolute and passive obedience to the monarch. Books VII and VIII of Richard Hooker's *Ecclesiastical Polity*, which carried discussion of political obligation well beyond crude assertions of obedience to authority, were not

[40] 34 & 35 Henry VIII c. 1.   [41] 1 & 2 Philip and Mary c. 3; 1 Elizabeth c. 6.
[42] 23 Elizabeth c. 2.

published until 1648. The most dangerous threat to government came from abroad, and neither Mary nor Elizabeth succeeded in stopping the flow of seditious or heretical literature from across the Channel. Mary's reign had seen the publication abroad of treatises advocating resistance to the monarch;[43] and under Elizabeth, presses in Antwerp and Louvain supplied English Catholics with a steady stream of religious works. In all, 223 Catholic books in English were published during Elizabeth's reign; and although it is not possible to tell how many of them were printed overseas, it is likely that the majority were produced in France and Flanders.

There were of course some notorious cases of censorship under Elizabeth. John Stubbs lost his right hand in 1579 for writing *The Gaping Gulf* against Elizabeth's proposed marriage with Anjou;[44] and John Penry was executed in 1593 for his part in the *Marprelate Tracts*. In the late 1590s, perhaps because of the stress of war and anxiety about the succession to the throne, censorship became stricter. Edmund Tilney, Master of the Revels, ordered the insurrection scene, concerning the 'Evil May-Day', to be excised from the play *Sir Thomas More* by Munday, Dekker, Chettle, and Shakespeare; the Privy Council closed the theatres for a few months after a performance of *The Isle of Dogs* by Thomas Nash and Ben Jonson; and the deposition scene from Shakespeare's *Richard II* was omitted from the quarto printed version and possibly for a time from performances.[45] History books and plays seem to have been the main target of the government, and the printing of books on English history without authority from the Privy Council was forbidden in 1599. Sir John Hayward, lawyer and historian, was sent to the Tower in that year for the first part of his *Life of Henry IV*, dedicated to Essex, and the second part of the book was banned from publication: he had been unwise enough to include the deposition of Richard II, always a sensitive topic with Elizabeth, but not one which he could have easily avoided, given his subject-matter. He commented on the issue some years later that

men might safely write of others in manner of a tale; but in manner of a history, safely they could not: because, albeit they should write of men long since

---

[43] For example, Christopher Goodman, *How Superior Powers Oght to be Obeyd* (1558); John Ponet, *A Short Treatise of Politicke Power* (1556); John Knox, *The Appellation of John Knoxe* (1558).

[44] John Stubbs, *The Discoverie of a Gaping Gulf whereinto England is like to be Swallowed by another French Marriage* (London, 1579).

[45] The text of *The Isle of Dogs* is lost and we cannot know what objections were made against it. On censorship of drama see Janet Clare, *'Art made Tongue-tied by Authority': Elizabethan and Jacobean Dramatic Censorship* (Manchester, 1990), *passim*. Above, Ch. 9 s. 4 for the connection between *Richard II* and the Essex rising of 1601.

dead, . . . yet some alive, finding themselves foul in those vices which they see observed, reproved, and condemned in others, their guiltiness maketh them apt to conceive, that, . . . the finger pointeth only at them.[46]

The Crown was not, however, the sole or the most effective censor. The City of London was consistently and aggressively hostile to the acting companies, and only the patronage of the Court enabled the drama to survive outside the City walls. The Protestant Church, too, was ill-disposed to the professional theatre and more effectively hostile to the mystery plays of the towns. These plays were still flourishing when Elizabeth came to the throne, but had totally disappeared by her death, probably some years before that. Archbishop Grindal, who had complained about the London players in 1564, had the York mystery plays suppressed in 1572; the Wakefield plays ended in 1576; and the last performance of the Coventry cycle came in 1579. With their death the professional companies were freed from competition: the loss of one great tradition may thus have helped in the creation of another.

Occasional resentment was voiced against the censorship, most notably by Ben Jonson, in *Sejanus*. In that play the Roman historian, Cordus, is indicted before the Senate and his annals ordered to be publicly burned. Sejanus, the instrument of Tiberius' despotism, attacked Cordus as one who

> . . . doth taxe the present state,
> Censures the men, the actions, leaves no tricke,
> No practice unexamin'd, paralels
> The times, the governments, a profest champion,
> For the old libertie.[47]

Ironically, Jonson got into some trouble with the Privy Council over *Sejanus*, in part because of the passage on censorship, in part because the Earl of Northampton considered the play to contain a hidden attack upon himself. Yet Jonson's career did not suffer, for he went on to become the Court's favourite author of masques; nor does the concern that he voiced over censorship seem to have been widespread.

One historian has seen in the censorship and responses to it an 'implicit social contract between authors and authorities . . . a fully deliberate and

[46] Hayward's work aroused enough public interest for three pirated editions to be published. A modern edition, *The Firste and Second Parte of John Hayward's 'The Life and Raigne of King Henrie the IIII'*, ed. John J. Manning, has been published by the Camden Society (4th ser., 42, London, 1991); the quotation is from introd., p. 1.

[47] *The Works of Ben Jonson*, ed. C. H. Herford and P. and E. Simpson (11 vols., Oxford, 1925–52), iv. 385.

conscious arrangement', under which authors used indirection and allegory to make and conceal their political statements.[48] The effect of Elizabethan censorship upon poetry and drama hardly seems sufficient to influence the whole strategy of literature; and allegory, obliqueness, and the use of complex symbols were too firmly a part of the literary conventions of the day to be explained or explained away by reference to censorship. Yet the great poems and plays of the era certainly did bear strongly, if often indirectly, upon political and social power, commenting upon it in a more revealing and subtle manner than did the formal works on authority. The remainder of this chapter is devoted to drawing out and identifying some of those revelations.

4. SOURCES OF IDEAS AND IMAGERY

Sixteenth-century authors drew on and deliberately imitated a very wide range of literary material; originality was not then prized as it has been since the Romantic era, and writers were open about the models that they used. Spenser proclaimed that he was emulating Homer, Virgil, Ariosto, and Tasso; and Philip Sidney based his *Arcadia* heavily on an earlier work of the same name by the Italian author, Jacopo Sannazaro, on the Spanish romance, *Amadis de Gaule*, and on many other sources. Writers expected their readers or listeners to catch the references and understand their implications—which makes their work difficult for present-day readers, who are usually less well versed than was the sixteenth-century public in medieval romance, classical literature, and the Scriptures.

Most remote from ourselves is the medieval chivalric romance, which formed the core of the epics of Spenser and Sidney. The essence of chivalry lay in knight-errantry, a code of violence and warfare, according to whose tenets knights performed heroic deeds in defence of Christendom, in search of the Holy Grail, or in rescuing high-born ladies in distress. The 'morality' of chivalry lay in knightly honour, which dictated that allegiance lay to the lord, to family and lineage, and to personal reputation; its outward expression was seen in tournaments and heraldry. The chivalric cult became immensely popular at the Court of Henry VIII, thanks in part to the courtly fashions inherited from Edward IV and his Burgundian connections, in part to the King's own predilection for jousting. Italian epics, especially

---

[48] Annabel Patterson, *Censorship and Interpretation: The Conditions of Writing and Reading in Early Modern England* (Madison, Wis., 1984), 17; a contrary view, which I have followed, is given in Blair Worden, 'Literature and political censorship in early modern England', in A. C. Duke and C. Tamse (eds.), *Too Mighty to be Free: Censorship and the Press in Britain and the Netherlands* (Zutphen, 1988), 45–62.

Ariosto's *Orlando furioso*, provided familiar, popular, and near-contemporary models for Elizabethan poets; and although the role of the armoured knight was already diminishing in Continental warfare, tournaments still had some relevance in battle-training, particularly in firing military ambition and temperament. However, the chivalric code was coming under direct attack from humanist writers. Castiglione, in *The Courtier*, heaped scorn on unlettered noblemen who could do nothing else but fight and incidentally warned young gentlemen against fighting with farm labourers, who might defeat them and inflict loss of face. In England Sir Thomas Elyot, in *The Boke Named the Governour*, stressed the importance of learning and public service against the ideals of knight-errantry. Roger Ascham, Elizabeth's tutor, went further still, condemning knightly feats as 'open manslaughter and bold bawdry'.[49] These attacks do not seem to have reduced enthusiasm for tournaments, although under Mary they were restricted to Anglo-Spanish occasions sponsored by Philip. Under Elizabeth tournaments were revived with a great display following her coronation, and gradually a pattern developed for the reign: two kinds of tournament were held, one for celebrating special occasions or foreign embassies, the other for marking the anniversary of Elizabeth's accession on 17 November.[50]

Elizabethan tournaments were bound up with the concept of courtly love. In this medieval tradition the beloved was a virtuous lady, usually married to another, whom the knightly lover wooed without hope of consummation. The love was ideally chaste and ennobling, reflecting Christian worship and demanding obedience to the beloved. Pursuing her, the knight was expected to perform honourable deeds on the tournament field or in battle. Under Elizabeth, the Queen herself was the focus for the courtly love of her young knights, who jousted for her favour. While the jousting was taken seriously enough, the surrounding ambience was equally, probably more, important: Royal Ascot comes to mind as a modern parallel. Scenic devices were highly regarded and the competing knights each carried an *impresa*—a motto and a pictorial device painted on a shield—to express their particular aspirations. The most famous of all the Elizabethan tournaments was mounted in April 1581, in honour of the Duke of Anjou, by the Four Foster Children of Desire (the Earl of Arundel, Lord Windsor, Philip Sidney, and Fulke Greville). The Foster Children besieged the Fortress of Beauty, in which the Queen was seated. She refused to yield and was protected by sixteen defendants. Jousting, prefaced by and intermingled

[49] Roger Ascham, *English Works*, ed. W. A. Wright (Cambridge, 1904), 230–1.
[50] Above, Ch. 5 s. 1.

with speeches, stretched over two days, at the end of which the attackers admitted defeat.[51]

Chivalric displays were not only presented at the royal Court. In 1596 the Earl of Pembroke, then Lord President of the Council in the Marches of Wales, held a Christmas feast in Ludlow Castle at which his guests played the parts of King Arthur's knights.[52] Knights and their exploits were pictured, not only in their own *imprese*, but also in some of the most striking miniatures of the time: Hilliard portrayed the Earl of Cumberland, richly dressed for tournament with his lance in his hand, and Thomas Cockson showed the Earl of Essex seated on a rearing horse (Plate 6). The aristocratic cult of tournaments was accompanied by popular versions of medieval epics, notably Anthony Munday's translations of *The Historie of Paladino of England* and *Amadis of Gaule*, which spread the appeal of chivalry beyond the immediate circle of the Court. Some Elizabethan buildings reflected chivalric notions: Leicester's fortified additions to Kenilworth were probably the earliest, serving as the background to pageants for the Queen. Geographically removed from the Court was Thomas Cecil's house at Snape, Yorkshire, transformed by him and his wife, Dorothy Neville, sister-in-law to the Earl of Northumberland, from a manor-house into a sham castle with crenellations and towers (Plate 9a). However, the most fully developed mock castles come from the reign of James I—Bolsover, Derbyshire, Ruperra, Glamorgan, Lulworth, Dorset, and Caverswell, Staffordshire.

During the Anglo-Spanish wars, Sidney died because he refused, with a chivalric gesture, to put on his thigh-plates, and in 1591 Essex challenged the enemy commander to single combat during the siege of Rouen. But knightly warfare was by then a thing of the past and the Elizabethan revival of chivalry was an exercise in make-believe. Artillery, sieges, new infantry tactics, and the emergence of the professional soldier put an end to that sort of fighting. Protestant zealots condemned unlicensed violence, and the demands of the state and of public service undermined the code of individual honour and knight-errantry. Yet the ideals of a transformed chivalry, softened by humanism, and mixed with the conventions of pastoral, served to protect traditional aristocratic values for a time, even if that time was not to last much longer. The honour code of the knight could still be reconciled with the Christian religion: Sir John Harington, writing to Robert Cecil in 1600, likened knighthood to baptism, since it impressed a character of

---

[51] This tournament carried a political message: that the fortress of the Queen should not be taken by the Duke of Anjou. See above, Ch. 8 s. 2.

[52] John Stradling, *The Storie of the Lower Borowes of Merthyrmawr*, ed. H. J. Randall and W. Rees, South Wales and Monmouthshire Record Soc. 1 (Cardiff, n.d.), 74.

honour into the recipient, as baptism impressed a mark of Christianity.[53]
Accommodated within the Protestant framework, the chivalric epic, mixed
with pastoral, provided the images and the structure of Sidney's *Arcadia*,
Spenser's *The Faerie Queene*, and many lesser works.

Loosely linked with the chivalric epic was national mythology. Geoffrey
of Monmouth, writing in the twelfth century, had devised the fictitious
history of a Britain founded by the Trojan Brutus and later ruled by King
Arthur, who defended it against the Saxon invaders. There was no historical foundation for any of this, but it appealed to sixteenth-century Englishmen and enabled later writers to locate British origins in a classical
civilization, provide a national hero in Arthur, and construct a royal descent
for Elizabeth. Intellectually battered by criticism at the beginning of the
sixteenth century, Geoffrey's myths nevertheless remained alive, though
with diminished credibility, until the end of it. In Book II of *The Faerie
Queene* Spenser described the arrival of Brutus and his pacification of the
island:

> Thus *Brute* this Realme unto his rule subdewd,
> And raigned long in great felicitie,
> Lov'd of his friends, and of his foes eschewd.[54]

British mythology moved across an ill-defined boundary into British
history. During the sixteenth century historical writing in England developed considerably in sophistication and popularity; and medieval chronicle-
writing was transformed by 1600 into something resembling modern
narrative history. The first changes came with *The History of King Richard
III* by Thomas More, written between 1514 and 1518, and the *Anglica
historia* of Polydore Vergil, an Italian humanist who came to England early
in the century and stayed for about fifty years. Between them they introduced the methods and approach of Italian historians of the fifteenth and
early sixteenth centuries. Polydore's work, wider in scope than More's, was
critical of the sources, especially of Geoffrey of Monmouth, and showed a
power of selection and organization that had been absent in the old chronicles; but his concept of causation was still tied mainly to the notion of
Fortune and divine intervention. His work lay behind the two principal
sources of Shakespeare's history plays, Edward Hall's *Union of the Two
Noble and Illustre Famelies of Lancastre and Yorke* (1st and incomplete edn.
1542; 2nd edn. 1550) and Ralph Holinshed's *Chronicles* (1st edn. 1577; 2nd

[53] *Letters and Epigrams of Sir John Harington*, ed. N. E. McClure (Philadelphia, 1930),
81–2.
[54] *The Faerie Queene*, II. x. Quotations are from *Spenser: Poetical Works*, ed. J. C. Smith
and E. de Selincourt (Oxford, 1912).

edn. 1587). Between Hall and Holinshed appeared the potent figure of John Foxe, whose *Actes and Monuments of these Latter and Perilous Dayes Touching Matters of the Church* or *Book of Martyrs* was published in Latin in 1559 and in English in 1563. Justifying the English Church by describing its ancient lineage and its divine guidance, Foxe combined prophecy and history to establish the idea of the English as God's people; and his voice was echoed in *The Faerie Queene*.

Under Elizabeth the growing popularity of history, especially of British history, was reflected in the foundation of the Society of Antiquaries in 1586 and in a wide range of publications, from the voluminous and expensive Holinshed to the pocket chronicles of Richard Grafton and John Stow. Parallel with these prose narratives there appeared a series of histories in verse, beginning with the *Mirror for Magistrates* (1559), a set of moral tales for rulers, moving on to historical romances like Samuel Daniel's *Complaint of Rosamund* and Michael Drayton's *The Barons' Warrs*. Yet the major achievement of historical writing in this period lay in the theatre, above all in Shakespeare, but also in Marlowe, Thomas Heywood, and others. They provided an organizing power and dramatic sense which was lacking not only in the medieval chronicles but also in the sprawling narratives of Holinshed.

Historical writing was used in part to rouse the spirit of the nation, in part to justify the English Church; and in those two aims it reflected the purposes of the state. However, it also reflected popular anxieties, not only about Spain, but also, in the 1560s and the 1590s, about the succession to the throne; it is no accident that many of Shakespeare's plays involved disputed claims to power. History, for playwrights and for historians, became a vehicle for presenting political problems and opinions that were aptly topical in the last years of Elizabeth.

The models supplied by the classical worlds of Greece and Rome were far more varied than those of chivalry or British history, though they provided little inspiration for painting, architecture, or music. The literary and intellectual texts of the classical world were transmitted by the humanists of the early sixteenth century, principally Erasmus and Vives, through the school curriculum that they and their followers had laid down, and through the many editions and translations of Greek and Roman texts that appeared throughout the century under humanist influence. The humanist principles of education depended on a close analysis of texts with a view to the pupil memorizing and imitating them; and imitation was the foundation of sixteenth-century literary creation, as Ben Jonson explained: 'The third requisite in our poet, or maker [after natural wit and exercise] is imitation, to be able to convert the substance, or riches of another poet, to his own use.

To make choice of one excellent man above the rest, and so to follow him, till he grow very he . . .'[55] Imitation was not mere copying, but the achievement of a true resemblance. As Petrarch had put it very clearly at an earlier date, in a letter to Boccaccio:

A proper imitator should take care that what he writes resembles the original without reproducing it. The resemblance should not be that of a portrait to the sitter . . . but it should be the resemblance of a son to his father. . . . Thus we may use another man's conceptions and the colour of his style, but not his words. . . . The first procedure makes poets, the second makes apes.[56]

The classical literary models most often venerated and exploited in the sixteenth century were Homer, Virgil, Ovid, and Cicero. Sir Guyon's voyage to the Bower of Bliss in Book II of *The Faerie Queene* dramatically recalls Odysseus' journeys between Scylla and Charybdis, and then past the island of the sirens, while the opening of the poem echoes *The Aeneid's* 'This is a tale of arms and of a man':

> Lo I the man, whose Muse whilome did maske,
> As time her taught, in lowly Shepheards weeds,
> Am now enforst a far unfitter taske,
> For trumpets sterne to chaunge mine Oaten reeds,
> And sing of Knights and ladies gentle deeds.[57]

As Virgil turned from pastoral to epic, so Spenser moved from *The Shepheardes Calender* to *The Faerie Queene*. Ovid, assisted by several Renaissance handbooks, gave the entry to the classical storehouse of mythology, and his *Metamorphoses*, splendidly translated by Arthur Golding in 1567, was perhaps the most popular of all classical poetry in the sixteenth century. Cicero was, for most of that century, the supreme model for Latin prose, his style elaborate, rounded, ornate. His influence can be seen, in an exaggerated and perhaps unfair form, in John Lyly's *Euphues* (1580) and, to better advantage, in Richard Hooker's *Of the Laws of Ecclesiastical Polity* (1593). Around the turn of the century the livelier, less rotund prose of Tacitus and Seneca began to provide an alternative model, seen in the sharp, crisp sentences of Bacon's *Essays*.

While sixteenth-century theology was obviously Christian, philosophical concepts were drawn largely from the pagan classical philosophers, especially from Aristotle, Plato, the Stoics, and their later followers.

---

[55] Isabel Rivers, *Classical and Christian Ideas in English Renaissance Poetry* (London, 1979), 145–6.

[56] Jones, *The Origins of Shakespeare*, 19.

[57] *The Faerie Queene*, I, ll. 1–4. Spenser adapted the 'cancelled' opening lines of the *Aeneid*, to bring out the parallel between his career and Virgil's.

Neoplatonist philosophy was the source of the principal concepts of Elizabethan cosmology. The universe, according to these beliefs, was divided into the heavenly spheres, which were ordered and unchanging, and the earthly, at the centre, which was corrupt and changeable. From God at the head of the heavenly order to the lowest beasts and the very stones on earth there stretched a hierarchy or chain of being, with man as its central link, his soul aspiring to heaven, his body tied to earth. In some versions man was fixed half-way up the ladder, in others he had no permanent position but the potentiality to become a beast or a god. This chain and the correspondences between the different planes of being provided some of the central precepts for Tudor government and order.

Neoplatonism also influenced sixteenth-century ideas of love. Platonic love stressed the importance of chastity, envisaging female virtue and beauty as the means by which man could ascend towards mystical union with the divine; and human love became a means of mediating between the two extremes of divine and animal love, the chaste woman combining the realms of spirit and of matter. Similar in its emphasis on chastity, and on the unattainably virtuous woman, but less mystical in its philosophy, was the legacy of the fourteenth-century poet, Petrarch, whose sonnets influenced European poets from his own day until the seventeenth century. The sonnet-sequences of the 1580s and 1590s, a major landmark for English poets, were his principal legacy in England. Many of the English sonneteers reacted sharply against the influence of Petrarch's continental imitators, but their use of imagery and of balanced antitheses, as well as of the sonnet form, recalls his work, sometimes consciously, as in Ralegh's sonnet prefacing *The Faerie Queene*:

> Methought I saw the grave, where *Laura* lay,
> Within that Temple, where the vestall flame
> Was wont to burne, and passing by that way,
> To see that buried dust of living fame,
> Whose tumbe faire love, and fairer vertue kept,
> All suddeinly I saw the Faery Queene:
> At whose approch the soule of *Petrarcke* wept.[58]

Classical writers as well as Christian ones created ethical models. Cicero's teaching in *De officiis* was transmitted to English audiences in part through Castiglione and Elyot, in part through intensive reading of his own works:

[58] Leonard Forster, *The Icy Fire: Five Studies in European Petrarchism* (Cambridge, 1969), *passim*; Arthur F. Marotti, ' "Love is not Love": Elizabethan sonnet sequences and the social order', *English Literary History*, 40 (1982), 396–428; *The Poems of Sir Walter Ralegh*, ed. Agnes M. C. Latham (London, 1925), 13; and below, p. 426, for a Petrarchan sonnet by Queen Elizabeth I.

Lord Burghley was said to carry with him always a copy of 'Tully's Offices'.[59] Cicero's ethics, derived in part from the Stoic philosophers, stressed the importance of public service and the necessity of a training in practical wisdom, eloquence, and rhetoric—the art of persuasion. His teaching was certainly not Christian, for he considered participation in public and political life to be essential to the good man, but it could be and was reconciled with Christian teaching by the humanists and their pupils. As an active politician, Cicero practised and taught the art of rhetoric, and his textbook on oratory and his speeches provided models for courtiers and statesmen in the sixteenth century. Rhetoric, the art of persuasion, became increasingly important in public life during the course of the century. Books like Thomas Wilson's *The Arte of Rhetorique* (1553) and Henry Peacham's *The Garden of Eloquence* (1577) minutely analysed rhetorical devices and figures of speech.

Classical history, Roman rather than Greek, was an important part of the school curriculum and an obvious source of material for plays. Sallust, Caesar, and Livy were the principal historians studied in school, while Plutarch's *Lives* was the main source for Shakespeare's Roman plays. However, they provided more than material for plays, for Plutarch and others were devoured by the political classes as handbooks of conduct.[60] The studies of Gabriel Harvey, lecturer in rhetoric at Cambridge and practitioner in civil law in London, exemplify the sixteenth-century approach to Roman history, especially to Livy. Harvey read the first three books of Livy with Philip Sidney, studying particularly 'the forms of states, the conditions of persons, and the qualities of actions'. His intention seems to have been to read Livy with nobles and courtiers, like Sidney and his uncle, the Earl of Leicester, in order to further his own career and to influence warfare and politics. Sidney himself drew out the principles of this enterprise, when he wrote to Sir Edward Denny just before the latter departed for Ireland in the retinue of Lord Deputy Grey: the foundation of study, wrote Sidney, lay in Scripture, but after that 'The second part consists as it were in the trade of our lives. For a physician must study one thing, and a lawyer another, but to you that with good reason bend yourself to soldiery, what books can deliver, stands in the books that profess the art, and in histories.'[61] In 1591

[59] Marcus Tullius Cicero, often referred to as 'Tully' in the sixteenth century, was active in Roman politics as a republican at the time of Augustus' triumph. He had a major influence on European culture through his *De officiis* (On Duties) and his *De oratore* (On Rhetoric).

[60] Plutarch, a Greek historian of the Roman Empire in the 1st century AD. His *Lives* were translated into English by Thomas North in 1579.

[61] Lisa Jardine and Anthony Grafton, ' "Studied for action": how Gabriel Harvey read his Livy', *Past and Present*, 129 (1990), 30–78, quotations from pp. 36, 39.

Henry Savile translated into English the *Histories* of Tacitus, chronicling the events of the Roman Empire from the death of Nero in AD 68 to the end of the first century; and Tacitus' English followers, notably William Camden and Sir John Hayward, set out to show not only what happened, but how things happened and how statesmen achieved or failed to achieve their aims. For them historical success and failure were no longer decided by Fortune or providence, but by the skill or the mistakes of the participants. For a short time Tacitean history was influential in the theatre, notably in Jonson's *Sejanus* and *Catiline*; but Jonson's scholarly attachment to his Roman sources proved too austere for the tastes of his audience.[62]

Although education at school and university was almost entirely classical, with Latin grammar providing the initial groundwork and Roman authors the models to be followed, Christian writings were obviously embedded in men's consciousness. Ecclesiastical and devotional writings made up the greater part of published works in the later, as in the earlier, sixteenth century. A division between these works and 'literature' in the modern sense would have then been inconceivable. Nevertheless, such a distinction is made here, unhistorical as it is, and this analysis is confined to the use of biblical and other Christian texts in the poetry and drama of the time.

The language of the English Bible had already been forged by William Tyndale in 1526, and subsequent translations up to and after the Authorized Version closely followed his text. Of all the books of the Bible the Revelation of St John the Divine, with the prophetic books of the Old Testament that lay behind it, was probably the most direct inspiration for Elizabethan poetry: Revelation acquired a special importance for English Protestants after it had been translated by John Bale in the middle of the century. It is echoed in the images and structure of Book I of *The Faerie Queene*, where Una, companion of the Redcross Knight, is identified with the 'woman clothed with the sun' of Revelation chapter 12; Duessa and Lucifera, her opponents, with the Great Whore of Babylon described in Revelation chapter 17 and Isaiah chapter 47; the dragon of canto xi with the beast from the sea of Revelation chapter 13. Furthermore, Spenser follows the book's narrative pattern: Redcross defeats the dragon as Christ destroys the beast in Revelation. Obviously the imagery, allegory, and parallels of *The Faerie Queene* are far more complex than that, and some of them will be more fully explored later; but for the moment it is enough to indicate the extent of biblical source-material in the greatest epic of the century.

---

[62] Cornelius Tacitus (AD *c*.56–*c*.117), wrote the *Annals*, covering AD 14–68, and the *Histories*, on AD 68–96, both periods of instability and corruption.

Spenser's use of Christian writing is obvious enough, even if interpretation of it has varied widely, but Shakespeare's is much less so. However, a convincing demonstration has been made of his debt to the medieval mystery cycles. Performances of the Coventry cycle were given up to 1579, when Shakespeare was 14, and it is likely that he would have seen some of them. Even if he did not, he was probably familiar with some of the other major cycles. The Passion sequence of the plays, leading from the conspiracy to capture Jesus, through his trial, to the Crucifixion, is paralleled by the death of Humphrey of Gloucester in one of Shakespeare's earliest history plays, 2 Henry VI. This reading is unavoidably speculative; but if it is correct it would help to explain both Shakespeare's early grasp of dramatic effect and the response to it of his audience.[63]

This section does not attempt to provide a complete genealogy of source-material for Elizabethan literature, for even if this were possible the result would be tedious and unilluminating: it sets out rather to indicate the variety of sources upon which writers could draw. These were not always easily compatible with one another: pagan Greeks and Romans were not obvious models for Christians; chivalric ideals were not exactly identical with Ciceronian. Yet the sources could be, and were, combined; and the tensions between them gave the plays and poems of the time freshness and edge. Obviously no literature springs from the imagination of writers without any reference to predecessors, and what matters is the way in which sources and tradition are used. Sixteenth-century authors were schooled— literally—in the doctrine of imitation, which, effectively used, gave their work an exceptional range and power.[64]

5. 'FEIGNING NOTABLE IMAGES'

The leading poets and critics of Elizabeth's last two decades had no doubt that poetry was intended to teach moral and political lessons. George Puttenham, in The Arte of English Poesie, drew a parallel between the arts of the poet and of the courtier. The poet at Court must retain the 'profession of a very courtier, which is in plain terms, cunningly to be able to dissemble'.[65] Admittedly, he went on to say that in England the courtly poet needed to dissemble only in his art and not in his conduct; but no one familiar with the Court of Elizabeth was likely to have been deceived by

[63] Jones, The Origins of Shakespeare, ch. 2.

[64] Jardine and Grafton, ' "Studied for action" ', passim, for an account of the way in which Elizabethan scholars and gentlemen read and imitated classical authors.

[65] Ed. G. D. Willcock and A. Walker (Cambridge, 1936; originally published 1589), 299 and passim.

that. Philip Sidney asserted that 'it is that feigning notable images of virtues, vices, or what else, with that delightful teaching, which must be the right note to know a poet by'. Of all kinds of poetry the best, according to Sidney, was the heroical: 'For as the image of each action stirreth and instructeth the mind, so the lofty image of such worthies most inflameth the mind with desire to be worthy, and informs with counsel how to be worthy.'[66] Spenser's 'Letter to Ralegh', appended to *The Faerie Queene*, claimed that he had written with two ends in view: 'to fashion a gentleman or noble person in vertuous and gentle discipline', and to praise Elizabeth, for 'in that Faery Queene I meane glory in my general intention, but in my particular I conceive the most excellent and glorious person of our sovereign the Queen, and her kingdom in Faery land'.[67] Neither Sidney nor Spenser consistently followed their proclaimed programmes, either in *Arcadia* or in *The Faerie Queene*, and there is much more to their works than didactic allegory; but however much these purposes may be obscured or, at times apparently forgotten, they remain important. Playwrights, by contrast, generally avoided pointing explicit moral and political lessons, for it was too dangerous to do this on an open stage. However, since a great many of the plays of Shakespeare, Marlowe, Chapman, Jonson, and others were concerned with kings and Courts, with noble men and noble women, political and social implications were inevitably present.

Sir John Harington, writing after Elizabeth's death, said of her, somewhat selectively that

Her mind was oftime like the gentle air that cometh from the westerly point in a summer's morn; 'twas sweet and refreshing to all round her. Her speech did win all affections, and her subjects did try to show all love to her commands; for she would say, 'her state did require her to command what she knew her people would willingly do from their own love to her'.[68]

Here was a classic statement of rule by queenly love. Panegyrics of Elizabeth celebrated the love and praise of subjects for their Queen as well as her love for them; but the praise and adoration involved more than simple eulogy. Both in the shows put on in London in 1559 and in the much more sophisticated allegories of Spenser, the panegyrics contained a pattern of

---

[66] Philip Sidney, *An Apology for Poetry* (1st edn. 1595. I have used the edn. by Geoffrey Shepherd, Manchester, 1973), 103, 119.

[67] Edmund Spenser, 'A Letter of the Authors', written to Sir Walter Ralegh, in *Poetical Works*, 407.

[68] *Letters . . . of Sir John Harington*, 122, quoted in Stephen Greenblatt, *Renaissance Self-Fashioning*, 168.

advice: Elizabeth was praised for her qualities and gently told what those qualities should be.[69]

The connections between love, the ceremonies of adoration, and political success were well understood. Sidney's *Arcadia* is a story of the loves of two young princes for the beautiful daughters of Basilius, Duke of Arcadia. Yet, according to Sidney's great friend Fulke Greville, the author's 'intent and scope was to turn the barren philosophy precepts into pregnant images of life, and in them . . . lively to represent the growth, state and declination of princes, change of government and laws, vicissitudes of sedition, faction, succession, . . . with all other errors or alterations in public affairs . . .'.[70] Sidney himself knew the value of ceremony: when, in the last book of the *Arcadia*, Euarchus, King of Macedonia, arrives to settle the disturbances, he 'did wisely consider the people to be naturally taken with exterior shows far more than with inward consideration of the material points' and 'would leave nothing which might be either an armour or ornament unto him; and in these pompous ceremonies he well knew a secret of government much to consist'.[71]

The ceremonies of adoration developed slowly during the first half of Elizabeth's reign. They were of course evident at its beginning, but with Sir Henry Lee's devising of the Accession Day Tilts in 1571 the cult began to grow into a distinctive pattern, and by the time of Anjou's visits in 1579–81 the full pageantry and symbolism of the Elizabethan tournaments could be displayed.[72] The symbolic apparatus of royal portraiture developed at about the same time. Early portraits of the Queen were not much different from those of her father and her brother. Henry VIII had been portrayed as both David and as Solomon; Edward, appropriately, as Solomon, David's son. In one of the most striking portraits of the time—by an unknown artist— Henry is shown on his deathbed, handing the succession to Edward, who presides over the collapse of the pope in the foreground and the destruction

---

[69] For the coronation procession through London see above, Ch. 7 s. 1.

[70] Fulke Greville, *A Dedication to Sir Philip Sidney*, in *The Prose Works of Fulke Greville, Lord Brooke*, ed. John Gouws (Oxford, 1986), 10. Greville wrote between 1610 and 1612, and may have attributed to Sidney views which he himself had come to hold under James I. The work has until lately been incorrectly called *The Life of . . . Sir Philip Sidney*.

[71] Sir Philip Sidney, *The Countess of Pembroke's Arcadia*, ed. Maurice Evans (Harmondsworth, 1977), Bk. v, ch. 4, pp. 806–7. There are two versions of the *Arcadia*: the *Old Arcadia*, not published for four centuries, is fairly short and less moralistic than its successor, *The Countess of Pembroke's Arcadia*, which was never finished. The published version, 1591, consists of Sidney's revised version of the first two and a half books joined onto the second half of the *Old Arcadia*.

[72] Above pp. 414–16, for tournaments.

of popish images in the distance (Plate 1). This traditional, biblical imagery was again adopted at the accession of Elizabeth, after an intermission under Mary. In Foxe's *Book of Martyrs* Elizabeth is pictured as a descendant of the Emperor Constantine, revered in Protestant mythology as the hero who established the authority of the secular arm over the pope; and in the frontispiece of the *Bishops' Bible* of 1568 she is shown, in a manner reminiscent of the pictures of Henry VIII, supported by the four virtues—Justice, Mercy, Fortitude, and Prudence—while on the title-page she is presented as Hope (Plate 2b). She was also represented as Deborah, Judith, and Esther from the Old Testament, and as 'The Woman Clothed with the Sun' from Revelation; and certain elements of the iconography of the Virgin Mary were transferred to Elizabeth, especially after her death. However, towards the middle of the reign there developed a more secular, and also more elaborate, form of royal portraiture. This is first marked by the publication in 1577 of John Dee's *General and Rare Memorials Pertayning to the Perfect Arte of Navigation*, whose title-page shows Elizabeth at the helm of the ship Christendom[73] (Plate 4a). While the older, biblical tradition of portraiture continued until the end of the reign, it was overshadowed by a succession of symbolic portraits, mostly based upon classical mythology. Elizabeth was shown with a sieve, casting her as a Vestal Virgin; with an ermine, the symbol of purity; with her feet on the map of England, storm clouds behind her and sunshine ahead; and with a rainbow, the symbol of peace. In the latter years of the reign it was fashionable to portray her as Cynthia or Diana, both embodiments of the same goddess, representing the moon and the seas, and also both beauty and chastity[74] (Plate 4b).

Elizabeth's appearance in these portraits was modelled on a pattern derived from the Petrarchan ideal of womanhood: her golden hair, her fair complexion, the red and white roses in her cheeks, the emblems of the sieve and the ermine, were all typical. She used the Petrarchan convention of the chaste beloved to form her own self-image, attracting suitors but holding them at a distance, and wrote verses in the style of Petrarch's imitators:

> I grieve and dare not show my discontent,
> I love and yet am forced to seem to hate,
>   ·   ·   ·   ·   ·
> I am and not, I freeze and yet am burned.[75]

[73] Below, Ch. 13 s. 2, for further comment on Dee.

[74] The identification of the sieve with chastity is derived from the story of Tuccia, the Vestal Virgin, who carried water in a sieve from the Tiber to the Temple without spilling a drop. The ermine was believed to prefer death to the dirtying of its white fur, and hence became a symbol of purity. In the person of Cynthia or Diana, Elizabeth could be credited with power over the cosmos.

[75] Forster, *The Icy Fire*, ch. 4, esp. p. 129.

From 1579 the poetic image of the Queen began to take shape, beginning in the April eclogue from Spenser's *The Shepheardes Calendar*:

> Of fayre *Elisa* be your silver song,
>> that blessed wight;
> The flowre of Virgins, may shee florish long,
>> In princely plight.
> For shee is *Syrinx* daughter without spotte.
> Which *Pan* the shepheard God of her begot:
>> So sprong her grace
>> Of heavenly race,
> No mortall blemishe may her blotte.[76]

Spenser's poem of praise was followed by a host of others, among them Sir John Davies's *Hymn to Astraea*, a rather pedestrian conceit in which each line starts with letters which, read downwards, form the words 'Elisabetha Regina'.

The creation of panegyrics for Elizabeth was, however, made difficult by her sex. Men were considered, at any rate by men, to be superior to women; and the virtues generally attributed to women—modesty, courtesy, silence, obedience—suited them to private life rather than public. During the reign of Mary, John Knox proclaimed in his *First Blast of the Trumpet against the Monstrous Regiment of Women* (1558) that the rule of women was 'monstriferous'; and although he was persuaded after the accession of Elizabeth to moderate his tone, he refused to retract his 'principal point'. In 1559 Calvin tried, in a letter to William Cecil, to moderate the Queen's anger against Knox. He wrote that two years previously he had had a conversation with Knox, who asked his opinion about female government: 'I frankly answered', said Calvin, 'that because it was a deviation from the primitive and established order of nature, it ought to be held as a judgement on man for his dereliction of his rights, just like slavery'; this was hardly likely to be helpful. Even John Aylmer, Bishop of London, attempting both to reconcile Protestants to the idea of a female ruler and Elizabeth to the English followers of Calvin, was tepid in his advocacy. If rulers were chosen by lot or suffrage, rather than by God, then, he wrote, 'I would not indeed [wish] that any woman should stand in the election, but men only: for I say with Aristotle, that . . . the male is in all likelihood meeter to rule, than the

---

[76] Spenser, *The Shepheardes Calendar* in *Poetical Works*, 423. Syrinx was a nymph of Arcady who, on being pursued by Pan, turned into a reed from which Pan made his pipe. According to Spenser's anonymous commentator, E.K., the shepherd singer of the eclogue did not intend to portray Pan and Syrinx merely as 'poetical gods', but to emphasize Elizabeth's divine origin, with Pan representing Henry VIII and Syrinx presumably as the 'immaculate conception' of Elizabeth: Anne Boleyn is written out of the script.

woman in many respects.' This was far from being whole-hearted support for a female monarch; but at least Aylmer accepted the notion that if God should send one, she must be obeyed.[77]

How could men be persuaded to revere and obey her? The strategy devised was to invoke the idea of the 'exceptional woman', endowed by God, like the prophetess Deborah, with qualities above those of ordinary women. Using the conventions of courtly love, Elizabeth herself admitted to 'sexly weakness'; but she also claimed to have the heart of a man, and indeed rhetorically manipulated both the supposedly 'feminine' virtues required of her as a woman and the supposedly 'masculine' qualities required of her as a ruler.[78] However, this did not entirely exempt her from criticism. Towards the end of her reign, Robert Cecil justified keeping his correspondence with James VI of Scotland secret from Elizabeth on the ground that her 'age and orbity, joined to the jealousy of her sex' would make her angry if she knew about it.[79]

The tension created by doubts over female rule and by the necessity of praising Elizabeth appears even in *The Faerie Queene*. In Book IV, Prince Arthur's squire, Timias, falls in love with Belphoebe, who 'figures' Elizabeth as a woman, as Gloriana 'figures' her as monarch. As a result of unrequited love, Timias withdraws from the world into a wood, where he is finally discovered by Arthur, 'Spending his daies in dolour and despair', having carved the name of Belphoebe on every available tree. The episode has been taken by some to represent Ralegh's 'courtship' and subsequent fall from favour; but even without that specific parallel, the effect of Belphoebe/Elizabeth's feminine charm upon the young knight suggests some doubt about the safety of adoring Elizabeth.[80]

The difficulty of reconciling the image of ideal woman with that of ideal ruler is presented by Spenser in the next book of *The Faerie Queene*. The hero of Book V, Sir Artegal, who stands for Justice, meets an Amazon, Radigund, and unwisely promises her that if she defeats him in battle, he will obey her. They fight, Radigund conquers Artegal by guile, and he not only allows himself to be disarmed, but also puts on woman's clothes:

> Of all the ornaments of knightly name,
> With which whylome he gotten had great fame:
> Instead whereof she made him to be dight

---

[77] Helen Anne Cobb, 'Representations of Elizabeth: three sites of ambiguity and contradiction' (unpublished D. Phil. thesis, University of Oxford, 1989), 28–33 for the quotations from Knox, Calvin, and Aylmer, and part i, *passim*, for the general problem of the woman ruler. I am most grateful to Dr Cobb for allowing me to read and to use her thesis, and for much helpful discussion.

[78] Ibid. 36–7.   [79] Ibid. 107.   [80] *The Faerie Queene*, IV. vii, stanzas 36–47.

> In womans weedes, that is to manhood shame,
> And put before his lap a napron white,
> In stead of Curiets and bases fit for fight.

This appalling fate is the consequence of allowing women freedom:

> Such is the crueltie of womenkynd,
> When they have shaken off the shamefast band,
> With which wise Nature did them strongly bynd,
> T'obay the heasts of mans well ruling hand,
> That then all rule and reason they withstand,
> To purchase a licentious libertie.
> But vertuous women wisely understand,
> That they were borne to base humilitie,
> Unlesse the heavens them lift to lawfull soveraintie.

The last line is of course crucial, for it allows the rule of Elizabeth, and also the rescue of Artegal by the female warrior, Britomart, who eventually marries him. She is the 'Magnificke Virgin', the mythical ancestress of Elizabeth, or Gloriana, whom she prefigures. After freeing Artegal and his fellow-prisoners, Britomart briefly rules in Radigund's place until her hero recovers, and then hands over authority to men.[81] One might say that the problems are just about resolved: the horrors of female rule have been revealed and then overcome by a woman who, through her marriage to Artegal, begins the royal line which eventually issues in Elizabeth. Nevertheless, this passage, like the previous one, raises doubts about Spenser's success in reconciling his general principle of female inferiority with specific endorsement of Elizabeth.

Sir Walter Ralegh was much more explicit in expressing disillusionment. Like other courtiers, he contributed his share of panegyric, figuring Elizabeth as Diana, the moon goddess, or as her *alter ego*, Cynthia; but in the *21st (and last) Book of the Ocean to Cynthia*, a poem that remained unpublished until the twentieth century, Ralegh's mood was sombre. Whether the poem was written after he had been imprisoned in the Tower following his marriage with Elizabeth Throckmorton, or whether he wrote it during his next stay in the Tower, under James I, does not affect the central point: that Ralegh was thrown into despair by his Queen. Admittedly, Elizabeth is praised:

> Such force her angellike aparance had
> To master distance, tyme, or crueltye,
> Such art to greve, and after to make gladd,
> Such feare in love, such love in majestye.

---

[81] Ibid. v. v–vii.

> My weery lymes her memory imbalmed,
> My darkest wayes her eyes make cleare as day.
> What stormes so great but Cinthias beames apeased?
> What rage so feirce that loue could not allay?

Then the reader is warned of the dangers hidden in Elizabeth's love and in loving her, for although she is capable of calming fear and allaying rage, she can be implacable. Total disillusionment sets in:

> Twelve yeares intire I wasted in this warr,
> Twelve yeares of my most happy younger dayes,
> Butt I in them, and they now wasted ar,
> Of all which past the sorrow only stayes.
>
> .   .   .   .   .
>
> But leve her prayse, speak thow of nought but wo,
> Write on the tale that Sorrow bydds thee tell,
> Strive to forgett, and care no more to know,
> Thy cares are known, by knowinge thos too well
> Discribe her now as shee appeeres to thee,
> Not as shee did appeere in dayes fordunn;
> In love thos things that weare no more may bee,
> For fancy seildume ends wher it begunn.[82]

The Ocean to Cynthia reveals a greater depth of despair than any other Court poem to Elizabeth. This is not surprising, for Ralegh had staked all his fortune upon the Queen's favour, had played the 'love game' to the full, and was thrown to the ground by the withdrawal of her favour.

Curiously disturbing reflections upon contemporary attitudes to Elizabeth are aroused by setting side by side the text of *A Midsummer Night's Dream* and the account of one of his own dreams by Simon Forman, Elizabethan astrologer and healer. In the play, Titania, whose name links her with Diana and thus indirectly with Elizabeth, is humiliated by Oberon, whose enchantments lead her to fall in love with Bottom wearing his ass's head. Direct reference to Elizabeth is carefully warded off by Oberon's account of Cupid aiming his bow at 'a fair vestal, throned by the west' and missing her. The 'fair vestal' plainly stands for Elizabeth, and we are then told that

> . . . The imperial votress passed on
> In maiden meditation, fancy-free.

---

[82] *The Poems of Sir Walter Ralegh*, ed. Latham, pp. 25–43; quotations from 'The Ocean to Cynthia' are from ll. 112–23, 213–20. It is likely that the '21st book' and a fragment of the '22nd' were all that Ralegh wrote of this poem; his numbering seems to have been a conceit.

That seems safe enough. However, Forman's dream on the night of 23 January 1597, a little after the most likely date for the first performance of *A Midsummer Night's Dream*, has strange echoes of the play. He dreamed that he was with the Queen, 'a little elderly woman in a coarse, white petticoat, all unready'; they walked through lanes and came to a meadow with many people in it including two men quarreling, one of whom was a weaver, a tall man with a reddish beard, 'distract of his wits', who took hold of the Queen and tried to kiss her. At this Forman took her away and they walked on, the Queen's clothes trailing in the dirt. He asked her if she would let him wait upon her, to which she agreed, and he then said to her: ' "I mean to wait *upon* you and not under you, that I might make this belly a little bigger to carry up this smock and coats out of the dirt." ' The weaver 'distract of his wits' sounds very like Bottom, and the sexual innuendo about waiting 'upon her' not unlike Titania's attempt to seduce Bottom with the roles reversed. The echoes thrown out by the play and the dream together suggest that male attitudes to Elizabeth may have involved more than simple reverence to a virgin queen.[83]

Elizabeth used fear as well as love to gain her ends. Sir John Harington, after writing of the mutual affection between the Queen and her subjects, continued: 'Surely she [Elizabeth] did play well her tables to gain obedience thus without constraint: again, she could put forth such alterations, when obedience was lacking, as left no doubtings whose daughter she was.'[84] The devotion was apparent; but so was the capacity to inspire fear.

The literature of praise and adoration for the Queen was genuine and pervasive; ceremony and art preserved the great and necessary illusion of her successful rule. Nevertheless, the picture was rather more complicated than that, strains and tensions being revealed that were not at first apparent; for her subjects' view of Elizabeth did not conform entirely to the idealized image presented in her portraits, Court ceremonies, or government propaganda. There was, for instance, a gap between the realities of her policy and the account given in *The Faerie Queene* of the destruction of Geryoneo, Grantorto, and the Catholic monster. In 1596, when England faced a powerful Spain and rebellion in Ireland, the Queen's response was not that of Arthur and Artegal, and for all his praise of her, Spenser knew that perfectly well: his aim was to urge her to follow the course taken by his

[83] Louis Montrose, ' "Shaping Fantasies": figurations of gender and power in Elizabethan culture', *Representations*, 1/2 (1983), 61–94; Shakespeare, *A Midsummer Night's Dream*, II. i. 155–74.
[84] Greenblatt, *Renaissance Self-Fashioning*, 169. Above, p. 424.

knightly heroes. The praise was real; but beneath it there sometimes lurked anxiety and frustration.

6. 'TO FASHION A GENTLEMAN'

In writing *The Faerie Queene* Spenser announced that he intended not only to praise Elizabeth but also 'to fashion a gentleman . . . in vertuous and gentle discipline'.[85] The production of role models for noblemen and gentlemen had long been a favourite occupation of sixteenth-century writers, their ideals based upon the writings of Cicero and Castiglione. The first part of Cicero's *De officiis*, his guide to duty, describes the four cardinal virtues—Wisdom, Justice, Fortitude, and Temperance—while part two is concerned with ways of securing advantage; part three provides guidance on conduct when duty and expediency are opposed to one another. This third part is lavishly illustrated with examples to show that 'What is morally wrong can never be advantageous': a comforting thought. Its emphasis lies upon the duty of public service; and it became a handbook for sixteenth-century courtiers, administrators, and statesmen, ironically so, for Cicero, now the mentor of servants of monarchy, had been a republican opponent of tyranny.

The other principal mentor in the century was Baldassare Castiglione, whose *Il Cortegiano*, written in Italy, takes the form of a fictional dialogue supposedly held at the Court of Urbino. Translated by Sir Thomas Hoby, Burghley's brother-in-law, *The Book of the Courtier* (1561) became the most influential guide to courtly conduct of its day. Basing himself upon Aristotle and Cicero, Castiglione presents an ideal picture of the courtier as skilled in all the courtly arts of dancing, music, learning, and love, as well as in war; his objective must be to please the prince so that he may give frank advice which the ruler will heed. In short, although Courts might be corrupt, the true courtier must be a paragon of all-round virtue.

In life the model held up to aspiring Elizabethan courtiers was Sir Philip Sidney. Thomas Nashe, writing in 1589, described a conversation that he had had with 'many extraordinary gentlemen, of most excellent parts, . . . touching the several qualities required in *Castalion's* Courtier . . . [and] this was the upshot, that England . . . never saw anything more singular than worthy Sir Philip Sidney'[86] (Plate 5c). Sidney's life, moulded and presented by imagination and art, became the ideal of nobility and courtliness; the story of his death was told by his friend Fulke Greville as an example to all; and his funeral provided a massive and expensive spectacle,

[85] Spenser, 'A Letter of the Authors', *Poetical Works*, 407.
[86] *The Works of Thomas Nashe*, ed. Ronald B. McKerrow (Oxford, 1966), i. 7.

the pictorial roll of the procession reaching a length of 38 feet, with 344 figures. Greville wrote, several years later, that Sidney's conduct and the reaction of his friends to his death showed that 'greatness of heart is not dead everywhere', and that 'war is both a fitter mould to fashion it than peace can be'.[87] Chivalry, played out on the tournament field and later in the battles of the Low Countries, was the training ground and the ideal for the nobility of Sidney's generation. For Sidney, embracing the code of chivalry did not involve the rejection of Christian humanism, and he tried both in his life and in his writings to expound a moral code that combined the two. His *Arcadia* tells the story of two princes, Pyrocles and Musidorus, who fall in love with the daughters of the Duke of Arcadia, pursue them by disguising themselves, one as an Amazon warrior, the other as a shepherd, attempt to seduce them, are tried for the murder of their father and for seduction of the princesses, and are finally saved by the sudden and improbable recovery of the Duke. The princes are models of chivalry performing valiant deeds, but also flawed models, who serve as negative examples and have to learn that passion must not be allowed to overcome virtue and reason.[88]

While Sidney expounds his moral theme under cover of a pastoral romance, intended to entertain as well as to instruct, Spenser sets out to provide in *The Faerie Queene* more elaborate and explicit models of conduct for the nobility of his day. In the opening 'Letter to Ralegh' he announces that he would treat of the twelve virtues named by Aristotle, assigning to each one a knightly exemplar.[89] Redcross Knight stands for holiness, Guyon for Temperance, Artegal for Justice, and so on. Whereas in Sidney's epic the Christian message is sublimated in a pagan world, Spenser is explicit. The first book tells of the pilgrimage of the Redcross Knight, accompanied by the lady Una, riding on an ass and leading a lamb, and symbolizing the true Church. At the end of the book Redcross is renamed St George and vouchsafed a vision of heaven:

> The new *Hierusalem*, that God has built
> For those to dwell in, that are chosen his,
> His chosen people purg'd from sinfull guilt
> With precious bloud, which cruelly was spilt.[90]

But Redcross only achieves this vision after he has purged his sins by repentance and undergone a course of moral surgery which involves fasting,

---

[87] Greville, *Dedication to Sidney*, 79.   [88] Above, n. 71.

[89] Spenser, *Poetical Works*, 407–8. Spenser only completed six out of a projected twenty-four books of *The Faerie Queene*. The relation between the 'Letter' and the poem is often confused: see C. S. Lewis, *Spenser's Images of Life* (Cambridge, 1907), 137–40.

[90] *The Faerie Queene*, I. x, st. 57.

removal of corrupted flesh with hot pincers, and whipping, followed by bathing in salt water,

> In which his torment often was so great,
> That like a Lyon he would cry and rore,
> And rend his flesh, and his own synewes eat.[91]

A similar pattern is followed by all Spenser's heroes. Although they are valiant and perform noble chivalric deeds, they are, like all men, subject to sin; and their weaknesses are revealed and purged in the course of the narrative.

While Sidney and Spenser elaborate the model of conduct represented by the noble, Christian warrior and courtier, who achieved his goal by the pursuit of virtue, Shakespeare presents another in his *Henry IV* and *Henry V* plays. Early in *1 Henry IV*, when Hal is left alone after Falstaff and his other disreputable companions have left the stage, he announces his intentions in a soliloquy:

> I know you all, and will a while uphold
> The unyok'd humour of your idleness.
> Yet herein will I imitate the sun,
> Who doth permit the base contagious clouds
> To smother up his beauty from the world,
> That, when he please again to be himself,
> Being wanted he may be more wond'red at
> By breaking through the foul and ugly mists
> Of vapours that did seem to strangle him.
> .   .   .   .   .
> I'll so offend, to make offence a skill,
> Redeeming time when men think least I will.[92]

Like Richard III and Iago, Hal is promising to offend, but doing so in order to serve good ends. In Part 2, Warwick allays the King's fears about his son and explains what is going on:

> The Prince but studies his companions
> Like a strange tongue, wherein, to gain the language,
> 'Tis needful that the most immodest word
> Be look'd upon and learnt; which once attain'd,
> Your Highness knows, comes to no further use
> But to be known and hated. So, like gross terms,
> The Prince will, in the perfectness of time,
> Cast off his followers, and their memory
> Shall as a pattern or a measure live

---

[91] *The Faerie Queene*, I. x, st. 28.   [92] *1 Henry IV*, I. ii. 190–212.

> By which his Grace must mete the lives of other,
> Turning past evils to advantages.[93]

At the end of the play Hal does exactly as Warwick has prophesied, when, after the death of his father, he meets Falstaff, who greets him royally. Hal, now King, replies:

> I know thee not, old man. Fall to thy prayers.
> How ill white hairs becomes a fool and jester!

He goes on to spell out his betrayal:

> Presume not that I am the thing I was;
> For God doth know, so shall the world perceive,
> That I have turn'd away my former self;
> So will I those that kept me company.
>
> . . . I banish thee, on pain of death,
> As I have done the rest of my misleaders,
> Not to come near our person by ten mile.[94]

In *Henry V* Falstaff dies of grief and Fluellen remarks at a later moment in the play that Henry has killed him when he 'turned away the fat knight with the great-belly doublet'.[95] Unlike the chivalric and moralized knights of Sidney and Spenser, and unlike Hotspur in *Henry IV*, Shakespeare's Hal is a Machiavellian schemer, who has planned from the beginning to betray his friends when they are no longer of use to him.

Shakespeare was not alone in presenting a calculating rather than a chivalric hero. The followers of the new Tacitean history, like Sir John Hayward, were concerned more with how things were done than with the morality of the actions. In *Sejanus*, Jonson, basing himself heavily on Tacitus, deals almost entirely with the rise and fall of scheming politicians, of whom Tiberius is the most ruthless and the most successful; the noble characters in the play are, without exception, ineffective. Chivalric knights and Machiavellian schemers could coexist in the culture of the Court for a time, but by 1603 chivalry was coming to seem outmoded, and writings on the Court tended to stress dissimulation and deceit more than had Castiglione; by the end of the following reign the chivalric ideal was near to death.

7. 'DEGREE, PRIORITY, AND PLACE'

The necessity for order and hierarchy was constantly proclaimed during the sixteenth century in visual images, in sermons and homilies, and in poems,

---

[93] *2 Henry IV*, IV. iv. 68–78.   [94] Ibid. v. v. 47–65.   [95] *Henry V*, IV. vii. 49–50.

romances, and plays. Costume announced the social status of men and women, statutes and proclamations minutely regulating their dress according to their station in life. Portraits of noblemen and courtiers were devised almost as carefully as those of the Queen to project a proper sense of power and position: Leicester appeared as the warrior courtier, Burghley as the sage councillor (Plates 5*a*, *b*). Tombs in cathedrals and parish churches testified to the honour of great families. When, early in the reign of Elizabeth, some of these were defaced by iconoclasts, a royal proclamation forbade such destruction, insisting that it was offensive to 'all noble and gentle hearts' and that 'the true understanding of divers families in this realm . . . is thereby so darkened as the true course of their inheritance may be hereafter interrupted'[96] (Plate 9*b*). Great houses, often dominating the landscape from hills and ridges, proclaimed the power and riches of their owners. Although Bacon urged that 'houses are built to live in, and not to look on', nothing could have been less true of the prodigy houses of his day, and it is significant that he felt the need to insist upon his point[97] (Plates 8*a*, *b*, 9*a*).

Tracts, sermons, and homilies expounded the notion of the great chain of being that stretched from the Almighty to the lowest animals and in which each man had his immutable place: 'Every degree of people, in their vocation, calling, and office, hath appointed to them their duty and order. Some are in high degree, some in low . . .'.[98] The Elizabethan preacher William Perkins insisted that 'God hath given these gods upon earth [kings and their lawful deputies]' their power and authority, and that disobedience to their commands is committed by 'profane men stirred up by the Devil'.[99]

In Book V of *The Faerie Queene* Spenser tells how the knight, Sir Artegal, representing Justice, encounters an assembly of people gathered round a giant holding a balance in his hand, with which, the giant claims, he will weigh the surplus portions of the world and restore each to his own:

> For why, he sayd, they all unequall were,
> And had encroched uppon others share,
> Like as the sea (which plaine he shewed there)
> Had worne the earth, so did the fire the aire,
> So all the rest did others parts empaire.
> And so were realmes and nations run awry.

[96] *Proclamations*, iii, no. 469 (p. 146).

[97] Sir Francis Bacon, *The Essays or Counsels, Civill and Morall*, ed. Michael Kiernan (Oxford, 1985), no. 45, 'Of Building'.

[98] E. M. W. Tillyard, *Shakespeare's History Plays* (London, 1944), 19, quoting from *An Exhortation Concerning Good Order and Obedience*.

[99] C. H. George and K. George, *The Protestant Mind of the English Reformation* (Princeton, NJ, 1961), 216.

> All which he undertooke for to repaire,
> In sort as they were formed aunciently:
> And all things would reduce unto equality.

Artegal points out that he is utterly mistaken,

> For at the first they all created were
> In goodly measure, by their Makers might,
> And weighed out in ballaunces so nere,
> That not a dram was missing of their right,
> . . . . . .
>
> Such heavenly justice doth among them raine,
> That every one doe know their certaine bound,
> In which they doe these many yeares remaine
> . . . . . .
>
> All change is perillous, and all chaunce unsound.
> Therefore leave off to weigh them all againe,
> Till we may be assur'd they shall their course retain.

One cannot help feeling that Artegal's answers to the giant do not fully meet his arguments; but whatever the relative strengths of the proponents in debate, the giant soon meets his appointed fate when Artegal throws him from the cliff into the sea. When his followers then attack, Artegal, disdaining to soil his hands with such base blood, sends his assistant, Talus the iron man, to destroy them with his flail: while a knight would fight another knight, a giant, or a dragon, he would not condescend to destroy the rabble himself.[100]

Famous lines upon the theme of hierarchy are spoken by Ulysses in *Troilus and Cressida*, and are often quoted to illustrate the devotion of Elizabethans to the existing order. When the Greek commanders lament the failure of the siege of Troy, which has withstood their attacks for seven years, Ulysses attributes it to the divisions in the Greek camp rather than to the strength of the Trojans:

> And, look, how many Grecian tents do stand
> Hollow upon this plain, so many hollow factions.

The withdrawal of Achilles and his Myrmidons has led to an infection of disrespect; degree and hierarchy are neglected, to the danger of all:

> The heavens themselves, the planets and this centre,
> Observe degree, priority and place,
> Insisture, course, proportion, season, form.
> . . . . . .
>
> ... O, when degree is shaked,
> Which is the ladder to all high designs,

---

[100] *The Faerie Queene*, v. ii, stanzas 29–54.

> The enterprise is sick! How could communities,
> Degrees in schools and brotherhoods in cities,
> Peaceful commerce from dividable shores,
> The primogenitive and due of birth,
> Prerogative of age, crowns, sceptres, laurels,
> But by degree, stand in authentic place?
> Take but degree away, untune that string,
> And, hark, what discord follows![101]

Certainly, these words reflect a view of nature and society held by many of Shakespeare's contemporaries; but they should not be taken as his own view nor as the unanimously held opinion of all Elizabethans. The lines are spoken by a man renowned as a subtle and persuasive manipulator, whose intention is, first, to blame Achilles for the misfortunes of the Greeks, and later, by rigging a ballot, to prevent Achilles from having the glory of fighting with Hector:

> . . . make a lott'ry,
> And by device let blockish Ajax draw
> The sort to fight with Hector; among ourselves
> Give him allowance for the better man.[102]

The whole play proclaims the absence, in a fallen world, of that order which Ulysses claims to uphold; and the one character who maintains its principles, Hector, is cruelly and treacherously murdered.

However, distinctions between gentlemen and commons were generally fixed and recognized as desirable, even if attitudes were more ambivalent than they appear at first sight. Differences of rank at the upper end of society were less clearly marked and harder to preserve. In 1579, at the time of the debate over the Anjou marriage, Philip Sidney, who opposed the match, became involved in a personal quarrel with one of its supporters, the Earl of Oxford. While Sidney was playing tennis one day, Oxford entered the court and ordered him to leave. Sidney gave a dignified refusal and high words were exchanged: Oxford called Sidney 'puppy', and Sidney replied that 'all the world knows puppies are gotten by dogs and children by men'. The Privy Council tried to reconcile them, but failed, and handed the matter over to the Queen. She saw Sidney and put before him 'the difference in degree between earls and gentlemen; the respect inferiors ought [=owed] to their superiors; and the necessity in princes to maintain their own creations, as degrees descending between the people's licentiousness and the anointed sovereignty of crowns'. She went on to complain that 'the

---

[101] *Troilus and Cressida*, I. iii.

[102] Ibid. I. iii. 369–72. For a traditional account of *Troilus and Cressida* see E. M. W. Tillyard, *The Elizabethan World Picture* (London, 1943), chs. 2, 7.

gentleman's neglect of the nobility taught the peasant to insult upon both'. Sidney's reply cannot have been wholly satisfactory to the Queen, for he told her that although Oxford was a great lord by birth, 'yet was he no lord over him', 'for the difference of degrees between free men could not challenge any other homage than precedency'. He went on to praise Henry VIII, 'who gave the gentry free and safe appeal to his feet against the oppression of the grandees'.[103] 'Degree, priority, and place' were a good deal less secure in the Elizabethan world order than, according to theories of the great chain of being, they should have been.

In a world governed by order and degree nothing could be worse than division and disobedience. The political anxieties of the middle and later years of the sixteenth century, in particular the constant uncertainty about the succession to the throne, focused attention upon the lessons of English history and the need to avoid a repetition of earlier strife. One of the earliest Elizabethan plays, *Gorbuduc*, first performed in 1561, describes the terrible consequences of a divided kingdom; its authors, Thomas Norton and Thomas Sackville, present Elizabeth with a direct and explicit warning about the dangers of leaving the succession undecided. It is not surprising that the play was reprinted in 1590, when the issue of the succession was again urgent. Nor is it surprising that Marlowe's *Edward II* and *The Massacre at Paris*, and Shakespeare's *Henry VI* sequence and *Richard III* should all have been written and performed at about this time. Shakespeare expresses the dangers of a divided kingdom in the opening scene of *3 Henry VI*, when Henry confronts York:

> K. HENRY. Thou factious Duke of York, descend my throne,
>   And kneel for grace and mercy at my feet;
> I am thy sovereign.
> YORK. I am thine.

Later in the play Henry tells of the consequences:

> O piteous spectacle! O bloody times!
>   Whilst lions war and battle for their dens,
> Poor harmless lambs abide their enmity.

And then he prophesies England's salvation by Henry Tudor:

> . . . If secret powers
> Suggest but truth to my divining thoughts
> This pretty lad will prove our country's bliss.[104]

---

[103] Greville, *Dedication*, ch. 6.   [104] *3 Henry VI*, I. i. 74–7; II. v. 73–5.

So indeed it proves at the conclusion of *Richard III*; but comforting as this resolution may have been, Elizabeth's refusal to name her successor was, in the light of these plays, far from reassuring.

Shakespeare's history plays, calling up England's past, appeal to patriotism as a defence of order. Gaunt's dying speech in *Richard II* is often taken as an affirmation of national pride:

> This royal throne of kings, this scept'red isle
> This earth of majesty, this seat of Mars,
> This other Eden, demi-paradise,
> This fortress built by Nature for herself
> Against infection and the hand of war,
> This happy breed of men, this little world,
> This precious stone set in the silver sea,
> Which serves it in the office of a wall
> .   .   .   .   .   .
>
> Is now leas'd out—I die pronouncing it—
> Like to a tenement or pelting farm.

Gaunt expresses, not pride, but shame that England

> Hath made a shameful conquest of itself

Amidst whispers of corruption at Elizabeth's Court and complaints against monopolies, his lament that the kingdom has been leased out may have had some contemporary meaning for his audience.[105]

Elizabethan attitudes—or, rather, the attitudes of some Elizabethans—towards rebellion were more complex than often supposed.[106] While the standard texts on government, such as *The Homily against Disobedience*, totally condemn resistance, advocate absolute obedience, and endlessly reiterate the dangers of allowing the feet to rule the head, the very strength of their language suggests some anxiety, and some literary works raise doubts. In *The New Arcadia* Philip Sidney expresses conventional views on revolt by the 'poorer sort'. The courtly dalliance of the two princes with their loves, and with Basilius' queen, is at one point interrupted by 'an unruly sort of clowns and other rebels which, like a violent flood, were carried they themselves knew not whither'. They are presented as entirely at odds among themselves, having no idea what they want: 'The peasants would have all the gentlemen destroyed; the citizens (especially such as cooks, barbers, and those other that live most on gentlemen) would but have them reformed.' They are confused and 'many-headed', and the princes—as

---

[105] *Richard II*, II. i. 31–68.

[106] For a rather different view on Shakespeare see Annabel Patterson, *Shakespeare and the Popular Voice* (Oxford, 1989), *passim*.

well, it would seem, as Sidney himself—treat them with disdain. A painter, who is swept along in the crowd, excited to see the action, has both hands cut off: 'And so', comments the author, 'the painter returned well skilled in wounds, but with never a hand to perform his skill.' The tone is cold-blooded, to say the least, and shows none of the sympathy towards the dispossessed which was characteristic of much writing in the reign of Edward VI.[107]

However, one major British theorist, George Buchanan, tutor to the young James VI of Scotland, asserts that rulers were established by the consent of the people, and that therefore the whole people, not merely the nobles, have the right to remove an oppressive ruler. Indeed, Buchanan even claims that a single individual has the right, in specific circumstances, to kill a tyrant. His writings were known in England, and seem to have had some influence in the circle of the Earl of Leicester, to which Sidney belonged. Sidney was certainly no friend to tyranny. Advising his brother Robert on foreign travel, he comments adversely upon the government of the Italian states, where, except for Venice, 'there is little . . . but tyrannous oppression, & servile yielding to them'.[108] Early in *The New Arcadia* Sidney describes the revolt of the Helots against the Lacedaemonians. The Helots 'were a kind of people who, having been of old freemen and possessioners, the Lacedaemonians had conquered them and laid not only tribute, but bondage upon them'. Lately, when the Lacedaemonians have become greedy and contemptuous, the Helots 'set themselves in arms'. Eventually, thanks to the intervention of the two heroes, an agreement is reached by which both sides are to be joined together in equality under the name of 'Laconians'.[109]

A more complex case is the revolt of Amphialus against Basilius in *The New Arcadia*. Describing the revolt, Sidney has the rebel leader declare that he is protesting, not against Duke Basilius, but against the delegation of all government to his officer, Philanax, and against the unsatisfactory arrangements made for the custody of Basilius' daughters. Amphialus puts forward his own claim to remedy the disorders of the realm by virtue of his being the next male heir and announces that when the realm is running to 'manifest ruin', the care of it 'did kindly appertain to those who, being subaltern magistrates and officers of the crown, were to be[?] employed as from the prince, so for the people'. His justification of rebellion is measured and in many ways convincing; but in the end, because his own motives are not pure (he is in love with one of the princesses), his rebellion fails.[110] The declara-

---

[107] Philip Sidney, *The New Arcadia*, Bk. II, chs. 25–7.
[108] *The Prose Works of Sir Philip Sidney*, ed. A. Feuillerat (Cambridge, 1962–3), iii. 127.
[109] Sidney, *The New Arcadia*, Bk. I, chs. 6, 7.   [110] Ibid. 453.

tion and the ultimate course of the revolt show the ambivalence of Sidney's attitudes. He uses the arguments employed by the Huguenots, with whom he was in sympathy, but then stops short of approving Amphialus' rebellion.

Sidney is unequivocal in his approval of monarchy. In Book IV of *New Arcadia*, when Basilius is thought to be dead, there is a debate about the form of government to be adopted. A few men recommend the 'Lacedaemonian government of few chosen senators; others, the Athenian, where the people's voice held the chief authority'; but these, says Sidney, are rather 'the discoursing sort of men than the active'; and those that 'went nearest the present case . . . were they that strove whom they should make prince'. Sidney dislikes those whom he calls 'discoursers', condemning Italians on the ground that 'from a tapster upwards they are all discoursers'.[111]

Spenser deals extensively with rebellion in Book V of *The Faerie Queene*. In fact, two rebellions are allegorically described: one is the revolt of the Irish against Elizabeth, the other of the Netherlands against Philip II. The first is unequivocally condemned, and is brutally repressed by Artegal and Talus; the other is approved and supported by Prince Arthur. Spenser was firmly committed to an active campaign against both the Irish rebels and the Catholic cause in Europe. In this he had become a principal mouthpiece of those politicians and soldiers, led first by Leicester and then by Essex, who urged on Elizabeth a more forward foreign policy.[112] In the last three cantos of Book V of *The Faerie Queene*, published in 1596, Spenser describes the actions of Prince Arthur in the Netherlands and Artegal in Ireland. The lady Belge has fallen under the tyranny of the giant Geryoneo; and Arthur, rather flatteringly representing Leicester, but also symbolizing knighthood and the ideal destiny of the English realm, comes to Belge's aid, slays Geryoneo and finally destroys a hideous monster lurking beneath an idol in the Church. The allegory is explicit, but of course Leicester's own exploits fell far short of this achievement and Spenser is not so much celebrating past events as pressing the Queen to take stronger action. Meanwhile, Artegal has gone off to rescue Irena, Ireland, from the tyrant Grantorto, Philip II under yet another name. Spenser, himself an officer and settler in Ireland, had just written his *View of the Present State of Ireland* in which he advocated a severe and ruthless transformation of native Irish society; and Artegal's actions are a poetic narrative of that policy. Artegal finally conquers the tyrant, introduces true justice into Ireland, and then sends Talus, his iron man, through the island

---

[111] Ibid. 767. *The Prose Works of Sir Philip Sidney*, iii. 127.
[112] For the political context see Chs. 8, 9.

> To search out those, that usd to rob and steale,
> Or did rebell gainst lawfull government;
> On whom he did inflict most grievous punishment.[113]

Unfortunately, before he can entirely reform the island, Artegal is recalled to the Court of the Faerie Queene. Spenser promises to tell us of Artegal's later adventures; but, as he did not complete his epic, we are left ignorant about the end of the story.

While Sidney and Spenser were certainly hostile to many forms of rebellion, they tolerated and even advocated others. Revolt by the lower orders of society was abhorrent to them, yet rebellion by a free people oppressed by a foreign conqueror was permissible, even admirable, unless the people happened to be Irish; tyrants could and should be overthrown, preferably by external intervention rather than by internal rebellion; but while Sidney presented the Huguenot arguments for revolt by a prince of the blood to remedy the deficiencies of government, he stopped short of approving them.

Complex as the attitudes of Sidney and Spenser may be, Shakespeare's is more elusive still; and he has been cast both as the upholder of the social and political order and as the champion of the people.[114] In *Julius Caesar* the issue of rebellion is confronted in Brutus' soliloquy in the orchard (Act II, sc. i), when he reflects on Caesar's ambition and its consequences:

> I know no personal cause to spurn at him,
> But for the general. He would be crown'd:
> How that might change his nature, there's the question.
> It is the bright day that brings forth the adder, . . .
>
> . . . . . .
>
> But when he once attains the upmost round,
> He then unto the ladder turns his back,
> Looks in the clouds, scorning the base degrees
> By which he did ascend. So Caesar may;
> Then lest he may, prevent. And since the quarrel
> Will bear no colour for the thing he is,
> Fashion it thus: that what he is, augmented,
> Would run to these and these extremities;
> And therefore think him as the serpent's egg,
> Which, hatch'd, would, as his kind, grow mischievous,
> And kill him in the shell.[115]

The course of the play demonstrates that Brutus is wrong and his enterprise ends in disaster; but he has uncomfortably raised the matter of

---

[113] *The Faerie Queene*, v. xii, st. 26.

[114] For the former view see Tillyard, *Shakespeare's History Plays*, *passim*; for the latter Patterson, *Shakespeare and the Popular Voice*, *passim*.

[115] *Julius Caesar*, II. i. 11–34.

tyrannicide and presented the argument in its favour to an Elizabethan audience.

Richard II raises the matter in a more direct way. At least one member of the public, Elizabeth I herself, saw the theme of the play as dangerous: she complained to the antiquary, William Lambarde, shortly after the Essex revolt, that 'I am Richard II, know ye not that'; and she protested that the play had been performed forty times in the streets of London. In the play, Richard's proposal to seize the property of his dead uncle, John of Gaunt, thus disinheriting Gaunt's son Hereford, gives rise to protest from his surviving uncle, the Duke of York:

> How long shall I be patient? ah, how long
> Shall tender duty make me suffer wrong?

When Richard asks him what was the matter, York replies:

> No afore God—God forbid I say true!—
> If you do wrongfully seize Herford's rights,
> Call in the letters patent that he hath
> By his attorneys-general to sue
> His livery, and deny his off'red homage,
> You pluck a thousand dangers on your head,
> You lose a thousand well-disposed hearts,
> And prick my tender patience to those thoughts
> Which honour and allegiance cannot think.[116]

When Hereford, by now called Bolingbroke, returns to England from exile, he makes those property rights the cause of his coming; and while Richard's deposition is condemned by the Bishop of Carlisle, the matter is treated in a surprisingly even-handed way: if Bolingbroke is wrong to depose his anointed king, Richard is wrong to tamper with the property rights of his subjects.

Even revolt by the lower orders is treated with sympathy, though not with approval, in one play in which Shakespeare had a hand, *Sir Thomas More*. The craftsmen who attack foreigners on the Evil May Day of 1517 are presented as misguided rather than wicked. The 'strangers' are mostly to blame for exploiting and stealing from Londoners, while English noblemen are castigated for failing to inform the King of the troubles:

> Men of your place and greatness are to blame.
> I tell you true, my lords, in that his majesty
> Is not informed of this base abuse
> And daily wrongs are offered to his subjects;

---

[116] *Richard II*, II. i. 163–4, 100–8. Cf.*Macbeth*, IV. iii, for a similar dialogue between Malcolm and Macduff.

> For, if he were, I know his gracious wisdom
> Would soon redress it.

Thomas More reprimands the rebels for their conduct, but promises that the King will pardon them, which he finally does, but too late for their leader, John Lincoln, who is hanged repenting of his folly:

> ... I had no ill intent
> But against such as wronged us over much:
> And now I can perceive it was not fit
> That private men should carve out their redress
> Which way they list.[117]

While Lincoln's own words condemn rebellion, the incident is treated with sufficient sympathy for the Master of the Revels, Sir Edmund Tilney, to order the 'insurrection' scene to be cut: dearth and high prices, combined with renewed hostility to foreign merchants, made it a sensitive matter in the 1590s.

In general, literary texts upheld the social and political order in Elizabethan England; Elizabeth is presented as an almost semi-divine being; rank and hierarchy are extolled; and resistance is condemned. Yet the very praise of Elizabeth raises some doubts about her; and anxiety about her death is apparent even while she is being spoken of as immortal. The arguments for order and degree sometimes, at least, allow some ambiguity: Spenser's giant presents a view which is only overthrown, literally, by the violence of Artegal and Talus. In expressing repugnance towards rebellion, Sidney and Spenser nevertheless admit that in some circumstances even tyrannicide may be permissible; and Shakespeare's characters engage in serious debate on the issues. While historians once spoke confidently of 'The Elizabethan World Picture', we can now see that there was more than one picture and that even a single text could contain within itself conflicting views.[118]

8. ÉLITE AND POPULAR CULTURE

This chapter has so far been largely confined to the art and literature of the educated élite. The country houses of nobles and gentlemen, the madrigals of the royal Court, the sacred music of the Chapel Royal, the portraits of monarchs and courtiers, the plays of the London stage, and the courtly poems of Spenser, Sidney, Ralegh, and their contemporaries were produced by the social élite and, with the exception of the plays, were mainly

---

[117] Munday, Dekker, Chettle, and Shakespeare, *Sir Thomas More*, I. ii. 64–70; III. i. 55–9.
[118] Contrast Tillyard, *The Elizabethan World Picture*, *passim*.

addressed to its members. Yet men and some women below this social group bought books and read them in increasing numbers; some plays were directed at merchants and craftsmen rather than at gentlemen or courtiers; and ordinary people had their games and festivals. Was this 'popular culture' of merchants, yeomen, artisans, apprentices, and their wives separate and distinct from the 'élite culture' of nobles and gentlemen?[119]

Popular culture is found in printed ballads, chap-books, and almanacs, in communal revels and amateur plays, and in the world of fairs and markets. Jonson's *Bartholomew Fayre*, first performed in 1614, reveals its rich vitality, with the hobby-horse seller, the gingerbread-woman, the ballad-singer, the pig-woman, the horse-courser, and the bawd. It is a world only partly accessible to historians, for much of the cheap printed material has disappeared and the performing arts of bear-baiters, clowns, minstrels, and other entertainers lose their effect and appeal when they are transmitted only through written accounts. The registers of the Stationers' Company list the titles of printed chap-books—small, cheap booklets sold by itinerant pedlars or chapmen—but few of the earliest ones have survived, for they were essentially discardable items, used as lavatory-paper or wrapping-paper, or simply thrown away. The best collections, made by Samuel Pepys and Anthony Wood, for the most part contain seventeenth-century editions, usually late seventeenth-century at that. Ballads, transmitted orally before 1550 and increasingly committed to print after that, have, however, survived in larger numbers than the 'little books' of the pedlars.[120] From the Stationers' lists and the surviving ballads we can at least get a broad impression of the range and variety of subjects covered by this cheap and popular literature. Many tell stories of romantic love: *A Newe Ballade of a Lover Extollinge his Ladye* speaks of it in conventional and simple terms:

> Alas, my heart doth boyle
> And burne within my breast,
> To show to thee, myne only deer,
> My sute and my request.

---

[119] 'Popular' and 'culture' are both slippery terms. By 'culture' I mean a network of shared values, together with the writings, pictures, performances, festivities, and so on in which they were embodied; by 'popular' I mean those parts of the culture accessible to people below the level of the élite—they may or may not have been part of the culture of the élite.

[120] The ballads discussed here were 'street ballads', written or printed in the sixteenth century; they were distinct from 'folk ballads', which had long been part of popular and élite culture and were sung by travelling minstrels. For discussion of the types of ballad see Tessa Watt, *Cheap Print and Popular Piety, 1550–1640* (Cambridge, 1991), chs. 1–3; and Natascha Würzbach, *The Rise of the English Street Ballad, 1550–1650*, trans. Gayna Walls (Cambridge, 1990), introd.

> My love no toung can tell,
>   No pen can well descrye;
> Extend thy love for love again
>   Or else for love I dye.[121]

Other ballads are explicitly bawdy. *A Ditty Delightfull of Mother Watkins Ale* tells, under the guise of providing a moral lesson, the lascivious story of a maid who says to herself 'I am afraid to live and die a maid'. She is overheard by a young man, who promises her

> For I will, without faile,
> Mayden, give you Watkins ale;
> Watkins ale, good sir, quoth she,
> What is that I pray you tel me?
> 'Tis sweeter farre then suger fine,
> And pleasanter than muskadine;
> And if you please, faire mayd, to stay
> A little while, with me to play,
>   I will give you the same,
>   Watkins ale cald by name,—

Watkins ale is duly provided and

> This mayden then fell very sicke,
> Her maydenhead began to kicke,
> Her colour waxed wan and pale
> With taking much of Watkins ale.[122]

Not surprisingly, Elizabethan moralists disapproved of this kind of ballad. Philip Stubbes, author of the *Anatomie of Abuses* (1583), complained that 'every town, city and county is full of these minstrels to pipe up a dance to the devil, but of divines, so few there be as they may hardly be seen'; and Sir John Harington, in *A Preface or Rather a Briefe Apologie of Poetrie* (1591) issued a cultural protest that the name of poetry was misused, since 'the common sort that term all that is written in verse poetry, . . . bestow the name of poet on every base rhymer and balladmaker'.[123]

However, many chap-books and ballads had a more serious end: among the earliest titles were listed *Devout Prayers*, *Ring of Righteousness*, *Sermon of Repentance*, and *Troubled Mans Medicine*; but none of these has survived.[124] However, some early ballads on religious themes remain, notably those dealing with the evils of popery: *The Brainless Blessing of the Bull*, for example, attacked the papal excommunication of Elizabeth:

---

[121] Joseph Lilly (ed.), *A Collection of Seventy-Nine Black-Letter Ballads and Broadsides, printed . . . between the years 1559 and 1597* (London, 1867), 24.

[122] Ibid. 251–9.   [123] Würzbach, *Rise of the Street Ballad*, 253–9.

[124] Spufford, *Small Books and Pleasant Histories*, 196.

O Sathans sonne! O pope puft up with pryde,
What makes thee clayme the clowdes where God doth dwel,
When thou art knowne the glorious greedy guyde,
That leades in pompe poore seely soules to hell?
The pumpe of ship hath not so fowle a smell
As hathe the smoke and fume that flames from thee.[125]

The message of repentance was hammered in by broadsides reporting monstrous births. One tells of the birth of a child to an unmarried woman in 1568: the child is hideously misshapen (the deformities are described in horrible detail) and lives for only twenty-four hours, 'which may be a terror to all such workers of filthiness and iniquity':

This monstrous shape to thee, England,
Playn shewes thy monstrous vice.[126]

The writer then proceeds to show exactly how each specific deformity reveals a particular vice of the times.[127]

Although a great number of ballads dealt with religious subjects, variety was provided by stories of heroism and chivalry, which already had a long history in the repertoire of minstrels and in communal plays. *Guy of Warwick*, for instance, can be traced back as an oral ballad to the fourteenth century and appeared in printed form in the sixteenth. The story has many variations, but tells essentially of a noble Saxon, Guy, whose father has lost his lands at the Norman Conquest. Guy serves the Earl of Warwick as his steward, enacts great deeds of heroism, and finally wins the Earl's daughter, together with her inheritance. The theme of the poor boy making good is common in this literature, but he usually turns out to come from noble stock; and the values expressed in the story are essentially chivalric.

Towards the end of the century a new genre of what may be called novels or romances emerged in London, describing and praising the people of the City. They were written mainly by men from gentlemanly families and were aimed at an urban readership. Thomas Deloney's *Jack of Newbury*, a prime example of the genre, was published in 1597. Unlike other contemporary writers in this genre, Deloney had been a silk-weaver and then a ballad-singer; and he turned to writing stories about craftsmen after he had incurred the anger of the Lord Mayor for a 'Ballad on the Want of Corn'. *Jack of Newbury* tells the story of a partly legendary weaver and clothier of the reign of Henry VIII, who has made a considerable fortune, yet still con-

---

[125] Lilly, *A Collection*, 224–7.   [126] Ibid. 194–7.
[127] Below, Ch. 11 s. 5, for a more serious religious ballad.

siders himself to be no gentleman, 'but a poor clothier, whose lands are his looms, having no other rents but what I get from the backs of little sheep'. However, he promises that he will still serve the king like a nobleman: ordered to bring six men to the field against the Scots, he brings 150, leading them himself 'in complete armour on a goodly barbed horse'. Later, Henry VIII in person is feasted by Jack and shown round the clothing establishment, where he finds a quantity of men and women working industriously at spinning, weaving, fulling, and dyeing. When Henry offers to give Jack a knighthood, the latter refuses, saying: 'I beseech your Grace let me rest in my russet coat, a poor clothier to my dying day.'[128] Jack proves the value, and the values, of industry, giving work to the poor and serving his sovereign. He is emphatically, perhaps over-emphatically, not a gentleman, but his values are those of the nobility, reflected in his war service and the conspicuous consumption at his banquet.

Thomas Heywood, Cambridge-educated son of a preacher, used the stage to praise merchants. In *1 Edward IV* (1592), he presents John Crosby, who has risen from being a foundling to become Lord Mayor of London. Crosby defends London against the rebellion of the Bastard Fauconbridge and reminds the merchants of the heroism of his predecessor, William Walworth, who stabbed Jack Straw in 1381. Like Jack of Newbury, Crosby feasts his sovereign, though his banquet ends unhappily, for at it Edward IV meets Jane Shore and discourteously leaves the table during the meal to pursue her. In *2 If you Know not me you Know Nobody* (1605), Heywood's hero is a man nearer to his own time: Sir Thomas Gresham, founder of the Royal Exchange. Heywood pays tribute to Gresham's extravagance by having him crush into powder a pearl worth £1,500, mixing it in his wine and drinking with it a toast to Queen Elizabeth.[129]

Jack, Crosby, and Gresham are merchant princes, real or legendary. The artisans who work for them receive less flattering treatment from early Elizabethan writers: at best they are clowns, at worst rebels. However, during the 1590s they are portrayed more favourably, for Deloney, in *The Gentle Craft* (1597), turns from praising merchants to extolling craftsmen and their world. His heroes, Simon Eyre and Richard Casteler, begin their lives as simple craftsmen and end up as rich merchants. Yet the world of shoemakers and weavers is harmonious and brave, a place where knights and lords can find contentment if they are down on their luck:

---

[128] Laura Caroline Stevenson, *Praise and Paradox: Merchants and Craftsmen in Elizabethan Popular Literature* (Cambridge, 1984), 114, 123, and *passim* on this genre of literature. For a convenient edition of *Jack of Newbury* see Paul Salzman (ed.), *An Anthology of Elizabethan Prose Fiction* (Oxford, 1987), 311–92.

[129] Stevenson, *Praise and Paradox*, 112–13, 117–18, 144–5 on these plays.

For evermore they still did find that shoemakers bore a gallant mind:
Men they were of high conceit, the which wrought many a merry feat;
Stout of courage they were still, and in their weapons had great skill . . .

The craftsmen were charitable to the poor and to one another:

Good houses kept they evermore, relieving both the sick and the poor,
         .   .   .   .   .

And never yet did any know, a shoemaker a-begging go;
Kind they are to one another, using his stranger as his brother.[130]

There was, then, an urban, 'ungentle' culture by the end of the century. However, its values did not differ greatly from those of the élite, or perhaps from those townsmen who wrote and performed the traditional plays of earlier times: knights could pretend to be shoemakers, just as they could, in pastoral romance, pretend to be shepherds; and war, chivalry, generosity, and conspicuous consumption were among the occupations and qualities shared by gentlemen, merchants, craftsmen, and apprentices. They also shared the central experience of the London theatre, at least in the closing decades of the century. Most of the 15,000 people who visited the two available theatres each week in 1595 would have come from the ranks of society below the level of the gentry. Knights and gentlemen may or may not have read the chap-books and ballads—it is impossible to say—but when they were in London they went to the same plays as did the citizens. After 1600 they tended to go to the more expensive hall-type theatres, but it was not for some time that the fare presented to the two groups was differentiated. However, playwrights do seem to have catered for a varied audience, including classical allusions for the learned which would have been missed by the majority.[131]

So far, when we have talked of a popular audience and a popular readership, we have been referring to books and plays which appealed largely to the literate, for chap-books and plays catered for men and women who could afford to buy the books and pay for admission to the theatres; and probably most of them could read. The culture, outlook, and values of the illiterate and the really poor—the greater part of the population—are revealed only in their traditional festivities.

The year was filled with festivities in town and country. Some, like the masques, were performed behind closed doors at Court, though these were less common under Elizabeth than they became under the Stuarts; others, such as the accession day tilts, were royal or aristocratic ceremonies at

---

[130] Stevenson, *Praise and Paradox*, 184.
[131] Above, pp. 408–10, on theatres and audiences.

which ordinary people were spectators; yet others mixed courtly and popular performance, as the Coventry townsmen did when they performed their Hock Tuesday play in the aristocratic setting of Kenilworth during Elizabeth's progress.[132] All these were occasional revels, designed for a particular purpose or for a specific moment. Most of the truly popular festivals had fixed days in the calendar, the 'ritual' part of the year being concentrated in the months between 24 December and 24 June. The first and longest period of festivity lay in the twelve days of Christmas, from 25 December to 6 January, celebrated with decorations, singing, visiting from house to house, plays performed by mummers, games of football, and so on, presided over in great households by a Lord of Misrule.[133] There followed a succession of festivals—Plough Monday, Shrove Tuesday, St Valentine's Day, Easter—before May Day, the day most enthusiastically celebrated in the villages and the occasion best documented by its enemies. Philip Stubbes, the most prolific of these opponents, described this, and other festivals, in his *Anatomie of Abuses*:

Against May, Whitsunday, or other time, all the young men and maids, old men and wives, run gadding over night to the woods, groves, hills and mountains, where they spend all the night in pleasant pastimes; and in the morning they return, bringing with them birch and branches of trees, to deck their assemblies withall, and no marvel, for there is a great Lord present amongst them, as superintendent and Lord over their pastimes and sports, namely Satan, prince of Hell. . . . But the chiefest jewel they bring from thence is their Maypole . . .

In painting the moral horrors of May Day, Stubbes unintentionally revealed its attractions. He seems, indeed, to have realized this himself, for he called the maypole 'this stinking idol' and compared the festival to the heathen dedication of idols. He added a practical warning that only one-third of the virgins who went to the woods returned home 'undefiled'.[134]

The festivals found their way into 'high culture', most obviously in plays like *A Midsummer Night's Dream*, where Theseus remarks on finding the lovers asleep,

> No doubt they rose up early, to observe
> The rite of May . . .

[132] Above, Ch. 5 s. 1, for details of the Kenilworth progress.

[133] For details of popular festivities see François Laroque, *Shakespeare's Festive World: Elizabethan Seasonal Entertainment and the Professional Stage*, trans. Janet Lloyd (Cambridge, 1991), *passim*; C. L. Barber, *Shakespeare's Festive Comedy* (Princeton, NJ, 1959), *passim*.

[134] Laroque, *Festive World*, 111, 116.

The action of the play reflects May Day, with the flight into the woods, the expectation of sexual licence, the transformation of Titania and Bottom, and the artisans' play in the final act.[135] People of most social classes seem to have participated in the rural and urban festivals, no doubt in different ways; and the rituals do not seem to have had the overtones of subversion sometimes apparent in carnivals in France and Italy.

They did, however, generate hostility from Protestant reformers, as the passage from Stubbes indicates. In his *Anatomie of Abuses*, he attacked every kind of popular indulgence. Plays, whether sacred or secular, were damnable: if on sacred topics they were sacrilegious; if on secular themes they 'nourish us in idolatry, heathenry and sin'. He went on to attack Lords of Misrule, May games, Church ales, and bearbaiting, the latter on the surprisingly modern ground that 'they [are] good creatures in their own nature and kind, and made to set forth the glory . . . of our God.' It is, he remarked, 'a common saying among all men . . . Love me, love my dog; so love God, love his creatures.'[136] Stubbes's campaign was enthusiastically taken up by Justices of the Peace in many counties. By this date the old mystery plays had largely gone, and it was the turn of secular entertainments to be attacked. Church ales were suppressed, maypoles pulled down, morris dances and Robin Hood plays forbidden; and the aldermen of London tried hard to close the professional theatres, successfully expelling them from the City itself. In many towns and parishes there was conflict between the reformers and upholders of the traditional order; but the divide did not usually lie along class lines. Noblemen protected and patronized the London theatre; and gentlemen often took part in country sports and sometimes defended them against attack. Nor was there a sharp divide between Church and alehouse, for religious texts and pictures were often painted on alehouse walls. The dispute lay essentially between those who believed that traditional games and festivals preserved harmony, and those preachers and godly laymen who considered that the revels and alehouses undermined discipline, encouraged popery, and subverted morality.

There was certainly a culture of the élite in sixteenth-century England. Sidney's *Arcadia* was intended to be read only by those few who had access to a manuscript copy; and even after it had been printed, against the wishes of its author, its readers are likely to have been found among men and women from the noble classes. *The Faerie Queene*, though certainly written for publication, was likely to appeal principally to leisured and courtly

[135] Shakespeare, *A Midsummer Night's Dream*, IV. i. 131–2.
[136] Philip Stubbes, *The Anatomie of Abuses* (London, 1583; facsimile of the 1585 edn., ed. William B. D. D. Turnbull, London, 1886), 160–2, 211.

readers, educated enough to decode its allusions and its imagery. Portrait miniatures were the hidden and secret objects of the closet. Yet the élite still participated in much of the culture of the literate populace, especially in the London theatre. Only in the course of the following century did the two worlds draw apart, so that the culture of the upper classes became largely isolated from the festivities of the common people, while the values of gentlemen, merchants, and craftsmen diverged.

There were, of course, strong regional variations. The Welsh preserved their own language, strengthened by the translation of the Bible and the Prayer Book; and the gentry of Wales were not yet Anglicized. Even within the same county in England distinct cultural patterns could be discerned: between, for instance, the traditional ways of the downland villages of Wiltshire, Somerset, and Dorset, and the more 'puritan' manners of the pastoral settlements of the same region.[137] Most distinct of all was the metropolitan culture of London. Here was the centre of the professional theatre and the printing press; its population was the most literate in Europe; but literacy, print, touring theatre companies, and travelling pedlars took its culture to the provinces. However, in spite of the printing presses, the oral culture of ballads and sermons remained strong, the spoken and the written traditions feeding upon and nourishing each other: popular ballads went into print, which helped to preserve, but also to transform, the older tradition. Popular and élite cultures were interlocking. There was an élite culture of the Court linked to a more broadly based culture of London. Some members of the élite still participated in the recreations of the people, although these were under attack; and metropolitan culture spread into the provinces through the trade in books and the mediation of nobles and gentlemen.

[137] For a development of this theme see David Underdown, *Revel, Riot and Rebellion: Popular Politics and Culture in England, 1603–1660* (Oxford, 1985), *passim*.

CHAPTER 11

Religion in Elizabethan England

1. BEGINNINGS

Mary's death on 17 November 1558 left the people of England and Wales
facing the likelihood of yet another turnabout in religion, reversing the
effect of the events of 1553. The prevailing uncertainty was reflected in the
will of William Woodman of Eye, Suffolk, who died two days after his
Queen, leaving 20 ounces of silver to his parish church 'if the laws of
the realm will permit and suffer the same'.[1] In Geneva John Pulleyne, an
Essex man, wrote to his fellow-exiles urging them to return home and to
recover the unity they had lost in their recent quarrels. The call to unity was
rejected by the rival congregations in Frankfurt and elsewhere; but the
exiles were quick to come back to England. They did not like what they
found: John Jewel, soon to become Bishop of Salisbury, told Peter Martyr
that ignorance had much increased in Oxford since Martyr had left the
university five years before; and his complaint was echoed by others. The
fears of the Catholics, the hopes of the returning exiles, and the bewilderment of many created an unstable and potentially dangerous situation. In
December the Crown forbade contentious preaching and ordered the continued use of the traditional Sarum rite, with only the Epistle, the Gospel,
the Lord's Prayer, and the Creed in English. Such a measure could only
hold off trouble for a short time. Elizabeth's illegitimacy in the eyes of
Rome determined that she must either secure a dispensation from the Pope
or once again detach the kingdom from papal jurisdiction. The former
course held risks and uncertainties, and she chose the latter, which almost
certainly appealed to her predilections.[2]

The Elizabethan 'settlement of religion' was based, with a few exceptions, upon statutes, liturgies, and injunctions promulgated under Henry
VIII and Edward VI; in consequence its legal foundations were laid rapidly,

---

[1] Eamon Duffy, *The Stripping of the Altars: Traditional Religion in England, 1400–1580*
(New Haven, Conn., 1992), 565.
[2] Above, Ch. 7 s. 1.

within six months of the accession of the new Queen. The creation of a Protestant Church and nation took a great deal longer. Two statutes of 1559, the Acts of Supremacy and Uniformity, established the royal authority and the liturgy; and on this groundwork were erected the royal Injunctions, issued in the summer of that year, the visitation to put them into force, and, later, the Thirty-nine Articles, devised in 1563 but not enshrined in statute until 1571.

The matter of ecclesiastical authority was central to the whole settlement and was defined in the Act of Supremacy, which made the Queen Supreme Governor of the Church, a title more acceptable than Supreme Head to foreign monarchs, Catholics, and Protestants alike.[3] All members of the clergy and royal officers were to take the oath of supremacy, acknowledging Elizabeth as Supreme Governor, an obligation extended to schoolmasters, lawyers, and MPs in 1563.[4] The fact that the settlement was authorized by statute suggested that the highest authority in the Church should be the Queen-in-Parliament. But that was not how Elizabeth saw the matter. In her mind Parliament, having laid the foundations, could now stand back and refrain from any interference. While she did not claim sacerdotal power, she did intend to govern the Church. Her bishops took a different view: to John Jewel, the leading defender of the settlement in the early part of the reign, the monarch was supreme in matters of ecclesiastical jurisdiction, but not in those of doctrine: 'touching the knowledge of God's word and cases of religion', he wrote, 'certain it is the king is inferior to a bishop'.[5] Yet in practice Jewel's distinction proved impossible to maintain, while Elizabeth's dismissive view of Parliament's role did not go unchallenged either in practice or in principle. MPs frequently voiced their opinions on religious issues, while Richard Hooker, writing at the end of the reign, claimed that

for the devising of laws in the Church, it is the general consent of all that giveth them the form and vigour of laws, without which they could be no more unto us than the counsel of physicians to the sick . . . Thus to define of our own Church's regiment [i.e. rule] the Parliament of England hath competent authority.[6]

It is not surprising that Book VIII of Hooker's *Ecclesiastical Polity*, from which this extract is taken, should have remained unpublished until 1648.

However, until the last decade of the century Elizabethan bishops took a relatively modest view of their status, accepting that their authority derived from the Crown and not considering themselves to be part of a divinely

[3] 1 Elizabeth c. 1.   [4] 5 Elizabeth c. 1.
[5] Claire Cross, *The Royal Supremacy in the Elizabethan Church* (London, 1969), 29.
[6] Ibid. 150.

ordained order separate from the rest of the clergy. This was true even of the authoritarian Whitgift; and although Richard Bancroft, Bishop of London in the last years of the reign, tentatively asserted a doctrine of the divine right (*jus divinum*) of bishops, in response to Presbyterian attacks, his was a minority view, even among the bishops themselves, until well into the reign of James. While the consequences of the doctrine of *jus divinum* were to be portentous under Charles I and Laud, it had little practical significance under Elizabeth.

The liturgy established in the Act of Uniformity and in the 1559 Prayer Book was based upon the second Book of Edward VI (1552) with some modifications.[7] The most important of these softened the impact of the sentences for the administration of communion: where the 1552 Book had here been uncompromisingly commemorative in its wording, the Elizabethan added at the beginning a clause from the 1549 Book.[8] In the administration of the bread two views of the eucharist were combined: '*The body of our lord Jesus Christ, which was given for thee, preserve thy body and soul into everlasting life*: and take and eat this, in remembrance that Christ died for thee, and feed on him in thy heart by faith, with thanksgiving.'[9] A similar sentence was prescribed for the administration of the wine. Although the change in the wording of the communion service in 1559 brought back some notion of the Real Presence of Christ, it could only be a spiritual, not a physical or material, Presence. The service could not be truly acceptable to Catholics since it implicitly denied the doctrines of transubstantiation and of the sacrifice of the Mass; but it did serve to reassure the more conservative, if not the strictly Catholic, subjects of the Queen. That the service was very far from being a mere remembrance is apparent from the words of the prayer of humble access: 'grant us therefore (gracious Lord) so to eat the flesh of thy dear Son Jesus Christ, and to drink his blood, that our sinful bodies may be made clean by his body, and our souls washed through his most precious blood.'[10]

For those who were attached to the traditional order or merely bewildered—or both—the 'ornaments rubric' of the Act of Uniformity gave some comfort. It provided that 'such ornaments of the Church and of the ministers thereof shall be retained and be in use as was in the Church of England by authority of Parliament in the second year of the reign of King

---

[7] 1 Elizabeth c. 2. *The Book of Common Prayer, 1559; The Elizabethan Prayer Book*, ed. John Booty (Charlottesville, Va, 1976), *passim*.

[8] Above, Chs. 2 s. 4, 3 s. 3.

[9] *Book of Common Prayer*, ed. Booty, 264. The italicized passage is that from the 1549 Book, the unitalicized that from the 1552 Book.

[10] Ibid. 263.

Edward the Sixth until other order shall be therein taken by the authority of the Queen's Majesty'.[11] In other words the clerical vestments and the liturgical furniture used in 1549 were to be preserved until the Queen ordered otherwise. Protestant reformers, especially those who had been in exile in Germany and Switzerland, wanted less ceremonial and ornamentation, fewer and simpler vestments; they both hoped and expected that it would not be long before these remnants of popery were swept away. However, they failed to understand that Elizabeth was firmly attached to these traditional ornaments and had no intention of allowing them to be abolished. In consequence, there was soon to be conflict between the Queen and the more ardent spirits among her clergy over this issue.

The settlement established by statute was fleshed out later in 1559 by royal Injunctions, issued on the authority of the Queen alone since no bishops had yet been appointed. These were based upon the 1547 Injunctions of Edward VI. They stressed the importance of preaching or the reading of prescribed Homilies, ordering that no one was to preach without licence from his bishop. Since licences were to be sparingly given, this meant that most churches would normally hear only readings from the printed Homilies, which were hardly fare to enliven the faithful. The Bible and the *Paraphrases* of Erasmus were to be placed in every church; and reluctantly Elizabeth allowed ministers to marry 'an honest and sober wife', but only after examination of the lady by the bishop and two JPs.[12] The Injunctions made some concessions to traditional religion: for instance, the holy table, which replaced the altar, was allowed to remain at the east end of the church, except during holy communion, when it was to be removed to the chancel. But the articles of inquiry, issued to visitation commissioners at the same time, were more uncompromising; and, more important, the commissions were dominated by returned exiles.

The commissioners were instructed to investigate the state of the clergy and to require their subscription to the Royal Supremacy, the Prayer Book, and the Injunctions. Articles of inquiry were issued to deal with the clergy's morality, their use of the Prayer Book, the preservation of images, and other topics. Unfortunately returns to the inquiry have survived only for the northern province, where, out of about 1,000 clergy, 300 were absent and only 90 refused to subscribe. In the southern province 1,800 subscribed, but we do not know how many were asked. However, although exact figures are not available for the whole country, it is evident that the lower clergy, unlike the bishops, were willing to conform even if their attachment to the new order was at best superficial and often reluctant.

[11] 1 Elizabeth c. 2 s. iii.   [12] Cross, *Royal Supremacy*, 181.

The doctrine of the Church was only gradually established and promulgated. Cranmer had laid its foundations with his Forty-two Articles of 1553, and the Elizabethan bishops drew on these to formulate the Eleven Articles of 1561, which received episcopal, but not royal, authority. These were mild and uncontentious statements, avoiding most issues of debate and broadly supporting the doctrinal tenets inherent in the Prayer Book. It was left to the Convocation of 1563 to produce the more comprehensive and contentious Thirty-nine Articles, which remain—in theory if not in any sort of reality—the doctrines of the Church of England today.[13] These, too, were based upon Cranmer's Articles, from which they deviated very little, mainly in condemning Roman Catholic tenets more strongly and in defining more closely the doctrine of the sacrament. Transubstantiation was firmly denied, but the Spiritual Presence of Christ in the communion was asserted against the Zwinglians, with the proviso (article XXIX) that he was present only to the faithful, a notion distasteful to Catholics and Lutherans. For some time the Articles had only a limited authority, since Elizabeth allowed the publication of a Latin version only, and that with article XXIX omitted; and she resisted their confirmation by statute, which was only achieved in 1571, when the Articles finally became the official, published doctrine of the Church.

The Church established under Elizabeth thus incorporated a diluted version of Henrician supremacy, a traditional episcopal structure of government, a liturgy which was not Roman but was far from pleasing to most reformers, and doctrines which were closer to those of Calvin than to any other Continental reformer but could only misleadingly be described as 'Calvinist'.

2. THE CHURCH ESTABLISHED

Although the great bulk of the clergy subscribed to the statutes of 1559, refusing to follow the course taken by the Marian bishops, the leaders of the Church faced a formidable task in turning statutes and ordinances into reality. Many of the clergy were attached to the old ways; the laity were mostly confused, indifferent, or plain hostile; and the resources in men and institutions needed for countering Catholic sentiment and instilling the reformed faith were weak.

The Queen was central both to the settlement itself and to its execution.

---

[13] Text in E. J. Bicknell, *A Theological Introduction to the Thirty-nine Articles of the Church of England* (London, 1925), *passim*. The text of the Articles may also be found in most editions of the old, i.e. the 1662, Prayer Book. Significantly, they are not to be found in *The Alternative Service Book*.

In principle she claimed only jurisdiction, not doctrinal authority; but in practice she exercised real power over matters of doctrine and liturgy, far more as it turned out than her bishops wished. Once the main lines of the settlement had been laid down she tried to give them as conservative a gloss as was possible. For instance, in selecting a model for the Church's Primer—a book of private prayers for the young—she chose a relatively traditional version drawn up in 1551 rather than a more reformist work of 1553. Her views on clerical marriage were notoriously grudging. Her farewell to Archbishop Parker's wife after a visit was typically forthright: '*Madam* I may not call you, and *Mistress* I am ashamed to call you, so I do not know what to call you, but yet I do thank you.'[14]

The most serious disputes with her bishops and clergy arose over images and vestments. A major row broke out early in the reign over her use of a silver crucifix in the Chapel Royal. To the bishops this seemed like the beginning of a campaign for the replacing of crosses in every church: in the words of Bishop Jewel, 'either the crosses of silver and tin, which we have everywhere broken in pieces, must be restored, or our bishoprics relinquished.'[15] More serious and prolonged was the dispute over vestments. The reformers had thought that the ornaments rubric in the Prayer Book would be temporary. However, Elizabeth intended not merely to preserve existing vestments but to restore others: for instance, she wanted cope and chasuble, as well as the surplice, to be used for communion. Looking back on the disputes in 1571 Bishop Horne of Winchester wrote that

our Church has not yet got free of the vestiarian rocks of offence on which she at first struck. Our excellent Queen, as you know, holds the helm, and directs it hitherto according to her pleasure. But we are awaiting the guidance of the divine Spirit, which is all we can do.[16]

Ultimately Elizabeth compromised on both issues. She kept her own crucifix, but did not allow or compel the restoration of images in other churches; and her demand for the chasuble was dropped, the cope being required only in cathedrals and collegiate churches. Elsewhere the surplice was sufficient, though it was to prove objectionable to many. On these matters the Queen had made some concessions, just enough to gain the support of her bishops. In practice images were more thoroughly destroyed than she may have wished during the visitation of 1559. The London visitors purged St Paul's of images and altars, and ordered the clergy to wear only surplices; roods

[14] William P. Haugaard, *Elizabeth I and the English Reformation: The Struggle for a Stable Settlement of Religion* (Cambridge, 1968), 200.

[15] Ibid. 189–90, quoting *The Zurich Letters*, ed. Hastings Robinson (2 vols., Cambridge, 1842–5), i. 67–8.

[16] Haugaard, *Elizabeth I*, 231.

and the rood-loft were removed from the cathedral and two great bonfires lit in Cheapside to burn 'all the roods and Maries and Johns and many other of the church goods'.[17]

Convocation retained some legislative authority over the Church. It was wholly excluded from any role in the settlement of 1559, since it was dominated by Marian bishops; but it played an important part in 1563, approving the Thirty-nine Articles and receiving petitions for reform. By 1583 its reforming zeal was largely spent, and reformers looked instead to Parliament. However, after 1559, and more particularly when Convocation became more conservative after 1583, Elizabeth insisted that the government of the Church was the province of herself and of the clergy in Convocation rather than of the laity in Parliament; but the former had little or no independent authority.

The day-to-day running of the Church was the affair of the bishops. By contrast with their predecessors of the pre-Reformation era, Elizabethan bishops were primarily pastors and divines rather than men who had risen in the service of the Crown: they were less secular-minded and less princely. Almost all the men appointed to sees in the early part of Elizabeth's reign were strong Protestants, most of them returned from exile under Mary; they were, with a few exceptions, zealous for more radical reform. One important exception was Archbishop Matthew Parker, who had stayed in England during Mary's reign: a man of academic distinction, he had been chaplain to Anne Boleyn and then Master of Corpus Christi College, Cambridge. He was not much involved in the dispute over the crucifix, but was deeply distressed by the Queen's views on clerical marriage: 'I can but lament', he wrote, 'to see the adversary so to prevail . . . I was in an horror to hear such words to come from her mild nature and Christianly learned conscience as she spake concerning God's holy ordinance and institution of matrimony.' He went so far as to write that 'I would be sorry that the clergy should have cause to show disobedience with "*it is better to obey God rather than men*".'[18] For such a man to hint at the possibility of disobedience was remarkable, for Parker usually stressed the importance of subjection to authority and due execution of the law. By the 1570s he had become isolated within the Church, worn out and embittered by his struggle with the puritans, sensing betrayal by his fellow-bishops and the councillors, complaining bitterly of 'this deep, devilish traitorous dissimulation, this horrible conspiracy'.[19]

In the long run a more important figure was John Jewel, Bishop of

---

[17] Patrick Collinson, *Archbishop Grindal 1519–1583: The Struggle for a Reformed Church* (London, 1979), 101.

[18] Cross, *Royal Supremacy*, 185–7.   [19] Collinson, *Grindal*, 219.

Salisbury, already encountered in the affair of the Queen's crucifix. He was the great defender of the English Church against Rome. Delighted that 'those oily, shaven, portly hypocrites', the popish priests, had been deprived, he saw a great reform dawning for the Church in spite of Elizabeth's attachment to tradition.[20] He took the leading role in controversy with the Queen over such matters as clerical marriage and images, and constructed the main intellectual justification of the Church in those early years.[21] Jewel's scholarship and intellectual attainments were allied to the work of Edmund Grindal, successively Bishop of London, Archbishop of York, and Archbishop of Canterbury. A devoted preacher and supporter of preachers, Grindal was sympathetic to radical reformers in the Stranger Churches of London—the congregations of French and Dutch Protestants. Determined to instil the true faith by sermons he introduced forty learned preachers into the northern province when he was Archbishop of York (1570–5). For him the crisis came when he was ordered by Elizabeth to suppress 'prophesyings'—gatherings of clergy to hear sermons, before a lay audience, followed by discussions restricted to the clergy. Grindal reacted by defending prophesyings as a form of instruction and edification, and by defying the royal order:[22]

I cannot with safe conscience and without the offence of the majesty of God, give my assent to the suppression of the said exercises . . . If it be your majesty's pleasure, for this or any other cause, to remove me out of this place, I will with all humility yield thereunto and render again to your majesty that I received of the same . . .

Bear with me, I beseech you, madam, if I choose rather to offend your earthly majesty, than to offend the heavenly majesty of God.

He was suspended from office by the Queen.

Elizabeth's early bishops had done much to frame the environment of the Church, removing images, resisting the Queen's objections to clerical marriage, and putting an emphasis upon preaching. Their efforts did not carry the Church as far in the Protestant direction as many reformers would have liked, but they took it further than Elizabeth herself wished.

However, from about 1576, the year in which Grindal was suspended from his see for disobedience over prophesyings, the character of the bench of bishops began to change. John Whitgift, appointed to Canterbury after Grindal's death in 1583, was a firm Protestant; but controversies with the

[20] Patrick Collinson, *The Religion of Protestants: The Church in English Society 1559–1625* (Oxford, 1982), 23.
[21] John Jewel, *An Apologie or Aunswer in Defence of the Church of England* (London, 1562; STC no. 14590). A Latin edn. was published in the same year (STC no. 14581).
[22] Cross, *Royal Supremacy*, 171–4.

puritans had left him more concerned with the imposition of discipline than with the pursuit of reform. While he resembled Parker in this, he had, unlike Parker, the will to execute his policies and the ability to carry the Queen with him. Tougher even than Whitgift was Richard Bancroft, who became Bishop of London in 1597, a man notorious for hunting and harrying puritan preachers. Yet, although the bench became more authoritarian and more conservative after about 1576, it was not uniformly so. Matthew Hutton, appointed to the see of Durham in 1589 and promoted to York in 1596, was a man cast in the mould of Edmund Grindal: he protected puritans and encouraged preaching. Elizabethan bishops were a varied team, but it is safe to say that they accommodated themselves more easily to the views of the Queen in the second half of the reign than in the first.

Whatever the attitudes and temperaments of the bishops they were all hindered by institutional weaknesses in their office. Episcopal wealth had been savagely depleted under Henry VIII and Edward VI. As Richard Hooker insisted, 'where wealth is held in so great admiration, as generally in this golden age it is . . . surely to make bishops poorer than they are were to make them of less account and estimation than they should be'.[23] They were compelled to maintain social responsibilities, keep up a high social rank, undertake tasks in secular government, and provide generous hospitality, all with a diminished income. Expected by reformers to be the model of the poor pastor and by government to live like noblemen, they were trapped between two conflicting views of their role. Although episcopal incomes improved after about 1580, and with them the status of the bishops, their standing was still a good deal lower than that of their predecessors before the Reformation. The relative poverty of their sees and of the Church generally forced them to spend much time on administration—looking to their revenues and maintaining the fabric of churches—to the detriment of spiritual affairs.

The main formal instruments for enforcing episcopal authority were the multitudinous Church courts, ranging from provincial courts—the Courts of Arches, of Faculties, and the Prerogative Court at Canterbury—to the diocesan bodies—the consistory courts of the bishops and the archdeacons' courts. These episcopal courts possessed two kinds of jurisdiction: over office cases, which were matters of discipline and morality; and instance cases, which involved disputes between private individuals over wills, titles, matrimony, and defamation. The procedure in instance cases seems to have been reasonably flexible and efficient; and the courts were not the monsters

[23] Felicity Heal, *Of Prelates and Princes: A Study of the Economic and Social Position of the Tudor Episcopate* (Cambridge, 1980), 210.

of oppression, corruption, and incompetence the puritans charged them with being and for which they have been condemned by some later historians.[24] Yet they lacked the authority to enforce the law: the censures of penance and excommunication no longer held the necessary terrors; morale was low. Certainly these were not bodies to transform the religion of England. The government met the problem by issuing ecclesiastical commissions to laymen and clerics for exercising a tougher jurisdiction: these commissions could fine and imprison offenders, and combined with recusancy commissions, issued towards the end of the reign, they were an effective weapon against Catholicism. However, by bringing laymen into the government of the Church they inevitably restricted the power of the bishops.

Ultimately the only way in which the bishops could raise standards in the Church was by putting suitable men into parish livings. Protestant doctrine emphasized the need for educated ministers who could teach true doctrine, instil faith by preaching, and provide examples of Christian living. The parish clergy at the beginning of the reign were very far indeed from meeting this ideal. The majority were poorly educated, badly rewarded, and bewildered by the frequent changes of the previous thirty years. In the see of Worcester only 19 per cent of beneficed clergy were graduates; in that of Oxford the figure was slightly higher—38 per cent. More alarmingly, of 36 candidates for ordination in Gloucester diocese in 1570 not one was a graduate. There was not merely a shortage of graduates, but a serious lack of clergy of any sort, and many parishes had no resident minister. To overcome this problem bishops were forced to ordain men whom they knew to be unsuitable. As Parker wrote to Grindal in 1560, 'occasioned by the great want of ministers, we and you both, for tolerable supply thereof, have heretofore admitted unto the ministry sundry artificers and others, not traded and brought up in learning, and, as it happened in a multitude, some that were of base occupations'.[25] When Whitgift much later lamented the lack of preachers in the 13,000 parishes of the realm, Elizabeth was astonished but unsympathetic: 'Jesus! Thirteen thousand! It is not to be looked for.' She was, as it happens, right to be surprised, for the true figure was nearer to 9,000: that the authorities were so hopelessly misinformed is yet another feature of the problem. The Queen's solution, however, was not one calculated to appeal to churchmen: bishops must lower their sights,

[24] For a reappraisal of these courts see R. A. Houlbrooke, *The Church Courts and the People during the English Reformation, 1520–1570* (Oxford, 1979), *passim*; and M. J. Ingram, *The Church Courts, Sex and Marriage in England, 1570–1640* (Cambridge, 1987), *passim*.

[25] Rosemary O'Day, *The English Clergy: The Emergence and Consolidation of a Profession, 1558–1642* (Leicester, 1979), 130.

cease to insist upon learned ordinands, and choose 'honest, sober and wise men and such as can read the scriptures and the homilies well unto the people'.[26] That might satisfy her, but it was not enough for her bishops, not even for more conservative figures like Whitgift.

Yet how could matters be improved? Livings were miserably poor—they often provided a stipend no better than that of a labourer—and men were not coming forward. Even if candidates were available, the bishops did not control appointments to livings: Bishop Bentham of Coventry and Lichfield was able himself to make only 5 out of 147 presentations to livings in his diocese during the period 1560–70. The right to present to the great majority of livings lay in the hands of lay patrons or of the Crown, which exercised its patronage through the Lord Keeper. While the Crown might have been expected to work in co-operation with the Church, it preferred in most cases to make appointments which pleased lay courtiers, landowners, and their protégés. The Church authorities tried to improve matters by imposing more rigorous tests for ordination and by providing 'in-service' training in the form of conferences of ministers. The first were opposed by lay patrons, who valued their right of presentation to livings as a means of rewarding friends and kinsmen, and the second met the dislike of the Queen. Even so, by the end of the century some improvement was in sight. The real incomes of ministers were increasing and more graduates were coming forward for ordination. However, only in the first quarter of the seventeenth century was real change apparent: by then a degree had come to be regarded as necessary for preferment, and, for better or worse, a graduate clergy was becoming a reality rather than a distant aspiration.[27]

The universities formed an essential element in the education and preparation of the clergy. Although by Elizabeth's reign they also served to educate the sons of landowners and merchants destined for secular careers, they were still primarily looked upon as 'nurseries of the clergy' and guardians of theological learning. The production of a graduate clergy was in their hands; so was the defence of true religion. Mary—or perhaps Cardinal Pole—had already seen the significance of this and had purged college fellowships of heretical incumbents. Elizabeth followed her example. Gradually Catholics were removed from their fellowships, college chapels were stripped of images and roods, strict inquisitions were made by college visitors, mostly bishops, into the life of the foundations; and a tighter structure of authority was imposed upon both Oxford and Cambridge. Men of power and influence—Leicester at Oxford and Burghley at Cambridge—

[26] Haugaard, *Elizabeth I*, 167.   [27] Below, p. 495, for the condition of the clergy.

were appointed to the office of Chancellor, each playing an active role in the running of his university; and greater authority was given to heads of colleges to impose discipline upon their fellows and students. By the end of the century the universities were under the tight control of Chancellors, visitors, vice-chancellors, and college heads: they were effectively bent to the service of the state. At the same time they were producing more graduates, many of whom went into the Church and provided an educated ministry.[28]

Discussion of patronage and of ecclesiastical commissions has already shown that the laity played a major role in the government of the Church. Great courtiers and statesmen interfered in the selection of bishops, deans, and heads of colleges—Leicester pre-eminent among them. As patrons of parish livings they were ubiquitous. There seems to have been no concerted campaign among puritan laymen to present doctrinally suitable men, but several nobles favoured radicals, among them Leicester himself, his brother Warwick, Bedford, and, above all, the Earl of Huntingdon, who placed many devout puritans in livings in Leicestershire and the north. Town corporations did not have much formal ecclesiastical patronage but often used their money to employ preachers and lecturers outside the normal parochial structure. As JPs and recusancy commissioners the gentry played a critical role in the enforcement of government policy, especially in the suppression and containment of Catholics; and at the bottom of the hierarchy churchwardens were crucial in the maintenance of buildings, the reporting of offenders, and so on.

Formally, supreme authority over the Church lay with the Queen, control of its normal running with the bishops and their officers. Yet the structure of the Church was far from monolithic: power and influence were shared by the monarch, Parliament, Convocation, the Privy Council, the bishops, the major preachers, lay landowners, and urban oligarchies; and while these often co-operated, they sometimes competed.

3. THE ENGLISH CATHOLICS

The one thing to be said with certainty about England in 1558 was that it was not yet Protestant. There was, to be sure, a Protestant minority, reinforced by the return of the exiles from Germany and Switzerland; but most men and women were not committed to reform. Some, bewildered by recent changes, were ready to accept any settlement that was imposed; others, perhaps the majority, would conform to a Protestant Church while

[28] Below, p. 471, for Catholics and the universities.

looking back nostalgically to traditional ways; and others again, a substantial minority, while not prepared to oppose the settlement, firmly preferred the Catholic religion. The bishops reported gloomily on the state of the parish clergy: Bishop Downham of Chester told the Privy Council in 1564 that many of the clergy in Lancashire were 'obstinate' or 'of unsound religion'; in the same year the Bishop of Hereford reported that 'all the canons residentiary (except Jones . . .) are but dissemblers and rank papists'; and in Sussex as late as 1569 the archbishop's commissary wrote that 'except it be about Lewes and a little in Chichester the whole diocese is very blind and superstitious for want of teaching'. Finally, the strongly Protestant Bishop of Norwich, Parkhurst, found himself confronted by a diocesan establishment that was largely Catholic: he described his archdeacons as 'popish lawyers or unlearned papists'.[29] The laity were even less conformable. Downham found that only five out of twenty-five JPs in Lancashire were favourably inclined to the established Church. In Suffolk a strong faction of Catholic gentry was protected by the dean and the archdeacons, while the Sussex gentry were similarly conservative. In the city of York the Archbishop considered only two out of thirteen aldermen in the early years to be 'favourers of religion'.[30]

The authorities had to face active and vigorous English Catholics overseas as well as conservatives at home. Early in the reign a group of scholarly controversialists settled at the University of Louvain, from which they launched attacks on the established Church. In 1568 one of their number, William Allen, founded a seminary at Douai for 'a perpetual feed and supply of Catholics, namely of the clergy'.[31] The college soon transcended its original modest aims and began to train priests for the establishment of a mission to England: the first missionary priest landed in England in 1574, and by 1580 100 had arrived. By that time the seminary, threatened by the religious troubles in the Netherlands, had moved to Rheims, while an English college had been founded in Rome in 1576, where, after severe birth-pangs and painful clerical disputes, it was taken over by the Jesuits in 1579.

The government's first line of defence against Catholics at home lay in the ecclesiastical courts, whose proceedings reveal wide resistance to the

---

[29] Christopher Haigh, *Reformation and Resistance in Tudor Lancashire* (Cambridge, 1975), ch. 14; A. Dures, *English Catholicism, 1558–1642* (Harlow, 1983), 188; Roger B. Manning, *Religion and Society in Elizabethan Sussex* (Leicester, 1969), 46; Diarmaid MacCulloch, *Suffolk and the Tudors: Politics and Religion in an English County, 1500–1603* (Oxford, 1986), 185–6.

[30] D. M. Palliser, *Tudor York* (Oxford, 1979), 244.

[31] John Bossy, *The English Catholic Community, 1570–1850* (London, 1975), 14.

settlement from an early date: there were many charges of recusancy and of refusal to take communion.[32] However, the consistory and archdeaconry courts were inadequate to deal with the task of enforcing conformity. Many officials—notably the archdeacons—were sympathetic to the Catholic cause; the courts themselves were too heavily loaded with other business to deal with recusancy; and when they did act they were able to inflict only negligible punishments. Very few of the unconforming clergy were deprived; and half the persons presented for recusancy in the archdeaconry of Norwich during the 1560s were dismissed without further proceedings against them. While the church courts were not wholly ineffective, they could do only a very little. The work of the ecclesiastical commissions, established early on in London and in York, and then in many other sees, was more impressive: with spiritual and secular members, a brisk procedure, and the power to fine and imprison, they were able to bring effective pressure to bear. So, later on, were the commissions for recusancy and the secular courts of Quarter Sessions and assizes.

At first, the government concentrated attention upon the clergy, letting lay Catholics alone unless their nonconformity was flagrant. The records of the High Commission in London for the early part of the reign have disappeared, but those of the commission in York have survived and reveal a relentless campaign against dissident clergy in the 1560s and 1570s: commissioners and their agents searched for and destroyed images, vestments, missals, and breviaries, prosecuting priests who failed to conform. Action against the laity was selective, but some prominent men were charged—for example, the son of Lord Hussey, who was put under house arrest for possessing popish books.

Gradually the government's measures increased in severity and widened in focus to catch the laity. A sterner line was provoked by the rising of the northern earls in 1569, the papal bull of excommunication in 1570, and the increasing evidence of widespread recusancy. Three statutes of 1571 made the laws against Catholics harsher: it became treason to bring papal bulls into the country; anyone leaving the realm without licence for more than six months was liable to forfeit his lands; and the treason Act of 1534, imposing the penalties of treason upon anyone who merely spoke treasonable words, was re-enacted.[33] Following the arrival of the missionary priests the laws were tightened still further: in 1581 the recusancy fine was raised from 12*d.* to £20 a month and it was made treason to withdraw subjects from their

---

[32] The term 'recusant' was applied to men and women who failed to attend the services of the Church of England; it usually referred to Roman Catholics, as I have employed it here; but it could also denote Protestant absentees.

[33] 13 Elizabeth cc. 1, 2, 3.

allegiance to the Queen.[34] A proclamation issued in 1582 declared all seminarists and Jesuits to be *ipso facto* traitors, without their having committed any treasonable act, and this became statutory in 1585: it was now treason to belong to a particular category of person, a remarkable extension of the law.[35]

Increased severity of the law was matched by stricter enforcement. All JPs were compelled to take the Oath of Supremacy in 1569. Six years later the Privy Council began to summon prominent lay recusants to appear before it and undergo interrogation; a census was conducted of all recusants in the inns of court, the universities, and the dioceses; and suspect JPs were removed from office. Missionary priests and their supporters were hunted down: the first missionary priest to suffer death, Cuthbert Mayne, was executed in 1577, his host, Sir Francis Tregian, being imprisoned for life. Stricter censorship was imposed on Catholic books, illicit presses were broken up, and houses were searched for unlawful literature.

The government naturally employed persuasion as well as repression. John Foxe's *Book of Martyrs* had been published in Latin in 1559 and in English translation in 1563. It went into many editions, having by law to be available in every cathedral, and being purchased by many parish churches. Foxe set the story of the Church of England in its historical context as the true Church and brought home the threat of popery through the lives and deaths of the Marian martyrs[36] (Plates 11a, b). Later, Burghley defended government policy with two works, *The Execution of Justice in England* and *The Copy of a Letter*, both designed to rebut the accusation that the Crown was condemning people for their beliefs, insistently arguing that the executions were for treason and not for heresy. The attractions of patronage were deployed to entice the laity into the fold of the Church: government offices gradually became closed to Catholics and the commissions of the peace were 'tuned'. A crucial part of the government's endeavour lay in the training and employment of a new, Protestant and educated, clergy. The old 'conservative' priests could not easily be removed, unless they were utterly recalcitrant, and there were at the beginning of the reign few men to replace them. The universities played a central role as 'nurseries' of the clergy and purges were duly carried out there from the start of the reign, more severely at Oxford than at Cambridge.

How effective was government action? Was the machinery of repression adequate for the task? Did persuasion and patronage provide sufficient

---

[34] 23 Elizabeth c. 1.   [35] 27 Elizabeth c. 2.

[36] The correct short title of Foxe's book is *The Actes and Monuments of These Latter and Perilous Dayes, Touching Matters of the Church* . . .

attraction to turn men towards the Protestant faith? The immediate impression given by the evidence is that government activity was hopelessly ineffective, for the numbers of recusants rose in almost every shire from the mid-1570s: in the West Riding of Yorkshire there were 271 recusants in the years 1575–80, 750 in 1582, and 1,136 in 1604; in Lancashire there were 304 in 1578 and no fewer than 3,516 in 1604. These figures are higher than the average, but nearly all counties show a considerable increase over the last twenty-five years of the reign, especially between 1580 and 1582; and we have to remember that there were probably as many 'church papists'—Catholic sympathizers who nevertheless attended their parish churches—as there were declared recusants. But these figures reflect greater vigilance as well as a possible rise in the actual number of Catholics, and they are a sign that the government was at least becoming better informed. Moreover, they need to be put into context: by 1603 there were perhaps 30,000–40,000 Catholics, including 'church papists', in a population of about 5 million. This is a small minority and remains so even if the Catholic community was much larger than this uncertain estimate.

From the point of view of government, the status and influence of Catholics were more important than mere numbers. By the middle of the reign they no longer occupied controlling positions in society, for gradually but effectively they were being removed from the county magistracies. In Suffolk the conservative position was defended in 1559 by a strong network of conservative landowners led by Sir Thomas Cornwallis and protected by the Duke of Norfolk. Ten years later many of them, including Cornwallis, had moved from being merely 'conservative' to becoming Catholic recusants, and their position, which was being undermined in the 1560s and early 1570s, was strengthened after 1575, when Edmund Freke became Bishop of Norwich and allied the episcopal establishment with the Catholics and conservatives against the county's puritans. However, when Elizabeth went on progress in the shire three years later she began to redress the balance, knighting five of the firmly Protestant group, while twenty-three of the East Anglian Catholics were summoned before the Privy Council in Norwich. Sir Thomas Heneage commented to Walsingham that 'by good means her Majesty is brought to believe right and entreat well divers most zealous loyal gentlemen of Suffolk and Norfolk whom the foolish Bishop had maliciously complained of to her Majesty as . . . favourers of preciseness, and puritans'.[37] Nevertheless the Catholic gentry hung on into the next decade and faction-fighting raged, with Whitgift, Freke, and the assize

[37] MacCulloch, *Suffolk and the Tudors*, 196–7.

judges supporting the conservatives, and the Privy Council backing the firm Protestants. However, when Freke departed for the diocese of Worcester in 1584 the tide turned, for by then the Catholic gentry were getting old and younger men were not coming forward to take over their cause in the battle for control of the magistracy. Puritan-minded gentlemen began to find favour and their leader, Sir Robert Jermyn, was appointed to the commission of the peace in 1593, becoming *custos rotulorum*—the chief member of the bench—a few weeks later. Thereafter Suffolk was dominated by committed Protestants, the Catholics retreated into passivity, and religious feuding ceased. Yet it is remarkable that, in a county often considered to be strongly puritan, the alliance of Catholics and conservatives should have held its own until the end of the third decade of the reign, partly thanks to the favour of archbishop and bishop, partly to the social influence of its own members.

A rather different pattern is apparent in Sussex. Here the Catholics were firmly entrenched at the beginning of the reign: about 40 per cent of the gentry were thought to be inclined to popery in 1559. Two strongly Protestant bishops of Chichester, William Barlow and Richard Curteys, were faced with a recalcitrant opposition and received less support from the Privy Council than they had hoped. When Curteys demanded of two leading JPs that they swear to keep 'no company with any that were backward in religion', they replied that 'we cannot take knowledge of every man's religion and conscience that cometh into our company': such a reply reflected too much tolerance of religious differences for the liking of the Protestants.[38] When Curteys pressed the point and summoned a group of gentry to appear before him in the cathedral, he was reprimanded for his tactlessness by the Privy Council, which could not afford in those early years of the reign to antagonize too many of the county's élite. But by the 1580s it was prepared to take stronger action, and the Sussex conservatives, unlike those in Suffolk, got no support from their bishops or from the Council. After 1585 the Protestant nobles and gentry controlled the county Lieutenancy and in 1587 only one suspected Catholic remained on the commission of the peace. In Sussex, as in Suffolk, the change was gradual, even cautious, but without the strife of factions that marked East Anglian politics, since the Catholics got no support from the bishop and the Council's task was to restrain an over-hasty prelate rather than overrule a conservative one.

Lancashire provides a contrast. According to the Bishop of Chester only six out of twenty-five JPs were favourable to the religious settlement in

[38] Manning, *Religion and Society*, 88.

1564. The civil and ecclesiastical powers were lax in their enforcement, and the Catholics were supported by a strong body of recusant priests who had survived from the previous reign. Of 129 families recorded as gentry in the heraldic visitation of 1590, seventy-four were counted as Catholics; and as late as 1598 fourteen out of forty-three JPs were 'church papists'. Yet, unlike Suffolk, Lancashire was little affected by factional strife, because the rival religions were geographically separate: the coastal deaneries of the west were strongly Catholic, that of Manchester was Protestant, and the northern parts of the county seem to have resisted the endeavours of both religions. Although by 1603 the commission of the peace was more conformist than it had been in 1559, the Church had still not gained control in Lancashire.

In the towns the position was much less favourable to Catholics. Admittedly the corporation of York was predominantly Catholic in 1559; but from that year on the city moved slowly towards conformity with the established Church under pressure from Archbishop Grindal and from the Earl of Huntingdon, Lord President of the Council in the North: Mayor Criplyng, who spoke 'very unseemly and foul words' against the clergy, was imprisoned by the Council in the North and on his release deprived by the corporation itself of his mayoral robes.[39] Other towns were Protestant from the beginning of the reign: Ipswich, for example, had ninety-eight inhabitants in hiding on account of their Protestant sympathies under Mary, and by 1564 there seems to have been only one conservative in the town's magistracy. London, above all, had strong underground Protestant congregations under Mary and in 1564 the bishop reported that its JPs were 'not to be misliked at this present', which was about as near as a bishop could get to expressing approval.[40]

Control of the universities was crucial to the process of weaning the Church from Catholic loyalties. Mary had removed heretic fellows from Oxford and Cambridge colleges, so that by 1559 they were thoroughly Catholic. John Parkhurst said of Oxford that 'it is as yet a den of thieves and of those who hate the light'; there were, he went on, 'few gospellers . . . and many papists'.[41] Elizabeth purged the colleges in turn, at least forty-three fellows of New College, Oxford, leaving or being expelled, probably for religious reasons, in the first twelve years of her reign. However, the pro-

---

[39] Palliser, *Tudor York*, 254.

[40] F. F. Foster, *The Politics of Stability: A Portrait of the Rulers in Elizabethan London* (London, 1977), 122.

[41] Penry Williams, 'Elizabethan Oxford: State, Church and University', in James McConica (ed.), *The History of the University of Oxford*, iii: *The Collegiate University* (Oxford, 1986), 405. See *Zurich Letters*, i. 11–12, 29, 33.

cess of conversion was slow, for new adherents to the Catholic faith came forward, like Edmund Campion at St John's and Robert Parsons at Balliol. But by 1577 a religious census showed that the established Church had almost gained control: only five colleges—All Souls, Balliol, Exeter, Queen's, and Trinity—contained any recusants, though the situation in the private halls was less satisfactory. While the government remained anxious, the Chancellor, Leicester, writing in 1581 that 'many papists have heretofore and may hereafter lurk among you, and be brought up by corrupt tutors', the Catholic strength of the previous decades had by then greatly diminished in both Oxford and Cambridge.[42]

Although Catholics had mostly been driven from positions of influence and power by the middle of the reign, recusancy was still an acute problem for the government and was to remain so until 1603 and beyond. Indeed the number of recorded recusants steadily increased. Why, when the Protestants had captured the high ground, should that have been so? The traditional view holds that, while Catholics maintained their preference for the old faith during the first eighteen or so years of the reign, they were not yet organized for positive recusancy; that except in a few counties, such as Lancashire, they were willing to attend the services of the official Church because they had not been taught that this was wrong; but that the missionaries, arriving during the 1570s and 1580s, transformed the body of ill-defined, poorly instructed, and unorganized Catholics into a hard core of recusants, with a more amorphous body of 'church papists' in support. This account has recently been challenged.[43] It is argued that there was a considerable body of recusants before the missionaries arrived; that this body had survived from the end of Mary's reign; that the increase in the number of recusants had begun before the great body of missionaries arrived in England; and that it was most marked in regions where they were least thick on the ground. There is little doubt that Catholic recusancy survived from Marian times into Elizabethan. From the beginning, there were priests who continued to say Mass, laymen who attended their services and stayed away from their parish churches. In Lancashire many priests were inspired by Laurence Vaux, Warden of Manchester College until 1559, who returned from self-imposed exile in Rome to tell English laymen that if they attended Anglican church services they 'do not walk in state of salvation'.[44] While

---

[42] Williams, 'Elizabethan Oxford', 427.

[43] I once held this view: Penry Williams, *The Tudor Regime* (Oxford, 1979), 265; but I now regard it as over-simplified. See Bossy, *The English Catholic Community*, ch. 1, for the most substantial expression of this opinion; and below, p. 577, bibliographical essay, for the key works in the controversy.

[44] Haigh, *Reformation and Resistance*, 249.

recusancy was admittedly less strong elsewhere during these early years, it was certainly present. Records of ecclesiastical courts reveal that prosecutions for recusancy were brought over most of England in 1569: there were 180 presentations of recusants that year in the archdeaconry of Norwich and 116 in Winchester in the following year. However, since convictions were rare, this evidence has until lately been overlooked. Recusancy was strongest during the 1560s in the regions where it most prevailed later; and there was no severance between the older tradition and the Catholicism of the missionaries. Even so, while it is now well established that the missionaries worked from a firm base in many parts of England, the increase in the official figures for prosecutions and convictions is striking. Why should it have occurred? The answer must almost certainly lie in the greater vigour with which the government and its agents pursued the Catholics once the missionary movement had begun.

Was the missionary movement then a failure? The seminarists and Jesuits have been criticized for concentrating their attention on the south, rather than on the more Catholic north, for cultivating the gentry instead of ministering to the masses, and for transforming Catholicism into a seignorial religion for landowners, neglecting the spiritual needs of the less well-to-do.[45] Yet they cannot stand guilty of seeking the protection of the gentry from fear for their personal safety: the overwhelming majority showed immeasurable courage and many sought martyrdom. If the mission was to survive it needed protection and in most regions that could best be found in the houses of the gentry. John Gerard, a Jesuit who landed in England in November 1588, commented that, although he had at first travelled in public, 'it could not continue for ever, since the danger of recognition grew as I came to know more people'. He therefore sought the protection of a Suffolk gentleman, Henry Drury, and lived in his house, where 'almost everyone was a Catholic and it was easier to live the life of a Jesuit, even in the external details of dress and arrangement of time'.[46] There were other religious reasons for seeking the security of the manor house. Gerard realized that if he and his colleagues were to convert, then they must do so through the gentry. Of East Anglia he wrote: 'the way, I think, to go about making converts in these parts is to bring the gentry over first, and then their servants, for Catholic gentle folk must have Catholic servants.'[47] He was surely right. Yet we need to remember that when he

[45] Haigh, 'From monopoly to minority: Catholicism in early modern England', *Transactions of the Royal Historical Society*, 5th ser. 31 (1981), 129–48.
[46] John Gerard, *The Autobiography of an Elizabethan*, trans. Philip Caraman (London, 1951), 24.
[47] Ibid. 33.

talked of making 'converts' he meant stiffening the resolve of 'schismatics' or 'church papists', turning them into recusants, and 'reconciling' to the Roman Church those who were in danger of lapsing. The conversion of real heretics was probably impossible and certainly dangerous.

As for the concentration of missionary activity on the south of England, it arose partly because most of the priests landed there, partly because the mission was organized from London. Moreover, it has also to be said that many of them did in fact work in Lancashire: of 452 priests sent to England before 1603, 66 had at some point operated in that county.[48] There they could move about freely: 'in Lancashire', wrote Gerard, 'I have seen myself more than two hundred present at Mass and sermon. People of this kind come into the Church without difficulty.'[49]

After the mission became organized in the 1580s under the direction of Southwell and Garnet, safe houses were set up and a network of priests and communications was established. While recusants had certainly existed before, the new priests stiffened resistance and sharpened religious boundaries which might easily have become blurred. Lord Montague of Cowdray in Sussex had been a devout Catholic—and a loyal subject of Elizabeth—since 1559, but, even so, had occasionally attended Anglican services. When a new chaplain arrived at Cowdray in the late 1580s he reproached Montague severely for this lapse, at which the Lord fell on his knees and 'piously promised never thenceforward to be present at heretical service, which all the rest of his life he exactly observed'.[50] The Catholicism of late Elizabethan England was firmly based upon the survival of the old faith from earlier reigns, but it was both strengthened and extended by the missionaries. Their efforts were by no means confined to the families of the nobles and gentry: Gerard wrote of reconciling to the Church not only members of landed families but also 'a large number of servants and poorer people';[51] and there were also devout Catholics among the merchants and craftsmen of London—the father, stepfather, and mother of John Donne were all strong Catholics, his maternal grandmother being the niece of Sir Thomas More. However, it is generally true that Elizabethan Catholicism became a religion organized in and around the houses of the gentry; and it is difficult to see how, in times of persecution, it could very well have been different, except in Lancashire, where priests were protected by the large numbers of the devout, and in London, where they could be more easily hidden than in villages and provincial towns.

---

[48] Haigh, *Reformation and Resistance*, 279.   [49] Gerard, *Autobiography*, 32.
[50] Manning, *Religion and Society*, 160–1.   [51] Gerard, *Autobiography*, 21.

Yet the role of persecution in frustrating the missionaries has recently been denied.[52] It is true that the number of executions fluctuated and that most were performed in the 1580s, easing off thereafter; true, too, that recusancy fines were levied with the maximum inefficiency. But the pressure was nevertheless great: 131 priests and 60 lay persons were executed between 1581 and 1603. The combined effect of fines, taxation for military levies, and the loss of opportunities for office could seriously damage a man's fortune: Sir Thomas Tresham was fined in all £8,000 between 1581 and 1605—a huge sum—and many Catholic families fell into financial trouble if not ruin. Searches of Catholic houses were brutal and degrading: Gerard describes a search at Braddocks, Essex, when the pursuivants burst open doors, locked the mistress and her daughters in her room, lifted tiles, knocked down 'suspicious-looking places', and stripped off plaster.[53] Horrific tortures were inflicted on a few to extract confessions; and conviction was often followed by a hideous death. While priests mostly met this with outstanding courage, the climate of fear and suspicion was often too much for ordinary men and women. John Donne's brother Henry harboured a priest in London, was arrested, imprisoned, and died in Newgate of the plague. Donne himself was profoundly marked and torn by the experience, for to desert the faith led to the fires of hell, while remaining within it exposed him to the fate of his brother; and, after undergoing intense inner conflict, he chose apostasy and thereafter reserved a special hatred for the Jesuits, who had, he believed, imperilled his family and forced his conversion.

The divisive impact of the mission left a dark legacy for English Catholics. Disputes had begun in the 1580s between secular priests and Jesuits in Wisbech prison. When an archpriest, George Blackwell, was appointed to England on the advice of the Jesuit Robert Parsons, the seculars protested vigorously to Rome, even though Blackwell was not himself a Jesuit. But the damage spread beyond the Catholic Church itself, for some of the seculars denounced the Jesuits to the English government and proposed that priests should sign a Protestation of Allegiance to the Queen. Although the Protestation was agreed by only thirteen priests, the desire of the secular appellants for toleration provoked a welcoming response among the gentry; and after 1602 the seculars and the Jesuits developed separate organizations. Even so, in spite of apostasy and division, Catholicism remained strong throughout at least the first forty years of the

[52] Christopher Haigh, 'Revisionism, the Reformation and the history of English Catholicism', *Journal of Ecclesiastical History*, 36 (1985), 394–406, esp. 401–2.
[53] Gerard, *Autobiography*, 58–63.

seventeenth century: it should not be described, as one historian has insisted it should, as a very small sectarian rump.[54]

4. THE PURITANS

Few terms have given historians so much trouble as 'puritan'. It was first used in the 1560s as a word of abuse: 'some hot puritans of the new clergy' was the disapproving phrase.[55] Other terms were used as synonyms—'precisians', 'precise folk', for instance—but 'puritan' is the word that has endured. Having begun life as a form of obloquy, it had no exact definition and never acquired one. Those to whom it was applied called themselves 'the godly' or 'the true gospellers', but for us to adopt that term would be to take them at their own valuation and to suggest that no one else deserved to be called 'godly'; 'nonconformist' is inappropriate, since the 'puritans' remained members of the Church and regarded themselves as conforming to its true doctrines; and 'radical Protestant reformers' is accurate but overlong.[56] In spite of its ambiguities, 'puritan' remains a convenient label for describing those who believed that the Church of England, while a true Church, needed to be further reformed in a Protestant direction: they would cleanse it of such popish elements as elaborate clerical dress, kneeling at communion, and the making of the sign of the cross; and they would emphasize more strongly than their opponents the edification of the people through the reading of the Scriptures and, above all, preaching. They were not a single, homogeneous, organized group, although there were such groups—the Presbyterians, for instance—among their number; but they recognized a common bond between those whom they called 'the godly'; and they also recognized a common antagonism towards those who will here be called 'conformists': men who, while remaining loyal Protestants, put order and obedience to authority above the reading of the Scriptures and preaching.

Conflict between the puritans and the government of the Church opened in the 1560s over their refusal to wear the surplice and the cope. In 1563 two Oxford heads of colleges, Laurence Humfrey of Magdalen and Thomas Sampson of Christ Church, protested against the government's insistence that, when conducting services, clergy should wear the surplice and, when not in church, the special outdoor dress prescribed by the royal Injunctions of 1559. When Archbishop Parker issued his *Advertisements* in 1566 a wider

---

[54] Haigh, 'From monopoly to minority', 130, 132.

[55] Leonard J. Trinterud (ed.), *Elizabethan Puritanism* (New York, 1971), 7.

[56] As used by C. M. Dent, *Protestant Reformers in Elizabethan Oxford* (Oxford, 1983), *passim*.

protest began under the leadership of Humfrey and Sampson. To these
men the surplice was reminiscent of their Marian persecutors: 'have you
forgotten', wrote William Turner, 'those cruel and popish butchers which
not long ago burned so many Christian martyrs, which had on their heads
such woollen horns?'[57] The issue was quickly broadened when some of the
protesters were deprived of their posts. Bishop Grindal of London encountered a crowd of Londoners who had held a wedding service illegally in
Plumbers' Hall: charged with absence from their parish churches and with
unlawful assembly, they replied that when 'all our preachers were displaced
by your law that would not subscribe to your apparel and your law . . . then
we bethought us what were best to do'.[58] They reminded Grindal that there
had been a secret Protestant congregation in London under Mary and that
exiles in Geneva had used a service book allowed by Calvin. For them the
issue had become one of obedience and authority, not merely of vestments.
To Grindal obedience was more important than costume: 'you see me', he
told them, 'wear a cope or a surplice in Paul's. I had rather minister without
these things, but for order's sake and obedience to the prince.'[59] While
Grindal was sympathetic to the puritan view but unwilling to tolerate
downright disobedience, Parker was much more rigid: 'execution, execution, execution of laws and orders must be the first and the last part of good
governance,' he wrote to Cecil, whom he suspected of leniency.[60]

The efforts of the early puritans foundered against Parker's obduracy
and the caution of reformers like Grindal; and the failure of their campaign to eradicate popery and to create a truly reformed ministry led them
into more extreme courses. By the early 1570s some of them were proposing
the establishment of a Presbyterian system of Church government. At
parish level, the discipline which the Church, as they saw it, lacked, would
be enforced by a consistory of pastors and lay elders; and in place of
bishops, the Church would be ruled by *classes*, meetings of ministers and
elders presided over by a moderator, whose office would rotate among
the senior ministers. The authority of Queen and hierarchy would be
abolished.

One of those who came to Presbyterianism through anger and impatience
with existing authority was Edward Dering, a distinguished Cambridge
scholar who was chaplain to the Duke of Norfolk and had been presented by
Archbishop Parker himself to a parish in Kent. Preaching before the Queen,
Dering told her that Church benefices were 'defiled with impropriations';
that patrons sold benefices or gave them to their children and servants; and

[57] Patrick Collinson, *The Elizabethan Puritan Movement* (London, 1967), 95.
[58] H. C. Porter, *Puritanism in Tudor England* (London, 1970), 82.
[59] Ibid. 89.   [60] BL Lansdowne MS 8, fo. 144.

that ministers of religion were but 'blind guides' and 'dumb dogs'. Then he addressed the Queen directly: 'yet you in the mean while that all these whoredoms are committed, you at whose hands God will require it, you sit still and are careless, let men do as they list.' Elizabeth let her reactions be known and Dering later wrote that the years had 'passed exceeding slowly . . . since first I heard how much your Highness misliked of me'.[61] His comments on the bishops were even more stinging: he wrote to Burghley that 'the lordship of the bishop hath been even a plague sore in the state of a kingdom and is at this day a swelling wound of corruption in the body of a commonwealth'.[62]

While Dering had moved to a radical position from a more moderate stance, others had been there all along, regarding government by consistory and *classis* as divinely ordained. Thomas Cartwright, Lady Margaret Professor of Divinity at Cambridge, was the scholar of the movement, who provided its scriptural foundation; John Field and Thomas Wilcox were its organizers and propagandists, who brought out the *Admonition to Parliament* in 1572. Field's invective was typical of much puritan polemic: he wrote of the Prayer Book that 'this book is an unperfect book, culled and picked out of that popish dunghill, the . . . mass book, full of all abominations'.[63] A popular foundation for the Presbyterian movement was provided by London congregations, some composed of those radicals who had come under attack in the previous decade, others of foreign exiles from persecution, who made up the 'Stranger Churches' of French and Dutch Protestants and provided models and teaching for their English friends. However, the power base of the Presbyterian movement was a narrow one, for many of those who had been involved in earlier protests against authority, like Laurence Humfrey and Thomas Sampson, now held aloof. When the Privy Council and Archbishop Parker again moved into the attack, radical London ministers were summoned for interrogation, several were imprisoned for disobedience to authority, and Cartwright was forced to escape into exile.

The apparent destruction of the Presbyterian movement was followed by a brief period of hopeful reform, when Grindal, backed by both Burghley and Walsingham, became Archbishop of Canterbury in 1576. The House of Commons presented a petition to the Queen humbly asking her to remedy the abuses of clerical ignorance, pluralism, and absenteeism, which were depriving many of the word of God. Now that the Commons had decided

---

[61] Patrick Collinson, *Godly People: Essays on English Protestantism and Puritanism* (London, 1983), 305.

[62] Peter Lake, *Moderate Puritans and the Elizabethan Church* (Cambridge, 1982), 21.

[63] Porter, *Puritanism*, 123.

to proceed by presenting a petition rather than by demanding legislation, which in her view encroached upon her authority, Elizabeth agreed to reform matters and to confer with her bishops; and the outcome was the issue of articles approved by Convocation and published with royal approbation. But they amounted to no more than a sop to the reformers.

More progress was being made at the grass roots through the occasions known as 'prophesyings'. These were not necessarily Presbyterian in tone and they won the approval of many bishops, including Grindal. However, there is evidence that they were being taken over in some places by radicals. The Earl of Leicester wrote to Thomas Wood, a puritan layman, that

I fear the over-busy dealing of some hath done so much hurt in striving to make better perforce that which is by permission good enough already as we shall neither have it in Southam [an important centre for prophesyings] or any other where else, and do what we can all, and those all you think more zealous than I. And this have I feared long ago would prove the fruit of our dissension for trifles first and since for other matters.[64]

Elizabeth, who had long been suspicious of prophesyings, heard of the matter and, possibly prompted by Leicester, ordered Grindal to suppress them. In a long letter to the Queen he refused. Suggestions for compromise—that the laity should be excluded from the audience—were turned down by him, and he was in consequence suspended from the execution of his office. His suspension marked the beginning of a change in the composition of the bench of bishops and the end of the brief era of co-operation between the authorities and the reformers.[65]

Bishop Aylmer of London did his best to silence unbeneficed preachers like Field, and Bishop Edmund Freke in Norwich diocese allegedly suppressed '19 or 20 godly exercises of preaching and catechising' in the city.[66] The puritans responded with more radical strategies, and repression led to a further development of the 'classical' movement. Conferences and *classes* were not necessarily Presbyterian in aims and outlook. The best known of them, whose minute-book has survived, was established at Dedham in Essex. There, ministers met to discuss points of doctrine as well as such practical issues as the observance of the sabbath; but they did not admit lay members to their conference and they did not all reject the authority of bishops. However, John Field, now returned to the scene of battle, very emphatically did. In 1583 he wrote to the moderate-minded leader of the Dedham conference, Edmund Chapman, urging the need to unite against

---

[64] Collinson, *Godly People*, 97.   [65] Above, Ch. 8 s. 1.
[66] A. Hassell Smith, *County and Court: Government and Politics in Norfolk. 1558–1602* (Oxford, 1972), 21.

Whitgift: 'Our new Archbishop, now he is in, sheweth himself as he was wont to be . . . He is eagerly set to overthrow and waste his poor Church.' All possible measures must be taken to hinder him: 'It will be too late to deal afterward. The peace of the Church is at an end, if he be not curbed.'[67] At the two universities, in London, and in Northamptonshire, Field established conferences with a firmly Presbyterian outlook. Elsewhere, while he had support from clergy and laity, the *classes* were not fully committed to the abolition of episcopacy.

Immediately after his enthronement Whitgift justified Field's warnings. In October 1583 he ordered the clergy to subscribe to three articles: that the Queen should properly have authority, ecclesiastical and temporal, over all her subjects; that the Prayer Book contained nothing contrary to the word of God; and that the Thirty-nine Articles were agreeable to the word of God. The second of these articles provoked opposition, for many reformers believed the Prayer Book to contain popish elements. Three or four hundred ministers refused to subscribe and were threatened with deprivation; and at this point their prominent lay allies in government came to their aid. Robert Beale, Clerk to the Council, commented that 'it is an easy thing to govern and reduce babes in colleges and perhaps some in universities to their opinions. But it is an unfit and undiscreet thing either to have the same opinion, or to attempt the same in the whole realm, without better matter than I can hitherto see.'[68] Beale was supported by Burghley, Leicester, and other councillors, and by gentlemen from the shires: thirty-eight Kentish landowners sent up a petition to the Privy Council complaining about the lack of preaching in their county. Faced with this opposition Whitgift retreated, withdrawing his demand that the clergy should subscribe to the contentious article and requiring only that they agree to use the Prayer Book. Most accepted this and subscribed to the other articles rather than divide the Church. Against the hard core of 'non-subscribers' Whitgift produced a new set of twenty-four articles, to be answered on oath, Burghley commenting that they were 'of great length and curiosity, formed in a Romish style' and comparable to the questions posed by 'the inquisitors of Spain'.[69] However, by now only a few clerics were standing out against Whitgift.

Yet a final Presbyterian drive was still to come. In the Parliaments of 1584 and 1586 the Presbyterians pressed for a 'Bill' and a 'Book': the 'Bill' was designed to erect strict discipline in a Church ruled by ministers and elders; the 'Book' was a liturgy based upon an English edition of the Genevan

---

[67] R. G. Usher, *The Presbyterian Movement in the Reign of Queen Elizabeth*, Camden Soc., 3rd ser. 8 (London, 1905), 96.

[68] Collinson, *Puritan Movement*, 254.   [69] Ibid. 270.

Prayer Book. Linked with these parliamentary proposals was a vigorous propaganda campaign. Petitions were sent up from the shires lamenting the wretched state of the Church, in particular the failure of the bishops to provide a preaching clergy and the persecution of the most worthy ministers. The petitions were supported by detailed surveys of the parochial ministry in several counties. 'Non-preachers' were carefully listed, the scandalous habits of some recorded in detail: Mr Ampleforth, vicar of Much Badow, Essex, 'had a child by his own sister' and was suspected of popery; Mr Ellis of Bowers was alleged to be 'a dicer, a carder, a pot companion, a company keeper of riotous persons, living very offensively to all men'. Probably some of these scandals were real enough; but it is essential to remember that these charges were part of a propaganda campaign and they should not be taken as an objective account of the Church. In spite of this outpouring of rhetoric and abuse the parliamentary measures secured little support.[70] Not only were they rejected in Parliament, they were even turned down by the Dedham conference; only in the *classes* of Northamptonshire and Warwickshire was there serious support. The collapse of the movement in Parliament was followed by a general erosion and retreat: Field died in 1588 and with him the leadership of the movement; and a series of prosecutions in Star Chamber brought the Presbyterian cause to an end. But more moderate puritans continued to minister and to preach.

Confrontation and campaigning were far from central to the lives of most puritans. William Perkins, one of the most revered puritan preachers and writers, was hardly involved at all in organization or propaganda, although he was called before Star Chamber in the 1590s. Interpretation of the Scriptures, establishment of true doctrine, preaching of the word, and practical moral conduct were the main and intense preoccupations of men like him. Their spiritual, mental, and moral concerns can be better understood from their pastoral tracts, sermons, letters, and diaries, and from the minutes of the Dedham conference, than from the polemical literature of the campaigns.

Predestination and election were central to the beliefs of puritans. Before the foundation of the world, God had made a double decree, predestining some to salvation, others to damnation, as Perkins vividly and unambiguously explained in his pastoral treatise *A Golden Chaine* (1591):

Predestination hath two parts: election and reprobation. Election is God's decree whereby of his own free will he hath ordained certain men to salvation, to the praise

---

[70] Albert Peel (ed.), *The Second Parte of a Register* (2 vols., Cambridge, 1915), i. 274–5; ii. 70 ff., esp. 162–3. Above, Ch. 8 s. 5, for the Parliament of 1586.

of the glory of his grace. This decree is that book of life wherein are written the names of the elect. . . . The decree of reprobation is that part of predestination whereby God according to the most free and just purpose of his will hath determined to reject certain men unto eternal destruction and misery, and that to the praise of his justice. . . . Further, whom God rejecteth to condemnation, those he hateth. This hatred of God is whereby he detesteth and hateth the reprobate when he is fallen into sin, for the same sin.[71]

God's unalterable decree separated the godly from the ungodly. While only he could distinguish with certainty between the two, the godly must nevertheless fight constantly with the ungodly: 'the destruction of God's enemies is a cause of rejoicing', wrote Abdias Ashton, fellow of St John's College, Cambridge. To win their battle the godly must always examine their hearts in order to know their faith and increase it; good works were necessary, not for salvation, but to assure a member of the godly of his election, to testify his faith to the world, and to persuade others to act to the glory of God. In the words of George Estye, preacher at Bury St Edmunds, 'we [must] always seek and labour for such a faith which may not make us idle but which may bring forth sweet and plentiful fruits'.[72] This was an active and combative faith, whose protagonists looked back for exemplars to the Old Testament, to the warlike people of Israel and their prophets.

The Old Testament lay behind another of the most powerful elements of puritan ideology: the doctrine of the covenant. God had made two covenants with man: one, of works, was formed with Adam before the Fall and obliged all men to live by God's law and perform good works; the other, of grace, was sealed by Christ and applied only to elect and regenerate Christians. In Perkins's words, 'God's promise to men is that whereby he bindeth himself to man to be his God, if he perform the condition. Man's promise to God is that whereby he voweth his allegiance to the Lord, and to perform the condition between them.'[73] Man's knowledge of grace and of the covenant led to the concept of sanctification, whereby the godly strove constantly to increase their faith, rid themselves of sin, and fight against Antichrist. Assurance of grace helped them to resist temptation with confidence; the idea of the covenant bound together the godly.

Puritans and conformists alike accepted the doctrine of predestination and the notion of the covenants. The doctrine of election had been declared, in a somewhat muted way, to be the faith of the Church in the Thirty-nine Articles; and it was more strongly reaffirmed in the Lambeth Articles of 1595, drawn up by Whitgift:

[71] William Perkins, *A Golden Chaine* (1591), in *The Work of William Perkins*, ed. Ian Breward (Abingdon, 1970), 197, 250 (chs. 15, 52).
[72] Lake, *Moderate Puritans*, 137, 159–60.   [73] Collinson, *Puritan Movement*, 434–5.

i. God from eternity has predestined some men to life and reprobated some to . . . death . . . iii. There is a determined and certain number of predestined, which cannot be increased or diminished . . . iv. Those not predestined to salvation are inevitably condemned on account of their sins . . . viii. No one can come to Christ unless it be granted to him, and unless the Father draws him; and all men are not drawn by the Father to come to the Son.[74]

These bleak statements fairly represented the doctrine of the Church, accepted by both Whitgift and the puritans. But they were repugnant to the Queen, who ordered the Archbishop to suspend them as involving 'a matter tender and dangerous to weak ignorant minds'.[75] For Whitgift and other bishops this did not involve a major problem, since the doctrine of election was not central to their beliefs; and indeed, since they had to minister to all members of the Church, godly and ungodly alike, it seemed to them best left in the background. For the puritans, on the other hand, these matters were central and must be applied with total commitment. Perkins emphasized the danger of a weak commitment to the doctrine: 'Men that live in the Church are greatly annoyed with a fearful security and deadness of heart, by which . . . they think it enough to make a common protestation of the faith, not once in all their lifetimes examining themselves whether they be in the estate of grace before the eternal God or not.'[76]

The struggle against the Pope, recognized as Antichrist, was another issue that involved all Protestants and all members of the Church of England. Yet some were prepared to tolerate ceremonies which the puritans saw as relics of the popish regime. The crucial distinction between puritans and conformists is seen in the conduct of Grindal, who disliked the surplice but would wear it out of obedience as a 'thing indifferent', while his opponents saw it and all the other 'rags of Rome' as abominations. For bishops, even for reforming ones like Grindal, some things must be tolerated for the sake of order within the Church, and only proven recusants should be condemned as papists; for the puritans anything which remotely smacked of popery was intolerable and anyone who did not belong to the godly community was at least a potential papist.

To increase their faith, to serve God, and to perform the good works which sprang out of his grace, the godly must learn how to live, how to teach others to do so, and how to support one another in faith. The divinity of the puritans was essentially practical: a matter of learning how to do God's will and to withstand temptation. The two essential instruments of the religious life were the exercise of godly preaching and the constant, deep study of the Scriptures, where God's will and law were revealed. Preaching of the word

[74] H. C. Porter, *Reformation and Reaction in Tudor Cambridge* (Cambridge, 1958), 371.
[75] Lake, *Moderate Puritans*, 228.   [76] *Work of William Perkins*, 357.

provided both a conduit for God's grace and instruction in the godly life. On preaching and prophesying Perkins wrote:

The dignity thereof appeareth in that, like a lady, it is highly mounted and carried aloft in a chariot, whereas all other gifts, both of tongues and arts, attend on this like handmaids, aloof off. Answerable to this dignity there is also a two-fold use: one, in that it serveth to collect the Church, and to accomplish the number of the elect; the other, for that it drives away the wolves from the folds of the Lord.[77]

Among the common errors of 'poor people', he listed the belief 'that a man which cometh at no sermons may as well believe as he which hears all the sermons in the world'.[78]

To be effective, preaching had to be grounded upon the Scriptures and to be directed at opening up the word to the godly; and therefore the true minister had to possess a thorough knowledge of the Bible. Indeed, only by constant study of the Bible could the godly, whether ministers or laymen, know God's will and purpose. Thomas Cartwright insisted on the need for the Scriptures to be available to all:

If (as hath been showed) all ought to read the scriptures, then all ages, all sexes, all degrees and callings, all high and low, rich and poor, wise and foolish have a necessary duty therein . . . For the scriptures declareth that women and children, and that from their infancy, that noble and ignoble, rich and poor, wise and foolish exercise themselves in the holy scriptures.[79]

Preaching and Scripture were the essential means of 'edification', the building of a true Church whose members were the godly.

The personal and communal preoccupations of Elizabethan puritans can be seen in two remarkable sources: the journal of Richard Rogers and the minute-book of the conference at Dedham in Essex. Rogers was born at Chelmsford (that 'dunghill of abomination' he called it), became a lecturer at Wethersfield, Essex, and wrote an important theological work, *The Seven Treatises*.[80] His journal is a record of his spiritual life, both his progress and his backsliding, and is obviously intended to aid the process of self-examination that was so strongly recommended to the godly. Rogers does not seem to have been much concerned with pastoral activity, although he was 'stayed' by the knowledge that God had brought many to the truth through his ministry. He found pleasure and joy in communing with other godly ministers, but otherwise gives an impression of intense and lonely introspection. Sometimes he felt a sweet peace, more often a 'sensible sorrow of

[77] *Work of William Perkins*, 331.
[78] Ibid. 143.   [79] Lake, *Moderate Puritans*, 288.
[80] *Two Elizabethan Puritan Diaries by Richard Rogers and Samuel Ward*, ed. M. M. Knappen (Chicago, 1933), 61.

my unworthiness', especially when he looked back and saw that 'my course hath been far unbeseeming one who hath given name to the gospel'. His commitment was to 'study'—study, that is, of the Scriptures. Any failure of concentration in himself was detected, noted, and lamented.[81] Marriage and family were one such distraction: he observed that when good men had families they delighted in them rather than in the Lord. When his own wife was in labour, he contemplated the possible implications of her death: among them were 'fear of marrying again'; 'want of it in the meanwhile'; 'care of household matters cast on me'; 'neglect of study'; 'care and looking after children'. His wife survived this crisis, but when she did die Rogers married again in spite of his own misgivings.[82]

A misfortune much worse than the death of his wife—from Rogers's point of view—nearly befell him when he was threatened with suspension from the ministry in 1589. It would, he wrote, be one of the 'greatest crosses' that could be laid upon him; he tried to 'stay up' his weakness with 'some strength of persuasions' that it was the will of the Lord, but also in part the result of his own shortcomings, 'seeing I did not honour God in studying for my sermons as sometime, and as I should have done'. It was, he insisted, sent by God to try him, 'seeing the lord will exercise my faith, patience, obedience, etc. hereby'. In the event, the blow did not fall and Rogers was able to continue his ministry, in which he found a role model in John Knewstub, a leading Suffolk puritan. Knewstub, according to Rogers, was unwearied in prayer, showed love to all, had rare humility joined with knowledge, was constant in his course to walk with the Lord, and prevented the subtleties of the devil. 'This glass', concluded Rogers, 'I desire to set before mine eyes daily.'[83]

The conference at Dedham began in October 1582 as a meeting of thirteen ministers from neighbouring parishes under the leadership of Edmund Chapman, who held an endowed lectureship in the parish. It was neither a separatist cell nor part of the Presbyterian network of *classes*; indeed its members disapproved of the proposals for the Book of Discipline. They met for mutual support and edification, and for discussion of scriptural and practical issues. Proceedings opened with an exposition of a biblical text by one of the members, followed by a 'censure' of his performance by the others after he had withdrawn. Certain days were appointed to be spent in prayer and fasting. The minutes themselves are mainly concerned with the discussion of practical pastoral issues. Should bastard children be baptized? What course should be taken with the multitude of rogues? Should the ministers subscribe to the articles presented by the

---

[81] Ibid. 55, 59.   [82] Ibid. 73–4.   [83] Ibid. 90–1, 95.

Archbishop? Should a member baptize a child of parents from another parish where there was an 'ill minister'? Should parishioners in hatred against one another for defamatory words be admitted to communion? Should the minister visit every family in his charge? Above all, how should the sabbath be observed?[84]

Two particular matters and one general issue illustrate the proceedings at Dedham. On 7 October 1588, the seventy-second meeting, Ranulph Catlin, vicar of Wenham, asked how he should deal with two people 'that were in hatred one against the other for words defamatory, viz. saying that he had killed a sheep'. Catlin asked whether he should admit them to holy communion, and was advised that 'if they would profess love one to another he might, because he cannot work love but only admonish them of the danger of it, but if they be in open hatred the book warrants him not to receive them'. Catlin also asked what he should do with some 'froward poor men' that were disordered: he was told to admonish them, and if they would not listen to him, tell them that they were no longer of his flock; but he should nevertheless continue warning them of the 'danger and misery' in which they stood.[85]

The general issue involved the debate over the sabbath. Three specific questions were raised: whether there was a sabbath; whether it involved the whole day; and whether Christians were bound to the same laws as Jews. Richard Crick, preacher of East Bergholt, and Henry Sandes, pastor of Boxford, were appointed to deliver the arguments. In essence, the dispute involved the nature of sabbath obligation: did it derive from divine command, as Sandes asserted, or was it a ceremonial matter, as Crick believed? In other words, was it a human institution, subject to the laws made by the Church, or were Christians bound by the Judaic laws of the Old Testament? The matter was debated several times in the conference without any firm conclusion being reached: the discussions are remarkable for the tolerance given to Crick's opinions, which appear to have been contrary to those usually attributed to puritans.[86] The openness of debate, the practical concerns of discussion, and the readiness to deal cautiously with the issues are striking features of the Dedham meetings, all of them contrasting with the dogmatic and often extreme utterances of puritan tracts and sermons.

The Dedham conference came to an end in 1589 'by the malice of Satan' and the death of some of the brethren; and the Presbyterian movement was crushed soon after that. But this did not mean the end of puritan activity; it merely enabled them to devote themselves more fully to writing and pub-

[84] Usher, The Presbyterian Movement, passim. [85] Ibid. 71.
[86] Ibid. 27, 28, 30–5, 47, 75–6; Kenneth L. Parker, The English Sabbath (Cambridge, 1988), 102–6.

lishing moral and devotional texts. The publications of William Perkins and puritan involvement in theological debate during the 1590s testify to their unflagging zeal.

There was no rigid body of doctrine that could be called 'puritanism'; but there were 'puritans'. Members of the godly, they shared many beliefs with conformists like Whitgift, but tended, in contrast to the establishment, to give total priority to the furtherance of reformation and the establishment of Christ's invisible Church on earth. While they did, usually, recognize one another as the 'godly', their views changed in the course of the reign and were, in part, formed by the attitudes and policies of their opponents, who often picked the field of battle.

5. A PROTESTANT CHURCH? A PROTESTANT NATION?

The identity of the Church of England and the measure of its success in establishing itself in the hearts and minds of the nation have been matters of debate since the sixteenth century. Some protagonists argue that there was no break in the tradition of the Church during the Tudor era; that the ambiguities of the Elizabethan 'settlement' and the preferences of the Tudor and early Stuart monarchs ensured continuity; and that the 'Arminian' policies of the 1620s and 1630s had their beginnings in the reign of Elizabeth. On the other side, such views are seen to derive from the claims of 'Arminian' churchmen in the seventeenth century and of High Church or Anglo-Catholic historians in the nineteenth; and insistence on continuity is thought to underestimate, even to deny, the Protestant credentials of the Elizabethan Church.[87]

No one disputes that the Church was a composite body, with a traditional structure of episcopal rule, a liturgy that owed something to Rome as well as to Geneva, little or nothing of the 'discipline' desired by the Presbyterians, but, on the other hand, a doctrine which was largely, though not completely, reformed. Its members ranged from Lancelot Andrewes, spiritual ancestor of the seventeenth-century 'Arminians', through conformist bishops like Whitgift and reforming bishops like Grindal, to puritans like Perkins and Presbyterians like Cartwright. Where, if anywhere, in this spectrum can the true Church be found? Can any one group within it be considered dominant? Was there any real consensus among its

---

[87] See below, bibliographical essay, pp. 576–7. The term 'Arminian' is, strictly speaking, applied to followers of the Dutch theologian Jacobus Arminius, who preached a doctrine of free will against the predestinarianism of Calvin's disciples. In English contexts the term is also used for the opponents of Calvinism, and particularly for Laud and his allies.

members? Is it right to claim that there was 'a Church establishment of senior clergy which was committed to a Protestant reformation, and which saw that reformation in terms of discontinuity rather than continuity'?[88] Some qualifications have to be made to this proposition. Elizabeth, while implacably hostile to Rome, did not intend further reformation, disliked Presbyterians as much as she did papists, and refused to commit the Church to the predestinarian tenets of the Lambeth articles.[89] She was, after all, Supreme Governor of the Church, and her will counted for more in its evolution than that of any individual bishop. Other exceptions to any consensus are found during the 1590s in men like Andrewes, who rejected the idea of further reformation, opposed the Calvinist emphasis upon election, and considered the sacraments more important than sermons; but, until the 1620s, their influence upon the Church was small.

The beliefs and attitudes of two men provide a key to the late Elizabethan Church: John Whitgift, Archbishop of Canterbury 1583–1604, and Richard Hooker, whose great work, *Of the Laws of Ecclesiastical Polity*, has been long regarded as a definitive treatise. Whitgift's position on central issues of doctrine is difficult to assess, since most of his writings were polemical in purpose, aimed at refuting the opinions of Cartwright. However, he accepted the doctrine of double election—of some to salvation and of others to damnation—as it was set out in his Lambeth articles; he acknowledged the unique authority of Scripture; he respected the opinions of Calvin; and he seems to have believed that preaching rather than the sacraments was the principal means of edification. But he differed from the puritans in his view of the Church. For them the true Church was the godly community, the invisible Church, consisting only of the elect; for Whitgift, the invisible Church existed only in Heaven, and the Church on earth comprehended sinners as well as saints. This profound difference opposed his way to theirs: he was concerned with unity and with ministering to all men; they were not. In a state Church, which necessarily included all the subjects of the realm, bishops, appointed by the monarch, were almost bound to give priority to the needs of the visible Church.

Hooker's beliefs are more easily discerned, for although he, like Whitgift, was engaged in controversy with the puritans, he was spared the burdens of office and free to develop his thought without concern for its immediate political consequences. Unlike both Whitgift and the puritans, Hooker considered reason as well as Scripture to be the source of ecclesiastical law and the means of coming to the knowledge of God; and this was perhaps his

---

[88] Diarmaid MacCulloch, 'The myth of the English Reformation', *Journal of British Studies*, 30 (1991), 1–19.

[89] Above, p. 483.

most important contribution to the ideological base of the Church of England. Further, he held that the Church of Rome was a true Church, however perverted it might have become, and that the Church of England had not broken with that true, traditional Church; and, in keeping with that view, he held that ceremonies, especially the Eucharist and baptism, could edify as much or more than sermons. Hooker seldom mentioned predestination and election in the *Laws of Ecclesiastical Polity*, and while his exact position on that doctrine is obscure, he certainly did not regard it as a central tenet. However, like Whitgift, he believed that the visible Church contained both saved and damned, and that it was obliged to minister to both, in part at least because it was not possible to distinguish between them. Some of Hooker's views were close to those of Whitgift and his fellow conformists; others were distinct and represented innovations in the doctrines of the Church. Yet, significantly, his works were not published until late in the reign of Elizabeth and some of them appeared later still: Books I–IV of the *Laws* were published in 1593, Book V in 1597, Books VI and VIII in 1648, Book VII in 1661. They had a restricted influence in Hooker's own day, were probably not much read until the seventeenth century, and were not even much acknowledged by the 'Arminians'.[90] Whether or not Hooker established the true faith of the Elizabethan Church, whether or not he was an innovator in that tradition, it is apparent that the beliefs of the clerical establishment, unlike the attitudes of the Supreme Governor, underwent considerable changes during the reign. Reformers like Grindal, opponents of Presbyterianism like Whitgift, 'proto-Arminians' like Andrewes, and advocates of reason and law like Hooker reflect different stages in the history of the Church under Elizabeth. Until 1603, and more uneasily until 1625, they could all be accommodated within the Church establishment.

Writing in the early seventeenth century, Arthur Dent, a respected and puritan Essex preacher, complained that the common people of England had no knowledge of true doctrine. They believed, he wrote, that 'if a man say his Lord's Prayer, his Ten Commandments and his Belief, and keep them, and say no body harm, nor do no body harm and do as he would be done, have a good faith Godward and be a man of God's belief, no doubt he shall be saved without all this running to sermons and prattling of the scripture'.[91] Such people may, in the opinion of one modern historian, 'properly be spoken of as "parish anglicans"'; 'they were not', he claims,

[90] Peter Lake, *Anglicans and Puritans? Presbyterianism and English Conformist Thought from Whitgift to Hooker* (London, 1988), ch. 4.
[91] Christopher Haigh, 'The Church of England, the Catholics and the people', in Haigh (ed.), *The Reign of Elizabeth I* (London, 1984), 214.

'Protestants at all'. Nor, he goes on, were they any longer Catholics: rather, they were 'spiritual leftovers', who attended Anglican services, defended the liturgy of the Church, but hankered after an older world of ceremonies and festivities.[92]

By about 1580 the established Church had won control of the commanding heights of society. But had it transformed England into a Protestant nation even by the end of Elizabeth's reign? Was its preaching a failure? Was a large part of the population marooned in a spiritual no man's land? Obviously there can be no complete or objective answers to such questions; and there are major difficulties in making general assessments. First, the date 1603 is in many ways inappropriate for discussing the matter, since the general state of the Church was not changed by the accession of James and the process of evangelism continued without a break; and we need therefore to consider as much the direction in which the Church was moving as its condition at any single moment. Second, there was much variation, not merely from one region or county to another, but from parish to parish. Third, the evidence is, to say the least, imperfect. Preambles to wills reveal something about belief and have often been used by historians as a measure of the progress of Protestantism; but as statistical gauges they are unsatisfactory, for we do not know whether the views expressed are those of the testator or his scribe. Prosecutions brought in ecclesiastical courts provide evidence about attendance at church and about morality; but like all court records they are biased and are often more reliable about the prosecutor than about his victim. The literature of denunciation is voluminous, but inevitably prejudiced. Letters, diaries, and spiritual biographies, more common in the seventeenth century than in the sixteenth, can be invaluable, but are more usually found in the upper levels of society. However, provided that these limitations and uncertainties are borne in mind, a tentative assessment can be made.

Not surprisingly, the denunciations of the preachers reinforce the pessimistic view of Arthur Dent. George Gifford, an Essex minister, lamented that 'let the preacher speak never so plain, although they [his listeners] sit and look him in the face, yet if ye enquire of them so soon as they be out at church doors, ye shall easily perceive that (as the common saying is) it went in at one ear and out at the other'.[93] Richard Greenham, minister at Dry Drayton, Cambridgeshire, left his parish after twenty years' service there because of the 'intractableness, and unteachableness of that people amongst whom he had taken such exceeding great pains'.[94] Yet such complaints

---

[92] 'The Church of England, the Catholics and the people', 219.

[93] Collinson, *Religion of Protestants*, 201.

[94] Margaret Spufford, *Contrasting Communities: English Villagers in the Sixteenth and Seventeenth Centuries* (Cambridge, 1974), 328.

should not be accepted without question as evidence of the failure of the Protestant mission, for puritans set a high standard for themselves and for the laity, and it would have been most surprising had such a standard been reached. Their consciousness of their own sin coloured their view of others and led them to a general belief in backsliding.

There is no doubt that the number of preachers and lecturers was increasing and was having its effect upon the upper ranks of society. Great noblemen like Leicester and his brother Warwick were accepted as the allies and protectors of puritans, although their religious commitment was sometimes ambiguous. The quality of the devotion of Henry Hastings, Earl of Huntingdon, was however unalloyed. Friend and supporter of such puritan writers as Anthony Gilby and John Field, Huntingdon sent his nephew and heir to be educated in Geneva under Beza, Calvin's successor. As patron of several livings in Leicestershire, he placed notable preachers in the parishes of the county, and as Lord President of the Council in the North he used his influence and authority to spread the word in Yorkshire, Lancashire, and Durham. His brother Francis Hastings has left a large body of letters, reflecting the attitudes of a puritan aristocrat. He makes it clear, especially to the Earl, that nobles have a special duty to use the wealth and property given them by God to advance true religion; and that involves, among other things, managing the family estates prudently—something that Huntingdon himself was little disposed to do.[95]

In many counties the leading gentlemen, as well as the peers, were converted to active Protestantism by the latter part of the reign. In Suffolk, for instance, Sir Robert Jermyn and Sir John Higham, both friendly to puritans, had come to dominate religious affairs. Jermyn presented to ten livings, Higham to four; and in thirty more parishes the gift of the living was in the hands of a puritan landowner. Much the same pattern had developed in Norfolk, Essex, and Northamptonshire; and the 'godly' had come to establish firm control in many towns of midland, southern, and eastern England. The corporations of Northampton, Colchester, and Shrewsbury—to name only three—all appointed a succession of worthy preachers; in Norwich the corporation and the preachers worked closely together, 'the magistrates and the ministers embracing and seconding one another, and the common people affording due reverence and obedience to them both'.[96] While that picture may be a little too good to be wholly true, it is not very far from the mark. In many shires and towns the preachers converted and advised the natural rulers, who in turn appointed and supported the preachers. Nobles, gentlemen, and borough merchants were not,

[95] *The Letters of Sir Francis Hastings, 1574–1609*, ed. Claire Cross, Somerset Record Soc. 69 (Frome, 1969), *passim*, esp. nos. 36, 39.
[96] Collinson, *Religion of Protestants*, 143.

of course, all devout Protestants, but those who were—and in some parts of England they were many—worked hard to advance religion, co-operated well with one another, and achieved preponderant influence.

While the lives of the 'better sort' are open to our inspection, the religion of humbler people is largely hidden. However, there is certainly evidence of popular Protestantism. A Catholic priest, William Weston, imprisoned in Wisbech Castle, described an open-air conference, seen from his prison window: 'from the very beginning a great number of puritans gathered here . . . eager and vast crowds of them flocking to perform their practices—sermons, communions and fasts . . . Each of them had his own Bible, and sedulously turned the pages and looked up the texts cited by the preachers.'[97] In villages, as in towns, the devout were beginning by the early seventeenth century to form conscious and coherent groups. This is reflected at Terling, Essex, by people linking together as witnesses and guardians of one another's wills. Admittedly, these bonds had become much more evident by the 1620s than they were at an earlier date; but the process that led to the formation of 'godly' groups may well have been beginning towards the end of the reign of Elizabeth. At Denham, Suffolk, a small and devout community had emerged before 1600 under the aegis of the lord of the manor, Sir Edward Lewkenor, his formidable mother-in-law, who was the daughter of Robert Jermyn and the wife of Thomas Higham, and the two preachers, Robert and Timothy Pricke, who were father and son. In East Bergholt, also in Suffolk, the parishioners themselves combined to choose a minister, promising him that after a trial period, if it were successful, they would submit 'to all that counsel of God which you shall truly deliver to us out of his written word'. Here is an example of that unofficial grouping together that has come to be called 'voluntary religion'.[98]

While such godliness was obviously pleasing to puritans, it was not to the taste of all. Bishop Fletcher of London described the dissensions created by puritan preachers in Essex: there were, he wrote, 'great quarrels and contentions, both in their civil bodies and among their ministers, the people divided and the priests taking part on both sides and at war with themselves, as well in matter of popular quarrels as points of doctrine'.[99] As an enemy of the puritans, Fletcher was naturally inclined to emphasize the divisiveness of their activity, but, even allowing for his partiality, there is no doubt that

[97] Spufford, *Contrasting Communities*, 262–3.
[98] MacCulloch, *Suffolk and the Tudors*, 318–19. On 'voluntary religion', see Collinson, *Religion of Protestants*, ch. 6. East Bergholt had an anomalous status as a chapel of ease, whose parishioners were able to exercise some choice of their pastor.
[99] William Hunt, *The Puritan Moment; The Coming of Revolution in an English County* (Cambridge, Mass., 1983), 153.

many rural and urban communities were polarized by religion. Some historians believe that the divide followed social and economic lines, but there is no good evidence that only the possessing classes were godly or that the poor were always profane.[100] Plenty of humble men and women were pious, many of the better off were licentious. If there were any social divide corresponding to religious differences it may have lain in the opposition of young and old. For while the young, at any rate in London, appear to have welcomed the early stages of the Reformation, by the end of the century they seem often to have been alienated from godliness, or at least from the moral demands of the stricter ministers, perhaps becoming more conformable in their conduct and attitudes as they got older.

Although there was often polarization, division, and tension, there was not, except in a very few instances, separation. The 'godly' might congregate together, but they stayed within the Church, hoping by their activity and example to purify it. In the words of one preacher, although the Church might be in many ways defective, 'so many parish assemblies of England as have any competent number of good Christians in them, united together for to worship God ordinarily in our society, so many have essential and integral form of a visible church'.[101] The achievement of the late Elizabethan, and even more of the Jacobean Church, was that many 'godly', while combining together, felt that they could remain within it. Although the variety of the Church did produce tension, as long as that was contained—as it generally was—it also produced strength.

What about those men and women, the great majority, who were not counted among the 'godly'? Were they ignorant of the faith, superstitious, religious only in a nominal and conventional sense? Most of them certainly believed in magic and witchcraft; and such beliefs were not confined to the poor, the simple, and the unlettered. People commonly went to 'cunning men', or practitioners of white magic, for protection against witches or for the recovery of lost or stolen goods. While practically all Christians believed in the power of magic, devout Protestants regarded it, whether white or black, as the work of the devil: magic and witchcraft must be attacked, not by countermagic, but by prayer, fasting, and exorcism, and puritans consequently rejected the use and power of holy words, ritual objects, and so on as safeguards against misfortune. However, their campaigns were unsuccessful, at least in the sixteenth century. George Gifford wrote that 'many in great distress have been relieved and recovered by sending unto such wise men or wise women, when they could not tell what should else become

[100] As argued by Keith Wrightson and David Levine, *Poverty and Piety in an English Village: Terling 1525–1700* (London, 1979), chs. 6, 7.
[101] Collinson, *Religion of Protestants*, 280.

of them and of all that they had'. Such remedies were, in Gifford's opinion, of no true value, for the devil 'doth cease from tormenting the body for a time, that he may enter deeper into the soul. He winneth this by driving out.'[102] Yet the practice continued in spite of all that Gifford and other preachers could do about it: in 1583–4 the churchwardens of a Berkshire parish even sent to a cunning woman to discover who had stolen the cloth from their communion table. But belief in magic, though widespread, did not set up a rival system of ideas to Christianity, for its existence was thought by many to be perfectly compatible with Christian faith, even if its practice was not; and cases of witchcraft were fairly rare in most English counties.

How true then is the picture presented by puritans and even by some later historians of a population largely untouched by Protestant Christianity? Undoubtedly there were many who were merely conformist and others who were semi-heathen, preferring the alehouse to the sermon. Parishes in which there was little faith and virtually no preaching can be set in the balance against such holy communities as Denham. Even in London, where the Reformation was probably more successful than anywhere else in England, attendance at communion was not remarkable. Evidence from London in the last years of Elizabeth's reign suggests that attendance varied greatly from parish to parish and that only 35–75 per cent of potential communicants actually took the sacrament in any one year, most of those probably communicating at Easter.[103] The 'religious', in any sense of the term, were a minority. Yet the evidence of wills, although of limited statistical value, suggests that while few men and women were firmly and explicitly Calvinist in their beliefs, many testators had thought carefully about their religion.

Popular literature testifies to a widespread concern with religion. From the very inception of the Stationers' Company register in 1557–8 cheap ballads and pamphlets were being published in large numbers. In the first part of Elizabeth's reign, from 1560 to 1588, a high proportion, some 35 per cent, of these had a religious content; but that proportion fell in the next forty years to 19 per cent. The fall probably results in part from disapproval of ballads by the educated élite, partly from the hostility of the Protestants to such profane associations; in spite of that, there remained a market for popular devotional literature. The ballads covered a range of topics: some attacked the pope and England's Catholic enemies; others lamented the

---

[102] Keith Thomas, *Religion and the Decline of Magic* (2nd edn., Harmondsworth, 1973), 314, 591.
[103] Ian W. Archer, *The Pursuit of Stability: Social Relations in Elizabethan London* (Cambridge, 1991), 87–92.

sinfulness of the time; others urged repentance as a means to salvation; and others again expounded stories from Scripture. One ballad, illustrated with woodcuts, told the story of the Duchess of Suffolk, who went into exile for the sake of religion under Mary:

> That for the love of God alone,
>   her Land and Goods she left behind:
> Seeking still for that precious Stone,
>   the Word and Truth so rare to find:
> She with her Nurse, Husband, and Child,
> In poor array their sighs beguil'd.[104] (Plate 14)

Some of the illustrations to ballads were traditional in content and imagery, although pictures of the Virgin and of the saints were rare after 1560. A print of 'The Daunce and Song of Death' (1568–9) shows a traditional theme with many of its religious elements removed: the message, however, is clear that a sinful life carries terrible dangers (Plate 12). More directly religious were the engravings of Gyles Godet, a French Protestant printer, who came to England in the 1540s and became a member of the French Church in London. He designed a series of narrative prints, concentrating upon stories from the Old and New Testaments. Illustrated ballads were hung up in private houses and biblical scenes were used to decorate inns: the separation of alehouse and church was not, perhaps, so strong as the godly liked to make out.[105]

Although wills and ballads indicate a genuine and widespread interest in religion they do not in themselves answer the charge that most people failed to understand true doctrine and were simply cast into the darkness reserved for 'spiritual leftovers'. Yet it is surely a mistake to divide the population sharply into two distinct categories of the 'godly' on the one side and the heathen or indifferent remainder on the other. It is more likely that there were gradations of belief, ranging from 'serious professors' of the gospel, through men and women of varying shades of goodwill, to the 'secret heathen' who were ignorant of Christ's teaching.[106] Just as the laity may not have fitted into one or two rigid categories, so there may have been many types of minister. Some men who were rejected by puritans as ungodly were revealed by other evidence to have been committed pastors to their flocks. Richard Fletcher, vicar of Cranbrook in Kent, was criticized by his church-wardens for defaming some of his congregation as schismatics: his target was evidently John Stroud, his curate, a puritan preacher. Yet while

---

[104] Tessa Watt, *Cheap Print and Popular Piety, 1550–1640* (Cambridge, 1991), 91–4.
[105] Ibid., *passim*.
[106] See Eamon Duffy, 'The godly and the multitude in Stuart England', *Seventeenth Century*, I/1 (1986), 38–40, for evidence from the early and mid-17th cent.

Fletcher was far from being a puritan himself, he is known to have been a very active minister of religion, vigorous in the prosecution of immorality.

William Shepard, rector of Haydon in Essex, was stigmatized as a papist in the puritan survey of the county; and he, too, was certainly no puritan. Yet he was a conscientious minister, who made many gifts to his parish and was remembered years after his death to have been 'a liberal man and good to the poor, and was a man . . . that did not seek to increase his living by that which to others pertained'. Although he was called a 'halting hypocrite' by the hot puritan Antony Gilby, Shepard was described by his own church-wardens as a minister who kept hospitality, was learned, and 'doth preach in his own cure'. Above all, he encouraged his congregation to listen to ser-mons. Men like Shepard, who had served under Mary as well as Elizabeth, did not win the approval of the godly—Shepard was eventually delated for popery and forbidden to preach—but their very conservatism may have been an advantage in winning men and women to the religion of the Prayer Book.[107]

By the last two decades of Elizabeth's reign the Prayer Book had become for many, though not for the godly, the repository of a comforting faith. Its ambiguities, so abhorrent to puritans, allowed the growth of a new form of traditional worship. The funeral rites, for instance, in spite of their predestinarian petition to God, 'beseeching thee, that it may please thee to accomplish the number of thy elect', were used, in the words of Bishop Pilkington of Durham, as 'a great comfort to all Christians . . . the want of them a token of God's wrath and plague'.[108]

Protestant pastors, whether or not they were counted among the 'godly' few, do seem to have been making some headway in the last years of Elizabeth's reign, although their progress was nothing like as rapid as they wished and was to become more marked under her successor. There is plentiful evidence of Protestant piety among the educated and the better off, but it was by no means confined to them; and however censorious the puritans may have been in their surveys and their castigations, there was a live religion of a Protestant flavour outside their ranks among both clergy and laity. The divisions in the upper ranks of the Church between conform-ists and puritans were echoed in the polarities within parishes between prayer-book Anglicans and the godly.[109]

---

[107] M. S. Byford, 'The price of Protestantism: assessing the impact of religious change on Elizabethan Essex: the cases of Heydon and Colchester, 1558–1594' (D.Phil. thesis, Univer-sity of Oxford, 1988), ch. 1.

[108] Duffy, *The Stripping of the Altars*, 590.

[109] The sexual morality of the laity is discussed below, Ch. 12 ss. 2, 6.

CHAPTER 12

Family, Kinsfolk, and Neighbours

1. THE FAMILY

Most families in Elizabethan England consisted of only two generations living under one roof: parents and children.[1] These 'nuclear' families of early modern England, and indeed of most of Western Europe, contrasted with the 'stem' families of Russia or of Asia, where it was common for married brothers, grandparents, and uncles to live within the same household. Only in the houses of great landowners would such extended family groups be found in England. In that respect—and in others—the families of Elizabethan England were not so different from those of our own day; and households were for the most part correspondingly small. A census taken at Ealing in 1599 shows that there were 404 persons living in 85 households, which gives an average, or mean, size of household as 4.75; and this figure from Ealing has been corroborated by larger samples from later dates. Obviously there were variations between households: the better off had several servants, the poor had none. A survey of Goodnestone, Kent, although taken in 1676, almost certainly reflects the pattern of the previous century and provides more detail than the Ealing census. There were then 62 households in all, of which the houses of the 12 poorest inhabitants contained only 25 residents between them, a mean size of 2.1. The 29 households of gentlemen and yeomen contained 178 people, a mean size of 6.1; one of the gentry houses contained 22 people, which somewhat increased the average. The yeoman households held an average of 2.5 children and 1.5 servants. In the whole parish there were 113 children, 51 servants, and only 5 resident relatives, the mean size of all

---

[1] In the 16th cent. the word 'family' denoted all those living under the same roof: husband, wife, children, and, in some instances, apprentices. However, for our purposes a distinction needs to be made between those people in the household who were related by blood or marriage and the others: 'family' will therefore be used of the former and 'household' of the latter and larger group. Beyond the confines of the household and of the 'nuclear' family of parents and children, there was a yet wider group of relatives; this will be described here as 'kin' or 'lineage'.

households being 4.5, only the household of the richest gentleman exceeding 12 people.[2]

Households did not remain constant in size. Children were born, grew up, left home to work or to marry—or died. The number of servants might well vary over time according to the demands of young children upon the mother. Fathers or mothers might die as the children were growing up; and the remarriage of the surviving parent would introduce new members into the family. So, given a mean size of 6 for yeoman households, we can assume that at some stage the number might be rising to 10 or even 12, and later falling to 4 or fewer; but the range of size for most yeoman households would probably lie between 4 and 8. Craftsmen and merchants in towns presided over larger households, since they usually employed several living-in workers and apprentices. A typical bakery in Jacobean London contained as many as 13 or 14 people, including 4 journeymen, 2 apprentices, and 2 maidservants; but such households were exceptional.[3] Even more exceptional were the households of the nobility, where dependent relatives, officials, servants, and retainers might raise the total to more than 100. Yet even their numbers were declining, and by the end of the century 30 or 40 was the more usual quota.

2. THE MAKING OF MARRIAGES

Families were formed by marriages. Yet the process of making a valid marriage was, to modern eyes, surprisingly vague. The full sequence prescribed by the Church involved four stages: first, betrothal or spousals between the man and the woman—these could be promises either *de futuro*, which could be revoked if the marriage was not consummated, or *de praesenti*, which could not be broken; second, the reading of the banns or, in special cases, the obtaining of a licence; third, the wedding in church before witnesses; fourth, consummation. Technically, solemnization in church was not essential to a valid marriage; and in earlier centuries marriages had sometimes been considered binding merely if the contract were properly witnessed and the marriage consummated. However, by the sixteenth century the blessing of the Church had come to be almost universally regarded as a necessary part of the process. Yet it was not entirely certain what constituted a valid contract; and some of the difficulties can be seen in the tale of Andrew Meten of Rampton and Agnes Cropwell of Cottenham, both in Cambridgeshire. Asked by Andrew to marry him, Agnes replied: 'you know I love you well and I can find it in my heart to take you to

---

[2] Peter Laslett, *The World We Have Lost: Further Explored* (London, 1983), 64.
[3] Ibid. 1.

my husband, if my mother's goodwill can . . . be gotten'. According to
Andrew's later evidence, they did not wait for the mother, and that evening,
in front of witnesses, they plighted troth to one another, each taking the
other as husband or wife and kissing, after which Andrew gave Agnes four
silver sixpences. Yet the touching story ends sadly, for Agnes later denied
her troth to Andrew and asserted that she was already contracted to another
man, whom she married in church before Andrew's case for breach of
contract came to court.[4] The pattern of decisions making up a marriage
could be obscure. Did spousals count as a marriage or not? Some of the
evidence about child-marriages may result from counting spousals as a full
marriage: but it is unlikely that such marriages were consummated, and
therefore completed, until both parties were older. Taking all social classes
together, the average age for completed marriages was 26 for women, and 27
to 29 for men, although there was a good deal of variation around the mean
and on the whole the children of the upper classes married earlier than
others. Landowners were generally anxious to get their heirs married
quickly so as to ensure the succession to the family estates; but most couples
had to wait until it was possible for them to set up a separate household.

The Church held that the consent of bride and groom alone was essential for a valid marriage: the agreement of others was not strictly necessary.
Yet Catholics and Protestants alike believed the consent of parents—even
sometimes of other close relatives—to be highly desirable. Certainly the
Church of England maintained that it would be wrong for children to
ignore the wishes of their parents. Some historians have regarded the
control of parents, especially fathers, as the principal and dominating force
in the choice of partners.[5] This was in practice very often, perhaps usually,
so in landowning families, and parental authority was reinforced by the
growing opposition of the Church to clandestine matches and its increasing
insistence upon church weddings, which made evasion of parental wishes
difficult. Sir Walter Mildmay, Chancellor of the Exchequer, demanded that
his son Anthony marry the 14-year-old girl selected for him, rather than
wait, as Anthony himself wished, until he knew more of the world.
Anthony, like many other dutiful sons, complied, although he probably did
have to wait for a time before he could consummate the marriage.[6] Joan
Hayward, chosen as wife for the heir of Longleat, John Thynne, was told

[4] M. J. Ingram, 'The reform of popular culture? Sex and marriage in early modern England', in Barry Reay (ed.), *Popular Culture in Seventeenth-Century England* (London, 1985), 141–2.
[5] Lawrence Stone, *The Family, Sex and Marriage in England, 1500–1800* (London, 1977), chs. 3–5, expounds this view.
[6] R. A. Houlbrooke, *The English Family, 1450–1700* (Harlow, 1984), 69–70.

that she and the young man could meet and see whether they could like one another; but they would, it was hinted, have to find good reasons for not doing so. Joan dutifully announced that 'I do put my trust in God and in my good father that God will put into my father's heart to choose me such a one as God will direct my heart not to dislike.'[7] However, even in the higher ranks of society parental dictates were sometimes resisted, and irregular marriages were occasionally made in very reputable circles. Thomas Thynne, heir to Longleat and son of the obedient Joan, went to Beaconsfield in 1594 to meet his close friend John Marvin, who happened to be the nephew of Sir James Marvin, confirmed enemy to the Thynne family. He also met—possibly by prearrangement—John's cousin Maria Audley. Her mother Lady Audley encouraged them to make a contract of marriage, and 'after the contract she caused a pair of sheets to be laid on a bed and her daughter to lie down in her clothes and the boy by her side butted and sported for a little while, that it might be said that they were abed together'. Since this version comes from Lady Thynne, Thomas's mother, it may be that more went on than butting and sporting. In any event, despite the indignant opposition and litigation of the Thynne parents, the marriage was held by the ecclesiastical courts to be valid.[8]

The children of prosperous yeomen and others of the 'middling sort' seem to have been free to begin courting without parental consent, but usually to have desired the approval of their parents and their 'friends', which normally meant other relatives, before marrying. Sometimes a relative or friend might be used as an intermediary in opening and facilitating negotiations, perhaps receiving some recompense for his (or her) efforts; but the professional marriage-broker, familiar and important in the peasant societies of Central Europe, seems to have been unknown in England. If parental approval was withheld, the marriage was often frustrated. However, couples sometimes went ahead without the agreement of their elders. When Hugh Harold and Rosa Clarke, a Leicestershire couple, determined to marry but found that they could not obtain the goodwill of their 'friends', Rosa declared to Hugh, 'you are the man that I do make choice of and therefore I do not care for their goodwills or consent', to which Hugh responded that 'when our friends or others will go about to break it they may not'.[9]

---

[7] Alison D. Wall (ed.), *Two Elizabethan Women: Correspondence of Joan and Maria Thynne, 1575–1611* (Devizes, 1983), pp. xix, 54–5.

[8] Ibid., pp. xxv–xxx, 9.

[9] Alan Macfarlane, *Marriage and Love in England: Modes of Reproduction, 1300–1800* (Oxford, 1986), 146.

Much depended upon the circumstances of the man and the woman. The daughters of the upper classes were carefully guarded—even the forward behaviour of Maria Audley was encouraged by her mother. In London, city-born girls from merchant families usually had their marriages arranged for them—and married younger than the average; but migrant girls from the country, who were generally domestic servants, had greater freedom of choice—and married later. Unmarried girls from families below the level of yeomen and merchants were fairly free in giving their favours on promise or expectation of marriage. In 1594 Alexander Best, a gentleman's servant from Wiltshire, and Alice Weaver were reported to have 'frequented each one the other's company in very friendly and familiar sort, both early and late, yea sometimes all night', in the presence apparently of the witness who reported the fact.[10] Richard Thomas of Portbury, Somerset, while sowing wheat with his father's maidservant Maud Methewaye, promised that if she conceived a child by him he would marry her; and he 'had carnal knowledge of the said Maud Methewaye's body diverse and sundry times' over the subsequent Christmas season.[11] A high proportion—about 20 per cent—of Elizabethan brides were pregnant at the time of their marriage; and, since the chance of conception from a single act of intercourse was low, the number who had pre-nuptial sex was probably even higher. Some, however, were cautious, like the Somerset girl who refused her lover with these words: 'no, truly you shall not lie with me till we be married, for you see how many do falsify their promises.'[12] Yet sexual conduct in English towns and villages was neither promiscuous nor unregulated, for local opinion was strongly hostile to open and widespread immorality, and towards the end of the century the Church was becoming stricter on the matter of pre-nuptial intercourse.[13]

Thus marriages were made, for most of the population, in a society that tacitly permitted, even if it did not approve, sex as a prelude to marriage, but strongly disapproved of promiscuity. The freedom allowed to these young men and women meant that many, if not most, couples made their own choice of partner, while hoping to receive parental consent and approbation. Sometimes they had to overcome the opposition of the parish notables and the minister of religion, who were known to refuse publication of the banns or even to stop the wedding ceremony if they feared that the children born to the marriage might become a charge on

[10] M. J. Ingram, *Church Courts, Sex, and Marriage in England, 1570–1640* (Cambridge, 1987), 226.
[11] Houlbrooke, *English Family*, 81.
[12] Keith Wrightson, *English Society, 1580–1680* (London, 1982), 86.
[13] See below, p. 513.

the parish. Such vetoes were, however, probably imposed only in the case of the very poor.

However, courtship and marriage nevertheless involved tension and anxiety, vividly revealed in the case-books of Richard Napier, a Buckinghamshire rector from 1590 to 1634. Napier was a physician, astrologer, and alchemist who built up a substantial medical practice, treating the rich and the humble, and dealing with mental as well as physical ailments.[14] Many young men and women came to him suffering from the heartaches of frustrated love. Thomas May, for example, threatened to kill himself if he could not marry his sweetheart: 'grief taken for a wench he loves', wrote Napier; 'he sayeth if he may not have her he will hang himself.' Ann Winch was unable to decide whether or not she loved the man who wished to marry her. Her father allowed her to live in the man's house for five weeks while she tried to make up her mind: 'hath been five weeks with him', Napier noted, 'and by fits careth much for him and sometimes will not have him.'[15] When the consent of parents was not forthcoming, couples might be cast into great distress: Mary Blundell, daughter of a minor gentry family, suffered 'much grief and sighing touching a young man that promised marriage of his own accord, and after . . . broken off by his father that would not consent'.[16]

This habit of marrying for love was observed with disapproval by some of those in authority. Archbishop Sandys warned in 1585 that 'there is a great fault in many at this day that . . . they dispose themselves in marriage as they list, without consent of their parents'.[17] The evidence of pre-marital pregnancies suggests that Sandys was right to say that couples were making their own marriages, though this was probably true at this date only of men and women in the lower strata of society.

3. HUSBAND AND WIFE

Once the marriage had been made, the rule of the husband was established. The Scriptures insisted upon the obedience of the wife, although they also demanded that the husband must show her respect. Wives had virtually no control over their own property, although they had their dower, a customary right to a share, usually one-third, in their husband's property; and in wealthy families they might have a jointure, generally a substitute for dower, stipulated in the marriage contract. Sir Thomas Smith wrote that 'the wife is so much in the power of her husband, that . . . her goods by

---

[14] Michael MacDonald, *Mystical Bedlam: Madness, Anxiety and Healing in Seventeenth-Century England* (Cambridge, 1981), 88–98, esp. 89.

[15] Ibid. 89, 90 and 88–98 *passim*.   [16] Ibid. 94.   [17] Ibid. 18.

marriage are straight made her husband's, and she loseth all her administration which she had of them'.[18] The *Homily on Marriage* stressed that 'the woman is a weak creature not endued with like strength and constancy of mind [to men]; therefore . . . they be the more prone to all weak affections and dispositions of mind, more than men be'.[19] William Gouge, author of *Domesticall Duties* (1622), wrote of the husband: 'he is the highest in the family, and has authority over all, and the charge of all is committed to his charge; he is as a king in his own home.'[20] Some historians have argued that Protestant, and especially puritan, moralists put stronger emphasis upon husbandly authority than Catholics. But there are plenty of pre-Reformation precedents for such views: William Harrington's *Commendations of Matrimony*, published in 1528, counselled wives to obey because 'the husband hath the pre-eminence and is master and ruler of his wife'.[21] The domination of husbands and total financial dependence on them could be a cause of bitter suffering for wives, who were expected to put up with any ill-treatment short of physical violence. Even Richard Napier, usually sympathetic to the unhappiness of his patients, tended to write severely of wives who wanted to leave their husbands: Alice Harvey was described as 'mopish', meaning inert or depressed, because she could not 'abide to be at home with her husband' and was living with her parents.[22] The insistence of the Church that wives must be totally obedient and yet create a loving and companionate marriage was not easily followed.

Yet in practice husbands did not always want—and did not always get—totally submissive partners: a contemporary proverb advised that it was 'better to marry a shrew than a sheep'.[23] The two Elizabethan wives of the Thynne family displayed a striking independence of mind and character. The elder, Joan Thynne, mistress of Longleat from 1580 until her husband died in 1604, so obedient at the time of her marriage,[24] was responsible for much of the running of the Longleat estate and for the armed defence of the family property at Caus Castle, Shropshire, against the attempts of Lord Stafford to gain possession. The letters of her daughter-in-law Maria to the

---

[18] Sir Thomas Smith, *De republica Anglorum*, ed. Mary Dewar (Cambridge, 1982), 131.

[19] Stone, *Family, Sex and Marriage*, 198.

[20] Kathleen M. Davies, 'Continuity and change in literary advice on marriage', in R. B. Outhwaite (ed.), *Marriage and Society: Studies in the Social History of Marriage* (London, 1981), 63.

[21] Ibid. 65. For the view that Protestants were more strict than Catholics, see Stone, *Family, Sex and Marriage*, ch. 5, esp. pp. 154–6.

[22] MacDonald, *Mystical Bedlam*, 102.

[23] Martin Ingram, 'Ridings, rough music and mocking rhymes in early modern England', in Reay (ed.), *Popular Culture*, 176.

[24] Above, p. 499, for the Thynne family.

husband with whom she was bundled into bed are loving but firm. 'Well, Mr Thynne . . .', she wrote, 'believe I am both sorry and ashamed that any creature should see that you hold such a contempt of my poor wits, that being your wife, you should not think me of discretion to order (according to your appointment) your affairs in your absence.' Her husband thereafter left much of the business of estate management to her when he was away from Longleat.[25]

Arranged matches were not necessarily loveless, for there is plenty of evidence that genuine affection grew between husband and wife, even when there had been no opportunity for any to develop before the marriage.[26] One example must serve for many. In 1584 Robert Sidney, younger brother of Philip, married a Glamorgan heiress, Barbara Gamage, fifteen days after the death of her father. Almost certainly she had never seen him before and the match was the outcome of some high-powered and rapid manœuvring at the royal Court. Yet theirs was a model of the companionate marriage. Sidney's first surviving letter to his wife begins: 'My most dear Barbara, think no unkindness I pray you at my long stay from you, since it doth no way proceed of want of desire to see you.' A few years later he ends with the words: 'Farewell sweet Barbara, and kiss your little ones from me.' Until he died in 1626 Robert Sidney wrote constantly to his wife from his military post in the Low Countries, usually addressing her as 'Sweet wench' or 'Sweetheart'. Ben Jonson epitomized her virtues in his poem 'To Penshurst':

> These, Penshurst, are thy praise and yet not all,
> Thy lady's noble, fruitful, chaste withall.
> His children thy great lord may call his own.
> A fortune, in this age, but rarely known.

A charming picture now hung in the gallery at Penshurst shows the fruitful Lady Sidney in the midst of her abundant family.[27]

The death of a spouse often produced heart-rending grief. Richard Napier's case-book records many instances. Margaret Langton 'took a great discontent and fretting by the death of her husband', even attempting suicide. John Flesher's wife died in childbirth, and the child died soon after. Napier described him as no longer taking 'that pleasure that he was wont, either in reading or working as heretofore he did. . . . Very

---

[25] Wall (ed.), *Two Elizabethan Women*, 32.

[26] For contrary views see Stone, *Family, Sex and Marriage*, 102–5.

[27] HMC, *Calendar of the MSS of Lord De L'Isle and Dudley at Penshurst Place* (3 vols., London, 1925–36), ii (1934), 101, 143–4, and *passim*; Ben Jonson, 'To Penshurst', ll. 89–93. For other examples of affectionate marriages see Houlbrooke, *English Family*, 102–5; Barbara Winchester, *Tudor Family Portrait* (London, 1955), 61–89.

heavy and apt to weep; and at other times very choleric and cannot endure crossing.'[28]

Loving and companionate marriages were possible, even quite common, in all ranks of society; but obviously, then as now, some marriages were unhappy and some disastrous. For both spouses, but especially for the wife, the rub lay in the very great difficulty of ending a miserable relationship. Divorce as such was not recognized; annulments could occasionally be obtained, but only with great difficulty and expense. Legal separation could be had in the courts, but not easily; the most common way of ending a marriage in practice was *de facto* separation, when the couple simply parted company; but the bond was not legally dissolved by this means. Among the poor, marriages were effectively broken by husbands abandoning their wives: a Norwich census of the poor in 1570 revealed that 8.5 per cent of the married women covered by the survey had been deserted by their husbands. Yet in all social classes marriages were prematurely broken more often by death than by annulment, separation, or desertion. The average duration of a marriage, before the death of one or other partner, was twenty years, although one-fifth of marriages lasted as long as thirty-five years. Widows and widowers usually remarried if they could, but this was much easier for men than for women and easier for those in comfortable circumstances than for the poor. In Norwich, among the poor, there were twelve times more widows or other unmarried women over 60 than there were men. Widows and widowers usually remarried fairly quickly if they did so at all, the mean interval between the death of a spouse and remarriage being thirty-six months for women and twenty-five for men.

There is a good deal of evidence available on the fate—or choices—of London widows. Since it was difficult, though not wholly impossible, for a woman to enter a craft or trade and engage apprentices, remarriage was an attractive way of continuing a deceased husband's business, and the widows of merchants or craftsmen were an enticing financial prospect: 45 per cent of *all* marriages by licence in London were remarriages for one or both parties; and 44 per cent of aldermen's widows are known to have remarried. They did so more quickly than widows elsewhere, for 37 per cent were remarried within six months, 67 per cent within a year. Generally they had few children in their second and later marriages. Ellen Battison was married to William Pearson for nineteen years and bore him ten children, of whom seven died under the age of 5. When William himself died, she married again six months later, at the age of 45, with three surviving daughters. She had no more children. Her story reflects the precarious outlook for the

[28] MacDonald, *Mystical Bedlam*, 104.

London family, where death was likely to strike more harshly at both adults and children than in the countryside. Remarriages were common everywhere, but especially so in the City.[29]

4. PARENTS AND CHILDREN

The only form of contraception believed in and practised at all widely in the sixteenth century was the prolonged suckling of babies, which is far from reliable, except by inhibiting intercourse. Upper-class families tended to avoid even this, sending their babies out to wet-nurses, partly because suckling interfered with the mother's social duties, partly also perhaps because husbands wanted sexual intercourse with their wives soon after childbirth and this was thought likely to curdle the mother's milk. The number of children born to a sixteenth-century family was therefore larger than today, and it was larger among the upper classes than among the rest. But the difference was not as great as we might expect. With a relatively late age of marriage, 23 to 27, and an early age of menopause, around 40, women could expect only fourteen to seventeen years of child-bearing. Births were widely spaced, in all but the better-off families, by the prolonged periods of suckling, and might be separated by twenty-four or even thirty months. The average woman might therefore hope for five to seven children. Of those born, many died young: more than one in eight died in their first year, and about one-quarter of all children died before reaching the age of 10. A married couple could expect four or five children to survive beyond that age, of whom only two or three might still be alive at the death of their parents.[30]

In the families of noblemen and gentlemen, parents often sent their children to other, socially respectable, households where they would learn good behaviour, though the practice was less common by the end of the century, when private tutors or boarding-schools were coming to be widely used. The children of yeomen and merchants would also often be sent away as apprentices; and yeomen's sons would usually have had to leave home to attend school; for, while merchants' sons could go to school from home, yeomen's sons would have had to board in town. Craftsmen and artisans generally apprenticed their sons to others rather than employ them at home; and usually could not afford to send them to school. The children of labourers were expected to start work in the household or in domestic

[29] Vivien Brodsky, 'Widows in late Elizabethan London', in Lloyd Bonfield et al. (eds.), *The World We Have Gained* (Oxford, 1986), 122–54. These figures may somewhat overstate the extent of remarriage.

[30] Laslett, *The World We Have Lost: Further Explored*, 112.

manufacture as early as 6 and went away as farm or domestic servants in their early teens.

One contrast with most modern families, therefore, was that those of the sixteenth century were constantly changing, as children were born, died, and left home. Perhaps the supposedly intense emotional bonds of the modern family did not have time to develop, but neither perhaps did the tensions and explosions. However, that is speculation: even if feelings existed at a rather lower pitch, they were still there. The treatment of children in the early modern period has been described as harsh and unfeeling; and some historians have suggested that affection between parents and their offspring was rare.[31] Ecclesiastical treatises on the upbringing of children certainly advocated severity as a means of expurgating original sin. But writers on education, such as Roger Ascham, one of Queen Elizabeth's tutors, opposed harsh punishments and urged a more lenient approach. It is unlikely that the practice of parents conformed to either 'ideal' and probable that most of them mixed severity and leniency in a wholly untheoretical manner. Burghley may have expressed a general commonsense attitude when he condemned both 'the foolish cockering of some parents and the over-stern carriage of others'.[32] The few diaries and autobiographies that have survived from the sixteenth and early seventeenth centuries record fairly mild regimes of discipline; but their testimony is too slender to be conclusive. Probably fathers were generally more strict than mothers, and sons were more severely treated than daughters. There might well be tensions between father and son, especially in the case of the eldest son, where there was property to inherit; and the threat of disinheritance could sometimes be used to discipline children if the estates had not been entailed. It is possible that upper-class parents preferred sons to daughters—or regarded them as more important—but there is no evidence that others did. The wills of peasants reflect a strong desire to provide something for all their children and not merely for the eldest son.

The high rate of child mortality did not deaden feelings of grief among parents at the deaths of sons or daughters. In his book of aphorisms the Elizabethan Marquis of Winchester wrote that 'the love of the mother is so strong, though the child be dead and laid in the grave, yet always she hath him quick in her heart'. Napier recorded the grief of many bereaved mothers who came to consult him: after the burial of her three-month-old baby, Elizabeth Foster was terrified by the cry of an owl and said that she had a sinking heart; Ellen Craftes 'took a fright and grief' when a door fell

---

[31] e.g. Stone, in *Family, Sex and Marriage*, 117, 215–18.
[32] Houlbrooke, *English Family*, 144.

upon her child, and soon she got so much worse that 'head, heart and stomach [became] ill, eyes dimmed with grief that she cannot see well'. Napier indeed considered a mother's inability to love her children to be a sign of mental disorder: he noted the symptoms of Elisabeth Clark as 'careth not for her children; can take no joy of her children; tempted to hang herself'.[33] There are fewer instances of men much stricken with sorrow at the deaths of their children, but nevertheless they exist. Ralph Josselin, the seventeenth-century vicar who left a highly detailed diary, recorded his sadness at the approaching death of his daughter and his son, but professed his willingness to give them up to God, for 'thou art better to me than sons and daughters, though I value them above gold and jewels'.[34] When preachers taught from the pulpit that God had taken the departed to himself and that the dead—provided that they were among the saved—were happier than they had been on earth, parents might find it difficult to give unrestrained vent to their affections or their sadness.

Most children experienced the death of at least one parent fairly early in life: about half of those who survived to the age of 25 had already lost one or both parents; and as many as one-fifth of children under 10 had suffered the death of either father or mother. What happened to the orphans? The bereaved parent would very likely remarry, and subsequent relations with stepfather or stepmother could well be difficult. Few children seem in fact to have lived with their stepparents. If they were heirs to property held in tenure from the Crown, they would become royal wards, and in most cases the Court of Wards would sell the wardship either to the stepmother or to another relative or to a royal official or courtier. Other children would probably go off to live with grandparents or with uncles and aunts.

In only about 6 per cent of households did grandparents and grandchildren live together, and this might lead one to suppose that married children were not expected to provide a home for their elderly parents. Yet the evidence of wills gives a quite contrary impression. While elderly married couples rarely seem to have lived with their children, single grandparents, especially widows, more often did so. Yeoman farmers and husbandmen usually made very careful provision for their widows. If the children were still young when their father died, the widow would continue to occupy the holding; and when the eldest son came of age, she would be given house-room: Grace Meade, of Orwell, Cambridgeshire, was left the right to use the little parlour 'with free egress and regress', together with furnishings, four acres of land, a load of hay, and some livestock. If the eldest son was already of age, the widow would be given house-room

[33] MacDonald, *Mystical Bedlam*, 82.   [34] Macfarlane, *Marriage and Love*, 52.

immediately: Margery Greville's husband, also of Orwell, left her a 'chamber . . . to her own use during her natural life, and also two acres wheat and iii acres barley'.[35]

The apparent contradiction between the evidence of censuses and that of wills can be satisfactorily explained, for widows and widowers made up only about 6 per cent of the total population; and it would seem that most of those whose grown-up children survived did live with them. Only a minority of men and women lived to be grandparents, but those who did seem usually to have established affectionate relationships with their children and grandchildren. However, not every widow had married children to whom she could turn, and the relicts of the labouring classes could not expect such provision. They appear mostly to have lived on parish relief, supplemented by wages from part-time work or by the meagre profits derived from selling ale. In 1594 the Privy Council recommended that licences to keep alehouses be given to 'the ancienter sort of honest conversation . . . that have no other means to live by'.[36]

Although the 'Elizabethan family' obviously differed from that of our own day, in neither century can one convincingly talk of a typical example: families and the relationships within them varied then as they do now. But the differences between the centuries were less marked than has often been supposed. Most Tudor households consisted simply of parents and children; more children would then be living at home at any one time than is now usual, but not many more; above all, emotional bonds between parents, sons, and daughters were often, perhaps usually, strong. The major contrast lies in the fragility and impermanence of the family in the sixteenth century: with so high a death rate, especially so many deaths of children, family life was always uncertain.

5. KIN AND LINEAGE

Beyond the 'nuclear' family of husband, wife, and children lay the wider ramifications of kinship: brothers, sisters, uncles, aunts, nephews, nieces, and cousins. Some historians, concerned mainly with the élite, have contended that the ties of kinship and lineage, though once of high significance, were being weakened in the sixteenth and seventeenth centuries under pressure from the state and the market economy.[37] Others, examining the middling and lower orders of society, have found little evidence that the

[35] Margaret Spufford, *Contrasting Communities: English Villagers in the Sixteenth and Seventeenth Centuries* (Cambridge, 1974), 113.
[36] Peter Clark, *The English Alehouse: A Social History, 1200–1830* (Harlow, 1983), 79.
[37] e.g. Stone, *Family, Sex and Marriage*, 29, 86, 123–9.

wider bonds of kinship ever mattered much in England, by contrast with countries across the Channel.[38] Among the nobility the strong and complex ties of lineage that had upheld the power and influence of such families as the Percies, the Nevilles, and the Talbots in the later Middle Ages were probably weaker by 1600 than they had been a century earlier: certainly these families no longer wielded the regional authority that had once been theirs. But landowning families in Elizabethan England continued to value such ties. William Cecil, Lord Burghley, fostered the members of his extended family, who also looked to him for office and patronage. Although he somewhat neglected the interests of his ablest relatives—his nephews Francis and Antony Bacon—perhaps because they were potential rivals to his son Robert, he made up for this by the generous favours that he bestowed upon the members of his 'lesser kin', especially those related to him by his first marriage into the Cheke family. Burghley could dispense large favours and it was natural that nephews and cousins should look to him for help. Although he advised his son not to employ kinsmen in household posts—'for they expect much and do little'—he seems often to have ignored his own advice. He was certainly well aware of the value of maintaining good relations with kinsmen: 'let thy kindred and allies be welcome to thy table', he advised Robert Cecil, 'grace them with thy countenance, and further them in all other honest actions for by this means thou shalt so double the bonds of nature as thou shalt find them so many advocates to plead an apology for thee behind thy back.'[39]

The gentry also valued their links with kinsfolk. The diary of Adam Winthrop, a Suffolk landowner, shows him to have been constantly entertaining his in-laws and cousins. On 10 May 1597, 'I did ride to my brother Mildmay's house': Thomas Mildmay was both his stepbrother and his brother-in-law. Next day he returned home and 'my cousin R[aven] did fall in my garden'; on 18 May 'my cousin [William] Alibaster came to my house'; on 29 May 'my cousin Bulwer came to my house'; and on 2 June 'I was at my Cousin [Joan] Muskett'.[40] Sir Thomas Meynell, head of a Yorkshire Catholic family, recorded in his commonplace book details of the family tree and made notes of the families with which his own had been allied: 'there was ever an ancient league of friendship betwixt the Consta-

---

[38] e.g. Keith Wrightson and David Levine, *Poverty and Piety in an English Village: Terling, 1525–1700* (London, 1979), 83–102.

[39] G. R. Morrison, 'The land, family and domestic following of William Cecil, Lord Burghley, *c.* 1550–1598' (D.Phil. thesis, University of Oxford, 1990), *passim*, esp. 124, 144. I am very grateful to Dr Morrison for allowing me to quote from his thesis.

[40] For extracts from Winthrop's diary, see Ralph Houlbrooke (ed.), *English Family Life, 1576–1716: An Anthology from Diaries* (Oxford, 1988), 222–7.

bles of Burton Constable and mine ancestors. The cause is now greater than before, for Sir John Constable, grandfather to Sir Henry that now is, married one of the daughters of . . . Lord John Scrope', who was the grandfather of Meynell's first wife; so 'Sir Henry that now is and my children are third and third in blood.'[41] In Wales the gentry displayed an intense passion for genealogy, which seemed excessive even to the English. Sir William Herbert of St Julians, Monmouthshire, stipulated in his will that his daughter should marry a gentleman bearing the Herbert name or be disinherited.[42] In the northern border country ties of kinship were still stronger, and the famous 'surnames', family groups led by a headman, dominated the wild country and perpetuated its feuds. However, by the second half of the reign of Elizabeth the surnames were in decline as the power of the great magnates, on whom they depended, was eroded. Socially, lineage was still important at the turn of the sixteenth century; politically it was less so and was declining.

It is much harder to assess the strength of kinship ties among the middling and lower orders of society. For them we have to rely largely on the evidence of wills, which point to a preoccupation with the immediate family. Indeed, many people had only their close blood relatives living in the same village: no more than 33 per cent of families in Terling, Essex, had relatives living there outside their own households. Bequests were overwhelmingly made to wives, children, and, to a lesser extent, grandchildren, while the witnesses to wills were usually neighbours rather than kinsmen. Elizabethan tradesmen and yeomen made more bequests to nephews, nieces, and cousins than did those social groups a century later, but that was simply because they had, in a time of rising population, many more relatives: members of this group in their fifties had on average 7.44 nephews or nieces, compared with only 3.56 for their counterparts in the 1680s. But the Elizabethans made bequests only to an average of 1.12 nephews or nieces, so most were left materially unrewarded. However, wills do not reveal everything, or even very much, about the depth and strength of such relationships. A letter written in 1638 by an Englishwoman living in Ireland to her distant relative, John Winthrop, in New England, spoke of his having 'done the part of a kinsman' for her emigrant son, 'as you promised'.[43] The role of such kinsmen was to provide help and favour when they were needed. Young girls migrating from the countryside to London contacted relations

[41] J. T. Cliffe, *The Yorkshire Gentry from the Reformation to the Civil War* (London, 1969), 10–11.

[42] G. Dyffnalt Owen, *Elizabethan Wales: The Social Scene* (Cardiff, 1962), 13.

[43] David Cressy, 'Kinship and kin interaction in early modern England', *Past and Present*, 113 (1986), 45. The statistics of wills are ibid. 55–9.

for help in making friends, getting jobs, and finding husbands. Tradesmen and farmers boarded their children with relatives in town when they were away at school. Merchants sometimes persuaded cousins to give them financial aid: George Gedge, an Essex clothier, left his house in Colchester to the 'eldest son of my cousin Thurston (of Ipswich) . . . in consideration of such travail and money as my cousin hath taken and disbursed about my affairs'.[44] Sometimes a man provided for a large family funeral dinner in his will: Thomas Harrison of Saffron Walden left money for one 'for such of my neighbours, friends and kinsfolks as shall then resort to the same'; George Derrington of Harlow not only provided for a funeral dinner 'for my kinsfolks and friends', but also left 20s. each to 'my wife's nephews, dwelling in Lincolnshire . . . at their coming to Harlow after my decease to visit their aunt'.[45]

Few people in Elizabethan England, other than landowners and merchants, wrote letters; and what letters they did write have probably for the most part perished. We should not therefore expect to find much evidence about the quality of relationships between kinsfolk at this time; but we should not on that account suppose that they were insignificant. Relatives would meet at weddings and at funerals; and they were there to give help when it was wanted. The situation was not so very different from that of today.

6. NEIGHBOURS

Late sixteenth- and early seventeenth-century villages have been described as places 'filled with malice and hatred', characterized by 'the extraordinary amount of back-biting, malicious slander, marital discord . . . and petty spying' which often worked their way into prosecutions for moral offences in the law courts of Church and state.[46] Those who have lived in the countryside know that strong feelings may be hidden beneath an apparently smooth surface. But they also know that one village may be very much less harmonious than the next and that generalization about social relations, even in twentieth-century communities, is difficult. In the sixteenth century it is far harder. With slight, patchy, and biased evidence, qualitative judgements are risky.

The inhabitants of small towns and villages had long been responsible for the regulation of economic, social, and moral conduct within their communities: there is no marked change in the nature of such regulation in the sixteenth century, although its intensity may have increased. Some of the

---

[44] David Cressy, 'Kinship and kin interaction in early modern England', 51.
[45] Ibid. 61.   [46] Stone, *Family, Sex and Marriage*, 98–9.

mechanisms of this control were official, such as the authority of constables and churchwardens. Others relied upon the informal pressures of local opinion, the most dramatic manifestation of which was the 'skimmington' or riding. A skimmington involved a mocking ride, to the accompaniment of a crowd playing 'rough music' on drums, pipes, and horns, and perhaps shooting off guns. The demonstration was directed against termagant wives and their downtrodden husbands. Sometimes wife and husband were forced to ride, seated back to back, and were pelted with filth; sometimes a neighbour acted as a surrogate or stand-in. The main target of the skimmington was not only the overbearing behaviour of the wife but also the unmanliness of the henpecked husband, who received abuse rather than sympathy. There were also often hints, in the shape of horns, that the man had been cuckolded as well as bullied. Skimmingtons were a communal protest against the overturning of the proper rule by husband over wife, and occasionally a condemnation of wifely adultery. They contained an element of penal action, derived from the punishments imposed by local courts, combined with the laughter of festival or charivari. Probably they were a fairly rare event, reserved for particularly notorious offenders, and seem, perhaps for that reason, to have been tolerated by the authorities.[47]

Less dramatic but much more common, and therefore more disruptive, were the mocking rhymes circulated by villagers about one another. These rhymes had a wider range of targets than skimmingtons, but were most often directed against adulterers, fornicators, and cuckolds. A cuckolded husband from a Wiltshire village was mocked with these crude verses in 1618:

> Woe to thee, Michael Robins,
> That ever thou wert born,
> For Blancute makes thee cuckold,
> And thou must wear the horn.
>
> He fetches the nurse
> To give the child suck,
> That he may have time,
> Thy wife for to fuck.[48]

Another rhyme, from the same county, held an erring wife up to ridicule— or worse:

---

[47] For examples of skimmingtons, see Ingram, 'Ridings, rough music and mocking rhymes in early modern England', 166–97; also id., 'Ridings, rough music and the "reform of popular culture in early modern England"', *Past and Present*, 105 (1984), 79–113. There is an account of a 19th-cent. skimmington in Thomas Hardy's *Mayor of Casterbridge*.

[48] Ingram, *Church Courts*, 164. There are ten more verses.

O hark a while and you shall know
Of a filthy beast did her breech show,
And of her doing and how indeed
In this her filthiness she did proceed.

She went and laid upon the ground
And tucked her coats about her round,
And because she is so brave and fine,
She tucked up her heels and said she would show the moonshine.

And so on.[49]

Such rhymes often gave rise, not surprisingly, to feud and friction, and then to suits in the ecclesiastical courts for slander and defamation: perhaps for that reason they were regarded less tolerantly by authority than were skimmingtons. Suits for defamation were frequent in the second half of the sixteenth century, and were increasing. While some involved accusations of drunkenness or witchcraft, most were for allegations of sexual misconduct. They were usually brought by women, who were the most common victims of sexual slander—perhaps because the double standard of morality allowed more licence to men. Often the suits arose out of local feuds. In the early seventeenth century a dispute broke out at Coulston, Wiltshire, between Alice Franklin and Maud Spender, after Alice had given hostile evidence against Maud in an earlier lawsuit. Maud then brought an action against Alice for calling her 'a fine whore, a burnt tailed whore, and a pocky whore'. These repetitive insults may well have been delivered, but the background to that particular defamation suit involves more than sexual misconduct and name-calling.[50] Yet the suits do reflect a real concern for moral reputation. While village communities were fairly tolerant of bridal pregnancy—given its frequency they could hardly be anything else—they strongly disapproved of adultery, and even more strongly of bastardy.[51]

Nevertheless bastardy was a serious problem for local communities. The proportion of illegitimate births to all baptisms—the illegitimacy ratio—was rising in Elizabethan England from about 1.9 per cent at the beginning of the reign to 3.0 at the end. Although this higher figure was only about half that calculated for the early nineteenth century, the number of bastards was still high enough to give alarm. Many of the bastard children were

[49] Ingram, 'Ridings, rough music and mocking rhymes in early modern England', 179.
[50] Id., Church Courts, 314.
[51] For a different view, see G. R. Quaife, Wanton Wenches and Wayward Wives: Peasants and Illicit Sex in Early Seventeenth-Century England (London, 1979), passim. Quaife portrays 'peasant' women as wanton in their conduct and careless of their reputation. His account, while colourful, is unconvincing: see Ingram, 'Reform of popular culture?', 154.

probably born to women who had expected to marry but had been disappointed by the faithlessness, death, or disappearance of their man; and in
the very straitened economic circumstances of the 1590s and subsequent
decades such disappointments may have been more common than before.
From about 1600 disapproval of adultery and fornication seems to have
become stronger, possibly because of this increase in illegitimate births.
While hostility to bastardy was generated partly by a fear that illegitimate
children would become a charge upon parish poor rates, condemnation was
not the result of economic concern alone. Francis Coggens of Hanney,
Berkshire, on learning that his sister had conceived a child out of wedlock,
furiously rejected the suggestion that she should name a false father: 'My
sister . . . hath committed an abominable fact already and if she should
father it to another man the plague of God would fall upon her and upon us
all for giving her such counsel.'[52]

Fear of direct and immediate punishment by the Almighty was often a
reason for castigating sin, even if it was less effective in persuading people
to avoid misdeeds. A petition from Castle Combe, Wiltshire, written in
1606 and signed by the minister, the churchwardens, the constables, the
overseers of the poor, and others, protested against a woman who had
committed a 'filthy act of whoredom . . . by the which licentious life of hers
not only God's wrath may be poured down upon us inhabitants of the
town, but also her evil example may so greatly corrupt others that great
and extraordinary charge for the maintenance of baseborn children may
be imposed upon us'.[53] Fear of the wrath of God and the financial balance
sheet nicely complemented one another.

From about 1600—a decade or so earlier in some places, a little later in
others—the inhibitions of popular disapproval were reinforced by rising
prosecutions in the ecclesiastical courts.[54] Fear of such prosecutions may
have been one reason for the parallel rise in suits for defamation, for if
adultery or fornication could lead to a penalty in court, then rhymes and
gossip became dangerous as well as unpleasant. However, it is unlikely that
such fear was the only reason behind defamation suits, for villagers seem to
have been genuinely concerned about their own reputations and about the
morals of others.

Was town life more private and anonymous, less censorious than that of
the countryside? The answer to this question would seem to be 'no'. Strict
regulation of morals began earlier in many English towns than it did in the
villages. In Colchester, for instance, the archdeacon's court operated along-

---

[52] Ingram, 'Reform of popular culture?', 154.   [53] Id., *Church Courts*, 261.
[54] Above, Ch. 11 s. 2.

side the borough courts of the town's JPs. These secular petty sessions dealt with an especially large number of sexual offences; and perhaps because they met twice a week competed successfully with the Church courts in securing business. The usual punishment for fornication was a ride in the tumbrel. When Thomas Faune, a newcomer, was found guilty of fornication with Helen Markham, both were sentenced to ride through the town in a tumbrel, wearing placards announcing their offence. Like the skimmington, the tumbrel was a 'shame' punishment, used to penalize the guilty parties and to 'terrify others from committing like offences'; unlike the skimmington it expressed official disapproval.[55] Even in London there was no escape from popular morality. On Shrove Tuesday, 1563, a skimmington was held at Charing Cross where 'there was a man carried of four men, and afore him a bagpipe playing, a shawm and a drum playing, and a twenty links burning about him, because his next neighbour's wife did beat her husband'. Evidently the neighbour had to perform as a surrogate for the unmanly husband, which seems hard.[56] Skimmingtons seem, however, to have been rare, or even unknown, in London after the middle decades of the century. Neighbourhood gossip provided a more common set of moral sanctions. Ralf Pollard, a wife-beater, described as 'a very bedlam and a hasty fellow, soon and for nothing set in fury and rage', was 'divers times' rebuked by his neighbours. Sometimes they took matters further than mere rebuke and reported offences, or supposed offences, to the courts: James Armes was summoned before the alderman's deputy because his neighbours had reported the resort of one Francis Kenninghall, a gentleman, to his house, Armes's wife being 'an evil and suspected person'.[57] These pressures were reinforced by a powerful network of courts, with the governors of Bridewell playing an active part in the punishment of fornication: they heard 232 such cases in 1559–60, 435 in 1576–7, and 312 in 1600–1.[58]

Did anything in English towns and villages offset the atmosphere of tension provoked by skimmingtons, rhymes, and gossip? Inevitably feuds and accusations leave more traces in the records than do instances of neighbourly help and communal support. But there is evidence that some people disapproved of mocking rhymes. A Wiltshire woman cried out in protest

[55] M. S. Byford, 'The price of Protestantism: assessing the impact of religious change on Elizabethan Essex' (D.Phil. thesis, University of Oxford, 1988), ch. 5. esp. 397. I am most grateful to Dr Byford for allowing me to use his thesis.

[56] Ingram, 'Ridings, rough music and mocking rhymes in early modern England', 169.

[57] Ian W. Archer, *The Pursuit of Stability: Social Relations in Elizabethan London* (Cambridge, 1991), 77.

[58] Ibid. 239.

when she heard a scurrilous verse: 'Fie upon it, what a beastly thing is this, burn it, for there will come anger of it.'[59]

More generally, local communities encouraged neighbours to fulfil their obligations, and they regularly attended at lying-ins, christenings, churchings, and funerals. William Harrison described the generous hospitality offered by husbandmen: '[they] do exceed after their manner [in feasting]; especially at bridals, purifications of women, and such odd meetings, where it is incredible to tell what meat is consumed and spent, each one bringing such a dish, or so many, as his wife and he do consult upon'.[60] Funerals, especially, were great occasions for communal gatherings. Not only the relatives of the dead person but friends and neighbours would come to the church in large numbers, often well over a hundred. After the service a 'drinking' would be held, sometimes in the churchyard itself, although this was disliked by the clergy. Even the funerals of paupers were accompanied by some conviviality, the parish bearing the cost. In well-to-do circles the 'drinking' would be followed by a banquet, usually provided only for family and the 'better sort' of tenants and neighbours. The cost of these affairs could be huge: that for Matthew Mennyer, Mayor of Sandwich, came to £42 in 1610. Gifts, usually gloves or ribbons, were given to the principal guests; and doles of money or bread were distributed to the poor. The entertainment and the giving helped to display the status of the departed, as well as assisting dependants to cope with grief and cementing the local community.[61]

Private charity was often very much a neighbourhood affair. Men and women gave more readily to the members of their own community than to strangers. London livery companies laid out increasing sums during the second half of the century to provide pensions for members or their families who had fallen into distress. Individuals often left bequests for providing loans to young men for setting up in business. Agnes Suckley, for instance, instructed the Merchant Taylors to give interest-free loans of £50 apiece to each of eight 'of the youngest occupiers . . . dwelling either in Watling Street or Candlewick Street or elsewhere in London, occupying the trade of retailing of woollen cloth'.[62]

Institutional aspects of communal life were centred upon the church and

[59] Ingram, 'Ridings, rough music and mocking rhymes in early modern England', 187.

[60] Felicity Heal, *Hospitality in Early Modern England* (Oxford, 1990), 353; see also Archer, *Pursuit of Stability*, 54, 95–6.

[61] Clare Gittings, *Death, Burial and the Individual in Early Modern England* (London, 1984), 157–64; also Heal, *Hospitality*, 371–6.

[62] Steve Rappaport, *Worlds within Worlds: Structures of Life in Sixteenth-Century London* (Cambridge, 1989), 373.

the alehouse. Churches and churchyards remained the sites of the principal parish festivals, religious and secular. In spite of the suppression of many holy days, most of the main festivals survived into the seventeenth century, and only then did they come under serious attack from puritans. John Aubrey was later to describe, perhaps with excessive nostalgia, the village festivals of his grandfather's day, when the poor were provided for by church ales at Whitsuntide:

In every parish is, or was, a church house, to which belonged spits, crocks, etc., utensils for dressing provision. Here the housekeepers met, and were merry and gave their charity: the young people came there too, and had dancing, bowling, shooting at butts, etc., the ancients sitting gravely by, looking on.

He comments that 'such joy and merriment was every holiday'.[63]

Alehouses were the humblest, but far and away the most numerous drinking houses in country and town. They sold ale or beer, with rough and ready food, to the poorer classes, while taverns catered for the moderately well-to-do and inns for prosperous merchants and gentlemen. Most alehouses were impermanent, small, and squalid. Yet they did a good trade, for the consumption of ale and beer was high: it was thought a sign of poverty to drink water. Andrew Boorde, the physician, commented that 'water is not wholesome sole by itself for an Englishman'.[64] Alehouses were constantly attacked by the propertied classes, Thomas Dekker complaining in 1603 that they 'hurt thousands and undo many poor men who would else follow their labours but now live beggarly, their wives . . . starving at home and their ragged children begging abroad'.[65] Yet, in spite of local hostility and attempts by Parliament and Crown to control their numbers, they flourished, and probably they provided a humble forum in which the poor men of a parish could congregate. However, they were too wretched and ephemeral to become, as some have claimed, the centres of an alternative culture or life-style.

Whether villages were really 'filled with malice and hatred' it is impossible to say. Certainly there was a good deal of feuding and gossip; but it is hard to tell how far this was outweighed by neighbourly instincts and support. We can, however, be sure that there was more interference, official and unofficial, in people's private lives that there is today. Sexual misconduct might be punished by mocking rhymes, shaming punishments, or prosecution in the ecclesiastical courts. Even so, it seems that the Church

---

[63] David Underdown, *Revel, Riot, and Rebellion: Popular Politics and Culture in England, 1603–1660* (Oxford, 1985), 45; also Heal, *Hospitality*, 354–65.
[64] Clark, *The English Alehouse*, 112.   [65] Ibid. 167.

courts were fairly discriminating in their attentions; and probably only the more flagrant offenders were delated and punished. There was some privacy in people's lives, though it was narrower than that to which we are accustomed.[66]

[66] Ingram, *Church Courts*, 238–45 for an assessment of privacy and the courts.

CHAPTER 13

England and the World

1. THE BRITISH PROBLEM

During the fifteenth century Ireland, Scotland, and Wales had threatened the political stability of England and its ruling dynasties; and the term 'The British Problem' has been given to the complex mesh of difficulties encountered by the English Crown in its dealings with those regions. The Welsh had shown their hostility to their English conquerors in the Glyndŵr rebellion and had continued to do so until the accession of Henry Tudor. Wales was a good recruiting ground and Welsh soldiers were prominent in the wars with France and in the subsequent civil wars in England: the Welsh Marches formed the most important power base of the House of York, and the House of Lancaster had strong support in the Principality itself and in the south-west. Although, after Bosworth, the region ceased to be a major political problem for the Crown, which had acquired almost all the major Marcher lordships by 1485, the corruption of Marcher officials and the deficiencies of the judicial system undermined any pretence at orderly government. The policies that culminated in the so-called Acts of Union of 1536 and 1543 assimilated Welsh government to English, gave administrative unity to Wales, and provided the region with a coherent judicial system. The authority of the Marcher lords was all but abolished and royal jurisdiction took its place. These measures were part of a wider policy adopted by the Crown to strengthen its control over such outlying areas as County Durham, the Anglo-Scottish border, Calais, and, above all, Ireland.

The policy of 'union' with Wales was in line with long-term developments there; it upset no powerful vested interests; and it satisfied the aspirations of most Welsh and Marcher gentlemen. In consequence, the political history of Wales between the second Act of Union in 1543 and the death of Elizabeth largely consisted of the implementation of the Henrician system. On the whole, it was successful in providing a more effective, less partial, and less corrupt system of government, while tightening royal control over the region. Although the Welsh language and Welsh identity were threatened by the abolition of specifically Welsh institutions, they were to survive in fair order into the seventeenth century. To balance the imposition of English as the language of government, the backing given by Parliament in 1563 to the translation of the Prayer Book and the New Testament, and Whitgift's support for William Morgan's translation of the whole Bible in 1588 not only preserved Welsh prose but helped it to develop into the medium of a whole literature. In the age of print and Protestantism Welsh poetry, largely bardic, underwent a gradual decline; but prose writing, especially religious prose, flourished. The loyalty of Welshmen to their language was reflected in the number of dictionaries and grammars published in the late sixteenth and seventeenth centuries. Furthermore, Welsh writers and gentlemen did not lose their national identity; indeed they usually gloried in it, while enjoying the advantages that Tudor rule brought them.

If Tudor government was successful in bringing a degree of order and law to Wales, it was less successful in converting the population to the reformed religion. The established Church was firmly in control, for it was part of the social and political order in Wales; and while the proportion of Catholic recusants in the population remained high, they were given little encouragement by missionary priests, who concentrated their efforts upon England. Yet Protestant evangelists were few in Wales, the parishes remained poor, the clergy uneducated, and the people little instructed in the Christian faith.

The social and economic benefits enjoyed by the Welsh gentry were not shared with the common people. The gentry built up their estates, achieving a prosperity well beyond the dreams of their ancestors. For the poor, however, times were harder than ever before, perhaps even harder than they were in England. A Welsh artisan of 1615, earning 9d. a day, would have taken forty-three weeks' labour to buy his yearly stock of provisions; an agricultural labourer, earning 7d. a day in summer and 6d. in winter, would have been unable to buy such a stock at all. No wonder that a Welsh poet wrote: 'And in every country the great kill the small completely.'[1]

While the fortunes of the Welsh might be mixed, those of the Irish were almost uniformly disastrous in the sixteenth century.[2] Politically, the de-

---

[1] 'Ag ymhob gwlad yn gyfan | Mae y mawr yn llad y bychan.' Quotation and statistics from Glanmor Williams, *Recovery, Reorientation and Reformation: Wales c.1415–1642* (Oxford, 1987), 394.
[2] For the events of Irish history, 1547–1603, see Chs. 3 s. 4; 4 s. 5; 7 s. 4; 8 s. 3; 9 ss. 4, 5.

mands made upon the government of Ireland always exceeded the resources available. These demands sprang in part from the ambition of English statesmen to bring the entire island under full royal control, in part from the Reformation, which made stronger authority essential, and in part from the threats presented first by France and then by Spain. Under Somerset and Northumberland the conciliatory policy of the latter years of Henry VIII was abandoned and the garrisons were increased from 500 to 2,600 men. By the reign of Elizabeth the number of troops stationed in Ireland nearly always stood at 1,500 or more, while the armies sent over to deal with major uprisings were much larger. Soldiers had to be paid for, and if the Irish Parliament would not agree to taxation, then the money would have to be levied by coercion. Only four Irish Parliaments met between 1543 and 1613—in 1557-8, 1560, 1569-70, and 1585-6—and coercion became the rule. Government by conciliation and consensus broke down: the Anglo-Irish lords and the landowners of the Pale, the Crown's traditional allies, were alienated by heavy taxes and by the 'invasion' of New English officials and settlers into lands and offices, robbing the Old English of wealth and influence. At the same time the Gaelic chiefs in Ulster and south-west Munster were provoked into rebellion by the intrusions of Crown and settlers into their lordships.[3]

This political alienation ensured that the campaign to establish Protestantism would fail. In 1547 Catholicism was probably no stronger in Ireland than it was in Wales; but whereas in Wales it was on the retreat after 1558, in Ireland it made headway from about 1580. Barnaby Rich, soldier of fortune, reported then that Ireland 'does swarm with Jesuits, seminaries and massing priests . . . and these do keep such continual and daily buzzing in the poor people's ears that they are not only led from all duty and obedience of their prince, but also drawn from God by superstitious idolatry and so brought headlong by heaps into hell'.[4] The Crown made little serious effort to encourage or support the conversion of the Irish to the Protestant faith; few of the preachers sent over could speak Gaelic; little was done to provide for education until late in the reign of Elizabeth; and, increasingly, Irish students went to the Continent, rather than to England. The political alienation of the Old English turned them, as

[3] Above, Ch. 8 s. 3. I use the term 'Old English' to denote the Anglo-Norman lords and the English who had settled in Ireland before the 16th cent., and who are referred to in earlier chapters as the 'Anglo-Irish'; from the reign of Elizabeth they are conveniently called 'Old English' to distinguish them from those who benefited from office and from plantations under her and her successors: the 'New English'. The former were predominantly Catholic from the early 17th cent.; the latter came to form the Protestant Ascendancy.

[4] Steven G. Ellis, *Tudor Ireland: Crown, Community and the Conflict of Cultures, 1470–1603* (London, 1985), 221.

well as the Gaelic lords, away from Protestantism. Even at the end of Elizabeth's reign, the Catholic Church had only an uneven hold upon the island, but the process had begun by which its people were to be divided by their faiths.

The third dimension of the British Problem lay to the north, in Scotland and on the border. Northern England has often been considered a world apart, but it is important to distinguish the three border counties— Northumberland, Cumberland, Westmorland—from the rest of the region. Durham, in the first half of the sixteenth century, had had a separate existence as a county palatine; but these rights had been eliminated under Henry VIII and Edward VI. While the northern part of Lancashire preserved some independence and some border characteristics, southern Lancashire and most of Yorkshire had more in common with the rest of England than with the border shires. True, the whole region was subject to the Council in the North, seated in York and established on a permanent basis in the 1530s; but that was largely a matter of convenience for governing counties distant from London. The specifically northern institutions were those of the border, headed, on the Scots side as well as on the English, by the Wardens of the three Marches, responsible for executing the border laws, maintaining order, and defending their side of the frontier against incursion.

Henry VIII and Cromwell had undermined the authority of major northern families like the Dacres, the Nevilles, and the Percies, and as a result the Crown was almost forced to rule through lesser landowners, appointing Sir Thomas Wharton, Sir William Eure, and Sir John Widdrington as deputy wardens of the three Marches, replacing the older families. The Dacres and the Percies made a brief recovery during the middle years of the century, when the fourth Lord Dacre was reappointed to the wardenship of the West March and the earldom of Northumberland was restored to the Percies by Mary. Elizabeth, however, again abandoned the policy of relying upon the great northern magnates. The seventh Earl of Northumberland was excluded from any of the major border posts, and after his rebellion in 1569 his heirs were effectively transformed into southerners, debarred from influence in their hereditary spheres. The Dacres lost the wardenship of the West March on the death of the fourth Baron in 1563; and the demise of the last Lord Dacre in 1569 (from falling off his rocking-horse) ended the dynasty, its lands passing into the hands of Lord William Howard, who had married a Dacre heiress. The wardenships of all three Marches were given by Elizabeth either to minor northern magnates like Lord Scrope, Lord Eure, and Sir John Forster, or to southerners like Lord Grey de Wilton, the

Earl of Bedford, Lord Willoughby, Lord Hunsdon, and his sons John and Robert Carey.

The disappearance of the great northern dynasties did not necessarily make governing the borders easier. Indeed, the southerners appointed to the wardenships resented their exile and found it hard to control the quarrelsome northern families without a landed base of their own in the region; and disorder was as bad or worse on the borders in Elizabeth's last years than it had been for decades. However, from the Crown's point of view the elimination of the northern magnate families lessened the danger of rebellion: the rising of the earls in 1569 was the last of the long series of northern baronial revolts.

The Crown's situation was also eased by the gradual improvement of relations with Scotland: from about 1570 the border was no longer a frontier to be defended. Henry VIII had tried to solve the problem of Scotland by the so-called 'rough wooing'—the attempt to coerce the Scots into accepting the marriage of the infants Prince Edward and Queen Mary Stewart. French influence had ensured his failure; and Somerset's continuation of the policy with the establishment of garrisons north of the border brought Scotland back to the 'auld alliance' with France, which became a serious threat to England when, in 1554, Mary of Guise, Mary Stewart's mother, became Regent.

The situation was saved by the growth of a Scottish opposition to the French and by its association with the Protestant movement. This in itself owed something to English influence, for Tyndale's New Testament was, until 1579, the only version of the Bible in the vernacular to be available north of the border. After initially appearing conciliatory to the Scots Protestants, the Regent Mary turned to the attack in 1559; and when French troops landed in Scotland in May of that year, Elizabeth was persuaded to take action: a fleet was sent to the Firth of Forth and a land force dispatched from Berwick. While the intervention of the fleet was not massive, it was sufficient to tilt the balance against the French, who withdrew. Ten years later, in 1570, Elizabeth again sent a limited force to help the Protestants after the assassination of Moray. But between 1578 and 1585, when the Marian party seemed likely to oust its rivals yet again, she did nothing to help the Protestants, who recovered by their own efforts. However, in 1586 James agreed to a league with England under which he was to receive a pension of £4,000 a year. After a brief and painful interruption following the execution of James's mother Mary Stewart in 1587, relations between the two countries remained reasonably harmonious until 1603, cemented by James's pension, the common interests of the monarchs, and James's hopes for the English succession.

The situation in the north, then, was transformed in the second half of the sixteenth century. The rule of the great magnates was brought to an end; the Scottish frontier ceased to be the 'postern gate' for England's enemies; and, if the borderland itself became no more orderly, it no longer threatened the political stability of the realm.

Under Elizabeth the British Problem had changed its nature. In her early years the preoccupations of the Privy Council had been heavily biased towards Scotland. If Ireland was then in confusion, it posed no serious danger to the regime. From 1586 the English government could be reasonably confident that the northern frontier was safe, but after 1595 it could have no such feelings about Ireland. The triumph of Tyrone, and with him the Spanish and Catholic cause, seemed only too likely. With Mountjoy's victory, that nightmare prospect was dispelled; and the destruction of Gaelic Ulster was begun. Thus the Crown's dealings with its 'Celtic' neighbours and its frontier provinces seemed vindicated. Wales was acquiescent in Tudor rule, its gentry positively enthusiastic; Ireland had been conquered by military force; and the accession of James Stewart brought a union of the crowns and the elimination of the northern frontier. However, in the long run the prospect turned out to be far from bright. Welsh assimilation to England continued, it is true; and if the later Anglicization of the Welsh gentry separated them from the peasantry, that did not disturb the Crown, which could not have prevented it even if it had wished to. But the victory in Ireland was bought at the heavy price of growing hostility from the Gaelic world and from the Old English to alien rule and the Protestant religion. The debt was to be called in during 1641. The union of the Scottish and English crowns turned out to present James I, and more particularly his son, with significant problems, especially over religion, foreshadowing eventual war in 1639 and 1640.

2. THE WIDER WORLD

Until about 1480 the globe was fragmented, economically and socially. The Amerindian societies of Central and South America were then still unknown to Europeans and themselves knew nothing of the world across the oceans; and while there had long been commercial links between Europe and Asia, there had been few direct contacts. In the half-century between 1500 and 1550 everything changed. Portugal, having already established bases in West and East Africa, achieved commercial hegemony over the Indian Ocean; and Spanish adventurers won for Charles V a new empire in the Caribbean and in Central and South America. Most of the societies which made up the human world had been brought finally and permanently into contact with one another; and European hegemony over the globe was soon to be established.

England at first played little part in these great events. After a few voyages to North America in the last decade of the fifteenth century and the first of the sixteenth, Englishmen seem to have withdrawn from the Atlantic world, showing little or no enthusiasm for exploration or oceanic trade until the reign of Edward VI. The revival of interest towards the end of that reign owes something to the personal encouragement of the Duke of Northumberland, more perhaps to the uncertainties of the Antwerp cloth market and the need to find wider outlets for English trade. Whatever the explanation, important ventures originated under Edward and were carried through under Mary, although the Crown seems to have given little support to these endeavours. In the next fifty years English sailors and adventurers penetrated into most of the oceans of the world and also made tentative, though unsuccessful, efforts to colonize. Under Mary and in the early years of Elizabeth, exploration and commercial expansion were the principal features of this movement. From 1568 plunder and piracy were dominant, together with some early schemes for settlement. After the defeat of the Armada, naval warfare against Spain combined with privateering to take English ships into the Indian Ocean and, above all, into the Caribbean.

The first major exploratory voyage of the mid-Tudor era left London in 1553, shortly before the death of Edward VI. It was commanded by Sir Hugh Willoughby, a soldier and gentleman, with Richard Chancellor, a skilled navigator, as its pilot. Its patron was the Duke of Northumberland; its inspiration was said to have come from Sebastian Cabot, now an old man; its backers were prominent London merchants; and its purpose was to find a north-east passage to the Indies. Clement Adams, printer and publicist, gave the main credit for its inception to the merchants, who, he wrote,

perceived the commodities and wares of England to be in small request with the countries and people about us and, near unto us. . . . Certain grave citizens of London . . . careful for the good of their country, began to think with themselves how this mischief might be remedied. Neither was a remedy . . . wanting to their desires, for the avoiding of so great an inconvenience: for seeing that the wealth of the Spaniards and Portingales, by the discovery and search of new trades and countries was marvellously increased, supposing the same to be a course and mean for them also to obtain the like, they thereupon resolved upon a new and strange navigation.[5]

Willoughby died in the course of the voyage; but Chancellor sailed on into the White Sea and eventually reached Moscow, where he was favourably

[5] Kenneth R. Andrews, *Trade, Plunder and Settlement: Maritime Enterprise and the Genesis of the British Empire, 1480–1630* (Cambridge, 1984), 65.

received by Ivan IV. He had failed to find a northerly route to the Orient, but he had opened up a commercial route; and a year after his return the Muscovy Company, a joint-stock venture, was formed for trading with Russia.

A few weeks after Willoughby and Chancellor had sailed, Thomas Wyndham, a naval commander and part-time pirate, set out for the Guinea coast, the region between Sierra Leone and Ghana, hoping to break his way into the Portuguese trade in gold and pepper. Where Chancellor's voyage had been peaceful, Wyndham's was violent and piratical. Although he himself died on the way, the expedition was profitable and was succeeded by several others. Portuguese resistance was, however, vigorous. Without an African base the English traders found the going hard, and in the early 1570s the trade was abandoned. Its cost was too heavy for the potential profit, and by then other opportunities were opening.

In 1562 John Hawkins launched a different African trade, this time across the Atlantic. He collected slaves from the upper Guinea coast and shipped them across to the Caribbean. The virtual extermination of the Indian population of Española and its disastrous decline in mainland America had left the Spanish colonists seriously short of labour.[6] Although the Portuguese had begun to take African slaves to the New World as early as the 1520s, their efforts by no means satisfied the colonists. Hawkins took advantage of the market and, in spite of opposition from the Spanish Crown, traded successfully for some years, with Spanish officials in the Caribbean mostly conniving at his intrusion. In 1568, on his fourth voyage, he put into the harbour of San Juan de Ulúa, on the Mexican mainland, having already sold the greater part of 500 slaves. There he met disaster, when the Spanish treasure fleet arrived under the command of the recently appointed Viceroy of New Spain, who was not prepared to wink at Hawkins's activities and ordered an attack. Three of the six English ships were lost and the rest of the fleet reached home battered and without most of its profit. Hawkins then abandoned slaving and peaceful trading in the Atlantic came to an end. In itself the incident at San Juan was as much symbolic as instrumental; for the growing hostility between England and Spain was increasing tension in the Atlantic and ensuring that the slave-trade would only be practicable with heavily armed vessels, which would make it less profitable. However, in the next few years, Hawkins and his associates, principally Francis Drake, were to find other and more attractive employment at sea.

[6] Española was the original name for the island now occupied by Haiti and the Dominican Republic.

In Africa and the Caribbean English merchants and seamen intruded upon areas that had already been explored and in which trade had been established. Even Chancellor had been preceded by others in his voyage to the White Sea, although he had led the way for England and had established a regular commercial route to Russia. One journey of real discovery was, however, made during these middle years of the century. In 1557 Antony Jenkinson, a merchant, was sent out by the Muscovy Company to find a route through Russia into Central Asia. He travelled on foot from Moscow to Bokhara, but found the latter a great disappointment, for 'these merchants are so beggarly and poor, and bring so little quantity of wares . . . that there is no hope of any good trade there to be had worthy the following'.[7] In 1561 he set out again and reached the Court of the Shah of Persia, only to be told that the Persians had no need of friendship with unbelievers. He was more successful with the ruler of Shirvan, but his hopes of establishing a trade with Central Asia that bypassed the Ottoman domains were never realized. Remarkable as were the journeys of Jenkinson and some of his successors, they did not add much to the reports and maps of Italians who had travelled in the region earlier, though these were not then known to the English. In the end English trade with Central Asia was established through the Ottoman Empire rather than by the lengthy route across Russia.[8]

In the twenty years between the disaster at San Juan de Ulúa and the defeat of the Armada, English sailors engaged in piracy, voyages of exploration, colonization, and the establishment of peaceful trade with the Levant. Expeditions for plunder and exploration were, without doubt, the most colourful and memorable of these endeavours. English pirates—they cannot be called privateers since they had no official authorization—had been actively engaged against French and Spanish shipping since the last years of Henry VIII; but resentment at the incident at San Juan de Ulúa combined with worsening diplomatic relations between England and Spain to stimulate greater activity. Francis Drake took the lead with three voyages to the Caribbean during the early 1570s. The third of these, in 1572, was the most dramatic and the best documented. Drake struck at the strategic isthmus of Panama, which linked the silver-mines of Peru to the Caribbean and thence to Spain. Making an alliance with runaway slaves, *cimarrones*, he succeeded in ambushing a mule-train of silver on its way from the Pacific coast to Nombre de Dios on the Caribbean, alarming the Spanish, who feared that he might combine with the negroes to take possession of the isthmus. In fact

---

[7] Andrews, *Trade*, 80–1.   [8] Below, p. 531, for the Levant trade.

the danger of an English occupation of Panama was slight; but Drake had shown the way to wealth through plunder, and in the years 1570–7 thirteen piratical expeditions, including his own, set out from England.

There followed Drake's voyage round the world in 1577, whose story has already been told.[9] Alongside projects for discovering the Asian entrance to the north-west passage and gaining access to Pacific trade with China and Manila, its main objectives were the plunder of the Spanish Main and the establishment of a colony in South America. Circumnavigation of the globe was not envisaged until after Drake had entered the Pacific, though that was to give the voyage its fame. While Drake gave confidence to English sailors and marked England's entry into the Asian world, he came nowhere near to establishing a colony or a trading base in South America. From 1578 Philip II began to look to his defences in the New World, sending a fleet to protect the coast of South America in 1581. It encountered an expedition under Edward Fenton two years later and forced him to retire. After that English plans to colonize in South America, either on its east coast or its west, came to an end.

Drake's exploration of the Magellan Strait was complemented by the voyages of Frobisher and Davis to find the north-west passage. Martin Frobisher was an experienced seaman, who had spent many of his early years in the hazardous Guinea trade. Backed by the Muscovy Company, he led three expeditions, between 1576 and 1578, to the north coast of Canada in the hope of finding a route to the east. At one point Frobisher thought that he had found gold and the object of his expedition turned from exploration to mining. In neither was it successful, for the gold was 'fool's gold' and the strait did not exist. Nevertheless hopes remained, and in 1585 John Davis, a fine navigator and geographer, set out on three further voyages into the Arctic regions. He found the mouth of the Hudson Strait and concluded that it could easily be entered and would then lead to Asia; but by then the Muscovy merchants had tired of supporting efforts to find the north-west passage and the quest was abandoned. Between them, Frobisher and Davis contributed much to geographical and ethnographic knowledege, even bringing some unfortunate Eskimos back to England. But they had been able to do nothing for English trade or colonization.

By this time ambitious schemes for colonizing North America were being developed by Humphrey Gilbert, a Devonshire gentleman, half-brother to Walter Ralegh. Gilbert had been involved in plans for plantations in Ireland in 1569, had brutally suppressed the Munster rising of 1569,[10] had led a force of volunteers to aid the Dutch against the Spaniards in 1572, and in

---

[9] Above, Ch. 8 ss. 1, 2.   [10] Above, Ch. 7 s. 4.

1578 received letters patent granting him the right to found a colony in
North America. He set out with a considerable fleet of ten ships, backed by
Walsingham and some prominent London merchants, accompanied by
some of his brothers and by various young courtiers. He himself got as far
as Ireland and remained there in government employ, while some of his
ships sailed off on piratical adventures. In 1583 he tried again, using his
earlier letters patent to grant 8.5 million acres in North America to some
loyal Catholic gentry anxious to escape from the growing persecution in
England, and to members of that hungry class, the younger sons of the
gentry. This time he reached Newfoundland, but after one ship sank and
two others deserted him, he sailed for home again, drowning when his own
ship went down.

Gilbert's schemes and voyages had an element of black comedy about
them; but he made up in boldness and vision for what he lacked in practical
sense and finishing power. Behind him were men with sophisticated knowledge of geography and navigation, inspired by a notion of English destiny.
In 1577 John Dee, astrologer, magus, mathematician, and geographer, published his *General and Rare Memorials Pertayning to the Perfect Arte of
Navigation*; part of a larger and unpublished work entitled 'Of Famous and
Rich Discoveries'. The title-page shows Elizabeth, at the helm of the 'Imperial Ship', being solicited by Respublica Britanica to found a strong navy[11]
(Plate 4*a*). Dee had given advice on navigation to Chancellor, Frobisher,
and Gilbert; he was deeply involved in the searches for the north-east and
north-west passages to Asia; and he was the first writer to use the term
'British Empire'. More influential even than Dee was Richard Hakluyt the
younger, author and publisher of *The Principal Navigations, Voiages and
Discoveries of the English Nation* (1589). He had a broad vision of the
expansion of English power overseas. By occupying a base in the New
World, Hakluyt argued, England would take away Spain's *nervus belli*, the
American silver, defeat the tyrannical purposes of Philip II, spread the true
religion, and make England rich by trade.

More promising for the future than Gilbert's projects was the planting of
the Roanoke colony, in what later became the colony of Virginia, by Sir
Walter Ralegh. Like his half-brother Gilbert, Ralegh had done service in
Ireland, fighting under Lord Grey of Wilton and carrying out Grey's orders
for executing the Italian and Irish prisoners taken at Smerwick in 1580.[12]
Like Gilbert, too, he carried the notion of plantation from Ireland across the
Atlantic to America. In 1585, having received a patent to colonize in the
previous year, he sent out a fleet to Virginia under Sir Richard Grenville,

---

[11] Above, Ch. 10 s. 5, for portraits of Elizabeth.   [12] Above, Ch. 8 s. 3.

another West Countryman. Ralegh himself never went to Virginia, but he was the master-mind behind this expedition and its successors. Grenville's men settled on Roanoke Island, while he himself sailed for home, leaving command of the infant colony to Ralph Lane, an army officer who had also served in Ireland. By June 1586 the colony was desperately short of food, having relied upon maize supplied by the Indians, who by now were becoming hostile. The chance of relief came when Drake reached Roanoke on his return from the Caribbean and gave the colonists a passage home.[13] Soon after they had left, Grenville arrived with a relief expedition, but finding the island deserted, he departed, leaving behind fifteen unfortunate men. Attacked by the Indians, they fled from Roanoke and were never seen again. In 1587, Ralegh sent out a new expedition under John White, a gifted artist who had probably been on one of Frobisher's expeditions, to settle at Chesapeake Bay, near Roanoke. Unlike Lane's colony, whose purpose was principally military, White's was essentially a farming settlement; but it was no more fortunate than its predecessor. After various catastrophes, White returned home to organize relief, but, with the Armada imminent, Elizabeth forbade the departure of more ships from England. When, in 1590, a ship did finally reach Roanoke, the colony was again found to be deserted, the settlers gone. So ended the Elizabethan attempts to establish colonies in America. Useful lessons were learned; and superb descriptions of the region and its people were produced by John White in his paintings, and by Thomas Hariot, Ralegh's adviser on navigation, in *A Briefe and True Reporte of the New Found Land of Virginia* (1588)[14] (Plates 17a, b). But the failure could not be disguised. Ironically, the colony, which had come into being as a result of hostilities with Spain, was weakened by those very hostilities. For the war diverted funds which might have been provided by the Crown and were essential to success, while the attractions of privateering distracted seamen from giving full co-operation.

The most positive English achievement overseas during the years 1568–88 was the least dramatic. After a long interval, English ships began once more to penetrate the eastern Mediterranean, when William Harborne, a merchant from Yarmouth, was sent to the Court of the Ottoman Sultan, where he negotiated privileges, or 'capitulations', for English merchants. In 1581 the Queen granted to the Turkey Company, later the Levant Company, the sole right to trade with the Ottoman ports, selling English woollen cloth in return for raw silk and currants. The Mediterranean trade was

[13] Above, Ch. 8 s. 5, for Drake's voyage of 1585.
[14] Paul Hulton and D. B. Quinn (eds.), *The American Drawings of John White* (2 vols., London, 1964), *passim*. Ralegh and his contemporaries normally referred to Roanoke as being in Virginia: it is now in the state of North Carolina.

highly profitable, probably outdoing all the overseas branches of English commerce apart from the traditional cloth trade with northern Europe; and profitable too were the depredations of English pirates, who found the Mediterranean as fruitful in pickings as the Caribbean.

Between 1588 and 1603 English overseas enterprise was dominated by the war at sea. As well as the main naval expeditions—to Portugal in 1589, to the Caribbean in 1595, to Cadiz in 1596, and to the Azores in 1597—there was waged the 'little war' of privateering, promoted and financed by rich London merchants and West Country gentlemen, conducted by professional sailors or noble amateurs, such as the Earl of Cumberland, and fought by the poor and unemployed who were suffering from the harvest failures of the 1590s. Between 1585 and 1603 there were seventy-four separate expeditions—excluding Drake's major campaigns—involving 183 ships. They probably imposed a heavier strain on Spanish resources and commerce than did the big expeditions, and they brought English merchants a considerable profit, which was later to be invested in oceanic trade, especially to Asia.

The first English expedition to the Indian Ocean sailed under James Lancaster in 1591; it was a complete failure, the crew having to return home in French ships. Dutch merchants were much more successful, dispatching profitable voyages to the East Indies in 1598 and 1599; and, spurred on by this, a group of Londoners established the East India Company, which was granted its charter in 1600, its first voyage, again under Lancaster, being launched early in the following year. Although this expedition saw some successful trading, the profits were disappointing to its backers, and no further venture was launched until 1604. The start was slow, hampered by the long wait for profits and the opposition of the Dutch; but the first steps had been taken on a road that was to lead to the Indian Empire.

One colonizing expedition, more dramatic than realistic, was made during the 1590s. In 1595 Sir Walter Ralegh led an expedition to Guyana. On his return he wrote an account of the voyage, *The Discovery of the Large, Rich and Beautiful Empire of Guiana*, in the hope of stimulating support, especially from the Queen, for a second attempt. If the expedition was a failure, at least it produced a marvellous piece of descriptive writing. This land of El Dorado, claimed Ralegh, could be easily conquered and equally easily held against the King of Spain.

Guiana is a Country that hath yet her Maidenhead, never sacked, turned, nor wrought, the face of the earth hath not been torn, nor the virtue and salt of the soil spent by manurance, the graves have not been opened for gold, the mines not broken with sledges, nor their Images pulled down out of their temples. . . . For whatsoever Prince shall possess it, shall be greatest, and if the King of Spain enjoy it, he will become unresistable.[15]

The sexual imagery is compelling and the warning powerful; but neither persuaded the Queen to support Ralegh in a further attempt.

Thus were the beginnings of an English overseas empire made in the second half of the sixteenth century. Some remarkable ventures were achieved: the voyages of Chancellor and Frobisher; Drake's circumnavigation of the world; Grenville's fight at the Azores. The literature of imperialism was enriched by Dee and Hakluyt; knowledge of the oceans and of other lands was gained. References to the Americas can be found in the works of Sidney, Spenser, Chapman, and, above all, Ralegh. Donne wrote in the 1590s or 1600s

> Let sea-discoverers to new worlds have gone,
> Let Maps to other, worlds on worlds have showne,
> Let us possess one world, each hath one, and is one.

and

> O my America! my new-found-land,
> My kingdome, safeliest when with one man man'd . . .[16]

Yet the 'new' worlds of America and Asia do not seem to have entered English consciousness very deeply before the successful foundation of the Virginia colony in 1607. It is significant that *The Tempest* was first presented at Court by Shakespeare's company in 1611. Some exotic plants and commodities were appearing from across the ocean in the second half of the sixteenth century: tobacco seems to have come into England in the 1560s, but did not become popular until the 1590s; the potato was first brought into Ireland and may have been taken thence by Ralegh. Again, the seventeenth century rather than the sixteenth sees the arrival of large-scale imports from America and Asia: tobacco, sugar, Indian silks, and so on.

Less colourful and romantic commercial developments were more important in the sixteenth century. Great trading companies, in particular the Muscovy in 1555, the Levant in 1581, and the East India in 1600, were then established.[17] The English merchant marine was greatly increased: in 1582

[15] Walter Ralegh, *The Discovery of the Large, Rich and Beautiful Empire of Guiana*, repr. in Sir Walter Ralegh, *Selected Writings*, ed. Gerald Hammond (Harmondsworth, 1986), 120, 123.
[16] John Donne, 'The Good-Morrow', in *Songs and Sonnets*; and 'To his Mistress going to Bed', in *Elegies*.
[17] Other trading companies founded during this period were the Guinea Company, the Barbary Company (trading with Morocco), the Spanish Company, and the Eastland Company (trading with the Baltic).

there were about 250 ships in England of 80 tons or more; between 1581 and 1597 133 ships of 100 tons or above were built. For all that, English commerce remained predominantly tied, as it had long been, to northern Europe, France, and, after 1604, Spain. Seen in the light of subsequent achievement, the sixteenth century was a seminal time in English imperial history; viewed from the perspective of 1603, England seems a relatively backward imperial nation, lagging well behind Spain, Portugal, and the Netherlands.

3. ENGLAND AND EUROPE

Whatever lay ahead in America, Africa, and Asia, England was still in 1603 a European nation: in many ways no more than an offshore island lying across the Channel from more powerful neighbours. In the reigns of Edward VI and Mary, when England finally lost her last possessions in France, she was a valuable strategic prize, the Imperial and French ambassadors competing for influence, while France strengthened her hold north of the border. With the expulsion of French troops from Scotland in 1560 and the outbreak, two years later, of civil war in France itself, the dangers of French intervention in English affairs receded. The French Crown was in no position to interfere directly and French politicians hoped to secure Elizabeth as an ally rather than to dominate the English—or for that matter the Scottish—realm. The situation of Philip II was different. His control over the Netherlands depended upon his communications by sea up the Channel. Elizabeth's seizure of the bullion destined for Alba's troops in 1569 demonstrated that the route was vulnerable, as indeed was the alternative—the Spanish Road from Italy, through the Alpine passes and along the eastern border of France to the Low Countries. Hence, after 1568, when Mary Stewart fled from Scotland, Philip's agents were behind most of the conspiracies which revolved around her.

In spite of repeated urging from some of her councillors, such as Leicester and Walsingham, that England should intervene more vigorously in support of the Huguenot cause in France and the Protestant cause in the Netherlands, Elizabeth, advised and supported by Burghley, avoided entanglement in Continental politics as long as she could. English intervention in Scotland, although relatively small in scale, shifted the balance of power in favour of the Protestants and against the French, ensuring that the Catholic cause north of the border would be defeated. Elsewhere England played a minor role. The expedition to France in 1562, in support of the Huguenots, was a humiliating failure, and thenceforward, until 1585, Elizabeth restricted her intervention to occasional loans to the Huguenots and the Dutch Protestants, while using the possibility of marriage to gain the support of Anjou. At sea, the depredations of English pirates forced Philip to look to his defences in the New World, and the activities of Drake and others thus diverted some Spanish resources from other theatres.

When, in 1585, Elizabeth decided to assist the Dutch directly, she committed herself to providing 6,400 infantry, 1,000 cavalry, and £126,000 per annum until the end of the war. The ineptitude of Leicester in 1585–7 ensured that most of this effort was wasted, but after Vere took over the English contribution became worthwhile. True, the Dutch were probably secure by 1590, after Parma's troops had been diverted to support the Armada and then to campaign in France; nevertheless, this English force was a valuable reinsurance. Furthermore, the dispatch of the Armada showed that Philip was sufficiently frightened of the English threat to his sea communications to use money, men, and ships on a risky enterprise. In France, Willoughby's expedition of 1591 enabled Henry IV to save Dieppe and helped him to strengthen his position in much of the north. While Essex's campaign to besiege Rouen was a failure—not entirely through the fault of its commander—Norris's small force of 4,000 men prevented the Spanish from securing control of Brittany. If the English commitment to France was smaller than that in the Netherlands, it was probably more important, since Henry's position, until his conversion to Roman Catholicism, was much more insecure than that of the Dutch.

At sea, the defeat of the Armada had a temporarily catastrophic effect upon the Spanish war fleet; but it was quickly rebuilt. The depredations of English privateers on the Spanish merchant marine were more serious. During the three years after the Armada English pirates inflicted damage upon Spanish commerce to a total of £400,000; and the English were later said to have attacked more than 1,000 Spanish and Portuguese ships over the whole war period. Iberian trade was seriously depleted, and with it the strength of the Spanish Crown, which was deprived both of customs revenue and of the sailors to supply its own ships.

Elizabeth's critics, men like Ralegh and Hawkins, claimed that she 'did all by halves and by petty invasions', failing to deliver the decisive blow against the King of Spain.[18] On land this was out of the question. At the time of the Armada Parma commanded 60,000 men in Flanders, while Medina Sidonia had another 19,000 on board ship. Against this, Elizabeth had 4,000 troops recalled from the Netherlands, 1,500 on her ships, and 26,000 wholly inexperienced men in the trained bands. In 1595 Spain had

---

[18] Ralegh's remark is quoted in R. B. Wernham, 'Elizabethan war aims and strategy', in S. T. Bindoff et al. (eds.), *Elizabethan Government and Society* (London, 1961), 340.

100,000 men under arms, England 20,000: the disparity was huge. However, Hawkins proposed in 1589 that Spain should be defeated, not by land battles, but by a silver blockade to starve her of treasure. At first sight this seemed more plausible. The English royal fleet was about the same size as that of Spain and, at the time of the Armada, was better armed. Moreover, Spain's vital line of communications across the Atlantic was badly stretched and apparently vulnerable. Yet, in the light of events, Elizabeth's caution, however annoying to her warriors, would seem to have been justified. An effective naval blockade was probably beyond England's powers in the sixteenth century: even the powerful Dutch fleet stationed in the Caribbean during the 1620s and 1630s, with the express objective of capturing the treasure fleet, only once succeeded. Furthermore, although the foundations of the Spanish monarchy looked fragile, it showed remarkable stamina. Confronted in the seventeenth century by both France and the United Provinces, Spain held out until 1659, even threatening Paris during the years of the Fronde.

The main objective of Elizabeth and Burghley in Europe was to give the Dutch and the French enough money and men to keep them in the war. There was not, it is true, much danger of the Dutch making a separate peace, and in the end they continued fighting longer than the English. But Henry IV was considerably less reliable and frequently threatened to come to terms with Spain if Elizabeth did not give him what he wanted. At Vervins, in 1598, he did just that. However, by then the financial position of Spain was such that she, too, was beginning to withdraw from the conflict, and the expedition to Kinsale in 1601 was something of a dying gesture. The English contribution was not massive in any theatre of war, and decisive only in Ireland. But we have to remember that England was fighting on four fronts: in the Netherlands, in France, in Ireland, and at sea. Cumulatively the war effort was considerable. In all, 106,000 men were sent overseas during the war years. If England was not the power she had been under Edward III and Henry V—as perhaps Shakespeare's audiences would have liked to believe—she was at least a significant second-division nation, which had to be counted in any international equation.

How did the power of English monarchs over their kingdoms compare with that of their Continental rivals? The kings of France and Spain apparently had almost sole personal authority over their realms. However, while their power at the centre of things was awe-inspiring, it reached much less effectively into the provinces. In France, provincial estates, local Parlements, and great magnates continued to hold considerable authority in the regions. Within the Iberian peninsula there were great distinctions between the kingdoms of Castile, Aragon, Catalonia, and Valencia, distinctions which Philip II did nothing to eliminate; and the Aragonese Corts tenaciously preserved their own significant privileges. In Scotland, in the middle of the sixteenth century, there were very few administrative institutions at all. The monarchy was institutionally weak, with a small income and little power to tax its subjects; effective government depended upon personal contact and the relations of the king with the great men of the realm. As the pressure of business increased in the second half of the sixteenth century, and with it the imposition of regular taxation, so a more elaborate and sophisticated administrative structure developed in Scotland; but Scottish government remained much less centralized than English. Of all the states in Western Europe the Low Countries were the least centralized. Under Charles V the separate provinces maintained their identities; and during the subsequent revolts Flemish and Walloon particularism constantly frustrated the Protestant cause. The constitution of the United Provinces, after the secession from Spain, was essentially federal: the power of the Estates General was limited and matters had constantly to be referred back to the towns. Yet the dominance of the province of Holland gave the new state cohesion.

England and Wales had been centralized at an earlier date and more completely than all these states. Although English monarchs had in theory a more restricted personal power, needing the consent of Parliament to make laws and to levy direct taxes, and were subject themselves in some degree to the common law, they had to contend with far fewer independent regional powers. There were no institutions remotely resembling the French Parlements, and, except in Ireland, there were no provincial estates. Furthermore, there was a single code of law throughout the realm. By the middle of Elizabeth's reign there was a more or less uniform system of county government, with Lords Lieutenant providing the essential link between the Privy Council and the shires. While there were powerful and independent English magnates, they possessed neither the territories, nor the judicial powers, nor the political authority of their counterparts in France and Spain: there was no English equivalent to the princes of Condé, the dukes of Guise, the dukes of Medina Celi, or the dukes of Alba.

Although there were regional institutions in Britain, like the Dublin administration and the Councils of the North and the Marches of Wales, they had little independence. The northern and Marcher Councils were in practice, though not strictly in law, extensions of the arm of the Privy Council; and their main function was to exercise jurisdiction over criminal and civil matters in regions remote from Westminster. However, if the English state was effectively centralized, it had only a small bureaucratic machine. By the early seventeenth century the French monarchy was served by some 40,000 paid officials, many of them operating in the provinces, and there were probably ten times more royal officials in France, in proportion to the population, than there were in England. In Spain, Philip II tried to develop a system of direct administration for collecting taxes and recruiting troops, and there was a multitude of petty officials. In England the tasks of local enforcement were carried through by nobles and landed gentry acting as Lords Lieutenant, Justices of the Peace, and *ad hoc* commissioners; and there were virtually no paid local officers. Yet the differences between the kingdoms were not so great as they seemed. The huge French bureaucracy proved as much of an obstacle as an assistance to royal control; and after 1580 Philip II was forced, against his will, to use grandees and towns for mobilizing resources for war. While government was more institutionalized in some countries than in others, monarchs everywhere relied upon the informal co-operation and goodwill of the great men of the localities, and probably this co-operation was more effectively secured in Elizabethan England than elsewhere.

The resources made available for war were, however, much larger, in proportion to the population and national wealth, in Spain than in England. Philip II extracted perhaps 10 per cent of Spain's national income for war, while Elizabeth took only 3 per cent of England's.[19] Philip's income was in the region of £2 million per annum, while Elizabeth's averaged not more than half a million, including taxes voted for war. Philip spent sums on war far beyond anything contemplated by the English Crown; but he achieved this only by heavy borrowing, which resulted in three royal bankruptcies.

By comparison with France and Castile, where representative assemblies were weak, the English Parliament was well entrenched, not as a rival to the Crown, but as an important partner in government. The English monarchy was not so much limited by Parliament as assisted in levying taxes and in enforcing the law by having the backing of parliamentary statute. However, in England the monarch was bound by law in a way in which the French and Spanish kings were not. The latter monarchs could imprison their subjects without trial—including in Philip's case even his own son, Don Carlos—they could issue decrees which had the force of law, and they could levy taxes without the consent of their subjects. In consequence, the French and Spanish realms were far more heavily burdened by taxation than was the English.

Partly as a consequence of this the English state was more stable in the second half of the sixteenth century than were its neighbours. France and

[19] As suggested in Ralph Davis, *The Rise of the Atlantic Economies* (London, 1973), 211.

the Low Countries were torn by civil war throughout that period; and Philip II faced two major rebellions, by the Moriscos in the 1560s and the Aragonese in the 1590s. By comparison, after 1554 the Tudors faced only very minor outbreaks within England itself, although Ireland was a different matter. If the low level of taxation was one reason for English stability, it was not the only one. English society was comparatively unified: English nobles did not have the privileges, especially the exemption from taxation, enjoyed by their counterparts on the Continent; and as a result the tax burden, while lighter, was also more evenly spread. Nor did England suffer from the major famines that struck France in the 1590s and which, together with the sufferings inflicted by religious war, led to the peasant risings of the Croquants. The system of poor relief and the regulations for supplying food in times of shortage helped to prevent, or at least to limit, destitution.

Finally, England was mercifully free from religious war, a blessing it shared with Spain and with Scotland. While the Protestant nobles were able to establish the Kirk in Scotland, they were careful not to antagonize the Catholics by adopting the rigorous and destructive policies demanded by the Protestant ministers: the monasteries, for instance, were allowed to stand. Scottish society, tightly bound together by the ties of kinship, survived the Reformation. France and the Netherlands were not so fortunate. In France, the weakness of the monarchy after the death of Henry II in 1559 allowed the Calvinists to recruit supporters in large numbers, while antagonism between the great nobles ensured that religious conflict would not be held in check. In the Netherlands, Philip II alienated his subjects by crude centralization, ruthless persecution, and burdensome taxes, while his own absence from the region robbed him of opportunities to use his personal influence to control the growing disaffection.

In England the combustible material for religious conflict existed, but did not ignite under the Tudors. Almost alone in Western Europe, apart from Scotland, England was free both from crippling foreign wars and from civil and religious strife. This freedom did not always appear secure to contemporaries, who feared Spanish invasion, Catholic plots, uprisings of the poor, and a disputed succession; but those very fears helped to unite the propertied classes in a common anxiety. More than that, the Crown was always strong enough to maintain its authority in religious affairs, while it avoided foreign adventures and the imposition of crushing taxation. A united kingdom, a strong monarchy, and a relatively cohesive society were the main ingredients for stability in an age of religious turmoil.

Glossary

advowson right of presentation to an ecclesiastical benefice

Arminian properly used of the followers of Jacobus Arminius, a Dutch theologian who preached a doctrine of free will against the predestinarianism of Calvin's disciples. In England it was applied to the opponents of Calvinism generally and, in particular, to Archbishop Laud and his allies

assizes judicial sessions held twice a year in each English county by circuit judges

cess tax imposed by the Dublin government in lieu of impositions in kind, such as purveyance (q.v.). See Ch. 8 s. 3

chap-book a small, easily transported book sold by travelling salesmen known as chapmen (e.g. Autolycus in *The Winter's Tale*)

classis under the Presbyterian form of government a *classis* was a colloquy of ministers and Church elders responsible for ruling the Church in a particular area. Under Elizabeth the term was applied to unofficial conferences of ministers, associated with Presbyterians. Ch. 11 s. 4

coign and livery general term for Irish exactions derived from a lord's right to billet followers on the country

copyhold copyhold tenants held their land 'by copy of court roll': that is to say, their tenures were subject to the customs of particular manors, which varied greatly

Fifteenths and Tenths taxes on property developed in the fourteenth century; in the sixteenth generally used in conjunction with the subsidy (q.v.)

First Fruits and Tenths ecclesiastical taxes, the former being a levy of the first year's income of any new incumbent, the latter involving a payment of one-tenth of his income. Both were payable to the papacy before the Reformation and were taken over by the Crown in 1534

gallowglass (galloglaich) Scottish mercenaries employed by Irish chiefs, named after the type of axe that they used. They had settled in Ireland before the sixteenth century; during that century other mercenaries, known as redshanks, came over, but did not settle

impropriation the term refers to the annexation of tithes by an individual or institution. Before the Reformation it was generally used of tithes taken over by monastic houses; after the dissolution of the monasteries it was applied to tithes attached to properties acquired by lay persons

latitat, writ of a writ designed, through a legal fiction, to extend the jurisdiction of the court of King's Bench. See *Middlesex, bill of*

letters patent open letters with the great seal attached, containing grant or instructions from the monarch. Copies were enrolled in Chancery, forming the Patent Rolls. Similar to, though technically different from, charters

Lords Lieutenant officials, usually nobles, appointed by the Crown to command the militia in one or more counties. First appointed temporarily under Edward

VI; became permanent after *c.*1585. Assisted by deputy lieutenants. Ch. 5 s. 7

marches; marcher lords 'marches' was the term generally applied to border-lands. It was more particularly applied to the counties on each side of the Anglo-Welsh and Anglo-Scottish borders. Marcher lords possessed wide powers in the lordships in the Marches of Wales up to the Acts of Union in 1536 and 1543, which much depleted their authority

Middlesex, bill of a real or fictitious bill brought against an individual with the purpose of bringing a case before King's Bench and extending the jurisdiction of that court. Often used in conjunction with writ of *latitat* (q.v.)

New English settlers and office-holders in Ireland from the reign of Elizabeth onwards. They later formed the Protestant Ascendancy. See *Old English*

Old English the Anglo-Norman lords and the English who had settled in Ireland before the sixteenth century; referred to above also as 'Anglo-Irish'. The term 'Old English' came into use under Elizabeth. See *New English*

oyer and terminer a commission to 'hear and determine' criminal cases

Pale, the the area surrounding Dublin in which the writ of the English government generally ran: the precise area varied but mainly consisted of the counties of Dublin, Meath, Louth, Kildare, and Westmeath

ploughland a term used in Ireland to denote an area of roughly 120 Irish acres

praemunire a writ deriving authority from statutes passed in the fourteenth century to protect the rights of the Crown against papal interference. In 1393 its scope was extended to cover all invasions of royal jurisdiction, and under Henry VIII it was used as a weapon against the King's opponents

Privy Chamber the king or queen's private apartments at Court; under Henry VIII and Edward VI the hub of Court politics. Ch. 5 s. 1

proclamation a formal command issued by the monarch or monarch-in-Council. The extent of legislative power of proclamation was debatable, but proclamations were certainly inferior to statutes. Chs. 2 s. 2; 5 s. 3

prophesyings conferences of preaching clergy for biblical exposition; often attended by other clergy and laity. Associated with puritans but not restricted to them. Suppressed by order of Elizabeth, though not completely. Chs. 8 s. 1; 11 s. 4

purveyance the right of the monarch, or his officers, to demand the sale of food and other goods for his household below market price. Purveyance was the object of much contention under Elizabeth I. In Ireland the right was extended to the Lord Deputy: see *cess*

recusant a man or woman who failed to attend church services; usually applied to Roman Catholics, but sometimes used of Protestant absentees

simony the buying and selling of ecclesiastical offices

skimmington a mocking ride, to the accompaniment of 'rough music', to shame termagant or unfaithful wives and their cuckolded husbands

subsidy a parliamentary tax on property

tanist the successor-designate of a Gaelic chief

transubstantiation the doctrine of the Roman Catholic Church that the whole substance of the bread and the wine are converted in the Eucharist into the body and blood of Christ, only the accidentals remaining

Walloons southern, French-speaking Netherlanders

wardship the right of the Crown to take over the estates of heirs or heiresses who were under age and held the property by 'feudal' tenure of the Crown. Wardship included the right to decide on the marriage of heirs or heiresses

Genealogical Tables

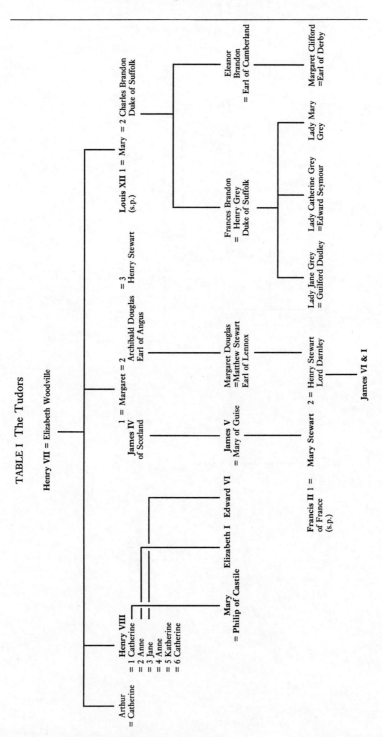

TABLE I The Tudors

Henry VII = Elizabeth Woodville

Arthur
= Catherine

Henry VIII
= 1 Catherine
= 2 Anne
= 3 Jane
= 4 Anne
= 5 Katherine
= 6 Catherine

Margaret 1 = James IV of Scotland
= 2 Archibald Douglas Earl of Angus
= 3 Henry Stewart

Mary 1 = Louis XII (s.p.)
= 2 Charles Brandon Duke of Suffolk

Mary
= Philip of Castile

Elizabeth I   Edward VI

James V
= Mary of Guise

Margaret Douglas
= Matthew Stewart Earl of Lennox

Frances Brandon
= Henry Grey Duke of Suffolk

Eleanor Brandon
= Earl of Cumberland

Francis II 1 = Mary Stewart 2 = Henry Stewart Lord Darnley
of France (s.p.)

James VI & I

Lady Jane Grey
= Guilford Dudley

Lady Catherine Grey
= Edward Seymour

Lady Mary Grey

Margaret Clifford
= Earl of Derby

TABLE II The Stewarts

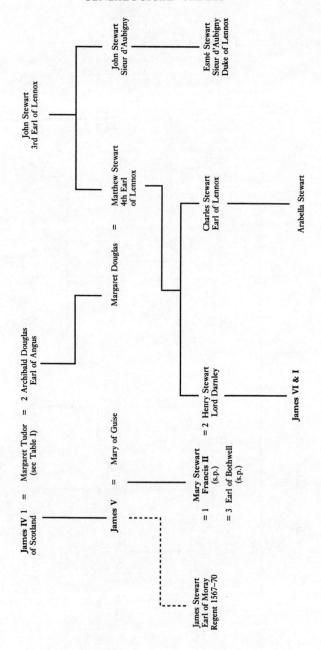

TABLE III The Dudley–Sidney–Herbert–Devereux Connection

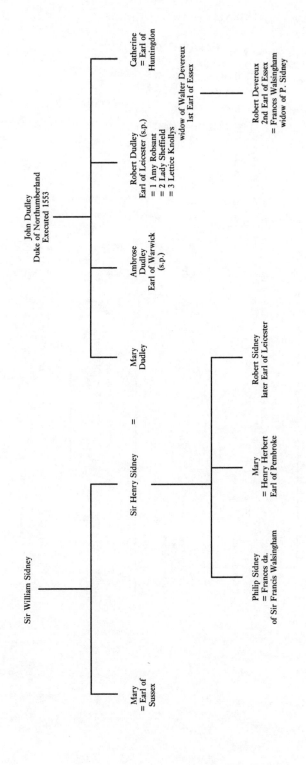

TABLE IV The Howards

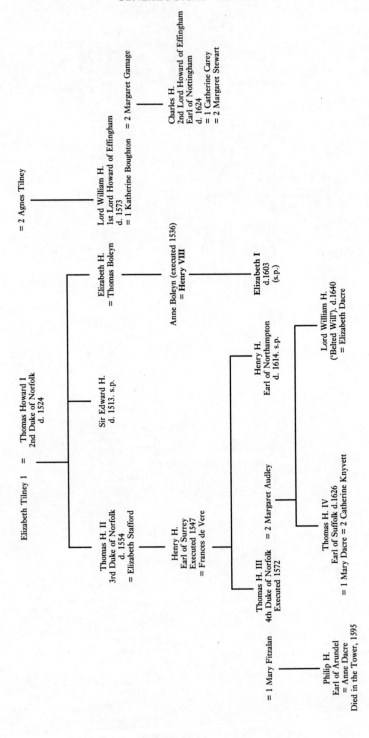

Chronology

The purpose of this chronology is to show the principal events described in the text and to relate them to selected events overseas. With the exception of a few happenings outside England, the relevant point in the text may be found by reference to the index. Reference to books and plays is selective, mostly confined to those mentioned in the text. The right-hand column includes matters involving English foreign policy as well as events in Scotland, Ireland, overseas countries, and the high seas.

Date	Domestic politics and religion	Legislation
1547	Death of Henry VIII; accession of Edward VI	Repeal Statute (1 Edward VI c. 12)
	Somerset made Protector	Communion in both kinds (1 Edward VI c. 1)
	Religious Injunctions	Dissolution of chantries (1 Edward VI c. 14)
		Vagrancy Act (1 Edward VI c. 3)
1548	Order of Communion	
	First Enclosure Commission	
1549	Execution of Thomas Seymour	First Act of Uniformity (2 &3 Edward VI c. 1)
	South-western revolt; Kett's revolt	
	Fall of Somerset	Marriage of priests (2 & 3 Edward VI c. 21)
1550	Warwick (Northumberland) made Lord President of the Council	Act against unlawful assembly (3 & 4 Edward VI c. 5)
	Somerset released from Tower; Cecil appointed Secretary	
	Bad harvest	
1551	Restoration of the coinage	
	Arrest of Somerset; Warwick created Duke of Northumberland	
	Deprivation of Gardiner	
	Sweating sickness	
1552	Execution of Somerset	Second Act of Uniformity (5 & 6 Edward VI c. 1)
		Poor Law (5 & 6 Edward VI c. 2)
1553	Forty-two articles of faith	Statute concerning financial courts (7 Edward VI c. 2)
	Edward's 'Devise' of the Crown; marriage of Lady Jane Grey to Guilford Dudley	First Statute of Repeal (1 Mary st. 2, c. 2)
	Death of Edward and brief reign of Lady Jane	
	Accession of Mary; Mary agrees to marry Philip of Spain	
	Pole appointed papal legate to England	
1554	Publication of royal marriage treaty; Wyatt's rebellion	Sedition statute (1 & 2 Philip & Mary c. 3)
	Execution of Lady Jane Grey	
	Religious injunctions issued	
	Marriage of Mary and Philip; arrival of Cardinal Pole	
1555	Burning of Rogers, Hooper, Ridley, Latimer, et al.; exiles multiply	Second Statute of Repeal (1 & 2 Philip & Mary c. 8)
	Philip's return to Netherlands	Heresy Act (1 & 2 Philip & Mary c. 6)
	Death of Gardiner; Westminster Synod	Treason Act (1 & 2 Philip & Mary c. 10)
	Mary's fourth Parliament: defeat of 'exiles bill'; restoration of First Fruits to Church	
	Revocation of privileges of Hanse	
	Year of dearth	

Publications, performances, etc.	Foreign policy, Ireland, Scotland, overseas	Date
Certain Sermons or Homilies; Sternhold and Hopkins, first book of Psalms	Invasion of Scotland	1547
	Death of Francis I; accession of Henry II	
	Battle of Muhlberg: victory of Charles V	
Hall, Union of . . . York and Lancaster	French troops land in Scotland; siege of Haddington; Mary Stewart taken to France	1548
	Bellingham appointed Lord Deputy in Ireland	
	Augsburg Interim: Religious settlement in Germany	
Cheke, The Hurt of Sedition; Book of Common Prayer	War with France; siege of Boulogne; Abandonment of garrison policy in Scotland	1549
Cranmer, Defence of the True Doctrine of the Sacrament; Crowley, Way of Wealth	Treaty of peace with France; Boulogne restored to French; withdrawal from Scotland	1550
	St Leger appointed Lord Deputy in Ireland	
Cranmer, An Answer to Stephen Gardiner; Robinson's translation of More, Utopia	Second Session of Council of Trent; war between France and Emperor Charles V	1551
	Croft appointed Lord Deputy	
Second Book of Common Prayer		1552
Wilson, Arte of Rhetorique	Failure of Charles V's siege of Metz	1553
	Willoughby/Chancellor expedition to north-east passage; Wyndham's voyage to Guinea Coast	
	St Leger appointed Lord Deputy	
		1554
	Election of Carafa as Pope Paul IV	1555
	Peace of Augsburg	
	Foundation of Muscovy Co.	

Date	Domestic politics and religion	Legislation
1556	Cranmer burned	
	Dudley conspiracy	
	Year of dearth	
1557	Return of Philip II to England (March); departure in July	
	Pole's legatine commission revoked	
	Stafford's landing at Scarborough	
	Viral epidemic: high mortality	
1558	Deaths of Mary Tudor and Pole; accession of Elizabeth (all on 17 Nov.)	
	High mortality	
1559	Coronation of Elizabeth; Parker made Archbishop of Canterbury	Act of Supremacy (1 Elizabath c. 1)
	Religious Injunctions	Act of Uniformity (1 Elizabeth c. 2)
		Restoration of First Fruits to Crown (1 Elizabeth c. 4)
		Act for exchange of episcopal lands (1 Elizabeth c. 19)
1560		
1561		
1562	Elizabeth ill with smallpox	
1563	Restoration of currency	Poor Law (5 Elizabeth c. 3)
	Meeting of Convocation; Thirty-nine Articles drafted; vestiarian controversy	Statute of Artificers (5 Elizabeth c. 4)
1564	Dudley created Earl of Leicester; proposed as husband for Mary	
1565		
1566	'Alphabetical' bills in Parliament	
	Parker's *Advertisements*	
1567		

Publications, performances, etc.	Foreign policy, Ireland, Scotland, overseas	Date
Huggarde, *The Displaying of the Protestants*; Harpsfield, *Life of More*; Ponet (Poynet), *Short Treatise of Politic Power*	Spanish invasion of papal states	1556
	Abdication of Charles V	
	Sussex appointed Lord Deputy; invasion of Ulster	
More, *English Works*; Tottel's *Miscellany*	War reopened between France and Spain; English declaration of war on France	1557
	Spanish victory at Saint-Quentin	
	Plantation of Leix and Offaly	
	Jenkinson's journey to Bokhara	
Knox, *First Blast of the Trumpet* and *Appellation*; Goodman, *How Superior Powers Oght to be Obeyd*	Fall of Calais	1558
	Marriage of Dauphin (Francis) to Mary Stewart	
	Death of Charles V	
Book of Common Prayer; *Mirror for Magistrates*	Treaty of Câteau-Cambrésis; death of Henry II; accession of Francis II	1559
	Protestant revolt in Scotland; landing of French troops in Scotland; English intervention in Scotland	
	Shane O'Neill in revolt	
	Treaty of Edinburgh; reformed Church established in Scotland	1560
	Death of Francis II; accession of Charles IX; Catherine de Medici regent	
Hoby's trans. of Castiglione, *Book of the Courtier*	Return of Mary Stewart to Scotland	1561
	Sussex's campaigns against O'Neill	
Jewel, *Apologia pro ecclesia Anglicana* Norton and Sackville, *Gorbuduc*	Civil War in France; English troops enter France under Ambrose Dudley	1562
	Opening of slave-trade by Hawkins	
Foxe, *Acts and Monuments*; Shute, *First Grounds of Architecture*	Treaty with O'Neill	1563
	Edict of Amboise ends fighting in France; withdrawal of English troops from France	
	Marriage negotiations between Elizabeth and Archduke Charles	
	Embargo on English trade to Netherlands	
	Departure of Sussex from Ireland	1564
	Treaty of Troyes	
	Mary's marriage to Darnley	1565
	Lifting of embargo on English trade to Netherlands	
	Sidney appointed Lord Deputy	
Harman, *Caveat for Common Cursitors*	Rioting in Antwerp	1566
	Murder of Rizzio	
	Birth of James (VI and I)	
Golding's trans. of Ovid, *Metamorphoses*	Revolt in Netherlands; Alba's march to Netherlands	1567
	Murder of Darnley; marriage of Mary and Bothwell; Mary's abdication	
	Arrest of Desmond; O'Neill killed by Macdonalds	

Date	*Domestic politics and religion*	*Legislation*
1568		
1569	Cecil's 'Memorial of the State of the Realm'; conspiracy against Cecil; proposed marriage of Mary and Norfolk; arrest of Norfolk; revolt of northern earls	
1570	Dacre revolt	
	Bull *Regnans in excelsis*	
1571	Revival of 'alphabetical bills' in Parliament	Treason Act (13 Elizabeth c. 1)
	Ridolfi conspiracy unearthed	Act against Bulls from Rome (13 Elizabeth c. 2)
	Cecil created Lord Burghley	Act for Thirty-nine Articles (13 Elizabeth c. 12)
1572	Execution of Norfolk	Poor Law (14 Elizabeth c. 5)
1573	Walsingham appointed Secretary of State	
1574	Arrival of first seminarist priests	
1575	Death of Archbishop Parker; translation of Grindal to Canterbury	
1576	Suspension of Grindal	Poor Law (18 Elizabeth c. 3)

Publications, performances, etc.	Foreign policy, Ireland, Scotland, overseas	Date
	Mary's defeat at Langside; flight to England	1568
	'Massacre' of San Juan de Ulúa	
	Seizure of Spanish treasure ships	
	Revolt of Moriscos in Granada	
	Execution of Egmont and Horn in the Netherlands	
	Fitzmaurice revolt in Munster	1569
	Assassination of Regent Moray; talks between Cecil, Mary, and Scottish commissioners; invasion of Scotland by Sussex; Lennox elected Regent	1570
	Treaty of Saint-Germain in France	
	Drake's first voyage to Caribbean	
	Battle of Lepanto	1571
	Suspension of talks with Mary and Scottish commissioners; death of Regent Lennox; Mar elected Regent	
	Marriage negotiations between Elizabeth and Anjou	
	Departure of Sidney from Ireland	
Admonition to Parliament	Death of Regent Mar; Morton elected Regent; English intervention in Scotland; Pacification of Perth	1572
	Dutch 'sea beggars' ordered to leave English ports; capture of Brille and Flushing by 'sea beggars'	
	Treaty of Blois between England and France	
	Massacre of St Bartholomew	
	Commercial relations restored with Spain	
	Drake's expedition to Panama	
	Attempted plantation of Ulster by 1st Earl of Essex	1573
	Death of Charles IX; accession of Henry III	1574
	Submission of Desmond	
	Treaty of Bristol between England and Spain	
Pettie, *A Pettite Pallace*	Civil War in France	1575
	Bankruptcy of Spanish Crown	
	Massacre at Rathlin Island; return of Sidney to Ireland; dispute over the cess	
Burbage's 'Theatre' built	Sack of Antwerp	1576
	Peace of Monsieur in France	
	Frobisher's voyage to find north-west passage	
	Death of Essex in Ireland	

Date	Domestic politics and religion	Legislation
1577	Execution of first seminarist priest (Mayne)	
1578		
1579		
1580	Arrival of Parsons and Campion	
1581	Drake knighted	Treason Act (23 Elizabeth c. 1)
	Capture and execution of Campion	Act against seditious books (23 Elizabeth c. 2)
1582	Proclamation declaring Jesuits traitors	
	Beginning of Dedham conference	
1583	Throckmorton plot	
	Death of Grindal; Whitgift appointed Archbishop	
1584	Bond of Association	
	Presbyterian campaign for 'Bill and Book'	
1585	Poor harvest	Act for Queen's surety (27 Elizabeth c. 1)
		Act against Jesuits (27 Elizabeth c. 2)
1586	Discovery of Babington plot; trial of Mary Stewart	
1587	Execution of Mary Stewart	
	Introduction of Presbyterian 'Bill and Book' into Parliament	

Publications, performances, etc.	Foreign policy, Ireland, Scotland, overseas	Date
Holinshed, *Chronicle*, including Harrison, *Description of England*; Peacham, *Garden of Eloquence*; Dee, *General and Rare Memorials Perteyning to . . . Navigation*	Pacification of Ghent and withdrawal of Spanish troops from Netherlands	1577
	Drake's voyage of circumnavigation	
Burbage's curtain Theatre built		
Lyly, *Euphues*	Don John's victory at Gembloux; Walsingham/Cobham embassy to the Netherlands; Dutch treaty with Anjou	1578
	Final departure of Sidney from Ireland	
	Gilbert's voyage	
John Stubbs, *The Discovery of a Gaping Gulf*; Gosson, *School of Abuse*; North's trans. of Plutarch, *Lives*; Spenser, *Shepheardes Calendar*	Anjou marriage negotiations reopened	1579
	Fitzmaurice/Desmond rebellion	
	Union of Utrecht	
Lyly, *Euphues and his England*	Death of Henry of Portugal	1580
	Fall of Regent Morton	
	Return of Drake	
	Baltinglass revolt; Smerwick massacre	
Campion, *Decem rationes*	Accession of Philip II to throne of Portugal	1581
	Walsingham's embassy to France; Anjou's visit to England	
	Execution of Regent Morton	
	Levant Co. founded	
	Return of Anjou to France	1582
	The Ruthven Raid	
Burghley, *The Execution of Justice in England*; Smith, *De republica Anglorum*; Philip Stubbs, *Anatomy of Abuses*	Desmond killed	1583
	Walsingham's embassy to Scotland	
	Gilbert's colonizing voyage	
	Perrott appointed Lord Deputy; survey of Munster	1584
	Deaths of Orange and Anjou	
	Treaty of Joinville allying Catholic League to Spain	
	Perrott's Parliament in Ireland; plantation of Munster	1585
	Acceptance by James VI of English pension	
	Treaty of Nonsuch with Dutch; fall of Antwerp; Leicester's expeditionary force	
	Submission of Henry III to Catholic League at Treaty of Nemours	
	Drake's expedition to Caribbean; Davis's voyage to north-west passage; establishment of Roanoke colony	
	Death of Philip Sidney; recall of Leicester	1586
	Abandonment of Roanoke	
2nd edn. of Harrison, *Description*	Leicester's second tour in the Netherlands	1587
Rose Theatre built	Preparation of Armada; Drake's expedition to Cadiz	
	Second Roanoke colony	

Date	Domestic politics and religion	Legislation
1588	The Armada Death of Leicester	
1589	Death of Mildmay	Husbandry Act (31 Elizabeth c. 7)
1590	Death of Walsingham Trial of Cartwright and other puritans	
1591	Death of Hatton Robert Cecil promoted to Privy Council	
1592	Plague	
1593	Dispute over office of attorney-general Lopez affair	Act against seditious sectaries (35 Elizabeth c. 1) Act against popish recusants (35 Elizabeth c. 2)
1594	First of four bad harvests	
1595	Second bad harvest	
1596	R. Cecil appointed Secretary of State Worst harvest of century; Oxfordshire 'rising'	
1597	Dearth Death of Lord Cobham Parliament: monopolies debate	Act against depopulation (39 Elizabeth c. 1) Tillage Act (39 Elizabeth c. 2) Poor Law and Vagrancy Acts (39 Elizabeth cc. 3, 4)
1598	Death of Burghley	

Publications, performances, etc.	Foreign policy, Ireland, Scotland, overseas	Date
Hariot, *Brief and True Reporte of the New Found Land of Virginia*; first Marprelate tracts; Morgan's trans. of Bible into Welsh	Capture of Paris by Guises; murder of Duc de Guise	1588
	Fitzwilliam appointed Lord Deputy	
Hakluyt, *Principal Navigations*; main Marprelate tracts; Nash, *Anatomy of Absurdity*; Puttenham, *Arte of English Poesie*	Deaths of Catherine de Medici and Henry III; disputed accession of Henry IV	1589
	Expedition to Portugal	
	Willoughby's expedition to northern France	
Munday's trans. of *Amadis of Gaul*; Peele, *Polyhymnia*; Sidney, *Arcadia*; Spenser, *Faerie Queen*, I–III	Spanish landing in Brittany; Henry IV's victory at Ivry	1590
Perkins, *A Golden Chaine*; Savile's trans. of Tacitus, *Histories*	Norris's expedition to Brittany; siege of Rouen by Essex	1591
Shakespeare, *2, 3, Henry VI*	Howard's expedition to Azores; fight of the *Revenge*	
	O'Donnell's escape from Dublin Castle	
Stow, *Annals*	Defeat of Anglo-French forces at Craon, Brittany; relief of Rouen by Parma; death of Parma	1592
Shakespeare, *1 Henry VI*; Heywood, *1 Edward IV*	Capture of *Madre de Dios*	
	'Spanish Blanks' affair	
Hooker, *Laws of Ecclesiastical Polity*, vols. i–iv	Conversion of Henry IV to Catholicism	1593
Shakespeare, *Richard III*		
R. Doleman (Parsons), *A Conference about the Next Succession*	Occupation of Paris by Henry IV; capture of Crozon by Anglo-French forces; coronation of Henry IV	1594
Munday *et al.*, *Sir Thomas More*; Shakespeare, *Richard II*		
Daniel, *Civil Wars*, i–iv; Sidney, *Apology for Poetry*; Spenser, *Colin Clout*	O'Neill revolt; Blackwater fort burned; arrival of Sir J. Norris; Bagenal defeated at Clontibret; Tyrone proclaimed traitor	1595
	Drake/Hawkins expedition to Panama; death of both men; Ralegh's voyage to Guyana	
	Henry IV's declaration of war on Spain; Unton's embassy to France	
Ralegh, *Discovery of Guiana*; Spenser, *Faerie Queene*, IV–VI	Fall of Calais to Spanish; bankruptcy of Spanish Crown	1596
Shakespeare, *A Midsummer Night's Dream*	Cadiz expedition	
	Spanish expedition to Ireland frustrated by storms; Tyrone pardoned	
Bacon, *Essays*; Hooker, *Laws of Ecclesiastical Policy*, v; Deloney, *The Gentle Craft* and *Jack of Newbury*	Triple Alliance of France, Netherlands, English; capture of Amiens by Henry IV	1597
	Azores expedition	
Nashe *et al.*, *The Isle of Dogs*; Shakespeare, *1, 2 Henry IV*	Burgh appointed Lord Deputy; death of Burgh	
Stow, *Survey of London*; Peter Wentworth, *A Pithie Exhortation*	Cecil's embassy to France; Edict of Nantes; Treaty of Vervins between France and Spain	1598
Globe Theatre built	Death of Philip II	
	Defeat of Bagenal at Yellow Ford; revolt in Munster	

Date	Domestic politics and religion	Legislation
1599	Buckhurst appointed Lord Treasurer; Cecil Master of Wards	
	Return of Essex from Ireland; under house arrest	
1600	York House trial of Essex; end of his lease of wine customs	
1601	Essex rising; execution of Essex	Poor Law (43 Elizabeth c. 2)
	Parliament: second monopolies debate	
1602		
1603	Death of Elizabeth (24 Mar.); accession of James VI and I	

Publications, performances, etc.	Foreign policy, Ireland, Scotland, overseas	Date
Hayward, *Life of Henry IV*	Essex appointed Lord Lieutenant; expeditions to Munster and Ulster; truce with Tyrone	1599
Shakespeare, *As You Like It*; *Henry V*; *Julius Caesar*		
Shakespeare, *Twelfth Night*	Mountjoy appointed Lord Deputy; campaign in Ulster	1600
	Foundation of East India Co.	
Fortune Theatre built	Siege of Ostend by Spanish	1601
	Spanish landing at Kinsale; Spanish/Irish army defeated; flight of O'Donnell	
Shakespeare, *Troilus and Cressida*	Surrender of Spanish in Ireland;	1602
Drayton, *Barons' Wars*	Submission of Tyrone	1603

Bibliography

BIBLIOGRAPHICAL ESSAY

The first *Oxford History of England* was planned before the Second World War: of the two volumes covering the sixteenth century J. L. Mackie's *The Earlier Tudors, 1485–1558* appeared in 1952 and J. B. Black's *The Reign of Elizabeth* in 1936, with a second edition in 1959. Since then a generation has passed, during which more primary sources have become available in print and a vast corpus of scholarly books and articles has been published. New approaches to the period have been explored and the emphasis has shifted.

Political history has been illuminated by the investigation of clientage, faction, and patronage. In *The Elizabethan Political Scene* (London, 1948), J. E. Neale established the importance of royal patronage for the working of the governmental system and stressed, perhaps exaggerated, the attachment of officials to leading statesmen. This process led, in his opinion, to a political structure dominated by the struggles of rival factions, pursuing different policies and seeking the favour of the monarch. Since then the concepts of faction and clientage have been applied to the reigns of Henry VIII, Edward VI, and Mary; they have also, more recently, been questioned.[1]

Much work has been done on Tudor parliaments. The discovery by Neale of hitherto unknown parliamentary diaries enabled him to tell the story of Elizabethan parliaments in dramatic detail. At the same time the application of prosopographical methods greatly increased our knowledge of Elizabethan MPs and their constituencies, a knowledge first revealed by Neale himself and more recently developed in the volumes published by the History of Parliament Trust.[2] Recently Neale's interpretation of Elizabethan parliaments in terms of conflict and biography has been questioned, and the emphasis has moved from confrontation to collaboration, and from the drama of debate to the enactment of legislation.[3]

The governmental system of Tudor England has been intensively explored by G. R. Elton in his *Tudor Revolution in Government* (Cambridge, 1953) and in subsequent studies. Following the tradition established by T. F. Tout for medieval England, Elton and his pupils have been concerned with a detailed investigation of administrative and judicial processes, putting the institutional history of the cen-

---

[1] See Simon Adams, 'Eliza enthron'd? The Court and its politics', in Christopher Haigh (ed.), *The Reign of Elizabeth I* (Basingstoke, 1984), 55–78; G. W. Bernard, 'Politics and government in Tudor England', *Historical Journal*, 31 (1988), 159–82. This introductory essay and its notes are not of course intended to do more than provide examples of recent literature.

[2] J. E. Neale, *The Elizabethan House of Commons* (London, 1949); id., *Elizabeth I and her Parliaments* (2 vols., London, 1953, 1957).

[3] e.g. G. R. Elton, *The Parliament of England, 1559–1581* (Cambridge, 1986).

tury on stronger foundations than before. This traditional approach has been complemented by studies of institutions as social groupings, operating within a social as well as an administrative context, an approach exemplified in Joel Hurstfield, *The Queen's Wards* (London, 1958).

Thanks to Patrick Collinson's *Elizabethan Puritan Movement* (London, 1967) and his *The Religion of Protestants* (Oxford, 1982), we are not only better informed than before about sixteenth-century Protestants, but have a greater insight into their minds. Local studies, such as Christopher Haigh's *Reformation and Resistance in Tudor Lancashire* (Cambridge, 1975), have brought us nearer to the grass roots and to Catholics and Protestants in the shires, shifting the emphasis away from the central institutions of the Church towards the parishes.

Local and regional history has, indeed, been one of the most fruitful concerns of early modern historians over the past thirty years or so. The pioneering work of A. L. Rowse and W. G. Hoskins has been followed by many studies of counties, towns, and parishes. Until about 1945 the tradition of writing and research on local history was largely 'antiquarian' in its approach. Since then local historians have examined the anatomy and metabolism of communities, relating their findings to wider and interrelated problems. At county level works like A. Hassell Smith's *County and Court: Government and Politics in Norfolk, 1558–1603* (Oxford, 1974) have analysed the government, politics, religion, and economy of individual shires. Studies of single villages have shown that more can be learned about the lives of peasants and labourers than was thought possible thirty years ago.[4] Urban history has become an autonomous province of the historical world, with its own professors and journals, and also its own self-doubts; we have had studies of towns like York and, more recently, of London.[5] Family history and demography have been rapidly growing and closely linked enterprises. E. A. Wrigley and R. S. Schofield, *The Population History of England, 1541–1871* (London, 1981) has put the study of population onto a firm foundation, while others have examined the personal relations of husbands and wives, parents and children.

Keith Thomas's *Religion and the Decline of Magic* (London, 1971) and his *Man and the Natural World* (London, 1983) have explored the *mentalités* of men and women in Tudor England. Within the last decade there have been some attempts to bridge the divide separating literary studies from history; most of these have begun on the 'literary' side, such as David Norbrook's *Poetry and Politics in the English Renaissance* (London, 1984), but there are signs of approaches from the 'historical' side as well.

Forty-five years ago the first rumblings were heard of the 'storm over the gentry'. Those growls of academic thunder have now been almost silenced, and few historians would today consider the question of whether the aristocracy fell and the gentry rose to be, in such simple terms, a matter for serious debate, since the distinction between the two groups is neither absolute nor realistic. But the controversy has produced work of lasting value, notably *The Crisis of the Aristocracy* (Oxford, 1965) by Lawrence Stone, himself one of the protagonists in the dispute.

[4] As in Margaret Spufford, *Contrasting Communities: English Villagers in the Sixteenth and Seventeenth Centuries* (Cambridge, 1974).

[5] Philip Abrams, introd. to Philip Abrams and E. A. Wrigley (eds.), *Towns in Societies: Essays in Economic History and Historical Sociology* (Cambridge, 1978).

Studies of estate management, rents, and conspicuous consumption have added to our knowledge of English landownership; and we also know more than we did about the education and social habits of the landed classes.

Finally, there has been a welcome and overdue revival of interest in the reigns of Edward VI and Mary. Until about 1965 these formed the dark age of Tudor history, often seen as periods of confusion and sterility, separating the more glorious epochs of Henry VIII and Elizabeth I. Recent work has shown that they are worth studying for their own sake.[6]

BIBLIOGRAPHIES AND GUIDES

Several excellent bibliographical aids are available to students of this period, in particular Conyers Read (ed.), *Bibliography of British History: Tudor Period, 1485–1603* (Oxford, 1st edn., 1933; 2nd edn., 1959). In view of this, the present bibliography concentrates upon works published since 1958, while including the more important items of an earlier date: the focus is on books rather than articles, although the latter have been cited when they are either particularly important or have not yet been incorporated into the main body of literature. The range of primary sources is so wide that only a brief sample of the main series can be included. A useful guide is G. R. Elton, *England 1200–1640* in the series The Sources of English History (London, 1969). A helpful supplement to Conyers Read is Mortimer Levine, *Tudor England (Bibliographical Handbook)* (Cambridge, 1968). *A Short-Title Catalogue of Books Printed in England, Scotland, and Ireland . . . 1475–1640*, comp. A. W. Pollard and G. R. Redgrave (2nd edn., 3 vols., London, 1976–91) is indispensable for a study of the contemporary literature. The Historical Association and the Royal Historical Society both publish annual bibliographies: the *Annual Bulletin of Historical Literature* and the *Annual Bibliography of British and Irish History* respectively. The *English Historical Review* carries notices of periodical publications in its July number each year, and the *Economic History Review* has a review of periodical literature each February.

Among many guides and works of reference are: Leslie Stephen and Sidney Lee (eds.), *The Dictionary of National Biography* (63 vols., London, 1885–1900, with subsequent supplements); G. E. Cockayne (ed.), *The Complete Peerage of England, Scotland, Ireland, etc.* (rev. edn. by V. Gibbs, London, 1910–49); E. B. Fryde *et al.* (eds.), *Handbook of British Chronology* (London, 3rd edn., 1986); C. R. Cheney (ed.), *Handbook of Dates* (London, 1945); S. T. Bindoff (ed.), *The House of Commons, 1509–1558* (3 vols., London, 1982) and P. W. Hasler (ed.), *The House of Commons, 1558–1603* (3 vols., London, 1981), both containing biographies of MPs.

THE PRINCIPAL SOURCES

Fundamental are the main PRO series: *Calendar of State Papers, Domestic: Edward VI, Mary, Elizabeth I* (12 vols., London, 1856–72); *Calendar of State Papers,*

---

[6] See e.g. D. M. Loades, *The Reign of Mary Tudor* (London, 1979); Jennifer Loach and Robert Tittler (eds.), *The Mid-Tudor Polity* (Basingstoke, 1980).

Foreign: Edward VI, Mary, Elizabeth I (25 vols., London, 1861–1950); *Calendar of State Papers, Spanish* (13 vols. and two supplements, London, 1862–1954); *Calendar of State Papers, Venetian* (9 vols., London, 1864–98); *Calendar of State Papers Relating to Scotland and Mary, Queen of Scots, 1547–1603* (13 vols., London, 1898–1969); *Calendar of State Papers Relating to Ireland, of the Reign of Elizabeth* (11 vols., London, 1860–1912); *Calendar of the Carew Manuscripts . . . at Lambeth, 1515–1624* (6 vols., London, 1867–73); J. R. Dasent (ed.), *The Acts of the Privy Council of England* (46 vols., London, 1890–1964). Outstanding among the volumes published by the Historical Manuscripts Commission, are: *Calendar of the MSS of Lord De L'Isle and Dudley at Penshurst Place* (3 vols., London, 1925–36); *Calendar of the MSS of the Marquess of Salisbury at Hatfield House* (24 vols., London, 1883–1976); *Calendar of the MSS of the Marquess of Bath at Longleat* (5 vols., London, 1904–80).

Older collections include Thomas Birch, *Memoirs of the Reign of Queen Elizabeth, from the Year 1581 till her Death* (2 vols, London, 1754); William Camden, *Annals of Queen Elizabeth*, trans. H. Norton (London, 1635); Samuel Haynes and William Murdin, *Collection of State Papers . . . Left by William Cecil, Lord Burghley* (2 vols., London, 1740–59); Walter Devereux, *Lives and Letters of the Devereux, Earls of Essex, 1540–1646* (2 vols., London, 1853); Simonds D'Ewes (coll.), *A Compleat Journal of the Votes, Speeches and Debates, Both of the House of Lords and House of Commons throughout the Whole Reign of Queen Elizabeth* (London, 1693); N. E. McClure (ed.), *The Letters of John Chamberlain* (2 vols., Philadelphia, 1939); Sir David Dalrymple, Lord Hailes, *The Secret Correspondence of Sir Robert Cecil with James VI, King of Scotland* (Edinburgh, 1766); Arthur Collins (ed.), *Letters and Memorials of State . . . Written and Collected by Sir Henry Sidney* (2 vols., London, 1746); John Strype, *Annals of the Reformation* (4 vols., Oxford, 1822–4); Thomas Wright, *Queen Elizabeth and her Times* (2 vols., London, 1838).

GENERAL HISTORY

The most recent general introduction to the Tudor period is John Guy, *Tudor England* (Oxford, 1988). See also on the whole period G. R. Elton, *England under the Tudors* (2nd edn., 1974); D. M. Loades, *Politics and the Nation, 1450–1660* (London, 1974); G. R. Elton, *The Tudor Constitution: Documents and Commentary* (2nd edn., Cambridge, 1982). General works on parts of the Tudor period are: C. S. L. Davies, *Peace, Print and Protestantism, 1450–1558* (London, 1976); G. R. Elton, *Reform and Reformation: England, 1509–1558* (London, 1977); G. R. Elton, *Studies in Tudor and Stuart Politics and Government* (3 vols., Cambridge, 1974–83); A. G. R. Smith, *The Emergence of a Nation State: The Commonwealth of England, 1529–1660* (London, 1984). D. M. Palliser, *The Age of Elizabeth: England under the Later Tudors, 1547–1603* (London, 1983), is primarily concerned with economic and social history. Useful essays on the whole period are to be found in the following: Peter Clark *et al.* (eds.), *The English Commonwealth, 1547–1640* (Leicester, 1979); E. W. Ives *et al.* (eds.), *Wealth and Power in Tudor England* (London, 1978); and Claire Cross *et al.* (eds.), *Law and Government under the Tudors* (Cambridge, 1988). C. H. Williams, *English Historical Documents, 1485–1558* (London, 1967) contains a valuable selection of sources.

THE REIGNS OF EDWARD VI AND MARY

The following cover both reigns: Jennifer Loach and Robert Tittler (eds.), *The Mid-Tudor Polity, c.1540–1560* (London, 1980); David Loades, *The Mid-Tudor Crisis, 1545–1565* (London, 1992); Mortimer Levine, *Tudor Dynastic Problems, 1470–1571* (London, 1973); R. B. Wernham, *Before the Armada: The Growth of English Foreign Policy, 1485–1588* (New York, 1966); Susan Brigden, *London and the Reformation* (Oxford, 1989); J. A. Muller, *Stephen Gardiner and the Tudor Reaction* (New York, 1926); Glyn Redworth, *In Defence of the Church Catholic: The Life of Stephen Gardiner* (Oxford, 1990); Jasper Ridley, *Thomas Cranmer* (2nd edn., Oxford, 1966); S. R. Gammon, *Statesman and Schemer: William, First Lord Paget* (Newton Abbot, 1973); F. G. Emmison, *Tudor Secretary: Sir William Petre at Court and Home* (London, 1961); Wilhelm Schenk, *Reginald Pole, Cardinal of England* (London, 1950); Dermot Fenlon, *Heresy and Obedience in Tridentine Italy: Cardinal Pole and the Counter-Reformation* (Cambridge, 1972); Diane Willen, *John Russell, 1st Earl of Bedford: One of the King's Men* (London, 1981); Mary Dewar, *Sir Thomas Smith: A Tudor Intellectual in Office* (London, 1964).

On **Edward VI**: W. K. Jordan, *Edward VI: The Young King* (London, 1968); and id., *Edward VI: The Threshold of Power* (London, 1970). A. F. Pollard, *England under Protector Somerset* (London, 1900) is interesting for reflecting an older view, contradicted by M. L. Bush, *The Government Policy of Protector Somerset* (London 1975). See also D. E. Hoak, *The King's Council in the Reign of Edward VI* (Cambridge, 1976); B. L. Beer, *Northumberland: The Political Career of John Dudley, Earl of Warwick and Duke of Northumberland* (Kent, Oh., 1973); C. S. L. Davies, 'Slavery and Protector Somerset: the Vagrancy Act of 1547', *Economic History Review*, 19 (1966), 533–49.

On **political manœuvring** in Edward's reign: Helen Miller, 'Henry VIII's unwritten will: grants of lands and honours in 1547', in E. W. Ives et al. (eds.), *Wealth and Power in Tudor England* (London, 1978), 87–105; E. W. Ives, 'Henry VIII's will: a forensic conundrum', *Historical Journal*, 35 (1992), 779–804; G. W. Bernard, 'The downfall of Sir Thomas Seymour', in G. W. Bernard (ed.), *The Tudor Nobility* (Manchester, 1992), 212–40; J. Berkman, 'Van der Delft's message: a reappraisal of the attack on Protector Somerset', *Bulletin of the Institute of Historical Research*, 52 (1980), 247–52; H. James, 'The aftermath of the 1549 coup and the Earl of Warwick's intentions', *Historical Research*, 62 (1989), 91–7; Robert Tittler and Susan Battley, 'The local community and the Crown in 1553: the accession of Mary Tudor revisited', *Historical Research*, 57 (1984), 131–9; J. D. Alsop, 'A regime at sea: the navy and the 1553 succession crisis', *Albion*, 24 (1992), 577–90.

The **rebellions of 1549** have been described in Barrett L. Beer, *Rebellion and Riot: Popular Disorder in England during the Reign of Edward VI* (Kent, Oh., 1982); Julian Cornwall, *The Revolt of the Peasantry, 1549* (London, 1977): Roger B. Manning, *Village Revolts: Social Protest and Popular Disturbance in England, 1509–1640* (Oxford, 1988); Frances Rose-Troup, *The Western Rebellion of 1549* (London,

1913); Joyce Youings, 'The south-western rebellion of 1549', *Southern History*, 1 (1979), 99–122; S. T. Bindoff, *Kett's Rebellion* (Historical Association Pamphlet, London, 1949); Diarmaid MacCulloch, 'Kett's rebellion in context', *Past and Present*, 84 (1979), 36–59, with further articles by J. Cornwall and MacCulloch in *Past and Present*, 93 (1981), 160–73, repr. in Paul Slack (ed.), *Rebellion, Popular Protest and the Social Order in Early Modern England* (Cambridge, 1984); and K. J. Allison, 'The sheep–corn husbandry of Norfolk in the sixteenth and seventeenth centuries', *Agricultural History Review*, 5 (1957), 12–30.

On **Mary** see first D. M. Loades, *The Reign of Mary Tudor: Politics, Government, and Religion in England, 1553–1558* (London, 1979) and id., *Mary Tudor* (Oxford, 1989), a life of the Queen. More specialized studies are: E. H. Harbison, *Rival Ambassadors at the Court of Queen Mary* (London, 1940); Jennifer Loach, *Parliament and the Crown in the Reign of Mary Tudor* (Oxford, 1986); Elizabeth Russell, 'Mary Tudor and Mr Jorkins', *Historical Research*, 63 (1990), 263–76; David Loades, 'Philip II and the government of England', in C. Cross *et al.* (eds.), *Law and Government under the Tudors* (Cambridge, 1988), 177–94; D. M. Loades, *Two Tudor Conspiracies* (Cambridge, 1965); M. R. Thorp, 'Religion and the Wyatt rebellion of 1554', *Church History*, 47 (1978), 363–80; C. S. L. Davies, 'England and the French war, 1557–9', in Loach and Tittler (eds.), *The Mid-Tudor Polity*, 159–85.

THE REIGN OF ELIZABETH

Detailed and up-to-date narratives are found in Wallace T. MacCaffrey, *The Shaping of the Elizabethan Regime: Elizabethan Politics, 1558–72* (London, 1969); id., *Queen Elizabeth and the Making of Policy, 1572–1588* (Princeton, NJ, 1981); and id., *Elizabeth I, War and Politics, 1588–1603* (Princeton, NJ, 1992). On the general history of the reign see also: Christopher Haigh (ed.), *The Reign of Elizabeth I* (Basingstoke, 1984) (the essays by Jones and Adams are important for political history; others will be mentioned in relevant sections). Conyers Read, *Mr Secretary Cecil and Queen Elizabeth* (London, 1955); id., *Lord Burghley and Queen Elizabeth* (London, 1960); id., *Mr Secretary Walsingham and the Policy of Queen Elizabeth* (3 vols., Oxford, 1925) are monuments of research. E. P. Cheyney, *A History of England from the Defeat of the Armada to the Death of Elizabeth* (2 vols., London, 1914, 1926) is still useful. The works of R. B. Wernham are invaluable. See R. B. Wernham, *Before the Armada: The Emergence of the English Nation, 1485–1588* (London, 1966); id., *After the Armada: Elizabethan England and the Struggle for Western Europe, 1588–1595* (Oxford, 1984); id., *The Making of Elizabethan Foreign Policy, 1558–1603* (Berkeley, Calif., 1980). Sadly Mr Wernham's *The Return of the Armadas: The Last Years of the Elizabethan War against Spain, 1595–1603* (Oxford, 1994) appeared too late for me to use. J. E. Neale, *Essays in Elizabethan History* (London, 1958); Norman Jones, *The Birth of the Elizabethan Age: England in the 1560s* (Oxford, 1993); S. T. Bindoff *et al.* (eds.), *Elizabethan Government and Society: Essays Presented to Sir John Neale* (London, 1961) are all useful.

Biographies of Elizabeth I abound. A short selection over a hundred years includes: Mandell Creighton, *Queen Elizabeth* (London, 1896). J. E. Neale, *Queen Elizabeth* (London, 1934); Paul Johnson, *Elizabeth I: A Study in Power and Intellect*

(London, 1974); and Wallace MacCaffrey, *Elizabeth I* (London, 1993). Christopher Haigh, *Elizabeth I* (Harlow, 1988) is an intentionally provocative study rather than a biography.

Special studies of the **political history** of the reign are: Mortimer Levine, *The Early Elizabethan Succession Question, 1558–1568* (Stanford, Calif., 1966); Susan Doran, 'Religion and politics at the Court of Elizabeth I: the Habsburg marriage negotiations of 1559–1567', *English Historical Review*, 104 (1989), 908–26; Mervyn James, 'At a crossroad of political culture: the Essex revolt of 1601', in M. James, *Society, Politics and Culture: Studies in Early Modern England* (Cambridge, 1986); Paul E. J. Hammer, 'The uses of scholarship: the secretariat of Robert Devereux, Second Earl of Essex, c.1585–1601', *English Historical Review*, 109 (1994), 26–51; Patrick Collinson, 'The monarchical republic of Queen Elizabeth I', *Bulletin of the John Rylands University Library of Manchester*, 69 (1987), 394–424; Howell A. Lloyd, *The Rouen Campaign, 1590–1592: Politics, Warfare, and the Early-Modern State* (Oxford, 1973); Charles Wilson, *Queen Elizabeth and the Revolt of the Netherlands* (London, 1970); G. D. Ramsay, *The City of London in International Politics* (Manchester, 1975); id., *The Queen's Merchants and the Revolt of the Netherlands* (Manchester, 1986); Neville Williams, *Thomas Howard, Fourth Duke of Norfolk* (London, 1964); A. G. R. Smith, *Servant of the Cecils: The Life of Sir Michael Hickes, 1543–1612* (London, 1977); Robert Tittler, *Nicholas Bacon: The Making of a Tudor Statesman* (London, 1976); Lawrence Stone, *An Elizabethan: Sir Horatio Palavicino* (Oxford, 1956); H. G. Stafford, *James VI of Scotland and the Throne of England* (New York, 1940).

On the **Armada**, Simon Adams, 'The Gran Armada: 1988 and after', *History*, 76 (1991), 238–49 provides a useful survey of recent literature. Garrett Mattingly, *The Defeat of the Spanish Armada* (London, 1959) is still valuable, as is Michael Lewis, *The Spanish Armada* (London, 1966). Important recent works are: Colin Martin and Geoffrey Parker, *The Spanish Armada* (London, 1988); Felipe Fernández-Armesto, *The Spanish Armada: The Experience of War in 1588* (Oxford, 1988); P. Gallagher and D. W. Cruickshank, *God's Obvious Design: Papers for the Spanish Armada Symposium, Sligo, 1988* (London, 1990); M. Rodríguez-Salgado, *Armada, 1588–1988: An International Exhibition to Commemorate the Spanish Armada: The Official Catalogue* (London, 1988).

THE MACHINERY OF STATE

General introductions are to be found in: G. R. Elton, *The Tudor Constitution* (2nd edn., Cambridge, 1982); Penry Williams, *The Tudor Regime* (Oxford, 1979); Christopher Coleman and David Starkey (eds.), *Revolution Reassessed: Revisions in the History of Tudor Government and Administration* (Oxford, 1986); Claire Cross *et al.* (eds.), *Law and Government under the Tudors* (Cambridge, 1988); Joel Hurstfield, *Freedom, Corruption and Government in Elizabethan England* (London, 1973), a collection of essays.

The Court: D. M. Loades, *The Tudor Court* (London, 1986); David Starkey *et al.*, *The English Court: From the Wars of the Roses to the Civil War* (London, 1987); Simon Adams, 'Eliza enthroned? The Court and its politics', in Christopher Haigh (ed.), *The Reign of Elizabeth I* (Basingstoke, 1984), 55–78; Penry Williams, 'Court and polity under Elizabeth I', *Bulletin of the John Rylands University Library of Manchester*, 65 (1983), 259–86; G. R. Elton, 'Tudor government: the points of contact. iii. The Court', *Transactions of the Royal Historical Society*, 5th ser. 26 (1976), 211–28.

The Council and executive government: D. E. Hoak, *The King's Council in the Reign of Edward VI* (Cambridge, 1976); id., 'Two Revolutions in Tudor Government: The Formation and Organization of Mary I's Privy Council', in Coleman and Starkey, *Revolution Reassessed*, 87–115; G. R. Elton, 'Tudor government: the points of contact: ii. The Council', *Transactions of the Royal Historical Society*, 5th ser. 25 (1975), 195–211; M. B. Pulman, *The Elizabethan Privy Council in the Fifteen-Seventies* (Berkeley, Calif., 1971).

Parliament: Good introductions are: Jennifer Loach, *Parliament under the Tudors* (Oxford, 1991); and M. A. R. Graves, *The Tudor Parliaments: Crown, Lords and Commons, 1485–1603* (London, 1985). More specialized are: M. A. R. Graves, *The House of Lords in the Parliaments of Edward VI and Mary: An Institutional Study* (Cambridge, 1981); Jennifer Loach, *Parliament and the Crown in the Reign of Mary Tudor* (Oxford, 1986); J. E. Neale, *The Elizabethan House of Commons* (London, 1949; rev. edn., 1963); id., *Elizabeth I and her Parliaments* (2 vols., London, 1953, 1957); and T. E. Hartley, *Elizabeth's Parliaments: Queen, Lords and Commons 1559–1601* (Manchester, 1992), which has an up-to-date bibliography. Accounts critical of Neale will be found in G. R. Elton, *The Parliament of England, 1559–1581* (Cambridge, 1986); D. M. Dean and N. L. Jones, *The Parliaments of Elizabethan England* (Oxford, 1990); M. A. R. Graves, 'The management of the Elizabethan House of Commons', *Parliamentary History*, 2 (1983), 11–38; J. D. Alsop, 'Reinterpreting the Elizabethan Commons: the parliamentary session of 1566', *Journal of British Studies*, 29 (1990), 216–40. *Parliamentary History*, 8 (pt. 2, 1989) consists of essays on 'Interest groups and legislation in Elizabethan parliaments' presented to Sir Geoffrey Elton. Patrick Collinson, 'Puritans, men of business and Elizabethan parliaments', *Parliamentary History*, 7 (1988), 187–211 strikes a judicious balance between Neale and his critics. T. E. Hartley (ed.), *Proceedings in the Parliaments of Elizabeth I*, i: *1559–81* (Leicester, 1981) publishes parliamentary diaries; P. W. Hasler, *The House of Commons, 1558–1603* (3 vols., London, 1981) provides a valuable collection of biographies of MPs.

Finance: F. C. Dietz, *English Public Finance, 1485–1641* (2 vols., Urbana, Ill., 1921; 2nd edn., London, 1964) remains the only comprehensive account, although in many ways out of date. Then see C. E. Challis, *The Tudor Coinage* (Manchester, 1978); J. D. Gould, *The Great Debasement* (Oxford, 1970); J. D. Alsop, 'Government, finance and the community of the Exchequer', in Haigh (ed.), *Reign of Elizabeth I*, 101–24; J. D. Alsop, 'The theory and practice of Tudor taxation', *English Historical Review*, 97 (1982), 1–30; id., 'The structure of early Tudor finance, c.1509–1558', in Coleman and Starkey (eds.), *Revolution Reassessed*, 135–62; C. Coleman, 'The reorganisation of the Exchequer of Receipt', in Coleman and Starkey (eds.), *Revolution Reassessed*, 163–98; Roger Schofield, 'Taxation and the political limits of the Tudor state', in Cross *et al.* (eds.), *Law and Government under the Tudors*, 227–55; Joel Hurstfield, *The Queen's Wards: Wardship and Marriage under Elizabeth* (London, 1958); R. W. Hoyle (ed.), *The Estates of the English Crown* (Cambridge, 1992); R. B. Outhwaite, 'The trials of foreign borrowing: the English

Crown and the Antwerp money market in the mid-sixteenth century', *Economic History Review*, 2nd ser. 19 (1966), 289–305.

Law: J. H. Baker, *An Introduction to English Legal History* (London, 1971; 2nd edn., 1979); Alan Harding, *A Social History of English Law* (Harmondsworth, 1966); J. Bellamy, *The Tudor Law of Treason: An Introduction* (London, 1979); R. W. Heinze, *The Royal Proclamations of the Tudor Kings* (Cambridge, 1976); F. A. Youngs, *The Royal Proclamations of the Tudor Queens* (Cambridge, 1976); W. R. Prest, *The Rise of the Barristers* (Oxford, 1986); C. W. Brooks, *Pettyfoggers and Vipers of the Commonwealth: The 'Lower Branch' of the Legal Profession in Early Modern England* (Cambridge, 1986); J. S. Cockburn, *A History of the English Assizes, 1558–1714* (Cambridge, 1972); J. P. Dawson, *A History of the Lay Judges* (Cambridge, Mass., 1960); W. J. Jones, *The Elizabethan Court of Chancery* (Oxford, 1967).

Many important studies of **regional and local government** have been appearing in recent years. J. H. Gleason, *The Justices of the Peace in England, 1558–1640* (Oxford, 1969), Joan Kent, *The English Village Constable, 1580–1642* (Oxford, 1986), R. R. Reid, *The King's Council in the North* (London, 1921; repr., 1975), Gladys Scott Thomson, *Lords Lieutenants in the Sixteenth Century* (London, 1923), and Penry Williams, *The Council in the Marches of Wales in the Reign of Elizabeth I* (Cardiff, 1958) all deal with local institutions, while id., 'The Crown and the counties', in Haigh (ed.), *The Reign of Elizabeth I* surveys some of the literature. For a stimulating reappraisal, Steven Ellis, 'Crown, community and government in the English territories', *History*, 71 (1988), 187–204. See also the sections of the bibliography on Towns and Rural Society (below).

Military and naval: C. G. Cruickshank, *Elizabeth's Army* (Oxford, 1946; 2nd edn., 1966); Lindsay Boynton, *The Elizabethan Militia* (London, 1967); David Loades, *The Tudor Navy: An Administrative, Political and Military History* (Aldershot, 1992); A. Hassell Smith, 'Militia rates and militia statutes, 1558–1663', in Peter Clark *et al.* (eds.), *The English Commonwealth, 1547–1640* (Leicester, 1979), 93–110; K. R. Andrews, *Elizabethan Privateering: English Privateering during the Spanish War, 1585–1603* (Cambridge, 1964).

THE ECONOMY: POPULATION, PRICES, INDUSTRY, TRADE

D. C. Coleman, *The Economy of England, 1450–1750* (Oxford, 1977); D. M. Palliser, *The Age of Elizabeth: England under the Later Tudors, 1547–1603* (London, 1983); and C. G. A. Clay, *Economic Expansion and Social Change: England 1500–1700* (2 vols., Cambridge, 1984) provide good general introductions. Peter Laslett, *The World We Have Lost: Further Explored* (London, 1983) is the revised edition of id., *The World We Have Lost* (London, 1965). Useful collections of articles are: F. J. Fisher (ed.), *Essays in the Economic and Social History of Tudor and Stuart England in Honour of R. H. Tawney* (Cambridge, 1961); D. C. Coleman and A. H. John (eds.), *Trade, Government, and Economy in Pre-industrial England: Essays Presented to F. J. Fisher* (London, 1976). R. H. Tawney and E. Power (eds.), *Tudor Economic Documents* (3 vols., London, 1924) is a classic collection of documents.

On **population** the authoritative study is E. A. Wrigley and R. S. Schofield, *The Population History of England, 1541–1871: A Reconstruction* (London, 1981).

Special studies are: F. J. Fisher, 'Influenza and inflation in Tudor England', *Economic History Review*, 2nd ser. 18 (1965), 120–9; John Walter and Roger Schofield (eds.), *Famine, Disease and the Social Order in Early Modern Society* (Cambridge, 1989); R. A. P. Finlay, *Population and Metropolis: The Demography of London, 1580–1650* (Cambridge, 1981); Vanessa Harding, 'The population of London, 1550–1700: a review of the published evidence', *London Journal*, 15 (1990), 111–28.

Money and prices: R. B. Outhwaite, *Inflation in Tudor and Early Stuart England* (Economic History Soc. pamphlet, London, 1982); P. H. Ramsey (ed.), *The Price Revolution in Sixteenth-Century England* (London, 1971); E. H. Phelps Brown and Sheila Hopkins, *A Perspective of Wages and Prices* (London, 1981); C. E. Challis, *The Tudor Coinage* (Manchester, 1978); id., 'The debasement of the coinage, 1542–1551', *Economic History Review*, 2nd ser. 20 (1967), 441–66; id., 'Currency and the economy in mid-Tudor England', *Economic History Review*, 25 (1972), 313–22; J. D. Gould, *The Great Debasement: Currency and the Economy in Mid-Tudor England* (Oxford, 1970). See the works by Rappaport and Archer in the section on London, and the chapter by Bowden in Thirsk, *Agrarian History*, in the section on rural society, below.

Crafts and industries: Joan Thirsk, *Economic Policy and Projects: The Development of a Consumer Society in Early Modern England* (Oxford, 1978); D. C. Coleman, *Industry in Tudor and Stuart England* (Basingstoke, 1975); id., 'An innovation and its diffusion: the "New Draperies"', *Economic History Review*, 2nd ser. 22 (1969), 417–29; S. M. Jack, *Trade and Industry in Tudor and Stuart England* (London, 1977); J. U. Nef, *The Rise of the British Coal Industry* (2 vols., London, 1932); G. D. Ramsay, *The English Woollen Industry, 1550–1750* (Basingstoke, 1983).

Trade: Ralph Davis, *English Overseas Trade, 1500–1700* (Basingstoke, 1973); G. D. Ramsay, *English Overseas Trade during the Centuries of Emergence* (Manchester, 1957); F. J. Fisher, 'Commercial trends and policy in sixteenth-century England', *Economic History Review*, 1st ser. 10 (1940), 95–117; G. D. Ramsay, *The City of London in International Politics at the Accession of Elizabeth Tudor* (Manchester, 1971); id., *The Queen's Merchants and the Revolt of the Netherlands* (Manchester, 1986); T. K. Rabb, *Enterprise and Empire: Merchant and Gentry Investment in the Expansion of England, 1575–1630* (Cambridge, Mass., 1967); T. S. Willan, *Studies in Elizabethan Foreign Trade* (Mancester, 1959); id., *The Early History of the Russia Company, 1553–1603* (Manchester, 1956); id., *A Tudor Book of Rates* (Manchester, 1962); K. R. Andrews, *Elizabethan Privateering: English Privateering during the Spanish War, 1585–1603* (Cambridge, 1964); P. J. Bowden, *The Wool Trade in Tudor and Stuart England* (London, 1962; 2nd edn., 1971); J. A. Chartres, *Internal Trade in England, 1500–1700* (Basingstoke, 1977).

ENGLISH SOCIETY

On **English society** generally: Keith Wrightson, *English Society, 1580–1680* (London, 1982); J. A. Sharpe, *Early Modern England: A Social History, 1550–1760* (London, 1987); and Joyce Youings, *Sixteenth-Century England* (Harmondsworth,

1984). Anthony Fletcher and John Stevenson (eds.), *Order and Disorder in Early Modern England* (Cambridge, 1985) is a useful collection of essays.

London: Steve Rappaport, *Worlds within Worlds: Structures of Life in Sixteenth-Century London* (Cambridge, 1989); Ian W. Archer, *The Pursuit of Stability: Social Relations in Elizabethan London* (Cambridge, 1991); F. F. Foster, *The Politics of Stability: A Portrait of the Rulers in Elizabethan London* (London, 1977); Susan Brigden, *London and the Reformation* (Oxford, 1989); A. L. Beier and R. A. P. Finlay (eds.), *London, 1500–1700: The Making of the Metropolis* (Cambridge, 1981); Valerie Pearl, 'Social policy in early modern London', in H. Lloyd-Jones *et al.* (eds.), *History and Imagination: Essays in Honour of H. R. Trevor-Roper* (London, 1979), 115–31; M. J. Power, 'London and the control of the "crisis" of the 1590s', *History*, 70 (1985), 371–85; F. J. Fisher, 'The development of London as a centre of conspicuous consumption in the sixteenth and seventeenth centuries', *Transactions of the Royal Historical Society*, 4th ser. 30 (1948), 37–50.

Provincial towns: Peter Clark and Paul Slack, *English Towns in Transition, 1500–1700* (Oxford, 1976) and id. (eds.), *Crisis and Order in English Towns, 1500–1700* (London, 1972) are useful introductions. On particular towns, see Alan Dyer, *The City of Worcester in the Sixteenth Century* (Leicester, 1973); D. M. Palliser, *Tudor York* (Oxford, 1979); W. T. MacCaffrey, *Exeter, 1540–1640: The Growth of an English County Town* (Cambridge, Mass., 1958; 2nd edn., 1975); C. Phythian-Adams, *The Desolation of a City: Coventry and the Urban Crisis of the Late Middle Ages* (Cambridge, 1979), important for the mid-Tudor years. For the debate on the rise or decline of towns, R. B. Dobson, 'Urban decline in late medieval England', *Transactions of the Royal Historical Society*, 5th ser. 27 (1977), 1–22; D. M. Palliser, 'A crisis in English towns? The case of York, 1460–1640', *Northern History*, 14 (1978), 108–25; Alan Dyer, 'Growth and decay in English towns, 1500–1700', *Urban History Yearbook* for 1979, 60–72; Peter Clark, 'A crisis contained? The condition of English towns in the 1590s', in P. Clark (ed.), *The European Crisis of the 1590s* (London, 1985), 44–66.

Rural society—general: the essential work is Joan Thirsk (ed.), *The Agrarian History of England and Wales*, iv: *1500–1640* (Cambridge, 1967), esp. chs. 1 and 4 (Thirsk), 5 (Batho), 7 and 8 (Everitt), and 9 (Bowden). Helpful introductions are found in D. C. Coleman, *The Economy of England, 1450–1750* (Oxford, 1977), and D. M. Palliser, *The Age of Elizabeth* (London, 1983). More specialized books on agriculture are: R. H. Tawney, *The Agrarian Problem in the Sixteenth Century* (London, 1912; repr. New York, 1967), a classic work criticized in Eric Kerridge, *Agrarian Problems in the Sixteenth Century and after* (London, 1969); see also E. Kerridge, *The Agricultural Revolution* (London, 1967). On enclosure, J. A. Yelling, *Common Field and Enclosure in England, 1450–1850* (London, 1977); on production, R. B. Outhwaite, 'Progress and backwardness in English agriculture, 1500–1650', *Economic History Review*, 2nd ser. 39 (1986), 1–18.

Nobility and gentry: Thirsk (ed.), *Agrarian History*, iv, ch. 5 (Batho) on landowners, for an introduction. For more detailed studies of the aristocracy see: Lawrence Stone, *The Crisis of the Aristocracy* (Oxford, 1965); id., *Family and Fortune: Studies in Aristocratic Finances in the Sixteenth and Seventeenth Centuries* (Oxford, 1973); Lawrence Stone and Jeanne Fawtier Stone, *An Open Elite? England 1540–1880* (Oxford, 1984); G. W. Bernard, *The Power of the Early Tudor Nobility:*

A Study of the Fourth and Fifth Earls of Shrewsbury (Brighton, 1985); id. (ed.), *The Tudor Nobility* (Manchester, 1992). On the gentry: Mary Finch, *Five Northamptonshire Families, 1540–1640*, Northants Record Soc. 20, (Oxford, 1956). See, more generally, J. P. Cooper, *Land, Men and Beliefs: Studies in Early Modern History* (London, 1983), a posthumous collection of essays.

Tenant farmers and labourers: Thirsk (ed.), *Agrarian History*, iv, ch. 7 (Everitt); Mildred Campbell, *The English Yeoman under Elizabeth and the Early Stuarts* (New Haven, Conn., 1942; repr. 1960); Ann Kussmaul, *Servants in Husbandry in Early Modern England* (Cambridge, 1981).

There are many good **local studies** at both county and village level. Examples are: A. L. Rowse, *Tudor Cornwall* (London, 1941; 2nd edn., 1969); Peter Clark, *English Provincial Society from the Reformation to the Revolution: Religion, Politics and Society in Kent, 1500–1640* (Hassocks, 1977); J. T. Cliffe, *The Yorkshire Gentry from the Reformation to the Civil War* (London, 1969); A. Hassell Smith, *County and Court: Government and Politics in Norfolk, 1558–1602* (Oxford, 1972); Mervyn James, *Family, Lineage and Civil Society: A Study of Politics and Mentality in the Durham Region, 1500–1640* (Oxford, 1974); Diarmaid MacCulloch, *Suffolk and the Tudors, 1500–1600* (Oxford, 1986); S. J. Watts, *From Border to Middle Shire: Northumberland 1586–1625* (Leicester, 1975) at county level. For villages see Margaret Spufford, *Contrasting Communities: English Villagers in the Sixteenth and Seventeenth Centuries* (Cambridge, 1974); David G. Hey, *An English Rural Community: Myddle under the Tudors and Stuarts* (Leicester, 1974); Victor Skipp, *Crisis and Development: An Ecological Case Study of the Forest of Arden, 1570–1674* (Cambridge, 1978); Joan Thirsk, *English Peasant Farming* (London, 1957); and Keith Wrightson and David Levine, *Poverty and Piety in an English Village: Terling, 1525–1700* (London, 1979).

For **rural buildings**: M. W. Barley, *The English Farmhouse and Cottage* (London, 1961); Mark Girouard, *Life in the English Country House: A Social and Architectural History* (London, 1978); id., *Robert Smythson and the Elizabethan Country House* (New Haven, Conn., 1983); H. M. Colvin, *The History of the King's Works*, iv: *1485–1660* (part ii) (London, 1982); W. G. Hoskins, 'The rebuilding of rural England, 1570–1640', *Past and Present*, 4 (1953), 44–59; R. Machin, 'The great rebuilding: a reassessment', *Past and Present*, 77 (1977), 33–56.

POVERTY, CRIME, AND DISEASE

Paul Slack, *Poverty and Policy in Tudor and Stuart England* (London, 1988) provides an excellent general account of the **poor and the poor laws**. See also A. L. Beier, *Masterless Men: The Vagrancy Problem in England 1560–1640* (London, 1985); K. Wrightson and D. Levine, *Poverty and Piety in an English Village: Terling, 1525–1700* (London, 1979); A. B. Appleby, *Famine in Tudor and Stuart England* (Liverpool, 1978); W. K. Jordan, *Philanthropy in England, 1480–1660* (London, 1959).

On **Crime**, see J. A. Sharpe, *Crime in Early Modern England, 1550–1750* (London, 1984) for an introduction; and then J. S. Cockburn (ed.), *Crime in England, 1550–1800* (London, 1977); Cynthia Herrup, *The Common Peace: Participation and* *the Criminal Law in Seventeenth-Century England* (Cambridge, 1987), very useful for the sixteenth century also; and Alan Macfarlane, *Witchcraft in Tudor and Stuart England: A Regional and Comparative Study* (London, 1970).

On **medicine and disease**: Charles Webster (ed.), *Health, Medicine and Mortality in the Sixteenth Century* (Cambridge, 1979); Paul Slack, *The Impact of Plague in Tudor and Stuart England* (London, 1985); Michael MacDonald, *Mystical Bedlam: Madness, Anxiety and Healing in Seventeenth-Century England* (Cambridge, 1981), relevant for the later sixteenth century; Michael MacDonald and Terence R. Murphy, *Sleepless Souls: Suicide in Early Modern England* (Oxford, 1990).

LITERATURE, ART, AND THE SOCIAL ORDER

I have not attempted in this section to provide even a selection of the huge number of literary texts from this period, and have concentrated upon selected secondary works. For an introduction to the literature, see C. S. Lewis, *English Literature in the Sixteenth Century, Excluding Drama* (*Oxford History of English Literature*, iii, Oxford, 1954).

Literacy, Education, and Language: David Cressy, *Literacy and the Social Order: Reading and Writing in Tudor and Stuart England* (Cambridge, 1980); Margaret Spufford, *Small Books and Pleasant Histories: Popular Fiction and its Readership in Seventeenth-Century England* (Cambridge, 1981); H. S. Bennett, *English Books and Readers, 1475–1557* (Cambridge, 1952); id., *English Books and Readers, 1558–1603* (Cambridge, 1965); and Caroline Lucas, *Writing for Women: The Example of Woman as Reader in Elizabethan Romance* (Milton Keynes, 1989) provide good introductions to literacy and reading. See also Keith Thomas, 'Numeracy in Early Modern England', *Transactions of the Royal Historical Society*, 5th ser. 37 (1987), 103–32. On **education**: H. F. Kearney, *Scholars and Gentlemen: Universities and Society in Pre-industrial Britain, 1500–1700* (London, 1970); Mark H. Curtis, *Oxford and Cambridge in Transition, 1558–1642* (Oxford, 1959); James McConica (ed.), *The History of the University of Oxford*, iii: *The Collegiate University* (Oxford, 1986); Lawrence Stone (ed.), *The University in Society* (2 vols., Princeton, NJ, 1975); Rosemary O'Day, *Education and Society, 1500–1800* (London, 1982); Joan Simon, *Education and Society in Tudor England* (Cambridge, 1967). On **language**, Richard Foster Jones, *The Triumph of the English Language* (Stanford, Calif., 1953; repr. 1966).

For **patronage**: Guy Fitch Lytle and Stephen Orgel (eds.), *Patronage in the Renaissance* (Princeton, NJ, 1981); Michael G. Brennan, *Literary Patronage in the Renaissance: The Pembroke Family* (London, 1988); John Buxton, *Sir Philip Sidney and the English Renaissance* (London, 1954; 2nd edn., 1964); David C. Price, *Patrons and Musicians of the English Renaissance* (Cambridge, 1981). On the **London theatre and its audiences**, Andrew Gurr, *The Shakespearean Stage* (2nd edn., Cambridge, 1982) and id., *Playgoing in Shakespeare's London* (Cambridge, 1987). Alfred Harbage, *Shakespeare's Audience* (New York, 1941) and id., *Shakespeare and the Rival Traditions* (New York, 1952) is contradicted by Ann Jennalie Cook, *The Privileged Playgoers of Shakespeare's London* (Princeton, NJ, 1981); for a balanced account of the controversy, Martin Butler, *Theatre and Crisis* (Cambridge, 1984).

For **censorship**: Janet Clare, *'Art Made Tongue-Tied by Authority': Elizabethan and Jacobean Dramatic Censorship* (Manchester, 1990); Annabel Patterson, *Censorship and Interpretation: The Conditions of Writing and Reading in Early Modern England* (Madison, Wis., 1984); Blair Worden, 'Literature and Political Censorship in Early Modern England', in A. C. Duke and C. Tamse (eds.), *Too Mighty to Be Free: Censorship and the Press in Britain and the Netherlands* (Zutphen, 1988).

There is a rapidly growing corpus of **historical and critical** work on the relations between literature, politics, and society. For good introductions, Julia Briggs, *This Stage-Play World: English Literature and its Background, 1580–1625* (Oxford, 1983); David Norbrook, *Poetry and Politics in the English Renaissance* (London, 1984); John N. King, *English Reformation Literature: The Tudor Origins of the Protestant Tradition* (Princeton, NJ, 1982); and John Buxton, *Elizabethan Taste* (London, 1963; repr. 1983). More specialized critical works are: Jonathan Dollimore, *Radical Tragedy: Religion, Ideology and Power in the Drama of Shakespeare and his Contemporaries* (Hemel Hempstead, 1984); Stephen Greenblatt, *Renaissance Self-Fashioning from More to Shakespeare* (Chicago, 1980); id., *Sir Walter Ralegh: The Renaissance Man and his Roles* (New Haven, Conn., 1973); id. (ed.), *Representing the English Renaissance* (Berkeley, Calif., 1988); Mervyn James, *English Politics and the Concept of Honour, 1485–1642* (*Past and Present*, supp. 3 (1978); repr. in id., *Society, Politics, and Culture: Studies in Early Modern England* (Cambridge, 1986)); Annabel Patterson, *Shakespeare and the Popular Voice* (Oxford, 1989); Robin Headlam Wells, *Spenser's* Faerie Queene *and the Cult of Elizabeth* (London, 1983) and *Shakespeare, Politics and the State* (Basingstoke, 1986).

On the **courtly background** to literature and art: Sydney Anglo, *Spectacle, Pageantry and Early Tudor Policy* (Oxford, 1969); Alan Young, *Tudor and Jacobean Tournaments* (London, 1987); Daniel Javitch, *Poetry and Courtliness in Renaissance England* (Princeton, NJ, 1978); Katherine Duncan-Jones, *Sir Philip Sidney: Courtier Poet* (London, 1991). See also the general works on the Court under 'Machinery of the state' (above, p. 567).

On the **intellectual background** to the period, see among others: Quentin Skinner, *The Foundations of Modern Political Thought* (2 vols., Cambridge, 1978). E. M. W. Tillyard, *The Elizabethan World Picture* (London, 1943) was a classic work in its day. More recent books are: David Bevington, *Tudor Drama and Politics: A Critical Approach to Topical Meaning* (Cambridge, Mass., 1968); F. J. Levy, *Tudor Historical Thought* (San Marino, Calif., 1967); Paul A. Fideler and T. F. Mayer, *Political Thought and the Tudor Commonwealth* (London, 1992); Isabel Rivers, *Classical and Christian Ideas in English Renaissance Poetry: A Student's Guide* (London, 1979); K. V. Thomas, *Religion and the Decline of Magic* (London, 1971); id., *Man and the Natural World: Changing Attitudes in England 1500–1800* (London, 1983).

Representations of the Tudor monarchs in portraiture and literature are treated in John N. King, *Tudor Royal Iconography: Literature and Art in an Age of Religious Crisis* (Princeton, NJ, 1989); Roy Strong, *The Cult of Elizabeth: Elizabethan Portraiture and Pageantry* (London, 1977) and id., *Gloriana: The Portraits of Queen Elizabeth I* (London, 1987). Margaret Aston, *The King's Bedpost: Refor-*

mation and Iconography in a Tudor Group Portrait (Cambridge, 1993) is a remarkable investigation into the origins of the picture of Henry VIII, Edward VI, and the Pope. The best guides to **painting and portraiture** in general are Roy Strong, *Tudor and Jacobean Portraits* (2 vols., London, 1969); id., *The English Icon: Elizabethan and Jacobean Portraiture* (London, 1969); id., *The English Renaissance Miniature* (London, 1983); Eric Mercer, *English Art, 1553–1625* (*Oxford History of English Art*, vii (Oxford, 1962)); On the 'cult' of Elizabeth I see also Frances A. Yates, *Astraea: The Imperial Theme in the Sixteenth Century* (London, 1975); Philippa Berry, *Of Chastity and Power: Elizabethan Literature and the Unmarried Queen* (London, 1989). A visit to the National Portrait Gallery, London, is essential.

Music of the period is best appreciated by listening to tape-recordings or compact discs of the work of Thomas Tallis, William Byrd, John Dowland, and others.

On **popular culture**, a good introduction is Peter Burke, *Popular Culture in Early Modern Europe* (New York, 1978). For England, François Laroque, *Shakespeare's Festive World: Elizabethan Seasonal Entertainment and the Professional Stage*, trans. Janet Lloyd (Cambridge, 1991); C. L. Barber, *Shakespeare's Festive Comedy* (Princeton, NJ, 1959); Barry Reay, *Popular Culture in Seventeenth-Century England* (London, 1985); Laura Caroline Stevenson, *Praise and Paradox: Merchants and Craftsmen in Elizabethan Popular Literature* (Cambridge, 1984); David Bergeron, *English Civic Pageantry, 1558–1642* (London, 1971); Margaret Spufford, *Small Books and Pleasant Histories: Popular Fiction and its Readership in Seventeenth-Century England* (Cambridge, 1981); Tessa Watt, *Cheap Print and Popular Piety, 1550–1640* (Cambridge, 1991); Natascha Würzbach, *The Rise of the English Street Ballad, 1550–1650*, trans. Gayna Wells (Cambridge, 1990); David Cressy, *Bonfires and Bells: National Memory and the Protestant Calendar in Elizabethan and Stuart England* (London, 1989).

RELIGION

General works: Claire Cross, *Church and People, 1450–1660* (London, 1976) sets the Reformation in a broad context; A. G. Dickens, *The English Reformation* (London, 1964; repr. 1989) gives a narrative up to 1558 from the 'Protestant' point of view, supplemented by his *Reformation Studies* (London, 1982), a collection of the author's essays. Four more recent works take the story beyond 1558 and present different interpretations from that of Dickens: Diarmaid MacCulloch, *The Later Reformation in England, 1547–1603* (Basingstoke, 1990); Christopher Haigh, *English Reformations: Religion, Politics and Society under the Tudors* (Oxford, 1993); Eamon Duffy, *The Stripping of the Altars: Traditional Religion in England, 1400–1580* (New Haven, Conn., 1992); J. J. Scarisbrick, *The Reformation and the English People* (Oxford, 1984). Useful collections of essays are: Felicity Heal and Rosemary O'Day (eds.), *Church and Society in England: Henry VIII to James I* (London, 1977); Christopher Haigh (ed.), *The English Reformation Revised* (Basingstoke, 1986).

On **religion under Edward VI**: Francis Proctor and Walter H. Frere, *A New History of the Book of Common Prayer* (London, 1932) remains valuable, supplemented by G. J. Cuming, *A History of Anglican Liturgy* (London, 1969); C. W. Dugmore *et al.*, *The English Prayer-Book, 1549–1662* (London, Alcuin Club, 1962); and C. W. Dugmore, *The Mass and the English Reformers* (London, 1958). On particular aspects of the Edwardian Reformation, see: Margaret Aston, *England's Iconoclasts*, i: *Laws against Images* (Oxford, 1988); Alan Kreider, *English Chantries: The Road to Dissolution* (Cambridge, Mass., 1979); Robert Whiting, *The Blind Devotion of the People* (Cambridge, 1989), on popular religion in the south-west; Jasper Ridley, *Thomas Cranmer* (Oxford, 1962; repr. 1966); Peter Brooks, *Thomas Cranmer's Doctrine of the Eucharist* (London, 1965); James Kelsey McConica, *English Humanists and Reformation Politics* (Oxford, 1965); Glyn Redworth, *In Defence of the Church Catholic: The Life of Stephen Gardiner* (Oxford, 1990).

On **Marian religion** see first D. M. Loades, *The Reign of Mary Tudor* (London, 1979), and also id., *The Oxford Martyrs* (London, 1970). C. H. Garrett, *The Marian Exiles: A Study in the Origins of Elizabethan Puritanism* (Cambridge, 1938; repr. 1966) has valuable information but a doubtful thesis. On Pole, R. H. Pogson, 'Reginald Pole and the priorities of government in Mary Tudor's Church', *Historical Journal*, 18 (1975), 3–20; id., 'The legacy of schism: confusion, continuity and change in the Marian clergy', in J. Loach and R. Tittler (eds.), *Mid-Tudor Polity, c.1540–1560* (London, 1980); and Dermot Fenlon, *Heresy and Obedience in Tridentine Italy: Cardinal Pole and the Counter-Reformation* (Cambridge, 1972). John Foxe, *Actes and Monuments of the English Church*, better known as *The Book of Martyrs*, remains indispensable. There are many editions since the first English one (London, 1563); references here are to that edited by Stephen Reed Cattley and George Townshend (8 vols., London, 1837–41). See also William Haller, *Foxe's Book of Martyrs and the Elect Nation* (London, 1963).

Elizabethan religion and the beginnings of the Church of England have been extensively and often acrimoniously discussed. Apart from the general works noted above, Patrick Collinson, *The Religion of Protestants: The Church in English Society, 1559–1625* (Oxford, 1982) is indispensable; id., *Godly People: Essays on English Protestantism and Puritanism* (London, 1983); id., *Archbishop Grindal, 1519–1583: The Struggle for a Reformed Church* (London, 1979) and id., *The Birthpangs of Protestant England: Religious and Cultural Change in the Sixteenth and Seventeenth Centuries* (Basingstoke, 1988) are also invaluable. On the settlement of 1559 see J. E. Neale, *Elizabeth I and her Parliaments*, i: *1559–1581* (London, 1953); W. S. Hudson, *The Cambridge Connection and the Elizabethan Settlement of Religion, 1559* (Durham, NC, 1980); Norman L. Jones, *Faith by Statute: Parliament and the Settlement of Religion, 1559* (London, 1982); William P. Haugaard, *Elizabeth I and the English Reformation: The Struggle for a Stable Settlement of Religion* (Cambridge, 1968); and Claire Cross, *The Royal Supremacy in the Elizabethan Church* (London, 1969).

There are two helpful review articles on the controversy over the nature of the Elizabethan Church, providing a guide to the literature: Diarmaid MacCulloch, 'The myth of the English Reformation', *Journal of British Studies*, 30 (1991), 1–19 (giving a Protestant view) and G. W. Bernard, 'The Church of England, c.1529–c.1642', *History*, 75 (1990), 183–206. Apart from works already mentioned above, especially Duffy, *Stripping of the Altars*, see Peter Lake, *Anglicans and Puritans? Presbyterianism and English Conformist Thought from Whitgift to Hooker* (London,

1988) and Christopher Haigh, 'The Church of England, the Catholics and the people', in C. Haigh (ed.), *The Reign of Elizabeth I* (Basingstoke, 1984), 195–220. The controversy is bound up with issues in Stuart historiography, for which see Nicholas Tyacke, *The Anti-Calvinists: The Rise of English Arminianism, c.1590–1640* (Oxford, 1987) and Conrad Russell, *The Causes of the English Civil War* (Oxford, 1990), chs. 3, 4.

The **institutions and clergy** of the Church of England are treated in R. A. Houlbrooke, *The Church Courts and the People during the English Reformation, 1520–1570* (Oxford, 1979); M. J. Ingram, *Church Courts, Sex and Marriage in England, 1570–1640* (Cambridge, 1987); Rosemary O'Day and Felicity Heal (eds.), *Continuity and Change: Personnel and Administration of the Church of England, 1500–1642* (Leicester, 1976); Felicity Heal, *Of Prelates and Princes: A Study of the Economic and Social Position of the Tudor Episcopate* (Cambridge, 1980); and Rosemary O'Day, *The English Clergy: The Emergence and Consolidation of a Profession, 1558–1642* (Leicester, 1979).

The standard work on **Elizabethan Puritanism** is Patrick Collinson, *The Elizabethan Puritan Movement* (London, 1967). See also: R. G. Usher (ed.), *The Presbyterian Movement in the Reign of Queen Elizabeth*, Camden Society, 3rd ser. 8 (London, 1905); C. M. Dent, *Protestant Reformers in Elizabethan Oxford* (Oxford, 1983); Claire Cross, *The Puritan Earl: The Life of Henry Hastings, Third Earl of Huntingdon, 1536–1595* (London, 1966); H. C. Porter, *Reformation and Reaction in Tudor Cambridge* (Cambridge, 1958); id., *Puritanism in Tudor England* (London, 1970); Leonard J. Trinterud, *Elizabethan Puritanism* (New York, 1971); Peter Lake, *Moderate Puritans and the Elizabethan Church* (Cambridge, 1982); id., 'Calvinism and the English Church, 1570–1635', *Past and Present*, 114 (1987), 32–76; P. S. Seaver, *The Puritan Lectureships: The Politics of Religious Dissent, 1560–1662* (Stanford, Calif., 1970); Kenneth L. Parker, *The English Sabbath* (Cambridge, 1988); G. J. R. Parry, *A Protestant Vision: William Harrison and the Reformation of Elizabethan England* (Cambridge, 1987).

On **English Catholicism** see first John Bossy, *The English Catholic Community, 1570–1850* (London, 1975); and then J. C. H. Aveling, *The Handle and the Axe: The Catholic Recusants in England from Reformation to Emancipation* (London, 1976); and Peter Holmes, *Resistance and Compromise: The Political Thought of the Elizabethan Catholics* (Cambridge, 1982). Recent controversy over the views of Bossy and others is found in Christopher Haigh, 'The continuity of Catholicism in the English Reformation', *Past and Present*, 93 (1981), 37–90; id., 'From monopoly to minority: Catholicism in early modern England', *Transactions of the Royal Historical Society*, 5th ser. 31 (1981), 129–48; Patrick McGrath, 'English Catholicism: a reconsideration', *Journal of Ecclesiastical History*, 35 (1984), 414–28; and *Journal of Ecclesiastical History*, 36 (1985), for reply by Haigh (394–405)and postscript by McGrath (405–6).

There is now a growing body of publications on the **local history** of religion. See especially: Susan Brigden, *London and the Reformation* (Oxford, 1989), which takes the story to 1559; Andrew Pettigree, *Foreign Protestant Communities in Sixteenth-Century London* (Oxford, 1986); J. E. Oxley, *The Reformation in Essex to the Death of Queen Mary* (Manchester, 1965); Christopher Haigh, *Reformation and Resistance in Tudor Lancashire* (Cambridge, 1975); Roger B. Manning, *Religion and*

Society in Elizabethan Sussex (Leicester, 1969); Diarmaid MacCulloch, *Suffolk and the Tudors: Politics and Religion in an English County, 1500–1600* (Oxford, 1986); D. M. Palliser, *Tudor York* (Oxford, 1979); Keith Wrightson and David Levine, *Poverty and Piety in an English Village: Terling 1525–1700* (London, 1979); Margaret Spufford, *Contrasting Communities: English Villagers in the Sixteenth and Seventeenth Centuries* (Cambridge, 1974); William Hunt, *The Puritan Moment: The Coming of Religion in an English County* (Cambridge, Mass., 1983).

The most significant work on **popular religion** is Keith Thomas, *Religion and the Decline of Magic* (London, 1971). See also: Tessa Watt, *Cheap Print and Popular Piety: 1550–1640* (Cambridge, 1991); Spufford, *Contrasting Communities* (above); Collinson, *Religion of Protestants* (above). See also the works on popular culture, above p. 575.

FAMILY, KINSFOLK, AND NEIGHBOURS

Ralph A. Houlbrooke, *The English Family, 1450–1700* (London, 1984) provides a good introduction and bibliography. Lawrence Stone, *The Family, Sex, and Marriage in England, 1500–1800* (London, 1977) is controversial and stimulating, as is Alan Macfarlane, *Marriage and Love in England: Modes of Reproduction, 1300–1800* (London, 1986). R. B. Outhwaite (ed.), *Marriage and Society: Studies in the Social History of Marriage* (London, 1981) contains useful articles. Martin Ingram, *Church Courts, Sex and Marriage in England, 1570–1640* (Cambridge, 1987) looks at the subject from a study of litigation. Lloyd Bonfield *et al.* (eds.), *The World We Have Gained: Histories of Population and Social Structure* (Oxford, 1986) contains interesting essays. Ralph A. Houlbrooke (ed.), *English Family Life, 1576–1716: An Anthology from Diaries* (Oxford, 1988) prints lively source-material. Finally, on the ending of marriages, Lawrence Stone, *The Road to Divorce: England, 1530–1987* (Oxford, 1990).

On **children and childbirth**: Philippe Ariès, *Centuries of Childhood* (London, 1962); Linda A. Pollock, *Forgotten Children: Parent–Child Relations from 1500–1900* (Cambridge, 1983); Peter Laslett *et al.* (eds.), *Bastardy and its Comparative History* (London, 1980); Ivy Pinchbeck, *Children in English Society*, i: *From Tudor Times to the Eighteenth Century* (London, 1969).

On **family and communal life** generally see Peter Laslett, *The World We Have Lost: Further Explored* (London, 1983), a revised edition of *The World We Have Lost*; Peter Clark, *The English Alehouse: A Social History, c.1200–1830* (Harlow, 1983); Barry Reay (ed.), *Popular Culture in Seventeenth-Century England* (London, 1985); Clare Gittings, *Death, Burial, and the Individual in Early Modern England* (London, 1984); Felicity Heal, *Hospitality in Early Modern England* (Oxford, 1990); David Underdown, *Revel, Riot, and Rebellion: Popular Politics and Culture in England, 1603–1660* (Oxford, 1985).

BRITAIN

Glanmor Williams, *Recovery, Reorientation, and Reformation: Wales, c.1415–1642* (Oxford, 1987) is comprehensive and essential for its subject. On the government of Wales, Penry Williams, *The Council in the Marches of Wales under Elizabeth I* (Cardiff, 1958); for the social order in Tudor Wales, Glanmor Williams (ed.), *Glamorgan County History*, iv: *Early Modern Glamorgan* (Cardiff, 1974); Howell A. Lloyd, *The Gentry of South-West Wales, 1540–1640* (Cardiff, 1968); G. Dyfnallt Owen, *Elizabethan Wales: The Social Scene* (Cardiff, 1962); and J. Gwynfor Jones, *Concepts of Order and Gentility in Wales* (Llandysul, 1992); and on religion, Glanmor Williams, *Welsh Reformation Essays* (Cardiff, 1967).

The best introductions to **Ireland** in this period are Steven G. Ellis, *Tudor Ireland: Crown, Community and the Conflict of Cultures, 1470–1603* (London, 1985) and T. W. Moody, F. X. Martin, and F. J. Byrne (eds.), *A New History of Ireland*, iii: *Early Modern Ireland, 1536–1691* (Oxford, 1976). Richard Bagwell, *Ireland under the Tudors* (3 vols., London, 1885–90) is still useful for detailed information. More specialized studies are: Brendan Bradshaw, *The Irish Constitutional Revolution of the Sixteenth Century* (Cambridge, 1979); Nicholas P. Canny, *The Elizabethan Conquest of Ireland: A Pattern Established, 1565–76* (Hassocks, 1976); id., *The Formation of the Old English Elite in Ireland* (Dublin, 1975); Jon G. Crawford, *Anglicizing the Government of Ireland: The Irish Privy Council and the Expansion of Tudor Rule, 1556–1578* (Dublin, 1993); Hiram Morgan, *Tyrone's Rebellion: The Outbreak of the Nine Years War in Tudor Ireland* (Woodbridge, 1993); Cyril Falls, *Elizabeth's Irish Wars* (London, 1950); David Beers Quinn, *The Elizabethans and the Irish* (Ithaca, NY, 1966); Michael MacCarthy-Morrogh, *The Munster Plantation* (Oxford, 1986). Useful essays are to be found in K. R. Andrews, N. P. Canny, and P. E. H. Hair (eds.), *The Westward Enterprise: English Activities in Ireland, the Atlantic, and America, 1480–1650* (Liverpool, 1978), especially the piece by Karl S. Bottigheimer; Ciarán Brady and Raymond Gillespie (eds.), *Natives and Newcomers: Essays on the Making of Irish Colonial Society, 1534–1641* (Dublin, 1986); Nicholas P. Canny and A. R. Pagden (eds.), *Colonial Identity in the Atlantic World, 1500–1800* (Princeton, NJ, 1987). Historical writing on the Tudor period in Irish history is rocked by controversy; for some guidance through this battlefield see Steven Ellis, 'Nationalist historiography and the English and Gaelic worlds in the late Middle Ages', *Irish Historical Studies*, 25 (1986), 1–18; Hiram Morgan, 'The end of Gaelic Ulster: a thematic interpretation', *Irish Historical Studies*, 26 (1988), 8–32; Brendan Bradshaw, 'Nationalism and historical scholarship in modern Ireland', *Irish Historical Studies*, 26 (1989), 329–51; and Steven Ellis, 'Historiographical debate: representations of the past in Ireland: whose past and whose present?', *Irish Historical Studies*, 27 (1991), 289–308. Lastly, R. F. Foster, *Modern Ireland* (Harmondsworth, 1988) sets the period in a general framework of Irish history.

On **Scotland** see: Gordon Donaldson, *The Scottish Reformation* (Cambridge, 1960); id., *Scotland: James V to James VII* (Edinburgh, 1965); Jenny Wormald, *Court, Kirk and Community: Scotland, 1470–1625* (London, 1981); id., *Mary Queen of Scots: A Study in Failure* (London, 1988); Michael Lynch (ed.), *Mary Stewart: Queen in Three Kingdoms* (Oxford, 1988), esp. ch. 9, 'Mary Stewart in England', by P. J. Holmes; Thomas I. Rae, *The Administration of the Scottish Frontier, 1513–1603* (Edinburgh, 1966); Christina Larner, *Enemies of God: The Witch-Hunt in Scotland* (Oxford, 1981).

THE WORLD OVERSEAS

There are two good introductions to British expansion overseas, both of which have helpful bibliographies: D. B. Quinn and A. N. Ryan, *England's Sea Empire, 1550–1642* (London, 1983); and Kenneth R. Andrews, *Trade, Plunder and Settlement: Maritime Enterprise and the Genesis of the British Empire, 1480–1630* (Cambridge, 1984). There is a large literature on the general background to oceanic voyages and colonization: C. R. Boxer, *The Portuguese Seaborne Empire, 1415–1825* (London, 1969); id., *The Dutch Seaborne Empire, 1600–1800* (London, 1965); Ralph Davis, *The Rise of the Atlantic Economies* (London, 1973); J. H. Elliott, *The Old World and the New, 1492–1650* (Cambridge, 1970); J. H. Parry, *The Spanish Seaborne Empire* (London, 1966); G. V. Scammell, *The World Encompassed: The First European Maritime Empires, c.800–1650* (London, 1981). Useful essays on transatlantic colonization are in K. R. Andrews, N. P. Canny, and P. E. H. Hair (eds.), *The Westward Enterprise* (Liverpool, 1978).

On **piracy and privateering**, see K. R. Andrews, *Elizabethan Privateering: English Privateering during the Spanish War, 1585–1603* (Cambridge, 1964); id., *Drake's Voyages: A Re-assessment of their Place in Elizabethan Maritime Expansion* (London, 1967); id., *The Spanish Caribbean, Trade and Plunder, 1530–1630* (New Haven, Conn., 1978).

On **England and America before 1603**: D. B. Quinn, *Ralegh and the British Empire* (London, 1947; repr. 1973); id., *England and the Discovery of America, 1481–1620* (New York, 1974); Paul Hulton and David Beers Quinn, *The American Drawings of John White* (2 vols., London, 1964).

Index